China

Tradition & Transformation

Items should be returned to the library from which they
were borrowed on or before the date stamped above,
unless a renewal has been granted. LM6.108.5

Wiltshire
COUNTY COUNCIL

BYTHESEA
ROAD

LIBRARY & MUSEUM SERVICE

TROWBRIDGE

China

Tradition & Transformation   *Revised Edition*

John K. Fairbank, *Professor Emeritus*

Edwin O. Reischauer, *Professor Emeritus*

Harvard University

Sydney
ALLEN & UNWIN
London   Boston

Revised edition first published in Australia in 1989 by
Allen & Unwin Australia Pty Ltd
An Unwin Hyman Company
8 Napier Street
North Sydney NSW 2059 Australia

National Library of Australia
Cataloguing-in-Publication entry:

Fairbank, John King, 1907-
   China, tradition & transformation.
   2nd ed.

   Index
   ISBN 0 04 374006 5

1. China — History. I. Reischauer, Edwin Oldfather, 1910 -,
joint author. II. Title.

951

Printed in Hong Kong

Contents

Maps and Charts

Preface

In the decade since 1978, the great Chinese revolution has turned another corner. Under Teng Hsiao-p'ing, the historical successor to Mao Tse-tung, Mao's Cultural Revolution of the period 1966–1976 has been repudiated. Teng's goal of economic modernization has replaced Mao's stress on class struggle. Foreign trade and investment, entrepreneurship in the countryside, less concern for ideology, and many other changes have shown China's vitality.

To understand China's potentialities, hopes, and limitations, a knowledge of history is more essential than ever. We have revised, expanded, and updated the chapter on the People's Republic in this new edition. This book is a slight reworking of the materials on China in the 1978 edition of *East Asia: Tradition and Transformation,* by the two authors of this volume together with Albert M. Craig. Half of Chapter 1 in this book and all of Chapters 2–6 are by E. O. Reischauer, while the other half of Chapter 1 and the other nine chapters are by J. K. Fairbank. Both authors, however, contributed advice, criticism, and at times revisions to each other's sections.

In writing a history of a quarter of humankind during a period of more than three milleniums, we have naturally relied on the work of a host of other scholars, both Asian and Western. Some have given us personal help and advice; far more have aided us through their writings. We are deeply grateful to all of them, but it would be impractical to attempt to list even the more important of these colleagues in our effort. Nor is it feasible to offer here a bibliography on this vast subject; any bibliography small enough to be included in this volume would have to be absurdly sketchy and soon would be quite out of date. Here we limit ourselves to expressing our special thanks to the late Professor Edward A. Kracke for help on Chapters 5 and 6 and Wilma Fairbank for aid in selecting the illustrations.

The Romanization system used in this book for Chinese names and words is that of Wade-Giles, generally considered standard in the English-speaking world for historical purposes. Common geographic names, however, are normally given according to the old Chinese Post Office system, which often followed southern Chinese pronunciations and not the Peking pronunciation of standard Northern Chinese. For example, the city that has been the capital of China for most of the past five and a half centuries is usually Romanized Peking and pronounced accordingly in the West, but the Wade-Giles Romanization of the name would be Pei-ching, and the real pronunciation is something like Bay-jing.

The Wade-Giles Romanization differs considerably from the *Pin-yin* system used by the People's Republic of China and also from what the sounds seem to be to the ears of English-speaking persons. In both Romanization systems the basic vowels and diphthongs are transcribed similarly for the most part and are in general pronounced as they would be in Italian, Spanish, or German. Examples are:

a as in f*a*ther

e as in *e*nd or the *u* in l*u*ng (the *-ien* combination of Wade-Giles appears as *-ian* in *Pin-yin*)

i as in *e*qua! (except that the *ih* of Wade-Giles has no English equivalent, though some English speakers try to approximate it by the *ir* sound in *stir;* it is transcribed simply as *i* in *Pin-yin*)

o as in *o*ld (except in some cases when it sounds like and is transcribed in *Pin-yin* as *e* and in other cases as *uo*)

u as in r*u*de (except after *ss, tz,* or *tz'* or corresponding *Pin-yin* forms, when there is hardly any vowel sound; it should also be noted that the *-ung* combination of Wade-Giles appears as *-ong* in *Pin-yin*)

ü as German *ü* or French *u*

ai as in t*ie*

ao as in c*ow*

ei as in w*ay*

ou as in *o*bey

ui, uei (or *wei*) as in w*ay*

Many of the initial consonants sound to the ears of English speakers much unlike their Wade-Giles Romanizations, and they are transcribed quite differently in *Pin-yin*. The following chart shows the major examples of these differences:

Wade-Giles	Pin-yin	Approximate Sounds in English
ch	*j, zh*	*j*
ch'	*q*	*ch*
hs	*x*	*sh*
j	*r*	*r*
k	*g*	*g*
k'	*k*	*k*
p	*b*	*b*
p'	*p*	*p*
t	*d*	*d*
t'	*t*	*t*
ts	*z*	*z*
ts'	*c*	*ts*
tz'	*c*	*ts*

J.K.F
E.O.R.

1. The Setting of Chinese History

For the people of the West the most important facts about China are, first, the vast numbers of people who live there; second, their very different ways of life, which have throughout history distinguished them culturally from Westerners; and third, the rapid growth and change that they are experiencing. In population and power, ancient China was the equal of the Roman Empire. Today China holds between one-quarter and one-fifth of the human race—some 900 or more million people. In the last few decades it has become clear that, in a rapidly shrinking world, relations with this vast segment of humanity can deeply affect the lives of Westerners. Three wars since 1941 in and around China have made this quite evident to Americans.

Mutual understanding between Westerners and Chinese is needed to form a basis for harmonious relations. But understanding must be based on a knowledge and appreciation of the other peoples' different customs, attitudes, ideals, and forms of self-expression. These are not easy to grasp from a distance. The cultural gap is enormous. Rapidly growing contacts during the past century have tended to lessen the cultural gap, but other factors have widened the gulf: first, a great upsurge of Chinese national consciousness and patriotic pride; second, a discrepancy in material standards of living between them and most Westerners; and third, a different experience of war and revolution. In part because of accidents of history and geography, Westerners have achieved a far more favorable balance between population and natural resources than has been the case in China, and this economic gap perpetuates and sometimes heightens the cultural differences. Americans in particular have not suffered warfare in their homeland as Chinese have, and the great changes in their lives have been evolutionary, not revolutionary. Not only their inherited culture but also their experience in modern times have set them apart from the Chinese.

The quest for peace is not the only reason for learning more about China. For the humanist interested in art, literature, philosophy, and religion, China's traditional society holds up a mirror to Western culture. It demonstrates alternate systems of value and belief, different traditions of aesthetic experience, and different forms of literary expression. For the social scientist, whether in anthropology, sociology, economics, political science, or history, the human record in China, in certain periods and in certain fields, is far fuller than that of the West.

China can best be understood through its history for a number of reasons. One is that the Chinese, more than the people of the rest of the world, see themselves in historical perspective. They are strongly aware of their heritage. To approach them through their history is to look at them as they see themselves. Secondly, their distinctive aesthetic, intellectual, and institutional achievements can best be studied as they evolved. They should be looked at separately from contemporary China. Only as one looks at the long flow of Chinese history can one perceive the direction of motion and have some understanding of what is happening in China now.

The essence of the present ferment in China is the interaction between new forces, many of which were derived from the West, and traditional habits and modes of thinking. Our story divides naturally into two major phases: the evolution of traditional Chinese civilization in relative isolation over three thousand years, and the upheavals and transformation of that civilization in recent times partly in response to contact with the modern Western world.

The Land, Peoples, and Languages of East Asia

China is the ancient source and today the central bulk of one of the great areas of civilization, which in recent years we have come to call East Asia. When Europeans first traveled far to the east to reach Cathay, Japan, and the Indies, they naturally gave these distant regions the general name "Far East." Americans who came westward across the Pacific might, with equal logic, have called it the "Far West." For the people who live there, however, it is neither "East" nor "West" and certainly not "Far." A better term for the area is "East Asia," which does not imply the outdated notion that Europe is the center of civilization.

China is so large a part of East Asia and was for so long so dominant in the region that any study of China involves some consideration of the whole East Asian area. In the remainder of this chapter we shall first discuss the broader East Asian setting of China and then proceed to a closer examination of China's geography and its traditional economy and society.

East Asia can be defined in three ways: in geographic terms as the area east of the great mountain and desert barrier that bisects Asia; in racial terms as the habitat of Mongoloid man (except for the Eskimo and American Indian branches of that race); and in cultural terms as the domain of a civilization rooted in that of ancient China. The last is the most restricted definition of the term, for it covers in addition to China itself only Japan, Korea, and Vietnam. It does not include two other large areas which are east of the great barrier and basically Mongoloid in population. One is Inner Asia, particularly Mongolia, Sinkiang (Chinese Turkestan), and Tibet. The nomadic peoples of these regions have seen their histories interwoven with that of China through commerce, war, and conquest. In the other area, Southeast Asia, much of the higher culture stemmed more from India than from China. In recent centuries, however, this region too has become increasingly linked with the rest of East Asia, economically, culturally, and strategically.

The Natural Environment.   One determining influence on East Asian civilization has been its relative isolation from the other great civilizations of mankind. Separated by great distances and formidable mountains and deserts, it developed distinctive cultural patterns that have been retained in large part until today. For example, the modern writing systems of all the rest of the world derive ultimately from a single series of inventions made in West Asia. Only in East Asia is there a writing system—the Chinese—which is based on entirely different principles.

Western civilization grew up in closely connected areas such as Mesopotamia, Egypt, and Greece. Only after it had spread to include most of Europe, North Africa, and Western Asia did it divide into its two present halves, Western Christian civilization and Islamic civilization. The Indus Valley in Northwest India (now a part of Pakistan) was the second great center of early civilization. Alexander's invasion of the Indus Valley in 327 B.C. is but one example of the close early contact between the ancient West and India.

The home of early East Asian civilization in North China was very much more isolated than were these other early centers. On one side stretched the seemingly boundless Pacific. On the other side rose the tremendous central massif of Asia—the Himalayas, the Tibetan Plateau, more than ten thousand feet high, and the huge mountain chains that radiate from this roof of the world. North of this massif lie the vast deserts and steppes of Central Asia—cold, inhospitable, and all but impassable for early man until he domesticated the horse and camel. South of the massif the rugged mountains and jungles of Southwest China and Southeast Asia are an even more formidable barrier. In ancient times this tremendous impediment of terrain and climate stretching

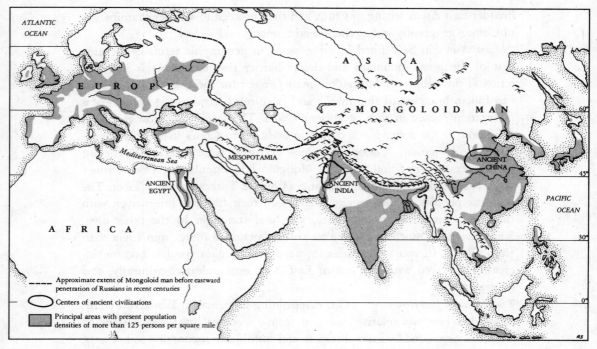

EURASIA

from the arctic wastes of Siberia to the jungles of Malaysia inhibited the free movement of men. Even today this barrier is crossed by only two railway lines and only a very few roads.

Climate also contributed to East Asia's cultural distinctiveness. Europe and West Asia have their weather determined largely by the Atlantic Ocean and receive the bulk of their rainfall in the cooler months. North Europe has relatively little sunshine, while the Mediterranean areas and West Asia receive relatively little rainfall. As a result the soils in Europe and West Asia are for the most part not cultivated very intensively. Usually only one crop can be grown each year.

The climate of East Asia, like that of India, is determined largely by the great land mass of Asia. In winter the air over Central Asia, far removed from the ameliorating influence of water, becomes very cold and heavy, flowing outward and bringing cool, dry weather to the southern and eastern fringes of the continent. In the summer the reverse takes place. The air over Central Asia warms up and rises, and moist oceanic air rushes in to take its place, dropping a heavy load of water on the continental fringes. As a result of these monsoon winds, most of East Asia and much of India have ample rainfall during the best growing months. This abundant water supply combined with the hot sunshine customary at these latitudes, far to the south of

Europe, permit intensive cultivation and, in many places, two crops per year.

This distinctive climate gave East Asia an agricultural pattern quite different from that of the West. Many of the principal crops and animals of East Asia, notably rice, the soy bean, the chicken, the water buffalo, and the pig, seem to have come from hot and humid Southeast Asia. In the West, cattle raising and sheep herding became a fundamental part of the economy, but in the more intensive agriculture of East Asia domesticated animals were used less and manpower more. The chief cereal of the West has been wheat, while that of most of East Asia and much of India has been rice, which grows best in flooded fields and is well adapted to the hot, wet summers of this area. Producing a much larger yield per acre than wheat, rice supports a heavier population on the land. Thus, right from the start of agriculture, there seems to have been a significant difference in the ratio between people and land in East Asia and India on the one hand, and in West Asia and Europe on the other. Even in recent times, when industrialization had added so heavily to the population of Europe, largely preindustrial East Asia and India continued to have greater densities of population.

The Peoples.   The area from the great Asian barrier eastward is for the most part the domain of Mongoloid man, while the area west of the barrier, including the greater part of India, most of the area of Islamic civilization, and the full zone of Western civilization, is the home of white or Caucasoid man. Negroid man, the third major racial type, occupies a discontinuous band of southerly areas in Africa, spots along the southern edges of Asia, and on the islands of Melanesia.

The origin of the races of mankind is still an unknown story. One of the predecessors of modern man in East Asia is Peking Man, whose skeletal remains were discovered in a cave near Peking in 1927. Living about 400,000 years B.C., he had tools, used fire, and was a hunter. He also had certain physical features that are more characteristic of Mongoloid man than of the other modern races. More recently a still earlier precursor of Mongoloid man, dating back some 600,000 years, has been found at a site in Lan-t'ien, near Sian in northwest China.

When the curtain rises on the first act of recorded history in East Asia, we find the Mongoloids already in a solid block covering almost the whole area. Their relative shortness of limb, which facilitates the retention of body heat, and their fleshy, narrow eyelids, which protect the eyes from snow glare, are thought by some to be the result of an original cold habitat in Northeast Asia. The range of skin color among Mongoloids, from very light in the North to dark brown in southern areas such as Indonesia, is clearly a product of environment, as is the comparable color range in the so-called white race. The other distinctive features of Mongoloid man are straight black hair, relatively flat faces, and dark eyes.

Mongoloids are not limited to East Asia. Some Mongoloids spilled westward north of the great barrier. The Eskimos represent a relatively recent incursion of the Mongoloid race into North America, while the American Indians themselves are thought to have come originally from Siberia by way of Alaska. Archaeology suggests the spread of the Mongoloids from the north and central parts of East Asia southward and outward to the offshore islands. The movement of the Thai people some seven centuries ago from Southwest China to their present home in Thailand was part of this great movement.

The Mongoloids were not, however, the sole occupants of this part of the world; the peripheral areas of East Asia contain many survivors of non-Mongoloid races. The most interesting of these are the Ainu, at present restricted to the northern extremities of Japan, who show certain traits of Caucasoid man. For example, they have considerable facial and body hair, a feature notably lacking in most Mongoloids.

The Sinitic Languages. The significant human divisions within East Asia, as in the West, are primarily linguistic rather than racial. In both East Asia and the West there is a common misconception that these linguistic differences correspond to racial divisions, but in fact there is no more a Chinese or Japanese race than there is a German or Hungarian race.

The largest linguistic division in East Asia is the Sinitic (or Sino-Tibetan) family of languages, which is comparable to the great Indo-European family that spreads over most of Europe and much of the Islamic and Indian zones of civilization. The Sinitic family of languages occupies a very solid block in the center of East Asia, covering all of China proper, Tibet, Thailand, Laos, most of Burma, and perhaps Vietnam. Except for the Tibetans, all the members of this language group appear to have been farmers since the Neolithic period, sedentary occupants of their part of the world, contrasting with the early Indo-Europeans, who often were nomadic, herding peoples and therefore wandered far afield.

Within the Sinitic group, Chinese is by far the largest linguistic subdivision. Chinese-speaking people have been in North China since the earliest recorded times. They have spread by emigration and also have assimilated culturally and linguistically allied groups. In time they came to occupy almost the whole of China proper and more recently Manchuria, much of Inner Mongolia, parts of Sinkiang, most of Taiwan (Formosa), as well as Chinese sectors in Southeast Asia, particularly Malaysia, where Chinese now constitute more than 40 per cent of the population, and Singapore, where they are the great majority.

In the course of this expansion the Chinese language divided into several mutually unintelligible languages, as distinct from one another as Spanish is from Italian, or Swedish from German. Chinese proper, which has been called Mandarin, is spoken as a mother tongue by more people than any other lan-

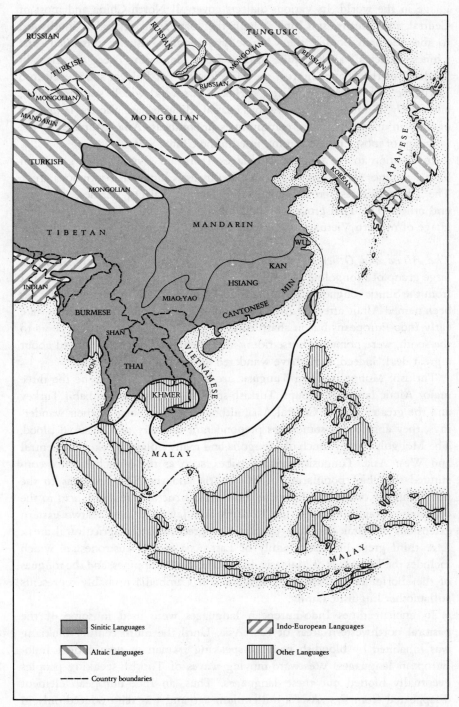

RUSSIAN

RUSSIAN

TUNGUSIC

TURKISH

MONGOLIAN

RUSSIAN

MONGOLIAN

MANDARIN

MONGOLIAN

TURKISH

KOREAN

JAPANESE

MONGOLIAN

TIBETAN

MANDARIN

WU

KAN

HSIANG

MIN

INDIAN

MIAO-YAO

CANTONESE

BURMESE

SHAN

VIETNAMESE

MON

THAI

KHMER

MALAY

MALAY

	Sinitic Languages		Indo-European Languages
	Altaic Languages		Other Languages
– – –	Country boundaries		

MODERN LINGUISTIC MAP OF EAST ASIA

guage in the world. Its various dialects cover all North China and most of Central and Southwest China. Along the coast from Shanghai southward to the Vietnam border, the Chinese-type tongues, usually miscalled "the Chinese dialects," are all quite distinct from Mandarin. There are the Wu "dialect" of the Shanghai area; the Min "dialect" of Fukien, subdivided into Fukienese and the Amoy "dialect"; Hakka in several widely scattered areas; and finally, Cantonese. These various coastal "dialects" are also the languages of Taiwan and the Chinese communities in Southeast Asia. Cantonese is the language of most Chinese communities in the United States.

In addition to the Chinese languages, there are several other groups of Sinitic tongues spoken by peoples in Southwest China and contiguous areas. The Tibeto-Burmese group includes the Tibetan dialects, Burmese, and several others. The Thai group of Thailand and Laos, and Vietnamese, the language of modern Vietnam, are usually included among the Sinitic languages.

The Altaic and Other Language Groups.   North of the Sinitic bloc is a large group of Mongoloid peoples who speak languages of a family as distinct from the Sinitic tongues as from the Indo-European. This linguistic family has been named Altaic after the Altai Mountains in Mongolia. These peoples, like early Indo-Europeans but in sharp contrast with their sedentary neighbors to the south, were nomadic, horse-riding sheepherders. They have moved about a great deal; indeed, some have wandered entirely out of East Asia.

Turkish, Mongolian, and Tungusic are usually considered to be the three major Altaic language groups. Turkish-speaking groups now inhabit Turkey and the greater part of Central Asia, although in the course of their wanderings, they absorbed a sometimes preponderant quantity of Caucasoid blood. The Mongols occupy much of Mongolia and many isolated pockets in Central and West Asia. Tungusic-speaking tribes, such as the Manchus, once constituted the chief population of Manchuria and the Siberian areas to the north. Since Korean and Japanese show close structural resemblances to the definitely Altaic languages, the Koreans and Japanese may be two eastern extensions of Altaic-speaking peoples into predominately agricultural areas.

A third great linguistic family of East Asia is the Austronesian, which includes the languages of Malaysia, Indonesia, the Philippines, and the tongues of the aborigines of Taiwan. The Khmer of Cambodia probably represents still another linguistic family.

In ancient times Indo-European languages were used in some of the pastoral northwestern areas of East Asia. Until the ninth century Sinkiang was inhabited by blondish peoples, speaking Iranian or now extinct Indo-European languages. Westward-moving waves of Turkish-speaking peoples eventually blotted out these languages. Thus, an Indo-European element disappeared from East Asia a millennium ago and was reintroduced only in the last few centuries by Russian colonization in Siberia.

China's Geographical Setting

China is geographically a less united area than either the traditional zone of Western civilization or India because it lacks the easy communications made possible by the Mediterranean or by the great plains of the other regions. The North China Plain is much smaller than the plain that extends across North India, to say nothing of the still greater North European Plain or the American Middle West.

China is broken up into a sort of checkerboard by two intersecting sets of parallel mountain chains. One major inland chain runs from southwestern China northeastward through Shansi and western Manchuria. A parallel coastal range extends from Canton northward to the Yangtze and then re-appears in the Shantung Peninsula and again in the mountains along the Korean-Manchurian border. Intersecting these two southwest-to-northeast ranges, three parallel mountain chains spaced at roughly equal intervals protrude from west to east toward the Pacific. The southernmost chain creates the watershed dividing the West River system of the Canton region from the Yangtze Valley. In the extreme north another east-west range divides North China from the Mongolian plateau. Between these two the important Tsinling range, the eastward extension of the massive Kunlun of northern Tibet, creates the watershed between the Yangtze and the Yellow Rivers and (together with the Huai River) marks the boundary between North and South China. This cross-hatching of mountain ranges has created a number of distinct geographical regions. It has given rise to problems of economic and political unity and has determined military strategy.

River Systems.   The great rivers of China water the centers of habitation which lie within the mountain ranges. The Yellow River (Huang Ho) is some 2700 miles in length. After it enters the North China Plain about 500 miles from the sea, it crosses a broad flood plain built up over the ages by its own silt. The river bed here slopes only about one foot per mile. In the summer flood season the waters from the great treeless mountain ranges to the west bring with them a heavy deposit of yellow silt which gives the river its name. Since the Yellow River constantly builds up its own bed, from earliest times Chinese administrators have had to construct dikes to keep it within its channel. Ordinarily the waters of "China's Sorrow" move across the plain within these dikes between ten and forty feet above the level of the surrounding land. A single breach in the dikes may spread a few inches or feet of water over hundreds of square miles and cut millions of farmers off from their sustenance. Years may elapse before flood-ravaged lands can be cultivated again. Meanwhile famine will have followed upon the flood. Only since 1949 have afforestation and dam building begun to conquer this age-old problem.

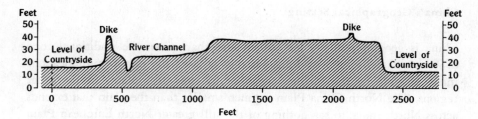

PROFILE OF THE YELLOW RIVER. *This diagram is a cross section with the vertical aspect greatly exaggerated. It shows how during flood season the river rises between its dikes above the level of the countryside.*

The vastness of the Yellow River problem has been graphically demonstrated by the historic shifts of its bed from the north to the south of the Shantung promontory and back again. From 1191 to 1852 its waters for the most part entered the ocean south of the peninsula; from 1852 to 1938 on the north; and from 1938 to 1947 again to the south. The present channel enters the ocean near Tientsin.

The Yangtze is a larger river than the Yellow. It is 3200 miles in length, with a catchment basin twice as large and receiving twice as much rainfall. It is also navigable, as the Yellow River is not. Steamers as large as 10,000 tons can in season ascend 630 miles to Hankow and smaller vessels another 1000 miles. In flood season the river rushes through the famous Yangtze gorges above Hankow at fourteen knots, and special steamers are required to make the ascent. Joined by a great network of tributaries, the Yangtze itself carries an enormous volume of silt into the China Sea, extending the Shanghai delta at the rate of about one mile in seventy years. Big lakes serve as storage basins for the lower Yangtze. Even so, the rainy season may raise the water level as much as forty or fifty feet between the dikes. Disastrous floods are not infrequent.

Climate.   China lies far south of most of Europe. Peking is south of both Naples and Madrid; Canton is in the same latitude as the Sahara Desert. China is further south than the eastern half of the United States, with Peking corresponding to Philadelphia, Shanghai to Mobile, and Canton to Havana, Cuba. The greater land mass to which China belongs gives it a more markedly continental climate, with much lower winter and somewhat higher summer temperatures than at corresponding latitudes in the United States. Peking in July can be as hot as Cairo and in January as cold as Stockholm.

China is a battleground between cold, dry, continental air and warm, humid, oceanic air, which brings it most of its rainfall. During the summer this sea air reaches further into the continent, sometimes as far as Mongolia. Most of the South receives more than sixty inches of rainfall a year. This ample water supply can be used not only for irrigating rice fields but also for transportation. Navigable streams and canals cover most of the central and lower Yangtze basin. In marked contrast, the Northwest receives less than the twenty inches minimum rainfall necessary for farming unirrigated lands and has little or no water transportation.

One important climatic boundary is the Tsinling Mountains. South of the Tsinling rainfall for the most part is over forty inches, making possible the irrigated rice economy that supports two-thirds of the Chinese people. North of this boundary stretch brown, parched lands used for dry field farming and traversed by cart or wheelbarrow tracks. (See page 908.) Another climatic boundary is between the farming areas of China proper and the steppe lands to the north that are too lightly watered to support any sort of agriculture. This has been sharply demarcated by the Great Wall, which the Chinese erected to defend themselves from their northern neighbors, pastoral, Altaic-speaking nomads.

Geologists speculate that in the last Ice Age the frozen interior of Asia sent forth tremendous winds which deposited the fine loess soil that covers about 100,000 square miles of Northwest China. The Yellow River has spread some of this soil over the North China Plain as alluvium. Fortunately the loess makes a fertile soil. In a region of light rainfall, it has remained unleached; that is, its mineral substances have not been percolated out by the constant passage of water through it. North China, however, despite its fertile loess, balances dangerously on the edge of famine. The growing season is short; precipitation is light and highly variable. Until the introduction of irrigation by electric pump, the Northern peasant faced a constant threat of drought. In the last 1800 years more than 1800 famines have been recorded.

South China soils have been leached by the heavier rainfall of that area. Moreover, only 15 per cent of its uplands are flat enough for cultivation. But since most of the area produces two crops a year, South China has a denser population than the North and higher standards of nutrition.

China's Traditional Economy and Society

China's greatest natural resource has always been her agricultural land. It is understandable therefore that climate and terrain have helped shape the economic and social institutions of Chinese life. Although the historical records of China, like those of most other countries, generally neglect the life of the common people, we can sketch certain features that have been typical of the life of the Chinese masses. First of all, China's vast population, now roughly four times that of the United States, must get its food supply from a cultivated area about one-half the size of that of the United States. The 80 per cent of the populace who live upon the soil and till it have been barely able to produce a food surplus adequate to maintain the other 20 per cent.

They have not been able to afford the raising of animals for food, aside from the scavengers, pigs and chickens. And because of the lack of animals, peasants have largely depended on human excrement, or "night soil," for fertilizer. At best, Chinese agriculture has always been a precarious business.

Secondly, China's economic life has been labor-intensive, that is, strongly dependent upon human muscle-power. The agricultural cycle requires the lavish use of human energy. In growing rice, for example, seed is thickly scattered in nursery beds. Meanwhile winter crops are harvested in the main fields, which are then cultivated and flooded in preparation for the rice. When the rice seedlings are about eight inches high after a month's growth, they are transplanted by hand to the main paddy fields, an activity roughly equivalent to the planting of the American wheat and corn crops by hand. Mechanization is difficult, not least because other work must be found for so many hands.

Similarly, the famous silk industry requires endless labor. A pound of silk-worms at hatching may number about 700,000 individual worms. Fed mulberry leaves by hand and carefully tended for five weeks until their maturity, the pound of worms will grow to a weight of some five tons, consuming about twelve tons of mulberry leaves in the process, but producing in the end only about 150 pounds of silk. The semimechanized reeling of silk cocoons to get their thread is only the last step after an enormous application of hand labor. The other traditional household industry of South China, tea production, involves a comparable use of hands to pick, sort, roast, pick over, re-sort, re-roast, and package the tea leaves.

The labor-intensive nature of the economy has been typified by the moving of irrigation water by human muscle, customarily with a simple foot treadle or even more simply by a bucket on ropes held by two persons. Transportation also has customarily been labor-intensive, using porters with carrying poles on mountain paths, men pushing wheelbarrows over the plains, boatmen sculling sampans on the waterways, chair-bearers with their palanquins in the cities (supplanted in recent times by rickshaw coolies and later by pedicab drivers). Even now bicycles seem to carry as many people as do motor vehicles.

Chinese farming from ancient times has applied large amounts of labor and, when possible, large amounts of water to small plots of land. Landowning has therefore been the main goal of economic endeavor and investment. Problems of landlordism and agricultural taxation have preoccupied both populace and officialdom in every generation. Moreover, the farmer's lack of capital and storage facilities kept him at the mercy of the middleman, who bought cheaply in the harvest season and lent capital in the off-season to the impoverished cultivator at rates of 2 per cent or more a month. Tenancy led to further exploitation. The farmer might have to pay as much as half his crop to the landlord.

Transportation of produce to market has always been a problem. A decentralized market pattern has therefore been typical, each village community

挿
秧

挿秧
晨雨麥秋潤午風
夏原溪南與溪北
歌挿新秧拋不停
千左右無亂行我敎
挿秧馬八勞民莫忘

TRANSPLANTING RICE. *With their bundles of rice seedlings, which
have already been grown in a seed bed, these farmers wade
backward ankle-deep in the flooded fields to transplant
the seedlings by hand in orderly rows. Communication paths
are on top of the field dikes. The bridge crosses the irrigation canal.
From* P'ei-wen-chai keng-chih t'u, *an early eighteenth-century
work extolling the imperial patronage of agriculture.*

exchanging its produce by barter at the local market town. A market center
and its surrounding villages within walking distance formed a unit that could
of course be wiped out by natural calamities such as flood or drought, but
conversely could live almost by itself as long as nature was kind. Thus the
fragmented and cellular nature of the traditional market center and village
economy enabled them to survive with a high degree of inertia, or persistence
in established channels, in spite of wars, invasions, and great social changes
in the cities and administrative centers where history was recorded. While the
recent decades of revolutionary effort have brought great changes—for

MAKING SILK. *Silk culture requires a maximum investment of hand labor. The silkworms are hatched from eggs and must be kept in the right condition of temperature and moisture. During their growth period they must be fed several times a day with fine-cut leaves from specially cultivated mulberry trees. The man and woman on the left are sorting the silk cocoons. A later stage requires that the strands of silk be unraveled from the cocoons in a pan of hot water. The woman in the picture on the right is collecting strands on a reel. This occupation also is suited to the lavish application of labor in a subsidiary handicraft industry within a farm household. These pictures show only two out of a dozen stages in the complex process of silk production. (Chinese woodcuts from the* T'ien-kung k'ai-wu *of 1637.)*

example, dams to accumulate water, more irrigation canals to distribute it, electrification to pump it onto the fields, afforestation, and improved crops— these improvements have only begun to remake Chinese life.

The Social Heritage.   While it would be misleading to generalize in brief terms about a society as large, ancient, and varied as that of China, there are

IRRIGATED AGRICULTURE. *Two men walk the treadles of a square-pallet chain-pump to lift water onto the fields, and another uses a windlass to distribute water to the various crops shown around the edge of the picture. (From T'ien-kung k'ai-wu, 1637.) Electric pumps now do this work.*

still a few major points for an outside observer to keep in mind. First of all, the family, rather than the individual, the state, or the church, has formed the most significant unit in Chinese society. Each individual's family was his chief source of economic sustenance, security, education, social contact, and recreation. Through ancestor worship, it was even his main religious focus. Of the five famous Confucian relationships—between ruler and subject, father and son, husband and wife, elder brother and younger brother, and friend and friend—three were determined by kinship. China's whole ethical system tended to be family-centered, not oriented toward God or the state.

The Chinese kinship group was extensive, reaching out in each direction to the fifth generation. The ideal was to have all the living generations reside in one great household, divided among the various courtyards of a big compound. Actually this was seldom achieved except by the rich. A typical household seems to have averaged around five persons and was in fact a family of a type familiar in the West, rather than the ideal extended Chinese family.

The family system was both hierarchic and authoritarian. The status of each person depended on his position by birth or marriage. Gradations of kinship were carefully spelled out in a complex terminology. The patriarchal father was the center of authority. At least in theory he controlled the family property and he arranged his children's and grandchildren's marriages. As an index of the subordination of the individual to the family, filial piety was the most admired of virtues. (See page 45.) The arrangement of marriages by the respective families, for which a good deal can no doubt be said when wise matchmakers were used, symbolized more clearly than anything else the individual's subordination. Marriage was more a union of families than of individuals.

Women traditionally obeyed their fathers in youth, their husbands in middle life, and their sons in old age. They were expected not to remarry if widowed, but men could take secondary wives and concubines into the household. Except for a dowry, women had no property rights and on marriage entered their husbands' families as humble newcomers. This tradition suggests the great potential for change that awaited China's modern revolution.

This authoritarian family pattern provided a basis for social order in political as well as in domestic life. The role of the emperor and his officials was merely that of the father writ large. A district magistrate was called the "father and mother" of the people.

In a pluralistic society, like that of the modern West, the many forces of church and state, capital and labor, government and private enterprise are balanced under a rule of law. Instead, in Chinese life the personal virtues of probity and loyalty, sincerity and benevolence, inculcated by the family system, provided the norms for social conduct. Law was a necessary tool of administration; but personal morality was the foundation of society. Far from being anarchic because of the weakness of the legal concept, Chinese society was firmly knit together by Confucianism. This great ethical institution occupied in China much of the place filled by both law and religion in the West.

As in most large-scale peasant societies, there was a wide gulf in power and prestige between the rulers and the ruled. Society was traditionally divided into four classes, which in descending order were the scholar-administrator (or warrior-aristocrat in ancient times), the farmer, the artisan, and the merchant. The scholar-administrator, as an educated man, was presumed to be morally superior. Exercising the supreme authority of the emperor, the paterfamilias of all Chinese society, the scholar-administrator came to dominate all aspects of public life, and also left us the voluminous record of Chinese history, which was naturally written from his ruling-class point of view.

2. Early China: The Birth of a Civilization

The Archaeological Record

Agriculture seems to have started in North China in the region of the great bend of the Yellow River, in a fringe area between wooded highlands on the west and swampy lowlands on the east, where hunter-fisher folk could domesticate animals and begin to cultivate plants for food. It then spread along the middle and lower course of the Yellow River and out over the North China Plain, which, despite severe winters, was well suited to agriculture in primitive times. In fact, this center of early Chinese civilization resembled in some ways the homes of other ancient civilizations—the flood plains of the Nile in Egypt, the Tigris and Euphrates in Mesopotamia, and the Indus in modern Pakistan. In each case, rainfall was too light to produce forests that had to be removed before tilling could begin, and the great river, if adequately controlled, provided ample water and replenished the soil's fertility with periodic floods.

It is significant that the North China Plain is the part of agricultural East Asia most accessible by land from India and West Asia. As far as we now know, many basic elements of ancient civilization appeared much earlier in West Asia and the Indus Valley than in East Asia and therefore may have spread slowly across the steppes and mountains of Central Asia to the North China Plain. Examples are the cultivation of grains like wheat; domestication of animals such as sheep, cattle, and horses; the wheel and chariot; bronze and iron.

Recent finds, on the other hand, have shown that pottery goes back as far in East Asia as anywhere in the world—perhaps some 10,000 years—and that bronze may have been produced even earlier in northern Thailand than in the Middle East. Rice, the chief cereal of East Asia today, is of South-east Asian origin, and its cultivation was well established in the Yangtze Valley by prehistoric times. The prehistoric Chinese also produced silk, which spread to the West very much later. Some important domestic animals were of different derivation—pigs, chickens, and dogs for food and the water buffalo for rice cultivation. The basic agricultural tool of East Asia has always been the hoe, in contrast to the plow of the West. The most characteristic Paleolithic remains are stone choppers; in the rest of the "old world" they are chipped stone axes. Neolithic remains in East Asia are typified by halfmoon-shaped stone knives and grey pottery with mat and cord markings, both quite different from Western Eurasian artifacts.

There is, thus, good reason to assume that in East Asia agriculture and early civilization developed quite independently of Western Eurasia. The culture that arose around the bend of the Yellow River in northwest China was probably based on this East Asian culture but seems to have also received enrichment from regions to the West. However, there is no evidence that these influences were brought by invaders or migrants, and the Neolithic peoples of North China and possibly their Paleolithic predecessors appear to have been the direct ancestors of the modern Chinese. Even at this early time the culture of North China showed distinctive East Asian features.

The Painted and Black Pottery Cultures.   Two distinct cultures, named for their characteristic pottery, occupied North China in late Neolithic times. They were first thought to show a clash between West Asian and local influences, but more recent studies have proved that the Black Pottery culture in large part followed the Painted, occupying most of its area.

The Painted Pottery culture, which is also known as Yang-shao from a type site in northwest Honan, is found throughout North China, except for Shantung province in the extreme east, and it lingered on longest in Kansu province in the northwest. Its most famous site is the partly excavated village at Pan-p'o near Sian (the ancient Ch'ang-an), which dates from the fifth millennium B.C. The culture is typified by large bulbous pots, painted in red and black, usually with bold geometric designs. While it bears some resemblance to the painted pottery of West Asia, one cannot assume that it was merely a cultural borrowing from the West, because there is no clear archaeological trail by which it could have come.

The Black Pottery culture, also called Lung-shan from type sites in Shantung, covered the same area as the Painted, except for the extreme northwest, and also extended into Shantung and the middle and lower Yangtze valleys. It is typified by a very thin, shiny, black pottery. This culture showed that since the time of the Painted Pottery new influences from West Asia, such as domesticated sheep and horses and the potter's wheel, had reached North China. It also showed strong cultural continuity with the following bronze

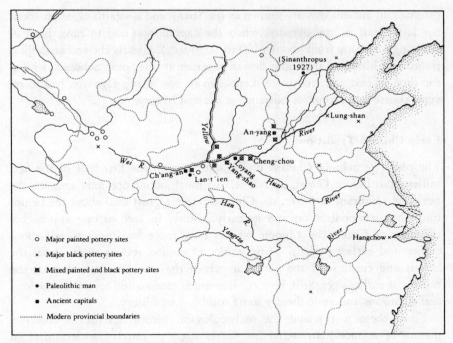

(Sinanthropus
1927)

Lung-shan

Yellow   An-yang   River

Wei R.   Loyang Cheng-chou
Ch'ang-an   Lan-t'ien   Yang-shao   Huai   River

Han R.

Yangtze   River   Hangchow

o   Major painted pottery sites
x   Major black pottery sites
⊠   Mixed painted and black pottery sites
•   Paleolithic man
■   Ancient capitals
·······   Modern provincial boundaries

NORTH CHINA IN PREHISTORIC TIMES

age. For example, it shared the same hollow-legged tripods, a common system of divination, and town walls of pounded earth, much like those that still may be found in North China today.

The Bronze Age.   Bronze casting by the piece-mold process, different from the method used in ancient West Asia, made its appearance in China by the middle of the second millennium B.C., if not earlier. The first known sites are found spread out in Honan south of the Yellow River from its great bend eastward, but the only bronzes they contain are small weapons. A second stage is typified by a site near Cheng-chou in the same area, which was a formidable capital city, surrounded by a pounded earth wall more than twenty feet high and a mile square. Outside the walls were two bronze foundries which produced elaborate ritual vessels.

The third bronze stage is best represented by a site near An-yang in the part of Honan north of the Yellow River. It was discovered by Chinese scholars who in 1899 became intrigued by what appeared to be ancient writing scratched onto the "dragon bones" that Peking apothecary shops were grinding up for medicine. They traced these bones to their source near An-yang and on further study discovered that they bore the earliest known form of Chinese writing and corroborated much of the early historical tradition.

The inscriptions contained the names of virtually all of the traditional rulers of an ancient dynasty known as the Shang and a wealth of detail about the latter half of the dynasty, when the capital was said to have been at An-yang (roughly from about 1400 to 1050 B.C.). Clearly the archaeological record and historical traditions flowed together at this point. Scholars, who at the time looked with complete skepticism on the Shang Dynasty, had to reverse course and accept its existence as verified history.

Early Chinese Traditions

The oldest remaining Chinese books, dating from the first half of the first millennium before Christ, do not tell us much about previous ages. In the next few centuries, however, the Chinese wrote a great deal about the beginnings of their civilization and its early history. In fact, as one approaches the time of Christ, the Chinese writers have more and more to tell about earlier and earlier periods. Their works, of course, tell us more about the beliefs and customs of the period in which they were written than of the history of earlier ages. Still, they contain much material on earlier mythology and traditions and undoubtedly some solid bits of history.

From these works and the archaeological record emerges a shadowy picture of a once matriarchal but increasingly patriarchal society, divided into tribal or clan-like units. From the clan name, the *hsing* or family name had already developed in ancient times. Then, as now, it always preceded a man's personal name, instead of following it as in the European tradition. There was a strong emphasis on exogamy, that is, marriage outside one's clan, which has persisted throughout Chinese history, so that even today Chinese feel that persons of the same surname, even though not actually related, should not marry.

Religious ideas centered on the clan and its deities, often identified as ancestors. Ancestor worship has remained ever since a characteristic of Chinese civilization. As was natural in an agricultural society, there was also strong emphasis on heaven as a controlling factor in agriculture, on the fertility of the soil, on grain gods, and on cosmological and calendrical lore. Authority was strongly religious, and the ruler was in a sense the chief priest and also calendar maker.

The Chinese early developed a strong feeling of history and the ideal of political unity. Unaware of the great cultures to the west, they considered China the unique land of civilization, surrounded on all sides by the "four barbarians." They therefore called it Chung-kuo, literally the "Central Country" but commonly translated the "Middle Kingdom." Chung-kuo is still the Chinese name for their land. The term *t'ien-hsia,* meaning "all under heaven," meant the world but came to be used for the Chinese Empire. Information and speculation about earlier ages was organized into a strict historical sequence of events attributed to rulers of a politically and culturally unified China that constituted the whole of civilization.

The Culture Heroes.   There are several versions of this early pseudohistory. The usual sequence is of three early rulers (*huang*) or possibly fraternal groups of rulers, followed by five emperors (*ti*), followed by three dynasties, which take us well into historical times. The three rulers and five emperors are often called "culture heroes," because to them and to lesser figures like them are attributed the early achievements of civilization, such as the discovery of fire, the origination of fishing, hunting, and agriculture, the devising of the calendar, the development of medicine, and the invention of writing. The wife of the first of the five emperors is credited with the development of sericulture, for silk production is typically the work of women.

The last two of the five emperors, Yao and Shun, are best known for having passed on their rule, not to sons, but to worthy ministers. Yao selected Shun, and Shun a man named Yü. The three together are known as the three model emperors. Yü is also famed as the hero who drained off the flood waters of the North China Plain and divided the empire into nine provinces. A Chinese reflection of the worldwide flood legend can be detected in this story.

The Early Dynasties.   With Yü also commences a somewhat more credible aspect of the tradition. He started a dynasty called the Hsia, which has been assigned the dates 2205–1766 B.C. (or 1994–1523 B.C. according to another source). The Hsia rulers are credited with reigns of reasonable length, in contrast to the Methuselah-like spans of the culture heroes.

The last Hsia emperor was so depraved that people revolted under the leadership of a man who founded a new dynasty, named Shang. The Shang, which is traditionally given the dates of 1766–1122 B.C. or 1523–1027 B.C., has been proven by archaeology to be fully historical, for the An-yang finds indubitably correspond to the second half of the dynasty and the Cheng-chou finds presumably to its earlier centuries. This raises the question of what actual facts may lie behind the tradition of the Hsia dynasty. Might it not correspond to the earliest bronze age, or perhaps the Black Pottery culture which preceded it?

The last of the Shang emperors was said to be a debauched tyrannical ruler—an allegation which the bone inscriptions from An-yang tend to substantiate. One of those who suffered most at his hands was a subject known to history as King Wen (Wen Wang) of the principality of Chou. His son and successor, King Wu (Wu Wang) eventually revolted, according to the tradition in either 1122 or 1027 B.C., and founded the third dynasty, which he called Chou after the name of his principality. His brother, the Duke of

Chou (Chou Kung), became the consolidator of the dynasty, as the wise and saintly councilor of King Wu's young son and heir.

While the story of the founding of the Chou bears the marks of later idealization, much of the record of the early centuries of the Chou is acceptable as history, because our earliest surviving books do date from this period. After 841 B.C. the traditional dating seems quite reliable, and in the next century we begin to encounter our first fully verifiable events—eclipses of the sun that did occur just when the Chinese records date them.

The Chinese Writing System

The outstanding feature of the late Shang finds at An-yang is the writing they contain; not only is it unmistakably the Chinese language but it is also an early form of the Chinese writing system that still dominates East Asian civilization. Some symbols are recognizable even to the untutored eye as identical with characters appearing in newspapers today. It is much as if the Arabic-speaking inhabitants of Egypt or Iraq were able to recognize in hieroglyphics or cuneiform the same language they now use and could point out occasional words that any schoolboy could read. The Chinese have always felt a complete cultural and racial identity with the ancient inhabitants of their land, and here is striking proof that they are right in doing so. They have good reason to feel a greater sense of direct continuity from the Shang than Westerners feel from the early Egyptians and Mesopotamians, or even the ancient Greeks and Romans.

One of the characteristics of the Sinitic languages, to which Chinese belongs, is that a relatively high percentage of their words are monosyllables. This is truer of ancient Chinese than of modern. Another feature of Chinese and most other Sinitic languages is the absence of inflections. The Chinese word *shan,* for instance, can mean "mountains" as well as "mountain." In the case of verbs, the difference from the languages of the West is even more marked. There are no variations like "go," "went," "gone," or even "look," "looks," "looked." Another feature of most Sinitic languages is their tonal character. Monosyllabic words which otherwise sound alike are distinguished from one another by the tone in which they are spoken, something like the differing inflections we use in conversation: "What's your name?" "Name?" "Yes, name." In modern Mandarin there are four tones. *Ma* pronounced in the first of these, for example, is an informal word for "mother," but in the second tone it means "hemp," in the third "horse," and in the fourth "to curse."

Chinese Characters. The monosyllabic and uninflected nature of the Chinese language helps account for the retention by the Chinese of a

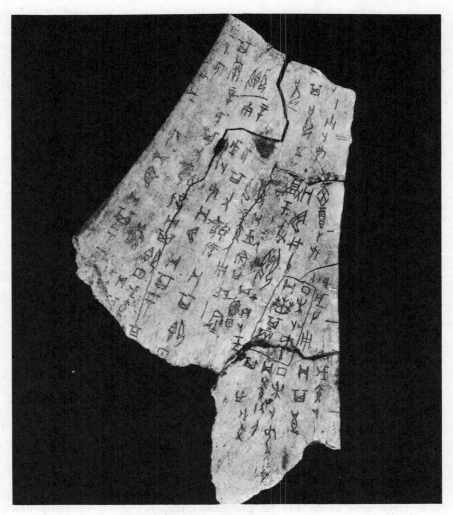

AN INSCRIBED AN-YANG BONE.

writing system which, like that of ancient Egypt, originated from pictographs but, unlike hieroglyphics, always remained true to the basic principle that each monosyllabic word should have its unique symbol, or
character. Inflections would long ago have forced the Chinese to a more
flexible phonetic system of writing.

The Chinese writing system encountered in the An-yang finds had
already undergone a long development and had progressed far beyond
simple pictographs. Antecedents for this writing, in fact, seem to exist in
sites of the fifth millenium B.C. The writing usually ran from top to bottom,
as remained the rule until recent years. The more than two thousand charac-

ters found in the Shang remains look for the most part quite different from modern Chinese characters, but almost all have been clearly identified with later forms, and all the principles to be found in the eight or nine thousand characters commonly used in modern times (dictionaries list up to fifty thousand characters and variants) were present in the Shang writing.

The many pictographs, though often very stylized, were for the most part more recognizable as pictures in Shang times than are their modern forms. For example, the character for "sun" (now 日) originally was a circle with a line in it; that for "moon" (now 月) was still quite recognizably a crescent moon; and "tree" 木 was written in Shang times 木 , a sketch representing both the branches and the roots of a tree. Some pictographs were quite complicated, as, for example, one of the words for "sacrifice," which showed two hands holding a bird upside down over a symbol that meant "the spirits."

There was, in addition, a large number of ideographs, that is, sketches of ideas rather than actual pictures. Perhaps the numbers "one" 一 , "two" 二 , and "three" 三 should be put in this category. "Above" 上 , originally a shorter line above a longer line, and "below" 下 , analogously formed, certainly belong to this group. So also do more complex characters, like those for "grove" or "forest" 林 , which is made up of two trees, and "bright" 明 , composed of the characters for "sun" and "moon." Many of the ideographs are very picturesque: a woman under a roof 安 means "peace" and a woman beside a child 好 means "good" or "to like."

A third category of characters was derived at least in part according to phonetic principles. Already by the Shang period many words were written with pictographs that actually represented some more easily depictable homophone, or word of identical pronunciation. Thus 來, which originally was a picture of some sort of grain, presumably pronounced *lai,* is the character used for the word *lai,* meaning "come."

A large subdivision of the phonetic category consists of compound characters made up of phonetics and significs. The phonetics are characters used to indicate the approximate sound of the compound character, and the significs, usually placed to the left or above the phonetic, show the category of meaning to which the word belongs. Thus hundreds of characters for words associated in some way with trees or wood, such as "maple," "pear," "branch," "to plant," "shelf," "spear," and "ladder," are made up of the character for "tree" combined with some other character used purely for its phonetic value.

The great majority of currently used characters belong to this compound type, and the significs in such characters have become the basis for the commonest system for classifying characters. In this system, 214 characters, largely made up of those commonly used as significs, are selected as "radicals," or classifiers, under which all characters are grouped and listed in

SHANG INSCRIPTION ON BONE. *The characters are to be read from top to bottom, but the lines in this particular case read from left to right. The meaning of the text is: "[On the day] hsin-mao, it is divined whether on this hsin day it will rain—or not rain."*
Most of the characters in this text are clearly identifiable from their modern forms. The second character in the second column is a picture of the sun with a spot in it, while the second character in the third column as well as the lower right-hand character show rain falling from a cloud. The upper right-hand character, showing a man's armpits (the two spots under the arms), was at this time a homophone for the undepictable word "also."

accordance with the number of brush strokes needed to write the rest of the character. Thus the word for "ladder" is classified under "tree" (radical 75) plus seven additional strokes. This is a very cumbersome system of classification as compared with alphabetic spelling, and many characters fit in only very poorly, but at least it achieves some order in what is otherwise an ocean of unique symbols.

Advantages and Disadvantages of the Writing System. The Chinese writing system has certain drawbacks when compared with the simpler phonetic systems of the West. It obviously takes a great deal more time and effort to master. The individual characters tend to be rather complex. The average character may require some twelve or thirteen brush strokes to write, and a few take as many as twenty-five. At least two or three thousand characters must be memorized before one can read even simple texts. The emphasis on rote memory work to learn all these characters may have had a limiting influence in Chinese education, putting a premium on memorizing ability.

The complexity of the system made literacy more difficult to achieve than it was in cultures with simpler writing systems, and thus helped limit upper-class life to the relative few who could find the time for protracted study. The writing system has become an increasing handicap in modern times as the need for widespread literacy has increased. Even though the Chinese invented printing, characters have made printing a much more difficult technique than in the West and so far all efforts to construct a Chinese typewriter that is anything less than a small printing press or electronic brain have proved unsuccessful. The recent simplification of some of the more commonly used characters, though helpful, has not solved the basic problems inherent in the writing system.

On the other hand, the Chinese writing system has certain merits that the Western systems lack. The very complexity of the characters and their graphic qualities give them aesthetic values far beyond mere phonetic scripts. Calligraphy is a great art in East Asia and the ancestor of all the graphic arts, for the writing brush is also the brush of the painter. A distinguished hand has always been considered the mark of a well educated man.

The characters themselves also have a sort of vitality lacking in phonetic scripts. Once they have been learned, who can forget that the character for "peace" is a woman under a roof and the character for "bright" a combination of "sun" and "moon"? Chinese characters seem to carry with them richer substance and subtler overtones than the oral words they were designed to represent, thus lending themselves to a terse vividness in both prose and poetry that is quite unattainable in our phonetically-bound writing systems. Once mastered, they can also be read more rapidly than a phonetic script.

It is easy to imbue the character with magic qualities, as the ancient Chinese undoubtedly did. The written word always took precedence over the spoken. Chinese history is full of famous documents—memorials to the throne, essays, and poems—but few great speeches. Everything written, and particularly that which survived from antiquity, was considered to be of almost sacred value. Such attitudes may help account for the high store the peoples of East Asia have placed on book learning and formal education. It may seem ironic but it is no accident that literacy rates in East Asia tend to run much higher than in other areas of comparable economic level but simpler writing systems.

Another great advantage of the Chinese writing system is that it easily surmounts differences of dialect or even more fundamental linguistic barriers. All literate Chinese, even if they speak mutually unintelligible "dialects," can read the same books and feel that classical written Chinese is their own language. If they had had a phonetic system of writing, they might have broken up into separate national groups, as did the Italians, French, Spanish, and Portuguese. The stature of China as the largest national grouping in the world is to be explained at least in part by the writing system.

The larger unity of East Asian civilization has also depended on it in great part. A love and veneration for Chinese characters has been a strong link between the various countries. Until a century ago, most books written in Korea and Vietnam and many of those written in Japan were in classical Chinese, not in the national languages. Even today educated Chinese, Japanese, and Koreans can recognize thousands of words written in characters in books from the other two countries, even if they all pronounce these words quite differently. If China had had a phonetic system of writing, East Asia would certainly not have become so distinct a unit in world civilization.

Shang Culture

Next to writing, the most remarkable finds at An-yang and other Shang sites are bronzes, consisting largely of weapons or elaborate ceremonial vessels, often of imposing size. The vessels are covered with rich designs in sharply incised lines or high relief, suggesting clay or wooden prototypes. Their beauty is enhanced by patination of varied shades of green produced by the chemical action of the soil in which they lay. The quality of bronze casting in the late Shang was extremely fine and has never been surpassed anywhere in the world. The designs appear to be entirely East Asian. There are bronze tripods, for example, which hark back to the hollow-legged tripods of the Black Pottery culture. Some vessels were cast in the shape of animals, such as the elephant, which still inhabited North China in this period when the climate was somewhat warmer and wetter than it is today.

The chief design element on the bronzes is the *t'ao-t'ieh* or animal mask. It is a frontal view of an animal head, such as a water buffalo or ram, portrayed with angular lines in a highly conventional manner. Similar designs are found at An-yang on bone artifacts and marble sculptures. The whole Shang approach to the problem of design is quite distinct from anything known in the prehistoric or ancient West, where animals were normally portrayed in profile. There are, however, parallels in other East Asian countries, in the South Pacific, and among the Indians of the Pacific Northwest. This has given rise to the concept of a Pacific Basin type of design, of which the Shang offers the earliest example.

Inscriptions occur on some early bronzes, but most Shang writing has been found incised on the "dragon bones." These are actually the undershells of tortoises, the scapulae or shoulder blades of cattle, and other flattish bones. Since they were used in a method of divination, also practiced in the Black Pottery culture, they are often called "oracle bones" and this method of divination, scapulimancy. A small groove was carved on one side of the bone and heat was then applied near this thin spot, producing cracks from which the diviner somehow derived "yes" or "no" answers to his questions.

About a tenth of the "oracle bones" have inscribed on them the questions asked, and a few also have the answer and sometimes even the eventual outcome. The questions cover such matters as sacrifices to the deities, the weather, crops, war, hunting expeditions, aid or injury by an ancestor to his living descendants, and the luck of the next ten-day period, which already had been established as the East Asian "week." We can see how significant an activity divination was from the fact that the chief ministers of the rulers all seem to have been diviners. Sacrifices were also extremely important. Usually animals were used, but sometimes liquor, probably a sort of beer, was poured on the ground in libation. Sacrifices were made to various nature deities, the cardinal points, and to Ti or Shang Ti (Supreme Ti), who may have been a "first ancestor" of the Shang people.

The Shang State and Society.   The Shang economy was mainly agricultural. The Shang also had sheep and cattle but already seem to have had the traditional Chinese abhorrence for milk and milk products. Since bronze was rare and costly, agricultural tools were made of wood or stone. Cowrie shells were used as a sort of primitive money. These shells from southern waters have left their mark on the writing system: many characters having to do with wealth and trade have the "shell" signific. Jade was highly prized, as it has been throughout Chinese history.

Succession among the Shang rulers was often from brother to brother (thirteen cases) rather than from father to son (seventeen cases). Two of the successive capitals of these rulers were undoubtedly the cities unearthed near Cheng-chou and An-yang. How far beyond their walls they actually ruled is not known. Shang cultural remains are found scattered over a wide area in North China from the great bend of the Yellow River to central Shantung; but much of this area may have been ruled by vassal or even rival states, and the effective area of Shang control may have been fairly small. The Shang rulers were frequently at war with nearby neighbors and marauding herdsmen.

On the other hand, the state was big enough to field armies of three thousand to five thousand men, and the remains at Cheng-chou and An-yang are impressive. The style of architecture was essentially the same as that of modern China, contrasting with the stone architecture of the ancient West. The roof was carried by rows of wooden pillars, and the walls, at first made of pounded earth but in later times usually of brick, were merely non-structural screens. The pillars rested on individual foundation stones set on

SHANG AND EARLY CHOU BRONZE RITUAL VESSELS.
*The left vessel, of ku shape, is from the Shang; the
upper right, of yu shape, from the Shang or early Chou;
the lower right, of kuang shape, from the early Chou.
The upper right, vessel has a t'ao-t'ieh (animal mask)
of a water buffalo with upward curving horns, the
lower vessel a t'ao-t'ieh of a ram with in-curving horns.
Note the elephant above the t'ao-t'ieh.*

a platform of pounded earth. As is still the custom in North China, buildings were carefully oriented to face south.

Unlike the palace buildings, the houses of the common people appear to have been crude pit dwellings, as in Neolithic times. The gap between ruler and ruled is further illustrated by the grandiose scale of the royal tombs at An-yang. These were great pits, as much as forty-three feet deep and covering up to five thousand square feet, subsequently filled with beaten earth. It was customary to bury with the corpse articles of use and value, presumably for the benefit of the deceased in some afterlife. In the tombs have been found war chariots, which show that Shang was part of the war chariot culture that in the middle of the second millennium B.C. swept over the civilized world all the way from Greece to China.

Many bodies of both aristocrats and humble followers were also buried with the rulers, and there were other forms of human sacrifice, usually in multiples of ten and sometimes hundreds at a time. Some historians have concluded that the Shang was a slave society. In any case, the cleavage between ruler and ruled was very great. The Shang sovereigns, who may have started as little more than chief shamans mediating between the people and their ancestors and deities, developed during the roughly five centuries of Shang ascendancy into rulers of very great authority. Thus the tendency of the Chinese to establish and accept a unified, authoritarian state goes back to very early times.

Origins of the Authoritarian Pattern.   The early Chinese pattern of political absolutism has given rise to some interesting theories. A virtual monopoly of bronze metallurgy, bronze weapons, and chariots probably gave the ruling class great power over the other members of the state in Shang times. Certain broader factors may also have been operative. As we have seen, the family pattern of China lends itself to authoritarianism. The development of an absolute centralized state may also have been fostered by the constant need the Chinese felt for unified defense against their nomadic neighbors, as is illustrated by the Great Wall.

Some scholars have seen the need for huge cooperative efforts to keep the Yellow River within bounds and to provide for necessary drainage and irrigation as another source for the authoritarian state in China. A few men had to direct the work of a great many in order to complete these undertakings. Wherever such water-control efforts were necessary on a large scale, it is argued, a despotic or "Oriental" type of society developed, with absolutist monarchs supported by a bureaucratic official class ruling over dense peasant populations, as was the situation in ancient Egypt and Mesopotamia.

The myth that Yü, the founder of the Hsia dynasty, controlled the flood waters of China fits this theory well, and great coordinated efforts at water control did take place in the years leading up to the founding of the first great Chinese Empire. But this was about a millennium after the Shang, who themselves depended on rainfall rather than irrigation for agriculture. The water-control theory thus cannot explain the centralized absolutism of the Shang state, although it may help explain the continuance and strengthening of this pattern in later times.

The Early Chou

The Chou State.   The Chou people, who conquered the Shang around 1050 B.C., lived in the Wei Valley west of the great bend of the Yellow River. Their capital was near the modern city of Sian. While the Chou were themselves an agricultural people, they lived close to the sheep-herding barbarians of the Northwest and were culturally quite distinct from the Shang. The old Neolithic Black Pottery culture seems to have persisted in the Wei Valley almost to the time of the conquest.

The Chou apparently had become vassals of the Shang, protecting the western marches of the realm, but under three successive leaders, King Wen, King Wu, and the latter's brother, the Duke of Chou, they destroyed the Shang and overran all of North China. In fact, the wide spread of early Chou remains suggests that they conquered a much larger area than the Shang had ever dominated, stretching from the Wei Valley to the eastern extremity of Shantung and from southern Manchuria to the middle and lower Yangtze Valley.

The primitive communications of the time by chariot or wagon made it impossible to administer directly so large an area. The Duke of Chou established a secondary capital at the modern Loyang in the old heartland of the Shang, but otherwise the Chou rulers delegated authority to a large number of vassals. These were for the most part their descendants or relatives, but included unrelated henchmen and local aristocrats who had acknowledged Chou suzerainty. In time these vassals became graded in a strict hierarchy of prestige with titles usually translated duke, marquis, count, viscount, and baron. Each principality was in essence a small city-state, consisting of a walled town and its surrounding countryside. How many such states there were is not known. In the eighth century, however, after many had been absorbed by others but new peripheral ones had also been added, the number seems to have been about two hundred.

Each lord, while supposedly recognizing Chou suzerainty, enjoyed autonomy within his realm. The system has often been called "feudal," and the East Asians use the same term for it as for medieval Western and Japanese feudalism. It seems dubious, however, that "feudalism" is the right word. Much of our view of the early Chou is colored by the attitudes of later Chinese thinkers, who took the early Chou as a sort of "golden age" and read back into it their own desires for political unity and organization and the emphasis on ritual, propriety, and morality that they felt should be the governing principles in politics. The resultant picture does bear some resemblances to Western feudalism, but the actualities were probably far different. Effective control depended more on bonds of blood or pseudo-blood relationships than on feudal legal principles. The Chou system was probably closer to the system of rule through satraps in West Asia of the same period than to the feudal organization of Europe two millenniums later.

The Chou, like the Shang, had a sharply divided class society, in which the hereditary lord, supported by his aristocratic warriors, ruled over the peasant masses and the outright slaves, who were used largely as domestic servants. Later writers claimed that in the early Chou eight peasant families, each with its own field, would cultivate among them a central field for the support of the lord. This system has been called the "well field" system, because the character for "well" 井 depicts the pattern of nine fields that made a unit. This is obviously a later idealization, but it may reflect a period when agricultural property and its produce were communally shared.

Chou Culture.   The cultural backwardness of the Chou conquerors is attested by the fact that in the early Chou period much of the Shang culture continued almost without a break. Imposing bronze ritual vessels continued to be cast, many with lengthy inscriptions, but the designs sometimes were cruder than those of the Shang, and as the period progressed the details became weaker and plainer, perhaps because they had lost their original religious significance and had become merely traditional. The writing system continued its uninterrupted evolution, and scapulimancy was still practiced, although in time other forms of divination took its place.

Unlike the practice during the Shang, succession was from father to son (the Duke of Chou's failure to ascend the throne is a key case in point), and the kings were buried under massive, square earthen pyramids. The chief Chou deity was T'ien, which came to mean "Heaven" but was obviously anthropomorphic in origin, since the character for T'ien was originally a rough sketch of a man. The Chou kings called themselves the "Son of Heaven" and justified their conquest on the grounds that they had received the "Mandate of Heaven." The chief ceremonial activity of the kings centered around their ancestor "Heaven," while each community conducted sacrifices to the life-giving soil. Later dynasties continued these ancient rituals up until the twentieth century, and a round altar of Heaven and a square altar of Earth, both imposing structures, still stand in Peking.

3. Classic China: The Golden Age of Chinese Thought

The Later Chou

We do not know how long the early Chou maintained effective control over their wide conquests—perhaps not for long or only sporadically. The original bonds of loyalty between the kings and their vassals probably weakened over time. In 841 B.C., the tenth Chou king was driven out of his capital by its citizens, and an interregnum of thirteen years ensued. Marxist Chinese historians make much of this event as the first popular uprising in Chinese history. It produced considerable disruption, and perhaps this accounts for the fact that traditional Chinese dating becomes reliable only after that date.

The next king managed to resuscitate Chou power and is said to have led armies of 3000 chariots and 30,000 men, as compared with the 350 chariots used in the original conquest. In 770 B.C., however, what remained of Chou power was extinguished when "barbarians" in alliance with rebel Chinese principalities destroyed the capital. Tradition says that the thirteenth king, by lighting the beacon fires, had repeatedly summoned his vassals' troops merely to amuse a favorite concubine, and now when help was really needed no one responded. The royal line was re-established at the subsidiary capital of Loyang to the east, but the Chou kings never again exercised any real political or military power, retaining only certain religious and ceremonial functions until their final extinction in 256 B.C.

The period before 770 B.C. is called the Western Chou from the location of the capital, and the period after 770, the Eastern Chou. The Chinese, despite a strong emphasis on the decimal system in counting (they had little

33

use for dozens, the seven-day week, and the like), have not traditionally counted time by centuries. Instead they have divided history into dynastic segments, such as the Western Chou and the Eastern Chou. The Chinese further subdivide part of the Eastern Chou into two shorter periods, the names of which will be explained later. These are the "Spring and Autumn" period, usually dated 722–481, and the "Warring States" period, commonly dated 403–221. The chronological chart included in this volume will help the reader coordinate the Chinese dynasties and periods with the Western system of counting years.

Technological and Economic Growth.   Later Chinese, imbued with the ideal of a unified empire, have looked back on the Eastern Chou as a period of hopeless disunity. But it was an age of dynamic growth, bursting energy, and tremendous creativity. Possibly the very lack of central authority and the multiplicity of rival states served as stimuli. In many ways the Eastern Chou is the most exciting and romantic phase of Chinese history.

In the eighth century B.C., China was still technologically behind West Asia, but by the end of the period it had largely caught up and already was the most populous land on earth. The seven largest of the Chinese states together may have had in the neighborhood of 20 million people—quite comparable to the whole of West Asia and the Mediterranean area. Iron, which had appeared about a millennium earlier in the West, became common in China by the fifth century B.C. Iron replaced bronze for weapons, and iron farming tools and the ox-drawn plow brought an agricultural revolution to China. Hitherto unfarmed areas in North China were brought under the plow, and the remaining islands of "barbarian" peoples were absorbed into the dominant culture. Grain yields were also greatly expanded by large-scale irrigation and other water-control projects, and great effort was devoted to the construction of transport canals, indicating the growth of the economic unit and the rising need to move large quantities of tax grains and other commodities over long distances.

The growth of production was accompanied by a rapid development of trade and a tremendous increase in wealth. As the Chou period progresses one hears more and more of wealthy merchants of all types. This newly risen class proved disruptive to the old aristocratic order, which perhaps in self-defense, propagated a theory that society consists of four classes: the warrior-administrators at the top, the peasants or primary producers next, the artisans or secondary producers third, and last of all the merchants, whose economic value seemed dubious to the aristocrats. However unrealistic this theory was even in late Chou times, it remained East Asian dogma for the next two millenniums.

While bolts of silk and ingots of precious metal had come into early use as media of exchange and continued to be used until modern times, copper coinage became prevalent at this time. At first the coins were in the shape of small agricultural tools in the western parts of the country and small knives in the east, but before the end of the Chou era the copper cash, a small round coin with a square hole for stringing purposes, had come into use, and it remained the standard Chinese coin until late in the nineteenth century. The late Chou also saw the appearance of other characteristic features of Chinese civilization, such as chopsticks and lacquer.

The States of the Eastern Chou Period.   Hand in hand with technological and economic progress went a steady growth of the effective political unit, as the great water-control activity of the latter centuries of the era clearly shows. Among the welter of petty city-states that covered the North China Plain, some ten already stood out by the eighth century B.C. as larger and more efficient units. These states, however, lost their leadership in later centuries to those on the periphery of the Chou cultural area. Crowded together in the center, they had less room for growth, and they were probably more constrained by tradition from making innovations in political, military, and economic techniques. The states of Lu and Sung, for example, despite the proud tradition that their rulers were descended from the Duke of Chou and the Shang royal line respectively, and despite their prominence in the early years of the Eastern Chou, gradually degenerated to the status of satellites of the peripheral states.

Ch'i was typical of the border states. Located on the eastern edge of the North China Plain, it extended its sway over the greater part of the hilly Shantung Peninsula, increasing its area sixfold in the seventh and sixth centuries B.C. and winning control over an area comparable to a modern Chinese province. On the north, in modern Shansi Province, the state of Chin carved out a comparable domain. Beyond it to the northeast, in the area around the modern Peking, was Yen, from which has been derived the literary name for Peking: Yen-ching, or the "Yen capital." In the west, Ch'in, regarded as semi-"barbarian" by the others, replaced the Chou in the Wei Valley.

In the south, the semi-"barbarian" state of Ch'u had by the eighth century built up a vast domain along the middle reaches of the Yangtze River. From the start it rejected the empty pretense of Chou rule by calling its own rulers *wang,* or "kings." To its east the state of Wu had by the sixth century come to dominate the area around the lower Yangtze. Recent archaeological discoveries indicate that it grew from an early Chou outpost among "barbarian" peoples. On the coastal region beyond Wu appeared the powerful state of Yüeh. Situated in a region of great lakes and navigable rivers, these three southern states were water powers, with fleets as well as armies. Wu is the origin of the name "Wu dialect" for the language of the Shanghai area, and in Yüeh we have the first appearance of a name that clung to the edge of the

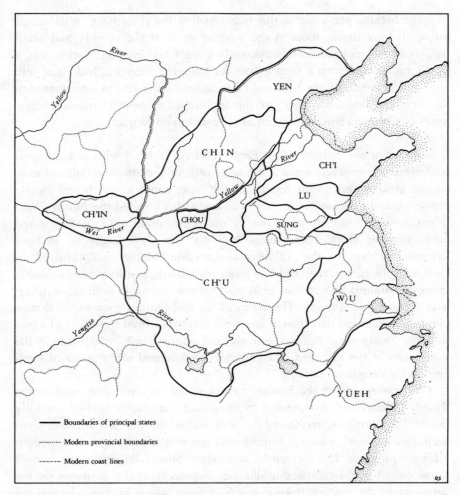

CHINA IN THE SIXTH CENTURY B.C.

advancing southern boundary of the Chinese cultural area, coming to rest eventually in Vietnam, or "Yüeh South."

The regions ruled by the great peripheral states fell for the most part within the area of the early Chou conquests, but they were in part inhabited by what people in the Chinese heartland considered to be "barbarians." On the north and west these "barbarians" presumably were pastoral folk, some perhaps already Chinese-speaking. In the south, they were agricultural people like the Chinese but were said to speak unintelligible tongues (though these were probably related Sinitic languages) and they clearly had many other distinctive cultural features. The incorporation of these "barbarian" peoples into the Chinese cultural area during the Eastern Chou period was the start of the great process of acculturation by which the originally non-

Chinese peoples of the Yangtze Valley and South China were gradually drawn into the main stream of Chinese civilization, except for a few still unassimilated remnants in the extreme southwest.

Political and Social Innovation.   The early Chou city-states were highly aristocratic societies. Their ruling lords claimed a sort of religious legitimacy as the maintainers of sacrifices to the common ancestors, and their warrior henchmen were largely their own relatives. But as technology advanced, wealth increased, trade grew, population rose, and the political unit expanded, this old form of aristocratic, almost tribal organization became outmoded. Many of the individual states became too large and complex for such family-like control.

The old communal use of land was gradually replaced by private ownership, and powerful new families, whose wealth was based on the lands they owned or on commerce, replaced the old aristocracy of close relatives of the lords. Newly risen families of this sort sometimes even overthrew and replaced the old rulers. One famous example of this was the split up of the northern state of Chin into the successor states of Han, Wei, and Chao. This occurred in 453 B.C. and was officially recognized by the Chou king in 403. Both dates are used as the start of the "Warring States" period.

If large domains were to be kept under control and if subjects were not to challenge the authority of their lords, there had to be stronger and more effective methods of rule than were used in the old aristocratic society. The result was the development of more impersonal political institutions and a greater centralization of power. Several important innovations of this sort are attributed to Duke Huan (685–643 B.C.) of the eastern state of Ch'i and his able minister Kuan-tzu, to whom a later book of this name is popularly attributed. They are said to have divided the population of Ch'i into geographic units controlled by the central government, instituted a uniform tax system, and reorganized the military forces by requiring that the various geographic subunits provide levies for a central army, instead of relying on such household units as the hereditary aristocracy might bring into the field. Ch'i is also said to have had an active economic policy, attempting to control prices, regulate weights and measures, and encourage trade. The first state monopolies of salt and iron production, which were to become major economic supports of centralized government in China, are also traditionally attributed to Kuan-tzu.

It is hard to say how many of these innovations actually date back to the seventh century B.C. or took place first in Ch'i. State monopolies probably did not develop that early, but all the reforms attributed to Kuan-tzu were important innovations that had appeared in China by the latter part of the Chou period. Unquestionably a major aspect of the centralization of power was the establishment of a uniform, centrally controlled system of local government and the development of a clear system of agricultural taxes. Another key factor was the appearance of bureaucratic administrators to replace the old related aristocrats as the aides of the ruler. Kuan-tzu himself is the first clear example of such a bureaucrat. Written law codes also came to replace the old system of personal rule on the basis of accepted tradition. The first known to history was that of Duke Wen (445–396) of Wei, one of the three successor states of Chin.

Military Development.   Meanwhile the scale and nature of warfare had also changed. In earlier times, strict rules of combat had apparently been observed, and there was a strong feeling that, even if subjugated, other noble lines should not be extinguished. Through this emphasis on legitimacy, the weaker central states may have sought to check the menace of the peripheral powers. But now warfare became much larger in scale and more ruthless. Conquered states were obliterated and turned into centrally controlled provinces of the victor. In the fourth and third centuries, all the principal states followed the lead of Ch'u in assuming the title of king for their rulers, thus indicating that they no longer recognized even the theory of Chou supremacy. While chariots continued in use until the late Chou, cheap iron weapons had led to a great increase in the size of fighting forces. Peasant foot soldiers replaced the aristocratic charioteers, who had been armed with expensive bronze weapons, as the backbone of the armies, which now numbered in the tens of thousands.

Another military innovation was the use of cavalry. Horseback riding, first developed by the pastoral peoples of Central and West Asia, had significant cultural influences on the Chinese wholly aside from its military impact. The greater mobility made possible by horseback riding speeded up communications between the agricultural civilizations of West and East Asia. This may account for the more rapid flow at this time of Western inventions and ideas to China, thus helping to close the technological gap that had once existed. Even in the field of the visual arts, for example, the Western emphasis on portrayal in silhouette, as transmitted by the intermediary nomads, came to replace the old Shang approach to design.

The use of the horse made the pastoral northern neighbors of China a greater military threat than they had been before. One result of this was the erection by the northern Chinese states of long walls, which when later unified became the Great Wall of China. Another result was the replacement of chariots by cavalry in Chinese armies. This change was perhaps hastened by the introduction of the crossbow, probably a local invention, which, together with the old native composite bow, made the cavalry a formidable force. Still another result of horseback riding was the introduction of close-fitting jackets and trousers, which were more convenient than the full sleeves and flowing robes of the traditional garb. The Chinese thus started on their way

Mounted archer design in silhouette, stamped on a late Chou tile.

to becoming the first great agricultural people to clothe both men and women in trousers.

The Search for Political Stability. The states of the Eastern Chou period, in the face of fading Chou authority and the growing ferocity of warfare, made many efforts to minimize fighting and stabilize the political situation. Bilateral or multilateral interstate conferences were held with considerable frequency; disarmament proposals were discussed; treaties were signed and alliances formed. Marriages between princely lines were an important means of strengthening alliances, while hostages were widely used to insure the loyalty of a satellite state.

The semi-"barbarian" state of Ch'u in the south posed a special threat to the states of the North China Plain, and they frequently leagued together against Ch'u. This league first took effective shape in 651, when Duke Huan of Ch'i was recognized as hegemon of the confederation. The system of hegemony, however, gave China only brief and sporadic stability, lasting no longer than the lifetime of each strong man who was able to establish himself as hegemon. After Duke Huan, the next to achieve this status was the duke of Chin in 632. The original purpose of the system was completely lost when the king of Ch'u became the third hegemon before the turn of the century. At times during the sixth century B.C. some stability was achieved through a formalized balance of power between Chin in the north and Ch'u in the south. Wu meanwhile had been rising rapidly on Ch'u's eastern frontier and in 482 won recognition as the paramount military power of China, only to be crushed and annexed in 473 by Yüeh, the most "barbarian" of all the states.

There were no further attempts to organize an interstate order in ancient China. Brute conquest had become the order of the day. After the breakup of Chin in 453 B.C., the chief contenders for supremacy were Ch'i in the east, Ch'in in the west, and Ch'u in the south. Ch'u exterminated Yüeh in 334 and the small central state of Lu in 249. Ch'i, surviving a usurpation of the throne, annexed the central state of Sung in 286, and Ch'in calmly exterminated Chou itself in 256. Finally, in a series of great campaigns between 230 and 221 B.C., Ch'in conquered all the remaining independent states, unifying China for the first time and opening a new phase in its history.

The Age of the Philosophers and the Classics

The Early Philosophers.   The Eastern Chou was a period of great economic growth, social change, and political development. The failure of old authority, both temporal and spiritual, as well as the current innovations, posed new problems. Time-worn traditions had to be discarded and new guiding values found. Men's minds could wander at will and did range more freely than ever again in East Asian history.

One is struck by the parallel in time between this intellectual outburst in China and the heyday of the Greek philosophers, the Hebraic prophets, and the historical Buddha and other early religious leaders in India. Throughout the whole civilized world it was a time of prodigious philosophical activity. One reason for this may have been mutual intellectual stimulation between the great centers of civilization in this age of accelerated communications. Another may have been that all these areas had by this time become wealthy enough to support large numbers of thinkers. Moreover, the increased pace of human invention was shattering traditional points of view, and therefore men everywhere were beginning consciously to grapple with the fundamental problems of the meaning and purpose of life and society. The challenge was the same, but the answers varied greatly, setting the civilizations of the Mediterranean, South Asia, and East Asia off in decidedly different directions. The contrasting philosophical attitudes developed during this great age of intellectual ferment still stand out among the factors that differentiate these major cultural zones.

Chinese philosophical interest from this time on centered primarily on man as a social and political animal. It was overwhelmingly "humanistic," or perhaps one should say "social," because the emphasis was more on society than on the individual. This was in sharp contrast to the emphasis on the divine and otherworldly in the traditional philosophies of India and the Mediterranean world. It is difficult to determine why Chinese thought took this particular direction. Possibly political and social problems posed themselves more vividly to Chinese minds because the interstate anarchy of the Chou period existed within a single large cultural unit.

The early Chinese philosophers, in any case, were first of all practical politicians. They were part of the new class of bureaucrats, produced by the spread of literacy and the needs of an increasingly complex political system. Such men often wandered from state to state, offering their services where they would be most appreciated. Great thinkers among them, whether successful or not as practical politicians, attracted followers and thus became teachers. Their disciples gradually formed into schools of philosophy, and from these schools the sayings of the original masters, as reworked and supplemented by many later hands, eventually emerged as the philosophical books of Chou times.

The Classics. Although the philosophers were often daring innovators, many of them looked to supposedly golden ages of the past for their inspiration, as have many other thinkers elsewhere in the world. In a civilization particularly concerned with the problems of society, it was natural that history, as the repository of human experience, should become the special focus of attention. This interest in the past, together with the peculiar Chinese respect for the written word, produced a tremendous veneration for the writings of earlier times. This, of course, has been a common trait throughout the world, but it seems to have been particularly strong among the Chinese. Confucius and other ancient Chinese philosophers looked upon the writings of earlier ages as classics from which they drew their own teachings, and this idea persisted in East Asia until recent times. For over two thousand years Chinese scholars, when faced with new problems, tried to wring the answers from reinterpretations of the classics.

To the Chinese, with their love of order and classification, "the Classics" is not just a vague term for ancient literature in general but means a clearly specified set of books associated with the dominant Confucian tradition. These works, together with the vast body of commentaries that has grown up around them, constitute the first of the traditional four divisions of Chinese literature. The various listings of the Classics were all made after Chou times and consequently contain works of diverse epochs, but the Five Classics, the earliest and most important listing, dating from the second century B.C., include the most ancient and most venerated works.

The first of the Five Classics is the *Classic of Songs* (*Shih ching,* also known as the *Book of Poetry*), which consists of 305 songs dating from the tenth to the seventh centuries B.C. Some are love songs, others political poems or ritual hymns, but all are characterized by such patterns of meter, rhythm, and rhyme that they clearly are not just folk songs but the products of a sophisticated literary tradition. Poetry was obviously an important part of Chinese culture even at this early time, and the ability to recite and also to compose poetry has remained ever since the mark of the educated man.

The *Classic of Documents* (*Shu ching,* also known as the *Book of History*) contains semihistorical documents and speeches dating from the early centuries of the Chou period, but a large part of the text is now known to consist of later forgeries. The development of two differing versions of the *Shu ching* in the second century B.C. and the problem of the forged portions of the work have led to endless philological and philosophical controversy ever since.

The *Classic of Changes* (*I ching,* also known as the *Book of Divination*) is another work of mixed age. It is built up around the eight trigrams and sixty-four hexagrams which developed as a system of divination alternative to scapulimancy. The eight trigrams, which are frequently portrayed in East Asian art, are all the possible permutations of three-line combinations of complete or broken lines. If six lines are used instead of three, the possible combinations number sixty-four. Probably by drawing odd or even numbers of stalks of the milfoil plant, a specific trigram or hexagram could be selected, and the *Classic of Changes* would then be consulted on this hexagram. It was, in other words, a diviner's handbook.

The *Spring and Autumn Annals* (*Ch'un ch'iu*) is a brief chronological record of major events that occurred in the state of Lu or were reported there. The period it covers from 722 to 481 B.C. became known as the "Spring and Autumn" period. The text is terse and entirely factual, but Confucius, according to tradition, and certainly later philosophers read great philosophical significance into the choice of words used to describe each event. The tradition that Confucius himself compiled this work, however, is undoubtedly false.

The last of the Five Classics, the *Record of Rituals* (*Li chi,* also known as the *Book of Rites*), is a compilation made in the second century B.C. out of earlier materials dealing with rites and rituals. These were, as we shall see, key elements in the whole Confucian concept of social order, and this classic clearly stems from the Confucian tradition. The others, too, became so closely identified with Confucianism that all five are commonly called the Confucian Classics.

More than a thousand years after the end of the Chou, four relatively short works were selected from the vast mass of classical literature as the supreme embodiment of Confucian teachings. These, known as the Four Books, included two chapters taken from the *Record of Rituals:* the *Great Learning* (*Ta hsüeh*) and the *Doctrine of the Mean* (*Chung yung*). The other two works were the *Analects* (*Lun-yü,* literally meaning "Conversations") of Confucius himself and a comparable work of his greatest successor, the *Mencius* (*Meng-tzu*). The *Analects* and *Mencius* together with the Five Classics and a few other early works are also commonly classified as the

A carved white jade showing the yin-yang *symbol (see page 49) surrounded by the eight trigrams.*

Thirteen Classics. In this grouping, the *Spring and Autumn Annals* counts as three works because of its three so-called commentaries. Two are simple exegetical works, but the third, the *Tso chuan* (*Tradition of Tso*), is an elaborate political history, containing much imaginative reconstruction of detail but constituting nevertheless the chief historical source for the period.

The writings of non-Confucian philosophers were never included among the Classics, and various other ancient works of comparable historical or literary interest to the Classics failed to win official acceptance. The most outstanding poetic collection of the late Chou period was the *Elegies of Ch'u* (*Ch'u tz'u*), made up largely of poems by Ch'ü Yüan, an aristocrat of the southern state of Ch'u who lived at the beginning of the third century B.C. His *Li sao* includes a fanciful flight through time and space that shows a rich imagination quite absent from the *Classic of Songs* and perhaps characteristic of the semi-"barbarian" peoples of the South.

Confucianism and Taoism

Confucius. It is fitting that the first man we know to have been a pro-professional teacher and philosopher in China should always have been recognized in East Asia as the greatest of all teachers and philosophers. We call him Confucius, the Latinized form of K'ung-fu-tzu (the *tzu* meant "Master"). He lived around 551–479 B.C., and what we know of him is largely drawn from the *Analects*. This work consists for the most part of Confucius' answers to questions, prefaced by the phrase, "The Master said." It was written by disciples or perhaps by disciples of disciples and includes many later additions.

Confucius was a native of the tradition-bound central state of Lu. He aspired to high political office and wandered in vain from state to state in search of appointment. Thus, in his chosen role as a practical politician, he was a failure; in his incidental occupation as a teacher, however, time proved him an unparalleled success. At first glance the concepts Confucius taught seem unexciting and flat. He showed the bias of his day in his paramount interest in political problems. While he fully recognized the spirits and Heaven (T'ien), sometimes showing a sense of mission derived from the latter, he was obviously not much interested in the suprahuman realm. To an inquiry about death, he replied, "Not yet understanding life, how can you understand death?" Even in the political sphere, he merely claimed to be a ·devoted student of antiquity and transmitter of the wisdom of the past. The disorder of his own day, he felt, could be corrected if men would return to the political and social order supposedly created by the founders of the Chou dynasty, King Wen and the Duke of Chou.

To return to the ancient Way, Confucius felt, men must play their assigned roles in a fixed society of authority. The idea is succinctly expressed in the statement: "Let the ruler be a ruler and the subject a subject; let the father be a father and the son a son." Later this concept was expressed by the term "the rectification of names" (*cheng ming*), by which Confucians really meant that society should be made to conform with theory.

All this sounds ultraconservative, but Confucius was in fact a great, though probably unconscious, innovator in his basic concept that good government was fundamentally a matter of ethics. He did not question the hereditary right of the lords to rule, but he insisted that their first duty was to set a proper example of sound ethical conduct. In a day when might was right, he argued that the ruler's virtue and the contentment of the people, rather than power, should be the true measures of political success. Chinese thought before Confucius might be characterized as premoral; it centered on auguries and sacrifices. Confucius was China's first great moralist, the founder of a great ethical tradition in a civilization which above all others came to concentrate on ethical values.

FILIAL PIETY. *Later Confucianists emphasized filial piety as a
cardinal virtue. A famous story, illustrated (top) in this Han stone
engraving (second century A.D.), tells of "Old Lai-tzu," who in
order to show his seventy-year-old parents that seventy is not old,
amuses them by dressing and playing like a small child. "Old
Lai-tzu" became one of the Twenty-Four Stories of Filial Piety,
memorized by every youngster. Dressed like a child (right),
he plays with toys (a Sung painting by Chao Meng-chien,
1199–1295), and in a Shanghai woodblock of 1873 (left) he
amuses his parents by purposely stumbling with his buckets.*

Confucius' ideal was the *chün-tzu,* literally "ruler's son" or "aristocrat,"
a term which at his hand changed its meaning from "a noble" to "a man
of nobility." It is perhaps best translated as "gentleman" in the sense of a
cultivated man or superior man. He had a great deal to say about the

virtues the "gentleman" should possess. These were uprightness or inner integrity (*chih*), righteousness (*i*), conscientiousness toward others or loyalty (*chung*), altruism or reciprocity (*shu*), and above all, love or human-heartedness (*jen*).

The necessary qualities of the "gentleman," Confucius felt, were not limited to these inner virtues. He must also have *wen,* meaning "culture" or possibly "polish," and *li,* literally "ritual," that is, an understanding of proper etiquette and social usage. Confucius was not interested in producing "diamonds in the rough." As he says, "Uprightness uncontrolled by etiquette becomes rudeness." Like Aristotle, he felt that proper music helped produce the proper ethical attitudes. His emphasis on the *li* of antiquity contributed to the tremendous importance of ritual and etiquette in later Confucianism and the reliance in East Asia on inculcating inner attitudes through the practice of external forms—a sound pedagogical principle that may be too little honored in the contemporary West.

The judicious balancing of inner virtues and external polish is characteristic of the moderation of Confucius in all his ideas. Great philosophers and religious leaders in India and in the West have commonly dealt in absolutes; that is, they have tended to emphasize logical and mathematical absolutes. Confucius was a relativist, thinking in social and human terms. He set the East Asian pattern of compromise, of always seeking the middle path. As the *Mencius* so aptly says, "Confucius did not go to extremes."

Moderation and balance may help explain the eventual triumph of Confucianism. Its basic political conservatism made it popular with most subsequent rulers in East Asia, and its high ethical principles gave political authority a stronger foundation than mere hereditary right and served as a constant stimulus for the improvement of government. Another basic reason for its success was its timeliness. A bureaucracy of the educated was slowly growing up in China in response to political needs, and this functional group required a philosophy, which Confucius admirably supplied. While never questioning the legitimacy of hereditary power, Confucius assumed that men of superior learning, whatever their original social status, had the right to tell the rulers how they should conduct themselves and their government. Confucius thus propounded the idea of a "career open to talent" —a concept that was essentially revolutionary and an implicit challenge to hereditary power.

Taoism. Next to Confucianism, the most important stream in Chinese thought is Taoism (pronounced *dowism*). It was in large part a philosophy of retreat and withdrawal on the part of thinkers who were appalled by perpetual warfare, instability, and death and so turned away from the struggle for power, status, and wealth. In the face of infinite time and space, they accepted the unimportance of individuality except as human beings are individual manifestations of vast cosmic forces. This philosophy constituted a protest of common men against the growing despotism of rulers. It also expressed the rebellion of the very uncommon man of intellect or sensitivity against the growing rigidity of the moralists, who were following in the footsteps of Confucius. Where both the moralists and the rulers sought to bring men into conformity with social patterns, the Taoists stoutly championed the independence of each individual, whose only concern, they maintained, should be to fit into the great pattern of nature. This was the *Tao,* literally the "Road" or "Way," a term used by Confucius to describe the social system he advocated but given a metaphysical interpretation in Taoism.

Some scholars have associated early Taoism with the state of Ch'u in the Yangtze Valley, suggesting that it may represent an enrichment of Chinese thought derived in part from "barbarian" sources. Its attempt to fit human life into nature's rhythms may also represent a philosophical expression of the interest of the early Chinese in nature deities, fertility cults, and the ruler's role as mediator between nature and man. Taoist mysticism, which may have been at the core of the movement, might also have derived from the early shamans. The latter, through self-induced trances, had communicated directly with the spirits; the Taoists, through "sitting and forgetting" and "fasts of the mind," experienced trance-like ecstasies in which they achieved the state of the "true man" and directly apprehended the oneness of the universe. Such practices may have been influenced by Indian yoga, for the Taoists, like the Indians, emphasized breathing exercises.

Our chief knowledge of Taoism of the Chou period is derived from three books of unknown authorship and somewhat doubtful date. The most venerated of these is the *Lao-tzu* or *Tao te ching (The Way and Power Classic).* It is a composite text, probably dating from the third century B.C., though attributed to a presumably mythical sage known as Lao-tzu, or the "Old Master," whose traditional dates have been fixed to give him a slight edge in seniority over Confucius. Terse and cryptic in style, the *Tao te ching* has given itself to diverse interpretations by later Chinese thinkers and a startling variety of translations into Western languages.

The second text is the *Chuang-tzu,* also probably of the third century B.C. but attributed to a man of this name of the late fourth century. Consisting of delightful parables, metaphors, and poetic passages, it is a work of high literary merit and represents the most important formulation of early Taoist thought. The third work, the *Lieh-tzu,* which in content and style is much like the *Chuang-tzu,* is variously attributed to the same period or to the third century A.D.

Like all mystics, the Taoists found it difficult to express their basic ideas in words. As they said, "The one who knows does not speak, and the one who speaks does not know." The *Tao* is founded on a nameless, formless "Non-being" which is, in essence, the totality of the natural processes. Despite constant flux, the *Tao* is unitary, having no distinctions of big or little, good or bad, life or death. The relativity of all things and the dependence of any quality on its opposite are constant Taoist themes. As they say, "Water, which is life to fish, is death to man," and "It is only because everyone recognizes beauty as beauty that we have the idea of ugliness."

The man who can transcend mundane human distinctions and become one with the *Tao* is "beyond all harm" and achieves "tranquillity in the midst of strife." The key to merging with the *Tao* is *wu-wei* or "doing nothing." By this the Taoists did not mean complete inaction but rather doing what comes naturally: "Do nothing and nothing will be not done." If left to itself, the universe proceeds smoothly according to its own harmonies. Man's efforts to change or improve nature only destroy these harmonies and produce chaos. There is a knack to all spontaneous accomplishment which conscious effort only mars. The sage knows no ambition and therefore experiences no failure. He does not even attempt to teach others. By this criterion, our Taoist authors are themselves clearly imperfect.

The Taoists were sufficiently in tune with the prevailing interests of the day to draw their own picture of a perfect society. Like other Chinese philosophers, they looked back to a golden age, but for them this past was a time of perfect knowledge, before the ancients even realized that "things had come into existence," much less had recognized the "distinction" between things or reached the consequent expression of "approval and disapproval." The concept of good and bad and the embodiment of this concept in rituals, they felt, were the real sources of human misery. The Confucian sages thus were the unwitting villains of history. The virtues they had invented were the reasons for the existence of vice. Law was the source of crime; without wealth there could be no stealing.

Primitivity was the ideal of the Taoists. Knowledge can only corrupt. In the *Chuang-tzu* we find the parable of Primitivity, whose two friends, Change and Uncertainty, decided to give him the usual seven apertures that are needed for seeing, hearing, breathing, and eating; this they did with success, boring one a day, but Primitivity died in the process. The Taoists laud the peasant who, though he knew of the water wheel, chose to carry water up from a well on his back, realizing that ingenious devices would lead to a devious mind. The political ideal of the Taoists was a small state from which the cocks and dogs of a nearby state could be heard, but whose people were so content that none had ever bothered to visit this neighboring village. Over such a primitive, passive society the Taoist sage would rule, without effort and without benevolence, accomplishing everything by doing nothing.

Taoism, as a school of philosophy, suffered serious debasement in later centuries, but its basic attitudes remained strong throughout Chinese history. It obviously supplied things which otherwise were weak or lacking in Chinese society. Growing political conformity and heavy Confucian morality were not conducive to aesthetic expression. The Chinese, however, have always had a strong aesthetic urge, which the individual freedom of Taoism and its mystical union with nature encouraged. Chinese artists and poets, however closely identified with the Confucian tradition, have usually been Taoists at heart.

Taoism, in fact, has served as an admirable balance to the dominant concepts of Chinese culture. The centralization of power placed sharp limits on human freedom; Confucian morality and insistence on social conformity were even more restrictive. But in Taoism the individual could achieve self-expression; his intellect was free to wander at will. Since neither Confucianism nor Taoism were jealously exclusive religions in the Western sense, the individual and even the whole of society could be Confucian and Taoist at the same time, achieving perhaps a healthier psychological balance on these two bases than could have been achieved on only one. The man in power was usually a Confucian positivist, seeking to save society. The same man out of power became a Taoist quietist, intent on blending with nature around him. The active bureaucrat of the morning became the dreamy poet or nature lover of the evening. This balanced dualism in philosophy and in personality has persisted until the modern day.

Other Philosophic Schools

The Naturalists and the Logicians. Confucianism and Taoism were by no means the only philosophies that flourished in late Chou times. With a characteristic love of categorizing, the Chinese have dubbed the proliferation of philosophical teachings in this period "The Hundred Schools."

One school, which might be called the Naturalists, consisted of men who attempted to explain nature's working on the basis of certain cosmic principles. One of their concepts was the basic dualism of nature: *yang* is male, light, hot, active; *yin* is female, dark, cold, passive. Unlike the dualism of the Mediterranean world, in which good and evil are in perpetual conflict, *yin* and *yang* are mutually complementary and balancing. The greater *yang* grows, the sooner it will yield to *yin*; the sun at noon is starting to give way to night. The interdependence of the two principles was well symbolized by an interlocking figure (see page 43), which today is used as the central element in the flag of the Republic of Korea. Actually, the *yin-yang* concept often seems more useful than Western dualism for analyzing nature and also human affairs. It neatly fits the rhythms of day and night, summer and winter, and the balancing roles of male and female. To apply it to the subject matter of this chapter, one might say that Confucianism is the *yang* of Chinese thought and Taoism the *yin*.

Another basic concept of the Naturalists was that all nature is made up of varying combinations of the "five elements" or "five powers": wood, metal, fire, water, and earth. The parallel to the four elements of the Greeks (earth, fire, air, and water) is striking. The "five elements" concept led in time to the development of an extensive pseudoscience that persisted through later ages. Cosmic correlations were worked out among the five elements and other categories of five: colors, tastes, sounds, planets, directions (including the center), and so on. With the addition of numerology and astrology, the possibilities became infinite. The ancient calendar signs were also incorporated into the system. These were the ten "heavenly stems" and twelve "earthly branches" (associated with the signs of the zodiac). When combined together in a sequence of pairs of characters, these formed the traditional cycle of sixty, which was used for counting time in periods of sixty days and sixty years. As applied to the lay of the land and the proper locations for houses, graves, and the like, this pseudoscience became geomancy (*feng-shui,* literally meaning "wind and water").

Another group of philosophers, the Logicians or School of Names, like the Sophists of Greece, were groping toward a system of logic by analyzing the meaning of words. For example, one of their most famous propositions propounded in the fourth century B.C. was that "a white horse is not a horse," presumably meaning that the adjective "white," in this phrase, makes "white horse" no longer applicable to the universal concept "horse." The ideas of the Logicians were condemned by later Chinese as frivolous and unprofitable.

Mo-tzu.   Confucianism's chief early competitor was the school of Mo-tzu, who was born around or soon after the death of Confucius. His teachings are found in a work known as the *Mo-tzu,* which contains essays, as well as dialogues like those in the *Analects.* Mo-tzu's concentrated attacks on Confucianism suggest that he may have represented a heretical offshoot of that school, while his interest in logic may have given rise to the school of Logicians.

In most matters Mo-tzu took a more extreme stand than Confucius. Where the latter advocated that men of learning should guide the rulers, Mo-tzu saw no reason why hereditary princes should not relinquish their thrones to their obvious superiors. While Confucius had been a traditionalist at heart, Mo-tzu was strictly a utilitarian. He advocated measures to enrich the country, increase the population, and bring order to the state. Anything that did not contribute to these ends he attacked with vehemence. Food, clothing, and housing should be limited to bare necessities. He had no use for any aesthetic expression and advocated the suppression of all emotions. Music and all the ceremonial *li* of the Confucianists were wasteful. In particular, Mo-tzu inveighed against elaborate funerals and the three-year period of mourning for one's parents, which were part of the Confucian system. Warfare was the greatest waste of all. His solution to the problems it poses was to develop the defense until offense became impractical. The history of the next two centuries presents overwhelming evidence of the failure of Mo-tzu's pacifistic views, and later ages esteemed his writings far less than they did the *Sun-tzu,* the late Chou classic on the military arts.

Mo-tzu did favor sacrifices to the spirits as bringing worldly blessings, and he accepted a moral Heaven which would provide the final sanction for his teachings by meting out appropriate rewards and punishments. There was thus a definitely authoritarian strain in his teachings. From his large following he demanded strict obedience, and he bequeathed his authority to a line of Grand Masters of the school. Not unnaturally, he envisioned a rigidly disciplined state, in which the subordinate at each level would follow the lead of his superior in all matters.

Mo-tzu's panacea for achieving his utilitarian utopia was the doctrine of universal love. The Confucians, accepting the family system and the complexities of society, were developing at this time a theory of graded love, dependent on the specific relationships among individuals. Mo-tzu felt that the interests of all would be better served if "everyone would love every other person as much as he loves himself."

It is an interesting question why Mo-tzu's school did not survive the third century B.C. He had a better organized following than Confucius, and for a while his ideas may have had greater currency. The Westerner recognizes in his "universal love," utilitarianism, pacifism, awareness of the other-worldly, and interest in problems of logic, concepts that could have greatly enriched Chinese thought. But Mo-tzu's ideas may have seemed too extreme to the Chinese of his time. They did not care for his austere utilitarianism and complete lack of psychological subtlety; they preferred the moderate but practical graded love of the Confucians to his lofty but seemingly impractical "universal love."

Mencius and Hsün-tzu. A philosopher who succeeded where Mo-tzu failed in passing on his doctrines to later ages was Meng-tzu, known to the West in the Latinized form, Mencius. His book, the *Mencius,* was in the twelfth century elevated to the status of a classic, second only to the *Analects.* A long work of great literary merit and deep psychological perception, the *Mencius* has left a profound mark on East Asian civilization.

Mencius, who lived around 370–290 B.C., came from an area near Lu. Like Confucius, he wandered from state to state seeking high government office without success. But he and his large retinue of disciples were well received by a series of rulers, whom Mencius treated with surprising disdain. Mencius considered himself merely a transmitter of Confucius' Way of the ancients, but in fact he added important new emphases. One was that man is by nature good. Anyone, he pointed out, will spontaneously feel alarm and pity if he suddenly sees a child about to fall into a well. (Such reasoning by example and analogy is typical of Mencius and most of the philosophers of his day.) This inborn goodness can be developed by inner self-cultivation and also by education. Men should consciously strive to extend their love to those beyond the narrow family circle, which spontaneously evokes this feeling.

In the political field, Mencius was even more insistent than Confucius that government was primarily an exercise in ethics. He identified Mo-tzu's utilitarianism with gross opportunism and maintained that the guiding principle of government should be not profit but what is right. He confidently believed that if any ruler showed himself to be a fully moral man the whole land would inevitably gravitate into his hands. This was the real "Kingly Way." The rule of the truly moral king, he argued, is characterized by his benevolence toward his people. He provides schooling for them and above all sees to their economic well-being. Mencius extolled the communal ownership of property under the "well field" system, as he interpreted this supposedly ancient institution. There is no way to become a true king, he reasoned, except by providing for the well-being of the people and thus winning their support. In fact, the "Mandate of Heaven," the basic justification for the ruler's power, manifests itself only through the acceptance of a ruler by his people; if the people kill or depose him it is clear that he has lost Heaven's support. In this way, Mencius took the argument that the Chou had used to justify their overthrow of the Shang and turned it into a justification of any successful rebellion.

Mencius' contributions to the main stream of Chinese thought were second only to those of Confucius. His concept of the goodness of human nature, which meant, in essence, that all men are created morally equal, contributed much to the egalitarianism of subsequent Chinese society. His insistence that government must be on behalf of the people and requires their tacit consent helps account for the high political ideals the Chinese were able to maintain throughout much of their history.

Hsün-tzu (about 300–237 B.C.) was another Confucianist who left a deep mark on Chinese civilization, though he was condemned by later men as unorthodox. In his day, however, he was a great success both as a politician and teacher, and sections of his book, the *Hsün-tzu*, which is made up of well-organized essays, were incorporated into the *Record of Rituals*.

Hsün-tzu flatly contradicted Mencius' basic tenet that man is naturally good. Human nature, he argued, is derived from an impersonal, amoral

Heaven; man's emotions and natural desires lead to conflict and therefore are bad. The cure for this situation is improvement through education. The teacher is all-important and therefore to be revered. The process of learning "begins with reciting the Classics and ends in learning the *li*." Hsün-tzu's concept of "the Classics" and *li* as the repository of all essential wisdom, the key role he assigned formal education and teachers, and his flat disbelief in spirits, all became accepted ideas in the Confucian mainstream. His emphasis on education, rituals, a hierarchic order, and strict rule through admonishments and punishments also seem to have contributed to a growing authoritarian trend in government.

The Legalists. These authoritarian tendencies and Hsün-tzu's pessimistic evaluation of human nature were developed further by a group of philosophers and practical politicians known as the Legalists, who for the most part were closely associated with the state of Ch'in. A leading thinker of this school, Han-fei-tzu (died 233 B.C.), and a prominent Ch'in statesman identified with it, Li Ssu (died 208 B.C.), were both disciples of Hsün-tzu. The Legalists may also have been influenced by Mo-tzu's utilitarian doctrine and his insistence on absolute obedience, as well as by the Taoist concept of an amoral natural order and their contempt for conventional ethics and book learning. Legalist ideas found fullest exposition in the *Han-fei-tzu,* which contains some essays by the philosopher of this name.

The Legalists believed that severe laws and harsh punishments, though hateful to the people, are the only means of bringing them the order and security for which they yearn. The people are like the baby who howls when its boil is lanced. The appeal of other philosophers to the Way of the ancients was dismissed by the Legalists: different times require different methods. Since the people are stupidly selfish and the bureaucrats untrustworthy self-seekers, the ruler cannot rely on their moral virtues but must control all alike by clearly defined rewards and punishments—in other words, by a detailed code of penal laws. Men should be judged not by their motives but by their accomplishments. Anyone who fails to achieve what he is assigned to do must be punished. People are to be made mutually responsible for one another's actions, and those who fail to denounce a transgressor are to be considered guilty of the same crime. If the penalties are made harsh, the people will be forced into such complete obedience that there will, in fact, be no penalties.

Right, to the Legalists, consisted simply in what the ruler desired. Though denying all hereditary rights except those of the ruler, they assumed hereditary kingship, and their whole philosophy was designed to aid the ruler in consolidating his position and power. They took for granted that the ruler's objective would be the creation of a prosperous and militarily strong state.

Merchants, intellectuals, and other unproductive and unmartial groups should not be tolerated. All aspects of life should be so regulated as to produce maximum wealth and military might for the state.

In recent years, the Legalists have often been called totalitarians. The name might be fully justified if they had had the technical means of popular control and propaganda of their twentieth-century counterparts. In terms of their own day, they were reactionary in their unquestioning acceptance of royal absolutism and an agrarian society of an earlier age. At the same time, they were undoubtedly part of the wave of the future in their emphasis on a universal system of law and impersonal, uniform relations between the government and the people it ruled. This emphasis, after all, was in large part the product of the needs of the larger, more complex political units of the day.

While the concept of law is one of the glories of Western civilization, in China, Legalism has been a despised term for more than two millenniums. This is because the Legalist concept of law fell far short of the Roman. Whereas Western law has been conceived of as a human embodiment of some higher order of God or nature, the law of the Legalists represented only the ruler's fiat. China developed little civil law to protect the citizen; law remained largely administrative and penal, something the people attempted to avoid as much as possible. Whereas Westerners have felt it safer to be ruled by impersonal laws rather than by fallible judges, the Chinese, presumably following Mencius in his estimate of human nature, have felt it safer to be ruled by ethically-minded adminstrators rather than by impersonal and, in their estimate, purely arbitrary laws.

Despite the condemnation of later ages, Legalism left a lasting mark on Chinese civilization. Through the triumph of Ch'in and the imperial system that Ch'in originated, it became an important part of the Chinese political tradition, partially accounting for the highly centralized government of later times and its harsh and often arbitrary rule. Legalism naturally leads us to the great political transition in Chinese history of the late third century B.C., when Ch'in unified the whole country and founded the Chinese Empire.

4. The First Chinese Empire: The Ch'in and Han Dynasties

Ch'in Creates the Empire

Ch'in's capital region was the Wei Valley, where previously the Chou had risen to power. The defense of this area was simple, because easy access to it from the rest of China was limited to the narrow strip of land between river and hills at the great bend of the Yellow River. The Wei Valley also was a peripheral area where there was room for growth at the expense of the nomads on the northwest and the less advanced agricultural peoples to the southwest. Ch'in annexed two semi-"barbarian" states in the Szechwan Basin in 318 B.C. Contact with the "barbarians" also maintained the martial arts. Ch'in, for example, developed cavalry in the fourth century B.C. Ch'in also faced a simpler water-control problem in the Wei Valley than did the states which sought to control the Yellow River. In the third century B.C. it built an irrigation and transport canal that greatly increased the productivity and population of the Wei Valley, and Ch'in engineers are credited with the marvelous irrigation system of the Chengtu Plain in Szechwan.

Another reason for Ch'in's triumph was its wholehearted application of the new techniques of political and military organization that the Legalists advocated. The first great surge forward took place under the leadership of Shang Yang, whose name has been incorrectly linked with a third-century Legalist work, the *Book of Lord Shang*. A native of East China, Shang Yang was the leading official of Ch'in from 361 until his disgrace and death in 338 B.C. He is said to have instituted a strict system of rewards and punishments, forced all persons into "productive" occupations, set up a system of mutual responsibility and spying among the people, and attempted to replace the old hereditary aristocracy by a new, purely honorary aristocracy based on military achievements.

The most important of Shang Yang's reforms was the effort to bring all the territory of the state under the direct control of the central government. For some time in Ch'in and some of the other larger states, newly acquired territories had been made into districts (*hsien,* sometimes translated "subprefectures" or "counties"). Each of these probably represented an old administrative unit of a walled town and its supporting countryside. Also, along the borders large military units had been set up under the name of commanderies (*chün*). In 350 Shang Yang divided the whole of Ch'in for the first time into thirty-one districts. These various measures, which centralized political control and maximized military power, enabled Ch'in to defeat a coalition of rival states. It then went on in 256 to exterminate Chou.

Unification under the First Emperor.   The unification of China was accomplished by a Ch'in king who ascended the throne as a boy in 246 B.C. He was assisted in his rule first by Lü Pu-wei, who had originally made his fortune as a merchant, and after Lü's downfall in 237 by Hsün-tzu's former disciple Li Ssu. The final unification came with amazing speed. Between 230 and 221, Han, Chao, Wei, Ch'u, Yen, and Ch'i fell in rapid succession. By 221 the King of Ch'in had created what he believed was a universal and everlasting empire. Grandiloquently he adopted the title *Shih Huang-ti,* "First Emperor," using for the new term "emperor" two words that previously had been used for deities and mythological early rulers.

It might have seemed natural for the First Emperor to parcel out his conquests among his relatives and generals as satrapies, as was the system in the newly risen empires of India and West Asia. On Li Ssu's advice, however, he applied the centralized system of Ch'in to the whole of his conquests, dividing the land into thirty-six (later forty-two) commanderies and these into districts. He also applied the Ch'in system of equal, impersonal laws and taxation to the whole land. He confiscated the arms of the states he had conquered and collected their hereditary aristocracies at his capital in the Wei Valley near the site of the ancient Chou capital. Here he built a great palace and erected a mausoleum within a veritable man-made mountain. Life-size ceramic figures of warriors, retainers, and horses by the thousands have recently been found nearby.

Not content with the conquest of the whole Chinese cultural area, the First Emperor sent his armies south, where they incorporated into the empire large numbers of the "barbarian" peoples of what is now South China and penetrated to the coast near modern Canton and into the northern part of the present Vietnam. Along the northwestern frontier the Ch'in armies drove back their old nomadic rivals, who in this period were themselves forming for the first time a large political union. To secure the border against the pastoral peoples of the steppe, the First Emperor had huge levies of forced laborers unite the walls built by the northern states into a single defense system stretching fourteen hundred miles from southwestern Kansu along the southern edge of Mongolia to southern Manchuria. This Great Wall was designed to be a permanent barrier separating the agricultural Chinese from the nomadic "barbarians." Properly manned, it could hold up raiding parties of nomad horsemen until adequate defense forces could be concentrated against them. Under later dynasties new walls were erected north or south of the old ones, depending on military and climatic conditions, and the simple earth construction of the Ch'in wall was later changed to more imposing brick, but the Great Wall always remained essentially the same unified defense system the Ch'in first created.

To consolidate his vast conquests, the First Emperor laid out a radiating system of roads, unified weights and measures, standardized the coinage, and even standardized the axle lengths of wagons. This last measure was important for communications in Northwest China, where wagon wheels cut miniature canyons through the loess soil. Li Ssu is also said to have standardized the writing system, for previously many different types of calligraphy had flourished in the politically divided land. As a result of his efforts and of the unifying influence of a centralized state, both the Chinese characters and the formal style of Chinese composition became standardized by the second century B.C. in what are essentially their modern forms.

The Ch'in rulers looked upon the writings of the philosophers, the ancient classics these men extolled, and the histories of the other princely states as subversive to their own system and therefore tried to wipe them out. Li Ssu started a literary inquisition in 213 B.C. in what has come to be called the "Burning of the Books." All books except useful ones, such as those on agriculture, medicine, and divination, as well as the collections in the hands of the central government, were to be destroyed and recalcitrant scholars banished or executed. Reportedly several hundred were actually buried alive. For this desecration of the written word, Li Ssu has won the opprobrium of later ages. His policy did indeed help put an end to the golden age of Chinese thought, but there were even more important factors at work, such as the violent wars that bracketed the brief supremacy of the Ch'in and the centralized empire itself, which had little room for cultural diversity. A great break resulted between pre-Ch'in and post-Ch'in philosophy, and the vigor and richness of Chou thought was seldom if ever again matched in Chinese history.

The Failure of Ch'in. Although the First Emperor thought that he had founded a dynasty that would endure "ten thousand generations," it survived his own death in 210 B.C. by only four years. His success had been

The First Emperor of the Ch'in attempts to recover the Chou ritual bronzes. (A Han stone engraving from the Wu family funerary shrines in Shantung, second century A.D.) The emperor stands on the bank of a river directing his men who are hauling on ropes to bring the bronze vessel up from the river bottom, but suddenly a dragon's head emerges from the vessel and snaps the ropes.

too sudden and his rule too severe. The upper classes of the states he had conquered were still pulled by loyalties to the old royal lines, and the best educated groups throughout the country were repelled by his effort to suppress the old philosophies. The common people felt heavily burdened by his drafting of men for campaigns abroad and unprecedented building programs at home: palaces, roads, canals, and the Great Wall. In proving the efficacy of Legalist concepts of rule, Ch'in also demonstrated the validity of one of Mencius' ideas: that government ultimately depends upon the tacit consent of the governed. The Chinese people simply deserted Ch'in, and the invincible empire collapsed.

The First Emperor had overcentralized the government, and a failure of leadership at the top immediately affected the whole. Though a prodigious worker and indefatigable traveler, he seems to have been a megalomaniac who hid his movements under an elaborate cloak of mystery. He also was obsessed with the idea of achieving physical immortality through magical practices, which was a rising Taoist concept of the time, and he visited magicians along the Shantung coast and dispatched expeditions to seek the "islands of the immortals" in the Eastern Sea. When he died, Li Ssu and others engineered the suicide of the heir apparent and the enthronement of a young and inexperienced son of the former ruler as the Second Emperor. Li Ssu himself soon fell prey to court intrigues, the Second Emperor was destroyed in turn, and by 206 B.C. Ch'in had disappeared entirely.

The First Emperor thus failed completely in founding a lasting dynasty, but the imperial system he created was to continue, though with occasional breaks, for more than two millenniums, proving to be the world's most durable political system. He has been excoriated as a tyrant throughout most of Chinese history, but Chinese scholars today quite rightly consider him the founder of China as a unified country. The name Ch'in quite fittingly is the origin of the Western name for China.

Han Receives the Mandate

The Founding of the Han. In 209 B.C., only a year after the First Emperor's death, a revolt broke out in the old Ch'u area, and rebellions followed in quick succession throughout the empire. Most of the rebel bands were led by turncoat soldiers or bandits, who commonly espoused the cause of the royal line of one or another of the states Ch'in had destroyed. When the leading rebel, Hsiang Yü, a descendant of Ch'u generals, finally wiped out the last of the Ch'in armies in 206, he enthroned a Ch'u prince as emperor, let the rest of the land be divided among supporters of the other royal lines, and declared himself Hegemon King. The old Chou system, however, could not be revived. Another rebel general, Liu Pang, who had seized the Wei Valley in 207, challenged Hsiang Yü, destroyed him in 202, and set himself up as emperor. He established his capital at Ch'ang-an near the old Ch'in capital in the Wei Valley and took for his dynastic name, Han, derived from a major tributary of the Yangtze River.

Liu Pang succeeded, where the First Emperor had failed, in creating a lasting dynasty. His descendants reigned for more than two centuries until 8 A.D. and then, after a brief usurpation, resurrected the dynasty as the Later Han, which lasted from 25 until 220 A.D. Corresponding roughly in time to the heyday of Rome, the two Han empires also paralleled Rome in power, prestige, and historical significance. Even today the Chinese refer to themselves as "men of Han," and the Japanese and Koreans call the Chinese writing system "the Han characters."

Liu Pang, like most later Chinese emperors, is best known not by his personal name but by his posthumous title, which is Kao Tsu ("High

Progenitor"). His success can be attributed to several factors: he could build on the work of the Ch'in; the wars that had swept all of China had further cut people off from the traditions of the Chou; and he himself represented an even more complete break with the past. Unlike the First Emperor, who was the scion of a long princely line, or the aristocratic Hsiang Yü, Kao Tsu had no contact with the aristocratic past but was of rough, plebeian origin. Most important, he was shrewd enough to move more slowly in consolidating his empire and push his subjects less hard. He reduced the severity of punishments and lessened the tax burden. As a result, the Chinese people gave a loyalty to Han they had denied Ch'in. In other words, Han won the Mandate of Heaven, as Mencius understood the term.

The early Han rulers for the most part continued the Ch'in system of government, but Kao Tsu made one notable and perhaps necessary retreat from centralized rule. He made some of his relatives and generals kings or marquises of vassal principalities. Subsequently, however, he eliminated the nonrelated kings and before his death in 195 B.C. established the rule that henceforth only members of the imperial clan could hold this rank. His successors whittled away the power of the remaining kings by reducing their territories, by dividing realms among the sons of the kings, and eventually by appointing officials of the central government to control each kingdom. The menace of the kings was eliminated in 154 B.C. when seven of the largest were destroyed. Kingdoms and marquisates continued throughout the dynasty, but at the end there were only 20 kingdoms as compared with 103 commanderies, and 241 marquisates as compared with 1314 districts.

A second menace to Han rule, and one which was to arise repeatedly in later Chinese history, was posed by the families of the empresses. Chinese emperors had many consorts, but when a child of one of them was made heir apparent that consort usually was recognized as empress, and on the accession of her son she, as the Empress Dowager, often became a dominant figure at court. This happened when Kao Tsu's empress became the real ruler of China on his death and came close to usurping the throne. Members of her family, surnamed Lü, dominated the court until her death in 180 B.C., whereupon they were massacred by loyal supporters of the Han line.

A third menace to the Han came from the pastoral peoples of the North, who at this time were known to the Chinese as the Hsiung-nu, an early form of the name later known to the West as Hun. By the third century B.C. these probably Turkish-speaking people had created a tribal federation that spread from western Manchuria through Mongolia and southern Siberia into Chinese Turkestan as far as the Pamirs, and their bands of mounted archers repeatedly raided and looted North China. Kao Tsu, after suffering a severe defeat at their hands, attempted to buy them off by giving their emperor a Chinese princess in marriage and sending annual tribute, but Hsiung-nu depredations continued.

Government and Society.   Despite all these difficulties, the Han rulers gradually established a firm and highly centralized government, and the whole country prospered greatly after centuries of almost uninterrupted warfare. By the first century B.C. the bureaucracy is said to have consisted of 130,285 officials. They and other persons of distinction held ranks in eighteen grades, which entitled them to reduced sentences for crimes and, in the higher brackets, to exemption from taxation. Although this bureaucracy can rightly be described as huge, it was small compared to the country it administered. A census of 2 A.D. reported a population of 59,594,978. Traditional Chinese population figures are notably unreliable. They were essentially tax registers, which might be falsified downward in an effort to escape tax responsibilities or upward to indicate administrative efficiency. But it seems safe to conclude that the Han ruled over a greater mass of people than ever recognized Rome's authority.

The Han administration was not constituted to provide what we today would consider the full services of government. It devoted attention primarily to the lavish support of the emperor and his relatives and the defense of the dynasty. The people were of major concern to the government only as taxpayers and *corvée* labor or as potential rebels. *Corvée* labor was a more important support of the central administration than were taxes. The government usually required each farmer to spend a month every year in local work on roads, canals, palaces, and imperial tombs, and various less frequent periods for military duties, frontier-guarding, and service at the capital. So long as the people met their tax and labor schedules and avoided all subversive activities, they were usually left free to administer their own village affairs and carry out their own customary justice. The government thus was a relatively small, highly centralized body that floated on a sea of semi-isolated peasant communities. The point of contact between the two was the district town, where a district magistrate and perhaps two or three other central government appointees dealt with the village heads, landed magnates, and other local leaders.

The ruling elite was in no sense a hereditary aristocracy like that of the Chou period. Even the families of the kings and marquises rose and fell with astonishing rapidity. The bureaucracy and the whole upper class consisted simply of those persons with sufficient talent, education, or wealth to play a part in the central government. The merchant class, however, was specifically excluded from leadership. The Han, like the Ch'in before it, and like most other despotisms based on agricultural taxes, had a strong prejudice against merchants. The class of wealth and education from which the bureaucracy was largely recruited, therefore, was primarily the richer landowners.

Except for the imperial clan at the top and a small number of slaves at the bottom, society seems to have been made up of two main groups: tax-

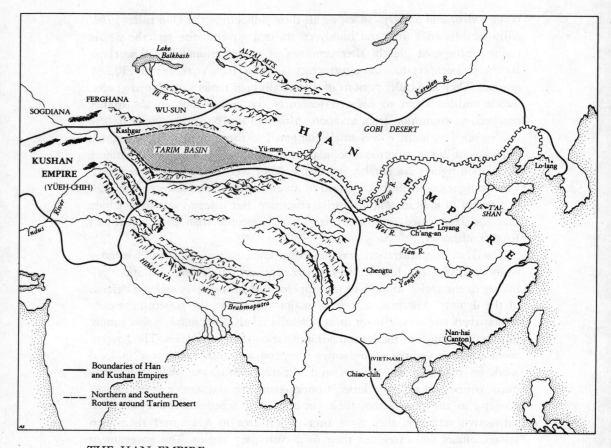

THE HAN EMPIRE

paying peasants and rich landowners. The latter were to some extent tax-exempt, provided the bulk of officialdom, and, as local leaders, served as the link between central government and the countryside. This remained the basic composition of Chinese society for the next two millenniums. These two groups were not castes as in India or even strict classes in the medieval European sense. A spin of the wheel of fortune could plunge a political leader into slavery or elevate a commoner like Liu Pang to the throne.

The Apogee of Han Power.   The first sixty years of Han rule were a period of national recuperation and dynastic consolidation. Then followed a sudden expansive burst of Chinese power such as had taken place under the First Emperor and was to be repeated under all of the stronger dynasties of later times. This occurred during the long reign of Wu Ti ("Martial Emperor"), which lasted from 141 to 87 B.C.

The government of the Chinese Empire has tended to alternate between periods of personal administration by dynamic emperors and periods in which the high bureaucrats were dominant. Under the former, policies could be more vigorously pursued, but, since the emperor was beyond criticism, there could be no check on his follies. Wu Ti was no exception to this rule. He reinstituted a major program of canal construction, connecting the capital directly with the Yellow River and thereby greatly facilitating the transportation of tax grain from East China to Ch'ang-an. He also embarked upon a long series of foreign conquests, while dealing harshly and unjustly with his generals and officials and being himself frequently the dupe of magicians.

Wu Ti greatly extended the Han Empire, filling it out to a much closer approximation of what appears on more recent maps as the Chinese Empire. He conquered native states along the southern coast in Chekiang and Fukien and moved their populations inland. In 111 B.C. he destroyed and annexed the semi-Sinicized state of Nan-yüeh (South Yüeh) in modern Kwangtung, Kwangsi, and northern Vietnam, inaugurating a thousand years of Chinese rule over the region around the modern Hanoi. In 108 he overthrew the semi-Sinicized state of Chosŏn in northern Korea and southern Manchuria, setting up at P'yŏngyang, the present capital of North Korea, the commandery of Lo-lang, which was to remain a flourishing outpost of the Chinese Empire until 313 A.D.

Wu Ti's greatest campaigns were against the Hsiung-nu on the northwest. These were in part defensive, for these highly mobile, warlike people constantly harassed North China. Wu Ti, however, may also have desired to control the lucrative trade with West Asia that passed through Central Asia, and he perhaps had the "Alexander complex," which lured some early Chinese leaders to distant conquests. Between 129 and 119 B.C. he dispatched a series of great armies, some numbering as many as 150,000 men, against the Hsiung-nu and managed to destroy their power south of the Gobi Desert, which bisects Mongolia.

Wu Ti's Hsiung-nu policy was not merely military. He also sought to find allies against them. As early as 139 B.C. he dispatched an officer, Chang Ch'ien, to make an alliance with a Central Asian people known as the Yüeh-chih. Probably an Indo-European people, the Yüeh-chih had been driven out of western Kansu by the Hsiung-nu and in Chang Ch'ien's time had moved all the way to Afghanistan and were on the point of invading India, where they subsequently set up the Kushan Empire. Chang Ch'ien, despite long years of captivity at the hands of the Hsiung-nu, finally reached the Yüeh-chih, but they had no interest in becoming embroiled again in wars in East Asia. He returned to China in 126 B.C. but was dispatched on a similar mission in 115 to another Indo-European people who occupied the Ili Valley of Central Asia. Although this effort also failed, Chang Ch'ien's two expeditions greatly increased Chinese knowledge of and interest in the regions to the west.

HAN MILITARY DEFENSE.
Miniature of a three-story Han watchtower, earthenware with green glaze, from a tomb in Honan. Note the horses at the door and the watchmen on the upper levels.

Wu Ti also tried to outflank the Hsiung-nu. He set up two commanderies between Tibet and Mongolia in what is now the western panhandle of Kansu and populated this area with 700,000 Chinese colonists. To protect this western protrusion of Chinese-speaking people, he extended the Great Wall westward as far as Yü-men ("Jade Gate"). Han rule was subsequently extended over the Indo-European populations of the small agricultural oases around the rim of the Tarim Basin in the heart of Central Asia, and the region was placed under a Protector General. These oases were important way stations on the ancient trade route between East and West. Chinese armies in 104 and 102 B.C. even crossed the mighty Pamirs to Ferghana in what is now Russian Turkestan.

The wars against the Hsiung-nu continued after Wu Ti's death, and eventually in 52 B.C. the ruler of the southern half of the Hsiung-nu horde submitted to Han. In 42 B.C. a Chinese army again crossed the Pamirs and penetrated as far as the former Greek kingdom of Sogdiana, where it crushed a force that may have included captive Roman soldiers. Thus Chinese armies, marching across all but impenetrable deserts and mountains, extended Han military might farther from their capital (over two thousand miles) than Roman legions ever reached from Rome, despite the much easier maritime communications of the Mediterranean area.

Han Thought and Scholarship

None of the pre-Ch'in schools of thought survived into Han times as distinct and mutually exclusive philosophical systems. This is the clearest evidence of how completely the successive triumphs of Ch'in and Han had destroyed the traditions of the past. But elements of the old thought survived piecemeal. Among these were the concepts of the late Chou Naturalists of *yin* and *yang* dualism and the "five elements." Closely allied with these ideas was the notion that unusual natural phenomena were portents which reflected the character of the ruler or foretold the future.

From such ideas there developed in the time of Wu Ti the practice of counting years by arbitrary "year periods" (*nien-hao*) chosen largely for their magical potency. A "year period" might last a long time if conditions were stable or might be abandoned within a few months if some disaster struck or a particularly propitious omen occurred. The result has been a chaotic method of counting years, which has made the Chinese all the more dependent on dynasties for reckoning time. Despite the drawbacks of this system, it still is widely used in East Asia. The only later advance has been to make year periods coincide with reigns, an innovation adopted by the Chinese in 1368 and by the Japanese in 1868.

The Taoist tradition survived the political upheaval of the late third century better than most schools of thought, but in the process the philosophy of the *Tao te ching* and the *Chuang-tzu* was almost lost among more primitive beliefs, particularly the search for long life and eventually for physical immortality. There was great interest in finding an elixir of life and in transmuting baser elements into gold, which apparently was the start of alchemy in the world. There was also much emphasis in this search for immortality on dietary regimens, such as the avoidance of cereals, and yoga-like breathing exercises. Various popular nature or ancestral cults also survived and developed a rich mythology, increasingly identified with Taoism. The old aristocratic cults had, of course, been obliterated, but their memory continued. In 110 B.C. Wu Ti was persuaded to revive them in mysterious form and on a grandiose scale, performing the sacrifice to Heaven on the summit of T'ai-shan, a sacred mountain in Shantung, and the sacrifice to Earth on a low hill at its foot.

At a higher intellectual level, men of scholarly bent busied themselves with the recovery of the writings of earlier times. After the Ch'in ban on philosophical and historical works was formally lifted in 191 B.C., some older scholars were apparently able to reconstitute certain texts from memory, while others were discovered hidden in walls. The result was sometimes two different versions of the same text, as for the *Classic of Documents,* which had an "old text," found in pre-Ch'in calligraphy, as well as the currently reconstituted text in the new standardized writing.

Han scholars showed little philosophic perception, lumping all the old writings together as equally valid expressions of the thought of antiquity. But they tried to bring order into the ancient writings by devising categories such as the Five Classics, and they devoted great efforts to attempting to explain these only imperfectly understood ancient writings. Their exegetical works, or commentaries, were the start of what has been ever since one of the major intellectual activities of China. The first great systematic dictionary, the *Explanation of Writing* (*Shuo wen*), also appeared around 100 A.D. In it more than nine thousand characters are listed under 540 radicals.

Han books were often decidedly eclectic in their philosophic content, as in the case of the *Huai-nan-tzu,* a compilation of cosmological, Taoist, and other lore, made under the patronage of a grandson of Kao Tsu. While most Han writing was scholarly or didactic, one important poetic genre developed during the period. This was the *fu,* which because of its irregularity of meter and rhyme has sometimes been called "prose poetry." Closely akin to the *Li sao* of Ch'ü Yüan, the *fu* were featured by long descriptions, rich in imagery and hyperbole, of capitals of China or beautiful landscapes.

The Writing of History.   The greatest literary achievement of Han times was in the field of historical writing. This is not surprising in a civilization that has so emphasized the record of the past. The Chinese have made history one of the four main categories of literature, the others being the classics and their commentaries, philosophical writings, and belles-lettres.

The *Historical Records* (*Shih chi*) of Ssu-ma Ch'ien (died about 85 B.C.) represents a great step forward in Chinese historical scholarship. A court astrologer, Ssu-ma Ch'ien claimed to be simply completing a history started by his father, but this may have been partly a pious excuse for what was in reality a most presumptuous undertaking—the continuation and amplification of what was supposed to be Confucius' greatest accomplishment, that is, the arrangement of the record of the past in proper form. Ssu-ma Ch'ien was obviously a man of great daring as well as prodigious learning. In 99 B.C. he came to the defense of a prominent Chinese general who had been forced to surrender to the Hsiung-nu, and Wu Ti repaid him for his audacity by having him castrated.

Ssu-ma Ch'ien not only set the pattern for most later Chinese historical works but also determined their style and scholarly approach. He limited

The archer Yi shooting nine of the ten sun crows which threaten to burn up the earth—a drought myth. Stone engraving on the wall of the Wu family shrines.

himself to a concise and straightforward statement of the facts as he knew them, quoting with a minimum of alterations those sources which he felt to be the most reliable. His book, therefore, is for the most part a complicated patchwork of passages and paraphrases from earlier books and documents. He thus set a standard for historical scholarship in China that was probably not equaled in the West until relatively modern times.

Ssu-ma Ch'ien was attempting to write universal history and came as close to succeeding as any man has. The *Historical Records,* which consist of 130 solid chapters, is a text of over 700,000 characters. Because of the conciseness of classical Chinese, this represents a work of close to ten times the content of the volume the reader has in hand. The first twelve chapters are "Basic Annals," which contain the main record of events from the time of the "culture heroes" through the kings of the three dynasties and the emperors of the Ch'in and Han dynasties up to Wu Ti. The next ten chapters are chronological tables of Chou princely houses and princes and high officials of the Han. Then follow eight essays on subjects that do not lend themselves to chronological treatment, such as rituals, music, the calendar, astrology, rivers and canals, and economic matters. The following thirty chapters are devoted to the records of the various states of Chou times. The last seventy chapters consist of biographies of important men and a few brief essays on other peoples and lands.

Many later Chinese historians followed Ssu-ma Ch'ien's model. Pan Ku (died 92 A.D.), together with his father and sister, compiled the second great history of this type, the *History of the Han.* A work of one hundred chapters, it differed from the pattern of the *Historical Records* largely in that it was limited to a single dynasty, the Earlier Han, and naturally has no section corresponding to that on the various states of Chou. Pan Ku also added very useful essays on literature and geography. The *History of the Han* became the prototype for all the later dynastic histories, which treat either one major dynasty or a group of smaller ones. The number of officially accepted "standard histories" of this sort had been twenty-four for some centuries until the President of the Chinese Republic accepted a "new" history of the Mongol dynasty in 1921.

The Triumph of Confucianism.   Wu Ti was almost as thoroughly a Legalist monarch as the First Emperor had been. It is commonly said, however, that during his reign Confucianism became the predominant philosophy of the Chinese court. Actually the triumph of Confucianism was a slow process, continuing over the whole Han period, and the Confucianism that won out was a curious synthesis of ancient philosophies and current superstitions, and not at all the pure, ethical teachings of Confucius and Mencius. But for all the eclecticism of Han thought, men of scholarly bent seem to have identified themselves increasingly with the Confucian tradition. This may have been because Confucianism was very specifically a philosophy for bureaucrats and educated men. Its very name suggested this: "the learning of the literati," or rather "weaklings," as the term *ju* originally meant. It was not so much that Confucian philosophy won over Han thinkers as that Han scholars gradually adopted Confucius as their ideal prototype.

At the same time scholarly men who identified themselves with the Confucian tradition were being brought into what had started out as a purely Legalist type of government. Kao Tsu, though himself untutored, had seen the need to utilize men of education in his government, and his successors had even held examinations to select qualified scholars for government service. By Wu Ti's time there was enough of a Confucian bias in the central government for the ruler to ban students of Legalist philosophy from the court. Two so-called Confucian scholars who rose to considerable influence under Wu Ti were Kung-sun Hung (died 121 B.C.) and his junior contemporary Tung Chung-shu. Both men were chiefly noted for their ability to interpret omens and for their analysis of the *Spring and Autumn Annals* as a book which supposedly indicated the moral judgments of Confucius through its choice of words. The pseudoscientific reasoning about the relationship between the "five elements" and historic events in Tung Chung-shu's writings on the *Spring and Autumn Annals* is a far cry from the thought of Confucius and Mencius.

In 136 B.C. Wu Ti set up at court five Erudites of the Five Classics, which were by then identified with the Confucian tradition, and in 124 B.C. he assigned fifty official students to these five Erudites, thus creating a sort of state university. This school is said to have grown to three thousand students in the second half of the first century B.C., and by 1 A.D. a hundred men a year were entering government service through the examinations administered by the official scholars. Thus, from Wu Ti's time on, a considerable portion of the lower bureaucracy was produced through a definitely Confucianist education at government expense.

Confucian precepts about proper rituals and etiquette were also gradually incorporated into law—a development quite at variance with the original Confucian emphasis on ethics in place of law. Confucianism was also beginning to be recognized as the official philosophy of the state. Great conferences of scholars were held under imperial auspices in 51 B.C. and again in 79 A.D. to determine the true interpretation of the Confucian Classics. In 175 A.D. the government had the approved version of the Classics carved on large stone tablets, which were erected at the capital. Meanwhile, in 58 A.D. all government schools were ordered to make sacrifices to Confucius.

The incorporation of Confucianism into the Legalist state was in many ways a strange phenomenon, but it helps explain the superior lasting power of the Chinese imperial system over all other empires. The land, though won by the sword, could be governed only by the writing brush. The Legalist conqueror needed the efficient civil administrator, and a place of responsibility and honor was, accordingly, created for him in the government. As a result, men of education became supporters rather than opponents of the state. More important, a start was made toward the development of an efficient bureaucracy through a system of education and selection of prospective officials. China in short was already beginning to develop a modern type of civil service system based on merit. It was almost two thousand years before the West adopted a system similar to, and in part inspired by, that of China.

It was fortunate for the Chinese that the Confucian tradition became the chief intellectual force among the educated classes. Although Han Confucianism was a strange mixture of ideas, the ethical concepts of the Chou founders of the school gradually reasserted themselves over the syncretic beliefs of the early Han scholars. The ruthless depotism that the Ch'in had created on Legalist principles, therefore, came increasingly into the hands of men who stressed moral virtues. The balance eventually achieved between the Legalist empire and its Confucian administrators once again illustrates the

Rubbing of a Han stamped tile showing a banquet scene. Note the full-sleeved flowing robes and kneeling position, no longer characteristic of China but still seen in Japan.

usefulness of the *yin-yang* concept of complementary, as opposed to conflicting, dualism. The Legalist victory, while seeming to destroy Confucianism, in reality created the stable society in which it could flourish. The Confucian victory, far from destroying Legalism, made the Legalist empire all but indestructible.

The Dynastic Cycle

The Chinese have traditionally interpreted their past as a series of dynastic cycles in which successive dynasties repeated a boringly repetitious story: a heroic founding, a period of great power, then a long decline, and finally total collapse. The Chinese practice of compiling history in dynastic chunks has contributed to this picture, as has their concept that the best that man could hope for was to recreate some golden age of antiquity. As a result, the tremendous growth and development of Chinese civilization has been all but hidden behind this apparent circular motion in human affairs, and the later history of China is made into a series of more or less successful attempts to repeat the story of the Earlier Han.

It must be admitted that there is some validity to the Chinese concept of a dynastic cycle, at least as a superficial political pattern that overlies more fundamental technological, economic, social, and cultural developments. The two Han dynasties both lasted about two centuries; the great dynasties of later times, existing under more advanced conditions, each tended to run about three centuries. And within each dynastic period, such matters as fiscal conditions, administrative efficiency, and military power showed remarkably parallel trends.

Personal Factors.   Chinese historians, influenced by the Confucian insistence on the ethical basis of government, have always emphasized personal factors in explaining the dynastic cycle. Founders of dynasties, who, like Kao Tsu, successfully claimed the Mandate of Heaven, were not portrayed just as strong men but as supermen. The last rulers, who lost the Mandate, were not considered just unfortunate or weak but were often described as evil and debauched, like the last kings of the Hsia and Shang. Actually, the imperial lines invariably did degenerate. The dynastic founder naturally had to be a man of great ability and force. Later rulers, raised in a luxurious and intrigue-ridden court, were more likely to be weaklings. Usually the dynasty produced at least one later strong man who either brought the regime to new power, as did Wu Ti, or gave it a sort of second start; but in general all the imperial lines showed a downward trend in ability.

The quality of the men around the throne was on the whole more important than that of the emperors themselves. Here the picture is less clear. Struggles over the succession and court intrigues between rival factions characterized the history of all the dynasties almost from beginning to end. In some of the later dynasties, factional quarrels at times centered on basic matters of policy, but throughout most of Chinese history they were simply struggles over power and rewards. In the latter years of a dynasty, when the central government was weakening for other reasons, the effect of such factional quarrels, *coups d'état,* and palace revolutions was naturally more deleterious than in the dynasty's heyday.

The most persistent factional problem was posed by the families of the empresses, as in the case of Kao Tsu's widow, who almost took the throne for her Lü family. High officials, generals, or great landed families might also take advantage of the weakness of an emperor or the disruption of his court to make themselves virtually independent power holders and in the end break up the empire.

Another type of factional struggle that was endemic in all dynasties was that between civil bureaucrats and eunuchs. The eunuchs were at court to guard and administer the imperial harem, but their functions spread to other fields, including the military. As men of low social origin without descendants who could rival the imperial line, they were the natural allies of emperors, who might need their help to curb overly ambitious or greedy officials. The bureaucrats naturally looked with keen disfavor on influential eunuchs, who lacked their own education, came from a different social background, and were their rivals for power and rewards at court. It was a eunuch who destroyed the Ch'in statesman Li Ssu in 208 B.C., and in 47 B.C. another eunuch got rid of his bureaucratic rivals at court. Since the writing of history was in the hands of bureaucrats, we find the eunuchs uniformly condemned by historians for their misrule.

Economic and Administrative Factors.   Despite the Chinese emphasis on individual morality and personality, the dynastic cycle is better explained in terms of problems of fiscal stability, administrative efficiency, and military power. All the great dynasties had an initial period of prosperity. The group that had seized the throne was relatively small and closely knit. The wars that had brought it to power had eliminated most of its rivals, and therefore the wealth of the nation poured largely into its coffers. The country prospered in its newly established peace, the population increased rapidly, and the treasuries and granaries of the central government were full.

But the excess of *yang* led to the rise of *yin*. The affluent central government built great palaces, roads, canals, and walls. The very military successes of the empire established far-flung defense lines that were costly to maintain. The imperial clan, the nobility, and the high bureaucracy grew in numbers and became accustomed to an ever more luxurious mode of life. More and more lands and their peasant-cultivators were used for the personal support of the ruling class and fewer and fewer tax-paying contributors remained to support the central administration. Because of constantly increasing expenditures and often a slight decline in income, every dynasty began to experience serious financial difficulties within a century of its founding.

Economic and administrative reforms were then carried out which sometimes halted the financial decline for a while. The downward trend, however, eventually reasserted itself. Economic and administrative difficulties accumulated. Official self-seeking and corruption became worse, leading to a decline in administrative efficiency and an intensification of factional quarrels at court. The potential rivals of the imperial family became politically and economically more independent of the central government and challenged it with greater impunity. To meet government deficits, the burden on the tax-paying peasant was increased to the breaking point. Because of the government's financial difficulties, canals and dikes were allowed to fall into disrepair, making floods and droughts more probable. Crop failures that once could have been offset by stores from the government granaries now resulted in famines, and these led to banditry and eventually to peasant uprisings. Inadequately maintained frontier defenses began to crumble. Provincial officials and their armies began to defect, and the central government started to go to pieces. Then followed the wars that liquidated the old regime and cleared the slate for a new dynastic beginning.

This downward economic and administrative spiral can be perceived in the histories of most of the long-lived dynasties. It was particularly clear in the Earlier Han. Wu Ti's canal-building program and foreign wars brought the dynasty to the height of its power but also produced a fiscal crisis. New revenues were desperately needed for the greatly expanded costs of government. Wu Ti's whole reign (141–87 B.C.) was characterized by a long series of efforts to redeem the finances of the dynasty.

The most important of Wu Ti's economic measures was the reinstitution of state monopolies, or rather licensing systems, for the production and sale of certain commodities from which large profits could be made with minimal effort. He restored the government monopoly on minting copper coinage, and in 119 B.C. he reintroduced the old Ch'in monopolies on salt and iron, later adding a monopoly on liquor. Such monopolies, though common throughout Chinese history, always remained highly controversial. As early as 81 B.C. a great court conference was held to discuss their propriety, and the largely condemnatory conclusions were put into book form a generation later under the title of *Discourses on Salt and Iron.*

In 110 B.C. Wu Ti introduced the so-called "leveling" system, by which the government purchased surplus produce in times or areas of glut to sell in periods or places of deficiency. This system may have helped stabilize prices, but the motive was profit for the treasury. Wu Ti also managed to tax commerce to some extent by special imposts, but others of his reforms were very unsound. He commuted some punishments to money fines; he sold court ranks for cash; and he debased the currency, making smaller coins and forcing worthless deerskin certificates on the wealthy.

Wang Mang's Usurpation. Wu Ti's fiscal efforts were on the whole successful and the government remained solvent for the next few decades. But meanwhile a serious problem had developed. The population had grown to such a point that the average peasant had less land to cultivate than had his ancestors. Moreover, a much larger proportion of the peasants were now on the virtually untaxed estates of the great landowners, and therefore the tax-paying peasants elsewhere were forced to carry a heavier load than before, on a smaller agricultural base. State revenues were declining and with them all the institutions of central government. A series of large-scale revolts commenced in 22 B.C.

At this critical juncture, Wang Mang, the nephew of an empress, rose

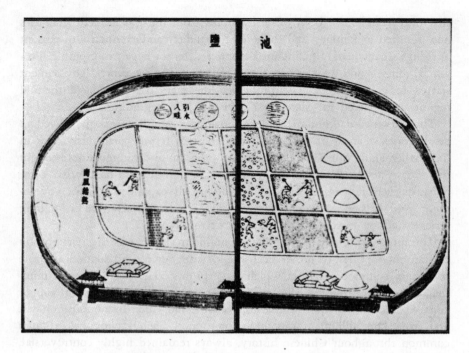

豐 池

THE SALT MONOPOLY. *Since salt was a necessity and its production easily monopolized, its production and distribution were ordinarily controlled by government licensing for the benefit of the central government treasury. This picture from an encyclopedia of 1637 (the* T'ien-kung k'ai-wu) *shows, from left to right, flat salt "pans" being smoothed, sea water being let in for evaporation, and the remaining salt pulverized and then collected in mounds for transportation, all within walls and gates for control purposes.*

to power and by vigorous reforms sought desperately to stem the tide. Eventually he usurped the throne in 8 A.D. and substituted his Hsin ("New") dynasty for the Han. (The date was January 10, 9 A.D., in the Western calendar, but the Chinese lunar calendar starts the year later in the winter.) Wang Mang seems to have been a sincere Confucian, and he saw his reforms as recreating the golden age of the Duke of Chou. With the aid of Confucian scholars, he focused attention on certain ancient texts that had hitherto been little studied, and he contributed greatly to the ultimate triumph of Confucianism. But his reforms actually were more in the Legalist tradition and were largely a revival or amplification of Wu Ti's policies. He built up the monopolies, reinvigorated the "leveling" system, and debased the coinage. He also instituted a policy of agricultural loans to peasants.

Wang Mang's most daring reform was a frontal assault on the major economic problem of his day. So many peasants lived on the tax-free estates that not enough of them remained as taxpayers supporting the central government. He therefore decreed an end to the great private estates by ordering in 9 A.D. that the land be "nationalized" and parceled out among tax-paying peasants and that private slavery be stopped. Such a drastic policy would have been extremely hard to carry out even in Wu Ti's time. Now, a century later, it was entirely beyond the power of the central government to enforce. While Wang Mang has been condemned by traditional Chinese historians for his usurpation, his effort to "nationalize" the land and free the slaves has won him the anachronistic title of "China's first socialist" and the praise of Marxist historians.

Wang Mang's daring effort to turn back the dynastic cycle and recreate the conditions that had existed at the beginning of the dynasty may have hastened the collapse of the central government. Already undermined by slow fiscal and administrative erosion, it now lost the support of the powerful families whose lands Wang Mang had sought to expropriate. A series of bad harvests and the breakdown of the water-control system also produced famines. A great peasant uprising broke out in Shantung in 18 A.D. and soon spread throughout the land. The rebels, who called themselves the Red Eyebrows from a mark used to distinguish them, had originated from a secret society with Taoist tendencies. As in many later popular uprisings that featured the closing years of dynasties, economic necessity was the real motivating force, but popular religious beliefs helped give the rebellion solidarity and lasting force. Meanwhile, the frontier defenses had crumbled, and the border states had reasserted their independence. The nomads invaded the border regions, the capital was sacked by rebels, and Wang Mang died at their hands in 23 A.D. The great centralized government that Kao Tsu had founded had finally collapsed in complete ruin.

The Later Han

The Reconstitution of the Empire.   Although the Red Eyebrows had laid waste the land, they, like the leaders of many popular rebellions, lacked the administrative experience and understanding to substitute a central government of their own for the one they were destroying. The task of re-creating the central power fell to the hands of better educated men. Various descendants of the Han emperors, usually great landowners themselves, had also risen in revolt, and one of them, Liu Hsiu, finally emerged victorious from the free-for-all that followed Wang Mang's downfall. He declared himself emperor in 25 A.D. and re-established the Han dynastic name, but since his capital was at Loyang to the east of Ch'ang-an, his dynasty is known as the Eastern Han as well as Later Han.

Liu Hsiu, who is better known by his posthumous title of Kuang Wu Ti

("Shining Martial Emperor"), unified and pacified the land by 37 A.D. and recreated a powerful central administration on the pattern of the Earlier Han. He was able to do this because he did not face the insoluble financial problem that had proved too much for Wang Mang. The wars had wiped out the Earlier Han aristocracy and some of the other great landholders. The new dynasty, moreover, was not as yet burdened with a large imperial clan and ruling class.

Kuang Wu Ti reconquered South China and northern Vietnam, and under his successor, Ming Ti ("Enlightened Emperor," 57–75 A.D.), a determined effort was made to restore Chinese control over Central Asia and the pastoral peoples of the north. Pan Ch'ao, the brother of the historian Pan Ku, was dispatched to Central Asia in 73 A.D. and eventually brought the whole of the Tarim Basin under his control, serving as the Protector General of the Western Regions from 91 A.D. until his death in 102. During this time he led an army across the Pamir Mountains and dispatched a lieutenant across intervening Parthia to the eastern regions of the Roman Empire.

In the meantime the Hsiung-nu had divided into northern and southern confederacies, and the southern group had submitted to the Later Han. In 89 A.D. Chinese armies marched across the Gobi Desert in Mongolia and administered a great defeat to the northern Hsiung-nu, which probably helped start them on their western migrations that were to bring them, under the name of Huns, to the southern Russian steppes in the late fourth century and into the heart of Europe a half-century later.

Cultural Growth.   Control over Central Asia during the two Han dynasties permitted a greatly increased flow of overland trade with the western regions. Contact by sea and a trickle of maritime trade with India and the Roman Orient also developed during these centuries. A group of jugglers appeared at the Chinese court in 120 A.D. claiming to be from the Roman Empire, and some merchants in 166 claimed, no doubt speciously, to be emissaries of Marcus Aurelius Antoninus. The Chinese obtained through this trade fine horses from Central Asia and various luxury goods from South and West Asia. They especially valued glass objects from the Mediterranean area. But Chinese silk was in even greater demand in the Roman Empire. In fact, so much silk was exported from China to the West that it contributed to an economically injurious drain of specie from Rome, and the route by which it came through Central Asia has been called the "Silk Road." The greater demand for Chinese goods abroad than for foreign goods in China was to remain characteristic of China's trade until the nineteenth century, in large part because of superior Chinese technology as compared with other areas during most of this period.

Stone engraving from the Wu family shrines (see pages 58 and 67). The upper register shows, left to right, guests arriving and then being served a banquet while sitting on the floor and watching acrobats perform. A gaming board is above the food trays. On the lower register servants prepare the banquet.

Trade with western areas brought to China various foreign influences in art and music and new agricultural products. The high level of Han astronomical and mathematical learning may have reflected stimulation from India or West Asia. But already by Han times the flow of cultural influences from China westward may have exceeded the flow toward China. Han textile techniques were centuries ahead of those of West Asia and Europe; in the Later Han the water-powered mill was invented; during the Han period the Chinese developed the shoulder collar that so greatly increased the efficiency of horses as draft animals; and at about the same time the technique of iron casting began to spread from China to the western regions.

Two of the greatest of all Chinese inventions, paper and porcelain, had their beginnings during the Han period. Pure rag paper dating from about 100 A.D. has been found in the remains of Han outposts in Central Asia. Naturally, paper soon replaced cumbersome wooden and bamboo slips for writing and also reduced the use of expensive silk cloth for this purpose. But it took more than a thousand years for the knowledge of paper-making to spread to Europe. Pottery glazes were already common during the Han, and toward the end of this period a sort of proto-porcelain appeared. The Chinese, in other words, were beginning to invent china. During the next several centuries they gradually developed the fine porcelains that the rest of the world eagerly imported and eventually copied in modern times.

Ch'ang-an and Loyang, no doubt, were cities that rivaled Rome, but little has survived from these great Han capitals. Their wooden architecture was too perishable and later inhabitants too numerous and destructive. Rich Han remains, however, are still to be found in Han tombs. From tombs at the Lo-lang commandery in Korea have emerged fine lacquer pieces made in distant Szechwan.

Dynastic Decline.   Despite the cultural brilliance of the period, the Later Han was never able to achieve the financial strength of the Earlier Han at its height. Too many of the large private estates of the first century B.C. had survived into Later Han times to allow the new dynasty the same clean slate, economically and administratively, that Kao Tsu and his successors had enjoyed. The position of the great landowners was quite secure. Land taxes in Han times were usually only about one-thirtieth of the yield, while rents ran about one-half. Thus they paid only an inconsequential land tax and could protect their wealth by holding high court posts. Although the central government repeatedly made efforts to build up an efficient bureau-cracy based on merit, the great majority of the officials achieved their posi-tions through inheritance, patronage, or the open manipulation of the official examinations by those in charge.

The financial and administrative weakness of the Later Han is reflected by the numbers of people on the tax registers. At their height in 105 A.D. the Later Han census roles did not quite reach the figures for the Earlier Han, and the decrease in tax-paying, *corvée*-serving peasants was greatest in North China and the northern border regions, where they were most needed for miltary defense and to support the capital. To maintain itself, the central government was forced to levy increasingly heavy taxes on the dwindling number of tax-paying peasants in North China. The burden eventually became unbearable, and many peasants fled to the less rigorously taxed South or into the estates of the great landowners, where the rents were less crushing than the taxes on free peasants. The result of such absconding was an inevitable increase in taxation on those who remained. The hard-pressed peasants thus were forced into banditry or open revolt, which further weakened the dynasty's finances. This downward spiral, once started, was not easily stopped.

As in the Earlier Han, the first major challenges to the imperial clan came from the relatives of empresses, but the emperors managed to suppress them with the aid of powerful eunuchs. The Tou family was put down in 89 A.D. and the Liang were exterminated in 160. The other great court families, supported by the students of the government university, who were said to number thirty thousand at the time, attempted to prevent the trium-phant eunuchs from monopolizing power, but the latter struck back, im-prisoning hundreds of officials and students in 166 and killing or imprisoning thousands of them again in 169.

The great purges carried out by the eunuchs were both symptomatic of administrative decline and contributory to a further disintegration of the government. By 184 two great rebellions had broken out, in East China and in Szechwan. Both were led by Taoist religious leaders of faith-healing sects. That in the East was called the "Way of the Great Peace" (T'ai P'ing Tao), but was popularly known as the Yellow Turbans for the yellow head cloths the rebels wore. In Szechwan the rebels were known as the Five Pecks of Rice band, because of the dues paid their cult masters. These popular Taoist rebellions raged for three decades, seriously disrupting the country.

The End of the First Chinese Empire

The Division of the Empire. The *coup de grâce* was given the Han by its own generals, as was often the case in later dynasties. The collapse of the tax-paying peasantry entailed the ruin of the *corvée* labor system and the peasant draft army associated with it. The professional armies that took its place tended to become the private forces of the rich, land-owning generals who commanded them. After the outbreak of the popular revolts, the generals became virtually independent warlords and soon completely overshadowed the central government. Gradually a three-way division of power developed among the leading generals, with Ts'ao Ts'ao, the son of an adopted son of a eunuch, in the North, Liu Pei in Szechwan, and Sun Ch'üan in the region of the lower Yangtze and the South. This division was geographically a natural one and was to reappear at various times in later Chinese history.

When Ts'ao Ts'ao died in 220 A.D., his son usurped the Han throne, naming his dynasty the Wei. The Later Han dynasty had been little more than a legal fiction for the past three decades, but this act brought it to an official end. The following year Liu Pei also assumed the imperial title, taking the dynastic name of Han, since he was a descendant of the old imperial line. His dynasty is called the Shu Han after the state of Shu which had once existed in Szechwan. In 222 Sun Ch'üan in the South followed suit, adopting the dynastic name of Wu after the Chou state that had once ruled the lower Yangtze Valley. The half-century during which China was divided between these three states is known as the Three Kingdoms (*San-kuo*) period.

The Breakdown of the System. According to the theory of the dynastic cycle one of the three succession states or some new rebel group should presently have reunited the country and started another two-century cycle of united rule, but nothing of the sort happened. Something much more profound than a mere administrative breakdown was occurring in China. The whole Han system of political and economic organization was going to pieces in somewhat the same way that the Roman Empire was starting to

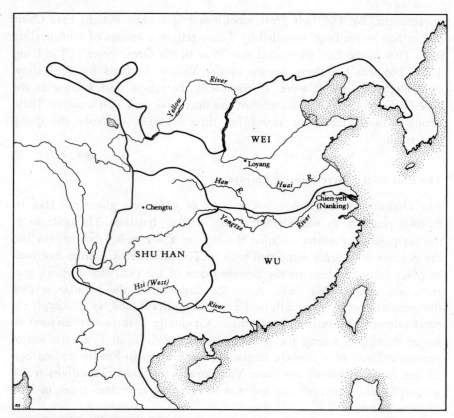

THE THREE KINGDOMS

disintegrate at much the same time. Existing at quite comparable technological levels, both Han and Rome proved incapable of adjusting to the increase in population, the growth of wealth, and the development of complex institutions that their great centralized rule had made possible.

The decline of the first Chinese Empire can be traced back to the financial difficulties at the time of Wu Ti. It became marked during the late first century B.C., when the great families consolidated their hold on their large estates. Kuang Wu Ti, in recreating the centralized state of the Later Han, had to make a greater compromise with large private holdings than had the emperors of the Earlier Han. From then on the decline was rapid, and the Later Han took no effective measures to check it. In fact, the centralized administration was its own worst enemy. Emperors awarded to their relatives, favorites, and outstanding generals and administrators huge grants of land and peasants in perpetuity. The great officials were unendingly avaricious in rewarding themselves and their relatives in similar fashion.

By the late second century the great local families were simply too rich and powerful to be curbed by the central government; in fact, they controlled it, and the division of the country into three separate empires after 220 A.D. was merely formal recognition of the fact that a truly united government was no longer possible. Nor was any of the three succession states an effectively united empire. All were more or less at the mercy of their own great families and generals. They and the dynasties that followed all sought to revive the Han imperial system, but none could achieve more than a pale imitation of it. Most of them were merely one-man dynasties, created by a strong general and lost within a generation or two by his heirs.

The Three Kingdoms period was a time of incessant warfare, which has seemed exciting and romantic to later Chinese. Finally in 263, Wei managed to destroy and annex Shu Han, but two years later, a Wei general usurped the Wei throne from Ts'ao Ts'ao's heirs and founded the Chin dynasty. Known to history as Chin Wu Ti ("Martial Emperor" of the Chin), he conquered the southern state of Wu in 280, uniting the country briefly, and he strove valiantly to restore the old Han system. No one man, however, could turn back the tides of history. The official census was down to 16,163,863, a sure sign that a large part of the population was beyond effective control or taxation by the government, and Chin Wu Ti made no real attempt to break up the estates and get the peasants back on the tax registers. The Chin, in fact, proved to be a typical one-man dynasty. Soon after Chin Wu Ti's death in 290, it fell apart in civil war.

"Barbarian" Invasions.   A new aspect of the disintegration of the imperial system now became apparent. China was all but defenseless against the pastoral peoples of the North. The pendulum of conquest, after swinging outward into the steppe land for centuries, was now beginning to swing back into China. This drastic shift in power relationship between the Chinese and the nomads can be explained in part by our useful concept of *yin-yang* dualism. The very subjugation of the pastoral peoples by the Han had sown the seeds for the "barbarian" conquest of China. Hsiung-nu bands that had surrendered were settled as semiagricultural tribal groups on the northern borders of China. The "barbarians," because of their horsemanship and martial traditions, also became important elements in the Chinese armies. Thus, the borderland and the whole Chinese defense system became permeated with semi-Sinicized "barbarians." The situation was not unlike that of late Roman times in Europe, when the borderlands and defense forces passed in large part into the hands of the Germanic "barbarians."

As the Chinese Empire disintegrated, the semiagricultural "barbarians" to the north and the still purely pastoral tribes beyond them found no difficulty in penetrating deep into China in their search for better pasture or booty. In 304 a Hsiung-nu band in North China declared its independence, and in 316 its armies sacked Loyang, the Chin capital, slaughtering thirty thousand of its inhabitants. For more than a century after that North China was fought over, despoiled, and ruled by rival "barbarian" groups. Only the mountain ramparts of Szechwan and the large river systems of the Yangtze Valley and the South preserved these regions from the ravages of the northern horsemen.

Huge numbers of Chinese, naturally, attempted to escape the depredations of the "barbarians" and the generally chaotic conditions in North China, fleeing southward to the safety of Szechwan and the area south of the Yangtze. As a result, the Chinese population in the South multiplied several times over between the third and fifth centuries, and the absorption of the non-Chinese peoples of the area was accelerated.

The Succession States of the South.   The year after the fall of Loyang, a Chin prince in South China declared himself emperor at Nanking. His dynasty is known as the Eastern Chin, in contrast to the first Chin dynasty, which is called the Western Chin. The capital at Nanking (appropriately meaning "Southern Capital," though this is actually a much later name for the city), grew into a great metropolis where the luxurious ways of the Han were continued. The government, however, was weak and continually at the mercy of its great generals, who repeatedly seemed on the point of snuffing out the dynasty. The Eastern Chin was obsessed with the idea of reconquering the North, but its various wars against the "barbarians" brought no permanent gains, and it was plagued at home by revolts and *coups d'état.*

Finally in 420 a general, Liu Yü, usurped the throne and founded the Sung dynasty, usually called the Liu Sung to distinguish it from the great Sung dynasty of later history. The next century and a half witnessed dismal repetitions of the same story. There were constant and usually unsuccessful wars with the "barbarian" states of the North, and one general after another seized the throne from the weak heirs of the preceding usurper. Usurpations followed in quick succession: the Southern Ch'i dynasty in 479, the Liang in 502, and the Ch'en in 557.

For more than three centuries, one dynastic founder after another had attempted to restore the great centralized empire of the Han, but all had failed. No dynasty had been more than a mere shadow of the old empire, perpetuating at most the conditions of ineffectual central government and complete dominance by the great families that had characterized the dying days of Han rule. A broken-down Han could be maintained for a while, much as Byzantium continued a degenerated Roman tradition for a much longer period in the West, but Han itself could not be revived—at least not by the Chinese alone. The later history of the Chinese Empire was to grow out of the amalgam of "barbarians" and Chinese in North China, as the later history of Europe grew out of the union of Latins and Germans.

5. The Regeneration of the Empire

The Challenge to the Chinese System

The Six Dynasties Period.   The epoch following the fall of the Later Han is called the Six Dynasties period (*Liu ch'ao*) after the six successive dynasties that had their capitals at Nanking between 222 and 589. This span of three and a half centuries is commonly treated as a single slice of history —a sort of dynastic cycle in reverse, in that it runs from unity through prolonged disunity back to unity again. During this period foreign peoples and influences challenged Chinese civilization more fundamentally than it was ever to be challenged again until the nineteenth century. Eventually the Chinese overcame this crisis by incorporating the challengers into the Chinese system. Out of this synthesis grew a new and richer Chinese civilization and a revivified empire that outshone the most glorious days of Han.

The challenge to classic Chinese civilization was posed most dramatically as a "barbarian" threat, for invaders overran North China and an alien religion, Indian Buddhism, menaced the ideological basis of Chinese society, but the challenge was more internal than external in origin. Only because the Han political system had collapsed of its own inner contradictions were the "barbarians" able to pour into China. Only because the Han synthesis of Confucian ideology, pseudoscientific superstitions, and Legalist practices had proved spiritually unsatisfying and politically inadequate were the Chinese receptive to Buddhism. In fact, thinking men first deserted Confucianism for Taoism before turning to Buddhism.

The Later Han and its aftermath saw the breakdown of a whole social order. Conditions were not unlike those in the Roman Empire at a slightly later date. They might even be described as protofeudal. As the central government weakened, the bulk of the land and its peasant cultivators gravitated into the hands of great landowners. These drew together for self-protection into extended family groups. They also consolidated their control over their subordinates. Tenant farmers gradually declined in status into virtual serfs. Impoverished peasants, fleeing the government tax collectors or the "barbarians," gave themselves and their services to powerful landowners in return for economic security and protection, becoming hereditary dependents or "guests" (*k'o*) of their patrons. Those among the dependents and serfs who had martial inclinations became the personal soldiers of the great landlords, and private armies replaced the former peasant levies. Each great family came to possess its own fortified manors and fortresses. The "barbarian" invasions, the constant wars and usurpations, and the movement of whole family groups to the South as organized military and economic units contributed to the militarization of society.

The large self-sufficient manor became the chief economic unit, and trade consequently languished. Administrative centers declined in size, and trading cities were drastically reduced. Copper coinage virtually went out of use in some regions, and barter, which had always persisted in rural areas, became again the rule throughout the country.

The Upsurge of Taoism.   The Confucian bureaucrat found only a shrinking role in the new society, and his scholasticism and preoccupation with rituals and the past proved of little help in meeting the problems of the day. During the Later Han the Confucian tradition had dominated society as never before, but as central government disintegrated, thinking men turned away from Confucianism's social teachings and began to look inward. Since society and government now seemed hopelessly degenerate, men again became interested in the old Taoist problem of the individual's relationship to nature and his personal perfection or salvation. This Taoist current of thought had no doubt always existed, particularly among the common people, but now it rose prominently to the surface of Chinese society. Wang Ch'ung (died about 100 A.D.), perhaps the most original thinker of Han times, had presaged the turning of educated men away from Confucianism in his iconoclastic and skeptical *Disquisitions* (*Lun heng*). The precocious Wang Pi (226–249), the most brilliant man of his day, showed the new interest in Taoism in his great commentaries on the *Tao te ching* and the *Classic of Changes.*

The outstanding expression of the Neo-Taoist intellectual current of the third century was called *ch'ing-t'an,* translated as "pure discussions" or "purity debates." The men in this tradition held themselves disdainfully aloof from unsavory politics and all other mundane matters. Their answer to the social and political disillusionment of the time was to develop their own aesthetic sensibilities and give individualistic expression to their every impulse. Typical of such men were the Seven Sages of the Bamboo Grove, a group of wealthy and eccentric recluses, living at the Western Chin capital, who loved to engage in philosophical debate, compose poetry, play the lute, enjoy nature, and drink to excess. A similar but even more eccentric group was the Eight Understanding Ones who lived at Nanking in the fourth century. In turning their backs on government, such men robbed society of some of its natural leaders, thus contributing to the general breakdown.

Another aspect of the Taoist resurgence was the growing interest in alchemy as a method of obtaining an elixir of life. A monumental work on alchemy, the *Pao-p'u-tzu,* appeared in the early fourth century. The search for elixirs probably led to the experimental eating of all sorts of organic and inorganic substances, which may have contributed to the extraordinarily catholic tastes of the Chinese and the richness of their culinary art. It also contributed to the development of medicinal knowledge through the discovery of many beneficial drugs and led to even broader protoscientific inquiry. One reason why later Chinese thinkers turned away from scientific experimentation was its association in their minds with Taoism.

A more widespread Taoist immortality cult centered on concepts of inner hygiene. By eschewing wine, meat, and cereals and by breathing exercises, practitioners supposedly cleansed the three "cinnabar fields" in their bodies, nurtured the 36,000 internal gods, and suppressed the three worms that were the causes of disease, old age, and death. This cult, which flourished between the third and sixth centuries, eventually evolved into the breathing exercises and general hygiene systems that are still popular among Chinese.

Popular Taoist Religion.   The most spectacular aspect of the upsurge of Taoism was its development as an organized popular religion. Very possibly the whole concept of collective worship and religious organization was derived from Buddhism, which was seeping into China at this time. Certainly many of the books of the huge Taoist canon that was later developed were nothing more than close imitations of Buddhist texts.

The revolts of the Yellow Turbans and the Five Pecks of Rice band in 184 A.D. were the first clear signs that Taoism had given birth to organized popular religions. Faith-healing was at the heart of both these religious movements. Popular Taoism in time developed an enormous pantheon, headed by a triad of deities and at the lower levels composed of immortals and historic human beings. It also borrowed heavily from Buddhism, eventually accepting the concept of the indestructible soul, an afterlife in heaven rather than corporeal immortality, and the value of good works as a means of reaching heaven and avoiding hell. In later centuries the distinctions between popular Taoism and popular Buddhism became vague, and the two tended to merge in a confused mass of mythology, superstitions, and magical practices.

After the suppression of the Yellow Turbans and the Five Pecks of Rice band near the end of the Later Han, the Taoist religions were never again reconstituted as effectively centralized churches, but individual parishes remained, and the movement flourished under their atomized leadership. The local priest was supported by gifts received at religious ceremonies and by the traditional tithes of five pecks of rice from his parishioners. Taoist monasteries and convents also developed in obvious imitation of Buddhist monasticism, but the monks were commonly allowed to marry, and the intellectual and moral standards of their communities tended to be very low. Taoist sects also appeared in great numbers, again under the influence of sectarian Chinese Buddhism.

Various efforts were made to unify the Taoist sects and parishes, but with no great success. An emperor of the "barbarian" Northern Wei dynasty was persuaded to proclaim Taoism the official religion of the state in 444, and various later rulers accorded it official recognition. In 1019 the hereditary leader of one of the Taoist sects, who claimed descent from Chang Ling, the second-century founder of the Five Pecks of Rice band, was granted a great tract of land in Kiangsi in South China and was invested as "Heavenly Master." In the late thirteenth century the Chang family was accorded official recognition as the leader of the Taoist church and during the next century was given a certain degree of official control over the Taoist priests of the whole land. The so-called Taoist "popes" of this line maintained some of their holdings and at least the theory of their leadership until 1927.

The Coming of Buddhism

Indian Buddhism.   The resurgence of Taoism in China at a time of political disruption is quite understandable; the even greater popularity of Buddhism is more surprising. The Indian religion flatly contradicted the dearest concepts and ideals of the Chinese. It constituted an even more direct challenge to Chinese civilization than did Western culture in the nineteenth century, and its adoption represented the greatest borrowing from abroad that the Chinese were to know before modern times. Buddhism is the chief cultural link between the peoples of East and South Asia, but its contrasting histories in India and China highlight the differences rather than the similarities between these two spiritual and psychological ends of the earth.

Indian Buddhism was based on a series of premises that the ancient Chinese would never have understood. It assumed that life was essentially painful. It also assumed that life was unending, since one existence was tied to the next by *karma,* a term literally meaning "act" but implying causality. Birth leads to old age, death, and further births in an endless chain of causality, which explains the differences in status and the seeming injustices one sees in the world. The Indian Buddhist, unlike the Chinese Confucian, was not interested in correcting these injustices and perfecting the social order but in escaping the painful cycle of existence.

The historic Buddha, known as Sakyamuni, lived around 500 B.C. in what is now the southern edge of Nepal north of India. Distressed by the suffering he saw around him, he abandoned his family and adopted an ascetic way of life, but found that this led nowhere. Subsequently, sitting in meditation, he achieved enlightenment, discovering the "Middle Way" between the extremes of self-indulgence and self-mortification. He thus became the Buddha, "the Enlightened One," and began to preach his wonderful discovery to a devoted band of disciples.

The essence of the Buddha's ideas was expressed in the Four Noble Truths: life is painful; the origin of pain is desire; the cessation of pain is to be sought by ending desire; and the way to this goal is through his Noble Eightfold Path—that is, his rules for right living. These constituted, from the Chinese point of view, an extremely ascetic way of life. The end objective was Nirvana, which was not the achievement of godhood or the salvation of the soul in the Western sense but merely the breaking of the chain of existence through the ending of all desires. Although literally meaning "emptiness," Nirvana was felt to be not simply extinction but something more, like the peaceful merging of a drop of water into the sea.

Buddhism early developed into a monastic church, and around the first century B.C. its hitherto oral teachings began to be written down in two closely related Indo-European languages. The Pali scriptures have been preserved in Ceylon, and the Sanskrit scriptures have been preserved largely through translations into Chinese and Tibetan. The Buddhist canon, known as the Tripitaka, or "three baskets," is traditionally divided into the *Vinayas* or "disciplines" for monastic life, the *Sutras* or "discourses," which constitute the major teachings, and the *Abhidharmas* or scholastic elaborations of the teachings. It is a huge collection of writings. The Chinese Tripitaka, for example, consists of more than sixteen hundred works in over five thousand sections.

The Spread and Development of Buddhism.   Buddhism is a universal religion, in which all men are equal in the Buddhist "law," or teachings. Like Christianity and Islam, the two great universal religions of the Mediterranean area, it spread widely. Indian traders and travelers carried it by sea throughout Southeast Asia and to South China. It also spread among the Greek kingdoms left over by Alexander's conquests on the northwestern frontiers of the Indian subcontinent. Gandhara in the border region between the present Pakistan and Afghanistan became a particular stronghold of Buddhism. The greatest monarch of the Kushan Empire of the Yüeh-chih, who ruled around 100 A.D. from North India to the Tarim Basin, also was an ardent patron of Buddhism. He championed the faith in Central Asia, and from there it spread into North China. A third wave of Buddhist propagation rolled northward a few centuries later, through Tibet and on into Mongolia. This was a late and degenerate form of Buddhism, which contained a large element of Hinduism and soon absorbed the popular demon worship of Tibet. The resultant Lamaism and the theocratic society it produced in Tibet and Mongolia bear small resemblance to the original teachings of the Buddha.

Even the purer forms of Buddhism divided at an early date into two major trends. These are usually known as Mahayana or the Greater Vehicle and Hinayana or the Lesser Vehicle, also called Theravada, "the doctrine of the Elders." Theravada, which remained closer to original Buddhism, is still the religion of Ceylon, Burma, Thailand, and Cambodia, while the Buddhism of China, Korea, Japan, and Vietnam stems largely from Mahayana.

The Greater Vehicle was "greater" in the sense of its all-inclusiveness. Since it distinguished between absolute and relative truth, it could tolerate even contradictory ideas as representing various degrees of relative truth accommodated to the different levels of understanding of its believers. Mahayana developed a vast body of metaphysical speculation and a huge pantheon. In place of the godless religion of the historical Buddha, the Mahayanists have myriads of godlike Buddhas in eons of time. They also developed a new type of deity, the Bodhisattva or "Enlightened Existence," who, though he has achieved the enlightenment of a Buddha, stays back in this world to help others to salvation before passing on into Nirvana himself.

Because of the concept of Bodhisattvas dedicated to saving other weaker creatures, the emphasis in Mahayana Buddhism shifted from enlightenment through "one's own strength" to salvation through "the strength of another." Faith was all that was necessary. The *Lotus Sutra,* a popular Mahayanist scripture, predicts the eventual salvation of all animal life. (Buddhism recognizes no division between humans and animals.) Naturally Bodhisattvas became the great popular gods of Mahayana Buddhism. For example, the Buddha Amitabha (Chinese: O-mi-t'o Fo; Japanese: Amida Butsu), who was a Bodhisattva in origin, became the great savior as the "Deity of the Western Paradise." Similarly Avalokitesvara (Chinese: Kuan-yin; Japanese: Kannon), gradually changing in sex, emerged as the benign "Goddess of Mercy." Mahayana thus provided compassionate, comforting gods for every human need.

Nirvana also gradually changed its meaning, at least for the less sophisticated Mahayanist believers. Increasingly, it came to mean salvation in a very definite afterlife in paradise. Descriptions and portrayals of this paradise became quite specific and those of hell even more graphic and gruesomely convincing. The Bodhisattva ideal of aid to others led to a strong emphasis

The Bodhisattva Kuan-yin carved in stone, from the Northern Chou dynasty (557–581 A.D.).

in Mahayana on charity—on good works to help others and to contribute to one's own salvation. Buddhism thus was turned somewhat from its original antisocial contemplative bent. The concept of charity made social work important; the possibility of salvation through faith made monasticism, celibacy, and asceticism less necessary.

The Introduction of Buddhism to China.   Many of these developments in Mahayana took place after Buddhism reached China, but the tolerance for other religious concepts and the wide inclusiveness of early Mahayana made it from the start more palatable to Chinese than the original religion would have been. Appearing to the Chinese at first as a variant of Taoism, it had a powerful appeal to a "barbarianized" North China and a demoralized South. To the superstitious it was a potent new magic, to the educated a stimulating new set of ideas. It was the first organized universal faith the Chinese had encountered. It had behind it the fruits of another great culture—the metaphysics and early science of India, a noble literature, a beautiful religious art, aesthetically satisfying ceremonials, the appeal of the peaceful

Nine-story brick pagoda erected at Cheng-ting in Hopei in 659 A.D.
and rebuilt in 1668.

monastic life in a troubled age, and the promise of personal salvation at a
time when there seemed to be no solution to man's worldly problems.

According to tradition, Buddhism was first introduced to China as the
result of a dream in 64 A.D. of the second emperor of the Later Han, Ming
Ti. The story is apocryphal, but already at this time there was a Buddhist
group at a noble's court in the lower Yangtze Valley, and by the next
century Buddhism had become entrenched in what is now North Vietnam.
Soon stupas, the Buddhist reliquary towers, were being erected by converts
in various parts of China. Modified by Chinese architectural concepts, these

stupas in time developed into the stone, brick, or wooden pagodas that have become so typical a part of the scenery of East Asia.

The first transmitters of Buddhism may have been traders, but the religion was soon being propagated more actively by missionaries. A Parthian prince, known to history by his Chinese name, An Shih-kao, was active as a missionary and translator of scriptures at Loyang during the latter part of the second century. An even greater transmitter of the faith was Kumarajiva, who was born in Central Asia to an Indian father, captured by a Chinese expedition around 382, and brought to China, where he headed a great translation project. No fewer than fifty-two of the ninety-eight scriptures he translated are still extant.

Chinese converts eventually became more important than the missionaries in transmitting the Indian religion to China. We have the names of close to two hundred East Asian monks, nine of them Koreans, who between the third and eighth centuries essayed the long and perilous trip to India to imbibe the Buddhist teachings at their source. This was the first great student migration of East Asian history. Fa-hsien, who left for India by way of Central Asia in 399 and returned by sea in 414, is particularly famous for the record of his trip that he left. Since the Indians, lacking much interest in history, rarely bothered to record dates, the carefully dated accounts of Fa-hsien and the other Chinese Buddhist pilgrims have proved invaluable in establishing Indian and Central Asian chronology. The most famous of the Buddhist pilgrims was Hsüan-tsang, who made the round trip to India between 629 and 645 by way of Central Asia. The account of his travels, the *Record of the Western Regions,* is the most important work of its sort. A third Chinese pilgrim, I-ching, who between 671 and 695 made the round trip to India by the southern route, compiled records of more than fifty other pilgrims.

Buddhism, unlike Christianity in the Roman Empire, apparently was taken up by the rich before it spread downward to the poor. At first it seems to have made more rapid progress in the "barbarian" North than in the South, perhaps because the non-Chinese rulers of this area felt no prejudice against it as a foreign religion. The greatest imperial patrons of the new religion were the emperors of the "barbarian" Northern Wei dynasty (386–534). Two groups of Buddhist cave temples, at Yün-kang near their first capital in northern Shansi and at Lung-men near their second capital of Loyang, contain some of the finest artistic remains of early Chinese Buddhism. By the sixth century, however, the South was as thoroughly permeated by Buddhism as the North.

Part of Buddhism's success was due to its readiness to compromise with Taoism and Confucianism, tolerating the former as an inferior level of truth and the latter as a political and social philosophy that was not incompatible with its own basic teachings. Ever since, there has been a strong tendency

*Stone bas-relief of the empress as a donor with attendants, from
the Lung-men rock temples (near Loyang) of the Northern Wei
dynasty (about 522 A.D.).*

among the Chinese to synthesize "the three religions" or to maintain them
side by side. At this time, however, Buddhism was definitely the dominant
member of the trio, and a great proportion of the higher intellectual capacities and artistic genius of the Chinese was devoted to the translation and
interpretation of its scriptures and the building and beautifying of its temples
and monasteries.

The whole epoch from the fourth century to the ninth might well be
called the Buddhist age of both Chinese and Asian history. During this
period, Buddhism blanketed the whole of the Asian continent, except for
Siberia and West Asia, giving to this vast area a degree of cultural unity
that has never again been matched. This, however, was but a brief moment
of religious unity. Buddhism began to decline in India as early as the sixth
century and by the fifteenth had virtually disappeared. It was wiped out in
Central Asia in the ninth century by the inroads of Islam. Meanwhile, the
Hinayana of Southeast Asia and the Mahayana of East Asia had begun to
drift apart, and a serious decline had commenced in Chinese Buddhism.

The "Barbarians" Restore the Empire

The Strength of the Imperial Tradition.   To an observer of world history in the fourth century it might have appeared that Rome would always endure but that the days of the Chinese Empire were over. North China, the heartland of the empire, was completely overrun by "barbarians"; South China was obviously incapable of restoring imperial unity; and the whole land was being swept by a foreign religion which had an otherworldly emphasis and a celibate, monastic ideal that cut at the roots of Chinese philosophy and the family-centered social system.

The Chinese Empire, however, was eventually reconstituted, while Rome faded into a mere memory. The "barbarian" conquerors of the North were no different from the "barbarian" conquerors of Rome in their hope that they could appropriate for themselves the empire they were defeating. They differed from their Western counterparts in that they eventually succeeded in this effort, recreating by the middle of the fifth century a fair facsimile of the old empire, which started a process that led by the seventh century to a Chinese Empire richer and stronger than Han had ever been. The contrast with the steadily sinking fortunes of Rome is striking and constitutes a sharp parting of the historical ways between the peoples at the two ends of the Eurasian continent.

There is no certain answer to the question why the Chinese Empire was restored but not the Roman. One reason may be that the southern dynasties maintained the old imperial tradition more fully than did Greek Byzantium and had a stronger influence on the North than Byzantium did on Italy or France because of the greater geographic compactness of China. Another reason may have been the superiority of the Han imperial ideal to the Roman. The concept of just and ethical rule by an emperor whose possession of the Mandate of Heaven demonstrated the support of his people and who exercised his power through a bureaucracy of educated men, chosen not by birth or by chance but because of merit, may have been more understandable to people of this age than was the Roman ideal of rule through impersonal law. The Chinese writing system also probably made for greater cultural continuity than did the Latin and Greek scripts of the West. The "barbarians" had to learn Chinese if they were to read and write, since Chinese characters could not be easily applied to their languages. Moreover, even the Chinese whose spoken "dialects" were mutually unintelligible had the written language in common. And finally, the very size and density of the Chinese population probably led to a more rapid and complete absorption of the "barbarian" invaders than happened in Europe. Since Chinese agriculture was more intensive than that of Europe, it produced a denser population, and the invaders thus were more rapidly submerged in the large numbers of Chinese around them.

The "Five Barbarians" and the Sixteen Kingdoms.   The Chinese tradition-ally describe the fourth-century invaders of North China as the "Five Bar-barians." These were the Turkish Hsiung-nu and another Turkish group; the Hsien-pei (or Hsien-pi), a Mongolian people from the northeast; and two groups of Tibetans from the west. The Hsien-pei overran the edges of the North China Plain as early as 281, and the Tibetans started their depredations in 296, but the main inundation came after the revolt of the Hsiung-nu in North China in 304.

During the period from 304 to 439 the Chinese throne in North China was claimed by a number of contending "barbarian" and Chinese groups, which historians have fittingly dubbed the Sixteen Kingdoms. The Hsiung-nu band that destroyed Loyang in 316 adopted the dynastic name of Chao. This kingdom is usually called the Earlier Chao in contrast to the Later Chao of one of their rebellious generals, Shih Lo, who destroyed the Earlier Chao in 329. Shih Lo attempted to restore a more strictly tribal rule than that of the more Sinicized Earlier Chao, and he treated the Chinese with great severity. Finally in 349 the people rose up and destroyed his successors.

Meanwhile a Chinese general had set up an Earlier Liang dynasty in the western panhandle of Kansu and Hsien-pei tribes had created the Earlier Yen in the Peking area, while in 351 a strong Tibetan leader, Fu Chien, set up the highly Sinicized state of Earlier Ch'in at the old historic capital of Ch'ang-an. Earlier Ch'in conquered Earlier Yen in 370, establishing a brief period of comparative peace and unity in North China.

This peace was shattered by the usurpation of the throne at Ch'ang-an in 384 by a Tibetan general, who founded the Later Ch'in, and in rapid succession Hsien-pei tribes founded Later Yen in the northeast and Western Yen in Shansi, while Tibetan groups founded Later Liang in the Kansu panhandle and Western Ch'in in the far west. All these were very short-lived kingdoms, and they were followed in turn by six other equally transitory so-called dynasties.

The Northern Wei.   Finally one "barbarian" tribe managed to establish a more lasting government and unify the North. This was the T'o-pa tribe of Hsien-pei, which had moved into northern Shansi as the Hsiung-nu had moved southward. The T'o-pa declared themselves the independent state of Wei (called the Northern Wei) in 386 and succeeded in pushing back some newly risen pastoral rivals on the northern steppes. By 439 they had also destroyed their "barbarian" rivals in China and had unified the North.

After the Northern Wei had incorporated under their rule the densely populated agricultural lands of the North China Plain, a subtle change began to take place in this originally "barbarian" empire. Like the Earlier Ch'in, the strongest of the previous "barbarian" dynasties, the Northern Wei from the start had been a semi-Sinicized state, but now the process of

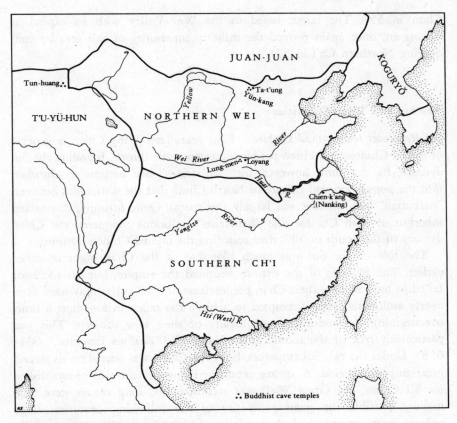

JUAN-JUAN

KOGURYŌ

Tun-huang

Ta-t'ung
Yün-kang

T'U-YÜ-HUN

N O R T H E R N   W E I

Wei River

Lung-men
Loyang

Huai R.

Chien-k'ang
(Nanking)

Yangtze River

S O U T H E R N   C H'I

Hsi (West) R.

∴ Buddhist cave temples

CHINA AROUND 500 A.D.

cultural absorption was accelerated. The agricultural lands were not divided among the T'o-pa tribesmen but were administered in the traditional Chinese manner, and the T'o-pa themselves were relegated to the status of a soldiery.

By the late fifth century, the process of acculturation had gone so far that the Northern Wei court embarked on a conscious policy of Sinification. In 493–494 the capital was moved from the present Ta-t'ung in northern Shansi to Loyang, which had been the capital of the Later Han and Western Chin. At about the same time, Chinese was made the only official court language, and the T'o-pa aristocrats were ordered to adopt Chinese dress, customs, and surnames and were encouraged to intermarry with the local population.

The complete Sinification of the court led to serious revolts in 524 by the still partly tribal military forces. The central government also found itself increasingly the prey of its own great families. In 534–535 it was divided under puppet emperors into Eastern and Western Wei dynasties, and through usurpations these became Northern Ch'i in 550 and Northern

Chou in 557. The latter, based in the Wei Valley with its capital at
Ch'ang-an, once again proved the military superiority of this area by conquering Northern Ch'i in 577.

The Sui and T'ang Dynasties

Sui Recreates the Unified Empire.   Four years later Yang Chien, a general
of mixed Chinese and Hsien-pei blood, usurped the throne, founding the Sui
dynasty. By this time, however, the "barbarians" had become so absorbed
into the population and culture of North China that the distinction between
"barbarian" and Chinese was largely theoretical. Quite fittingly, this mixed
inheritor of both Chinese and "barbarian" traditions conquered the Ch'en
dynasty of the South in 589, thus restoring the unified Chinese Empire.

The role of the Sui was much like that of the Ch'in eight centuries
earlier. The founder of the dynasty reunited the empire, but his successor
failed to hold it. Like their Ch'in predecessors, the Sui rulers may have been
overly ambitious. They attempted to achieve too much in too short a time,
overstraining the endurance and loyalty of their new subjects. This was
particularly true of the second ruler, Yang Ti ("Zealous Emperor," 604–
618). Under the two Sui emperors, however, China was started on its second
great imperial period. A strong centralized government was re-established
for all China; the Great Wall was reconstructed; long canals were dug,
making possible the great prosperity of the following centuries; huge
palaces were erected; and the prestige of the Chinese Empire was fully
restored.

Once again, the pendulum of conquest swung outward from China into
the lands of the "barbarians." The *yin* of "barbarian" rule in China, by
infusing new blood and new martial ardor into China, had produced once
again the *yang* of Chinese imperial conquest. Chinese control was re-
established over northern Vietnam and expeditions were sent against the
Cham state in southern Vietnam and to Taiwan. In the north, the T'u-chüeh,
the earliest known form of the name Turk, had overthrown their nomad
masters but had split into eastern and western confederations in 581. The
Eastern Turks now acknowledged the suzerainty of China, and in 609 Sui
also conquered a mixed Tibetan and Hsien-pei state (called T'u-yü-hun) in
northern Tibet.

Yang Ti, however, alienated his people because of his endless wars and
the tremendous labor needed for the construction of canals, walls, and
palaces. The prestige of the dynasty was also seriously tarnished by a
disastrous campaign in 612 against the Korean kingdom of Koguryŏ in
North Korea and South Manchuria. Serious revolts broke out, forcing him
to terminate inconclusively his campaigns of 613 and 614 against Koguryŏ.

Stone relief from the tomb of the T'ang emperor T'ai Tsung (626–649), depicting one of his battle chargers attended by a bearded "barbarian" groom.

In 615 he was badly defeated by the Eastern Turks, who had hitherto been his loyal vassals. The empire then started to disintegrate, and Yang Ti fled to South China, where he was assassinated in 618.

The World Empire of T'ang.   The man who emerged victorious from the free-for-all that followed the collapse of Sui was Li Shih-min, who was a prominent official and general of mixed Chinese and "barbarian" blood from Shansi in the North. He captured the capital, Ch'ang-an, in 617 and the next year founded the T'ang dynasty, placing his father on the throne. After eliminating his brothers, he had his father abdicate in 626 and thereafter ruled in his own name until 649. He is known to history as T'ai Tsung ("Grand Ancestor") and his reign (626–649) is considered the first great high point of the T'ang dynasty. The whole T'ang dynasty, like the Earlier Han, is regarded as one of the two golden ages of the Chinese Empire.

In 630 T'ai Tsung subjugated the Eastern Turks, and in great campaigns in 639–640 and 647–648 he wrested the Tarim Basin from the Western Turks. He was aided in this victory by the Turkish Uighur tribes, which at this time broke away from the Western Turkish Empire to become the loyal allies of the T'ang and their chief source of military power in Central Asia. Chinese suzerainty was gradually extended beyond the Pamirs over the states of the Oxus Valley. In 657 the Western Turkish Empire was finally broken up, and various Turkish groups were pushed southward into India and westward into West Asia and Europe.

Tibet, which had been unified for the first time in 607, also came under Chinese suzerainty, and from there a Chinese emissary, leading Tibetan troops, pacified a part of North India, bringing back to Ch'ang-an in 648 a captive Indian princeling. This incident was the only military encounter between China and India before recent years, and its uniqueness illustrates the effectiveness of the mountain barrier between these two great masses of humanity. T'ai Tsung's armies were twice repulsed by the Korean state of Koguryŏ, but in 668 his successor, Kao Tsung ("High Ancestor," 649–683), succeeded with the help of the southeastern Korean kingdom of Silla in crushing a coalition of Koguryŏ, Paekche (in southwest Korea), and Japan. Thereafter a unified Korea under Silla remained a loyal vassal of T'ang.

T'ang power extended over a vast area from southern Siberia to Southeast Asia and westward through Tibet and Central Asia to the Caspian Sea. Around the borders of China proper clustered vassal states, controlled by six protectorates. Four of these were named for the cardinal points, as in An-hsi ("the pacified west") in the Tarim Basin, An-tung ("the pacified east") in the Korean area, and An-nan ("the pacified south"), from which Annam, the usual Chinese name for Vietnam, was derived. Beyond these vassal states were others, such as Japan and various kingdoms in Southeast, South, and West Asia, which recognized a vague Chinese suzerainty by occasionally presenting tribute. T'ang rule thus, from the Chinese point of view, was virtually worldwide.

The T'ang, like the Han before it, was almost brought to an end by an empress. The Empress Wu dominated Kao Tsung's later years and after his death ruled for a while through puppet emperors. Then in 690 she assumed the title for herself—the only time a woman ever did this in China—and changed the dynastic name to Chou. As a usurper, and a woman at that, she has been severely condemned by Chinese historians, but actually she was a strong and able ruler, and she greatly furthered the supremacy of the merit bureaucracy over the aristocracy. The Empress Wu was set aside in her eighties in a palace *coup d'état* in 705, but after a few years of confusion another able ruler came to the throne in 712. He is known to history as Hsüan Tsung ("Mysterious Ancestor") or Ming Huang ("Enlightened Emperor"), and his long reign (712–756) represents the second blossoming of the dynasty.

Actually T'ang was by this time a far more populous and richer empire

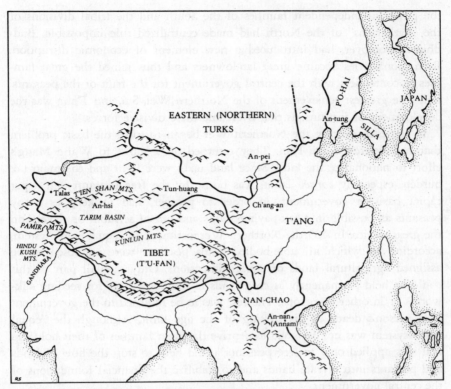

THE T'ANG EMPIRE IN THE EARLY EIGHTH CENTURY

than it had been in the days of T'ai Tsung. But it had also started to show signs of decay. Financial problems multiplied, and the pendulum of conquest started to swing back against China. In 747 Kao Hsien-chih, a Korean general in the service of T'ang, led an army across the Pamirs and the Hindu Kush to break up an attempted juncture between the Arabs and the Tibetans, but this was the last highwater mark of T'ang power. In 751 he was disastrously defeated by the Arabs at Talas, north of Ferghana, and Hsüan Tsung's reign ended a few years later in rebellion and an apparent breakup of the empire. With the aid of its "barbarian" allies, the dynasty was restored and continued for another century and a half, but it never again showed its earlier power and verve.

The Revival of Centralized Rule

The Landholding and Military Systems. The reunification of China by force of arms in the sixth century and the conquest of a far-flung empire in the seventh were merely the surface manifestations of a much more profound process—the restoration of a stable centralized government. For centuries the powerful independent families of the South and the tribal divisions of the "barbarians" of the North had made centralized rule impossible. Buddhism, moreover, had introduced a new element of economic disruption. Rich monasteries became great landowners and thus joined the great families as contenders with the central government for the fruit of the peasants' toil. The greatest achievement of the Northern Wei, Sui, and T'ang was the development of institutions that overcame these divisive forces.

In the fifth century the Northern Wei began to solve the basic problem that had destroyed the Han. They returned, in a sense, to Wang Mang's effort to nationalize the land. Since land taxes were light and the main tax burden, especially *corvée* labor, was borne by the free peasantry on a per capita basis, a government, in order to prosper, had to keep as many peasants as possible in a tax-paying status and out of serfdom or slavery on the great estates. In 485 the Northern Wei instituted an "equal field" system, according to which all able-bodied adult peasants were supposed to be assigned agricultural lands of equal dimensions. Only a small part of this could be held permanently as crop lands in mulberry trees for feeding silkworms or in other tree crops. The rest was to be returned to the government at a person's death or his passing of the age limit. Although the "equal field" system was not designed to deprive the great families of their holdings and was applied only to free peasants, it did help to stop the flow of lands and peasants into private hands and to stabilize the financial foundations of the central government.

The Northern Wei also reinstituted a system by which the people were divided into groups that were mutually responsible for one another's conduct and tax payments. This sort of collective-guarantee system had been used in one form or another since antiquity, and it was continued in more recent times as the *pao-chia* system for maintaining local order. This system sets neighbors to watching neighbors, since they are all held accountable for one another.

During this period also, self-supporting military colonies of soldier-farmers were set up along the northern frontier. Similar colonies had been created during the Han, but from the Six Dynasties period on they became a permanent element in the defense of the empire. Another important military institution—the militia system—was inaugurated by the Western Wei (535–557) and Northern Chou (557–581), the successor states to Northern Wei in the Ch'ang-an area. Able-bodied peasants were given military training and organized into regular forces like the tribal soldiery. Under the T'ang this militia service became part of the tax burden that peasants bore as landholders under the "equal field" system.

During the Sui and T'ang dynasties the "equal field" system was greatly elaborated. The Sui applied it to the whole country and forced the great families to fit into the system by assigning their holdings as "rank lands," scaling downward from a maximum of about 1370 acres for the highest rank. In the T'ang the great families and officials were assigned similar "rank lands" and in addition "office lands" varying in size according to the specific government positions they held. Organs of local government were supported by "office fields." The bulk of the land, however, was divided equally among the peasants. Each able-bodied male between the ages of eighteen and fifty-nine was supposed to receive about 13.7 acres, of which only one-fifth could be permanently owned "mulberry" land. On this economic base, he was to pay the government in taxes a fixed amount of grain; a certain amount of silk or hemp, depending on the type of textile produced in his region; and twenty days per year of *corvée* labor for the central government and other periods of labor for the local organs of government. This *corvée* labor was sometimes communted into textile or money taxes. In addition, certain able-bodied peasants who were exempted from other taxes and levies had to render periodic military service, usually without pay and at their own expense.

To operate this complicated landholding system, a careful census and land register were necessary for the whole country. Remaining examples of such surveys show that every piece of land was indeed allotted by specific category to individual taxpayers. This was perhaps as complicated a system of landholding and taxation as was to be found anywhere in the world before the late nineteenth century, but it worked reasonably well for about a century, supporting the Chinese Empire during an outstanding epoch.

T'ang Prosperity.   During the early T'ang, the central government had an ample tax income, which was equaled by expenditures only after the imperial clan and the organs of government had undergone a long period of growth. With their characteristic genius for organization, the Chinese at this time developed units of measure of approximately equal value for the principal commodities in the economy. Thus, a string of one thousand cash, an "ounce" of silver, a "bushel" of grain, a "bolt" of silk, and a "weight" of silk floss were all roughly equivalent in value. Counting by this standard "unit" of value, the tax income of the central government, according to one of several such listings, amounted to over 52 million "units." In addition, the central government enjoyed as a part of the tax system the free labor and military service of its millions of peasants.

The government unquestionably was far more affluent than it had ever been under the Han. Advances in technology and administration were probably responsible for part of this gain, but the chief reason was the great growth in population of the Yangtze Valley during the intervening centuries. Although the government remained in the Northwest and in the hands of a military aristocracy from that region, the chief breadbasket was no longer the dry wheat and millet lands of the Wei Valley and the North

China Plain but the rich rice-growing paddy fields of the lower Yangtze region.

This situation explains the great canal-building activity of the Sui. An efficient transport system was necessary between the South and the capital and frontier areas in the North to enable the empire to take full advantage of its rich southern provinces. Yang Ti, by connecting various older canals and building new ones, constructed by 610 a Grand Canal system stretching from the Hangchow area south of the Yangtze to the Yellow River and from there westward to Ch'ang-an and northward to the Peking area. The modern Grand Canal was identical with this first system as far north as the Huai River but then cut directly across the North China Plain to Peking.

In theory the "equal field" system rested on the periodic redistribution of the bulk of the farm land among the tax-paying peasants, but it is doubtful that there was ever much actual redistribution. The population grew quickly because of domestic peace, and the peasantry thus increased faster than the land resources. The result was that most peasants received from their fathers less than their full quota of land, and most of this came to be registered as permanent possessions. At the same time, cumulative imperial grants, as in the Later Han, reduced the total quantity of land available to the tax-paying peasants. By the first half of the eighth century the whole system was obviously breaking down. The collapse of the T'ang government toward the close of Hsüan Tsung's reign may be attributed in part to the failure of the landholding and tax system. In any case, the system was abandoned at this time and was never again attempted on the same scale.

The Bureaucracy and the Examination System.   A dependable bureaucracy was indispensable for the centralized government. After the Han system of government schools and examinations had decayed, the Wei and Western Chin dynasties of the third century attempted to secure efficient administrators by having local authorities classify men of merit in nine grades and recommend the best for government service, but the powerful local families perverted the system by putting their own members and henchmen at the top of the lists, which became in time merely rankings of social status.

It was not until the Sui and T'ang that Chinese rulers were able to reconstitute a system for recruitment of officials that would help preserve the central government from the complete domination of the rich, aristocratic families. The first Sui ruler restored the old Han emphasis on Confucian traditions as being the most suitable ideological basis for a centralized government. He also reinstituted—though on a much more elaborate scale—the Han system of examinations for would-be bureaucrats based on a Confucian curriculum, and he reasserted the principle that the officials of the prefectures and districts should not be local aristocrats but appointees from the central government.

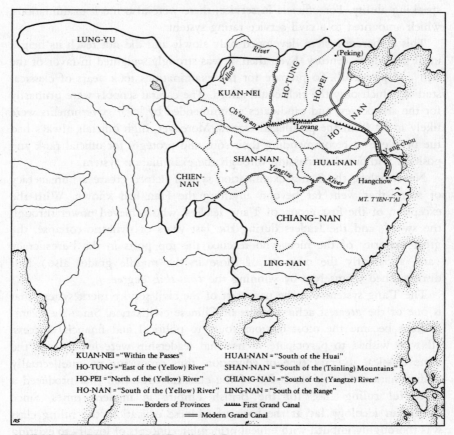

LUNG-YU

KUAN-NEI

HO-TUNG

HO-PEI

(Peking)

Yellow River

Ch'ang-an

Loyang

HO-NAN

Yang-chou

SHAN-NAN

HUAI-NAN

Yangtze River

Hangchow

CHIEN-NAN

MT. T'IEN-T'AI

CHIANG-NAN

LING-NAN

KUAN-NEI = "Within the Passes"
HO-TUNG = "East of the (Yellow) River"
HO-PEI = "North of the (Yellow) River"
HO-NAN = "South of the (Yellow) River"

HUAI-NAN = "South of the Huai"
SHAN-NAN = "South of the (Tsinling) Mountains"
CHIANG-NAN = "South of the (Yangtze) River"
LING-NAN = "South of the Range"

········· Borders of Provinces
᠊᠊᠊ First Grand Canal
═══ Modern Grand Canal

CHINA PROPER AROUND 700 A.D.

T'ang continued and expanded the government schools and examination system of the Sui. There was a series of specialized national schools at the capital, and the prefectures and districts also maintained institutions where local students could pursue their studies. Government examinations were held for the students of the capital schools and for nominees from the local governments. The Ministry of Rites administered these examinations amidst elaborate rituals. There were several different categories of examination degrees, such as "flowering talent" (*hsiu-ts'ai*) for current political problems, "presented scholar" (*chin-shih,* implying presentation to the emperor) for letters, and also examinations in classics, law, calligraphy, and mathematics. The last three, however, were considered merely technical skills leading to low positions, and in time the *chin-shih* degree became the most prestigious and the chief route to high government office. Before appointment, those who had passed the *chin-shih* examination faced a second series of examinations, administered by the Ministry of Personnel, in which they were judged not only on their written answers but on their personal appearance and speaking ability. For officials in service, there were also merit examinations, which amounted to a civil service rating system.

This elaborate system developed only slowly and did not reach its height until the eighth century. Even then, it was strongly weighted in favor of the rich and powerful. To prepare for the examinations took years of classical studies, which only the rich could afford. The capital schools were primarily for the aristocracy, and candidates recommended by local governments were likely to be from the privileged classes. Moreover, high officials always had the privilege of recommending their sons and protégés for official rank and position without their passing through the examination system.

Nevertheless, the T'ang examination system helped create a bureaucracy of merit that went far beyond anything the Han had known. With the exception of the first group of T'ang leaders, who achieved power through the sword, and the leaders during the last years of dynastic collapse, the great majority of the men who reached the top posts in the bureaucracy (and apparently the majority of those in the middle grades also) first distinguished themselves by winning the *chin-shih* degree.

The T'ang system was the true start of the civil service merit system that is one of the greatest achievements of Chinese civilization. Since the examinations became the most obvious route to political and financial success, all who wished to participate in national leadership were led to seek the same classical, literary type of education, thus producing an intellectually unified nation. One is reminded of the classical education that produced a successful ruling class for the British Empire in modern times. Since Confucian ideology lay at the basis of Chinese education, the ruling class was thoroughly imbued with ethical principles, concepts of loyalty to existing authority, and a strong sense of the value of rituals and decorum. Men of intellectual ability, singularly favored as they were by the system, became the strongest supporters of the government, instead of its critics, as has happened in so many other societies. The system even won the support of the lower classes for the established order, because there was always the possibility that a man of humble birth might pass the *chin-shih* examination and eventually become one of the emperor's chief ministers.

Of course, the examination system had its weaknesses too. The resulting prestige of scholarship, combined with the traditional prestige of political office, helped perpetuate a division of Chinese society by education into two major strata long after the power of the medieval aristocracy had faded. The emphasis on literary, historical, and scholarly subject matter in the examinations may also have given the ruling groups an overly scholastic, literary, and antiquarian bent, to the detriment of other more practical qualities. The system, while helping to produce extraordinary stability in China over the next millennium, may also have contributed to a slowing down of change and progress.

The Structure of Government. The Sui abolished the old commanderies (*chün*) and divided the country into a more uniform system of districts (*hsien*), grouped together in prefectures (*chou*). The T'ang added to this system by grouping prefectures together as provinces, called "circuits" (*tao*), of which there were originally ten and later fifteen.

To bind the empire together, T'ang also created an elaborate system of post-stations on the roads and waterways that radiated out from the capital. Commonly located at ten-mile intervals, these post-stations maintained inns for official travelers provided with government tallies and furnished them with horses or boats. The post-station system remained thereafter a standard part of Chinese government. T'ang also established barriers on the principal trade routes and strictly controlled city marketplaces as a way to tax and regulate trade. Despite this interest in taxes on trade, however, it showed the traditional Chinese scorn for merchants.

In T'ang times the top organs of the central government were the Imperial Secretariat, the Imperial Chancellery, and the Department of State Affairs. The first was the chief originator of government policies and imperial orders; the second, a stronghold of bureaucratic power, had the right to review these orders, thus serving as a check on the emperor's authority; the third carried out the orders agreed upon by the other two. This three-way division of power and the collegial sharing of leadership among high officials in each of these bodies ensured a division and balance of power in the high bureaucracy beneath the throne. Under the Department of State Affairs were Six Ministries or Boards (*Pu*): Personnel, Revenue, Rites, Military, Justice, and Public Works. This sixfold division of adminstration persisted in Chinese government down to the twentieth century.

An office that deserves special mention was the Board of Censors. It had the duty of ferreting out cases of treason or misgovernment and reporting them directly to the emperor. Its members were also to point out to the emperor (at no little risk to themselves) any imperfections in his conduct. The Board of Censors remained an important organ in the Chinese imperial government in later dynasties.

Ch'ang-an was both the focus and symbol of the highly centralized T'ang Empire. The eastern terminus of the great overland trade routes across Central Asia as well as the capital of the largest empire the world had yet seen, Ch'ang-an was thronged with people from all over Asia. The population of the capital district, including the city, its suburbs, and a little surrounding countryside, rose to 1,960,186. Its walls formed a great rectangle of slightly more than five by six miles. The city was laid out in modern checkerboard fashion. Broad and straight north-south and east-west thoroughfares divided it into 110 blocks, each of which was an administrative "village," with its own internal alleyways. A 500-foot-wide central thoroughfare led from the central southern gate of the city to the Imperial City (government head-

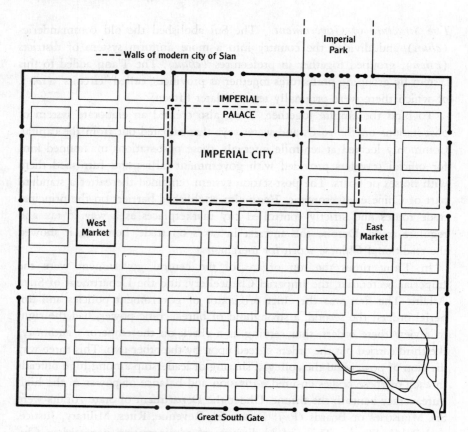

Imperial Park

Walls of modern city of Sian

IMPERIAL
PALACE

IMPERIAL CITY

West
Market

East
Market

Great South Gate

PLAN OF CH'ANG-AN DURING THE T'ANG

quarters) and beyond it the Imperial Palace at the north, dividing the city into eastern and western administrative halves, each with a large government-operated marketplace.

The whole plan and organization of Ch'ang-an illustrate the strict and careful control that the early T'ang maintained over society. The size and grandeur of the city suggest the dynasty's power and wealth. China during the seventh century towered high above all other political units of the time. During the Han dynasty China had drawn abreast of the Mediterranean world. Now it was starting on what was to prove to be almost a millennium of pre-eminence as the strongest, richest, and in many ways most advanced country in the world.

The Absorption of Buddhism

The Development of Sects.   Just as the Chinese incorporated the "barbar-ians" into a new and greater Chinese Empire, they also gradually absorbed

Buddhism, deriving cultural enrichment from it but neutralizing its challenge to Chinese values. Buddhism flourished economically and intellectually under the imperial patronage of the Northern Wei and in the early T'ang. It perhaps reached its apogee in China around 700 under the zealous patronage of the Empress Wu, who had once been a nun. The Buddhism that flourished from the fifth to the eighth centuries, however, was being steadily reshaped into a set of ideas and institutions that bore little resemblance to primitive Buddhism but fitted easily into the Chinese system.

The Indian love of philosophical speculation had given rise to numerous schools of thought; the Chinese love of classification now resulted in the organization of some of these different philosophical tendencies into sects. Some sects were direct philosophic transplants from India, as in the case of Fa-hsiang (Japanese: Hossō), brought back in 645 by the great traveler Hsüan-tsang. Those sects that prospered most, however, stressed elements that were native to Chinese thinking. One of these was T'ien-t'ai (Japanese: Tendai), founded by Chih-i (538–597) and named for its mountain head-quarters in Chekiang. Its popularity was based on its typically Chinese eclecticism, love of compromise, and skill at classification. It developed the Mahayana concept of relative truths, organizing the vast body of conflicting Buddhist doctrines into different levels of truth, each valid in its own way. T'ien-t'ai became the leading sect in the eighth and ninth centuries and helped establish the *Lotus Sutra* as the most popular scripture of East Asian Buddhism.

Another sect that came to the fore at much the same time was Chen-yen, the "True Word" (Japanese: Shingon). This was an esoteric or secret doctrine, strongly influenced by the Tantric cults of Hinduism. It taught that ultimate reality could not be expressed by words but was best suggested by magic signs and symbols. The incantations, magic formulas, and ceremonials that Chen-yen emphasized were readily appreciated by the Chinese, who were familiar with such things from Taoism and from the Confucian emphasis on ritual. Chen-yen masses for the dead, in particular, became extremely popular, because they fitted in well with traditional ancestor worship. Chen-yen's schematic cosmological drawings, known as *mandala* (Japanese: mandara), had great influence on later Chinese Buddhist art.

The Mayahana concept of salvation through faith also became the basis of a strong sectarian movement known as "Pure Land" (Ching-t'u; Japanese: Jōdo), a name for the Western Paradise of Amida. This sect stressed the simple act of faith of calling on the Buddha's name (*nien-fo;* Japanese: *nembutsu*). By the fifth century these ideas were entrenched in China. Popular rebellions from Sui times on drew spiritual inspiration from such forms of Buddhism, rather than from Taoism. The "Pure Land" sect appealed to the common man and became numerically the greatest force in East Asian Buddhism.

The last of the sectarian movements proved ultimately the most significant.

This was the Meditation sect, or Ch'an, better known by its Japanese name, Zen. It appeared in China in early T'ang times but did not become prominent until the ninth century. Zen was close to primitive Buddhism in its stress on meditation and intuitive insight or "enlightenment," but it derived perhaps even more from philosophical Taoism, which had also stressed these qualities. It taught that the only true reality was the Buddha nature within each person's heart. Though it derived a sense of the otherworldly and the infinite from India, this mysticism was applied in typically Chinese fashion to the mundane life of the individual. The meditative life became in China a life of hard work and rugged self-reliance. Zen's antischolastic, antitextual bias was pure Taoism. Instead of texts, it stressed oral instruction, particularly through the posing of outwardly nonsensical questions meant to shock the student out of his dependence on ordinary logic. In its love of nature and rustic simplicity, Zen was merely the old Taoist tradition in a new guise, and it therefore quite naturally became a major inspiration for artistic and poetic creativeness.

Although Zen never formed a well-organized church in China, its discipline of meditation and emphasis on self-reliance gave it much greater strength than the other sects derived from their monastic rules or intricate philosophies. Zen was the only type of Buddhism that continued a vigorous intellectual life after the T'ang. Gradually, the rest of Chinese Buddhism was absorbed either by Zen or by the popular "Pure Land" sect, and in time even these two lost their distinctiveness, merging in the vague mixture of superstitions into which Chinese Buddhism eventually degenerated.

Buddhism's Role in Society.   While the Chinese were modifying Buddhist ideas, they also were remolding its institutions to better fit Chinese society. Buddhist monasteries began to take on social functions as inns, public baths, and even primitive banking institutions. They also took over the burial of the dead until recent times. Celibacy, which was regarded by the Chinese as the most antisocial aspect of Buddhism, was in time relaxed to permit the marriage of the clergy and thus the continuation of the family.

The rich holdings of the great Buddhist monasteries presented the Chinese state with the only true church problem it ever faced. Monasteries were built and endowed by rulers or prosperous individuals and tended to accumulate more riches through further gifts of land or treasure from pious believers. They also expanded their holdings through usury and the various other legal or illegal methods by which the great families amassed their landholdings. Thus they constituted in the eyes of the rulers a fiscal menace to the state, removing land and men from the tax registers. The idea therefore developed that the number of monasteries and monks and the size of their holdings should be limited. This was paralleled by the concept that, if Buddhism were indeed of value to society, it should not only be regulated by the state but also supported by it as a sort of spiritual branch of the administration. Nothing could have been further from the original role of Indian Buddhism.

The southern dynasties could no more control the Buddhist monasteries than they could the great families, but in the North a regulatory system did develop. By the fourth century, rulers were appointing "bishops" to control the church, and the Northern Wei fixed limits on monasteries and their lands. The T'ang had the theory that there should be one official monastery, with thirty monks, per prefecture and by 729 had inaugurated a clerical census every three years to help enforce this system. By 747 the government itself was issuing ordination permits to limit the number of new monks. Attempts to control the number of monasteries and monks, however, always failed in the long run. Devout rulers and government officials were constantly breaking their own regulations, and secret ordinations were common.

Occasionally the effort to regulate the Buddhist church escalated into harsh persecution. Many Chinese resented Buddhism as a foreign religion or abhorred some of its practices, such as self-mutilation and cremation as well as celibacy, which were felt to threaten family continuity and to violate the body one had received from one's ancestors. The jealousy of Taoist priests was also sometimes a contributing factor. But the chief reason for Buddhist persecutions was the financial need of the government. Persecutions were chiefly efforts to return the lands and monks of the monasteries to the tax registers and seize their gilt-bronze images and other wealth for the imperial treasury. Individual believers were not seriously bothered.

There was a persecution of Buddhism under the Northern Wei in 446 and another, including Taoism, under the Northern Chou in 574. The greatest and most significant persecution occurred in 841–845 under a half-insane T'ang emperor who had become a fanatic Taoist. According to the official accounts, 4600 monasteries and 40,000 shrines were destroyed, and 260,000 monks and nuns and their 150,000 slaves were returned to the tax registers. This persecution proved a crippling blow to Buddhism because the Indian religion was already losing its inner vitality. The examination system had again focused attention on the Classics and Confucian ideas, and the upper classes, as a result, were losing interest in Buddhism. Zen continued its growth and influence for a few more centuries, but the other forms of Buddhism rapidly fell into decay.

Fortunately, before the intellectual and artistic glories of Chinese Buddhism were irretrievably lost, it left a permanent shrine at Tun-huang near the western extremity of the Kansu panhandle in the far northwest. Here, among the elaborately decorated, rock-hewn temples known as the "Caves of the Thousand Buddhas," a great Buddhist library was sealed shut around 1035 to save it from raiding Tibetans. Not reopened until 1900, this library, with its thousands of manuscripts, many in various Central Asian languages, proved to be a unique repository of the Buddhist age in China.

*T'ang paintings of Buddhist deities, saints, and angels on the walls
and ceiling of a grotto at Tun-huang.*

Although Buddhism was a major component of Chinese culture during
one of its most brilliant epochs, it left relatively little permanent impress on
Chinese civilization. Its lasting contributions tend to be additions to traditional
Chinese culture rather than fundamental alterations of native values. It was
the source of much of the popular religion and mythology of the common
people. It added a metaphysical dimension to Chinese thought and greatly
enriched Chinese literature and art. It thus embellished Chinese culture, but
it did not remold the whole civilization, as did Christianity in Europe.

The Growth of Chinese Culture

Contacts with the Outside World.   During the Six Dynasties period and the
early T'ang, China was pervaded by a spirit of cultural tolerance. The "barbarian" invasions left the North wide open to foreign influences; Buddhism
was both a vehicle for and a stimulus to close cultural contacts with distant
areas; interregional trade by sea and by land was growing far beyond anything

known in Han times; and the early T'ang Empire brought the Chinese into direct contact with the great centers of civilization in India and West Asia. Never again until the twentieth century was China to prove so responsive to foreign influences.

Foreign contacts brought many new agricultural products and some inventions. Tea, for example, was introduced from Southeast Asia. Valued at first as a medicine and as a stimulant for meditation, it had by late T'ang times come into more general use and subsequently spread from China to become the world's most popular drink. The chair was also introduced from the west and over the centuries gradually replaced sitting pads and mats. More technological advances came from China itself. The earlier inventions of paper and porcelaneous ware were greatly developed, and gunpowder was discovered, though it was still used only for fireworks. Another invention was the wheelbarrow, which became a major means of transportation on China's narrow footpaths but did not spread to the West for many centuries. Coal came into use as early as the fourth century in North China, though it was still a marvel to the European Marco Polo in the thirteenth century.

Trade and foreign embassies brought thousands of foreigners to the T'ang capital, and these people brought with them their many religions. Zoroastrianism (or Mazdaism), the fire-worshipping religion of Persia, reached China by the sixth century. Manichaeism, which included Zoroastrian and Christian elements, came in the early T'ang, as did the Nestorian branch of Christianity. A great stone stele was erected at the Nestorian church in Ch'ang-an in 781 and rediscovered only in the seventeenth century. All three of these religions from the west were virtually wiped out in the religious persecutions of 841–845, but two others survived. Judaism continued in small isolated communities until the nineteenth century, and Islam grew steadily until it embraced many millions, largely in Chinese Turkestan and in the northwest and southwest corners of China proper.

T'ang, as the greatest empire of its day, was assiduously imitated by many neighboring peoples. Never before or again did such a large proportion of mankind look to China not only as the paramount military power of the time but as the obvious model for government and culture.

The first unified Tibetan government, established in the seventh century, and the state of Nan-chao, founded by Thai groups in Yunnan around 740, were both directly inspired by the T'ang system of rule. The T'ang political and cultural pattern was even more fully adopted by the peoples to the east. The various kingdoms of Korea had for centuries shown strong Chinese influence, and Silla, after uniting the peninsula in 668, became a veritable replica of the T'ang in miniature. The Tungusic kingdom of P'o-hai, which flourished in the woodlands of southern and eastern Manchuria and northeastern Korea from 713 to 926, also closely copied certain T'ang institutions. The efforts of the Japanese in the seventh and eighth centuries to create another small T'ang in their remote islands was an even more remarkable example.

The Arts.   Buddhist psalmody had a profound influence on Chinese music, and during this period the music and instruments of Central Asia virtually displaced the older musical traditions of China. In art, and particularly in sculpture, foreign Buddhist influence was also strong. In fact, the Buddhist demand for religious images made this the greatest age of Chinese sculpture. What had been a minor art form in earlier periods rose to great heights for a few centuries, and then declined with Buddhism after the T'ang.

Chinese Buddhist sculptures, as preserved in such successive shrines as the rock temples of Yün-kang, Lung-men, and Tun-huang, show diverse artistic strains. Some influences came directly from India, but the most important artistic traditions in North China during the Six Dynasties period were those of Central Asian Buddhism, which had been derived in turn from the strongly Hellenistic Buddhist art of Gandhara and surrounding areas in what is now northwest Pakistan and Afghanistan. The early Buddhist sculpture of China, however, was quite different from the Greek in spirit, as was to be expected in a deeply religious art. The human figures, far from being naturalistic, were stiff, austere abstractions of deity, and Greek realism was limited to such superficial elements as the folds of their clothing, By the T'ang, however, Chinese humanistic interests had made the Buddhist concept of deity more intimate, and this change was reflected in sculpture. Images became much plumper and more lifelike, closely approximating T'ang concepts of human beauty. There was also great secular sculpture during this period, and large numbers of beautiful pottery figures of dancing girls, camels, horses, Central Asian grooms, and the like were made for burial in tombs.

Little remains of the Buddhist painting of the Six Dynasties and T'ang periods, except for the murals of the Tun-huang caves, but the Buddhist influence on Chinese painting was tremendous. Though most of the artistic genius of China during this time was probably devoted to religious art, secular painting also flourished, and South China saw the beginnings of artistic trends which were to grow into the great painting traditions of the late T'ang and following periods. Though, again, little remains today of this secular art, Ku K'ai-chih, who flourished around 400 A.D., is honored as the first great figure in Chinese painting, while Wang Hsi-chih (321–379) is considered the greatest name in calligraphy.

Except for brick and stone pagodas, not much remains of either the secular or religious architecture of the T'ang or earlier periods. Buddhist temples built in the Chinese style in Japan during the seventh and eighth centuries, however, have survived, giving us some idea of the classic simplicity and balance of Chinese architectural forms at this time.

Giant guardian deities carved in a cliff at Lung-men around
672–676 A.D. *Note the square holes and niches made to support*
the wooden structures that once enclosed these images.

Seventh-century pottery figure of a lady polo player, about ten
inches high.

0   5   10   15   20   25 FEET

CHINA'S OLDEST WOODEN BUILDING. *Front elevation and cross
section of the main hall of the Fo-kuang-ssu ("Monastery of the
Buddha's Halo") on Mount Wu-t'ai, dating from the T'ang dynasty.*

Literature and Scholarship.   During the Buddhist age a large proportion of
the best literary and scholarly talent naturally was devoted to Buddhist works,
which later generations of Chinese have generally ignored, but there was
also much endeavor along more traditional lines. Literary writing for the
most part continued to be an essentially aristocratic art. The *fu* poetic form
remained in fashion during the Six Dynasties period and was paralleled in
prose by an elaborate balanced style that featured carefully paired verbal
patterns, commonly in four- and six-syllable phrases (*p'ien-t'i-wen*). The
most important verse form of the Six Dynasties period was the *shih,* a lyric
in five-syllable meter, which first appeared in the late Han. It was typically
Taoist in its laments over the corruption of the world and its assertation of
the individual's independence of society. The greatest *shih* master of the
time, T'ao Ch'ien (also known as T'ao Yüan-ming, 376–427), was a south-
erner who in characteristic Taoist fashion found his personal elixir in wine.

Works of literary criticism began to appear as early as the third century,
and in the sixth Hsiao T'ung (501–531), the heir apparent to the Liang
throne in the South, compiled the *Literary Selections* (*Wen hsüan*), China's
most famous anthology. There was no falling off in the output of standard
histories, commentaries on the classics, and other traditional types of scholarship. Around the year 500 there appeared a curious work much used in later
Chinese elementary instruction. This was the *Thousand-Character Classic,*
which summarizes Chinese history and Confucian philosophical views in a
thousand characters, none of which is repeated.

One new aspect of Chinese scholarship, which in later periods grew to
colossal proportions, was the compiling of works of an encyclopedic nature.

These were of many different types, but one of the commonest, usually called local gazetteers, concerned the history, natural features, and political and social institutions of a single local administrative unit, such as a district or prefecture. The earliest surviving work of this sort dates from the fourth century.

All these new literary and scholarly trends grew out of earlier Chinese traditions and were continued and expanded under the T'ang. In higher culture the Six Dynasties period thus represented no great break with the past and led on smoothly into the T'ang and later periods. This was perhaps because of the broad overlapping in time of the old and the new. The continuing Han cultural tradition of succession states in South China and the rising new semi-"barbarian," semi-Buddhist culture of the North remained for a long time contemporaneous. Despite the challenge to Chinese society of "barbarian" invaders and a foreign religion, there was much greater cultural continuity between Han and T'ang than between Rome and medieval Europe.

6. The Late T'ang and Sung:
The Flowering of Chinese Culture

The Transition from Classic to Early Modern China

To divide a dynasty between two major periods goes against the whole cyclic interpretation of Chinese history. The traditionalist may be especially outraged when the dynasty so divided is the T'ang, perhaps the most resplendent in all Chinese history. But this is necessary if we are to see the more fundamental trends that underlay the dynastic cycle.

We are accustomed to thinking of great cultural and social changes as occurring during times of military defeat or political breakdown. But nothing produces change more inevitably than growth, and growth in population, production, trade, culture, and institutions takes place more easily in peaceful times than during periods of disruption. This is what happened during the T'ang. The Sui and early T'ang saw the re-creation of the classic empire, though in a more perfected form. A century of relative peace and prosperity then brought growth that lifted China to a significantly higher level than that attained by the Han. There was an institutional and cultural break-through, which in turn produced more growth.

The Six Dynasties period and early T'ang were in many ways the last phase of ancient Chinese history; the late T'ang and the Sung (960–1279) which followed it formed the first phase of later Chinese history. One might, in fact, call this period the "early modern" phase, for the culture which evolved at this time was to remain characteristic of China until the opening decades of the twentieth century. Much of what has proved most typical of China during the past millennium appeared at least in embryo by late T'ang times and came into early bloom under the Sung.

The cultural and institutional level achieved during the late T'ang and Sung was not greatly changed during the next several hundred years. This period proved to be a plateau in time, with the Chinese at first well above Western attainments but in later times technologically below them. In post-Sung times, China seems to have changed more slowly than in earlier centuries and certainly much less rapidly than the Occident, where the rate of change accelerated in modern times.

The period of transition between late classic China and the early modern period centered around the eighth century. The decay of the T'ang dynasty at this time and the start of a long swing of the pendulum of conquest back against China were typical of the dynastic cycle and earlier trends in relations with the northern "barbarians," but there were also other more subtle changes in progress which were to remake Chinese society and culture. The intellectual leadership, for example, started to reject Buddhism and return to Confucianism, but with such decidedly new emphases that post-T'ang Chinese philosophy is usually called Neo-Confucianism. The Chinese also re-emphasized the strongly secular bias that has distinguished East Asian civilization from the civilizations of South Asia and the West during the past millennium. Moreover, in their rejection of foreign religions and in their losing battle with the "barbarians," they gradually lost the cosmopolitanism and cultural tolerance they had shown in the Six Dynasties period and early T'ang and became much more narrowly ethnocentric.

In the eighth century a fundamental change also was made from a per capita based system of taxation to taxation of land areas, and this together with a tremendous increase in both domestic and international trade during the T'ang period made the government's subsequent financial and administrative problems quite different from those of earlier dynasties. These economic changes also contributed to a great shift in society. Until the early T'ang the ruling class had been composed of powerful aristocratic families, largely of military origin. But gradually leadership devolved upon a much broader class of landowners, often with mercantile backgrounds, who have commonly been called the "gentry."

With the decline of the old aristocracy came the real triumph of the bureaucratic system. Or, to put it the other way, with the appearance of the fully developed examination system in the T'ang, the decline of aristocratic society commenced. Until the seventh century the organized bureaucracy, itself drawn largely from a hereditary aristocracy, had been used to buttress the rule of a military empire of aristocratic traditions. In post-T'ang times, Chinese or "barbarian" warriors continued to found dynasties by force of arms, but for the most part government and culture became dominated by bureaucrats who owed their position more to their own talents than to birth. This meant the acceptance of a basically egalitarian ideal that had always been implicit in Confucianism but did not really triumph in Chinese society until the late

T'ang and Sung. It also meant the shift from an essentially military leadership to one that was basically civilian. By Sung times the civilian point of view had become predominant, and there was a growing contempt for the military profession.

A parallel change was the displacement of the center of gravity in China. While the capital usually remained in the North, where the major defense problem existed, the lower Yangtze Valley became the economic heart of the country, and men from this region increasingly dominated both the culture and the government. The cultural center of gravity also moved from rural China to the cities. The new gentry class did not necessarily live on its agricultural holdings and lead a rural life, but often joined the officials and merchants in the cities and towns, leaving junior members to manage estates in the countryside.

The higher culture was naturally affected by all these trends. There was a growing sophistication of scholarship, literature, and art and a tremendous expansion in scope and sheer quantity of production. Most of this activity grew out of earlier traditions, but it was richly creative, producing the artistic and literary forms which have seemed most typically Chinese ever since. In fact, the patterns set during the late T'ang and Sung in art and literature, as well as in society and government, were to dominate Chinese civilization until the early twentieth century. In this sense, the period from the eighth to the thirteenth centuries was a second golden age of Chinese culture.

The Late T'ang

The Degeneration of the System.   Naturally, the great changes outlined above took place slowly, and some of them had only just begun by the late T'ang. Still, the reign of Hsüan Tsung (712–756) was perhaps the key period in the transition from ancient to early modern China. It was also, and more obviously, the crucial turning point in the dynastic cycle, which revolved as inexorably during the T'ang as in the Han.

Under Hsüan Tsung the dynasty reached its second great peak. In wealth, grandeur, and cultural brilliance his reign far outshone that of T'ai Tsung a century earlier. But the costs of maintaining the imperial family and the government had multiplied many times over, and income had by no means kept pace. The whole system of government was operating less smoothly and was beginning to break down in such vital sectors as taxation and military defense, much as had happened in the Han. The "equal field" system (see pages 100–101) slowed the descent but could not stop it.

The rapid increase of population and the habit of emperors of rewarding their ministers with grants of lands and people—as many as fifteen hundred households at a time—made it impossible to redistribute the land to the peasants and assign each family an adequate share, as was called for in the "equal field" system. The tax burden, including *corvée* labor and military service, fell on a progressively shrinking proportion of the peasantry, whose holdings were growing steadily smaller. When the burden became unbearable, peasants would flee their farms or transfer their holdings through shady deals to the estate of some wealthy man, where the 50 per cent of produce paid in rent would actually be less oppressive than the government taxes. This only aggravated the situation for the remaining free peasants.

As the "equal field" system collapsed, the yield from the per capita tax system associated with it declined drastically, and the government had to find substitute forms of income. For example, the very light land tax, which applied to the estates as well as to peasant holdings, was gradually increased, commercial taxes were developed, and a tax on all households, divided into nine categories according to wealth, was instituted. Such tax reforms, however, could not save the *corvée* and militia systems. Bit by bit *corvée* labor was eliminated from the key function of transporting tax grain up the Grand Canal to the North. By 723, some 120,000 mercenaries had taken the place of the militia in the capital guards, and professionals had also begun to replace the militia in the frontier armies. Although both the *corvée* and militia systems were to continue in use in various forms until recent times, they were never again as important to the central government as they had been up through the seventh century.

While these changes in part represented an institutional advance connected with a developing money economy, they entailed some grave difficulties. Paid workers and mercenaries meant increased government expenses. Moreover, professional soldiers, who were commonly recruited from the dregs of society or from "barbarian" tribes, might not prove ardent defenders of China, and because of their long terms of service they frequently developed a primary loyalty to their generals rather than to the dynasty. This situation allowed ambitious generals to become virtually independent local warlords.

The defeat in 751 of Kao Hsien-chih by the Arabs at Talas west of the Pamirs was a turning point in East Asian history. It marked the end of Chinese control over Central Asia and the beginning of five centuries of steady military decline for the Chinese Empire. It also marked the beginning of Islamic penetration of Central Asia. At much the same time the Turkish language also began to replace the Indo-European tongues in the oasis states of the Tarim Basin.

Not long after the defeat at Talas, T'ang collapsed internally. Regional commanders had by Hsüan Tsung's time become more or less permanent officials controlling the civil as well as military affairs of ten large border regions. One of these regional commanders, a man of Turkish origin named

An Lu-shan, came to control three regions and won power at court through the patronage of Hsüan Tsung's favorite consort, Yang Kuei-fei ("Consort" Yang), who adopted him as her legal son. An Lu-shan came into conflict with Yang Kuei-fei's brother over control of the central government and revolted in 755. He captured the capital, and the fleeing emperor was forced by his discontented soldiers to execute Yang Kuei-fei and her brother, who were blamed for the catastrophe. This pathetic story has been a favorite theme for Chinese poets and writers. An Lu-shan was killed by his own son in 757, and the same fate befell his successor, another "barbarian" general. Meanwhile Hsüan Tsung had abdicated, but loyal armies, with the aid of the Uighur Turks, managed to restore order to the country by 762. The earlier grandeur of T'ang, however, was never restored.

Political Disunity and Fiscal Reforms.   The rebellion of An Lu-shan was a serious blow to centralized government, as was reflected in the drop of the official census figures from 52,880,488 in 754 to a mere 16,900,000 in 764. The dynasty also remained entirely dependent on foreign troops and never again exercised any real power outside of China proper. The Uighurs continued to dominate much of Central Asia, until they were supplanted around 840 by the Kirghiz. T'ang control over China proper also weakened. The system of regional commanders was extended to the whole country, and many of the commanders turned their areas into personal satrapies. Their positions in some cases became virtually hereditary, and on occasion they openly rebelled against the court.

The central government was wracked too by internal dissensions. Already in Hsüan Tsung's reign there had been a growing struggle for power between the old T'ang aristocracy and the newer bureaucracy. A century of successful use of the examination system and the strong patronage of the Empress Wu had made the bureaucrats powerful enough to challenge the old sources of power. After An Lu-shan's revolt the now dominant bureaucracy itself broke up into quarreling factions. The eunuchs, as in the Later Han, also became powerful, contending with the bureaucrats for leadership, and they dominated most of the T'ang rulers during the ninth century.

Despite these conditions the T'ang managed to survive for a century and a half after An Lu-shan's revolt. The central government, moreover, was not as feeble nor were conditions as chaotic as has usually been supposed. Such matters are always relative. The Japanese monk Ennin, during his stay in China between 838 and 847, described in his diary a prosperous and well-ordered society with a degree of bureaucratic meticulousness and centralized control that probably was not matched in other parts of the world until much later times.

One fundamental reason for this situation was the new financial basis of government developed during the restoration that followed An Lu-shan's revolt. The transport of grain from the Yangtze Valley to the capital was improved and put fully into the hands of professional workers. The old system of government monopolies was revived, and those in salt, tea, and liquor became important sources of revenue. In 780 various land, personal, and household taxes were consolidated into the so-called Double Tax, levied twice a year on land areas, regardless of ownership, rather than on peasants as individuals.

This reform capped an epoch-making transition which had been a century under way. Thenceforth in Chinese history land areas rather than individuals were the basic units of agricultural taxation, and the collecting of taxes became much simpler. The central government could be less concerned about the development of private holdings, for such holdings no longer represented a menace to the financial underpinnings of the state. In fact, the whole landholding system of China changed. Landowners no longer needed to be politically powerful in order to protect the virtually tax-free status of their estates but could simply be landlords of tenant-operated, tax-paying farms. This was, in other words, the beginning of the type of landlordism that was to characterize China's rural economy from then until the twentieth century.

The Final Breakup: The Five Dynasties Period.   A simpler landholding and tax system than in earlier times, together with a more diversified fiscal foundation for government and an improved administration based on the examination system, may account for the ability of the T'ang and later dynasties to run a cycle of three centuries, compared to the two-century cycle of the Earlier and Later Han. But it was inevitable that sooner or later the long enfeebled T'ang would collapse completely. The final breakup started with great uprisings in the North in 874. One of the rebel leaders, Huang Ch'ao, an unsuccessful candidate in the government examinations, even captured the capital, but the revolt was finally suppressed in 884 by a general of Turkish origin. All semblance of control over the regional commanders had been lost, however, during the revolt, and in 907 one of them, who once had been a supporter of Huang Ch'ao, usurped the throne, bringing the T'ang to a formal end.

There ensued a more complete but much briefer disintegration of centralized rule than had followed the collapse of the Later Han. Central and South China and parts of the North were divided among a number of former regional commanders, each claiming to be the emperor of China. There were, in all, fourteen such kingdoms, though the official histories have grouped them together as the "Ten Kingdoms." Meanwhile in North China, five ephemeral dynasties, for which the Five Dynasties period (907–960) is named, followed one aonther in rapid succession, as a series of ambitious generals usurped the throne and tried without success to found lasting regimes. None lasted more than sixteen years. The last, the Later Chou (951–960),

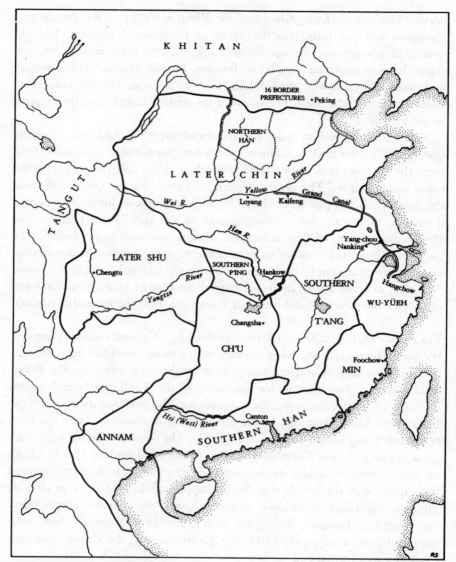

CHINA AROUND 940 A.D.

is remembered chiefly for a great persecution of Buddhism it carried out in order to strengthen its financial position.

Three of the five usurping generals were "barbarians"—two Turkish and one perhaps an Iranian. Thus once again the Chinese Empire had drawn "barbarian" soldiers into its heart. Meanwhile tribal "barbarians" were pressing in again on China's borders. The Khitan Mongols of southern Manchuria, in return for helping the Later Chin (936–946), the third of the "Five Dynasties," achieve the throne, were given sixteen border prefectures around the present Peking. Although they subsequently destroyed Later Chin and over-ran North China, they proved unable to hold onto it. Their control of the sixteen border prefectures, however, has given their Liao dynasty (947–1125) a place in official Chinese histories. Incidentally in Kitai, a later form of Khitan, we find the Russian name for China as well as the origin of Cathay, the medieval European term for the country.

The Sung Dynasty

The Founding of the Sung. The most significant fact about the disunity of the Five Dynasties period is that it lasted only half a century, in contrast to the three-and-a-half centuries of political division during the Six Dynasties period. Perhaps the traditions and techniques of centralized rule had become so much stronger by the tenth century that a long multiple division of the country was no longer possible. In any case, it should be noted that China was never again divided into a number of competing political units for even so long as half a century. Foreign conquest was to divide it between a purely Chinese South and a "barbarian"-ruled North, but not until the collapse of the old system in the early twentieth century was the empire again broken up into a number of independent or autonomous units. In other words, China since the T'ang has proved to be a virtually indestructible political unit.

In 960, only fifty-three years after the end of the T'ang, another general, Chao K'uang-yin, carried out the sixth usurpation of the throne in the North, and this time the effort succeeded. Known to history as T'ai Tsu ("Grand Progenitor"), he founded the Sung dynasty, which was to last until 1279. Before his death in 976 he had extended his rule over all but two of the other Chinese states, and these last two were incorporated into the empire in 978 and 979 by his brother and successor T'ai Tsung ("Grand Ancestor," 976–997).

T'ai Tsu's successs in establishing a lasting dynasty can be attributed in large part to the determination with which he tackled the gravest political problem of his day—the almost unrestricted power of local military commanders. He managed to transfer his own leading generals to minor posts or to retire them with suitable rewards. In the provinces he limited the regional commanders to a single prefecture and, as they died or retired, replaced them with civil officials from the central bureaucracy. He also followed a policy of transferring the best military units to the capital armies, and he placed all military forces directly under the central government. In these various ways he assured the central government of preponderant military power and eliminated the warlordism that had destroyed the T'ang and kept China unstable and divided during the Five Dynasties period.

T'ai Tsu's success in carrying out these military reforms, however, may have contributed to what became the Sung's greatest problem—military weakness in the face of the "barbarian" menace. The Sung never achieved the military prowess of the Han and T'ang. It was unable to reincorporate Northern Vietnam (Annam) into the empire or extend its control over any part of Central Asia or the northern steppe. It even failed to win back the sixteen prefectures lost to the Khitan Liao in 926, and in 1004 it agreed to pay the Liao an annual sum of 300,000 units of silk and silver. On the northwest, Sung was hard pressed by Tangut tribes of Tibetans. These had established a strong state in the Kansu panhandle and the Ordos region inside the northern loop of the Yellow River, and in 1038 they assumed the Chinese dynastic name of Hsia (called in history the Hsi Hsia, or "Western Hsia"). After a serious defeat, the Sung started in 1044 to pay an annual sum to the Hsi Hsia too. Thereafter a three-way military and diplomatic stalemate developed between the Sung and their two predatory northern neighbors.

The Government and Civil Service. T'ai Tsu and his successors set up at the capital a series of administrative offices that were more directly under the personal control of the emperor than the T'ang organs of government had been. For example, two minor offices, close to the throne, which had appeared in the second half of the T'ang, were now made into major government agencies and continued to have an important role in later Chinese history. The first was the Board of Academicians, originally a sort of document-drafting body, which now became a major advisory group to the emperor. The other was the Bureau of Military Affairs. The Secretariat-Chancellery continued the names of two of the three highest bodies of the T'ang, and under it operated the six ministries and lesser administrative offices, as they had under the Department of State Affairs in the T'ang. Two other important organs of government were the Board of Censors, which in time developed an elaborate system for checking on all the operations of government, and the Finance Commission, which handled the treasury, taxes, monopolies, and other financial matters. The Sung, unlike the T'ang, kept close and direct control over the entire tax yield of the empire. Because of this and also because of general economic growth, the government's income in the early eleventh century was three times that of the T'ang at its height, and a huge surplus was soon built up.

The administration of the whole empire in the Sung was more thoroughly centralized at the capital than ever before in Chinese history. The capital, as during most of the Five Dynasties, was at Kaifeng. Located near the juncture of the Grand Canal system with the Yellow River, it was still in the old northern heartland of China but almost three hundred miles closer than Ch'ang-an to the rich rice-producing areas of the lower Yangtze. The Sung continued unchanged the T'ang system of prefectures and districts but increased the number of provinces or "circuits" (*tao*, later called *lu*). These were given greater supervisory authority over the prefectures than the T'ang

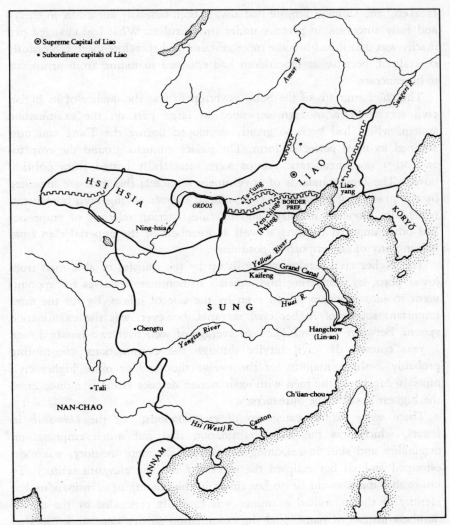

CHINA AROUND 1050 A.D.

"circuits" had possessed, and in order to insure that they would not fall under military dominance, as had happened in the T'ang, they were given functions and areas of supervision clearly differentiated from those of the military authorities.

The conscious effort of T'ai Tsu and his successors to gather the reins of administration into their own hands and concentrate control of the whole country at the capital made the Chinese government thenceforth not only more centralized but also, in a way, more autocratic. The following millennium of Chinese history, therefore, is often called the age of "autocracy," as opposed to the preceding "aristocratic" age. The term, however, is misleading. Despite the right of rebellion implicit in the theory of the "Mandate of

Heaven," the Chinese Empire had always been basically autocratic in theory and fully autocratic in practice under strong rulers. What had changed primarily was that it had become more efficient, and therefore more successfully centralized, because its officialdom had changed in nature from aristocrats to bureaucrats.

The chief strength of the Sung government was the quality of its higher civil service. This in turn depended in large part on the examination system, which had been so greatly developed during the T'ang and now attained its most perfected form. The palace eunuchs around the emperor and other nonbureaucratic groups were successfully barred from political power. The high standards of government service at this time are indicated by the practice of prohibiting close official contact among high bureaucrats related by blood or marriage and by rules barring relatives of empresses and other imperial consorts as well as members of the imperial clan from holding any of the important positions.

The higher civil service was built up by the transfer of able men from lower posts, by permitting high officials to nominate relatives for appointment to junior positions, and even by the sale of offices. By far the most important source of higher civil servants, however, was the examination system. Between 997 and 1124 an average of well over two hundred men a year entered the civil service through the examinations, constituting probably a slight majority of the twelve thousand or more higher civil officials. Moreover the men with examination degrees virtually monopolized the highest posts in the bureaucracy.

There were various categories of examinations, but the *chin-shih* in letters, which was the only examination that put much emphasis on originality and skill in reasoning rather than on mere memory, was most esteemed and all but eclipsed the others by the late eleventh century. To insure that there would be no favoritism in the grading of examinations, the identity of the individual examinee was carefully concealed by the use of numbers instead of names and the examination papers were copied so that the handwriting could not be recognized.

After 1065 the examinations were held regularly every three years. There were three successive levels of examinations. First came the examinations held by the individual prefectures or government schools. Scholars who passed these, reportedly varying between 1 and 10 per cent of the candidates, went on to an examination given by the central government at the capital. About 10 per cent of these were passed and were then subjected to a "palace examination," which rejected a few more and gave rankings to the others that helped determine their initial appointment to office. Unsuccessful candidates usually took the examinations time after time. As a result, those who passed might range in age from the late teens to the seventies, though they probably averaged around thirty-five.

The promotion of officials depended on several factors—the length of their tenure of office, a system of merit ratings, special examinations for certain specific assignments, a candidate's rank in the original examinations, and the sponsorship of higher officials. According to the sponsorship system, certain higher officials had ths duty of nominating for promotion promising junior officials who might otherwise be overlooked. The protégé could not be a relative of the sponsor, but the latter was responsible for his protégés and could be punished for their misdeeds.

The civil service system succeeded in bringing a large measure of talent into government. It also helped keep men of ability out of subversive activities by opening a more attractive door to them. The degree to which the examination system discovered new talent is suggested by the lists of successful candidates in 1148 and 1256, which reveal that more than half of the men came from families with no record of civil service status in the paternal line during the three preceding generations.

In large part because of the civil service system perfected under the Sung, the Chinese government became so stable that Chao K'uang-yin's usurpation in 960 was to prove to be the last in Chinese history. In earlier periods emperors had repeatedly been robbed of the throne by their great generals, empresses, or other powerful subordinates. After 960 this never happened again. Dynasties continued to be destroyed by foreign conquest or popular revolution, and members of the imperial family stole the throne from one another, but no subject ever again succeeded in usurping the imperial prerogative.

Economic Problems. While the Sung was more prosperous than any previous dynasty had ever been, the usual administrative decline and financial difficulties of the old dynastic cycle had reappeared by the end of its first century. Government income had risen rapidly during the first six decades to a high point in 1021 of 150,850,000 units, each roughly equivalent in value to a string of a thousand cash, but thereafter receipts gradually dropped off, until by 1065 government income had fallen by nearly a quarter.

One underlying cause for this decline may have been the increase in population. In a basically agrarian economy, population growth swelled tax resources up to a certain point, but beyond that point it tended to outrun the increase in yield from the limited land resources. As a consequence, the more mouths there were to feed, the less surplus remained for the tax collectors. Another factor may have been the increasing concentration of farm land in the hands of the bigger landowners. Although taxes had been levied since the middle T'ang primarily by land areas rather than on a per capita basis, the burden still fell most heavily on the small peasant, who had the least financial resources. Population increases meant smaller farms and overworked soil, with the result that many small peasants were reduced to pauperism or were driven into tenancy on the holdings of the landlord class. The latter, though theoretically subject to the same taxes as the peasants, frequently enjoyed exemptions or were able to escape part of the burden through their government connections, and thus the state's income tended to decline as landlord holdings increased.

Government expenditures, however, could not be tailored to fit declining receipts. As in past dynasties, the costs of government steadily grew as the court became larger and more luxurious, government organs proliferated, and the bureaucracy expanded. Some historians have attributed the financial difficulties of the Sung to the appeasement payments paid to the Liao and Hsi Hsia, but this was only a minor factor. While the payments came to total 1,500,000 units of silk and silver, this never amounted to even 2 per cent of the government budget. A much more serious drain was military expenditures. The professional armies that had replaced the comparatively inexpensive militia system of the T'ang had proved not only ineffective but costly. Ill-equipped with horses and recruited largely from among paupers, the Sung forces were no match for the spirited cavalry of the northern "barbarians." The only answer seemed to be to increase the size of the military, until by 1041 it numbered 1,259,000 men and absorbed close to 80 per cent of the government budget.

The Reforms of Wang An-shih. Because of its financial difficulties, the government allowed official salaries to become inadequate, which in turn hurt morale, encouraged the misuse of office, and may have stimulated the growth of the bureaucratic factionalism that bedeviled the remaining years of the Sung. A more fundamental reason for this factionalism, however, was that the bureaucrats, rather than aristocratic families, empresses, or eunuchs, were now in control of the government and they faced very difficult financial problems and a precarious military situation. They not unnaturally became deeply divided over policy issues, but there was no mechanism for resolving these policy differences, except through factional strife and imperial whim.

In 1069 the new young emperor, Shen Tsung ("Inspired Ancestor," 1067–1085), appointed as Chief Councilor the able but opinionated Wang An-shih (1021–1086). Wang was the champion of a reformist faction that was opposed by the traditionalists, who supported established bureaucratic procedures as they had developed in recent decades. He immediately embarked on a series of sweeping reforms to bolster the government's finances and strengthen its armies.

Wang plunged the government into economic manipulations of a sort that had not been tried for several centuries. He had the government buy the specialized products of one area for sale in other regions, thereby helping to stabilize prices and making a profit for the government. He instituted government loans to peasants at 20 or 30 per cent, a very low rate for the time, thereby possibly helping poorer farmers to maintain themselves but certainly diverting the profits of moneylending from private usurers to the treasury. He had new land surveys made to eliminate old inequities and established a graduated scale of land taxes according to the productivity of the soil. He commuted the remaining *corvée* services into taxes. He also had all personal wealth assessed for tax purposes, attempted to regulate prices, extended relatively cheap credit to small enterprisers through government pawnshops, and carried out needed water control.

On the military side, Wang An-shih revived under the name of *pao-chia* the old collective-guarantee methods of the Six Dynasties period, and decreed that the various units under this system were to provide at their own expense certain quotas of trained and armed militia. To build up a cavalry, he had horses procured at government expense and assigned to the peasant families of North China, in return for which one member of each family was to serve with his horse in cavalry militia in time of need.

Wang also expanded the number of government schools to compete with the endowed private academies (*shu-yüan*) that dominated education at this time, and he insisted that the government examinations should be less tests of memory and literary ability and should be directed more toward practical problems of policy and administration. Like Wang Mang in Han times, he claimed the support of the Classics for his reforms.

Wang An-shih, again like Wang Mang, has been both castigated and praised as a socialist, but he was no more motivated by concepts of social equality than was his famous predecessor. Some of his reforms, such as the graduated land tax, cheaper credit systems, and the complete abandonment of the *corvée*, obviously were steps forward economically and administratively. Other measures, such as price regulating, government commodity controls, and the collective-guarantee and militia systems, were merely revivals of earlier institutions. The reforms naturally roused the determined opposition of the groups they hurt—large landowners, big merchants, and moneylenders. The bulk of the bureaucracy, drawn as it was from the landowning class, was also in opposition. Most of the great scholar-statesmen of the day, such as Ssu-ma Kuang, Ou-yang Hsiu, and Su Tung-p'o, were ranged against the innovations, and Wang has been roundly condemned by traditional Chinese historians.

This bureaucratic and scholastic opposition, however, was probably not basically a matter of class interests. It more fundamentally reflected the natural administrative inertia of a bureaucratized state—a growing inflexibility which was to characterize the Chinese government from this time on. The reforms also had produced considerable confusion and transgressed various checks and balances in the established system. For these various reasons, even though the reforms were not really very revolutionary

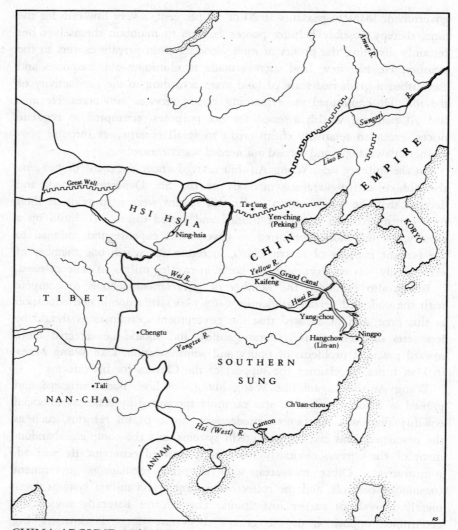

CHINA AROUND 1140 A.D.

and were often merely a reversion to older practices, they stirred up intense
partisan politics during the next several decades, and partisan debate has
raged ever since. On Shen Tsung's death in 1085, the traditionalists came
back to power and vitiated Wang's reforms. Thereafter reformists and traditionalists alternated in power, nullifying through their bitter struggles whatever financial and military benefits the reforms might have produced, until
this bureaucratic battle was itself submerged in a greater disaster.

The Southern Sung. The emperor Hui Tsung ("Excellent Ancestor,"
1100–1125), a great patron of the arts and himself a talented painter,

presided over a culturally brilliant and luxurious court that further strained government finances. During the latter years of his reign, the empire was wracked by popular uprisings, but the chief blow came from outside. Beyond the Liao, Tungusic tribes known as the Jurchen (Ju-chen in Chinese) had gradually risen to power in northeastern Manchuria. In 1114 the Jurchen rebelled against the Liao and the next year adopted the Chinese dynastic name of Chin (1115–1234), meaning "Golden." The Sung, intent on regaining the sixteen border prefectures lost to the Liao two centuries earlier, unwisely allied themselves with the Chin against the Liao. The Chinese armies, however, met with no success, while the Jurchen hordes completely destroyed the Liao by 1125. When Sung showed itself dissatisfied with its meager share of the spoils, the Jurchen swept on to capture Kaifeng in 1126 and pursued the Chinese armies across the Yangtze. The many rivers and canals of the South, however, made it unfavorable terrain for their cavalry, and they eventually withdrew from the South, though they retained their hold over most of North China.

A son of Hui Tsung, known to history as Kao Tsung ("High Ancestor," 1127–1162), managed to restore Sung rule in the South, establishing his capital in 1138 at the modern Hangchow in Chekiang. Henceforth the Sung Empire was limited to the area south of the Huai River and consequently is known as the Southern Sung (1127–1279), as opposed to the Northern Sung (960–1126), which had ruled from the North over almost the whole of China proper.

For a while the Southern Sung fought desperately to recapture the North under the able general Yüeh Fei (also pronounced Yo Fei), who has been extolled by modern patriots as a symbol of national resistance to foreign domination. A peace party under Ch'in Kuei, however, eventually won out, executed Yüeh Fei, and concluded a treaty with the Chin in 1141. This treaty stipulated that the Sung was the vassal of the Chin and should pay an annual tribute of 500,000 units of silver and silk. An unsuccessful attempt by the Chin to conquer the South led to the reduction of the sum by 100,000 units in 1165 and the dropping of the Sung's status of outright vassalage, but an even less successful effort by the Sung to conquer the Chin led in 1208 to an increased annual payment of 600,000 units and a special indemnity of 3,000,000 units.

While the Southern Sung was geographically a rump state and its government remained torn between war and peace factions, it was in most ways a wealthier country than the Northern Sung had ever been. It occupied what had become the economic heartland of China, and this was a period of rapid economic growth. The Southern Sung had a much higher military budget than the Northern Sung and supported a larger bureaucracy. Its capital at Hangchow was a far grander city than Kaifeng had been. Even after Hangchow had passed its peak and had fallen into the hands of "barbarians," it struck Marco Polo as "beyond dispute the finest and noblest city" in the world.

The Southern Sung during its century and a half of existence was no more impervious to the dynastic cycle than previous dynasties had been. The administrative decline continued throughout the period. Even so, the government, because of its sound financial base and strong civil service, showed no sign of collapsing from inner pressures. As in the case of the Northern Sung, it was destroyed only by a powerful foreign enemy, the Mongols, and only after many years of large-scale warfare.

The Commercial Revolution

The political history of China shows a steady military decline from the high point of empire in the eighth century to the eventual conquest of all China by the Mongols in the thirteenth; but this was nonetheless a period of significant institutional and cultural growth. Underlying this growth was such a great expansion of the Chinese economy, and particularly its commercial aspects, that it might not be inappropriate to call it the "commercial revolution" of China. This rapid growth brought China up to an economic level that was distinctly higher than that of earlier ages and produced economic and social patterns that remained in many ways unchanged into the nineteenth century.

One of the reasons for this spectacular development of the economy was probably a general increase in population. Chinese census figures, as we have seen, are generally more indicative of administrative than of demographic conditions, but they suggest a considerable growth in population at this time. In fact, the population of the South seems to have tripled between the eighth and the eleventh centuries, and the total population of China may have passed the 100 million mark during the Northern Sung.

Technological Advances.   There also appears to have been a considerable increase in agricultural productivity during the Sung period. For example, the introduction in the early eleventh century of a more quickly maturing strain of rice from Champa in South Vietnam greatly increased agricultural yields in the South by making double cropping possible. Another factor was the large number of major water-control projects undertaken during the Sung, which added significantly to the total area devoted to irrigated paddy fields. The cultivation of tea on hillsides also increased, and around the twelfth century cotton began to be a common crop, expanding the textile resources of the country.

There were also technological advances in fields other than agriculture. Already highly developed skills, as in textiles, lacquer production, and porcelain making, were further perfected. The abacus came into use in

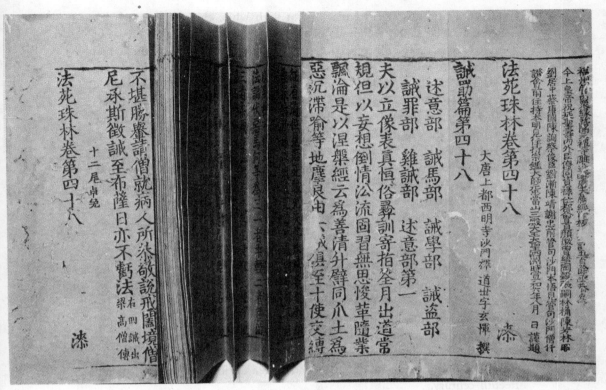

SUNG PRINTED BOOK. *Page from a Buddhist book compiled in 668 A.D. and printed in 1124, more than three centuries before the Gutenberg Bible. The vertical lines are to be read from right to left. The small type on the right lists the reasons for the project and also its patrons. The first large line of type gives the chapter heading, followed by a smaller line identifying the author.*

late Sung times and ever since has been the chief calculating device of East Asian merchants. Another step forward in technology was the use of gunpowder for explosive weapons. By the early eleventh century, mines, a type of hand grenade, and other explosive projectiles had been developed, helping the Chinese to compensate for the weakness of their cavalry.

The most important technological advance, though it contributed only indirectly to economic growth, was the development of printing. This great invention was originally motivated by the desire to establish and spread authentic versions of important books. It may have been inspired by the practice of making "rubbings" from texts carved on stone tablets. This was done by making a thin, dampened sheet of paper adhere closely to the stone and rubbing the higher surfaces of it with lampblack, thus producing a primitive sort of block print with white characters on a black background. The actual technique of printing, however, probably grew out of large carved seals for official use. By the seventh century these had developed into full-page woodblock pictures or texts. A series of consecutive printed blocks produced whole books in scroll form. When such a long sheet of consecutive printed blocks was folded at regular intervals and then stitched together on one side, the result was the standard Chinese printed book with its continuous double-folded pages.

A whole Buddhist sutra had been printed in China by 868, and in the middle of the tenth century the printing of all of the Classics and the whole of the Buddhist Tripitaka was undertaken by some of the independent regimes in Szechwan and South China. During the Sung, printing became extremely widespread, and printed books of all types appeared in large numbers.

Because of the huge number of Chinese characters, the Chinese usually found it simplest to have a whole block of wood carved as a unit for printing. When in the fifteenth century this invention reached the West by way of Central Asia and the Middle East, the Europeans quickly discarded woodblocks for movable type, because of the small number of writing symbols they employed. But movable type in wood, porcelain, and copper had actually been developed long before in East Asia, appearing in China around 1030 and being much utilized in Korea during the first half of the fifteenth century.

The Growth of Trade.   The most important reason for the great economic growth of the eighth to thirteenth centuries was probably the tremendous expansion of trade, which permitted much greater local specialization and therefore increased overall production. The early T'ang, with the traditional Chinese contempt for commerce, had attempted to control and restrict trade, but during the late T'ang and Sung it broke out of this government strait jacket. It spread beyond the old government marketplaces, and by Sung times the main streets of the cities were lined with shops, as in modern China. Great commercial cities also began to appear for the first time—that is, great population centers which, unlike earlier Chinese cities, were not largely centers of political administration but were primarily great emporiums of trade.

The interregional exchange of goods in earlier times had been conducted in large part by the government through taxation, the operation of monopolies, and other measures of economic control, with private traders serving mainly as dealers in luxury goods. During the late T'ang and Sung, however, there was so great a development of private trade that it came to overshadow the government's operations. Wholesalers or brokers gathered the local surplus of agricultural or manufactured goods for sale to transport merchants. The latter ranged from itinerant peddlers to large-scale, monopolistic operators, served by an extensive network of inns. The large transport merchants disposed of their goods through local brokers to a multitude of individual shops and peddlers.

The growth of commerce was accompanied by a proliferation of trade guilds. These were known as *hang* (later called *hong* by Westerners), because they had grown out of the merchant associations grouped by streets (*hang*) in the marketplaces of early T'ang times. The more important guilds were usually those that transported and sold such basic commodities as grain, salt, tea, or silk or had the banking functions of storing and lending money. The scale of operation of the larger guilds is indicated by the case of a guild of one hundred grain transport merchants in the capital region during the eleventh century which reportedly did an annual business worth 10 million units.

Foreign Trade.   Growth in foreign trade was one of the clearest indications of the mercantile expansion of the time and presumably was a major stimulant to the whole commercial revolution. Trade with the West by way of Central Asia had gone on since Han times, and now there was a great increase in overland trade with China's immediate neighbors to the north and northwest. The peoples of these areas had acquired a taste for Chinese products, such as silk and tea, and the incorporation of millions of Chinese into the empires of the Liao, Hsi Hsia, and Chin greatly heightened the demand for these goods. Profits from these exports made it possible for the Sung both to make appeasement payments to the northern empires and to purchase from the steppe lands the horses needed for China's defense.

Overseas trade seems to have been an even greater stimulus to the economic development of China at this time. A significant maritime trade with India and the Middle East had existed since the Later Han, but in the eighth century it began to grow very rapidly, ushering in what might be called the first period of great oceanic commerce in the history of the world. The entrance of the Europeans in the early sixteenth century into this lucrative trade along the southern littoral of Asia was to mark the beginning of the oceanic phase of Western history.

Improvements in the techniques of shipbuilding and navigation help account for the increase in maritime commerce. Large vessels, relying on both sails and oars, had come into use, and a system of transverse water-tight bulkheads had been developed, making ships much less likely to sink. The Chinese had known of magnetic polarity at least as early as the third century A.D., and a Chinese text clearly indicates that the compass was in use in this southern trade by 1119, several decades before it was introduced to Europe by the Arabs. Another factor in the growth of oceanic commerce may have been the outburst of energy in West Asia following the rise of Islam. In fact, the overseas trade of China was at first largely in the hands of Muslim Iranians and Arabs. But the greatest spur to this trade was probably the unprecedented prosperity of China under the T'ang and Sung, which inevitably drew traders to Chinese ports and created an insistent demand for Chinese manufactures all the way from Japan to East Africa.

The rise of oceanic commerce in time altered the orientation of China toward the outside world. The eastern and southern coasts, which had once been distant and unimportant regions, gradually became the chief areas of foreign trade and contact, while the northwestern provinces, once the front door of China, started to sink to the status of a remote hinterland. During the Sung, overseas trade was concentrated at a few large ports along the south coast and on the lower Yangtze, where it was supervised by the Superintendencies of Merchant Shipping. The system of limiting foreign trade to certain official ports where custom duties could be collected had started in the eighth century, and during the Sung these custom duties became an important source of government income. The bulk of foreign trade flowed through Canton during the late T'ang and the Northern Sung, but, under the Southern Sung, Ch'üan-chou (Marco Polo's Zayton), situated near the great tea- and porcelain-producing areas in Fukien, became the leading port.

Koreans seem to have dominated the trade with Korea and Japan in the ninth century, and Arabs and Iranians controlled most of the trade with South and West Asia. These foreigners, who occupied designated quarters in the port cities, lived under their own customary laws, under a system analogous to the extraterritoriality of modern times but without its implications of foreign cultural superiority. The West Asians brought Islam with them and erected mosques. The foreign trade communities seem to have been quite large, and already in the eighth century the records tell of "thousands" of foreigners in Canton and in Yang-chou, a great city on the lower Yangtze. Gradually during the Sung, the Chinese began to take a larger part in overseas trade and by late Sung times had come to dominate commerce with Korea and Japan. Thus the originally land-locked Chinese were becoming a more maritime people, and their ships began to venture overseas and in time all the way to Africa.

The nature of China's foreign trade at this time indicates the leading role China had come to occupy in the world's economy. Except for fine cotton textiles, China's imports were largely raw materials—horses and hides from the steppe lands, and gems, spices, ivory, and other luxury goods from the tropics. On the other hand, except for some minerals, Chinese exports were largely manufactured goods. Books, paintings, and art objects were eagerly sought in areas such as Korea and Japan, which had derived their higher culture from China; Chinese copper cash was in great demand throughout East and Southeast Asia; and silk textiles and porcelains were highly prized everywhere. Fragments of Sung porcelains are to be found as far afield as Zanzibar, and the ruins of the medieval trading cities of the Persian Gulf and Egypt are said to be littered with them.

The Advanced Money Economy.   One of the clearest signs of the economic growth that took place in China during the late T'ang and Sung was the great expansion of the currency system. Copper cash had appeared as early as the late Chou and had been used extensively ever since, but there was now a huge increase in the quantity of currency minted, a great development in the complexity of the currency system, and a corresponding rise in the role of money in trade and government finance.

Annual tax receipts in cash, as opposed to textiles or grain, had amounted to only 2 million strings of a thousand cash each in 749, but by 1065 the Sung was receiving 37 million strings of currency a year in payment of taxes, and in the Southern Sung the government's income in money completely overshadowed its grain and textile receipts. The early T'ang, like most previous Chinese regimes, had relied almost exclusively on agricultural taxes, but during the Northern Sung income from government monopolies and various commercial taxes began to outbalance agricultural taxes, and in the Southern Sung state revenue came overwhelmingly from commercial sources. Although later dynasties were to prove more dependent than the Sung on agricultural taxes, the great development of commercial sources of revenue during the Sung gave to Chinese regimes from this time on a second major financial support and therefore greater fiscal stability than earlier dynasties had enjoyed.

The rapid growth in the use of money during the late T'ang and Sung put a heavy strain on China's currency resources. Under the T'ang, the minting of cash had averaged between 130,000 and 310,000 strings per year. By the late tenth century production was around 880,000, and in the eleventh century it rose to as much as 1,830,000 strings a year. Even then the demand for cash commonly outstripped production. To meet this demand the government sometimes tried to limit the use of copper to coinage or attempted a sort of debasement by reducing the number of coins in a string of cash. It also attempted to bar the export of cash and, when this proved ineffective, to place a 50 per cent export duty on coinage. In border areas such as Szechwan and Shansi it even experimented with iron coins in a vain effort to erect a sort of "iron curtain" between China and the purses of its "barbarian" neighbors. The use of gold and silver—gold dust by weight and silver in the form of ingots of supposedly standard weight and purity—helped relieve the pressure on copper coinage, but curiously the Chinese only rarely minted these precious metals.

The most interesting solution to the currency problem, and the one that best illustrates the growth of an advanced money economy, was the development of paper currency. Both the government and the great transport merchants faced the problem of transferring large sums of money over great distances. Copper cash were too bulky for convenient transfer, and consequently various types of paper credit and paper money were developed to meet the need. As early as 811 the T'ang was issuing so-called "flying cash" to pay for goods acquired in distant areas. These money drafts were reimbursable at the capital. The system proliferated under the Sung, which put out many separate issues of this sort. Because of their convenience, such government money drafts were exchanged between merchants who wished to transfer credits.

Meanwhile, another type of paper money was being developed by private bankers, who issued certificates of deposit which could be cashed for a 3 per cent service charge. Such certificates, because of their convenience, came to circulate freely at face value. Those issued by the bankers of Chengtu in Szechwan were among the most famous, and when they were taken over by the government in 1024 they became the world's first genuine paper money. Issued in denominations of between two hundred and a thousand cash (or one string), these government notes were subject to the usual 3 per cent service charge, and they were limited to three years' validity because of the deterioration of the paper.

The Chengtu paper money was at first limited to 1,256,000 strings in value and in the early days was soundly backed by 360,000 strings of cash. The Sung also put out various other local issues of paper money. When in financial trouble, however, the government could not resist the temptation of printing more paper money than it could redeem, thus starting what was to become in time a worldwide phenomenon. In currency development and in many other features of the economy, the Sung achieved a level that was not always equaled and was not significantly surpassed in China before the nineteenth century.

Society and Culture

The Gentry Class. China's commercial revolution did not produce as great a change in society and government as did the later commercial revolution of Europe. This was probably because it took place within a highly organized, bureaucratic empire which easily adjusted to and drew new strength from this economic growth, whereas the feudal social and political institutions of Europe were quite incapable of accommodating great changes in the economy and therefore collapsed, leading to far more basic alterations of society in Europe than occurred in China. On the other hand, very significant changes in society and culture did accompany the great economic growth of the eighth to the thirteenth centuries in China.

Since the society that emerged at that time was to remain characteristic of China until the nineteenth century and since it included many features that appear characteristic of modern urban civilization, it can in a sense be considered "early modern." In any case, while the twelfth-century culture of Europe seems only a rather remote ancestor of the nineteenth-century West, the twelfth-century civilization of China appears to be only a younger and more exuberant stage of the China that the West came to know in the nineteenth century.

One of the major factors in the transformation of the highly aristocratic society of the Six Dynasties period and early T'ang into the essentially nonaristocratic and more egalitarian society of the Sung was the shift in the landholding and tax system. Before this change the land was divided for the most part between the free peasants, who gave virtually the whole of their surplus produce and labor as taxes to the government, and the estates of great families, who could protect their lands from most taxes, could count on the political and military support of their subordinates on their estates, and could influence government because of their wealth and independent base of power. After the change, the government no longer opposed the private accumulation of agricultural land, and so private holdings could be preserved without exceptional power and influence. As a result large numbers of small and medium landowners appeared. On the other hand, the new simplified tax system made it more difficult for the old aristocrats to maintain their tax-free status.

The rapid rise of commerce and a money economy also made the old type of self-sufficient estate no longer an efficient economic unit, and at the same time the political power of the great landowner was diminished by the growing role of the examination system in producing political leadership and the increasing concentration of power in the hands of the emperors and their bureaucracy. Gradually the old aristocracy merged into a much broader gentry or landlord class, scattered parcels of land became a more common landholding pattern than large estates, and the farmers living on the property of the landlords took on the character of tenants rather than of retainers.

The new gentry class depended much less on agricultural wealth than had the old aristocracy. Actually agriculture seems to have become economically a losing proposition from Sung times on. Because of the prestige of owning land and its relative safety from government confiscation, surplus capital was usually invested in land, but the wealth of the gentry landowners seems to have been often of merchant origin, and it could best be protected by high government office. Another reason why the gentry was not simply a landowning class was that its wealth could be effectively translated into power in the central government only through education and the achievement of high political office by way of the examination system. The gentry as a class gained national political influence directly from intellectual accomplishments and only indirectly from wealth and property.

Still another contrast with the old aristocracy was that by Sung times hereditary status had become relatively unimportant. Social mobility had greatly increased in an economically more diversified society and had become justified by a greater acceptance of egalitarian principles. Thus the whole tone of society was different, and this in turn affected the spirit of the higher culture.

The Urbanization of Society.   Another feature of the new society was its growing urbanization. At the beginning of the twelfth century there were fifty-two large urban prefectures with more than 100,000 households, compared to twenty-six in the middle of the eighth century. The real urbanization of Chinese culture, however, was not so much a matter of numbers as it was the domination of society from this time on by city and town dwellers. The new gentry, unlike the old aristocracy, lived to a large extent in cities and towns, being thus more like absentee landlords than country squires. Since nearly all officials and rich merchants also lived in cities and towns, a large proportion of the leadership group was concentrated in urban areas. The higher culture, therefore, naturally became heavily urbanized, developing interests and attitudes that seem more characteristic of city people than of rural populations.

The triumph of the civilian as opposed to the military point of view was one of the chief characteristics of the new urban culture. While the Chinese until the early T'ang had exulted in military power as much as other strong peoples, from the time of the Sung, Chinese civilization has been characterized by an overwhelming emphasis on civil accomplishments and a contempt for the martial life, as also appears to be the case in modern urban societies in the West. Military service, it was felt, was fit only for the dregs of society; or, as the Chinese put it, the best men were no more to be used for soldiers than the best iron for nails. It is significant that of the four great dynasties since the T'ang only the two "barbarian" ones conquered far afield.

In an urban environment, the higher culture became much more sophisticated and diversified than before, and a broader swath of the population participated in it. The urban way of life and citified amusements naturally came to the fore. While rural pleasures such as hunting and horseback riding have persisted among certain groups in the West until the present, most cultivated Chinese turned their backs on such rustic pastimes almost a millennium ago. At the same time, and somewhat paradoxically, the Chinese began to show the romanticized love of the beauties of nature characteristic of the West as it began to urbanize.

City life in the Sung was free and luxurious. Cities were no longer

Scene from "Spring Festival on the River," a long scroll painting from the twelfth century. Note the street stalls, a sedan chair on the bridge, and boatmen lowering their mast to pass under the bridge.

conglomerations of walled villages dominated by the imperial palace or some other center of political authority. Amusement quarters, instead, were now the centers of social life. Here were to be found countless wine and tea shops, restaurants specializing in various types of cuisine, and houses featuring professional female entertainers comparable to the geisha of a later period in Japan. Both these houses and the restaurants frequently shaded off into brothels. There were also theaters, puppet shows, jugglers, storytellers, and various other entertainments.

The evils of urban society also first made themselves felt in this age. Absentee landlords and tenancy created problems in Chinese agriculture that continued until contemporary times. Widespread pauperism also ap-

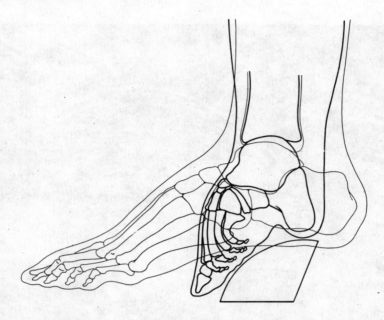

A BOUND FOOT. *This diagram shows the twisted and cramped bone structure of a bound ("lily") foot, as compared with that of a normal foot. Bound tightly with cloth from the age of five, a little girl's foot grew painfully into this deformed but erotically admired shape.*

peared among the city proletariat. Private charity agencies came into being in the late T'ang, performing such services as caring for orphans and indigent old people or burying dead paupers. These institutions were nationalized and greatly extended in the early twelfth century. The Sung army was the chief means of taking care of the unemployed, but the government also provided work relief and special granaries for the support of the poor.

A change in the position of women may also have been associated with the urbanization of culture. Women had always been subservient to men, but the concentration of the upper classes in cities, where the work of women was less essential than on the farm, may have contributed to a further decline in the status of women over the next few centuries. This change is suggested by the growth at this time of the institution of concubinage, the strengthening of the social rules against the remarriage of widows, and the custom introduced among the upper classes of binding the feet of women. When still quite young, girls would have their feet tightly wrapped and gradually bent until the arch was broken and the toes, except for the big toe, were turned under. This produced a "lily-foot" only about half the normal size, virtually crippling girls for life and thus accentuating the wealth of the men who could afford such useless play-things. While foot-binding and the resultant stiff walk of Chinese women have appeared repugnant to foreign observers, bound feet developed strong erotic associations for Chinese men. The custom gradually spread through-out society and lasted down to the present century.

Artistic Trends.   Despite the far conquests of the T'ang and the wide commercial contacts of the Sung, the culture of the eighth to thirteenth centuries showed relatively few new foreign influences. It was characterized instead by a rich and sophisticated reworking of native traditions. This was as true in the arts as in other fields. Architecture remained close to its original post-and-lintel construction, though multistoried buildings became more common and the original straight lines of the tile roofs increasingly curved upward at their ends. Religious sculpture, which had flourished under the influence of Buddhism, achieved a high point of realism in the Sung and then rapidly declined. The industrial arts all prospered greatly, and the celadons and other porcelain wares of the Sung became famous all over the world.

Painting, however, showed the richest development, and ever since the Sung most Chinese have felt, with good reason, that it is the greatest of their fine arts. Drawing from a rich, continuous tradition stretching well back into the Han period, Chinese canons of painting became fully established during the Sung, and painting itself reached a level of per-fection that was probably not surpassed in later dynasties. Looked at closely, subsequent Chinese painting reveals great variety and vitality but, scanned more broadly, it seems to be largely variations on themes already well developed by Sung times.

Buddhist painting, with its strong iconographic elements, remained prominent through the Sung, though it was fast losing place to purely secular art. In the latter, the emphasis shifted from figures and depictions of human events to landscapes, in which the human element was at most a small detail, or to vignettes of nature, such as a spray of bamboo. The approach was impressionistic rather than realistically complete. Color was felt to be unimportant and monochrome paintings predominated. The artist was selective in detail and concentrated on what he felt was the true essence of his subject. A landscape represented nature as a whole; a spray of bamboo was a microcosm of the universe. The Taoist or Zen inspiration of this art is obvious.

The genius of Sung painting is revealed by the fact that, as compared with the art of medieval or Renaissance Europe, it seems to us extremely modern. The whole Sung attitude toward art also appears essentially modern. It was no longer the handmaiden of religion. Paintings were not merely icons or architectural adornments but were valued for their own aesthetic

Detail of an eleventh-century ink and tint painting on silk by Kuo Hsi.

qualities. Painters were not nameless craftsmen but were known and respected artists—usually men of broad education and high social status.

The names of famous late T'ang and Sung artists are legion. Among the greatest were Wu Tao-hsüan (or Wu Tao-tzu) of Hsüan Tsung's time, Mi Fu (or Mi Fei, 1051–1107) of the Northern Sung, and the Southern Sung landscapists Ma Yüan and Hsia Kuei. The Chinese love of classification was applied to art, and there was much written about Southern and Northern schools of landscape painting. There was also a great antiquarian interest in art and archaeology. Great public and private collections were assembled. Famous collectors affixed their seals to important paintings as indications of authenticity as well as ownership, thereby increasing rather than detracting from the value of the works. Detailed catalogues and learned critiques of art were written. The antiquarian interest also stimulated the faking of antiques, a minor art in itself.

Literature.   While the ability to paint was a prized talent among the elite of China, beautiful calligraphy and literary skill, especially the ability to

Landscape painted on a round fan by Ma Yüan in the late twelfth or early thirteenth century.

compose poetry, were virtual necessities. The written word had always been accorded great respect, and the development of the highly literary examinations as the chief doorway to fame and fortune further enhanced its prestige. There was a great increase in the tenth century in private schools and academies (*shu-yüan*), and the spread of printing naturally contributed to the availability of written materials of all sorts and thus to a general spread of literature and learning.

The lyric poetry known as *shih,* which had been popular since the Six Dynasties period, flourished in the T'ang, becoming freer and less bound by form. It perhaps reached its apogee in the eighth century at the hands of Li Po (or Li T'ai-po, 701–762) and Tu Fu (712–770). Li Po was a Taoist wine lover and carefree, though melancholy, wanderer. The apochryphal story of his death characterized his attitudes: he is said to have drowned while boating when he reached out in drunken ecstasy for the reflection of the moon in the water. Tu Fu was more the grave Confucian moralist, deeply aware of the suffering of humanity and the injustices of life.

Literally thousands of other T'ang and Sung poets have left their names to posterity. Po Chü-i (772–846), who wrote in a simple style not far removed from the vernacular, became vastly popular throughout East Asia. By Sung times the *shih,* through constant repetition of its themes, had become more stereotyped and lost some of its vigor, but there were still great poets of this form, such as Su Shih (better known as Su Tung-p'o, 1036–1101), who was also a famous calligrapher, great prose stylist, and philosopher.

As the *shih* declined in freshness, a new form of poetry, the *tz'u,* which originated in the lyrics of popular songs, rose to prominence. The *tz'u* had a great variety of patterns and made free use of the colloquial language. At first it was looked down on by literary men, but by the Sung all the major poets, including Su Tung-p'o, wrote *tz'u.* But this form too in time became more stereotyped, and a new type of song lyric, *san-ch'ü,* began to take its place and became the favorite song form of the succeeding Mongol and Ming periods.

The late T'ang and Sung was also the golden age of formal prose writing. Han Yü (768–824), rejecting the ornate, balanced prose style that had flourished since the Six Dynasties, returned to a simple and straightforward style. It was, however, slightly archaic and tended to fall back on ancient models, in this way widening the gulf between literary and colloquial Chinese. But the fight to free prose writing from cramping artificialities was continued. Ou-yang Hsiu (1007–1072), a leading historian and thinker of his day as well as a composer of *tz'u,* felt that writers should be entirely free to express ideas in whatever form seemed best. Back of such a concept, no doubt, was the rising use of the vernacular for philosophic writings and for the recorded dialogues of Zen masters.

This period also saw the beginnings of two entirely new literary currents —popular theater and romances or tales. Though traditionally depreciated by well-educated Chinese as plebeian and vulgar, these were in time to achieve great literary heights, growing into the full-fledged drama and novels of later periods. The appearance of these popular literary forms at this time is clearly to be associated with such factors as the spread of literacy and the general urbanization of Chinese culture.

An outstanding characteristic of the literature of the late T'ang and Sung is that most of the great poets, prose writers, and scholars were also officials, even if sometimes relatively unsuccessful ones, as in the case of Li Po and Tu Fu. Conversely, most of the great statesmen were also distinguished men of letters. Wang An-shih was a poet of note as well as the leading political personality of his day. In earlier periods, the roles of poet, scholar, and statesman had been relatively distinct; but the ideal Confucian type that had evolved by the Sung was that of the "universal man" who was scholar, poet, and statesman all at the same time, and possibly philosopher and painter as well.

Scholarship. The late T'ang and Sung saw a tremendous expansion and enrichment of earlier forms of scholarship. Standard histories were compiled with even greater enthusiasm and care than before and were supplemented by new types of historical work. The historical record had grown to such enormous size that a new effort at a single comprehensive history of China's past seemed necessary. The *Tzu-chih t'ung-chien,* by Ssu-ma Kuang (1018–1086), a statesman and leading opponent of Wang An-shih, was the first effort at a comprehensive history since Ssu-ma Ch'ien's time. It is a strictly chronological presentation covering the years 403 B.C. to 959 A.D. in 294 chapters. Its name reveals the whole philosophy of the Chinese historian, for it literally means *The Comprehensive Mirror for Aid in Government.*

The materials of this bulky book were abridged and reworked in the twelfth century under the direction of the famous philosopher Chu Hsi. In the resulting *Outline and Details of the Comprehensive Mirror,* the main points of history were sorted out from the supporting factual data, and a great deal of emphasis was given to moral judgments. *Narratives from Beginning to End from the Comprehensive Mirror* by Yüan Shu (1131–1205) was another reworking of the same materials but was divided up by major incidents more in the manner of the modern historical writings of the West. These three works became the chief introductions to history for later generations of Chinese students.

The earlier tendency toward encyclopedic compilations was also greatly developed during this period. The *Comprehensive Compendium (T'ung tien),* completed in 801, and the *Selected T'ang Documents (T'ang hui yao),* a great collection of materials on T'ang government and economics, completed in 961 on the basis of earlier compilations, became the prototypes for whole new categories of encyclopedic works, which thenceforth supplanted the standard histories as the chief sources of information on the political institutions and economic developments of the past.

Neo-Confucianism

New Currents of Thought. In intellectual attitudes and formal philosophy, the late T'ang and Sung saw the clear appearance of patterns that were to remain characteristic of China until the nineteenth century. The philosophical synthesis, known in the West as Neo-Confucianism, which emerged from the intellectual ferment of these centuries was to be the almost unchanging core of Chinese thought from then until its collapse under the impact of Western thought and revolutionary political and social changes in the twentieth century.

Two basic factors lay behind the revived interest in Confucian philosophy. One was the turning inward of the Chinese during their long losing battle with the northern "barbarians." In the early T'ang the Chinese, confident in their power, were inquisitive and tolerant toward the outside world. When the first ambassadors from the Islamic caliphate came to China in 713 and refused on religious grounds to prostrate themselves before the emperor in the traditional kowtow, the Chinese readily waived the requirement, in significant contrast to their rigidity on this point with European embassies in recent centuries. By the late T'ang, however, a growing fear and resentment of the "barbarians" was becoming evident. Buddhism had always been criticized on the grounds that it was a foreign religion, but now attacks of this type became more common and had greater influence. A sign of the times was a famous memorial presented to the throne in 819 by the great scholar and essayist Han Yü, criticizing the emperor for paying honor to the supposed fingerbone of the Buddha. Two decades later came the great persecution of 841–846.

The other basic reason for restored interest in Confucianism was the obvious success of the old Chinese political ideal. The political disillusionment of the Six Dynasties period had now receded into the dim past. The need for an educated officialdom in the revived bureaucratic state had led to the re-creation of the examination system and a re-emphasis on the Confucian writings and ideas on which the examinations focused. Confucian concepts, of course, had never died out even at the height of the Buddhist age, but after the reunification of the empire they grew steadily in strength and popularity. By the ninth century the educated classes were so thoroughly imbued with Confucianism that they increasingly rejected the antipolitical concepts of Taoism and condemned what they regarded to be the antisocial aspects of Buddhism.

The Neo-Confucian upsurge, however, was not simply the continuation of Confucian concepts as they had existed in the Chou or Han. It was in part an exciting rediscovery, in part a creative new movement. It was obvious to scholars that the society in which they lived was quite different from that described in the Classics. The Neo-Confucians hoped to recapture the original vision—to recreate the ideal Confucian society that they believed had existed in ancient times—but they did so in terms of the attitudes and interests of their own day.

The Neo-Confucian thinkers were strongly influenced by some of the Buddhist concepts that had been so important in Chinese thinking for the past few centuries. Many of them had been students of Buddhism or Taoism before they turned to Confucianism, and some had even lived in Zen monasteries. Buddhism had conditioned men to think in metaphysical terms, and one of the things that was new about Neo-Confucianism was that it developed a metaphysics for Confucianism, freely utilizing Buddhist ideas and Taoist terminology.

Neo-Confucianism thus was drawn from the diverse intellectual currents of the day, just as Han Confucianism had been eclectic in its time. Essentially, however, it was a rejection of the Taoist search for immortality and the Buddhist concern with the divine and the afterlife. It returned to the ancient Chinese emphasis on mundane social and political matters, particularly ethics, and it reasserted the old agnostic, nontheistic tendencies of Chinese thought.

The Neo-Confucianists and Their Thought. Han Yü, the distinguished prose stylist and critic of Buddhism in the ninth century, might be called the first of the great Neo-Confucianists. The eleventh and twelfth centuries, however, were the period of greatest philosophical ferment, when many different schools of thought appeared. For example, Lu Chiu-yüan (or Lu Hsiang-shan, 1139–1192) developed a Zen-like emphasis on personal intuition that was to reach its height under the Ming. In the eleventh century, the great reformer Wang An-shih represented a pragmatic, activist type of Confucianism, while his contemporaries, the scholar Ou-yang Hsiu and the poet Su Tung-p'o, were leaders of other important philosophical trends.

Among the opponents of Wang An-shih there was one particular school of philosophy which was eventually to win out as Neo-Confucian orthodoxy. The first major figure in this line of thought was Chou Tun-i (1012–1073), who took from the essentially non-Confucian *Classic of Changes* the term *T'ai-chi,* or "Supreme Ultimate," and devised a cosmological chart showing how *yin* and *yang* and the five elements derived from it. The brothers Ch'eng Hao (1031–1085) and Ch'eng I (1032–1107) elaborated this metaphysics. Ch'eng I was also largely responsible for selecting two works which in a sense had been rediscovered by Han Yü—the *Mencius* and the *Great Learning* from the *Record of Rituals*—and adding to them another chapter from the latter work, the *Doctrine of the Mean,* and the *Analects* of Confucius to form the category known as the Four Books, which became thereafter the central scriptures of Confucianism and the core texts for traditional Chinese education.

The final synthesizer and organizer of this school was Chu Hsi (1130–1200), who has been compared with Aquinas and was in any case the perfect Confucianist. He was a famous historian, as we have seen, and played briefly a dramatic role as statesman, but above all he was a great commentator on the Classics and China's leading philosopher after the classic age. He put his stamp so heavily on Neo-Confucian thought that in East Asia it has often been known as Chu Hsi-ism.

In the Neo-Confucian metaphysics of Chu Hsi's school, all varieties of things were thought to have their respective *li,* or fundamental principles of form, and their *ch'i,* literally "ether," or what we might call "matter." While *li* provides the pattern of a house, actual houses are made out of the *ch'i* of wood or bricks. All the many *li* are part of the limitless, time-less, unitary Supreme Ultimate, which "is not cut into pieces; it is merely like the moon reflecting itself in ten thousand streams."

The influence of Buddhist concepts is obvious. The Sung Neo-Confucianists were close enough to Buddhism to put much emphasis on this sort of metaphysics, and they carefully elaborated and schematized the relationships between the Supreme Ultimate, *yin* and *yang,* and the five elements and developed cyclical theories of change reminiscent of Buddhist ideas. But the heart of Neo-Confucianism, like that of all earlier Confucianism, was the application of its ideas to ethics and to social and political institutions. To later generations, who were ready to accept Sung metaphysics without question, perhaps in part out of apathy, the ethical and social concepts of the school were what was truly important.

The old conflict between Mencius' belief that man is by nature good and thus only needs teaching and self-development and Hsün-tzu's view that man is by nature evil and thus needs strict control and indoctrination came to a head during the Sung. Chu Hsi and his school settled the argument in Mencius' favor. The *li* of man's nature, they argued, is of course pure and good. It is the origin of the five basic virtues, which can be translated as love, uprightness, propriety, knowledge, and reliability. But the pearl of man's *li* is always found in the mire of his *ch'i.* It needs polishing to be given its full potential luster. Thus, education is desirable, though self-cultivation is even more important.

Confucianism, as it has been known during the past millennium, came into full flower under the Sung Neo-Confucianists. The emphases were essentially those of Mencius and of the scholar-bureaucrats of Sung times. There was the particularistic, family-centered ethic, stressing the five human relationships first spelled out in the *Mencius.* These were between the ruler and his minister or subject, between father and son, husband and wife, elder brother and younger brother, and friend and friend. It should be noted that, except for the last, all of these were relations of authority and obedience. Next there was the Confucian political ideal of benevolent paternalism. The state was regarded as the family writ large. The authority of the ruler, like that of the father, was considered to be essentially ethical, as Mencius had insisted. Finally there was the bureaucratic ideal, institutionalized in the civil service and the examination system. Moral, scholarly men, trained in the classical principles of right conduct and good government, should guide and administer society. They bore a responsibility to put public service above private interest and to advise the Son of Heaven with rectitude, even at personal risk.

Cultural Stability. After Chu Hsi's death, his Neo-Confucian synthesis gradually became established as a rigid orthodoxy. By 1313 his commentaries on the classics had been made the standard ones to which all answers in the civil service examinations had to conform. Thus Chu Hsi's great scholarship and philosophic comprehensiveness became a check on further Chinese intellectual development. Strengthened by the traditional respect for both the past and the written word, Chu Hsi-ism, once established as orthodoxy, proved to be a sort of intellectual strait jacket, reinforcing the growing rigidity of Chinese society.

Neo-Confucianism thus helped create the uniquely stable and traditionalist society of early modern China—a society which changed so little, in comparison with Europe, that both Occidentals and Chinese came to accept the myth that China has always been "unchanging." The relative slowness of cultural and institutional change in China after the Sung left the country weak in the nineteenth century before the cultural onslaught of the West, which had grown so spectacularly during that same period. China's comparative inertia during these centuries, therefore, is usually viewed as an historic tragedy, if not a cause for national shame. It can, however, be looked at in an entirely different perspective. For the successive generations of Chinese who lived during this long period, the high degree of political, social, and spiritual stability that they enjoyed was probably preferable to the constant turmoil of life and thought during these same centuries in Europe. Modern man, living in the notably unstable world civilization that has grown out of the rapidly changing culture of the West, may also look with envy at the peace and stability of China between the thirteenth and nineteenth centuries.

The question remains how China was able to achieve so long a period of cultural stability. The chief reason may have been the balance between political, social, and intellectual forces that China had achieved by the thirteenth century—a sort of perfection within the bounds of the ideas and the technology of that time. The balance was so firm that it took massive blows from the outside to destroy it in the nineteenth and twentieth centuries. The Chinese are perhaps right to view with great pride the golden age of their culture which produced a degree of stability no other high civilization has ever been able to approach.

7. China and the "Barbarians": The Mongol Empire

From the thirteenth to the nineteenth centuries the Chinese way of life showed great stability. Three ruling houses held power during three dynastic periods: Yüan (1271–1368), Ming (1368–1644), and Ch'ing (1644–1912). Disorder occurred principally during the years of dynastic decline and change, in the fourteenth, seventeenth, and nineteenth centuries.

Yet this stable political record has a puzzling aspect. The Yüan and the Ch'ing were non-Chinese dynasties of conquest who ruled over the immensely more populous Middle Kingdom as legitimate holders of the imperial power. Plainly, the Chinese Empire included not merely the agricultural area within the Great Wall but also the peripheral regions of Inner Asia, especially Mongolia and Manchuria. A strong Chinese dynasty, such as the Han, T'ang, or Ming, would dominate these regions. But periodically, the *yang* of Chinese expansion would give way to the *yin* of "barbarian" invasion. Tribal peoples outside the Wall would seize power and rule part of the empire. Yet invariably they would make use of its traditional political institutions, which supported centralized imperial rule through a great and largely Chinese bureaucracy. The stability of the Chinese political order lay partly in its capacity to let non-Chinese, when they were strong enough, rule over it without changing its fundamental features.

The chart of Central Asian peoples and kingdoms on page 153 indicates the names and habitats of the major groups of "barbarians" who have appeared and disappeared in the grasslands on China's northern horizon

CENTRAL ASIAN PEOPLES AND KINGDOMS

(Note: The data below are not by any means permanently established, many points being still in dispute among scholars.)

People	Language Group	Period and Region
Hsiung-nu (Huns?)	Turkish	Founded first steppe empire in third century B.C.; conquered by Han in first century B.C. and first century A.D.
Yüeh-chih	Probably Indo-European	Second century B.C., sought by Han China as allies against Hsiung-nu; migrated from Kansu to Ili to Bactria, thence to Northwest India and set up Kushan Kingdom.
Hsien-pei	Mongolian	Third century A.D., in eastern Mongolia; invaded China in fourth century A.D.
Tabgach (T'o-pa)	Largely Mongolian	Founded Northern Wei dynasty, 386–534 A.D., in North China.
Turks (T'u-chüeh)	Turkish	Empire established c. 552; split into Eastern Empire (c. 600–744) on the Orkhon River, and Western Empire, in contact with Sassanians in Persia; groups penetrated India and Europe after 659.
Uighurs	Turkish	Conquered Eastern Turks and set up empire on the Orkhon River, 744–840; forced out by Kirghiz, set up empire in Tarim basin (Turfan) during 840 and after.
Khitan (Ch'i-tan)	Mongolian	Founded Liao dynasty in North China and adjacent area, 947–1125; driven west by Jurchen; set up Kara-Khitai (Western Liao) Empire in East Turkestan, 1124–1211.
Jurchen (Ju-chen, ancestors of the Manchus)	Tungusic	Founded Chin dynasty in North China, 1122–1234.
Tanguts	Tibetan	Founded Hsi Hsia Kingdom in Northwest China, 1038–1227.
Mongols	Mongolian	Founded Yüan dynasty over all China, 1271–1368.

throughout history. A westward drift characterizes this record, one people after another being driven by the Chinese or by their own nomadic successors toward the west. The earlier peoples belonged generally to the Turkish-speaking language group, while the Mongolian-speaking peoples became dominant later. From these tribes of the steppe emerged periodically leadership groups and fighting forces that succeeded in ruling part or all of China.

This ever-present "barbarian" influence on China's political life was based upon a major geographical fact—the close juxtaposition of the steppe and the sown areas, of two irreducibly different ways of life and two contrasting types of social organization suited to these different geographical regions. Underlying this contrast was the difference in rainfall. The aridity of the Inner Asian steppe, from which no rivers flow out to the sea, has made extensive agriculture impossible. Lacking adequate water resources, the high uplands of Tibet and the grasslands of Mongolia have had a very sparse population. The "barbarians" lived in areas roughly twice the size of China, but had perhaps no more than one-fortieth of the population. The source of "barbarian" power is therefore a very interesting question. The military superiority of the "barbarians" was frequently demonstrated when their mounted archers came within the Wall. But what lay behind this capacity to produce fierce and mobile fighting men?

The Society of the Steppe

In the grasslands, life was sustained primarily by the raising of animals rather than crops. The full nomad lived on a sheep-and-horse economy. Sheepskins formed his clothing. The wool made felt for his tents. He ate mutton and from the milk of his horses and sheep made cheese and butter. His women gathered dung for fuel. He used his horses for transport and the management of his flocks, and also for hunting and warfare, supplemented by camels for crossing deserts and by oxen for pulling his carts. His pastoral economy had little need of agriculture so long as it could maintain a minimal trade with settled areas in order to secure grain and also textiles, tea and other "luxuries," and metals to make weapons. Thus the nomad of the open steppe was self-sufficient in the short run, but could not be wholly cut off from commercial centers.

Since cities could not flourish on the grasslands, there were strict limits to culture and technology. Wealth was stored in the silver ornaments worn by the women. The chief art form was the so-called Scythian or animal style of metal work found all across the Eurasian steppe from the lower Volga and the Caspian Sea to the Amur River. Literacy and literature remained undeveloped. The religion of the tribes was a primitive shamanism, practiced by medicine men, not unlike that of those far-distant cousins

LIFE ON THE STEPPE. *A Mongol camp near the Altai Mountains with yurts, sheep, horses, pasture, and a brackish lake of surface water (on right).*

of the Tungusic peoples, the American Indians. The one great deity of the steppe was the Eternal Heaven.

The nomad's migration was not an aimless wandering but occurred on a seasonal basis, usually to move his flocks and herds from summer pasture on the open plain to winter pasture in some more sheltered area such as a mountain valley, and back again. His essential rights were those of movement for pasture rather than of land control for agriculture. The tribal chieftain sought the right to perform a cycle of migration using certain grasslands at certain seasons. He had little interest in the settled activities of plowing, reaping, house construction, and road building. He remained precariously dependent upon nature, for a severe winter could destroy his flocks. The seminomads, who lived on the fringes of sedentary agricultural societies, shared this constant economic instability. Their lack of accumulated resources gave both types of nomads a periodic incentive not only for increased trade but for military expansion. The nomads were the have-nots of antiquity, always poor in comparison with peoples in more thickly populated farming regions.

"SCYTHIAN" BRONZE. *A horned herbivore attacked by a feline beast. Bronzes in this so-called "Scythian," "Sino-Siberian," or "animal" style have been found throughout the northern areas of Asia which were accessible to the steppe peoples.*

Unlike peasants, who could seldom leave their fields without loss of production, the herders and huntsmen of the steppe could be quickly mobilized. From boyhood they spent their lives in the saddle. Their energies could be turned in a moment from the care of their flocks or the pursuit of game to the destruction of enemies. Their active outdoor life produced a type of individual (not unlike the early American cowboy) who was independent, self-reliant, and omnicompetent. The herdsman-hunter-warrior of the steppe had to be ready for anything. His capacity for warfare was increased by the fact that his women managed the camp and could handle all the problems of nomad life except war and politics.

The social organization of the tribes contributed to their military strength. Their clans were under chieftains who rose through personal prowess. When old or weak, they would be displaced. Personal relations of fealty and protection were reciprocally maintained between major and minor chieftains as well as among warriors, and so a strong personality could rise rather quickly to the top of a hierarchy of personal relationships.

Nomad striking power came from a combination of many factors. One technical element was the iron stirrup, which came into use in the early centuries A.D. and gave the cavalryman a firmer basis for mounted archery. Securely mounted on a well-trained horse and armed with a compound bow small enough for use from the saddle, he now had a tactical military superiority over the peasant foot soldier. For the next thousand years (ca. 400–1400), until the introduction of firearms, the balance of military technology in Asia remained in favor of the horseman.

The Great Wall boundary, where cultivator and herdsman met, remained unstable. Rainfall was marginal and farming met periodic disaster. Chinese trade with the nomad—in grain, silk, and later tea—in exchange for horses, easily became intermixed with politics. Seminomads on this frontier might settle down as Chinese vassals and even become Sinicized. Conversely, if Chinese rule proved ineffective, the mixed Sino-"barbarian" populace of the frontier might give allegiance to a rising nomad leader. The secret of such a leader's rise lay usually in his capacity to learn Chinese ways of administrative organization, so that he could set up a hybrid regime based on control of merchants, farmers, and tribal warriors. Chinese inevitably played a part in the rise of such a "barbarian" ruler on the frontier. In this uneasy partnership the alien rulers functioned in special roles—as fighters and power-holders.

The Khitan Empire. The Liao Empire of the Khitan tribes (947–1125) illustrates the characteristic features of a dual state. Their empire extended over much of Manchuria, Mongolia, and the northeast corner of China proper. Thus it included an agricultural area in North China and southern Manchuria, grasslands in western Manchuria and Mongolia, and the forested valleys of eastern and northern Manchuria. The non-Chinese part of this kingdom included several tribal groups. In eastern Manchuria were the Tungus (ancestors of the Manchus), who lived by a combination of hunting and agriculture together with pig-raising. On the Mongolian steppe to the west were Turkish tribes, full nomads who had neither agriculture nor pigs, but many sheep, horses, and camels. In between were the semi-nomadic Khitan people, who lived by a mixed economy in which agricultural crops, camels, pigs, horses, and oxen all played a part. These Khitan tribes in the central region of mixed economy led the way in building the empire, beginning with a nucleus of eighteen tribes which eventually grew to a total of fifty-four.

Khitan society was headed by one clan, divided into eight main lineages, who regularly got their wives from another major clan. Non-Khitan tribes were incorporated into the society as was also the settled Chinese population of agricultural villages and cities. The status of the Chinese varied all the way from slavery, through various forms of bondage and partial freedom, to complete freedom. At the bottom of the social scale were the conquered peoples of the state of P'o-hai (713–926) in eastern Manchuria.

Unlike the Chinese clan system, in which an unbroken line is maintained indefinitely, most of the Khitan clans lacked clan names and tended to lose their identity after several generations. Ancestral sacrifices were maintained only by the ruling clan, following the Chinese example. Marriage followed the tribal custom, which was quite at variance with Chinese practices. That is, a man might marry his mother's or his father's sister, or his brother's widow, in complete disregard of the Chinese rules of generation.

By 907 the Khitan had formed a tribal confederation comparable to that of the Hsiung-nu of earlier times. In that year the chieftain declared himself emperor of the Khitan. Soon he set up a dynasty with his son as heir apparent but was involved in constant warfare, not least with his own brothers. As the empire expanded, it firmly adopted the Chinese system of hereditary monarchy.

Next to their capacity for central leadership, the Khitan owed their empire to their cavalry. The ruler's mounted archers were organized in his *ordo,* which formed his camp bodyguard and was the prototype of what Westerners later called a "horde." As early as 922 he had some two thousand braves in this elite guard drawn from all the tribes. Beginning as a bodyguard like those of Western emperors, this elite cavalry grew to include some fifty to seventy thousand horsemen.

In warfare the cavalryman might use three horses (leading two remounts). He wore some armor and in battle used two kinds of bows and carried an ax, a sword, a rope, and dried food. Training was in the form of hunting exercises in units of five or ten horsemen, strictly disciplined to follow their leaders. On the open plain, the Khitan warriors developed a clock-like precision of organization based on units of tens, hundreds, and thousands, with a vanguard, wings, a center, and an imperial guard. Their army was preceded by a scouting force, perhaps ten thousand strong, and they used night patrols and complicated signals consisting of beacons, drums, horns, banners, shouted code names, gongs, and even birdcalls. They avoided close combat with superior numbers but would cut off the enemy's supplies and use tactics of ambush and maneuver. In siege operations they made the Chinese populace fill in moats and used Chinese catapults to break down walls. In storming a city they would drive Chinese captives ahead against their own townsmen and relatives.

The Liao Dynasty. By 947, the Khitan had extended their power southward over the sixteen prefectures in North China already mentioned and had captured towns and cities. In that year they adopted a Chinese dynastic title, as the Liao dynasty. Taking advantage of the collapse of the T'ang, they had now created a dual state of "barbarian" elements in the north and Chinese in the south. In this they had essential help from Chinese advisers who joined their cause, bringing with them the culture of cities and the methods of bureaucratic government.

The Liao administration was organized under five capitals, among which the Supreme Capital was north of the Wall. Each capital was the center of a circuit with a hierarchy of territorial units below it and with its own military commanderies, forts and fortified cities to protect it. Each half of the dual government had its own prime minister, chancellery, and ministers. The heads of both governments held office at the Supreme Capital. The government of the southern region inherited forms of the T'ang, such as the Six Ministries and the Board of Censors. The Chinese examination system was adopted after 988 to determine eligibility of Chinese for office. In making the Liao monarchy into a Chinese type of ruling institution, the Khitan took over the Chinese custom of naming year periods, selected an heir apparent, made Confucius the supreme sage of the state, practiced Confucian ancestor worship, used the Chinese language and script as their administrative *lingua franca,* and even wore Chinese clothes when in the southern region.

To offset this Sinification, the Khitan retained their own tribal organization and rites and, in the main, their own style of food and clothing. Unlike earlier "barbarian" invaders they consciously avoided taking over the Chinese spoken language as their own tongue, lest they be submerged in the sea of Chinese. They developed two forms of writing for their own type of Mongolian speech, the smaller one being alphabetical and the larger one based on Chinese characters. (See page 161.) The two Khitan scripts were used for administration, but no true literature developed in them.

The Liao Empire seems never to have had a population of more than about 4 million, very small in comparison with the Northern Sung. Indeed, the actual Khitan population was only about 750,000. Constituting only one-fifth of the population of their empire, the ruling Khitan tribesmen had to be on their mettle to maintain control. In the end they were overwhelmed not by Chinese but by another tribal people at their rear.

The Hsi Hsia Kingdom.   The Sung had been able to withstand the Liao partly because a three-way division of power had developed in the northwest. A Tibetan people, the Tanguts, had built in the area of modern Kansu a kingdom known as Hsi Hsia, or West Hsia. Their capital at Ning-hsia, on the Yellow River, stood between Mongolia and the Central Asian trade route to the west. They had a semioasis economy, combining irrigated agriculture with pastoralism and trade. After sending tribute to the Sung, the Tangut ruler in 1038 declared his independence, proclaiming himself emperor of the Hsia. He had a new writing system invented for his people which used extremely intricate Chinese-type characters to record the Tangut speech. The resulting literature remains today still largely undeciphered. The Tanguts modeled their government and education on that of China but made Buddhism their state religion.

The Chin Dynasty of the Jurchen.   The Jurchen tribes of northern Manchuria were Khitan vassals who became restive because they were prevented from moving down into the attractive southern region of Manchuria. They rose to power after an outstanding leader unified them in 1115, declared himself emperor, and quickly seized the Supreme Capital.

The Liao collapsed, but a remnant of the regime fled westward and set up another nomad empire. This was the Kara-Khitai, or "Black Khitan," which styled itself the Western Liao Empire (1124–1211). It established its control over the oases both east and west of the Pamirs, from the borders of the Hsi Hsia in Kansu across to the Amu-Daria (the Oxus River of Western antiquity), but was finally overwhelmed by the Mongols in 1211.

The Jurchen, unlike the Liao, were not confined to the northern borders of China but overran most of North China and captured the Sung capital Kaifeng in 1126. Their armies pushed all the way south to the Yangtze but the boundary with the Southern Sung was eventually stabilized roughly along the Huai River, at the approximate northern limit of major rice cultivation (see map, page 130).

The Jurchen named their dynasty the Chin ("Golden," 1122–1234), after a river in their homeland. Compared with the Chinese population they ruled, they were proportionally even fewer than the Khitan had been. They inherited the dual administration and hybrid culture of the Khitan rulers but were inevitably drawn further into the Chinese pattern. At their main capital, Yen-ching, on the site of modern Peking, they built up a Chinese-type bureaucratic state, divided into nineteen small provinces and subdivided into prefectures and subprefectures (*hsien*) on the model of the Sung and governed by the Six Ministries in the style of the T'ang. Chinese officials eventually outnumbered non-Chinese three to two.

The Jurchen, like the Khitan, sought both to rule over a large mass of Chinese subjects and to preserve their own culture in the face of the Chinese tradition. These post-T'ang non-Chinese peoples are in this respect reminiscent of the European tribal peoples who asserted their nationality as Frenchmen or Germans against the tradition of the Roman Empire. Thus the Jurchen used the Khitan alphabetic script and also devised two styles of Jurchen script, one alphabetic and one in characters derived from Chinese (see page 161).

At first, the Jurchen tribesmen, together with Khitan and other non-Chinese allies, were kept in readiness for instantaneous warfare, but this nation-at-arms, once settled in farming households on Chinese soil, could not remain effective warriors. Through economic relations with Chinese, they often became tenants on their land and sometimes paupers. Inter-marriage between the two peoples was eventually permitted. Peace with the Southern Sung in 1141 confirmed the nominal suzerainty of the Chin and facilitated extensive trade. While Jurchen nobles fought among themselves over the succession, their Chinese subjects creatively pursued the arts of peace, in printing, scholarship, painting, literature and also the theater. The Chin rulers themselves came to follow Confucian norms, studying the Classics and writing Chinese poetry. After 1189, the Chin became involved on two fronts in exhausting wars with the Mongols and

CHARACTER SCRIPTS				ALPHABETIC SCRIPTS				
Chinese	*Khitan*	*Jurchen*	*Hsi Hsia*	*'Phags-pa*	*Syriac*	*Uighur*	*Mongolian*	*Manchu*

夫優曇現瑞普獲馨香善逝真旨豪演教世出世間決生

解脱為大事因緣演教世出世間決生

Scripts Used or Created By Inner Asian Peoples. *These examples are given to show form without any reference to meaning. For each type of script two columns are shown. All of them usually read from top to bottom and from right to left, although there are sometimes exceptions. For example, Syriac and Uighur almost always read from top to bottom in the Far East and in Central Asia, but they normally read horizontally from right to left in the Near East. The scripts in non-Chinese characters are believed to have been developed mainly on the model of Chinese, but are still largely undeciphered. The alphabetic scripts (except 'Phags-pa) trace back indirectly to Aramaic, which had a common origin with our own alphabet. The 'Phags-pa script was derived from the Tibetan which ultimately was derived from the Sanskrit.*

the Southern Sung. They inflated their paper currency, which they had inherited from the Northern Sung, with the usual unfortunate consequences. By 1215, under Mongol pressure, they were forced to move their capital south from Peking to Kaifeng, where the Mongols extinguished the Chin dynasty in 1234.

The Mongol Empire

In the history of the Northern Wei, the Liao, and the Chin we can see a number of repetitive features which become still clearer in the periods of Mongol and Manchu conquest: (1) Invaders seized power in North China usually during periods of disorder. (2) The "barbarians" enlisted Chinese advice and aid, especially from Chinese of the border region. (3) The superior "barbarian" cavalry was supplied with more and better horses from the steppe than could be maintained in an agricultural region. (4) Through a policy of tolerance, if not appeasement, local Chinese leaders were attracted and used to enlist a larger corps of Chinese tax collectors and administrators. (5) The invaders made use of the Chinese institutions of government and also let the traditional administration and Chinese social and cultural life continue. (6) But for themselves the invaders maintained a homeland of their own beyond the Wall in order to preserve their own conscious existence as a people and avoid absorption. (7) A dual, Sino-"barbarian" administration was conducted at the local level, largely by Chinese under the supervision of the conquerors. (8) The invaders also employed other foreigners in their administration. (9) They preserved control through military force held in reserve—including both a territorial army into which Chinese could be recruited, and units of the invading horde, which garrisoned the capital and key areas. (10) Toward tribal peoples in Inner Asia, dynasties of conquest developed a divide-and-rule policy. (11) In the long run, the invaders in the midst of overwhelming numbers of Chinese subjects would begin to borrow elements of Chinese culture: food, clothing, names, and even the language. (12) The result was eventual absorption or expulsion. All these features were illustrated during the Mongol conquest.

The Mongol people lived in small groups of a few families, each family in its felt tent, or yurt. At times of seasonal migration these scattered units might form larger groups of several hundred yurts. The basic social and political units were patriarchal clans. Spiritual life was focused on loyalty to clan, expressed in a cult of the hearth. A group of clans, bound together by blood relationships, formed a larger tribal unit. Within this social framework, two members of different clans might become "sworn brothers." Meanwhile, polygamy heightened the demand for wives to be acquired from outside the clan. Consequently, wives were often obtained by seizure, which fostered feuds, raids of vengeance, and petty warfare. As a result clan groups would become vassals of other clans, and whole tribes subordinate to other tribes, enhancing their power. A hierarchy of feudal-type relations of fealty and protection among "lords," "knights," "commoners," and "serfs" (to borrow European terms which are not entirely appropriate) thus developed among the Mongols. Through these personal relationships a strong personality might rise to a commanding leadership.

The Career of Chinggis Khan. When Chinggis Khan (also spelled Genghis, Jenghiz, etc.) was born, about 1167 (some say earlier), the Mongolian-speaking tribes still lacked a common name. He became their great organizer and unifier. His personal name was Temüjin. He was of aristocratic birth but his father had been slain when he was a boy, and he struggled through hard times to avenge him. He rose only slowly, for the establishment of personal loyalties was a gradual process. Rebelling against his overlord, he subjugated first one tribe and then another. Finally, in 1206 at a great meeting of the Mongol tribes on the Kerulen River, he was confirmed in the title of Chinggis Khan, which seems to have connoted "universal ruler." From the few accounts written long afterward by Persian, Chinese, and Arab chroniclers, we can see Chinggis' methods of organization. To secure a religious sanction, he asserted his own divine mission, delegated to him by the Eternal Heaven. His political structure was organized on the family principle, families forming clans, clans forming tribes, and so on. He drew up as a permanent basis of rule, superior to the Khan himself, an imperial code of laws or Great Yasa, first promulgated in 1206 and further developed before his death in 1227. While no complete text has survived, we know that it formulated the basic rules of organization. One source of the strength of this untutored nomad chieftain lay in his ability to learn from others. In building a civil administration, he used Uighur Turks, who were a commercial people, many of them Nestorian Christians, centered around the oasis of Turfan. The Mongols adapted the alphabetic Uighur script to write down Mongolian speech.

Chinggis' personal bodyguard eventually grew to an elite corps of 10,000, recruited from the sons of clan leaders, generals, and kinsmen. From this group, comparable to a modern officer training corps, Chinggis chose his generals and top administrators. The army was organized in units of tens, hundreds, and thousands, with clan members carefully intermixed. The whole force in 1227 amounted to about 129,000 men, a huge army by nomad standards but small for China. The total population of the Mongols cannot have exceeded 2,500,000 and perhaps was closer to 1,000,000 at this time. The Mongol cavalry fought under hereditary, aristocratic leaders. Clad in leather and furs, leading extra horses as remounts, living in the saddle as long as ten days and nights at a time, these troops could cover incredible distances, such as 270 miles during three days in Hungary. Since the troops lived mainly on their plunder, bases of potential supply ahead of them were a constant incentive for expansion.

In battle the Mongols used flying horse columns to encircle and compress the enemy just as they compressed the game caught in the ring of a great hunt on the steppe. Their heavy bows, more powerful than the English longbow, could kill at six hundred feet. As masters of deception, they would get their enemies to pursue, and then turn back, surround, and cut them up. "In this sort of warfare," Marco Polo remarked, "the adversary imagines he has gained a victory, when in fact he has lost the battle." In another tactic, heavy forces concealed on the wings would wait for the enemy to be enticed through the center and so expose his flanks. Through mobility and coordination, crushing force could be concentrated against a weak point. The Mongols thus brought offensive power to its height in the age before firearms. They were also masters of espionage and psychological warfare. From spies among merchants on the trade routes, the Mongols learned about their victims. By putting cities to the sword, they let terror run ahead of them. To capitalize on this terrorism, they also spread fair promises of toleration for religious minorities and freedom for merchants, providing all surrendered without delay.

Chinggis subjugated the Hsi Hsia kingdom in the northwest of China between 1205 and 1209, and it was finally extinguished in 1227. His first campaign against the Chin Empire in 1211–1215 destroyed their capital and also gained the services of Chinese who knew how to besiege cities and to govern them. The most famous of these was a descendant of the Khitan royal house, Yeh-lü Ch'u-ts'ai (1190–1244), who persuaded his new masters that it would be more profitable *not* to turn North China into an empty pasture! Instead he taught them to levy taxes on agriculture and foster the existing mines and industries. Chinggis then overran the Turkish empire of Khorezm (in Russian Turkestan) in 1219–1221. He acquired not only rich, irrigated oasis-cities like Bokhara and Samarkand, centers of handicraft production, caravan trade, and Islamic culture, but also the services of Muslim merchants and financiers. Turkish tribes were also incorporated into the Mongol horde.

Thus Chinggis before his death in 1227 had established the basis of a far-flung Eurasian empire by conquering its inner zone across Central Asia. Many have speculated as to Chinggis' true personality. For all his ability, his motives apparently were simple. "Man's highest joy," he reportedly said, "is in victory: to conquer one's enemies, to pursue them, to deprive them of their possessions, to make their beloved weep, to ride on their horses, and to embrace their wives and daughters." Both in Europe and in Asia the Mongols have been remembered for their wanton aggressiveness, and this trait was certainly present in Chinggis.

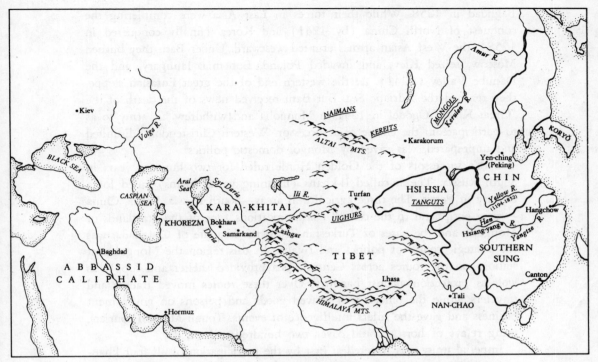

ASIA ON THE EVE OF THE MONGOL CONQUESTS (AROUND 1200)

The Four Khanates. In the tribal fashion, Chinggis divided the empire among the four sons of his principal wife. After his numerous grandsons had helped to expand it, the empire was composed of four main khanates (the asterisks denote grandsons of Chinggis):

(a) *Great Khan* (East Asia): Ögödei (third son of Chinggis), 1229–1241; Möngke (Mangu),* 1251–1259; Khubilai,* 1260–1294 (ruled over all China after 1279); Mongols expelled from China by Ming, 1368.

(b) *Khanate of Chaghadai (Djakhatai,* in Turkestan): Chaghadai (second son of Chinggis), 1227–1242; western part incorporated after 1370 in empire of Timur or Tamerlane (1336–1405).

(c) *Khanate of Persia* (Il-khans): built up by Hülegü*; capture of Baghdad, 1258; dissolution after 1335.

(d) *Khanate of Kipchak* (Golden Horde) on lower Volga: built up by Batu,* 1227–1255; dominated Russia; conquered by Tamerlane and broken up in fifteenth century.

In their expansion over most of the known world, mixed Mongol-Turkish armies overran Persia by 1231 and extinguished the Abbassid Caliphate at

Baghdad in 1258. While their forces in East Asia were completing the conquest of North China (by 1241) and Korea (finally conquered in 1258), the West Asian armies erupted westward. Under Batu they burned Moscow, seized Kiev, and invaded Poland, Bohemia, Hungary, and the Danube Valley (1241). At the western end of the great Eurasian steppe, they reached the Adriatic Sea. But Batu received news of the death of the "Great Khan" Ögödei in 1241 in Mongolia and withdrew his army so as to participate in the choice of a successor. Western Christendom, disunited and unprepared, was saved by Mongol domestic politics.

Batu's successors of the Golden Horde ruled for two hundred years in South Russia. The so-called Il-khans (meaning vassal khans) ruled for a century in Persia. The three agricultural areas—South Russia, Persia, China —were peripheral to the central communications zone of the grasslands of Mongolia and the oases of Turkestan. Thus the khanate of Chaghadai was the strategic center of politics and rivalry. In this region the Mongol post stations on the routes across Central Asia provided shelter and supply as well as protection against banditry. Over these routes moved traders and travelers while the official post moved goods and persons on government business and gave the rulers intelligence of events. Tough Mongol couriers, using relays of horses, could cover two hundred miles a day.

Imperial unity was fostered at first by the participation of all four khanates in each conquest. But the descendants of Chinggis soon yielded to centrifugal forces within their far-flung domains. Mongol rulers in West Asia accepted Islam while in China they became Buddhist believers and Confucian statesmen. The Chinese, Persian, and Russian states had their separate languages, cultures, official systems, court politics, and local needs, all bound to create disunity among the relatively few Mongol-Turkish overlords. The local bureaucratic administrations were oriented inward, toward their domestic problems. The Mongols' conglomerate superstate held together for only a century.

Conquest of the Southern Sung.   The Mongols' takeover in China occupied more than a generation up to 1279 and left a correspondingly deep impress on Chinese life. The Southern Sung repeated its earlier mistake of aiding Chin against Liao by joining the Mongols against the Chin, thus helping to remove the buffer between themselves and their eventual conquerors. Yet the conquest of South China took several decades, which is clear evidence of the strength of the Southern Sung—a much more difficult conquest for the Mongols than the empires of West Asia.

The invaders' strategy was to outflank the Southern Sung on the west. In 1253 they took over the non-Chinese kingdom of Nan-chao with its capital at Tali in Yunnan, making this region for the first time an integral part of China. The conquest of the Southern Sung was completed under

Chinggis' ablest grandson, Khubilai (1215–1294), who became Great Khan in 1260 and ruled for thirty-four years. Khubilai built up Peking as his winter capital. His forces moved down the Yangtze and took the Sung capital at Hangchow. Next they took Canton, southwest of which the remnants of the big Sung fleet (most of which had already defected to the Mongols) were finally destroyed in 1279. Khubilai, in 1271, had adopted the Chinese dynastic name of Yüan, meaning "The First Beginning" or "The Origin," the first dynastic name not derived from a place name.

Conquest having become a way of life, Mongol envoys and expeditions went on to penetrate outlying parts of East Asia, using the naval power inherited from the Sung. Large but unsuccessful armadas comprised of thousands of vessels were sent against Japan in 1274 and 1281. At least four land expeditions invaded Vietnam and five penetrated Burma. Envoys visited Ceylon and South India by sea. In the 1280's ten states of Southern Asia sent tribute. In 1292 a Mongol fleet attacked Java but without permanent success. This continued effort to conquer the known world is all the more remarkable in view of Khubilai's long struggle with the rebellious leader of a western branch of the imperial clan. This rival, a grandson of Chinggis' successor, Ögödei, revolted in 1268, seized the khanate of Chaghadai, and remained until his death in 1301 a continual threat to the Great Khan in China.

China under Mongol Rule

Only gradually did the Mongols face the fact that conquered Chinese villagers, merchants, and city artisans could not be incorporated into the Mongol tribal society. Yeh-lü Ch'u-ts'ai, as chief minister in the conquered parts of North China after 1230, set up schools and held examinations to recruit Chinese into a bureaucracy. But the Mongols, like the Jurchen, found they could not use the rather simple dual type of divided Sino-"barbarian" administration that the Liao had developed. The Yüan therefore continued the administrative structure of the T'ang and Sung, particularly the sixfold division under the Six Ministries at the capital. During the thirteen hundred years from the early T'ang to 1906, this basic structure remained the same. The Yüan also continued a threefold division of central government among civil administrative, military, and supervisory (censorial) branches. Innovation was greater in provincial administration, where they followed the Chin example and made provincial governments into direct extensions of the central chancellery, an important step in perfecting the Chinese imperial structure.

The Mongol conquerors faced the age-old problem of how to rule in a Chinese fashion and still retain power. The Chinese populace had to be persuaded to acquiesce in foreign rule. To accomplish this, an alien dynasty had to maintain local order, give Chinese talent the opportunity to rise in bureaucratic political life, and lead the scholar-official class by fostering Confucian ideology and culture. For this exacting task the rank and file of Mongols were unprepared. Much of their success in the early Yüan era must therefore be ascribed to the commanding personality of Khubilai and his use of Confucian principles and collaborators.

The Mongols differed from their subjects in very striking ways, not only in language and status. For costume, they preferred the leather and furs of steppe horsemen. For food they liked mare's milk and cheese, and for liquor the fermented drink made of mare's milk. Bred on the almost waterless grasslands, the Mongols were unaccustomed to washing. They lacked even surnames. Their different moral code gave greater (and in Chinese eyes, immoral) freedom to women. Moreover, the Mongols' non-Chinese traits were constantly reinforced by their contact with a vast area outside China. They were the only *full* nomads to achieve a dynasty of conquest. The gap between them and the Chinese was thus greater culturally to begin with and was more strongly perpetuated politically. To make the division between conquerors and conquered even more complete, the recruiting of Southern Chinese talent for the Yüan bureaucracy was impeded by the heritage of Sung hatred for the plundering "barbarian." Later Chinese chroniclers, who have always had the last word on their conquerors, depicted the Mongols as primitive savages capable only of destruction and orgiastic excess. One later Chinese account states, "They smell so heavily that one cannot approach them. They wash themselves in urine."

In the face of native hostility, the Mongols in China as elsewhere employed many foreigners, particularly Muslims from Central and Western Asia. As Marco Polo recorded, "You see the Great Khan had not succeeded to the dominion of Cathay by hereditary right, but held it by conquest; and thus, having no confidence in the natives, he put all authority into the hands of Tartars, Saracens, or Christians, who were attached to his household and devoted to his service, and were foreigners in Cathay." The Mongols set up a hierarchy of social classes: they were the top class, and their non-Chinese collaborators second, followed by the Chinese of the North who had capitulated earlier, and, at the bottom, by those of the South, who of course outnumbered all the rest. Meanwhile the Mongol ruling class remained separate from Chinese life with separate systems of law for Chinese and for Mongols. The Great Khan kept his summer residence north of the Wall at Shang-tu (Coleridge's "Xanadu," meaning "Superior Capital"). His alien rule injected a heightened degree of centralized and ruthless despotism into the traditional Chinese Empire.

Life Under the Yüan Dynasty. Khubilai on his accession had protected the Confucian temples, and he soon revived the state cult of Confucius.

Later he exempted Confucian scholars from taxation. But on the more fundamental issue of recruitment for government service, Khubilai did not seek out the talent of South China. The examination system had ceased to function in the North after 1237 and in the South after 1274. Its revival was delayed until 1315. Chinese clerks of course staffed the bureaucracy, but Confucian scholars did not often rise to the top.

The scholar class was antagonized also by the Mongols' patronage of foreign religions. In Persia many had embraced Islam, and in Central Asia, Nestorian Christianity. In China religious establishments of the Buddhist, Taoist, Nestorian, and Islamic faiths, like the Confucian temples, were all exempted from taxation. The Chin and Yüan periods saw many new Taoist monasteries built in North China. This multiple religious growth was a distinct setback for the Neo-Confucian doctrines of the Chu Hsi school.

The superstitious Mongols, with their background of shamanism, tended to accept the debased form of Buddhism that had developed in Tibet, namely Lamaism. Buddhism was introduced into Tibet according to tradition from northwest India in the eighth century. Once introduced, it was influenced by the native Tibetan cult known as Bon, which made much of magic and divination. The fusion which resulted is called Lamaism (the term "lama" means "superior one"). In the thirteenth century it spread rapidly into Mongolia and also China, with imperial support.

Khubilai was hailed by the Buddhist clergy in China as an ideal Buddhist monarch. Under his patronage the number of Buddhist establishments, including the great mountain retreats at Mount Wu-t'ai in Shansi, rose to 42,000 with 213,000 monks and nuns, a great many being Lamaists. All this patronage of a religious cult could not be offset, in the eyes of the Confucian scholar class, by the emperor's performance of Confucian ritual. He lacked the personnel and the policies to patronize Chinese accomplishments in literature, the arts, and thought. Instead of performing this function of upper-class leadership in China, the Mongols maintained a cosmopolitan regime, under which the Chinese bureaucratic class was given little scope.

In fostering the people's livelihood, on the other hand, Khubilai had some temporary success. The landholding element of the Southern Sung was not dispossessed, taxation of land and labor and the usual government monopolies were developed, and trade was facilitated by the far-flung contact with the rest of Asia. Arab and Persian seafarers and merchants frequented the great port cities like Canton and Ch'üan-chou (Zayton). Foreign trade by land was chiefly conducted by Muslim merchants of Central Asian origin. Their corporate groups not only served as trading associations but also became tax-farmers for their Mongol patrons. These merchant "companies," whose members guaranteed one another, played a key role in collecting the agrarian surplus of the Yüan Empire and channeling some of this accumulated capital into an expanded commerce. They also shared in the inordinate graft and corruption which accompanied Mongol rule. Commerce was aided eventually by a unified nation-wide system of paper currency. Marco Polo, coming from a much less economically advanced Europe, was amazed at this use of paper for money.

Khubilai moved the Great Khan's capital from Karakorum in Outer Mongolia to Peking, where the main entrance through the Great Wall leads down to the North China Plain. There he built a new city called Khanbaligh (Marco Polo's "Cambaluc"), meaning in Turkish, "city of the Khan." Within it was a palace enclosed by double walls and complete with parks, treasuries, a lake and a big hill dredged from it. (See page 181.) To feed the new capital, grain was transported from the lower Yangtze by extending the Grand Canal north to Peking from the Yellow River. On the stone embankments of this second Grand Canal system ran a paved highroad from Hangchow to Peking, a distance of eleven hundred miles, which took forty days to traverse.

Khubilai's grandson Temür, who succeeded him in 1294, maintained a strong central administration, but after his death in 1307 the Mongols' hold on China rapidly weakened. In the next twenty-six years, seven rulers occupied the throne. Open civil war began after 1328. Meanwhile paper money, which had earlier stimulated trade, was now issued in increasing quantities without backing, and so paper notes were no longer accepted for tax payments and steadily depreciated. In addition, the Yellow River was causing recurrent floods which ruined the well-watered productive areas of northern Anhwei and Kiangsu and southern Shantung. Financial, moral, and political bankruptcy thus came hand in hand.

The First Direct Contact with the West.   The Mongol Empire's control over the Central Asian trade routes permitted the travel of many Europeans to the court of China. Marco Polo was only one of many who brought back direct word of "Cathay" (the name derived from "Khitai" and referring specifically to North China). The century from about 1240 to about 1340 was an interlude between earlier and later eras in which Arab-Turkish control of Central Asia and the Near East kept a barrier between China and the West. During this Mongol century, European travelers reached Cathay by several routes: either through South Russia and Ili across the steppe, a hard journey; or across the Black Sea and through the Central Asian oases of the ancient Silk Route, the way taken by Italian merchants like the Polos; or by sea to Syria and the Latin states set up by the crusades, and thence through Baghdad and Central Asia; or, finally, by the sea route through the Indian Ocean and around Southeast Asia to the ports of South China, a passage made difficult by Arab obstruction. Over these routes, thronged by people of West Asia, many Europeans reached China and a few left accounts of their travels. They recorded the presence of many Greek Orthodox Christians at the Great Khan's court, mainly captured Russian artisans or soldiers.

Contact between medieval Christendom and East Asia was facilitated by the fact that the heretical Nestorian Christian faith had earlier penetrated the region from Persia. Although it had died out in China, it was revived among the Khitan and Jurchen and became widespread among the Uighur Turks and several Mongol tribes. Khubilai's own mother was a Nestorian Christian. The Nestorian church had some twenty-five metropolitan sees; in 1275 its patriarch at Baghdad created an archbishopric at Peking. Though deemed heretical, the Nestorian church had contact with the papacy.

Meanwhile, Western Christendom was absorbed in the fervor of the crusades. The stage was thus set for diplomatic relations between Western Christendom, the Mongols, and Islam. Saracen envoys sought French and English help against Mongol expansion in the Near East and, after the Mongols' conquest of Persia and Baghdad, their Il-khans sent at least seven embassies to the West between 1267 and 1291 to get help against Islam. On its part the papacy, when the Mongol threat to Europe had receded after 1241, sent a notable series of Franciscan monks on diplomatic and evangelical missions to Persia, Mongolia, and China, evidently to explore the possibility of obtaining Mongol help against the Saracens. While no diplomatic result was achieved by these envoys between East and West, the papal missionary effort finally established a Roman Catholic outpost in China under John of Montecorvino. Under the Great Khan's protection he preached, built a church with help from an Italian merchant, and taught 150 choirboys, whose Gregorian chants pleased the imperial ear. Six thousand converts were baptized in Peking in 1304, many of them probably non-Chinese. Roman Catholic missions made increasing progress toward the end of the Yüan period in China only to be snuffed out afterwards.

Western merchants must have greatly outnumbered the friars who crossed Asia, but Marco Polo was the only one to leave a record. He set out in 1271 with his father and uncle, Venetian merchants on their second trip to China. After reaching Shang-tu ("Xanadu") and Peking ("Cambaluc"), Marco spent seventeen years in Khubilai's service (1275–1292), returning to Venice in 1295. His *Description of the World* was dictated to a professional romance writer in a Genoese prison. It is not a travelogue but a systematic, scientific treatise, well informed and objective. (The original has not survived, but about 120 manuscripts, containing many variations, have been found in Italian, Latin, French, and other languages.) No other traveler has ever had so great a tale to tell as Marco Polo. His was the first connected exposition of the geography, economic life, and government of China to be laid before the European public. It was more than could be believed, for the China of the late thirteenth century was

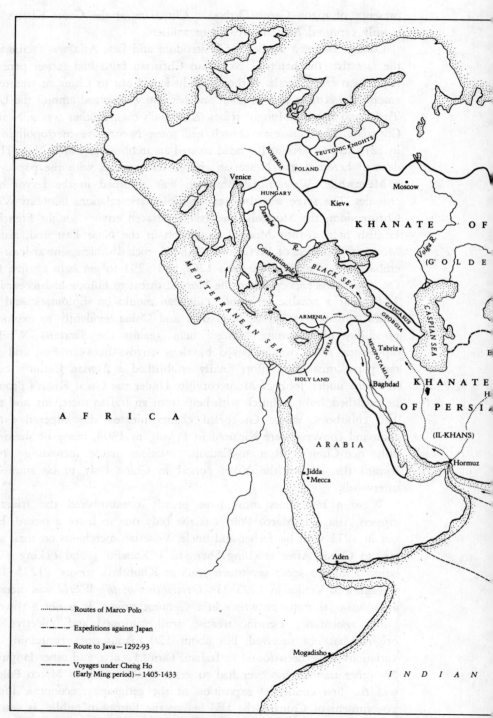

THE MONGOL EMPIRE (LATE THIRTEENTH CENTURY)

BOHEMIA

TEUTONIC KNIGHTS

POLAND

Moscow

HUNGARY

Venice

Kiev

Danube R.

K H A N A T E   O F

Volga R.

Constantinople

BLACK SEA

(GOLDE

MEDITERRANEAN SEA

CAUCASUS

GEORGIA

CASPIAN SEA

ARMENIA

SYRIA

Tabriz

MESOPOTAMIA

HOLY LAND

Baghdad

K H A N A T E

A F R I C A

O F   P E R S I A

ARABIA

(IL-KHANS)

Hormuz

Jidda

Mecca

Aden

Mogadisho

I N D I A N

·········· Routes of Marco Polo

—·—·— Expeditions against Japan

———— Route to Java — 1292-93

– – – – Voyages under Cheng Ho
(Early Ming period) — 1405-1433

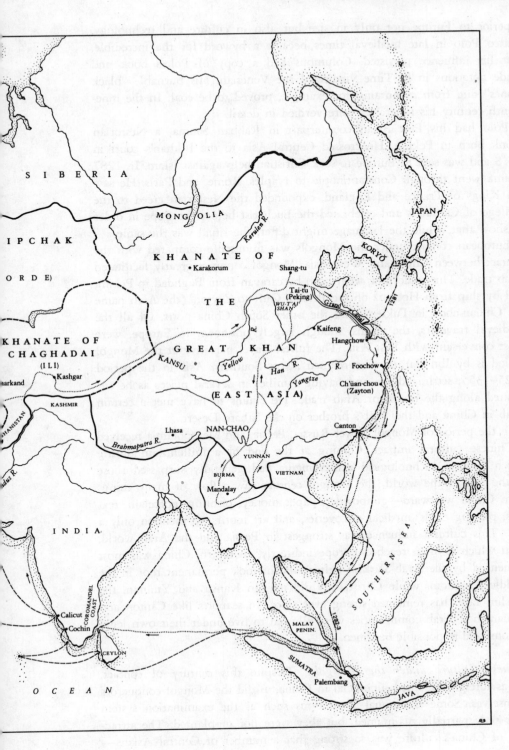

superior to Europe not only in size but also in culture and technology. Marco Polo in late medieval times became a byword for the incredible. Yet his influence persisted. Columbus had a copy of Polo's book and made notations in it. Time vindicated the Venetian. His burnable "black stones" dug from mountains, for example, proved to be coal. In the nineteenth century his itineraries were verified in detail.

Polo had his East Asian counterpart in Rabban Sauma, a Nestorian monk born in Peking. He crossed Central Asia to the Il-khan's court in 1278 and was sent to Europe to seek Christian help against Islam. In 1287 Sauma went through Constantinople to Naples, Rome, and Paris. He saw the Kings of France and England, expounded the Nestorian creed to the College of Cardinals and celebrated the Eucharist before the Pope in order to show that, while the language might differ, the ritual was the same.

European contact under the Mongols was minuscule compared with the contact between China and West Asia. Mongol conquest greatly facilitated Arab trade. This trade now went both by caravan from Baghdad to Peking and by ship from Hormuz on the Persian Gulf to Zayton (the Arab name for Ch'üan-chou in Fukien) and the other South China ports. Of all the medieval travelers, the Arabs, though largely unknown to Europe, were most conversant with East Asia. The fullest travel narrative of the Mongol period is by Ibn Batuta, who roamed across Southern Asia in the period 1325–1355, settling down and having families in several places as he circulated along the routes of Arab trade. He claims to have met a certain Arab in China and the Arab's brother on the Sahara Desert.

In the period of Mongol power Russia, Persia, and Mesopotamia received a Chinese cultural impact. Coming at the end of a millennium during which Chinese technological achievements had generally surpassed those of the rest of the world, the Mongol century saw a flow of many things from China westward—gunpowder, paper money, printing, porcelain, textiles, playing cards, medical discoveries, and art motifs, to mention only a few. This cultural influence was strongest in Persia and the Arab world, from which it often reached Europe indirectly. In return, China was most influenced by the Arab-Turkish culture. Islam took permanent root in the Middle Kingdom, while Christianity did not. In Kansu and Yunnan, the Muslim faith has remained strong ever since. In seaports like Canton and Ch'üan-chou Arab communities were allowed to live under their own legal customs and responsible headmen.

Chinese Culture under the Mongols. Despite this century of contact, things foreign remained superficial in China, as did the Mongol conquerors themselves. Some traditional institutions such as the examination system were only partially maintained, but they were not supplanted. The attraction of China's culture was so strong that a number of Central Asians—

ILLUSTRATION FROM THE SHUI-HU-CHUAN. *Outlaws, led by one of their number who wields an ax, ambush an official (with black hat, on horse) and his entourage, in order to rescue a comrade who is being led to execution. From a Ming woodblock of a type easily reproduced for wide distribution.*

Tanguts and Uighurs, Nestorian Christians, and Muslims—made their mark as Confucian scholars or as typically Chinese painters and calligraphers. Compiling of the official dynastic histories of the Sung, Liao, and Chin went forward under a Mongol as head of the bureau of historiography. Chinese scholarship did not flourish notably, but neither did it wither away. The great traditions of landscape and nature painting were brilliantly maintained.

Two new literary forms, the drama and the novel, were connected with the increased use, during this period, of the written vernacular (*pai-hua*) in place of the traditional literary language. Both had to use a form closer to everyday speech in order to reach the wider urban audiences of the day. The Yüan administration itself used a more vernacular style in its documents so that these would be more easily intelligible to the many officials who lacked a Chinese classical education. Chinese scholars on their part, finding less opportunity in official life and less patronage of classical studies, turned their talents to purely literary endeavor. Playwriting had begun to flourish in the twelfth century, both at Peking under the Chin and at Hangchow under the Southern Sung. Titles of nearly a thousand plays survive from this period. From the Yüan there exist the printed librettos of many plays. Their themes, typically Chinese, involve conflicts of human passion with the social bonds of filial piety, fidelity, or loyalty.

The Chinese drama was semioperatic, with orchestral music to accompany a great deal of singing and dancing. Scenery and realistic properties were not used, as in Elizabethan England. In their place was developed a great variety of conventions—stylized movements of the hands, sleeves, eyes, and feet, as in stepping over an imaginary doorsill, climbing nonexistent steps, or mounting an imaginary charger. Female roles generally came to be played by men, whose falsetto singing, dancing, and delicate gestures were especially appreciated. Romantic plots, technical virtuosity, humorous dialogue, brilliant costuming, and violent action all combined to create an urban art of wide popularity.

While the drama grew up primarily at the capital cities, the novel was created by professional storytellers among the populace. The Buddhist wonder stories of T'ang times grew into historical or purely imaginative love and adventure tales, which professional storytellers developed into long, loosely constructed sagas. Prompt-books for itinerant storytellers were the earliest written form of these episodic tales, and when gradually filled in with details by many different hands, became the early novels. Most are of prodigious length. The heroes usually are not scholar-bureaucrats but men of low class or military origin. All the novels are written in a style close to the vernacular of the day. The later ones were usually the work of single authors, men of education and literary talent, though they often concealed their identity. (The principal novels are discussed more fully on pages 235–237.) Although most of the major novels attained their mature form, or were actually first composed, in the Ming and Ch'ing periods, their roots go back to the Yüan or earlier.

The novel became the kind of literature that the majority of literate Chinese could most readily appreciate. Though customarily disesteemed by the scholar trained in the Classics, it became a principal literary form, with wide influence as a repository and mirror of social values. The emergence of both the novel and the drama in the Yüan period illustrates the vitality of Chinese culture as well as the frustration of the scholar class under the Mongols.

8. State and Society under the Ming

Chinese "Culturalism"

The Ming period from 1368 to 1644 is one of the great eras of orderly government and social stability in human history. A population averaging around 100 million lived during 276 years in comparative peace. The subsequent change from Ming to Ch'ing rule was relatively easy. The decline of Ming power and the Manchu capture of Peking in 1644 were followed by the Manchu conquest of all China. But this warfare and its devastation seem limited in comparison with the organized looting and massacres of contemporary European armies during the Thirty Years' War of 1618–1648. In any case, so stable was the political and social order of the Ming that it persisted, basically unaltered, under the alien Ch'ing dynasty for another 267 years from 1644 to 1912. Thus from the middle of the fourteenth century to the beginning of the twentieth, China followed traditional ways.

Unfortunately for the Chinese people of recent times, this remarkable stability was maintained during those very centuries that saw the dynamic rise of modern Europe — the Renaissance, the Reformation, the growth of national states, their expansion into the New World and over the earth, followed by the French Revolution and the Industrial Revolution. None of these fundamental Western transformations of the last six centuries had a real counterpart in China's own experience. China remained outside the turbulent stream of Western history, which was moving to engulf the world, and consequently by the nineteenth century had fallen behind the

177

West in many aspects of material culture and technology as well as in economic and political organization. This long period of stability in East Asian civilization left it comparatively "backward" or "underdeveloped." But this comparison with the expanding West should not stigmatize the Ming and Ch'ing periods as retrogressive or overshadow their real achievements. As we learn more about these centuries, we may expect to find many evidences of innovation and growth. Chinese society was far from unchanging, but the pace was slower and the degree of change less than in the West.

One factor creating stability was the Chinese view of history as "change within tradition." The leaders of society were devoted to tradition; anything that happened in the present had to be fitted into the rich pattern of experience inherited from the past. Instead of the ideal of progress, which Westerners today have inherited from the nineteenth century, the Chinese of the Ming and Ch'ing saw their ideal models far in the past.

This turning back for inspiration to the great ages of Han, T'ang, and Sung was accompanied by a deep resentment against the Mongols. Alien rule had inspired hostility toward alien things in general. Gradually this view hardened into a lack of interest in anything beyond the pale of Chinese civilization. This turning away from the outside world was accompanied by a growing introspection within Chinese life. We have already seen this in the antiquarian interest in art and in the burst of historical scholarship in the Sung. From that time on a degree of mingled fear and contempt for the outside world and a narrow concentration on the exclusively Chinese way of life produced a growing ethnocentrism. Eventually it dominated China's foreign relations and gave her an intellectual and psychological immunity to foreign stimuli.

This attitude had much in common with modern nationalism. But there were differences. A nationalist group asserts its own distinctiveness and superiority because it fears not only political but also cultural inundation by some other group. Nationalism thus seems closely tied to a general feeling of competition and insecurity. It is commonly asserted by a cultural subunit, particularly a linguistic subgroup, against other subunits within the same culture, as in the rise of national states within the common culture of Western Christendom. The Chinese, by contrast, showed no sign of a feeling of cultural inferiority. Political subjugation may have been feared, but cultural conquest was unimaginable. Thus Chinese xenophobia was combined with a complete confidence in cultural superiority. China reacted not as a cultural subunit, but as a large ethnocentric universe which remained quite sure of its cultural superiority even when relatively inferior in military power to fringe elements of its universe. Because of these similarities to and differences from nationalism, we call this earlier Chinese attitude "culturalism," to suggest that in the Chinese view the significant unit was really the whole civilization rather than the narrower political unit of a nation within a larger cultural whole.

Underlying this devotion to the Chinese way of life was one primary political fact, that the whole Middle Kingdom remained an administrative unit under a central government. This remarkable cohesiveness, compared with the constant disunity among the relatively smaller European states, cannot be attributed to geography. It normally took a month or so for the emperor's writ to be carried by horse to the borders of the realm in Kwangtung, Yunnan, Central Asia, or the Northeast, farther than any distances in Western Europe. China's inveterate unity must be explained on institutional grounds, by the habits of thought and action that had become established in the society. The Chinese state was regarded as coterminous with Chinese culture. There was such a close identification of the entire way of life with the unified empire that the one implied the other. It was as if the Roman Empire had persisted in the West and had prevented the rise of France, England, and the other nations. The identity of culture and polity made the Chinese leadership of the Ming and Ch'ing periods uninterested in, and at times hostile to, things foreign. Culturalism thus was a pervasive attitude throughout the period.

Government under the Ming

The Founding of the Ming Dynasty. The weakening of Mongol rule was hastened by fratricidal rivalry within the imperial clan. Fifteen years of frequent famine in North China after 1333 were capped by severe floods of the Yellow River. Flood and famine depleted the granaries. During the 1340's, uprisings occurred sporadically in nearly every province. In 1351–1353 several major rebel leaders emerged, and a typical interdynastic contest began among them to determine who should survive as the fittest to inherit the Mandate of Heaven. Some of these men claimed descent from the Sung emperors, some invoked a religious sanction by prophesying the advent of the Bodhisattva Maitreya, the Buddha of the Future, and others had the help of secret societies. The most famous of all secret societies has been the White Lotus Society. Its origin as a sect of T'ien-t'ai Buddhism has been traced back directly to the first half of the twelfth century. As with any group that opposed the ruling dynasty, this society had to be secret in order to survive.

The eventual winner among all these Chinese rebel heroes was Chu Yüan-chang (1328–1398), whose name ranks with that of Liu Pang, the founder of the Han, as a humble commoner who through native ability in a time of opportunity became the Son of Heaven. He was born in the Huai River region northwest of Nanking. Left an orphan, he entered a Buddhist monastery as a novice, which gave him a chance to become literate. For a time he even begged for a living. But in 1352, at the age of twenty-five, he joined a rebel band. (Probably he also joined the White Lotus Society, but he later denied this—it was an unwise precedent to leave in the historical record.)

Chu and his band crossed the Yangtze and in 1356 seized Nanking, a strategic base close to the key economic area of the Yangtze delta. By 1367, after defeating rival regimes both upstream and downstream, he controlled all the Yangtze Valley. Meanwhile, the Mongol commanders, instead of attacking the Chinese rebels, fought among themselves. In 1368 Chu Yüan-chang seized Peking but continued to use Nanking as his capital. He proclaimed himself the first emperor of the Ming ("Brilliant") dynasty, and chose Hung-wu ("Vast military power") as the name of the "year period," but, by keeping it for his whole reign, the first Ming emperor transformed it into his reign title. This set a fashion throughout the Ming and Ch'ing, of using only one year-period name during a whole reign, so that emperors of this era are generally known by their reign titles.

A second strong ruler was Yung-lo (reigned 1403–1424). The fourth son of Hung-wu, he had his base of power in Peking, where he rebelled against his nephew, Hung-wu's grandson, who had inherited the throne at Nanking. He waged a devastating civil war until he finally captured Nanking, and as a usurper at the age of forty-three took as his reign title Yung-lo ("Perpetual Happiness").

Nanking had been built up by Hung-wu as the imperial capital, with a city wall sixty feet high and over twenty miles around, the longest city wall in the world. Yung-lo in 1421 moved the Ming capital to Peking, leaving Nanking as the subsidiary capital. He rebuilt Peking on a more extensive plan than that of the Mongols. The main city walls, forty feet high and more than fourteen miles around, formed a square with nine gates, each one protected by an outer gate. In the center stood the walls of the Imperial City, some five miles in perimeter. Within it, in turn, were the high red walls of the Forbidden City, the imperial palace itself, surrounded by a moat about two miles around. Running from south to north through the palace, on the main axis of the whole capital, are the imposing throne halls with their gold-tiled roofs, each one rising from a terrace of white marble. Much of this great architectural creation of the Ming still stands today as an unparalleled monument of empire. The walls of the southern city of Peking with their seven additional gates were added in the sixteenth century.

Ming Despotism.   The seventeen Ming emperors reigned during a series of recognizable phases: (1) the inaugural era of founding and consolidation under Hung-wu (1368–1398); (2) the vigorous building and expansion under Yung-lo (1403–1424) and his successors, which, however, by the

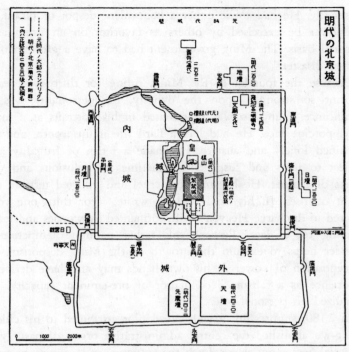

PEKING UNDER THE MING AND CH'ING. *Top and center: Site of Yüan capital, Tai-tu, of which the northern walls were razed by the Ming. Center: Inner City surrounds Imperial City which encloses lakes on left and Forbidden City or Palace on main axis, with Prospect Hill (dredged from lakes) on north. Bottom: Outer city (under the Manchus, the "Chinese City") with Altars of Heaven (right) and of Agriculture (left). Outside the main city on east, north, and west, respectively, are Altars of the Sun, Earth, and Moon. (From Wada Sei,* Tōyō bunkashi taikei.)

middle of the century had overstrained the imperial resources; (3) a century of gradual decline of imperial power both at home and abroad; (4) in the latter part of the sixteenth century a period of reform; and (5) by the early seventeenth century an intensification of evils and final collapse.

This profile was studied intensively by moralistic Confucian scholars in the late Ming, who saw the Chinese state collapsing. They and their successors in the Ch'ing made a moral interpretation of the dynastic decline, analyzing the personal failings of successive emperors, the errors of their officials, and the factionalism which rent the bureaucracy. Today, our basic political criticism might be that the emperor was subject to no higher law or constitutional checks. Power was concentrated in him personally. He had to be either a benevolent despot or tyrant, or else let his power be exercised by others as favorites on an irregular, unstable, personal basis. The Ming government had to have a great man at its head or face disaster.

Because the founder of the Ming, ruling for thirty-two years, left his imprint so strongly upon the dynasty, his personality was of special significance. Hung-wu was represented in his portraits as a man with an ugly, porcine face. He had had a hard life in his youth, and as emperor remained lonely and austere. He made a fetish of frugality and became subject to fears and suspicions, sometimes to delusions and violent outbursts of temper. He became very cruel and inflicted terrible tortures for slight offenses. In his final will he wrote: "For thirty-one years I have labored to discharge Heaven's will, tormented by worries and fears, without relaxing for a day." Perhaps this rather paranoid temperament of the founder helps to explain the growth of the Ming despotism. Hung-wu's concentration of power in his own hands may also have derived from his experience as a self-made conqueror of pre-eminent capacity. He institutionalized his personal role.

In 1380, suppressing a widespread plot attributed to his chief minister, Hung-wu abolished the central administrative organ of past dynasties, the Imperial Secretariat. Henceforth the emperor's rule was to be personal and direct. This institutional change gave the emperors of the Ming and also the Ch'ing periods a more autocratic role. In his personal administration Hung-wu, however, made use of Grand Secretaries, who handled the flow of official memorials (as many as a hundred a day) and drafted the imperial edicts in reply. Eventually they became institutionalized informally as the Grand Secretariat, a sort of cabinet, superior to the Six Ministries. But the Grand Secretaries remained merely aides of the ruler, unable to take executive action on their own initiative.

One group who eventually acquired considerable power were the eunuchs. Hung-wu had warned vigorously against this very possibility. He erected in the palace a metal tablet three feet high reading, "Eunuchs must have nothing to do with administration." He limited their numbers, ranks, titles, and style of clothing, forbade their handling documents, dismissed those who commented on government affairs, and decreed that they should remain illiterate. Nevertheless the eunuch institution remained an integral part of the Inner Court, based on the emperor's need of male descendants and his consequent maintenance of a harem. Later emperors grew up in the Inner Court, often personally devoted to eunuchs who had been their childhood companions or preceptors. The eunuchs' ranks and duties proliferated within the palace, and their influence gradually extended into the entire administration. In the 1420's a palace school was set up for them. The number of eunuchs increased to thousands. In a central office in

THREE MING EMPERORS. *Left: The founder Chu Yüan-chang who reigned as the Hung-wu emperor, 1368–1398. Center: The consolidator, the Yung-lo emperor, 1403–1424. Right: A source of disaster, the Wan-li emperor, 1573–1620.*

Peking (the Eastern Yard), they kept secret files on official personnel, accessible only to the emperor. They became, in effect, a separate echelon of administration, not unlike a present-day security system. This was because eunuchs, as palace inmates, lacking family loyalties and completely dependent upon their master, had a unique inside position, closer to the imperial person than any of the scholar-officials. Eunuchs consequently gained great influence as trusted agents of the emperor, even becoming commanders of military forces or inspectors in the provinces. The Ming saw a constant struggle for power between the eunuchs and the Grand Secretaries within the palace, and also between these groups of the Inner Court and the top officials of the imperial bureaucracy, or Outer Court, at the capital.

The arbitrariness of the emperor's rule was visibly demonstrated in another custom, the corporal punishment of high officials at the court. Hung-wu had early followed the Mongol precedent of having officials publicly and ceremoniously beaten with the bamboo. He had a dozen officials executed at various times on suspicion of having inserted derogatory puns in their congratulatory memorials. Such treatment contravened the Confucian doctrine that punishments are for the unlettered masses while the superior man is to be moved by the power of the ruler's moral example. The Ming regime, famous for exalting the letter of the Classics, became notorious for contravening their spirit.

Another phenomenon of the Ming court was factionalism. Cliques of officials became violently involved in one dispute after another, hating their opponents, appointing members of their own faction to office when they could, accusing those in power when they were not. However, the unconfined power of the emperor and the factionalism of officials were active mainly at the level of the imperial bureaucracy, which was spread very thinly over the empire. At the local level was a stable social order in which the emperor's power was held in reserve and seldom exercised.

The Structure of Government.   The Ming emperors retained the inherited structure of central government: first, a civil bureaucracy under the Six Ministries and other organs; second, a centralized military hierarchy; and third, a separate hierarchy of censors. In Western eyes the Board of Censors is perhaps the most interesting of the three. Its chief bureau at the capital had a staff of 110 "investigating censors." In addition, each ministry had a special censorial staff that watched its operations. Censors drawn from the general civil bureaucracy were typically younger officials of rather low rank, selected for personal qualities of probity. When sent into the provinces, often on one-year tours of duty, they investigated the conduct of justice and of ceremonies, the condition of granaries and of schools, and received reports from officials and complaints from the public. Their power came from their having direct access to the throne, both to impeach other officials and to remonstrate (at their peril) with the emperor. These broad powers were limited by the fact that censors usually returned to the regular civil bureaucracy after a tenure of nine years or less; like all officials, they depended upon the imperial whim. Protected neither by life tenure nor by immunity from their master's wrath, these "eyes and ears of the emperor" were in reality bureaucrats like all their fellows, concerned for their own safety, dependent upon favorable merit ratings from their superiors, and sometimes open to bribery or intimidation.

This threefold administration of the Ming and Ch'ing has an interesting comparability with the recent regimes of the Kuomintang and the Chinese Communist Party. Since 1928, China has been governed through the three principal echelons of party, army, and government. The modern governing parties in China may be viewed as the successors of the dynastic families, from whom the rulers were chosen and to whom they answered. The party apparatus, running parallel to army and civil administration, has also inherited some of the ancient censorial functions. This Chinese trinity is not a separation or balance of powers, like that under the Constitution of the United States, but perhaps we may call it a system of balanced administration. The military forces kept the regime in power, the civil bureaucracy carried on the government, and the censors (and also the eunuchs) kept watch on everything.

The territorial civil administration of the Ming was divided into 15 provinces, which the Ch'ing later increased, by subdivision, to 18. Each province was divided into local units composed of still smaller units— prefectures, of which there were, generally speaking, 159 in the Ming Empire; subprefectures or departments, of which there were 234; and counties (hsien), which totalled 1171. Under the Ch'ing these totals expanded to roughly 183 prefectures and 1470 counties (also called districts). The local administrative hierarchy of magistrates, according to the law of avoidance, were never permitted to serve in their own native provinces lest they be seduced into collusion with kinfolk and local friends. These officials in ascending order were the hsien magistrate, the subprefect, and the prefect. Their administration was headed by a provincial administrative commissioner. There was also a judicial commissioner or judge, with his own staff. A third top official was the provincial military commander. Thus each province was under a collegial group of officers who represented the same threefold administrative, military, and supervisory functions as in the capital. A governor was eventually added as a coordinator at the top of each province. The administrative hierarchy was also watched, as already noted, by censors on tour.

The Ming military system developed by Hung-wu was based on guards units of 5600 men. Each unit was divided into five subunits of 1120 men, who were registered professional soldiers. By 1393 there were 493 guards units under the Ministry of War, stationed at strategic spots on the Inner Asian frontier and the seacoast, along the Grand Canal and at the capital, under five main regional commands. The original guards units had thus become garrisons, independent of the local civil administration. The positions of the registered soldiers were hereditary, and many were given land on which to farm for their livelihood, in the hope of realizing the ancient ideal of a self-supporting army of farmer-soldiers. But inevitably, these Chinese garrisons, even more than Khitan, Jurchen, or Mongol troops, found it difficult to remain effective soldiers in a nonwarlike society.

As at the capital, new administrative organs in the provinces began informally and later became institutionalized. Among these were the intendants of circuit (*tao-t'ai*, Anglicized as taotai), first appointed to handle special functions connected with the salt monopoly, police,. customs, river conservancy, or the like. Eventually, the provinces were each divided for these various purposes into a number of circuits, which formed a new

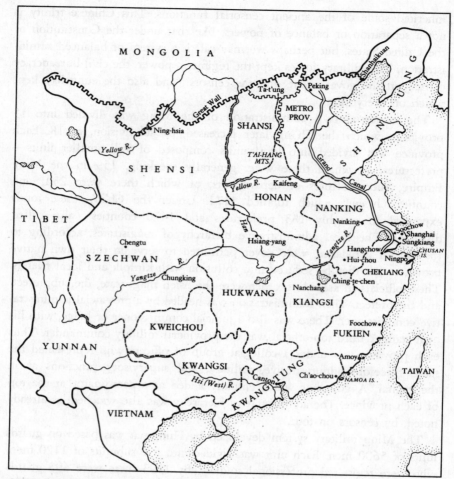

CHINA UNDER THE MING

administrative level between the provincial and the prefectural levels. Another development was the sending of new traveling inspectors and special commissioners from the capital to check corruption and misgovernment. Such officials were given certain administrative, censorial, and military powers within designated areas, so as to introduce a more unified executive capacity into the territorial administration. From them developed, by the middle of the Ming era, the office of provincial governor, already mentioned, as well as that of governor-general, an official normally in charge of two provinces.

Land, People, and Taxes. The Ming government's control over the land and the people was signalized by the drawing up of detailed registers of land and of population. In 1393 the population registers gave an estimated total of 10 million households and 60 million persons. This registration, not based on a modern type of census, produced a total no greater than that of the Han period. We can only wonder whether the population in 1393 may not have been double this figure. The land registers in 1393 recorded a total of roughly 129 million acres of land in use, less than half the estimated acreage of cultivated land in recent times. Each holding was classified according to type and productivity and was taxed accordingly.

Taxation followed the tradition which went back to the Double Tax of the eighth century (see pages 120–121). The Ming Summer Tax was collected in the eighth month on the supplementary crops grown during the winter and harvested in early summer. The Autumn Grain Tax was collected in the second month on produce grown during the previous summer and harvested in the autumn, above all on the great rice crop of the Yangtze Valley. The usual government monopoly taxes on tea and salt were also maintained. The Ming continued to issue paper money, as the Sung and Yüan had done, but made it unconvertible into metal currency (copper cash or silver bullion), so that it became worthless and had to be abandoned by 1450.

Households were classified into three, five, or nine grades (there were many complexities) and were obliged to provide labor service according to the number of registered adult males between sixteen and sixty years of age. One kind of labor service was to bear local responsibilities in connection with tax collections and public works. This service was organized under the *li-chia* system. Ideally, each 110 neighboring households formed a unit (*li* or village). Within this unit each year one of the ten leading families superintended one-tenth of the 100 remaining households to form a *chia* or section, which bore the responsibility for local labor service during the year. The others served in rotation over a ten-year period. Thus the *li-chia* system had common features with but was separate and distinct from the *pao-chia* system of mutual guarantee which had been inherited from the Sung (pages 100 and 129). Another kind of labor service, also apportioned among the male adults, involved prescribed tasks in the big government offices (*ya-men,* Anglicized as yamen), or else money payments for supplies for the yamen. Still other forms of labor service, apportioned among the populace, required service at the government post stations and in the local militia.

The Ming legal system showed the same pattern of reapplying traditional principles with a new thoroughness. A comprehensive body of administrative and criminal law was first published in 1397.

Yet the early Ming government remained, by modern standards, superficial. It claimed the prerogative of organizing and controlling all aspects of society. But in practice it did not interfere with the Chinese people in their daily lives. There were in the provinces only about two thousand principal posts. If one adds minor incumbents, the total of civil officials in the Ch'ing Empire as late as 1800 was only around twenty thousand. The control of the country by such a small number of mandarins, as Chinese officials came to be called by Westerners, was feasible only because of the functions performed by the dominant elite in each locality, that is, the degree-holders or gentry.

Society and Culture under the Ming

The Examination System.   In the Ming revival of a purely Chinese rule over China, the animating spirit had been to return to the pre-Mongol institutions of the T'ang and Sung. This soon built up the importance of the examination system. Under the Ming and Ch'ing there were three main levels of examination activity: First were preliminary examinations in the county (*hsien*), which qualified one to compete in examinations held during two out of every three years at the prefectural city (*fu*). This gave one the lowest principal degree, that of licentiate or bachelor, called by the ancient name of *hsiu-ts'ai,* "flowering talent." This admitted one to the privileged class of literati, who enjoyed exemption from labor service and corporal punishments. In order to retain this lower-gentry status, the degree-holder had to pass routine examinations, usually every three years. For the second level another preliminary test led to the great triennial examinations at the provincial capitals, where thousands of candidates would spend several days incarcerated with brush and paper in the long rows of individual cells at the examination field. One out of every one to two hundred competitors became a provincial graduate or "recommended man" (*chü-jen*), eligible to compete at the third level in the triennial metropolitan examinations at Peking. If successful at the capital, he became a metropolitan graduate or "presented scholar" (*chin-shih*), went to the palace for a final test by the emperor himself, and then received his official ranking and appointment to a post.

The bureaucratic system flexibly permitted some men to advance without examination. One means was the inheritance privilege, by which a son of an official of high rank could receive degree status and sometimes even official position in consideration of his father's merit. Another means under the Ming and Ch'ing, as in all previous dynasties, was to let men secure degree status by purchase. This was done by making a contribution to the imperial treasury. Generally the purchaser was allowed to obtain only degree status, not an actual official post. This admitted him to the gentry class, but not into officialdom. Thus degrees acquired by purchase, clearly designated as such, admitted certain men of wealth, mostly merchants or landlords, to the scholarly elite, giving them, in return for their

THE IMPERIAL GOVERNMENT'S EXAMINATION SYSTEM. *Thousands of cells standing in a vast enclosure at Nanking, as in other provincial capitals.*

payments, a qualified recognition within a framework that still gave the genuine scholar the highest prestige. The sale of degree status in this fashion was partly a safety valve, letting ambitious nonintellectuals into the establishment, and partly a source of revenue, which tempted a dynasty particularly in time of need. In the nineteenth century roughly a third of the lowest level degree-holders got them by purchase.

Generally speaking, the examination system brought in the great bulk of the bureaucracy and succeeded in recruiting the best talent of the country for government service. Quotas limited the number who could succeed in each county and province, so as to ensure geographical representation. Candidates' papers were sometimes copied, without their names, before being read in order to ensure anonymity and impartiality. For the provincial examinations, the examiners were sent out from the capital. The system was managed by the Ministry of Rites, instead of the Ministry of Personnel which supervised the officials' later careers. All these practices ensured the impartial universality of the selection process.

One weakness of the system was its restriction of subject matter to the Four Books, which had been selected as the essence of Confucianism in the Sung, and the Five Classics, again as interpreted by the Sung scholars of the school of Chu Hsi (see pages 149–150). In its passion for formal organization, the Ming adopted finally in 1487 a set form for writing examination papers under eight main headings, with not over seven hundred characters in all and with much use of balance and antithesis. This was the famous "eight-legged essay" style, later denounced as imposing a tyranny of literary structure over thought.

The institutions which prepared examination candidates included so-called government schools, which were ordered to be set up at the county and prefectural levels. But their chief function was to enroll the scholars and hold periodical examinations, not to provide organized instruction or residence facilities. The actual preparation of scholars began in the family or sometimes in a clan school. This gave the advantage to youths from extended families that could afford tutors, specifically from scholar-official families, in which parental example and family tradition provided incentive and guidance.

The chief primer, memorized by many millions during the Ming and Ch'ing eras, was the *Three-Character Classic* produced in the thirteenth century. It gave in jingle form a concise summary of basic knowledge and doctrine in 356 alternately rhyming lines, each of three characters. The opening lines, when understood, convey the prime doctrine of Mencius that human nature is fundamentally good, an idea universally accepted in China, which was to prove a stumbling block to Western missionaries convinced of original sin. Thus the process of elementary learning was at the same time a process of philosophical indoctrination.

Scholarship. At the top of the intellectual pyramid under the Ming stood the Hanlin Academy, a carefully selected body of outstanding metropolitan graduates, who performed important literary tasks for the court. The ethnocentric reaction of the early Ming centered in this citadel of Confucian doctrine. In addition some 300 private academies (*shu-yüan*) were founded in various parts of the country, on the model of the Sung, as centers of scholarly study, discussion, and compilation, usually under the patronage of high officials or rich merchants; some also received imperial encouragement. They brought together eminent scholars, students who received free maintenance and tuition, and small libraries. Academies also published scholarly works and stored the wooden printing blocks.

The emperor's sponsorship of letters and the arts was an important means of maintaining his position as head of the Confucian state and culture. This tradition produced in 1407 the great *Encyclopedia of the Yung-lo Period* in 11,095 volumes—a compilation of all the principal

三字經 章炳麟重訂

人之初 性本善 性相近 習相遠
苟不教 性乃遷 教之道 貴以專
昔孟母 擇鄰處 子不學 斷機杼
孟母姓仇曾三遷其居以教孟子孟子廢學母斷
織以警之孟子懼旦夕勤學卒成大儒
荀季和 有義方 教八子 名俱揚
荀季和東漢時潁陰人名淑桓帝時補朗陵侯相
蒞事明理稱為神君子八人並有才名時謂之八

THE THREE-CHARACTER CLASSIC (SAN-TZU CHING). *The first page of a modern edition, with the title of the book at the upper right-hand corner and the text itself starting on the third line. The commentary appears in smaller type.*

works on history, government, ethics, geography, etc., inherited from previous ages. Compiled by more than two thousand scholars, it was too large to print. Fewer than four hundred manuscript volumes have survived. The next two centuries saw a continued flood of publication sponsored by the court, by officials, and by academies and families. To try to describe this literature, its great compilations, the myriad monographic treatises, the many genres of belles-lettres, would be no easier than to attempt to describe the literature of all Europe in the same period. To cite one example, after several smaller works had led the way, one scholar (Li Shih-chen) spent twenty-six years compiling an illustrated *materia medica* which described almost two thousand animal, vegetable, and mineral drugs and gave over eight thousand prescriptions. Completed in 1578, it described smallpox inoculation and the uses of mercury, iodine, chaulmoogra oil, ephedrine, and other items of a rich pharmacopoeia upon which the modern world is still drawing. Again, a well-illustrated handbook of industrial technology (by Sung Ying-hsing, printed in 1637; see pages 14, 15, and 74), describes methods and instruments used in producing rice, silk, salt, pottery, metals, coal, paper, weapons, and many other products of China's premodern technology.

The vitality of Ming scholarship reflected processes of social growth of the same sort that had flowered in the Sung. Two centuries of domestic peace under the Ming brought substantial economic growth—big increases

The Ming official and philosopher, Wang Yang-ming (Wang Shou-jen), 1472–1529.

in farm production and population as well as in trade and industry. City life flourished accordingly, accompanied by more printing and distribution of books, more widespread education, and a more refined and also more democratized urban culture. Out of this came a larger scholar class as well as an enlarged bureaucracy; yet the problems of Chinese life also proliferated and taxed the powers of Confucian thinkers to maintain an integrated view of society and define the scholar's role in it.

The Ming philosopher most influential on later generations in China and Japan was Wang Yang-ming (1472–1529), a successful high official who went beyond the orthodoxy of Chu Hsi by advocating both spiritual enlightenment through meditative self-examination and a vigorous ethical activism within society. Wang carried further a line of Sung thought (see page 149), the Neo-Confucian school of Idealism or of the Mind which had stemmed from a contemporary of Chu Hsi as a minority school opposed to the dominant Chu Hsi school of Rationalism. In general, this School of the Mind was inclined to deny the dualism of Chu Hsi's system, the sharp distinction between Heaven and man and therefore between "Heavenly Principle" (*t'ien-li*) and "human desire." Instead, it viewed them both as parts of a single realm, which brought it closer to Buddhism. Building on this tradition, Wang Yang-ming's teaching represented a sort of Zen revolt within Confucianism: it put greater stress on meditation and intuitive knowledge. Chu Hsi's interpretation of the classical phrase (from the *Great Learning*) about the "extension of knowledge through the investigation of things" could thus be revised. Wang advocated instead "the extension of intuitive knowledge," which could be achieved through the investigation of one's own inner mind, the *li* within one. The process for doing this, as in Zen Buddhism, was essentially meditation, leading to a sort of enlightenment. But Confucian self-cultivation sought to eliminate not all desires, as in a Buddhist nonattachment to the world, but only selfish desires, the better to achieve one's dutiful harmony with others and with all creation. This led Wang to stress the "unity of knowledge and conduct." As he put it, "Knowledge is the beginning of conduct; conduct is the completion of knowledge." This has remained a Chinese and Japanese ideal down to the present day.

The Gentry Class.   The metropolitan graduates totaled only 25,000 men during the whole Ming period. But the degree-holders of the lower ranks probably numbered at any one time about half a million. These degree-holders of all ranks have been known in Chinese as "officials and scholars" (*shen-shih*). In English the term gentry has been applied to them, but this term requires careful definition. It is ambiguous, for it is applied both to individuals and to families, and may have either a political-social or an economic connotation. Strictly defined, the gentry were individual degree-holders. Yet in China where the family overshadowed the individual, the existence of gentry families (i.e., families that had members who were degree-holders) was to be expected. Individuals became gentry by securing degrees. Yet, in a crowded society based on farming, where landowning was a chief economic support for scholarly study, landlord-gentry families were very common. Degree-holders and landlords overlapped to a considerable but imprecise extent.

The peculiar strength of Confucian government lay in the fact that the gentry performed so many public functions in the local community without official remuneration. They commonly lived in their big houses in the market towns but also maintained contacts or establishments in the administrative cities. As men of influence, they assumed responsibility for many activities which today are performed by officials. They raised funds for and supervised public works, such as the building and maintenance of irrigation ditches and canals with their dikes and dams, and roads with their bridges and ferries. They took responsibility for public morals, maintaining the local Confucian temples and ceremonies. They supported schools and academies. They compiled the local histories or gazetteers. In time of plenty they sponsored orphanages and care for the aged. In time of disaster they provided relief. In the face of disorder, they might get permission to organize local militia as defense forces. In most of these activities they received official encouragement or recognition but not specific appointment to office or any pay. A loose comparison might be made

GENTRY IDEALS. *From an eighteenth-century work* (Pin-feng kuang-i) *illustrating the rewards of virtue. The caption (not shown) for the illustration on the left says: "In the tenth month winter cold sets in. The diligent have ample food and clothing. They feast with wine, play games, and entertain relatives. Parents live in comfort while sons pursue learning." The illustration on the right is for the eleventh month and shows a winter scene. Within their apartments women who have done their weaving sit warmly clothed around a brazier enjoying wine. On the street people who have been indolent suffer from the cold.*

with other classes that have functioned in very different societies, such as the equestrian order of ancient Rome, the modern American business class, or other nonofficial groups that have provided local community leadership.

The interest of the government was to maintain morale and a type of public spirit among the gentry, as opposed to selfish opportunism. To this end the Confucian doctrines were recited in the local Confucian temples and the Son of Heaven issued his moral exhortations. The six imperial injunctions of Hung-wu were ordered posted in all villages in 1397. These said, in effect, "Be filial, be respectful to elders and ancestors, teach your children, and peacefully pursue your livelihood." Thus the great tradition of learning, under the patronage of the head of the state, was used to indoctrinate the common people, while the gentry class as the local elite in turn provided leadership in the orderly life of the villages. Though not aristocratic in a hereditary sense, this was indeed an elitist system, for the degree-holders with their immediate families formed certainly no more than 2 per cent of the population but held the highest social authority outside the small official class itself.

Foreign Relations

The Tribute System. Upon gaining the throne, Hung-wu immediately tried to re-establish the grand design of the Chinese state in his foreign relations as well as at home. He sent envoys to the peripheral states, Korea, Japan, Annam (Vietnam), Champa, Tibet, and others, announcing his accession. Tribute missions soon came from these states and from others to which Mongol expeditions had been sent almost a century earlier, on the established routes of China's overseas trade.

The suzerain-vassal relationship between the ruler of China and rulers of other countries expressed the traditional "culturalism" in which China was assumed to be not only the largest and oldest among the states of the world but indeed their parent and the source of their civilization. Tribute relations involved not only performance of the kowtow, the "three kneelings and nine prostrations," but also many other aspects of interstate relations: the exchange of envoys and conduct of diplomatic relations, repatriation and extradition of persons, regulation of Sino-foreign trade, and special Chinese efforts at self-defense through intimidating, cajoling, or subsidizing foreign tribes and rulers. In short, the fitting of foreign potentates into a hierarchy of superior and inferior, and the expression of this in ritual observances, was merely an extension to the outer world of the "Confucian" social order which the ruler of China sought to maintain at home. The vassal king was given an official patent of appointment and a seal to use on his memorials, which were to be dated by the Chinese ruler's year period. The Son of Heaven affected a paternal interest in the orderly government of the tributary state, confirming the succession of new rulers, sometimes offering military protection against attack, usually conferring the boon of trade with China, and in any case sending down moral homilies and exhortations. This was not an aggressive imperialism. Rather, it was a defensive expression of culturalism: foreign rulers, if they wished contact with the Middle Kingdom, had to accept its terms and acknowledge the universal supremacy of the Son of Heaven. Trade with China might be of great value. Tribute formalities were the price to be paid. Like so many grand designs, this one failed of perfect execution. Yet Chinese chroniclers, by maintaining the forms of tribute at least in the

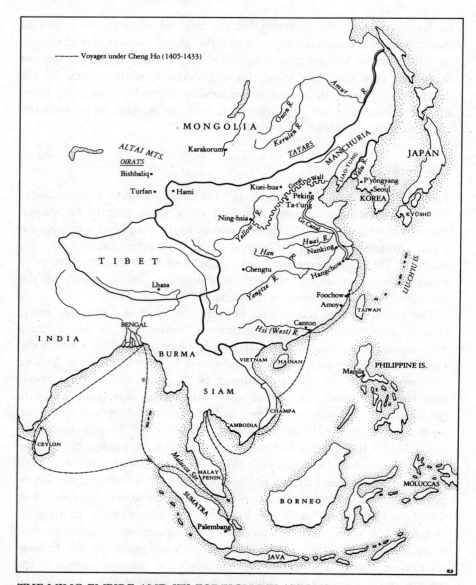

------ Voyages under Cheng Ho (1405-1433)

THE MING EMPIRE AND ITS FOREIGN RELATIONS

record, made it seem important. It was often regarded quite differently by
the tributaries.

The tribute system served many purposes. To get the "king of Japan"
to curb Japanese pirates who were raiding Chinese ports, Hung-wu sent
three missions to Japan in 1369–1372, using various inducements—
repatriation of captured pirates, threatening rescripts from himself, and
Chinese monks as envoys, but all to no avail. Japanese piracy continued.
Though tribute missions came, they were not always submissive, nor were

they from the Japanese sovereign. "You stupid eastern barbarians!" wrote Hung-wu to the Ashikaga shogun, the feudal ruler of Japan. "Living so far across the sea . . . you are haughty and disloyal; you permit your subjects to do evil." The Japanese replied in kind: "Heaven and Earth are vast; they are not monopolized by one ruler."

The high point of tributary activity under Yung-lo saw a brief period of professed Japanese fealty to China, expressed in very dutiful terms but regarded by the Japanese feudal rulers as merely a means of monopolizing the lucrative Chinese trade for themselves. Yung-lo in 1403 reopened the three Superintendencies of Merchant Shipping in the southern coastal provinces, which had been closed in 1374, and built hostels at each to entertain tribute envoys. Japanese missions now came annually for several years. In the usual fashion the Chinese court prepared a series of numbered paper passport tallies, tore them from their stub books, and sent them to the vassal ruler, retaining the stub books. When a mission came to the designated Chinese port to bring tribute and to trade, its ships, goods and persons were all specifically limited by statute. They were recorded on one of the numbered tallies, which could be verified by its fitting into the stub books. Thus all envoys were given bona fides, and imposters were checked. The Japanese shogun could maintain his trade monopoly and the Chinese could identify pirates. Between 1433 and 1549, eleven large Japanese missions, usually of several hundred persons, came to the Chinese court under the tally system, by way of Ningpo. Innumerable problems arose—rivalry in Japan to get possession of the official tallies, conflicts in China with disorderly Japanese warriors, prolonged haggling at Peking over the prices to be paid for trade goods, which included copper ore and sulphur by the hundreds of tons and Japanese swords by the thousand. Members of missions also carried their own goods for private trade. In addition, they received gifts from the emperor, as did the shogun, in lavish quantity.

The Maritime Expeditions.   One of Yung-lo's major undertakings was to incorporate the states of South and Southeast Asia into the tribute system. While his motives still remain a matter of speculation, this ambitious venture was marked by seven great maritime expeditions which were begun in 1405, and continued until 1433. They were led for the most part by a Muslim court eunuch named Cheng Ho, who came originally from Yunnan and as a Muslim was well fitted to deal with the Islamic rulers of South Asia. (See map, pages 172–173.) The first fleet sailed in 1405–1407 with sixty-two vessels carrying 28,000 men, and reached India, as did also the second and third. The fourth voyage in 1413–1415 reached Aden and the head of Asian circum-navigation at Hormuz on the Persian Gulf. A fifth voyage also went as far as Aden. The seventh voyage started out with 27,500 men and reached Hormuz again in 1431–1433. Chinese vessels visited far down the east coast of Africa, where chinaware and copper cash had been known for centuries. Seven Chinese reached Mecca.

The world had never seen such large-scale feats of seamanship. These Chinese armadas sailed all across the Indian Ocean almost a century before the Portuguese in 1498 reached India by sailing around Africa, and a century and a half before the Spanish Armada of 1588 made Western history by its short voyage around England. Cheng Ho's voyages were made possible by the development of Chinese shipbuilding and techniques of navigation on the Asian sea routes. His seagoing junks were of considerable size, some over four hundred feet in length, with four decks and up to a dozen watertight compartments. They navigated by detailed sailing directions and also used the compass. These remarkable expeditions penetrated to the sources of China's maritime trade not only along the Southeast Asian coasts but also in Ceylon, on both coasts of southern India, and in the Middle East and East Africa. In addition to customary tributaries, like Vietnam and Siam, some fifty new places were visited, and their rulers enrolled as tributaries. Missions from Hormuz and the African coast came to China four times, from Bengal eleven times. Rulers in Sumatra and Ceylon were brought back by force. Back also came ostriches, zebras, and giraffes, the latter touted as the auspicious "unicorn" of Chinese fable.

These spectacular maritime expeditions expressed the exuberance of an era of great vitality. For the eunuch leaders, they brought adventure, fame, and presumably profit. Commercial interests were also no doubt at work on the well-established routes of earlier trade, where Chinese migration had already created large overseas Chinese communities in Southeast Asian ports. Another motive seems to have been broadly political, to bring all the known world within the Chinese tributary scheme of things. Far-distant places trading by land were regularly enrolled as tributaries. Why not those trading by sea? This grandiose concept had been in the minds of Mongol emperors and was implicit in the idea of the universal rule of the Son of Heaven.

Speculation as to the causes of the Ming expeditions raises the question of why they were suddenly stopped and never resumed or imitated later. One reason for their cessation was their great cost, at a time when the early Ming campaigns against the Mongols and the building of Peking had begun to deplete the imperial coffers. The great fleets could be criticized as expensive adventures, largely unproductive except for pageantry and strange tales. They were also promoted particularly by court eunuchs, whose activities were opposed by the scholar-officials—so much so that Cheng Ho's feats were practically suppressed in the historical record.

These demonstrations of the early Ming capacity for maritime expansion were all the more dramatic because Chinese ideas of government and official policies were fundamentally indifferent, if not actually opposed, to such an expansion. The contrast between capacity and performance, if looked at by our modern world of trade and overseas expansion, is truly striking.

Chinese seapower, based upon the fishing fleets and trading junks of Canton, Amoy, Ch'üan-chou, and Ningpo, had been steadily increasing. China was on the verge of becoming a naval power that could dominate East Asia. The Ming fleets were developing the nautical and logistic capacity to bring military force and trading goods in overwhelming volume to any point in the Eastern seas. But after 1433 this beginning was cut short. No Henry the Navigator came to the Chinese throne. The Ming court, unlike that of contemporary Portugal, had no sustained interest in seafaring, no grasp of the possibilities of seapower. The Ming voyages were not followed up but remained isolated *tours de force,* mere exploits.

Ming Anticommercialism. This contrast throws light on the nature of Chinese society. Cheng Ho lived and sailed a century and a half before Sir Francis Drake and the other captains of Queen Elizabeth began to lay the foundations of the British Empire. The Chinese Empire was then greater than all of Europe in size and in the volume of her domestic, if not also her foreign, commerce. Yet Ming China, having shown her capacity to do so, failed to become a maritime power. Through this default, the Eastern seas and even the China coast soon came to be dominated by a succession of non-Chinese seafaring peoples—the Japanese, the Portuguese and Spanish, the Dutch, and finally the British and Americans. Out of this commercial and naval domination of East Asian waters emerged eventually those forces of imperialistic expansion which finally humbled the traditional Chinese Empire and led to its disintegration. Cheng Ho, as a court eunuch and high dignitary, lacked precisely those motives which later inspired the merchant-adventurers of Europe. His power and advancement, even as he cruised the Indian Ocean, still depended upon the emperor. Cheng Ho was an organizer, a commander, a diplomat, and an able courtier, but he was not a trader. No chartered companies grew out of his expeditions, empowered like the Virginia Company or the East India Company to found colonies or establish governments overseas. The migration of Chinese into Southeast Asia was already under way, and the Chinese in that area would always outnumber the Europeans who might come there. But the Chinese state remained uninterested in these commercial and colonial possibilities overseas. The Ming and Ch'ing governments got their major sustenance from the land tax, not from trade taxes. They refused to join in the great commercial revolution which was beginning to sweep the world.

To understand this anticommercialism we may suggest several approaches, institutional, economic, ideological, and strategic. The institutional explanation goes back to the early environment of ancient China on the North China Plain far from the sea, where the official class came into being as tax-gatherers, fostering agriculture and gathering its products to maintain themselves and the state. In this agrarian-bureaucratic society merchants were kept subordinate to officialdom and utilized by it. The economic interests that did grow up were centered in domestic, not foreign, commerce simply because the Chinese subcontinent, then as now, was so relatively self-sufficient. But after the growth of commerce during the T'ang, Sung, and Yüan, why did the Ming and Ch'ing governments revert to the traditional agrarian-centered attitudes of an earlier era? Perhaps one reason was the culturalism we have already mentioned, in particular the establishment of the Neo-Confucian orthodoxy as the matrix of Ming thought. This revived the classical values, including the ancient disesteem of commerce. Foreign trade was left to powerful eunuchs, which made it all the more distasteful to the official class. Another explanation was presumably strategic—the Ming determination to prevent a repetition of the Mongol conquest.

The Mongol Problem. Hung-wu's preoccupation with breaking the Mongol power remained the chief focus of early Ming foreign relations. His aim was not to subjugate the whole of Mongolia but rather to destroy the unity of the tribes, which gave them their striking power. Even before China had been unified, Ming armies crossed the steppe to break up the Mongol forces, twice seizing Karakorum. Mongol chieftains pacified by defeat, intimidation, purchase, or other means were put in charge of Mongol settlements on the border and given titles, honors, emoluments, and opportunities for trade. Using a divide-and-rule policy, the Chinese tried to keep the seminomads of Inner Mongolia as border allies against the fully nomadic and mobile tribes of Outer Mongolia.

In the Central Asian khanate of Chaghadai, the last great successor of Chinggis, the conquerer Timur, known to Europe as Tamerlane (1336–1405), rose to power in 1369. From his capital of Samarkand, he expanded violently in all directions, overrunning Persia and Mesopotamia, defeating the Golden Horde in southern Russia, even briefly invading northern India. Tamerlane had some contact with the Chinese court and conceived the ambition to take it over. When he died in 1405, he had a vast army already on the way eastward to conquer China and make it an Islamic state. His death, however, marked the end of the Mongol era, particularly of the Mongol capacity to keep Central Asia united and so to threaten the agricultural civilizations that bordered on it. The end of a united Central Asia also diminished the trade and contact across it between East and

West. Under the Ming and Ch'ing, this land route was severed, and the tribes of Mongolia became more dependent on trade with China alone.

By the early fifteenth century the Mongol tribes were split (see map, page 196): in eastern Mongolia were the Tatars (*Ta-tan* in Chinese, corrupted by Europeans to "Tartars"), in western Mongolia, the Oirats. Chinese strategy was to play each off against the other. The Yung-lo emperor rose to power by leading expeditions against the Mongols and also by finding allies among them on the border. After his usurpation in 1403, Yung-lo personally led five expeditions far out across the steppe. In 1410 he mobilized over 100,000 men with 30,000 cartloads of supplies, overawed the Oirats, gave them gifts and secured their neutrality, crossed the Kerulen River, and defeated the Tatars. However, when the Oirats expanded eastward in 1414, Yung-lo led an army back to the Kerulen and this time defeated the Oirats. Both these Ming expeditions used cannon. Soon the Tatars ventured to raid the border. In 1422 Yung-lo led forth another host of 235,000 men with a supply train of 117,000 carts and 340,000 donkeys. The Tatars escaped westward, however, and further campaigns in 1423 and 1424 were unable to catch them.

Already Yung-lo's removal of the capital in 1421 from Nanking to Peking had symbolized the Ming preoccupation with defense against the Mongols. Imperial strategy centered on the frontier, where Peking stands guard near the principal gateway (the Nan-k'ou Pass) leading from Mongolia down onto the North China Plain. The capital of the great Ming Empire thus was located a scant forty miles from the traditional northern boundary of China, the Great Wall. This site has been used by dynasties oriented toward Inner Asia—the Liao, Yüan, Ming, and Ch'ing, as well as the Chinese People's Republic since 1949. Southern capitals have been used by regimes originating in the south or oriented toward overseas trade—Hangchow under the Southern Sung; Nanking in the early Ming, under the Taiping rebels (1853–1864), and under the Nationalist Government after 1927. Peking was far from the centers of Chinese population and production. Its strategic vulnerability to nomad inroads and its dependence on grain shipments from the lower Yangtze via the Grand Canal, are startling facts—too startling to be mere accidents. The explanation is that the capital of China had to serve also as the capital of the non-Chinese areas of Inner Asia. The "barbarians" were a constant military and therefore political component of the Chinese Empire; its capital was drawn outward to the border of China as a result.

The Ming expeditions to chastise the Mongols had been part of the effort to keep them harmless by carrot-and-stick methods. The Oirats, for example, had established tribute relations in 1408 and sent missions almost every year, which became a thinly veiled means of keeping them pacified through subsidies, a sort of tribute in reverse. Their annual missions to Peking sometimes totaled two or three thousand persons, including several hundred merchants from Central Asia. Passing through the Great Wall at Ta-t'ung in northern Shansi, this host had to be quartered and banqueted by the local authorities, for, like cultural delegations invited to Peking today, tribute missions were guests of the Middle Kingdom. As tribute, the Oirats presented their chief native product, horses, and received in return imperial "gifts in reply," mainly silk and satin textiles. A few days of free trade in the market followed the presentation of tribute within the Forbidden City. In this context of profitable exchange, the "barbarians" acquiesced in the "three kneelings and nine prostrations" as a traditional court ceremony. While gaining the nomads' submission, China had to suffer their depredations on the route between the border and the capital, and their drunken roistering at Peking. For the Mongols, the trip spelled glamour and profit, from fees paid them by the Muslim traders to whom their tribute missions gave cover. Many bearers of "tribute" were actually merchants claiming to represent distant and sometimes nonexistent potentates. The Ming *Collected Statutes* listed thirty-eight countries of the Western Regions which submitted tribute by way of Hami, the natural funnel for the caravan trade. Among them, for example, the Kingdom of Rum in Asia Minor (i.e., the long defunct Roman East) was recorded as presenting tribute as late as 1618. The Ming viewed this thin trickle of Central Asian tributary trade as having political rather than fiscal value, as it kept troublesome warriors quiet on the frontier.

In the late 1430's, just as the overseas expeditions came to an end, the Inner Asian frontier saw a violent recrudescence of the Mongol threat. A new chieftain of the Oirats subjugated Hami, then extended his influence over the tribes to the east all the way to Korea, and in late 1449 mobilized his horde along the border, threw off the forms of tribute, and approached Ta-t'ung. The Ming emperor, a product of palace life, was under the ill-advised domination of his chief eunuch, who took the emperor into the field and foolishly advanced toward Ta-t'ung to do battle. The Oirats advanced, defeated, pursued, and destroyed the Chinese force, and captured the emperor. But when they came to Peking, they found that the war minister and others had prepared a defense with cannon, enthroned a new emperor, and affected no interest in the former one. After several days before the walls, the Oirats went back to Mongolia. Next year they sent back the useless emperor and soon resumed their profitable tribute relations.

Ming-Mongol relations during the next century were a mixture of border raids and tribute missions. In 1550 a new leader, Altan Khan of the eastern Mongols, united a large striking force, came through the Wall from the northeast, and pillaged around Peking again for several days before withdrawing. Ming defenses of walls, beacon towers, and military agricultural colonies on the frontier were offset by Chinese deserters who aided the raiders. Such Chinese helped Altan Khan try to establish a settled administration. He built a capital city at Kuei-hua outside the Wall, northwest of Ta-t'ung. Eventually in the 1570's he was pacified and given the hopeful title of "Obedient and Righteous Prince" (Shun-i Wang). Until the rise of the Manchu Empire, however, Mongol freebooting continued to harass the Chinese border.

Troubles with Japan. From the cost of the Japanese and the Mongol tribute missions, we can see why the Ming court may have preferred to let the tribute system rest in comparative abeyance overseas after the first half of the fifteenth century. The expense of maintaining, transporting, and bestowing gifts upon hundreds of functionaries and merchants who came to Peking was not compensated by the trade they conducted. Missions from Southeast Asia grew fewer and fewer. The Ryūkyū Islands alone remained a regular maritime tributary on a biennial basis, serving actually as an indirect channel for Sino-Japanese trade. In this context of fading grandeur and frontier disorder, the first Europeans to reach China by sea, Portuguese adventurers in 1514, seemed to the Chinese only a small increment in a general growth of piracy and unwanted relations on the China coast.

In Japan a growing maritime capacity had produced overseas adventurers a full century before the Elizabethan age glorified the somewhat comparable exploits of gentleman-pirates from England. Like Drake and Hawkins, the Japanese could trade or loot by turns, as opportunity offered. Their bigger ships could carry three hundred men. Landing suddenly and attacking villages with their great swords, the pirates would seize provisions, hostages, and loot and make their getaway. Although known in Chinese records as "Japanese pirates" (*Wo-k'ou,* or in Japanese, *Wakō,* a term with pejorative connotations of "dwarf"), these raiders actually included many Chinese. Unlike the Mongol raids, the disloyal Chinese in these forays were not so much advisers as principal participants. By the latter decades of Ming rule, Chinese actually formed the majority among the "Japanese pirates."

The Ming response to this growing disorder, the prohibition of maritime trade, reflected the court's agrarian-minded and land-based unconcern for foreign commerce in general. The prohibition had the effect of forcing crews and captains into smuggling or buccaneering for a livelihood. Pirate raids after 1550 became actual invasions. The pirates based themselves on Chusan Island south of Shanghai, which was later to be the British base in 1840, and in 1552 they attacked inland cities in Chekiang, while others went up the Yangtze. In defense, Ming pirate-suppressors bought over the leading renegades with rewards and pardons and attacked the pirate lair on Chusan. But the scourge increased. Japanese harassment

of the South China coast declined only with the political reunification of
Japan in the late sixteenth century. However, this reunification concentrated
Japan's military energies in a form even more menacing and exhausting to
the Ming court.

Peking learned of Japan's intent to invade China by way of Korea
through spies in Japan as well as from Korea. In 1592, when the Japanese
attack on Korea came, the court debated whether to send a fleet from the
southern provinces to attack Japan, or to put an army on the Korean frontier, or to negotiate for peace. In the end the court decided it had to fulfill its
suzerain duty to aid Korea in order to defend Southern Manchuria and North
China. Ming forces did not cross the Yalu until after the whole peninsula was
in Japanese hands. The Chinese attacked P'yongyang in mid 1592, were badly
defeated, and started negotiations to gain time. Early in 1593 they surprised the Japanese, drove them out of P'yongyang, and advanced to the
outskirts of the capital, Seoul, but were ambushed and again defeated. The
short swords of the Chinese cavalry proved no match for the long swords,
spears, and guns of the Japanese infantry. Negotiations and exhausting conflict continued until the Japanese finally withdrew in 1598 (after a second
invasion in force in 1597). The total Ming expenditure to meet the first
Japanese invasion of Korea must have come to over 10 million taels, with
a comparable sum required later to meet the second invasion. The administration was already close to bankruptcy, after constant subsidies to the
Mongols and rebuilding of Peking palaces. Japan's invasions of Korea were
a final strain on Peking's dwindling resources and prepared the way for the
rise, after 1600, of bandits within and "barbarian" invaders from without.

The Ming Economy

Economic Growth. In studying China's economic history, we must constantly distinguish between the imperial regime and the country as a whole.
We have noted the court's anticommercial attitude and approach to final
bankruptcy. But if we look at the late Ming economy as a whole, we find
much evidence of growth in almost all its aspects—population, area of
cultivated land, volume of foreign trade, production of handicraft and industrial goods, and even, perhaps, in the use of money.

Tax grain (called by Western writers "tribute rice") had to be transported from the rice baskets of the Huai River and lower Yangtze to feed
the new capital at Peking. Sea transport around Shantung was increasingly
hindered by Japanese pirates, and was in any case expensive. Yung-lo therefore dug out the unused "Connecting Canal" in western Shantung that
Khubilai Khan had first constructed as part of the second Grand Canal
system, and installed fifteen locks. Three thousand or more shallow boats

were now used on the canal route, and after 1415 sea transport was given up. But transport of tax grain to collecting depots on the canal, still part of the labor-service obligation of the peasantry, became a heavy burden on them. Yung-lo's successors therefore placed the task of transportation entirely on certain military transport divisions of the local garrisons, which had to be increased from 120,000 to 160,000 men. From the 1430's this new system supplied usually over 3 million Chinese bushels (say roughly 200,000 tons), and sometimes over 5 million, to the capital every year.

Trade between North and South China was stimulated by the growth of Peking and the canal system. Trade on the Yangtze and in South China also increased. For example, merchants in the southernmost part of modern Anhwei spread their operations widely into other provinces. Called, from an old place name, "Hsin-an merchants," they traded in all manner of commodities—porcelains from the nearby production center at Ching-te-chen in Kiangsi, teas and silks locally produced, salt, timber, and comestibles. Naturally they developed the close relations with officialdom that such extensive operations required for their protection.

Specialized handicraft production grew up for this enlarging market and even some larger-scale manufacturing. At Ching-te-chen the imperial kilns produced great quantities of porcelain for the palace and also for upper-class use and even for export. The particular clay now known as kaolin (named for *Kao-ling,* "High Ridge," a hill east of Ching-te-chen; a hydrous silicate of alumina), when properly prepared with other substances and heated to about 1400 degrees Centigrade, becomes white, translucent, and so hard that steel will not scratch it. This porcelain was a truly superior product in the eyes of Europeans, who lacked the technique and who properly called it "chinaware." Again, Soochow became a national center of trade, finance, and processing industries, particularly the weaving and dyeing of silk. The nearby Sungkiang region, inland from Shanghai, became a late Ming center for cotton cloth production, using raw cotton from other provinces both north and south, and sending its product back for sale there. Canton iron pans (shallow cooking pans for use directly over fire) were exported widely throughout China, overseas, and to Central Asia.

This domestic commercial growth led to the setting up in the sixteenth century of numerous regional guilds with guild halls in major centers, especially Peking. These bodies were created chiefly by officials and merchants who came from a common region—a province, prefecture, county, or city—so as to have a convenient center of contact and mutual aid in a distant place, pre-eminently at the capital.

Meanwhile China's maritime trade developed steadily in the late Ming outside the framework of the tribute system. Missions from Southeast and South Asia became fewer, while Chinese merchants who went overseas became more numerous. In short, foreign trade was no longer brought to

China principally by intermediaries, like the Arabs, but was now carried by Chinese merchants who went abroad with Chinese products and on their return with foreign wares entered easily into the stream of China's coastwise junk traffic. The government did little to encourage this trade and sometimes banned it, but it continued to grow.

The Single-Whip Reform.   The traditional taxes on land and labor underwent a gradual reform during the sixteenth century, which reduced them to money payments and simplified them by combining many small items into one. The whole movement has become known as the "Single-Whip" reform. (The name is a pun, since *i-t'iao-pien,* meaning "combination in one item," sounds also like "a single whip.")

The evils in the land and labor taxes had begun with the falsification of local records. As we have seen on pages 186–187, both landholdings and households early in the Ming period were classified into grades and remained supposedly subject to reclassification every ten years or so. Each man's tax burden depended first of all on his classification in the local registers. But responsibility for management of the system was placed on the leading households—the wealthier families, who thus had an opportunity to escape their allotted burden by falsifying the records. By collusion and bribery, these interested parties could reduce their own tax liability, providing they could increase that of the poorer households to meet the overall tax quota of the area. Many methods could be used: concealing the number of male adults, removing land from the record altogether, registering land under the name of a servant or tenant, or registering private land as government land or private persons as officials. Because of the special privileges enjoyed by wealthier families, smaller households often sought their protection, transferring the nominal ownership of their land in order to escape the tax burden, for a consideration paid privately to the large household. As a result, the official registers within a few generations became meaningless, while taxation became chaotic—a racket levied by the powerful upon the weak. Revenue collections ran short, the government above suffered loss, and the poorer peasants beneath were milked harder than ever, while the large households and petty officials in between benefited from their mutual arrangements. Since this middle stratum of leading families in the countryside provided many of the degree-holders through examination or purchase, they became all the more a "landlord-gentry" ruling class.

The confusion of this situation was compounded by the variety of taxes. The forms of landholding were complex: rights to the subsoil might be held by one person but rights to the use of the surface by another, who might lease the use of the surface to a tenant, who could sublet in turn. Tenantry assumed many forms. The labor service charges became even more complex. They were apportioned on the basis of a factor less stable than land, namely, the number of male adults, and might vary according to local needs and by decision of the local powerholders. As the institution became more corrupt, demands for labor services bore so hard on the poorer peasantry that first households, then sections (*chia*) of villages, and finally whole villages (*li*) began to abscond. Since tax quotas were seldom diminished, this increased still further the burden on those left behind. Finally, as more and more items became commuted to money payments, the tax collectors had every opportunity to add surtaxes and extra fees, commute labor into silver inequitably, and maintain assessments after the need for the original services had passed. The result was a limitless web of money taxes entangling the peasantry, levied in all seasons of the year for myriad nominal or alleged purposes, inequitably assessed and imperfectly recorded, according to no general scheme and under no superior control or direction.

The Single-Whip reform was carried out gradually by many hard-pressed provincial officials in one area after another, in a desperate effort to maintain a reliable tax structure and regular collections. It occurred chiefly in the period 1522–1619, that is, in the final century of effective Ming administration. It consisted of two principal tendencies—to combine all the various items of taxation under one or a few headings and to collect them in silver. One basic reform was to simplify the land classification so that in place of as many as a hundred different land tax rates, there were only two or three rates. Another reform was to unify the land taxes, combining sometimes thirty or forty different taxes into two or three items. Labor services were similarly unified. Next, the two major categories of land tax and labor service were sometimes combined to make a single item. Finally, dates of collection were unified, as well as the apparatus for it, which reduced the opportunities for extortion and fraud.

The resulting fiscal situation was probably no simpler than it would be to have a separate income tax law for each county in the United States. The Single-Whip reform was only a partial step toward a modernized tax structure. After the reform, the government used its tax receipts in silver to pay wages to hired laborers, who performed the labor service tasks formerly required of the common people. Communities were no longer required to transport their tax grain to a government granary. The reform also abolished the former indirect payment of taxes through the section and village heads. Instead, the taxpayer now put his tax silver directly into the government collector's silver chest in front of the local yamen and got an official receipt.

Several earlier dynasties had begun by relying at first on taxes and services in kind, only to have the system deteriorate, until a reform simplified it by a greater recourse to tax collections in money. In the late Ming this increased use of money was related to the vigorous economic growth already mentioned and in particular to the inflow of silver from abroad.

The End of Ming Rule

Even if we make allowance for human frailty among historians—their capacity to find in the voluminous record of history the evidence they may seek for almost any interpretation of events—still the drama of the late Ming has all the classic features of a dynastic decline: effete and feckless rulers, corrupt favorites misusing their power, factional jealousies among officials, fiscal bankruptcy, natural disasters, the rise of rebellion and, finally, foreign invasion. These evils in the last decades of Ming rule were highlighted by the fact that they followed a vigorous reform effort under Chang Chü-cheng, one of the great ministers of the era, who rose to supreme power as senior Grand Secretary during the first decade (1573–1582) of the Wan-li reign. Chang was on good terms with the Outer Court and influential with the young emperor. He tried to increase the land tax revenue by getting exempted lands taxed again. He tried to restrict the ever-growing perquisites and privileges of the official class and the imperial family. Yet Chang, for all his efforts, could not check the emperor's greed. After his death in 1582, Wan-li, reigning for another thirty-eight years until 1620, became utterly irresponsible. He avoided seeing his ministers for years on end, refused to conduct business or make needed appointments, let evils flourish, and squandered the state's resources. The fifteen-year-old emperor who ascended the throne in 1620 was a dimwit interested mainly in carpentry. He let his nurse's close friend, the eunuch Wei Chung-hsien (1568–1627), who had been butler in his mother's apartments, take over the government. Wei brought the eunuch evil to its highest point. Backed by a small eunuch army to control the palace and a network of spies throughout the empire, he recruited unprincipled opportunists among the bureaucracy, purged his enemies in official life, and levied extortionate new taxes in the provinces.

Factionalism: The Tung-lin Party. The Confucian resistance to these evils was carried on mainly by a group of scholars, whose long struggle and eventual failure make a poignant chapter in the annals of Chinese politics. Tung-lin (literally, "Eastern Forest") was the name of an academy at Wusih on the lower Yangtze. Led by a dozen scholar-ex-officials, most of whom had been dismissed during factional controversies at the court, its members lectured at affiliated academies nearby, and soon spread their influence among scholars and officials elsewhere in a moral crusade to reassert the traditional principles of Confucian conduct. They condemned the philosophical eclecticism that had grown popular in the sixteenth century since the time of Wang Yang-ming, and that seemed to confuse Confucianism, Buddhism and Taoism. They stressed the supreme importance of moral integrity and denounced various holders of power, both Grand Secretaries and eunuchs.

The Tung-lin reformers of course had an incomplete monopoly on virtue. By 1610 they were being denounced in turn as a *tang* (the modern word for "party"), that is, an organized clique of the sort traditionally anathematized as subversive of imperial authority and bureaucratic harmony. The factional struggle was conducted in terms less of state policies than of the moral qualities of ministers. Denouncing and being denounced, the Tung-lin crusaders had their ups and downs. They became dominant in the years 1620–1623, just before the eunuch Wei Chung-hsien achieved complete power. In 1624 a Tung-lin leader accused Wei of twenty-four high crimes, including murders and a forced abortion of the empress. Wei mobilized the enemies of the reformers and retaliated with terror. Blacklists were compiled of some seven hundred Tung-lin supporters. Leading figures were denounced, condemned, dismissed, disgraced, imprisoned, tortured, and beaten to death. The Tung-lin group had been practically wiped out by the time Wei fell from power in 1627. This eunuch's manipulation of the sacred office of the Son of Heaven for evil ends had completed the moral degradation of the Ming regime.

The Rise of Rebellion.   Yet the Ming collapse was perhaps due less to misgovernment than to nongovernment, less to eunuch immorality than to the regime's failure to keep up with its problems. The real problem was not that tax burdens were oppressive but that tax revenues were inadequate. The administration suffered less from tyranny than from paralysis.

When Shensi in the Northwest was hard hit by famine in 1628, a postal employee named Li Tzu-ch'eng was thrown out of his job by unwise government economies. Li joined his uncle, who was already a bandit, and made his lair on the edge of the North China Plain in the mountains of southern Shansi, the same area where the Japanese during World War II proved unable to dislodge the Chinese irregular forces. Li Tzu-ch'eng raided Honan and Szechwan, acquiring more followers, and eventually some of the forms of an organized government. At least two scholars joined him and advised him how to win popular support. They spread songs and stories about his heroic qualities, helped him distribute food to the starving, appoint officials, proclaim a dynasty, confer titles, and even issue his own coinage. By 1643 Li Tzu-ch'eng held much of Hupei, Honan, and Shensi. Early in 1644 he descended on Peking from the northwest, just as the last Ming emperor hanged himself on Prospect Hill, overlooking the Forbidden City.

Meanwhile Li's chief rival, another rebel named Chang Hsien-chung, had acquired a great reputation more as a killer than as an organizer of men. From about 1630 he had raided widely through North China, plundering with hit-and-run tactics. Finally in 1644 he invaded Szechwan and set up a government, complete with Six Ministries and a Grand Secretariat, headed by genuine metropolitan graduates who held examinations and minted money. But Chang's main concern was stamping out opposition with terror tactics, used especially against the gentry. He lost gentry support, and the Manchus killed him in 1647.

Thus the Ming dynasty was destroyed by Chinese rebels before it was superseded by "barbarian" invaders. But the Manchu conquerors preserved and used the major institutions of government that had functioned for more than two centuries under the Ming. The downfall of Ming rule must therefore be attributed less to the structure of these institutions than to their malfunctioning under the accumulated stresses that typify the end of a dynastic cycle.

9. Traditional China at Its Height under the Ch'ing

The Rise of the Manchu Dynasty

The Ch'ing dynasty began in the early seventeenth century, contemporary with the American colonies, and lasted until 1911. Thus it spanned the greater part of modern times and yet was dominated by a regime and social order that changed relatively little. The Ch'ing period saw both the zenith and the nadir of the traditional Chinese state. In the eighteenth century the population and territory of the empire were the largest they had ever been, and the finesse and stability of administration were at a high point. Yet the nineteenth century brought unmitigated disaster.

Here we are concerned only with the first act in this drama, the success of the Manchus in presiding over the Chinese state and society up to the beginning of the nineteenth century. In studying their achievement, however, we cannot help wondering to what extent their very success in maintaining the traditional order may have been a factor in its later collapse. So well established was the Chinese tradition that a thoroughgoing change of institutions and values could not easily be imagined. The Manchus were more successful as inheritors than as innovators; it was not in them to remake the Chinese scheme of things.

The success story of the Manchus was like that of the Mongols under Chinggis Khan: a powerful leader at a propitious time united his people, giving them a common name, and set them on the march until his descendants ruled all China. The Manchu nation-at-arms sprang from Jurchen tribes of the same Tungusic stock as the founders of the Chin dynasty (1122–1234). They rose to power on the fringe of Chinese culture and administration where they could learn both from their predecessors the Mongols and from China on a selective basis without being completely subjugated or Sinicized.

Southernmost Manchuria, or Liaotung ("East of the Liao River," including the Liaotung Peninsula), had been part of ancient China, suited to the same kind of intensive agriculture as North China and administered within the Han Empire. It communicated easily by sea with the Shantung peninsula and under the Ming was part of Shantung province. But Liaotung, being vulnerable strategically, was a hostage to fortune. No natural barriers defended it from the north. On the other hand, like all Manchuria, it could easily be cut off from land contact with China at Shanhaikuan ("the mountain-sea pass"), where the Great Wall meets the coast. Anyone who can hold a few miles of level land between mountain and ocean there can control access to or from Manchuria like a cork in a bottle. Consequently Liaotung, though Chinese, was a place where Chinese and "barbarians" interpenetrated, where strong "barbarians" could control an agricultural Chinese population, and so rival the ruling dynasty.

The Chinese defense against this was to rely not on static walls but on human relations, to establish China's political hegemony over the tribes by "subduing them with a loose rein" (*chi-mi*). Hung-wu created commanderies on the Mongol border and Yung-lo extended this system to the tribes of Manchuria also. In the Yung-lo period alone 178 commanderies were set up, an index of the Chinese divide-and-rule tactics. These commanderies were tribal military units under their own hereditary tribal leaders. These chieftains were given official titles and seals and expected to send yearly tribute. A chieftain's family might be given a Chinese surname and his daughter might be taken into the imperial harem. Surnames of course facilitated compilation of genealogies and fostered concepts of legitimacy and inheritance. Meanwhile the bestowal of honors and decorations from the emperor, like those still conferred throughout the British Commonwealth, served to bind the "barbarians" into the empire. Another policy was to let a tribal chieftain become an absentee, moving his own residence into the pleasanter circumstances of a Chinese town or even the capital, and so become Sinicized.

The first Jurchen commandery was established on the northeast of Liaotung in 1403. As the Manchurian tribes grew in numbers, groups of two hundred to six hundred tribesmen at a time would parade annually to Peking, harassing the populace en route. The Ming opened a horse market on the northern border of south Manchuria near Mukden (modern Shenyang) so as to obviate this travel inside the Wall. It was on this frontier that the Manchu power arose as the Ming grew weak. China's defense required the Sinicizing of the "barbarian" to make him a loyal subject of the empire; yet this process gave the "barbarian" his chance to combine

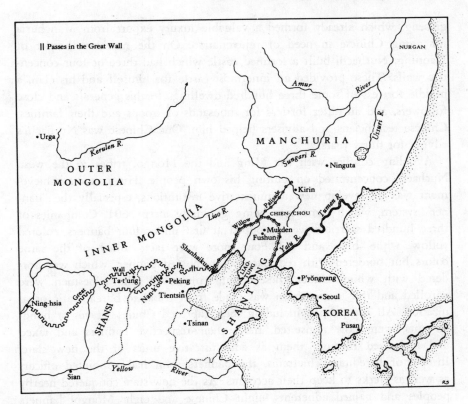

THE RISE OF THE MANCHUS

his native fighting strength with all that he could learn of Chinese ways. The result in Manchuria was a formidable synthesis of institutions and a new state power.

The Creation of a Sinicized Manchu State.   Nurhachi (1559–1626), the founder of the Manchu state, followed the tradition of Chinggis Khan in fighting his way to power on the pretext of avenging the deaths of his father and grandfather. They had been killed in a fight which involved the Chinese commander of Liaotung and an allied Jurchen chief, who therefore became Nurhachi's immediate target. While accepting the Chinese appointment to succeed his father, Nurhachi is said to have mobilized his family and tribe and exterminated this rival by 1586. He fortified his home, married the daughter of one powerful chief and the granddaughter of another, suppressed bandits, and earned Chinese commendation. Through thirty years of negotiation, arrangements of marriages and alliances, and sporadic warfare, Nurhachi united the four main Jurchen tribes to the north and rose to a position where he could defy the Ming. Meanwhile, he traded at the horse market and dealt in the supposedly medicinal root ginseng, which already formed a valuable luxury export from Manchuria for aging Chinese in need of rejuvenation. On the northeast border of Liaotung, Nurhachi built a fortified castle which had three or four concentric walls. These provided an innermost castle for himself and his clan, a middle fortress of some three hundred dwellings for his generals and close followers, and an outer fortress for thousands of troops and their families. Chinese technicians and advisers helped him. One Chinese was Nurhachi's adviser for thirty years.

Avoiding conflict with the Ming and the Mongol tribes to the west, Nurhachi concentrated on uniting his own people. His greatest achievement was to develop new administrative institutions, especially the "banner" system, which came into being gradually after 1601. Companies of three hundred warriors were grouped at first under four banners, colored yellow, white, blue, and red. Four more were later added, of the same colors but bordered with red, except for the red banner, which was bordered with white. Under these eight banners all the tribesmen were enrolled and thus a transition was made from tribal to bureaucratic organization. All the people, including their captured Chinese slaves or bondservants, were now registered under their respective banners and taxed and mobilized through them as administrative units of the new state. Instead of hereditary chieftains, the banners soon had appointed officers as well as clerks to keep their accounts. As the new state conquered nearby peoples and gained adherents, eight Chinese and eight Mongol banners were added, making a total of twenty-four. By 1644 there were 278 Manchu companies, 120 Mongol, and 165 Chinese, making an army of about 169,000, with the Manchus forming less than half the total.

Banners and their component companies did not fight as units. Rather, each company contributed a certain quota of men to make up the needed task force. For the expedition of 1634 into Inner Mongolia, for instance, each company provided twenty cavalrymen and eight guards, making a force of about 11,000. The banners differed from the Ming garrisons in that bannermen were allotted lands scattered in diverse places and intermixed with holdings of nonbannermen. The banners thus were not attached to one place, even though they had their own lands and got sustenance from them.

Another of Nurhachi's achievements was to develop a writing system for administrative purposes. He had his interpreter write Jurchen words in a modified Mongolian alphabet to which diacritical marks (dots and circles) were later added beside the letters. The *Mencius* was soon available in written Manchu. Thus the new writing made possible a rapid borrowing of the Confucian ideology of the state.

In 1616 Nurhachi took the title of emperor of the Later Chin, as though to continue the Chin dynasty of 1122–1234. In 1618 he openly attacked the Ming, took part of Liaotung, and developed a civil administration with Chinese help. In 1625 Nurhachi moved his capital southeast to Mukden. After his death in 1626 he was given the posthumous title of T'ai Tsu ("Grand Progenitor"). He was followed by three other capable leaders: his eighth son, Abahai (1592–1643), his fourteenth son, Dorgon (1612–1650), who dutifully refused the imperial title in favor of Abahai's six-year-old son but actually ruled as regent, and finally Nurhachi's great-grandson the K'ang-hsi emperor, under whose sixty-one-year reign from 1661 to 1722 the dynasty was firmly established.

To establish their leadership, the early Manchu rulers first had to subordinate clan government by group decision to a new principle of monarchy. The imperial clan leaders were brought into a state council and subordinated to it. Eventually the Manchu imperial clan was kept out of administration entirely, but its members nonetheless were concentrated at the capital. Their primary state function was to put a strong ruler on the throne and avoid the twin evils of government by women and by eunuchs.

On their part, the Manchu rulers absorbed the Confucian style of government far better than had their Mongol predecessors. Their success depended upon organizing state power in a Chinese fashion and using Chinese collaborators. As bureaucracy supplanted tribalism, literate clerks and administrators were recruited from among the Chinese of Liaotung, who numbered about 3 million, some ten times the estimated number of the Manchus at this time. These Chinese were attracted by the prospect of taking part in a strong and successful "Confucian" type of government. In 1631 the Six Ministries were set up at Mukden, a simulacrum of those at Peking. A censorate and other offices were also established, all on the Ming model.

The joint Sino-"barbarian" nature of the Manchu regime in its formative years is indicated by the number of Liaotung Chinese who rose in the Manchu service. For example, three Ming officers from Liaotung went over to the Manchus about 1633. Later, all three led armies to conquer South China. All three were made princes. One of these Chinese had twenty-three sons, of whom eleven became generals under the Ch'ing and three became state councilors.

The Manchu Conquest.   By building up their military and administrative capacities, the early Manchu rulers had made themselves leading contenders for the throne at Peking. Abahai attacked Korea in 1627 and again in 1636–1637, making it a vassal state. He led expeditions through the passes in the Great Wall to descend on North China in 1629, 1632, and 1634. He defeated the Inner Mongols and made them his vassals. Four expeditions brought the Amur region under his control. During this furious expansion, Abahai in 1636 renamed his dynasty the Ch'ing ("Pure").

The key figure in the Manchu conquest of China in 1644 was a Ming general, Wu San-kuei (1612–1678), who was a native of Liaotung. As the rebel Li Tzu-ch'eng (see page 209) approached Peking, the Ming emperor summoned Wu to the rescue. The capital fell before his arrival, however, and Li Tzu-ch'eng advanced against him. Instead of surrendering to a Chinese bandit rebel, Wu preferred to surrender to the Manchu, Dorgon, whose banners were waiting east of the pass. He did so and together they defeated Li, drove him from Peking and wiped him out. Thus the non-Chinese rebels on the frontier were able with Chinese assistance to eliminate the rebels within the country. Seizure of the throne proved easier from outside the Wall than from within. The Manchu state, in its defensible external base, had been able to develop as a rival imperial regime, while rebels within China had hardly been able to rise above the bandit level.

For three decades after the capture of Peking, Wu San-kuei helped install the Manchu dynasty while gaining great power for himself. He built up his own satrapy in Yunnan and Kweichow, developed his own trade monopolies, and yet milked the central Ch'ing treasury to support his armies. Two other satrapies were built up by Liaotung Chinese generals in Kwangtung and in Fukien. For many years South China thus remained under the Manchus' Chinese collaborators, whose local power rivaled that of Peking. When Wu rebelled against the Ch'ing in 1673, the other two satraps soon followed suit, in the so-called Revolt of the Three Feudatories (*San-fan*). This major civil war caught the nineteen-year-old K'ang-hsi emperor by surprise and threatened to oust the Manchu dynasty. It was not suppressed until 1681.

The last part of China to be taken over was the island of Taiwan, as it is known in both Chinese and Japanese, or Formosa ("The Beautiful"), as it was christened by the Portuguese. Although frequented by traders and pirates and colonized from Fukien, Taiwan had not been brought under Ming administration. From 1624 to 1662 the Dutch East India Company from Batavia (modern Djakarta) maintained several posts on the island. The last anti-Manchu resistance was maintained in Taiwan by Cheng Ch'eng-kung (1624–1662) and his family. This man's father had risen as an adventurer in maritime trade and piracy. He was in contact with the Portuguese at Macao (who baptized him a Christian), the Spanish at Manila, and the Japanese at Hirado, where he acquired a Japanese wife who bore him Cheng Ch'eng-kung. The son became a favorite of the refugee Ming court at Nanking and then at Foochow and received from it the imperial surname Chu and hence the popular title *Kuo-hsing-yeh* ("Lord of the Imperial Surname"), from which the Dutch derived "Koxinga." From 1646 to 1658 he controlled much of the Fukien coast, basing himself on the Amoy region, including Quemoy.

The Ch'ing tactics in dealing with Koxinga's maritime power were in

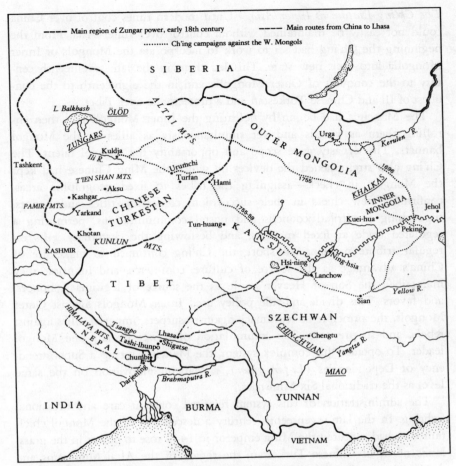

CENTRAL ASIA UNDER THE CH'ING (TO AROUND 1800)

the landbound tradition of the past. Echoing the Ming tactics toward Japanese pirates, they restricted foreign trade. Koxinga retaliated with a massive attempt to seize Nanking. Defeated, he descended on Taiwan in 1661 with some nine hundred ships and expelled the Dutch, who sent a fleet to help the Ch'ing against him in 1663–1664. After Koxinga's death, a son maintained his regime. The Ch'ing now resorted to a drastic policy of trying to force the population along the Chinese coast to evacuate the islands and move inland a distance of ten miles or more, behind a patrolled barrier, so as to cut Taiwan off from its mainland sources of manpower, food, and trading silk. The Taiwan regime was little damaged by these efforts, but finally became involved in supporting the Revolt of the Three Feudatories. After suppressing this, the Ch'ing occupied the island in 1683. Thus the Manchu conquest, in spite of the sudden success of 1644, actually occupied two generations, from 1618 to 1683.

The Ch'ing Empire in Inner Asia.   Until modern times control over China could not easily be maintained without control over Inner Asia. From the beginning the Ch'ing had set to work to incorporate the Mongols of Inner Mongolia into their new state. This led them in the late seventeenth century to the conquest of Outer Mongolia and in the eighteenth to the conquest of Ili and Chinese Turkestan and a protectorate over Tibet.

The Manchus had begun by defeating the Inner Mongols and then enrolling them as vassals and yet simultaneously as allies in the Mongol banners. The dynasty gave scope and opportunity for Mongol talent. The Ch'ing also strengthened the devices by which the Ming Chinese had kept the Mongols in check—assigning the tribes to fixed geographic areas, confirming new chiefs in their successsion, conferring titles and honors, supervising intertribal councils and postal communications, permitting a regulated trade at fixed markets, and bestowing the customary gifts on regular tribute missions. In short, the Ch'ing continued to make use of China's advantage as the source of culture, commerce, and luxuries; they maintained the Son of Heaven's role as the source of legitimacy, honors, and favors. This divide-and-rule policy used Inner Mongols against Outer Mongols, the principle of legitimacy against usurpers, imperial allies against rebels, and so prevented the accumulation of power by any one Mongol leader. To operate this complex system, the Manchus set up a Superintendency of Dependencies (*Li-fan yüan*), a Manchu innovation on the same level as the traditional Six Ministries.

The administration of this system required constant care and occasional fighting. In the late seventeenth century a descendant of the Mongol chieftain who had captured the Ming emperor in 1449 rose to power in the grasslands north of Chinese Turkestan, the region of the Altai Mountains and the Ili River valley, a common route of access to West Asia. This new leader was Galdan, khan of the Zungars, one of the tribes of the Western Mongols. Galdan had been educated as a lama at Lhasa, and he received valuable moral support from Tibet. In the 1670's he took over the oases and Muslim population of Chinese Turkestan as far east as Hami. Eventually he crossed Outer Mongolia and pillaged the Eastern Mongols as far as the Kerulen River. The K'ang-hsi emperor of the Ch'ing mobilized accordingly, and at length in 1696, like Yung-lo of the Ming, he personally led some eighty thousand troops in several columns to the Kerulen River. Galdan's power was destroyed in a great battle south of Urga, in which the Ch'ing use of artillery foreshadowed the end of a millennium of nomad cavalry power.

The final settlement came in the 1750's. After a long series of Mongol tribal rebellions, murders, usurpations, invasions, and migrations, Ch'ing forces occupied the Ili region three successive times in the years 1755–1757, practically wiped out the Zungars, and in 1758–1759 also sup-

CONQUESTS OF THE EMPEROR OF CHINA. *To celebrate the conquest of Ili and Chinese Turkestan, Emperor Ch'ien-lung had sixteen drawings by Catholic missionaries at Peking sent to Paris for copperplate engraving. This one (1772) shows a Manchu army camp in 1758. In the central pavilion the commander, with his officers on either side, receives a kneeling delegation, while wrestlers, lancers, and archers perform.*

pressed a Muslim rising in Chinese Turkestan and established control over Aksu, Yarkand, Kashgar, and the other oases. Following the precedent of the Han, T'ang, and Yüan, this was the fourth major period in which the Son of Heaven in China ruled over the Tarim basin as far as the Pamir massif.

Incorporation of Tibet in the Empire. In the process of subduing the Western Mongols, the Ch'ing rulers also had to establish their control over Tibet, because the Lamaist church centered at Lhasa had become a potent influence not only in Tibetan life but also among the Mongols. For several centuries the Tibetans had played a role on the periphery of the Chinese Empire. During the T'ang they emerged as a small but strong military power capable of making devastating raids into India or into China as far as Ch'ang-an. In the Yüan period the vogue of the Lamaist faith had spread rapidly among the Mongols (see pages 98, 111, and 169). The early Ming had regularly recorded tributary relations with Tibet, and Yung-lo in particular received Tibetan envoys, conferred titles, and confirmed appointments. During the Ming, however, a reform movement had arisen in the Tibetan church: one lama who did not come to China was Tsong-kha-pa (1357–1419), a great religious reformer who aimed at restoring monastic discipline within Tibetan Buddhism by such measures as enforcing celibacy and prescribing the various routines of meetings, confession, retreat, and other aspects of monastic life. His reform movement is generally known from the color of the vestments of its adherents as the Yellow Sect, as distinct from the older Red Sect. During the late Ming its influence spread over Mongolia, and so the Mongols became involved in the politico-religious competition between the established Red Sect of Lamaism and the new reforming Yellow Sect.

According to the Lamaist belief in reincarnation, Tsong-kha-pa's successors as head of the Yellow Sect were found in new-born infants. When his third successor went to Mongolia, a powerful prince of the Eastern Mongols gave him the impressive title of Dalai ("All-Embracing") Lama, and when he died there in 1588, his successor was found reincarnated in a Mongol baby. In this way the Eastern and Western Mongols and the two Tibetan sects all were drawn into religious power politics. The second dignitary in the Yellow Sect was the Tashi Lama, generally known as the Panchen Lama, of the great monastery called Tashi-lhunpo, west of Lhasa. A third figure emerged about 1600 as a permanent patriarch of the church in Outer Mongolia, the so-called "Living Buddha" (in Mongolian, *Hutukhtu*) at Urga, modern Ulan Bator.

Order was eventually imposed upon this Inner Asian field of religious politics when, first, the Dalai Lama became the temporal ruler of Tibet, and second, the Ch'ing rulers of China established a protectorate over him. Though long recognized as head of the Yellow Sect, the Dalai Lama achieved his temporal power in Tibet only by degrees and by making skillful use of Mongol and Manchu support. Even before the Manchu conquest of China, a Western Mongol tribe had intervened at Lhasa in 1641 on behalf of the Yellow Sect. It crushed the Red Sect supporters, unified the country under foreign Mongol rule, and put the fifth Dalai Lama (1617–1682) on his spiritual throne in Lhasa, where he rebuilt his great palace, the Potala.

When the K'ang-hsi emperor confronted the Western Mongols, he naturally regarded the Dalai Lama as one key to the control of Mongolia, where Lamaist monasteries were already absorbing large numbers of young men into the peaceful life of the church. The upshot of K'ang-hsi's concern was another Mongol intervention at Lhasa, with Ch'ing moral support, in 1705. This was followed by anti-Ch'ing counterintervention by the Zungar

CH'ING PATRONAGE OF LAMAISM. *Above: The Potala, the monastery or palace of the Dalai Lama at Lhasa, rebuilt by the Fifth Dalai Lama (1617–1682). Below: The miniature Potala erected by the Ch'ing emperors at their summer residence at Jehol (Ch'eng-te) north of Peking, as an aid in their relations with the Mongols as well as Tibet.*

tribe of the Western Mongols which in turn inspired in 1720 the first direct Ch'ing intervention in force. Soon a violent Tibetan civil war in 1727–1728 brought in a second Ch'ing army of fifteen thousand. The Dalai Lama's administration was now taken under the supervision of two Ch'ing imperial residents (*amban*) and a garrison. The third Ch'ing intervention was precipitated by a revival of Zungar intrigue and multiple murders in 1750. The Ch'ing solution to this breakdown of political control was to establish the Dalai Lama finally in a position of full temporal power under a continued Ch'ing protectorate. He ruled thenceforth through a council of four ministers under the supervision of the imperial residents and a Ch'ing garrison of fifteen hundred men. Thus after a good deal of trial and error, the political power in Tibet was firmly incorporated in that of the Ch'ing Empire.

Ch'ing Rule over China

The Preservation of Manchu Power. The Manchus' basic problem in China was to preserve themselves as a cohesive minority capable of keeping its grip on power. Since their numbers totaled at most 2 per cent of the population of their empire, this was a formidable task. They had to preserve their special status, privileges, and emoluments, keep themselves separate from the Chinese, and so maintain their racial consciousness and identity.

One method to maintain the ruling family's power was to build up its material resources. Its own revenues accumulated from extensive landholdings, special taxes, and investments rivaled the ordinary state revenues but were kept under separate and secret management of the Imperial Household Department. Such funds supported not only the palace but also the imperial clan, which was governed through a special office and organized in twelve main ranks from princes on down. The rank inherited by a son was one grade lower than that of his father, giving the son an incentive to prove himself. There was also the Manchu aristocracy, ranked in thirty-one grades of nobility, who received investiture and stipends from the throne.

The remainder of the Manchus were all bannermen, given land to till and also stipends, and exempted from Chinese local jurisdiction. For all the Manchus there was a ban on engaging in trade or labor, intermarrying with Chinese, or following Chinese customs. The traditional clan system was preserved and education in the Manchu language was compulsory. On the other hand, all Chinese were required to braid their hair in a queue and shave the rest of their heads like the Manchus, as a symbol of submission.

To preserve Manchu military control there were the banner forces. On the official rolls these grew from some 169,000 in 1644 to about 350,000 listed in the eighteenth century, although this listed strength was not maintained in practice. The banner forces were distributed in a network under Manchu generals-in-chief, whom Westerners called "Tartar generals." Garrisons were located in three sectors—first, twenty-five small posts around Peking; second, in strategic spots in the northwest against incursions from Central Asia; and third, in major Chinese centers of population (Chengtu, Nanking, Hangchow, Foochow, Canton), and at strategic spots in the South. The banner garrisons, of about 4000 men, were each set apart with their families in their own fortified residential quarter of a city, instead of being outside it like their Mongol predecessors of the thirteenth century.

The remnants of the Ming military system and additional Chinese levies were absorbed into a Chinese constabulary, the "Army of the Green Standard." In the late seventeenth century it totaled 594,000 men, and by the early nineteenth century 640,000 men in 1202 battalions, decentralized in scattered small units and posts. As a local police force designed to suppress banditry, its troops were seldom concentrated and never expected to have the offensive power of the bannermen. In general, the military command was carefully divided—between Chinese and Manchus, between the Ministry of War and troops at the capital and the garrisons in the provinces, and between the high civil and military officials all over the empire. Together with the meagre funds for army maintenance, this prevented the growth of any military power independent of the court.

As a major way of preserving themselves and their control of China, the Manchus also maintained their homeland as a base separate from Chinese life and culture. Sinification seemed to be overtaking them after the conquest: Manchus in China were learning the Chinese language, while Chinese from Liaotung were pushing northward in Manchuria. To stop this, north and central Manchuria were closed to Chinese immigration in 1668. The Willow Palisade (a ditch with willows planted along it, begun by the Ming) was extended several hundred miles from Shanhaikuan to the north of Mukden and then down to the Yalu, to mark the statutory limit of Chinese settlement. Most of Manchuria, with its hunting lands, forests, and streams, was thus preserved for the tribal peoples. One pecuniary motive in closing off this area came from the official ginseng monopoly. This theoretically medicinal root was gathered in the hills along the Ussuri and other streams and special officials annually sold licenses to some ten thousand ginseng collectors, following the general model of the salt monopoly system.

How could a limited number of Manchus rule a people some fifty times as numerous? Modern Chinese have felt humiliated by this historic fact. There are several lines of explanation. First, non-Chinese like the Manchus were as much a part of the great "Chinese" Empire of East Asia as were the Chinese themselves. The small "barbarian" Inner Asian component of this empire was specialized for fighting and for holding power. The Man-

MANCHU RULERS ON VACATION. *Beaters have maneuvered a stag into being fair game for the emperor's bow, while courtiers look on.*

chus were just numerous enough to provide the imperial clan, the top supervisors and the garrisons for an empire embracing both China and Inner Asia. Like Europeans in their nineteenth-century colonies, the Manchus bore the burden of governing and were also exhausted by it. Others have stressed a different aspect—that China under the Ch'ing was still ruled about 90 per cent by Chinese, that the Ch'ing regime was from the first not purely Manchu but a Manchu-Chinese synthesis, that the Manchu rulers stayed in power only by becoming as Chinese as their subjects.

These two views are not incompatible with each other, nor with a further consideration, that the Chinese state was an autocracy in which political life was monopolized by the bureaucracy so that the mass of Chinese had little to do with it in any case, no matter who was in power. The imperial government was superficial, confined to the upper layer of society, not present in the villages. The Chinese polity was a synthesis of state and culture. Its state sector was highly centralized while the culture was thoroughly diffused among the populace. The state could be dominated by an alien autocracy, while China's cultural life continued firmly rooted among the people.

The Ch'ing Administration.   In ruling China within the Wall, the Ch'ing altered the Ming administrative structure only to insert Manchu power and dynastic control into the established edifice. The three ingredients of Ch'ing rule were ultimate military force, kept in reserve; ultimate political power, exercised by the Son of Heaven; and Manchu supervision of Chinese collaborators in administration. The Manchu rulers from the first conciliated the Chinese upper strata of landlord-gentry families, local scholar-gentry leaders of community life, and Ming officials. Local landlords and administrators were generally let alone, providing they submitted. The Manchus raised no flag of social or agrarian revolution. On the contrary, they buried the Ming emperor with honors at Peking and claimed they had come to suppress the anti-Ming rebels and bring China peace and order. This persuaded most local officials in the North to accept the new dynasty. A leading example of this class was Hung Ch'eng-ch'ou (1593–1665), a metropolitan graduate who had risen to be Ming governor-general of five provinces. Transferred in 1639 to subdue the Manchus, he was captured by them and well treated. After Peking fell, he was made a Grand Secretary and from 1645 to 1659 Hung played a principal administrative role in mobilizing the resources needed for the Ch'ing campaigns in South China.

The Peking administration after 1644 became a Manchu-Chinese dyarchy. Of the six Grand Secretaries, three were Chinese and three Manchu. The Six Ministries each had two presidents, one Manchu and one Chinese, and four vice presidents, two Manchu and two Chinese. Since this produced a collegial body in place of one minister at the head, the Six Ministries under the Ch'ing have been called by Western writers the "Six Boards." Manchus (together with some Mongols) were similarly interlarded among Chinese at the top of the provincial administrations. In the early years primary reliance was placed on Chinese who were either bannermen or actually bondservants (originally household slaves) of the Manchus. The Ch'ing completed their system of dual control by appointing equal numbers of Manchus and Chinese to the Board of Censors. In the provinces fifty-six

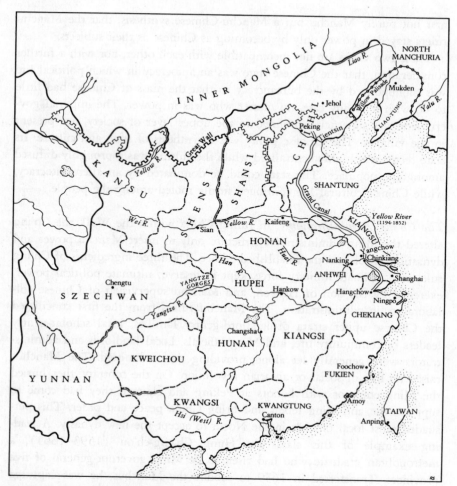

CHINA PROPER UNDER THE EARLY CH'ING (TO AROUND 1800)

censors were divided under fifteen circuits. Manchus and Chinese worked side by side. In general the dyarchy was made secure by using many Chinese bannermen loyal to the Ch'ing among the Chinese appointees.

The Ch'ing divided three of the fifteen Ming provinces to make a total of eighteen within the Wall. A single governor was now put over every province (except Chihli and Szechwan) on top of the territorial hierarchy—namely, county (*hsien*) magistrates, subprefects, prefects, intendants of circuit (or taotais), and the four heads of province-wide administrations, civil service, judiciary, examination system, and salt monopoly). A governor-general, often called "viceroy" by Europeans, was put over every two provinces, with some exceptions. Important business from all provinces that were under both a governor and a governor-general had to come to the emperor from the two officials jointly. Provinces were typically administered by a

Chinese governor and a Manchu governor-general working together. Each had his own troops, but the chief provincial force was usually of bannermen under a Manchu general.

The bracketing of Manchus and Chinese at first created a problem of interpretation and translation. The early Ch'ing regime was bilingual. Chinese interpreters, usually Chinese bannermen, were at first appointed to assist all high Manchu officials. Until its last days, the Ch'ing continued to go through the formality of elaborately translating Chinese documents at Peking into Manchu, but the need for bilingual procedures collapsed rather early, for the Manchus learned Chinese. The Manchu dictionary compiled under K'ang-hsi to help keep the language in use served chiefly to embalm it for posterity. Meanwhile, local government throughout the Ch'ing period was carried on in Chinese; local magistrates were almost all Chinese.

Ch'ing Absolutism. The gathering of power into the emperor's hands was a continuing tendency during the Yüan, Ming, and Ch'ing periods. Under the Ch'ing all important and many unimportant decisions, executive, legislative, and judicial, had to come from the emperor himself. A further step in this centralization of power in the emperor's person was taken under K'ang-hsi's successor Yung-cheng, who reigned from 1723 to 1736, and perhaps grew in part out of the circumstances of his accession to the throne.

K'ang-hsi from the age of thirteen had produced uncounted daughters and thirty-five sons, of whom twenty grew up. When the son who had been designated heir apparent grew mentally unbalanced, intrigue arose among his brothers over the succession. Yung-cheng became emperor by having military support on the spot at Peking when K'ang-hsi died and boldly announcing his own accession. It was rumored by the jealous opposition that he had disregarded his father's wishes, perhaps even killed him. At any rate, Yung-cheng took every means to safeguard his imperial power. Five of his brothers died in prison, and their supporters were victimized. He further divorced the imperial princes from control of the banner forces. He forbade the naming of an heir apparent, leaving the succession to the emperor's deathbed decision. Yung-cheng made widespread use of spies and secrecy in administration. He arranged that "palace memorials," a new type of document, should be opened only by himself and returned directly to the senders, so that he could get secret reports direct from trusted officials all over the empire.

The main Ch'ing addition to the Ming administrative machine was made in 1729 when Yung-cheng set up a Grand Council (*Chün-chi Ch'u*) as the top organ of policy decision. The Grand Secretariat (*Nei-ko*) continued to handle most routine business while the new Grand Council (literally, "Military Plans Office," sometimes called "Privy Council") worked directly with the emperor on urgent matters, using less formal documents and less complex procedures. Among the Grand Councilors, usually five or six, there were often two or three who were concurrently Grand Secretaries, providing some identity between the two bodies. The council met with the emperor every day at dawn. Its business was handled by thirty-two specially selected secretaries, half Manchu and half Chinese.

The emperor was a hard-working and hard-worked man. Yung-cheng wrote his personal comments on an inordinate mass of documents. Ch'ien-lung, during most of his long reign from 1736 to 1795, was equally conscientious. "Ten or more of my comrades," wrote one of the Grand Council secretaries, "world take turns every five or six days on early morning duty and even so would feel fatigued. How did the emperor do it day after day?"

The Unity of State and Culture.   The insertion of a Manchu controlling element into the inherited administration was only the first requirement for successful Manchu rule. The second was the wide recruitment of Chinese talent through the examinations. This ramified and exacting system of successively higher competitions winnowed out both the weak and the unorthodox. Under the Ch'ing, county (*hsien*) examinations, held two years out of every three, provided each time a total of about twenty-five thousand degree-holders at the lowest regular level. In the triennial examinations at provincial capitals, there were usually about fourteen hundred successful provincial graduates and something over two hundred successful metropolitan graduates (*chin-shih*) in the subsequent tests at Peking. The latter, normally in their mid-thirties, were the pick of the land, bearers of a title twelve hundred years old, and fit for appointment as county magistrates.

By presiding over the palace examinations at the summit of the system, the emperor personified a sage-teacher who rewarded assiduous and loyal scholars. Once admitted to the elite, scholar-officials still looked to their imperial master as the font of ethical instruction and the patron of learning and the arts. The real test for the Manchu emperors was whether they could become such patrons of Chinese scholarship that the state and culture would remain unified, under the sole headship of the Son of Heaven. To rule the Middle Kingdom called for cultural as well as political and military leadership.

Both these aspects of leadership were well typified by the K'ang-hsi emperor (reigned 1661–1722). Inheriting the throne at the age of seven, he began to rule in person at thirteen. By the time he was twenty-seven, he had met the crisis of the Revolt of the Three Feudatories and won an eight-year civil war (1673–1681). He led great armies into Mongolia (page 220) and fostered the warrior-huntsman tradition among the Manchus, building up his summer capital at Jehol, north of the Wall. As ruler of China he made six great tours to the south as far as the lower Yangtze

PEKING STREET SCENE. *From a scroll celebrating the K'ang-hsi emperor's birthday (1713). Note barrows, one-man and two-man carrying poles, Peking carts, shop lanterns, and pennants.*

provinces, the stronghold of the scholar-gentry. On these imperial progressions he devoted special attention to the efforts to check the flooding of the Huai and Yellow River systems and maintain the grain transport by canal to Peking. The sixteen moral maxims that he laid down in 1670, which became known as the *Sacred Edict,* were to be expounded semimonthly by officials and gentry in the villages to inculcate proper conduct.

K'ang-hsi's chief ideological success was with the Chinese scholar class. He was well-versed in the Classics himself and had strong intellectual interests. A number of leading scholars refused all cooperation with the Manchus, but in 1679 K'ang-hsi held a special examination to select the compilers of the *Ming History* and succeeded in getting 152 top scholars to take it, out of 188 whom he invited. He also selected Chinese scholars, calligraphers, and artists to serve within the palace. Important works were produced under his patronage, often with a preface by him. These included the famous *K'ang-hsi Dictionary,* an administrative geography of the empire, and the complete works of Chu Hsi. He also supported a massive encyclopedia, *Synthesis of Books and Illustrations of Ancient and Modern Times (Ku-chin t'u-shu chi-ch'eng),* a good deal larger than the *Encyclo-*

paedia Britannica. It was finally printed in five thousand volumes. Thus the Manchu emperor had become as ardent and magnificent a patron of scholarship as any Ming emperor had ever been.

Control over the local populace was not merely a physical matter of inculcating fear of punishments, but included cultural measures and a good deal of moral exhortation. There were the network of official granaries to control famine; the academies and local "schools" to spread classical learning; the system of official honors to be paid to the aged and virtuous; official sacrifices to local spirits; and official lecturers who expounded the *Sacred Edict.*

The mixture of Confucian and Legalist devices is best illustrated by the system of mutual responsibility for groups of neighboring families. As we have seen (pages 53–54 and 187), this originally Legalist institution was used by the Ch'in and had been inherited by the Han, Northern Wei, T'ang, and Sung with more variations in terminology than in practice. Known by Sung times as the *pao-chia* system, it was particularly suited to a static agrarian society rooted in the land. The Ming had used mutual responsibility within village units to maintain order by identifying all persons and encouraging neighbors to inform on all suspected evildoers.

The Ch'ing perfected the *pao-chia* structure. Ideally, one hundred households formed a *chia,* and ten *chia* a *pao.* The headmen of each were selected by the villagers, and could not be gentry. They became responsible for the local registry of population and for seeing that each household kept on its door placard the correct information as to who dwelt within. This was less a form of "self-government" than an officially imposed but unofficial arm of the state. Through it the government and local ruling elite used the family system for police purposes.

Culture in Late Imperial China

Scholarship: The School of "Empirical Research." The major fact confronting Chinese scholars of the seventeenth century was the failure of Chinese rule under the Ming and the re-emergence of "barbarian" conquerors. The dynastic change-over, occupying most of the century, raised many moral problems, such as how to uphold Confucian ideals against eunuch corruption at the late Ming court and whether to transfer one's loyalty from the old dynasty to the new. Scholars of the late Ming, who still worshiped the culture of T'ang and Sung and abominated the Mongol tyranny, were deeply disturbed by the repetition of alien conquest. They rejected any idea that the non-Chinese warrior peoples outside the Middle Kingdom could have an organic political function as potential holders of power over it. Many remained staunchly loyal to the Ming and refused to serve under the Manchus. Instead they held the traditional assumption that foreign aggression was made possible only by domestic disorder and they sought to discover the reasons for the moral decline which alone, they felt, had opened the door to "barbarian" invaders.

One leader in this new scholarship was Ku Yen-wu (1613–1682), a Ming loyalist who fought against the Manchus, was persecuted by personal enemies, and from about 1650 lived a life of intermittent travel and study. This took him widely over North China and brought him into intimate contact with problems of farming, trade, and banking, and even industry and mining. His travel notes and researches resulted in a major geographical work and also a widely-read collection of essays on many topics.

Refusing to serve the Ch'ing, Ku developed a trenchant thesis as to the cause of the Ming collapse. He blamed the sterile and abstract philosophizing of the dominant Ming school of Sung Neo-Confucianism—the so-called "Sung Learning" or "Rationalism" of Chu Hsi. He also attacked particularly the metaphysical branch of Neo-Confucianism, which had been further developed by the influential Wang Yang-ming (see pages 192–193). Ku correctly discerned in Wang's idealistic stress on intuition and self-cultivation the actual influence of Ch'an (Zen) Buddhism, rather than of the Classics. He attacked the routine acceptance of preconceived ideas which had resulted, and their propagation through the Four Books and the examination system as a prefabricated, orthodox interpretation of the Classics. This, he felt, had so confined Chinese thinking within set patterns that it had become incapable of facing political realities or of saving China from "barbarian" conquest. The "eight-legged essay" had done more harm, he claimed, than the First Emperor's burning of the books.

To remedy this intellectual failure of the Chinese scholar class, Ku advocated the pursuit of "knowledge of practical use to society." But this attack on the "Sung Learning" was by no means an attack on the Classics. To the contrary, Ku Yen-wu was the chief founder of the great Ch'ing school of Han Learning, which sought to restudy the classical inheritance by going back to writings of the pre-Sung period. The commentaries of the Han scholars, who had been closer in time to the sages and lacked the metaphysical preconceptions of Neo-Confucianism, were thought to be a more accurate reflection of the wisdom of the Classics. The Sung Learning, as the established orthodoxy now under attack, gave ground only slowly, but the fresh ideas of the Ch'ing period came mainly from adherents of the new Han Learning.

This new approach brought with it the use of the inductive method, assembling evidence from a broad range of sources, not from a few selected texts, and making new hypotheses to test against the evidence. This was applied first in the field of phonetics (studying the rhymes of ancient poetry to determine the ancient pronunciations) and led into broader studies of philology, etymology, and textual criticism. It was called the method of "empirical research" and greatly enlarged the subject matter of classical studies. Indeed, studies of this sort made it possible to determine the authenticity of ancient texts. One great scholar, for example, after studying the *Classic of Documents* for thirty years, proved by textual analysis and historical reasoning that the so-called "old text" of this venerated classic, accepted for over one thousand years and used in the official examinations, was really a forgery. Thus the Han Learning, through the many scholars who came after Ku Yen-wu, achieved a new critical mastery of the great corpus of Chinese classical literature.

This work has been hailed by some as a growth in premodern China of the scientific method, but this term can apply only to the limited field of literary studies, not to natural science and technology. The many protoscientific discoveries and inventions in China were associated more with the nature-loving Taoists than with the scholarly Confucians. The promising beginnings of nature lore in China were never consciously rationalized and institutionalized like modern science in the West. Ch'ing scholars continued to be divorced from the practical inquiries and manipulations of the workshop.

The Ch'ing reappraisal of Neo-Confucianism had its effect on formal philosophy. Tai Chen (1724–1777), for example, attacked Chu Hsi's dualism, which consisted of the two elements of form (*li*) and material stuff or ether (*ch'i*), as based on a misreading of the Classics. The Sung philosophers, having been misled by Taoist and Buddhist concepts, had accepted the *li* as transcendent, superimposed on man's physical nature, and setting proper limits to his physical desires. Instead, Tai Chen asserted that *li* is the immanent, internal structure of things, inherent in the processes of life, including the desires. He denied the Neo-Confucian contention that one can grasp the *li* through introspective meditation and achieve sudden enlightenment. Instead, he argued that the *li* exists objectively and can be grasped only through study, by "wide learning, careful investigation, exact thinking, clear reasoning, and sincere conduct." Although a few words cannot do justice to Ch'ing philosophy, it is plain that systematic thinkers like Tai Chen were modifying the great Sung tradition, not subverting it. Their contribution was still "change within tradition."

The Official Domination of Learning.   Much of the intellectual activity of the eighteenth century was carried on in the shadow of the imperial institution. Yung-cheng subsidized academies to give employment to scholars. Ch'ien-lung, who reigned from 1736 to 1795 and actually held power for sixty-three years, sponsored some fifty-seven large publications compiled by a host of learned editors. Ch'ing scholarship was dependent upon official life, even if indirectly. For example, Tai Chen, the son of a cloth merchant, found his livelihood mainly as tutor or editor in the homes of leading officials. He was one of the leading scholars appointed by Ch'ien-

IMPERIAL PATRONAGE OF LEARNING: THE FU-WEN ACADEMY.
*This woodcut shows the orderly arrangement of academy
buildings in a natural setting, on the Peak of Myriad Pines in the
Phoenix Mountains beside a lake in Chekiang. Subsidized by
Emperor Yung-cheng in 1733, the academy was visited by Emperor
Ch'ien-lung on his fourth southern tour, when he composed
poems for the scholars to match.*

lung in 1773 to compile a great imperial manuscript library called *The
Complete Library of the Four Treasuries* (*Ssu-k'u ch'üan-shu*), that is, the
four branches of literature—the Classics, history, philosophy, and belles-
lettres. This marked a high point in the tradition of bringing together a
number of works previously produced, sometimes on a common theme, and
republishing them as a collection. Ch'ien-lung's super-collection of the *Four
Treasuries* employed as many as fifteen thousand copyists and lasted nearly
twenty years. The compilers began by copying rare works from the great
Ming *Encyclopedia of the Yung-lo Period* (see page 190). But where the
Yung-lo collection had produced 11,095 manuscript volumes, the *Four
Treasuries* now comprised more than 36,000 volumes, containing about
3450 complete works. Seven manuscript sets were made. A printed cata-
logue gave comments on about 10,230 titles.

The emperor's domination of the Chinese learned world was demonstrated in the literary inquisition which for some fifteen years paralleled the compilation of the *Four Treasuries.* The searching out of all major writings afforded an opportunity to suppress objectionable works. Some 2300 works were listed for total suppression and another 350 for partial suppression. The aim was to destroy writings that were anti-Ch'ing or rebellious, that insulted previous "barbarian" dynasties, or that dealt with frontier or defense problems. All the works of certain authors, even inscriptions by them on monuments, were destroyed, as were works that seemed heterodox in general, or merely unliterary. "Although there is nothing that shows evidence of treason in this work," wrote the censors in one case, "still the words are in many cases lying nonsense, fishing for praise. It should be burned." This literary despotism may be illustrated by one case among many, that of an unfortunate dictionary-maker who disrespectfully printed in full the forbidden characters for the personal names of Confucius and the Ch'ing emperors. He and twenty-one members of his family were arrested and sent to Peking. He was executed; two sons and three grandsons were sent into slavery.

The Cultured Life.   In pre-empting intellectual talent for official projects, the Ch'ing government drew upon the gentry class. The common people did not bulk large in the cultural record. For them, Taoism and Buddhism still supplied the principal explanations of the cosmos, and the family and village still were the focus of their lives. But it is not yet possible to reconstruct the daily life of the Chinese villager in the premodern centuries. We know most about the ruling class who lived off the peasantry usually as landlords. They were an educated, urban upper class, who had the means and leisure to enjoy their own private gardens or collections of *objets d'art,* and practice their own calligraphy and painting. They also, without boasting about it, read novels and joined the city crowd at the theater. Porcelains from the imperial kilns at Ching-te-chen in Kiangsi, which reached their height of perfection with Ming blue-and-white and Ch'ing polychrome wares, were of course prized by Chinese connoisseurs long before they became a European vogue. These inheritors of the great cultural tradition were first of all collectors, connoisseurs, and critics, with a strong antiquarian interest. Their amateur ideal was a natural result of their classical education. Their purpose was humanistic, to perceive the principles and proper values of the tradition.

This life of culture, though widespread, centered in the commercial cities of the lower Yangtze delta, in direct descent from the Southern Sung. Hangchow was famous for its beautiful West Lake, its wooded hills, and many temples. Soochow women were the empire's most beautiful. The proverb went, "Above is paradise; here below, Soochow and Hangchow."

One major avocation of cultivated men was painting, in which the trends already well established in the Ming period were continued in the Ch'ing. The names of over one thousand Ming painters have come down to us and of course many more from the Ch'ing. The Ming emperors patronized artists, and Hsüan-te (who ruled from 1426 to 1435) was himself a talented painter. One conservative style followed the landscape painting of the Southern Sung, with the misty distances, the angular pine trees, and broken cliffs of masters like Ma Yüan and Hsia Kuei. Another community of painters centered at Soochow. The amateur ideal of these scholar-gentlemen-artists was expressed by the wealthy critic Tung Ch'i-ch'ang (1555–1636), who summed up the view that painting together with poetry and calligraphy were the highest expressions of the human spirit, reflecting man's communion with the forces of nature. Mastery of technique and the taste to avoid the vulgar or sentimental both had to be gained through close study of the old masters. This view combined the appreciation of nature with the study of tradition. The artist paid minute attention to method. The famous seventeenth-century *Mustard Seed Garden Painting Manual,* for example, illustrated the painter's vocabulary of techniques. Tung and his fellow critics appraised and classified the whole inheritance of Chinese painting. Under the Ch'ing, private collections were absorbed into the palace at Peking, where Ch'ien-lung, with great zeal if not taste, made an imperial collection of some eight thousand paintings.

Chinese painting is only the most obvious of the humanistic arts that embody the spirit of Taoism and Buddhism rather than Confucianism. The institutions of political and economic organization, so heavily stressed in this volume, formed the framework of Chinese life but by no means summed it up. The public scene was dominated by the Sage, to be sure, but not the private thoughts of most individuals. Consequently, the day-to-day life of the upper class may be approached more closely through some of the books they read for amusement.

Literature.   One widely read work was *Strange Stories from a Chinese Studio* by P'u Sung-ling (1640–1715), which continued the T'ang tradition of tales of the marvelous and supernatural. Consider, for example, the typical story of a lonely young man visited alternately by two beautiful girls, each more eager than the other to please him in every way, who turn out, after he is nearly dead from exhaustion, to be actually a ghost in human form and a fox-fairy (fox-fairies are mischievous creatures who live as foxes in their holes but often appear among mankind in the form of beautiful women). In such a story neither the situation nor the action is in the Confucian vein, to say nothing of the actors. But since the author wrote in a classical style with a wealth of literary allusions, it was intelligible only to the educated elite, with whom it was actually very popular.

CH'IEN-LUNG AS A CHINESE RULER. *Surrounded by a scholar's*
objets d'art, *the emperor is shown with his portrait.*

For a broader public, the vernacular novels supplied a wealth of fiction,
romantic in theme and realistic in detail. The plots derived in part from the
late Sung and Yüan, but most of the great novels were written during the
Ming. One of the most popular, *Shui-hu chuan* (translated as *All Men Are
Brothers* and as *Water Margin*), originated in legends concerning a bandit
who lived about 1121. With thirty-six companions he probably had his lair
in a great marsh near the juncture of the Yellow River and the Grand
Canal. Professional storytellers developed the exploits of this band in a
narrative interspersed with verses to be sung by the raconteur. Playwrights
of the Yüan also used these themes. Several story sequences were recorded
about 1300 in a prompt-book by members of the storytellers' guild. By this
time the bandits had become "faithful and just" heroes, champions of the
oppressed common people, victimized by evil and corrupt officials, and
their number had grown to 108. *Shui-hu chuan* in its final written form was
the work of several authors in succession and was a truly popular novel,
developed gradually in response to public taste during several centuries—
an example of the extensive literature of protest which the Confucian system called forth but tried to ignore. (See page 176.)

The first great realistic novel, created by a single (although still unknown) author, was *Chin P'ing Mei* (translated as *Golden Lotus*), written in the late Ming. Its story of the pursuit of pleasure in an everyday urban life avoids overtones of popular legend, heroic adventure, or the supernatural, and treats women characters convincingly as individuals. Its value as a reflection of social manners and family life is not obscured by the fact that it is also pornographic.

The Chinese family system has its greatest monument in *The Dream of the Red Chamber* (*Hung-lou meng*) by Ts'ao Hsüeh-ch'in, whose forebears had grown rich in the service of the Manchus. The founder of the family had been captured by the Manchus and enslaved as a bondservant under the imperial household. His descendants held lucrative posts so that Ts'ao's grandfather was wealthy enough to play host to K'ang-hsi on four of his southern tours. He was both a calligrapher and writer and also a patron of literature who printed fine imperial editions of T'ang poetry. Small wonder that his debts survived him! The Yung-cheng emperor collected some of these debts owed to the imperial court by confiscating the family property in 1728. At the time the household comprised 114 persons, including servants, with some thirteen residences in Nanking and about 300 acres of land. Ts'ao lived meagerly with his early memories of this vanished household. He portrayed in his novel, written mainly in the 1750's, the varieties of personality and of incident, the strengths and weaknesses of character, which attended the gradual decline of a well-to-do gentry family. The frustrated love story of two cousins forms only the most tragic of several interwoven themes.

While the professional storytellers' tales in the marketplace had gradually been developed by talented writers into the vernacular (*pai-hua*) novels, the drama remained less developed and less widely read as literature. Its combination of singing, dancing, violent action, and earthy humor left little chance for the few spoken lines of the libretto to develop into a literary form of interest to the scholar class.

Present-day impressions of the culture of late imperial China will be modified as studies of these five-and-one-half centuries approach the thoroughness and detail already achieved in studies of the same centuries in Japan. Yet our overall impression of the Ming and Ch'ing is of a rich culture so firmly imbedded in its inherited tradition that it is more critical than creative and, in some cases, even repetitive and decadent. In architecture, for example, the grandeur of the palace buildings at Peking derives from an ancient and well-proved formula—white marble terraces, red pillars and beams supporting massive gold-tiled roofs. Under the broad eaves the beams are brilliantly colored, yet their construction betrays the decadence of the architectural style. T'ang and Sung buildings had carried the weight of the heavy tiled roof down to the pillars through a complex series of large wooden brackets. The large, twin-armed brackets of the

T'ang style, still visible at Nara in Japan, were both functional and decorative, lending rhythm and grace to the wooden construction by which an imposing roof was supported on a few columns. By Ming and Ch'ing times, however, the brackets had become smaller and more numerous, set in a continuous series and performing no more function than a cornice—in short, vestigial ornaments instead of important structural components.

The Beginning of Dynastic Decline

Military Deterioration.   Certain preliminary signs of decline had appeared by 1800 in at least three forms—military ineffectiveness of the banner forces, corruption at the top of the bureaucracy, and difficulties of livelihood among a greatly increased population. The banner forces which had dominated continental East Asia for almost two centuries were losing their vigor. Under Ch'ien-lung, the Ten Great Campaigns were much celebrated in the official annals, yet most of them were in a different category from the early Manchu conquests.

The Ten Great Campaigns included three already mentioned—two against the Zungars and the pacification of Turkestan, strategic achievements of the 1750's which enlarged the area of Ch'ing control in Central Asia. But the other seven campaigns were more in the nature of police actions on frontiers already established—two wars to suppress rebels in Szechwan, another to suppress rebels in Taiwan (1787–1788), and four expeditions abroad to chastise the Burmese (1766–1770), the Vietnamese (1788–1789), and the warlike Gurkhas in Nepal on the border between Tibet and India (1790–1972), the last counting as two. Ch'ien-lung's generals, almost all Manchus, led busy lives. For example, Fu-k'ang-an (died 1796) commanded forces in Szechwan, Kansu, Taiwan, and against the Gurkhas. To fight the Gurkhas, who had invaded Tibet, he led an army over a thousand miles across the roof of the world in 1792 and drove the invaders back through the Himalayan passes into their homeland of Nepal, which thereafter sent tribute to Peking every five years until 1908.

All these later campaigns took place on the periphery of the empire, were conducted by a group of professional Manchu generals, and required large expenditures of funds, often through the hands of these generals. For example, the rebels in the mountains on the Szechwan-Yunnan border, although they totaled fewer than thirty thousand households, built thousands of stone forts in the rocky defiles of their homeland and were eventually dislodged only with cannon. The second campaign against them took five years and seventy million taels of silver, equal to more than two years of the cash revenues normally received at Peking. Until the mid-Ch'ing campaigns are thoroughly studied, we can only speculate as to the corrupt pecuniary motives that may have played a part in their prosecution. The large alloca-

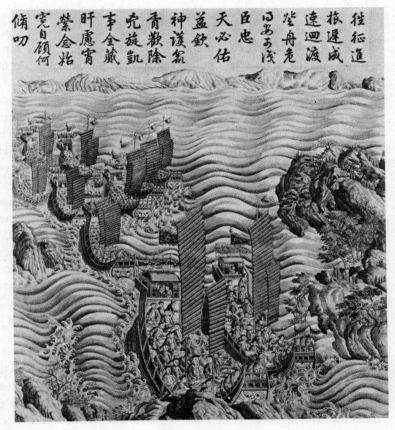

備叨　寬自顧何　縈念怗　旰應宵　事全臧　尤旗凱　膚歡除　神護氣　益欽　天必佑　臣忠　㠯安吾淺　登舟免　速迴渡　振遲咸　往征進

The great Manchu general, Fu-k'ang-an, invading Taiwan to suppress a Triad Society rebellion, 1787. Emperor Ch'ien-lung's autographed poem celebrates the victory.

tions of imperial funds necessary in each case may have created a vested interest in the prolongation of operations. Fu-k'ang-an, we know, was not only governor-general over various provinces continuously from 1780 to 1795, but also a henchman of Ho-shen (1750–1799).

Ho-shen was the classic type of evil courtier, reminiscent of infamous eunuchs of earlier times. His rise was a symptom of the emperor's senescence. With great prudence the Manchus had succeeded in forestalling the rise of most of the evils which had beset the leadership of earlier dynasties. Imperial princes, military commanders on the frontier, new "barbarian" invaders, great landed families entrenched in the provinces, eunuchs at the court, empresses and their relatives, even factionalism among the officials— all had been sedulously guarded against, so that the centralized power of the state might remain undiminished in the emperor's hands. The one thing that could not be prevented was the aging of the emperor himself. When

Ch'ien-lung was sixty-five he became much impressed by a handsome twenty-five-year-old bodyguard, a clever and unscrupulous Manchu who became his favorite and chief minister and plundered the state for the next twenty years. Ho-shen rose like a meteor in one year from the fifth rank to Grand Councilor. Thereafter he got his hands on the principal posts in charge of revenue and personnel, betrothed his son to the emperor's youngest daughter, and entrenched himself in as many as twenty different positions at a time. He built up his clique of similarly corrupt henchmen all over the empire and levied a squeeze upon the whole officialdom. The private wealth attributed to him by his enemies after his fall was alleged to be worth some one-and-a-half billion dollars.

With Ho-shen leading the way at Peking, we can more easily understand how military corruption went hand-in-hand with its civilian counterpart. The banner forces became gradually ill-supplied, poorly trained, and demoralized. Officers and troops on stipends were both under the pressure of rising prices. Impoverished bannermen who tried to subsist on rice stipends in their garrisons were forced to become artisans, petty traders, or evildoers to eke out a living. Finally, after more than a century of comparative peace within China, the deterioration of the Manchu military machine was startlingly exposed in a big peasant rebellion.

The White Lotus Rebellion. In the mountainous border region bounded by Hupei, Szechwan, and Shensi, the relatively inaccessible area between the upper waters of the Han River and the Yangtze gorges, a great uprising, called the White Lotus Rebellion, occurred during the years 1796–1804. Here a migration of poor settlers from the crowded lowlands had created new communities on infertile mountain soil, on the margin of subsistence. Though encouraged by the government, this immigration had not been accompanied by an equal extension of civil administration, communications, or military control. The expression of discontent, evidently aroused by the exactions of petty tax collectors, was led by men who claimed the mantle of the ancient White Lotus Society (see page 179), a religious cult that had been active in the late Yüan and Ming periods. It now promised its followers the advent of the Buddha, the restoration of the Ming, and personal salvation from suffering in this world and the next. Once started, the rebellion became violently anti-Manchu, but it achieved no further ideological development and did not create a government administration or claim a dynastic title. During its early years the rising was an inconclusive contest between ill-organized bands of rebels and inefficient imperial forces who struggled for control of the mountain villages and thus of the sinews of local military power—the supplies of men and food. However, the corrupt administration dominated by Ho-shen, who held power until the retired Ch'ien-lung emperor died early in 1799, hamstrung the military effort.

The suppression of the White Lotus Rebellion, after both sides had harassed the local scene for several years, showed many classic features. The first requirement was to restore discipline and morale to the banner forces. This became possible after the Chia-ch'ing emperor came into effective power in 1799 and supported more vigorous Manchu commanders. A systematic program was also pursued of "strengthening the walls and clearing the countryside," that is, collecting the farming populace in hundreds of walled or stockaded villages and removing all food supplies from the open fields. The local manpower, thus concentrated, was organized into garrisons of self-defense corps paid and fed partly by the government. Recruitment of this militia was made easier by the devastation and poverty that the rebellion had brought. Some militia were also trained as a striking force to pursue the rebels. With its campaign of pursuit and extermination, the government combined a policy of conciliation, trying to split followers from leaders by offering amnesty to the rank and file who surrendered and putting a price on the heads of rebel commanders. The Ch'ing suppression thus was many-sided, starving the rebels of food and new recruits, organizing military strength among the villages, and encouraging desertion from the rebel ranks. This program was eventually effective, and the banner forces, after their initial failure, somewhat redeemed themselves. But the Manchu fighting man had lost his reputation for invincibility. The government's victory, such as it was, was really due to its use of some three hundred thousand local militia, whom the government subsequently had to try to disarm.

Population Growth.   Behind this popular rising at the turn of the century lay an era of unparalleled domestic peace, prosperity, and population increase. The growth of numbers, however, eventually destroyed both the prosperity and the peace which had made it possible. The official population estimates record a year-by-year increase from 142 million in 1741 to 432 million in 1851. Such an increase might be possible in a new country where immigration and industrialization were both at work, but in an ancient and thickly populated agricultural state like early modern China such figures are amazing.

The ritualistic, rather than statistical, nature of the Ch'ing population figures seems evident from the way they were compiled and reported. From 1741 this was done by the *pao-chia* headmen in the villages. Population figures recorded on the door placards of each household were only one of their many concerns. They also had to report on local irregularities of all sorts—such as burglary, gambling, harboring criminals, illegal coinage, illicit sale of salt, gang activities, or the presence of strangers. Moreover, procedures were neither uniform nor reliable for reporting births, deaths, females, children, non-Chinese minority peoples, and migrants. Premodern

China did not, in short, achieve a modern census. On the contrary, annual reporting of population figures became routinized and ritualized. Some provinces reported regular increases year after year, often a fixed percentage, say 0.3 or 0.5 per cent, over the previous year. As Ch'ien-lung remarked, "The number increases the same year after year. This is absurd."

This literary nature of the Ch'ing figures suggests that the steep curve of increase should be flattened out, that the Chinese population was greater at the beginning and probably less at the end of the Ch'ing period than the figures indicate. For example, the totals of population estimated in the Ming do not exceed 60 million, the figure reached by the Han dynasty some fifteen hundred years earlier. We may guess that the Ming population actually approached 150 million by 1600 and this total was inherited by the Ch'ing. In the early eighteenth century came an important administrative change that combined the head tax and the land tax and decreed that the quotas of these taxes to be collected in the provinces should remain fixed forever at the levels of 1711. This may have reversed the incentives in the estimating of population totals. Where formerly an official in charge of an area might have held his estimates down to avoid raising his tax quota, normally set according to population and land totals, now he might aim to please the throne by reporting a prosperous increase of the people under his care. Imperial demands for careful reporting called forth great increases. By 1800 the total population may have been about 300 million, rather than the 350 million reported to the emperor.

Even so, this was an extraordinary growth in an ancient farming country where industrialization had not yet commenced. Historians have accounted for it mainly by citing the domestic peace and order of the eighteenth century and the increase of food supply through cultivating more land and planting faster-ripening types of rice. In ancient times, after transplanting from nursery beds into paddy fields, rice had required about 150 days to reach maturity. Importation and development of earlier-ripening varieties from Champa (in what is now South Vietnam) had gradually reduced this growing time to 100, then to 60, 40, and, in the nineteenth century, even 30 days. This made possible double- and even triple-cropping. Another factor was the use of new food crops. Maize, sweet potatoes, tobacco, and peanuts all were introduced into China from the Americas in the sixteenth or early seventeenth century. The sweet potato became the poor man's food of South China, for it could be grown on sandy soil, useless for rice, and provided more food energy per unit of land than most crops. Other factors in population growth presumably lay in the area of hygienic practices affecting public health, in the increase of foreign trade and of handicraft production and trade attending it, and in other domestic economic developments as yet unexplored.

Whatever the causes of China's demographic growth, it was not paralleled by comparable growth of the Ch'ing administration. The populace may have doubled, but not the official class and its services for the people, nor the military forces which maintained peace and order. On the contrary, the Ch'ing government in all its aspects seems to have grown less effective just at a time when its domestic problems were increasing. The two developments were of course interrelated. Bad government and unsolved problems exacerbated each other in a vicious downward spiral, such as China's long history had seen so often before. This time, however, because of new factors from abroad, the process was to culminate during the late nineteenth and early twentieth centuries in an unprecedented crisis for the whole traditional system of government and society. The process was complicated, some say "distorted," by the intrusion of the West.

Early Western Contact

The expansion of Europe is an oft-told tale. In the parochial Western perspective, the Europeans going out to conquer the globe in early modern times were impelled by their superior culture, which stemmed from the Greco-Roman and Judeo-Christian traditions and created the modern European nations. Europeans trace the rise of their modern power to the growth of towns after the Dark Ages that were contemporary with the glory of T'ang. They stress the influence of the Crusades, the growth of a merchant class, the commerce of Venice and Genoa with the eastern Mediterranean, and the Italian-Iberian rivalry to control the spice trade from the Indies. In a Chinese perspective, the Europeans on their northwest Eurasian peninsulas seem have-not peoples, too far north (between 35 and 55 degrees) to produce much rice, sugar, tea, or cotton and so impelled to trade and drawn like many barbarians before them to the Middle Kingdom.

From any point of view, it is plain that China under the T'ang and Sung and right down to Marco Polo's day was a far greater civilization in both size and accomplishment than its contemporary, medieval Europe. As one index, consider how the main flow of influences over the long course of history had been from China to Europe, not the other way: first, the silk trade across Central Asia to Rome, then the great series of inventions emanating from China—paper and printing that spread literacy, porcelain (chinaware) so easy to keep hygienically clean, the crossbow used by the Han armies, cast-iron, canal lock-gates, the wheelbarrow, the stern-post rudder to steer ships at sea, the compass to navigate them, gunpowder, and all the rest. This material technology was paralleled by the Chinese primacy in the methods of bureaucratic government, including civil service examinations, to say nothing of such arts as painting. In short, the expansion of the Europeans reflected not only their greed, curiosity, zeal and patriotism but also in some ways their backwardness.

Portuguese adventurers, from a tiny nation of perhaps one and a half million persons, set the tone for Sino-European relations. After rounding Africa in 1498, they took Malacca on the Malay Peninsula in 1511 and by 1514 reached the southeast coast of China, where only pirates, like those from Japan, had previously caused trouble. Their assertion of equality with the Chinese seemed unjustified. Many arrived in Chinese junks with Chinese pilots. Most Europeans of the time were unaccustomed to daily bathing, and they commonly emerged from their cramped and fetid ships' quarters not only with more body hair than most Asians but also with more body odor.

The first Portuguese explorers in China's waters accomplished little to prove Europe's cultural equality. In 1517 the Portuguese sent an embassy from the "King of Portugal" to the "King of China." On reaching Canton the mission fired a salute of cannon in proper Western style, which outraged the Chinese sense of etiquette and required an immediate apology. The envoys were housed in the office of the Superintendent of Trading Ships, like any tribute mission, and were taken to Peking in the usual Chinese manner. Meanwhile other Portuguese built an island fortress outside the Canton River mouth and mounted cannon in *their* usual fashion. Hindering trade and flouting Chinese law, these semipirates were accused of robbery, blackmail, and buying Chinese children from Chinese kidnappers. All Portuguese were expelled from Canton in 1522, and their first envoy died in prison there. Not until mid-century did they get local Chinese permission to base their trade on the small peninsula of Macao. The peninsula was walled off by Chinese authorities, who continued (until 1887) to collect land and customs taxes while letting the Portuguese run their own local government. Meanwhile in late Ming times the Portuguese in Asia were generally eclipsed by the Dutch, who took Malacca in 1641 but devoted their main effort to the East Indies.

The Jesuit Success Story. The Europeans met the Chinese on two fronts —trade and evangelism—but the religious contact was at first more active than the commercial. During the Ming decline and Ch'ing conquest, a handful of Jesuit missionaries became versed in Chinese culture, secured the patronage of high officials, and gained court positions at Peking.

The greatest of these Jesuit pioneers, Matteo Ricci (Chinese name, Li Ma-tou; 1552–1610), was assigned to China in 1582. Ricci was an Italian of impressive personality, tall and vigorous, with a curly beard, blue eyes, and a bell-like voice. Guided by their experience in India and Japan, where they gained admittance earlier than in China, Ricci and his colleagues accommodated their message to the local scene. In China as in Japan they worked from the top down, appealing to the upper-class elite. They adopted Chinese forms as far as possible, avoiding all open connection with the

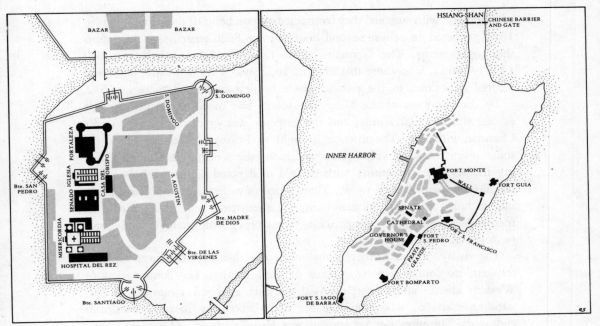

LEFT: THE PORTUGUESE STRONGHOLD AT MALACCA.
RIGHT: MACAO IN THE 1840'S.

Portuguese traders at Macao. They soon abandoned the Buddhist monk's costume for the Confucian scholar's gown. Instead of preaching, they held conversations with Chinese scholars, arousing their curiosity with demonstrations of prisms, clocks, and geographic knowledge. Above all they became fluent in Mandarin, or standard North Chinese, and literate in the Chinese Classics. This enabled Ricci to represent Christianity as a system of wisdom and ethics compatible with Han Confucianism.

By 1601 Ricci, like a Chinese man of talent, had secured the patronage of high officials and was able to establish his residence at Peking. When he presented two clocks and a clavichord, which caught the emperor's fancy, he and his colleagues were brought into the palace to show how these mechanisms operated. Ricci finally got himself out of the category of tribute-bearer and was given an imperial stipend as a scholar. Within a few years he and his colleagues had made some two hundred Christian converts, including even ministers of state.

Ricci's successors found that they could make themselves most useful by applying their Western knowledge of astronomy to the revision of the Chinese calendar. The Son of Heaven had a special responsibility to maintain a calendar which would accurately foretell the positions of the heavenly bodies and the timing of the seasons—no easy matter. In the astronomical bureau at Peking, the Muslim astronomers, as well as the old-style Chinese astronomers with whom they competed, were behind the times and in 1610 predicted an eclipse several hours wrong. Such errors gave the Jesuits their opportunity. The German Jesuit, Johannes Adam Schall von Bell (1591–1666), who came to China in 1622, was a trained astronomer and secured a position in the palace, where he first celebrated mass in 1632.

By the last years of the Ming, the Jesuits had made numerous converts among the imperial family, and the emperor was gradually coming under Christian influence. The mission brought to Peking a Western library of some seven thousand volumes on which to base writings in Chinese. During the seventeenth century with the aid of devoted Chinese scholars they produced some 380 such works. These writings were mainly on Christianity, but included treatises on astronomy, mathematics, geography, medicine, meteorology, mechanics, pharmacology, anatomy, zoology, logic, and European government and education.

The decay of the Ming regime made the dynasty, for many Chinese scholars, no longer a worthy focus of their loyalty. The combination of Western science and Christian moral teaching attracted a number of outstanding converts, who were capable of collaborating in truly bicultural endeavors. The most famous convert was Hsü Kuang-ch'i (Christian name, Paul Hsü; 1562–1633), who became a Christian even before he passed the highest examination and entered the Hanlin Academy in 1604. With Ricci he completed the translation of the first six books of Euclid's geometry. Hsü was made a Grand Secretary in 1632. He gave the missionaries an entrée into high official circles and helped them to present Christianity through Chinese writings that had literary polish. Both Paul Hsü and Adam Schall also helped the Ming court obtain Western arms. To fight off the Manchus, Schall in 1636 set up a foundry and cast some twenty big guns. Western technology, in short, gained acceptance more readily than Western religion.

After the Manchu conquest of 1644, the Ch'ing kept Schall as chief astronomer. The young emperor for several years saw much of him, called him "grandpa," and permitted the building of a Christian church at Peking. During the middle decades of the long reign of K'ang-hsi the Jesuit mission at Peking reached the height of its influence. The missionaries enjoyed intimate contact with the emperor, seeing him sometimes almost daily. They once gave him a new drug, "Jesuit's bark" or quinine, and were commissioned to survey and map the Chinese Empire using Western methods. Their position was that of courtiers to the emperor, performing the kowtow with complete servility like other officials, displaying knowledge with finesse, presenting gifts and making friends at court.

Sino-European Cultural Relations. The Jesuits were pioneers in contact between two great cultures. Facing two ways, they eventually suffered

THE JESUITS IN PEKING AS DEPICTED IN EUROPE. *1. Ricci and his chief convert. Left: "Fr. Matteo Ricci of Macerata, of the Society of Jesus, the first propagator of the Christian Religion in the Kingdom of China." Right: "Paul Li {error for Hsü}, Great Colao {i.e., Grand Secretary} of the Chinese, propagator of the Christian Law."*

2. Fr. Adam Schall with his astronomical instruments. Director of the Imperial Board of Astronomy, he wears on his cap the colored button and on his gown the "mandarin square" of a Ch'ing civil official. Illustrations published in 1673.

attack on both fronts. Significantly, however, the main attack came from their European competitors.

Europe, having initiated the contact with China, received at first the greater impact from it. The image of China conveyed through the influential Jesuit writings from Peking figured in the Enlightenment as an example of an ancient society which had a natural morality quite independent of revealed religion. In the philosophical debate over the relationship between morality and religion, the China depicted by the Jesuits was cited approvingly by Voltaire and the Deists, and also by the Physiocrats. Eighteenth-

EMPEROR CH'IEN-LUNG RECEIVES MONGOL HORSES. *Painted by the Jesuit lay brother G. Castiglione (Chinese name: Lang Shih-ning, 1688–1766), who reached Peking in 1715 and was court painter to three emperors.*

JESUIT ARCHITECTURE AT CH'IEN-LUNG'S SUMMER PALACE. *This European engraving (ca. 1786) of the Hall of Peaceful Seas (Hai Yen T'ang) shows Chinese-style tile roof surmounting pilasters and "Chinese rococo" details, combined with Western perspective and staircases reminiscent of an Italian villa.*

century Europe enjoyed a vogue of things Chinese, not only an idealized image of rational Confucian ethics and benevolent despotism in government but also a craze for *chinoiserie*, the Chinese style in architecture, porcelain, furniture, and decoration.

At Peking the Jesuits continued to serve the emperor as astronomers, interpreters, cartographers, painters, engravers, architects, and engineers— the first technical experts from West to East. At the old summer palace near Peking, the Yüan Ming Yüan, they designed baroque buildings and banks of fountains for a miniature Versailles, as part of a minor European vogue at the court. But the Jesuits were primarily missionaries, and their effort to apply the universal principles of Christianity to the concrete realities of China led them into the path of cultural accommodation—in short, Sinification. Accommodation in fact had been the secret of the Jesuit success in Asia generally. In China, as Paul Hsü put it, Christianity "does away with Buddhism and completes Confucianism." Christian faith could be added to Confucian practice. The cornerstones of this position were the acceptance of the Confucian canon in its textual form in the Classics as "ancient wisdom"; the rejection of much of the great corpus of Chinese interpretation and comment upon the Classics, constituting principally what we now call Neo-Confucianism, as unsound and misguided; and an attack upon Taoism and Buddhism as idolatry.

This Jesuit compromise did not go unchallenged by missionaries in the field. Should the ritual performed in veneration of ancestors before the family altar be regarded merely as a "civil rite" and therefore permissible to Christians, or was it really "pagan worship," which could not be allowed? What about the state cult of Confucius and a magistrate's prayers for rain? To many theologians it seemed plain that the Jesuits' compromises went too far, that in making Christianity acceptable to Chinese classical scholars the early Jesuits had destroyed its essential monotheistic articles of faith. Since the pagan world, after all, had no idea of the true God as a spiritual substance, its classical expressions could not be used to describe Him.

By the 1640's the controversy over the rites to be permitted had been referred to Rome by mendicant friars of the Dominican and Franciscan orders from the Philippines who got a foothold in Fukien. They had an utterly different approach to mission work, based on their experience in less culturally resistant lands like Mexico and the Philippines, where there were no powerful local bureaucracies to prevent a direct and uncompromising evangelism among the common people. Consequently they followed the order of poverty and preached in the streets, disregarding most of the lessons the Jesuits had learned. By 1701 there were in China fifty-nine Jesuits, twenty-nine Franciscans, eighteen Dominicans, fifteen secular priests, mainly from the French Society for Foreign Missions, and six Augustinians. The Jesuits alone had 70 mission residences and 208 churches or chapels.

The total Christian community was estimated at 300,000, but its leadership was split. The "Rites Controversy" boiled along for a full century (ca. 1640–1742), both within and between the various orders and missions in China and their supporters in Europe, eventually even between the Pope and the Ch'ing emperor.

The Confucian scholars' hostility to Christianity, meanwhile, was based on several points of view—rational skepticism about such doctrines as original sin, the virgin birth, and the divinity of Jesus; a culturalistic defense of Taoism, Buddhism, and the Confucian teachings; and a positive aversion to such alleged Christian practices as sexual promiscuity, kidnaping of children, and extraction of the eyes and hearts of the dead. The leading Chinese opponent of Christianity, Yang Kuang-hsien (1597–1669), was a highly emotional but articulate xenophobe. Appealing to Chinese pride, he cited Jesuit writings that depicted the Chinese as minor descendants of the Hebrews who had anciently worshiped God but had lost the true way until Ricci's arrival. He also accused Father Schall of having cast evil spells on the recently deceased Shun-chih emperor. This alarmed the Manchu court, which had an inherited belief in the spells of shamans. Schall, sentenced to death, was saved by a providential earthquake, indicative of cosmic disapproval of the sentence, but five Chinese Christian astronomers were executed. Christianity remained suspect because of its convert's private organization in an esoteric cult, like a secret society but with foreign connections, truly subversive.

The Jesuits' eclipse was precipitated by action in Europe. During a controversy at Paris in 1700 the Jesuits at Peking in self-defense secured a rescript from K'ang-hsi which supported their view of the Chinese rites. This threw the fat in the fire, for K'ang-hsi had now been brought to pronounce on theology, the prerogative of the Pope. Christian priests, representing the interests of Portugal and France, or of the rival orders, now began to destroy the hard-won Christian position at Peking. In the trial of strength between emperor and Pope, the Jesuits were largely on the side of the emperor. K'ang-hsi sent Jesuits to Rome with sixty-nine documents to lay before the Pope. But the Pope responded with a bull of 1715 reaffirming the anti-Jesuit position.

The Jesuit compromise with Chinese practice had been accepted at the court of Peking for over a century, and K'ang-hsi had found the missionaries useful and reliable throughout his long reign. The papal attack on the Jesuits came now as an affront, difficult to believe, impossible to accept. K'ang-hsi sent a Jesuit emissary to Rome via Russia, but the only papal reply was a heightened denunciation. After 1722 the Yung-cheng emperor turned against the missionaries, who had been unable to avoid involvement in palace politics, and began an active suppression of Christianity in China. Many churches were seized for civil purposes, and missionaries were forced into hiding, except at Peking. In 1724 Yung-cheng added a commentary to his father's *Sacred Edict* to denounce Christianity as a heterodox sect, which remained the Ch'ing policy for over a century. In 1742 another papal bull settled the Rites Controversy for the next two centuries. It required (until 1938) a strict oath by Catholic missionaries to forbid all Christian practice of "the Rites and Ceremonies of China." Under Ch'ien-lung, missionaries outside Peking suffered continued persecution. They were obliged to live and travel in disguise and to keep out of cities. Congregations shrank. The anti-Christian folklore became implanted in the popular mind.

Early Sino-Russian Relations.   European contact with China by sea and the Jesuit letters from Peking overshadowed in Western thinking the other early approach to China that was made by the Russians overland across Siberia. On this route the Russians of course faced much greater logistic problems. The Westerners' ships could bring them to Malacca or Canton in full force, self-sufficient, mobile, with their own armament, and without the necessity of passing through foreign kingdoms. Sea power could bring great force to bear suddenly. The carracks of the Portuguese or the East Indiamen of the Dutch and English could also carry more goods than camel caravans.

Characteristically, the Russian colonizing expansion across the endless stretches of Siberia was slow and gradual but also relatively permanent. The Russians reached the Pacific by 1637, almost as early as the English founding of New England, but their penetration of East Asia subsequently lagged far behind the Westerners who came by sea. British fleets might descend upon East Asia like a typhoon, irresistible but impermanent. Russian colonists advanced like a glacier. Americans today have inherited the West European tradition of sea contact with the Far East. The Russian tradition is different.

Beginning with the penetration of the Ob River basin about 1580, the Russians traversed the closely adjoining upper waters of the great rivers (Ob, Yenisei, and Lena) that flow northward to the Arctic. Climate and terrain were inhospitable and there were no centers of population. The administration of this vast region set up by officials from Moscow was parasitic, collecting its tribute of furs and skins from the local tribes through a network of fortified out-stations joined by post routes. Since the food supply was precarious, the Russian explorers sought a grain-growing area, and inevitably were attracted to the Amur River, on which barges in summer and sledges in winter could reach more productive country and, eventually, the sea. After 1643, Cossack raiding parties from Yakutsk began to go down the Amur, fighting the local tribes and establishing fortified posts. Other Cossack expeditions, coming from Yeniseisk by way

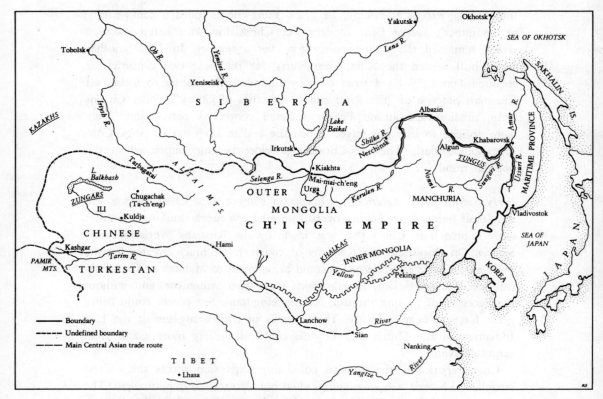

EARLY RUSSIAN-CHINESE CONTACT

of Lake Baikal, founded in 1656 a post at Nerchinsk on the main tributary of the Amur. A permanent outpost and a fortress were established to the east at Albazin in 1665.

These posts within the Amur watershed brought the Russians into conflict with the Ch'ing Empire. The tribes of northern Manchuria appealed to their overlords of the new dynasty at Peking. However, during the first generation of Manchu-Russian relations, the Ch'ing rulers were not in a strong position. Their conquest of China was not really completed until 1681, and meanwhile their hegemony over the Mongols was formidably challenged by the rise of the Zungar tribe in the far northwestern Ili region. Western Mongol tribes were already in contact with the Russians on their north in Siberia, and Eastern Mongols were already trading with the Russians at Nerchinsk. The K'ang-hsi emperor's aim, therefore, was not only to eject the Russians from the Amur but also to forestall their growing closer to the Mongols.

Diplomatic relations had begun informally as early as 1619. A more formal attempt was made in 1654 when the tsar sent an envoy to Peking with a letter to the emperor of China. The envoy's aim was to get trade without acknowledging Chinese suzerainty; he therefore refused to perform the kowtow. The officials in charge of him were not interested in trade, and the Russian envoy's stubborn demand for the European type of interstate equality threatened the ideological basis of Ch'ing power over East Asia. He was sent away without being received at court. Another Russian envoy was the colorful N. G. Spathar-Milescu ("Spathar" was actually a title), an intellectual Greek educated in Constantinople who had had wide experience in Western Europe. He reached Peking in 1676 bearing credentials for the first time in Latin and got the Jesuits to serve as interpreters. He was sent away for refusing to kneel when receiving the emperor's presents for the tsar.

After the consolidation of his rule within China in the early 1680's, K'ang-hsi proceeded systematically to develop post routes by land and water from South Manchuria to the Amur region, setting up stations, establishing granaries and military colonies, and creating a naval force to operate on the Manchurian river system. The Russians were soon ejected from the lower Amur. A superior Ch'ing army laid siege to the one remaining small fortress of Albazin. Under this pressure the Russian court decided to negotiate and sent an ambassador to Nerchinsk. The time was favorable, for the Ch'ing position was still threatened by the Western Mongols. Following the precedent of Spathar-Milescu, K'ang-hsi deputed two Jesuits to act as interpreters and advisers in negotiating with the Russians. After much confusion, suspicion, and bargaining, during which the two Jesuits crossed the river repeatedly between the rival camps, agreement was reached, and the Jesuits drew up official copies of a treaty in Latin, with other copies in Manchu, Chinese, Mongolian, and Russian. This treaty of Nerchinsk of 1689 was in terms of equality. It checked the Russian advance into the Amur region but gave Russia a stable basis for trade by caravan at Peking. The Russians agreed to destroy Albazin and withdraw from the Amur watershed. The treaty delimited the North Manchurian boundary but left its western end, between Mongolia and Siberia, uncertain.

By the Treaty of Nerchinsk, K'ang-hsi had forestalled Russian aid to the Eastern Mongols. In the decade after 1689 he achieved the final defeat of Galdan (see page 218) and began to assert his control over the Western Mongols. Russian trade caravans now crossed Mongolia via Urga to Peking under official passports, usually accompanied by envoys with a semicommercial, semidiplomatic status. Under the Superintendency of Dependencies (*Li-fan Yüan*), this early caravan trade fitted into the Chinese tributary pattern. Missions were nominally limited to two hundred persons, and eventually were conducted under a system of numbered tallies. At Peking they were kept under guard in a Russian Hostel similar to the Hostel for Tributary Envoys. Russian envoys performed the kowtow.

Sino-Russian relations continued to be important in the complex Ch'ing strategy for the control of Inner Asia. In the early eighteenth century the Zungars still fought, traded, and negotiated with the Russians, who under Peter the Great were encroaching steadily on their western frontier. On their part the Russians wanted a permanent commercial-diplomatic foothold in Peking, with their own interpreters, independent of the Jesuits. This effort resulted in a Russian Orthodox ecclesiastical mission, whose ostensible purpose was to minister to the spiritual needs of a small Russian emigré community at the Ch'ing capital. In the 1690's Moscow began to use it as a pretext for sending Russian Orthodox priests to Peking along with the trading caravans. The Yung-cheng emperor after 1722 welcomed the establishment of the Russian ecclesiastical mission to offset that of the Jesuits. He also wanted to prevent a Russian-Zungar alliance in the west and to eliminate Russian influence among the Eastern Mongols.

These Russian commercial interests and Manchu strategic interests produced another important settlement in 1727. The Russian ambassador brought fifteen hundred troops and a retinue of one hundred persons. After negotiating for six months in Peking, he withdrew to Kiakhta on the Mongol-Siberian border north of Urga. The treaty signed there delimited the boundary between Russia and the Ch'ing Empire and Russia was definitely excluded from Mongolia. In return the Russians gained a regular trade at Kiakhta. The Russians were allowed to send official caravans triennially to Peking and to maintain there a Russian Orthodox ecclesiastic-diplomatic mission, building their own church and sending language students. But whereas a score of Russian missions had reached Peking in the century before 1730, only half a dozen came in the century following. The Ch'ing court was not interested in trade but wanted political stability, and for this the best policy was isolation. Ch'ing realism was illustrated in two embassies sent to secure Russia's neutrality toward the Western Mongols, one to Moscow in 1731, the other to St. Petersburg in 1732. The Manchu envoys performed the short kowtow, kneeling and bowing three times, a ceremony which the Russian court expected of Oriental envoys, just as the Ch'ing expected Russian envoys to perform the kowtow in Peking. This realistic Ch'ing diplomacy was successful. By 1760, Ch'ing power had been firmly established over Tibet, the Western Mongol menace had been destroyed in Turkestan, and Russian contact was being held in check on distant frontiers.

The Canton Trade.   The Ch'ing foreign policy of stability through limitation of contact was less easy to achieve in the maritime trade at Canton. In the eighteenth century China faced new and more powerful forms of European expansion. The British East India Company, like its Dutch counterpart and like the other chartered companies that settled Virginia or Massachusetts Bay, was a private association that brought extensive capital resources under a central control, yet by its royal charter acquired wide powers of government abroad, monopolizing the national trade in certain areas. It built and armed its outposts, exercised jurisdiction over its countrymen there, developed navies as well as carrying fleets, and had in fact the prerogatives of both a merchant and a government. Eventually it ruled India, until the end of its charter in 1858. The expanding British trade with China was based on India, where the commercial spirit remained dominant in the Company's activities. When the British public developed a great demand for China teas, England, India, and China soon became joined in a triangular trade. And so the revenue of British India began to depend partly on commerce at Canton.

A British factory or trading post was established at Canton in 1699. During the next sixty years the Anglo-Chinese trade gradually became institutionalized into what we may call the Canton system. In this evolution, the British finally concentrated all their business at Canton, and their export trade came to center on teas and silks. During the eighteenth century, the tea trade became a great vested interest which stimulated further developments—the British effort to monopolize it for profit at home and to finance it abroad through trade from India to China, and the Ch'ing effort to regulate it at Canton and profit from it at Peking.

On the Chinese side, maritime trade increased so greatly during the Ch'ing period that it outgrew the framework of the tribute system. The European trade at Canton was only one of the two great commercial interests that expanded outside the system—the other was the trade of Chinese merchants with Southeast Asia. These Chinese traders had actually led the way in expanding beyond the tribute system and the Westerners merely moved into channels they had created. In this Chinese "junk" trade (as the Europeans called it, "junk" being a Malay word for "ship"), the Chinese vessels compared in size with their European counterparts and far outnumbered them. The biggest junks might be of 1000 tons burden, carrying a crew of 180 men. An average-sized junk of 150 tons, high-sterned, with lateen sails held out by battens to take a following wind, could make six or even eight knots, which compared well with the East Indiamen. Hundreds if not thousands of these sturdy merchantmen plied annually between Amoy or Canton and the Straits of Malacca, south in winter and north in summer. They followed detailed sailing directions through numerous ports of call. Since this trade with Southeast Asia was carried in Chinese vessels, it could not be regulated under the old forms of tribute. Instead, the Ch'ing officials used a traditional device. They appointed merchant firms (*hang,* anglicized as "hong"; see page 135) to be licensed brokers responsible for the conduct of the trade.

In a similar way the Chinese merchants that handled Canton's trade with the Europeans gradually became organized into a merchant guild called by Westerners the Cohong (from *kung-hang,* meaning "officially author-ized merchants"). It consisted of half-a-dozen to a dozen firms who were given a monopoly of the Western trade. This was the same type of regula-tory mechanism used for trade within China—a guild monopoly, licensed by and responsible to the officials, with little room left for free private enterprise. In charge of taxing the foreign trade at Canton was a high officer specially deputed from the Imperial Household Department at Peking, whom the foreigners called the "Hoppo." The Chinese merchant firms or hong merchants paid large fees to the Hoppo and bore responsibility for the foreign ships and traders. Every ship entering Canton was guaranteed or "secured" by one of them acting as its "security merchant." On the foreign side, the British East India Company's Canton committee took responsibility for all British vessels and persons. In this way by 1760 the British and other European trade was brought under Chinese control.

The foreign merchants were restricted by numerous regulations (not to bring in foreign wives, not to ride in sedan chairs, etc.). They were kept outside the city walls of Canton, confined to the riverbank area known as the "Thirteen Factories," that is, the establishments of foreign business agents or "factors." Their trade was legally confined to the Cohong. Mean-while, all foreigners remained subject to the procedures of Chinese criminal law, which gave the individual few civil rights and might subject him to arbitrary imprisonment and torture.

The picturesque life and trade at Canton became a legend. For the young Western trader ensconced in the Thirteen Factories, there was the prospect of large profits in exotic surroundings and occasional contact with famous hong merchants. The concentration on trade made it hardly necessary to speak more than pidgin (i.e., "business") English, a lingua franca using a limited number of foreign words in Chinese word order, which can still be heard in Hong Kong. The young men quickly made fortunes, if they did not die of the ague, but they learned little of Chinese culture. Anglo-Chinese relations at Canton were relatively easy, handled by a trading company, not a sovereign government, without raising the question of equality between sovereign states.

Canton had thus been drawn into world trade, though the Chinese Em-pire remained intellectually unaware of it and politically cut off. Breaking down the traditional Chinese indifference to trade expansion seemed less urgent to the East India Company, conservatively intent on current profits, than to government leaders seeking outlets for British manufactures. Al-ready free trade was being advocated in place of mercantilism, East or West. In 1784 enterprising young Americans began to compete at Canton. Private traders were agitating for access to the Indian market and abolition of the Company's monopoly. This was the background of the Macartney embassy of 1793.

Though paid for by the East India Company, this embassy came from the King of England in a ship of war to Tientsin. Macartney asked for permission to trade at Ningpo, Tientsin, and other northern places, access to one or more island depots where British goods might be stored and ships refitted, and a regular printed tariff instead of the Chinese system of personal presents or "squeeze" in addition to more formal fees. From the beginning, the embassy struck the problem of fitting into the tribute system. It brought magnificent presents which the Chinese officials labeled "tribute presents." They also urged Macartney to practice the kowtow, which he stoutly refused to do. The emperor issued an edict commending King George III for his "respectful spirit of submission" but pointing out that "our celestial empire possesses all things in prolific abundance." From this direct contact the British gained some knowledge of China but no change in the Canton system. The dogma of tribute was confirmed in the Chinese records. A Dutch embassy of 1795 reinforced this idea, for the Dutch envoys found themselves lined up with those of the outlying dominions at the Chinese New Year, and performed the kowtow on numerous occasions.

Behind the failure of the Macartney embassy lay the vested interests of the merchants and officials at Canton. So strong was this interest and so cautious did the Company become in its last years that the Canton system continued unchanged by any diplomatic effort. The Amherst embassy in 1816 was less well prepared than Macartney's and had the misfortune of arriving just as the British were fighting with Nepal, a Chinese tributary. Amherst when he reached Peking was misrepresented by his Chinese escorts and querulously ordered away by the emperor without an audience.

By the second quarter of the nineteenth century, when European expansion was about to take on a new and overwhelming vigor, the West had no more contact with Peking than in the seventeenth century. The Ch'ing rulers, inheritors of China's imperial tradition, had perfected their institutions of domestic control and had stabilized their relations with non-Chinese in Ili, at Lhasa, at Kiakhta, and at Canton. Europe and even North America had achieved contact with China, but the first three centuries of this contact had been successfully contained. The Chinese way of life remained essentially undisturbed.

10. Invasion and Rebellion in Nineteenth-Century China

Traditional China's Resistance to Change

In the middle decades of the nineteenth century, China, Japan, Vietnam, and Korea were each in turn confronted by the expanding Western nations and forced into greater contact with them. The Victorian era, so exhilarating for Englishmen, brought dismay and disaster to the peoples of East Asia. This was especially true in the great Chinese Empire, which had slipped into the downward phase of a dynastic cycle just as the Western powers began to beat upon the gates. Domestic and foreign troubles came hand in hand, as the nineteenth century advanced, each abetting the other. One chief problem for the student of this period is to discern the complex interaction between the rise of rebellion within China and the impact of the Western invasion from without. How far one process "caused" the other is an all-but-meaningless question, inasmuch as both went on for an entire century, mutually interacting from moment to moment.

The main fact influencing China's modern transformation was that China's center of gravity lay deep within. Her long history as the ancient center of East Asian civilization had given her people an inborn sense of superiority to all outsiders. The inertia and persistence of traditional patterns and both material and intellectual self-sufficiency all made China comparatively resistant and unresponsive to the challenge of the West. In Japan an economic and social ferment was already at work. Partly in response to Western contact, this ferment would develop into a full-scale political and social transformation. Within the much larger Ch'ing Empire no such transformation occurred. Scholars are still debating why it was so long delayed.

The Ruling Class and Its Agrarian Outlook.   One cause of China's inertia was the world view or self-image of the ruling class which intervened between the great mass of the peasantry and the rather small imperial government. This Chinese ruling stratum of the Ming and Ch'ing eras was, to be sure, a composite of several types of persons—rent-collecting landowners, merchants, degree-holding literati, officials not in office. All together they formed the local elite in the market towns of the countryside and in the administrative centers, the local ally of the Manchu dynasty.

The ruling class was knit together and set apart from the peasantry by its possession of literacy and the higher culture that went with it. It derived strength from the extended family system, indeed, the upper class consisted of large successful families that sought by every means to preserve themselves and their status. The leading elders of a clan lineage or common-descent group (*tsu* or *tsung-tsu*) managed its common property, recorded its genealogy and performed the rites of ancestor reverence in the clan temple, dispensed welfare aid, provided schooling for talented sons, and disciplined its wayward members to keep them out of the magistrate's court and jail. Marriages were arranged between families, and not by the individuals concerned, with an eye to sustaining the family-clan structure. It did, of course, cut across class lines and relate poor families to rich, providing channels of contact and cohesion between the landlord families and the tenant families within a clan. This facilitated upward mobility into the ruling class but a downward pull was exerted by the parceling of land-holdings divided up among a family's sons in an era of population growth. In general, the kinship relations of the local elite seem to have given it balance and continuity, allowing just enough mobility to keep the underprivileged but talented and energetic members within the system.

The ideal of this gentry elite was agrarian rather than urban, frugal rather than expansive. The Confucian teachings extolled the cultivation of the land and decried the parasitic manipulations of merchants. "Acknowledgment of limits leads to happiness" was an old adage. Ideally, one should be content amid one's fields, close to nature, almost like the Taoist worthies who lived their lives hearing the dogs bark in the next village but never going there.

This bucolic and nostalgic view of the world was kept vigorously alive by the fact that the local elite were mainly supported by landholding and were oriented to seek advancement through the examination system. Confucianism taught that self-cultivation, especially through learning based on study of the Classics, would enable one to be a superior man and possibly, through the government examinations, to become a degree-holder and even an official. This ideal was kept alive by the way in which the examination system accommodated even nonscholars who were rich enough to buy their way into it and thereby supported the system. The lower-level degree-holders, lower gentry not yet qualified for appointment to office, included two types: the great majority were genuine scholars who had passed the preliminary examinations (and were called *sheng-yüan*). But about a third were usually degree-holders by purchase (*chien-sheng*) whose "contributions" had been rewarded by degree status. As in earlier dynasties, a few degrees were also acquired by inheritance or by recommendation. As of 1800 this lower level totaled altogether something more than a million persons and formed a reservoir from which emerged the upper stratum of higher gentry and officials. The upper level, consisting of persons qualified for appointment to office, together with officials in office and in retirement, totaled somewhere around 125,000 persons and had special privileges which set them apart from the lower level. Thus the examination system was flexible, permitting upward mobility into the ruling class for people who could pay their way, and yet ensuring in normal times that the scholars, being the great majority especially at the higher levels, would predominate and set the tone among the actual holders of power. This in turn ensured the continued domination of orthodox ideals.

China's Premodern Economy.   Western contact came earliest in the form of commerce; trade was important long before diplomatic relations or Western ideas. Yet the Chinese economy, like the ruling class, was slow to respond. This was because of its large size and great self-sufficiency. In the early nineteenth century some 300 million people lived in rural China, at least four-fifths of the population. Their capital wealth consisted chiefly of the land itself, improved over the centuries by an arduous investment of labor to create paddy fields with embankments and irrigation channels; terraces even in the Northwest, where irrigation was often impossible; waterways both for transport and for irrigation, with dikes and sluiceways and the equipment of foot treadles, buckets, and wheels for moving water onto the soil. This farm economy represented a great investment of past labor and presupposed a continued heavy application of manpower to keep it working. Other types of capital equipment—draft animals, tools, buildings, storage facilities—were rather meager. Unexploited natural resources, assuming no revolution in technology, were limited. Labor resources, on the other hand, were plentiful. Rapid population growth in the eighteenth century had put a high proportion of the populace in the younger age brackets. Thus land was limited and capital scarce, while labor was plentiful and generally skilled in the traditional methods of production. There was little means or incentive for labor-saving innovation in technology. Innovation was also inhibited by the sharp functional distinction between hand-workers and brain-workers, who lived at different social levels. Farmers and artisans remained generally illiterate, while men of learning seldom came up against the practical, mechanical problems of field and shop.

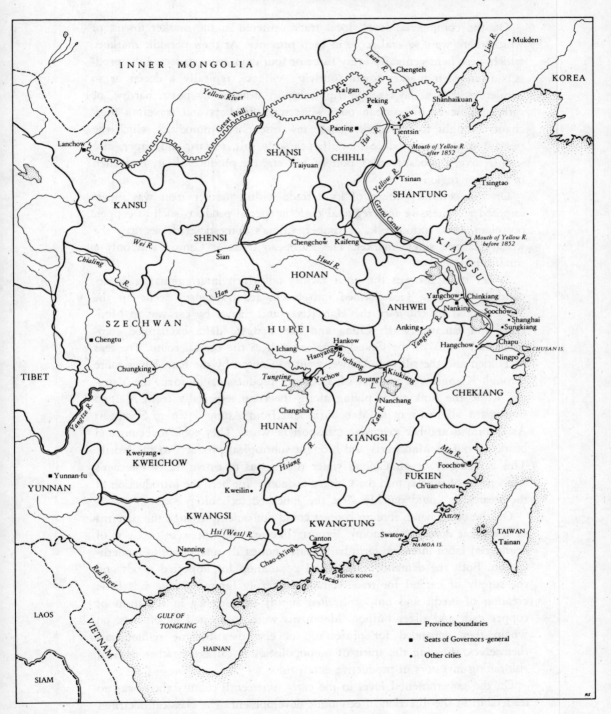

INNER MONGOLIA

• Mukden

KOREA

Luan R.

Liao R.

• Chengteh

Yellow River

Kalgan

Great Wall

Peking ★

Taku

Shanhaikuan

Lanchow ▪

Paoting ▪

Hai R.

Tientsin

Mouth of Yellow R. after 1852

SHANSI

CHIHLI

Taiyuan •

Yellow R.

• Tsinan

• Tsingtao

SHANTUNG

KANSU

Grand Canal

SHENSI

Wei R.

Chengchow • Kaifeng

Mouth of Yellow R. before 1852

Sian •

Chialing

Huai R.

HONAN

KIANGSU

R.

Han R.

Yangchow • Chinkiang

Nanking ▪ Soochow •

• Shanghai

Anking • Sungkiang

• Shanghai

SZECHWAN

HUPEI

ANHWEI

Chengtu ▪

Ichang •

Hankow

Yangtze R.

Hanyang Wuchang

Hangchow •

Chapu

Ningpo

CHUSAN IS.

Chungking •

Tungting L.

Yochow •

Poyang L.

Kiukiang

TIBET

Yangtze R.

Changsha •

Nanchang •

Kan R.

CHEKIANG

HUNAN

KIANGSI

Kweiyang •

Min R.

KWEICHOW

Hsiang R.

Foochow •

FUKIEN

Yunnan-fu •

Kweilin •

Ch'üan-chou •

YUNNAN

KWANGSI

KWANGTUNG

Amoy •

TAIWAN

• Tainan

Nanning •

Hsi (West) R.

Canton ▪

Swatow •

NAMOA IS.

Red River

Chao-ch'ing •

Macao • HONG KONG

LAOS

VIETNAM

GULF OF TONGKING

—— Province boundaries

▪ Seats of Governors-general

• Other cities

SIAM

HAINAN

RS

ADMINISTRATIVE AREAS UNDER THE CH'ING DYNASTY

On the commercial level, local trade centered in the market towns, of which there were several score in each province. At their periodic markets, which were held generally every three or four days, were collected the products from each market town's outlying villages, typically a dozen or so hamlets within a day's round-trip transport distance by beast, barrow, or carrying-pole or by sampan on a waterway. Peddlers and traveling merchants brought to the market those few essential commodities which the peasant could not produce himself, primarily salt, metals, and paper, also simple luxury goods, textiles, pottery, tea, and the produce of city craftsmen or of other regions.

On this cellular pattern of local trade within market areas was superimposed an extensive interregional trade in special products such as copper, porcelain, furs, cotton, silk, or timber. China's domestic trade serviced the world's largest single market. The European trade at Canton was only a small offshoot of it.

Water transport was the great facility on which interregional trade depended. Brick tea (tea formed into bricks for transport) went up the Yangtze and its tributary the Han River and thence by caravan to Mongolia and Russia. North China and the Yangtze delta exchanged commodities by way of the Grand Canal as well as the coastal route. The teas of Fukien and the silks of Anhwei went to Canton by the Kan River route through Kiangsi. All manner of Szechwan products came down the Yangtze, while the junk fleets plying along the coast, especially from Ningpo northward all the way to Manchuria and from Amoy down to Southeast Asia, formed another extensive transport network. They took soybeans and beancake out of Manchuria and brought subtropical products to the North. This carrying trade on China's water routes was to prove the Westerner's main point of ingress into the Chinese economy, for here the introduction of the steamship could quickly alter the inherited technology.

On the other hand, foreign contact could not quickly change the patterns of the great domestic economy. Exports like tea and silk were products of traditional labor-intensive farm handicrafts, not easily susceptible to modernization. Both the demand of the local population for imported goods and the supply of capital for trade remained sharply limited. There was little creation of credit and only a limited supply of currency in the form of copper cash and silver bullion. Merchants were dominated by officials, on whom they depended for protection, or else they became semiofficials themselves, showing the spirit of monopolistic tax-gatherers rather than of risk-taking investors in productive enterprise.

On the governmental level in the early nineteenth century there was no leadership in the direction of economic development. The classical doctrines of the state gave little thought to economic growth and stressed the frugal use of agrarian taxes rather than the creation of new wealth. It was assumed that there was a fixed volume of trade. Customs were levied on exports at the same rates as on imports. There was no mercantilist concept of maximizing the national wealth through exports. Official monopolies and license systems reduced competition.

In sum, the Chinese economy around 1800 was not only at a different stage of development from that of Europe, it was also differently constructed and was thought of in entirely different terms. First, China regarded herself as—and in fact was—a relatively self-sufficient economic entity. Trade, both foreign and domestic, was neither formally encouraged nor heavily taxed. Second, China had not yet institutionalized science and invention, as Europe was in the process of doing, and so the development of new technology was negligible. Third, lacking the stimuli of both foreign trade and new technology and suffering from the government's readiness to monopolize or tax exorbitantly any newly profitable economic undertaking, the type of entrepreneurship so important in Britain's industrialization was quite impossible in the Middle Kingdom. Capital accumulation was precarious except under the wing of officialdom. Legal safeguards, an investment market, and the forms of the joint-stock company were all lacking. Finally, the application of abundant manpower to all processes— irrigation, rice culture, transport, handicrafts, and the like—had reached a high degree of efficiency in the use of resources but was at a stationary level of technology. Population growth tended to eat up any increase in production. Production, in short, was generally absorbed completely in consumption, in an endless circular flow just to keep people alive, so that net saving and investment were all but impossible.

The Inertia of Government.   A similar unresponsiveness to foreign stimuli characterized the Ch'ing administration, beginning with the fact that it had to be quite passive at the local level because it was spread so thin. The typical county magistrate had charge of an area of three hundred square miles and a population of a quarter of a million people. A minor official in the government, faced with a large administrative task, he was in no position to coerce a defiant populace or the local gentry, or initiate new policies, nor would his philosophy of government have permitted him to attempt such things. The local magistrate was aided by his private secretaries or advisers and by personal servants whom he brought with him and paid himself. With their help he had to deal with the local yamen staff of semipermanent government clerks and various underlings—runners, jailers, police, and miscellaneous attendants. The magistrate was caught up in a web of responsibility for all that occurred within his area. His jurisdiction was territorial and complete rather than functional and specialized.

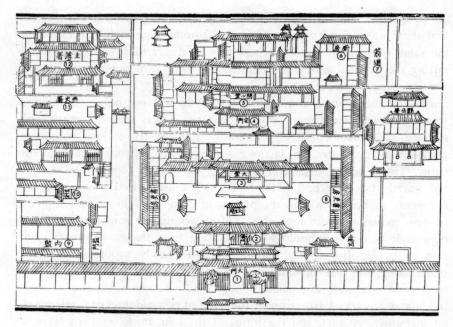

YAMEN OF THE SHANGHAI DISTRICT MAGISTRATE (from the
Shanghai gazetteer of 1871). *On the main axis, reading upward,
are the (1) main entrance, (2) ceremonial gate, (3) main hall,
(4) residence gate (to the magistrate's personal quarters) and his
(5) meditation hall, and (6) kitchen (right top), adjoining (7) an
archery butt. Right and left of the main hall are (8) clerks' offices.
Far right is the small yamen of the assistant district magistrate.
At left, reading upward, are (9) jail, (10) "ever-normal" granary,
(11) jail warden's office, and (12) registrar's office.*

Since his own virtuous conduct was supposed to set the example, he was to
blame or praise, almost in a ritual manner, for all that took place within
his jurisdiction, just as was the emperor within the empire. This doctrine of
what we might call ritual responsibility made officials seek by all means to
avoid the appearance of trouble. Looking forward to transfer to a new post
within three years, local officials were more interested in avoiding immediate
embarrassment within their areas than in fostering their long-term development. To have. to suppress disorder and so acknowledge its existence
might be more disastrous to one's personal career than to have it continue
unreported. Better to buy off bandits by enlisting them in the local militia
than to oppose them publicly. The result was a deeply ingrained tendency
to compromise, to harmonize the elements of the local scene, not to change
them. The spirit of Chinese official life was therefore passive. Officials
waited for things to happen, hoping they would not.

The government structure of checks and balances was designed to keep the ship of state on its traditional course, not to steer it in new directions. Even at the very top, the personal rule of the emperor was passive. His function was to serve as a glorified clearing-house rather than to initiate policy. Business was initiated in memorials addressed to the emperor; it was concluded by edicts from him. The volume of business became so great that the emperor was forced more and more to be a mere transmitter and selector of proposals rather than a maker of them. Here was one reason for the Chinese state's incapacity to change when confronted by the Western challenge: leadership was stultified below and worn out at the top. Officials on the spot in the provinces could not easily innovate, while the emperor in Peking was much too busy to do so. The broad responsibilities of the bureaucracy were not matched by a capacity for local initiative and innovation; the cumbersome safeguards which preserved the imperial power robbed it of adaptability.

Enfeeblement by Corruption. Fiscal administration further limited the government's responsiveness, because it permitted a growth of organized corruption that by the middle of the nineteenth century robbed the Ch'ing dynasty of its financial resources. Officials were still tax-farmers, expected to maintain both their public offices and their private establishments out of the revenues they collected. This confusion of public and private funds, as it would be considered today, reflected the very personal nature of the official's administration and responsibility, and also the fact that his revenues were not collected entirely in money (some being in kind or in labor), were not accounted for in a system of budgeting and auditing, and were produced by the infinitely complex interplay of personal relationships, haggling, and bargaining that characterized the old China on all levels. The actual amounts of tax payments were not fixed but resulted in each case from an interplay of interests, including those of the taxpayer, the tax collector, and his superiors, as well as the state. The custom of receiving unofficial fees or "squeeze" was well established. Genuine "corruption" appeared only when the customary limits of squeeze were exceeded.

Central government revenue figures give us only the most superficial view of how the ruling class and government together lived off the peasantry. In times of peace and good crop weather, all three might make ends meet. But with any decline in the self-denying Confucian morality of the ruling class, the interests of the government and the local elite tended inevitably to diverge. The instinct of the local landlord class was constantly to increase their private exactions. If unchecked this would make the government responsible for ever-increasing burdens upon the populace and lose it the Mandate of Heaven. The official quotas collected and reports made to Peking were thus a façade behind which the triangular struggle between landlords, officials, and populace went on without ceasing.

For example, in the lower Yangtze Valley, a chief area of surplus rice production, the land tax included chiefly two items. First was the fixed land-and-capitation tax, a combination of a tax on acreage and a tax originally levied on males between sixteen and sixty, but which had become since the early 1700's purely a fiscal quota of revenue to be collected from each administrative area. The second item, also to be collected by quota, was the grain tribute for Peking, either in kind or in money. The collecting officers not only added to the established quotas a number of further charges, but also found ways to profit through the process of collection. In general this profit was achieved by bold-faced methods, whereby several pecks might be discounted, i.e., "squeezed," from each bushel of rice; or silver payments substituted for the rice might be demanded at higher than the current market price; or copper payments in lieu of silver might be demanded at more than the current copper-silver exchange rate. The extra charges and discounts might total ten times the stated tax. These personal takings of the tax collectors usually had to be split with certain local gentry who cooperated in the system and with the higher officials. Collectors, gentry, and higher officials formed a corporation, living on the "sweat and blood" of the farmer. The underlings and clerks got their squeeze by manipulating a variety of charges for porterage, inspection, stamping, gate money, and the like.

In all this institutionalized corruption, the most significant feature was the alliance between the officials and the "big households." In general, big landlords, who usually had gentry status, paid their taxes at lower rates than the middle and poor peasants. This made the tax system "regressive," bearing more heavily on the poor, rather than "progressive," like a modern income tax. The wealthier a family was, the better arrangement it could make with the officials. Gentry degree-holders in the community, even if they were not landlords, through their access to officialdom could similarly oblige the tax collectors to give them favorable arrangements. That the well-to-do paid at lower rates than the poor can be documented in each province. Where a big house might pay four thousand cash to discharge a tax of one bushel, a small village household might have to pay twenty thousand. Yamen runners were usually ready to help landlords by coercing defaulting tenants. The consequence was that the poorer households sought the protection of the bigger, so as to make their payments on the latter's more favorable terms. On their part, the big gentry households were happy to make these payments on behalf of their smaller neighbors and take a profit on the transaction. Big establishments that paid taxes for others were known as "tax-farming households." Thus the landlord gentry got their middlemen's profit, the state was defrauded of revenue, and the little people were defenseless against the dominant landlord-official combination.

In the preceding we have offered different explanations of China's peasant impoverishment in the early nineteenth century: one, that the farming masses lacked the economic resources (especially capital and technology) to improve their lot; second, that the corrupt maldistribution of their product left them exploited by the landlord-official ruling class. These explanations are of course not incompatible. Future research will highlight many regional variations in the diverse and as yet barely studied Chinese landscape.

Scholarship and Thought

The "New Text" and "Statecraft" Schools. After the White Lotus Rebellion (1796–1804), the customary symptoms of dynastic decline could not be lost upon the scholar-official class, who were from their training particularly aware of, and believers in, the operation of a dynastic cycle. Corruption and rebellion had shortened the life span of earlier dynasties. How could the Ch'ing escape?

This concern prompted a new growth of scholarship. By the nineteenth century the Han Learning (see page 231) had become firmly established as a new orthodoxy, but now two new trends became important. One was a continuation of the "new text" school of classical criticism. The orthodox Han Learning, as its name implies, studied texts of the Later Han period, when the "ancient text" versions of the Classics were allegedly discovered and in time became accepted as orthodox. However, in the late seventeenth century, the so-called "ancient text" of the *Classic of Documents* (also known as the *Book of History*) had been shown to be a forgery. Now bold and vigorous scholars began to question other "ancient text" versions of the Classics and found in them further proofs of forgery or editorial tampering. Thus the "new text" school, paradoxically, espoused the older texts which had been recovered and accepted in the Earlier Han, alleging that they were older and more authentic than the orthodox "ancient texts" accepted ever since the Later Han period. At the same time it found in these "new text" versions of the Classics, especially in the *Kung-yang Commentary* on the *Spring and Autumn Annals (Ch'un-ch'iu)*, radically new meanings which had implications for the hitherto taboo subject of politics and seemed relevant to the course of events in the nineteenth century. In brief, the concept of change in the *Kung-yang Commentary* could be used as a basis for advocating institutional reform. This prepared the way for a wholesale attack at the end of the century upon the classical tradition, which would open the door for reform and indeed revolution at the very center of the tradition itself. Until the 1890's, however, the "new text" movement was still gradually gathering momentum.

The other new trend of the early nineteenth century was likewise a revival of an earlier approach. This was the school of "statecraft" (*ching-shih*), which aimed at the application of scholarship to the problems of government administration in reaction against intuitive knowledge, speculative philosophy, and formalism. This revival of concern with the policies and processes of administration was stimulated by the evidences of dynastic decline. The dominant tradition of Ch'ing scholarship, confined to the study of classical antiquity and especially philology, had provided detailed information on the imperial institutions of earlier eras, including the sacrifices, funeral dress, conveyances, and even the styles of headgear, but it offered little wisdom on how to meet the pressing problems of government in the late Ch'ing period. As the portents of decline became more obvious, reflective minds began again, as they had during the disorder of the Ming-Ch'ing changeover in the seventeenth century, to blame the impracticality of the scholars and their absorption in dry-as-dust and useless book-learning. The writings of Ku Yen-wu (see page 231) provided a special stimulus. The slogan of the new movement was "learning of practical use to society" (*ching-shih chih yung*). Its leaders set themselves the task of studying how to maintain the economic and political institutions of the empire.

The efforts of the school of "statecraft" are illustrated in the career of Wei Yüan (1794–1857), a wide-ranging and practical-minded scholar-administrator from Hunan. He had studied the Neo-Confucianism of the Sung and the Han Learning at Peking, and his criticism of these orthodox traditions contributed to the rise of the "new text" movement. He also became a leading advocate of the application of the scholar's talents to the urgent practical problems of administration. When the Grand Canal became blocked, Wei Yüan in 1825 wrote a treatise advocating the transport of rice to Peking by sea. His admirer, a reforming governor of Kiangsu, put this plan into effect in 1826, for one year only, sending fifteen hundred shiploads to Tientsin. During the 1830's Wei helped the reform of the North Huai salt monoply. Later, in 1850, Wei himself administered part of this salt region, with exemplary results. Thus he was a scholar with practical experience.

In 1826 Wei Yüan was invited to edit a work called *Collected Essays on Statecraft under the Reigning Dynasty* (*Huang-ch'ao ching-shih wen-pien*) in which were reprinted over two thousand essays on economic and other administrative topics. This became the prototype for an entire genre of such collections, of which more than a dozen continuations or supplements later appeared, in order to make readily accessible the ideas of scholar-officials concerned with governmental problems. Wei Yüan next secured a post under the Grand Secretariat at Peking, with access to the archives, where he saw the vast sea of unpublished proposals, studies, reports, and decisions accumulated under the Ch'ing administration. He began to compile a large work of recent history on the campaigns of the Ch'ing period, the *Record of Imperial Military Exploits (Sheng-wu chi),* in which he set forth the impressive record of Ch'ing subjugation of China, Mongolia, Tibet, Sinkiang, and Taiwan and defeat of the Russians, Burmese, Vietnamese, and the White Lotus rebels. He completed this work in 1842, the very moment of unprecedented disaster at the hands of the British.

There were others like Wei Yüan concerned with current policy, but unfortunately they were a small leaven in a large mass. The Ch'ing dynasty's consistent policy of wooing the scholars, while at the same time suppressing dissent and forbidding scholarly discussion of official policy outside government channels, had diverted the early vigor of political thought, manifested in the period of the Manchu conquest, into orthodox textual research or fact-gathering for its own sake. Skepticism and criticism had been largely confined to matters of etymology and exegesis of the Classics. The scholarly talent of the day was absorbed in narrow bibliographical or purely classical literary activities. This may be illustrated in the case of Juan Yüan (1764–1849), a famous bibliophile and promoter of scholarly enterprises, who served as governor-general at Canton in the crucial decade from 1817 to 1826. Juan Yüan had been several times a governor and governor-general, had founded several libraries and academies, and had published at least a dozen large works—catalogues of art objects, anthologies of poetry, dictionaries and commentaries on the Thirteen Classics, collections of rare works, and the like. During his decade at Canton, when the disastrous conflict with Britain was taking shape there, Juan Yüan established another academy, edited the provincial gazetteer, printed in 366 volumes a collection of 180 works of classical commentary, published some fifty chapters of his own poems, prose, and bibliographical notes, and brought out an anthology of Kiangsu poets in 183 chapters. He also made important contributions to the study of Chinese painting, mathematics, and ancient inscriptions on stone and bronze. All this time he was the top official in charge of China's relations with the West. Small wonder that his policy toward the Westerners at Canton was generally one of compromise and passivity.

China's Image of the West. With scholar-officials like the orthodox and assiduous Juan Yüan setting the example, there was little opportunity or incentive for trained minds to pursue a curious interest in the overseas peoples. The inherited lore of the Ming era, when Cheng Ho sailed west and Europeans first came to China, was laboriously copied out—errors, garbles, and all—and set forth as information about the Europeans of 1800, one outdated source being copied into another in endless succession. Aside from this lore, the only other source of information was the Westerners themselves who came to Canton; but they were few in number and more accessible to merchants than to scholars. In the absence of more precise

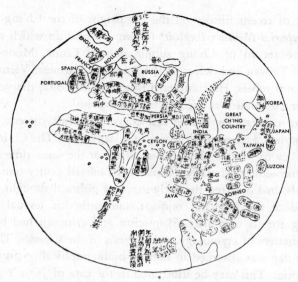

CHINA'S PREMODERN VIEW OF WORLD GEOGRAPHY. (English captions superimposed) *Round map is "A General Sketch of the Four Seas," from the widely used* Hai-kuo wen-chien lu, *ca. 1730. Among many anomalies, the Black Sea is labeled "Dead Sea," the Indian Ocean almost disappears, and both places marked * are labeled No-ma ("Rome"). Square map is Wei Yüan's map of Europe from* Hai-kuo t'u-chih, *1844. In it, Germany is "now divided in 24 parts," Italy into "9 countries," England is large and Denmark expanded. "Sweden"* (Shui-tien) *and "Switzerland"* (Shui-shih) *are confused, both being simply "Shui country." Such maps gave Commissioner Lin his view of East and West.*

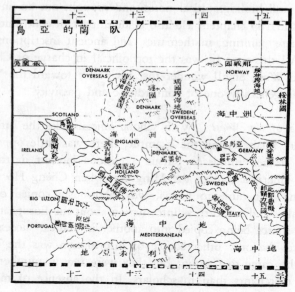

information, Chinese observers of the early nineteenth century applied to the Europeans and Americans many of the stereotypes that had been developed during millenniums of contact with neighboring peoples in Asia. Just as the pastoral tribes of the Inner Asian steppe constantly waxed and waned, changing their names and locations, so the Western peoples whose traders came to Canton, as recorded in Chinese writings, shifted about and changed identity like phantoms. Their names had become thoroughly confused. In the Kwangtung provincial gazetteer, edited under Juan Yüan in 1819–1822, the account of the Spaniards in the Philippines was sandwiched in between Quilon (in southern India) and the Moluccas, and dealt with the Ming period only. Portugal was stated to be near Malacca. England was another name for Holland, or alternatively a dependency of Holland. France was originally Buddhist, and later became Catholic (it had become a common belief in China that Christianity was an offshoot of Buddhism). Finally, France was said to be the same as Portugal.

One is left with the impression that the scholars were not interested in learning about the West. When exceptional men like Wei Yüan sought to do so, they had to seek translations of Western writings. The facts were not to be found in China. The expansive West caught China by surprise, and ways of handling foreign relations which had worked reasonably well for four centuries suddenly became useless.

The Collapse of the Canton System

Country Trade and Private Traders.   Private enterprise in India was from the first an indispensable extension of the East India Company's operations, necessary to connect them with the local Asian sources of trade and revenue. This enterprise took the form of the so-called Country trade, that is, trade conducted by private individuals within the commercial domain of the Company's charter. Country trade grew up first within and around India, where the British Company sold bills of exchange, payable in Calcutta or London, to the Country traders, both British and Indian, and so were able to use the traders' profits as a means of making Company remittances. The Country trade expanded eastward in response to greater opportunities for profit. The supply of Bengal opium, for example, was monopolized by the Company, sold by it at auction, bought by Country traders, and exported by them, mainly at first to the Straits of Malacca and Indonesia. The Country trade was facilitated by private firms of Englishmen and Scotsmen, who formed "agency houses" which not only invested in shipments themselves, but also handled cargoes, ships, warehouses, insurance, and sales for other private parties on a commission basis. They were the cutting edge of the commercial, financial, and industrial expansion of Britain and the modern international economy.

"ILLUSTRATIONS OF TRIBUTARIES" FOR THE CH'IEN-LUNG
EMPEROR. *"A 'Barbarian' from Sweden"* (left) and *"An Englishman"* (from Huang-Ch'ing chih-kung t'u, *Palace edition, 1761*).

The Country trade from India was soon extended to China. Enterprising British subjects as early as the 1780's had begun to remain at Canton as nominal representatives of other European governments, in order to avoid the control of the British East India Company. This became an established custom—in 1823, for example, James Matheson was Danish consul and Thomas Dent was Sardinian consul. To succeed in this kind of private business required little capital but a great deal of enterprise and ingenuity. Thus Dent, Matheson, and the other "private English" at Canton soon began to acquire fleets, set up insurance companies, and carry on banking operations. The private traders were the Far Eastern correspondents, friends, and often relatives of merchants in the similar but bigger agency houses in India, which had become well established after the Company ceased to monopolize British trade in India in 1813. These houses in turn, like those at Canton, dealt with the hub of Britain's worldwide economic expansion in London. In this expansion, the Country trade by providing (after about 1817) three-quarters of the British imports at Canton, accomplished two things at once: it gave an outlet for Indian produce, remitting profits to India, and it continued to finance the East India Company's purchase of China's teas, which were as usual profitably taxed by the British government in London.

A similar growth of commercial interests occurred on the Chinese side, although they have not yet been as fully studied. Canton was an outlet for tea and for silk and cotton textiles, mainly produced by handicraft industries on the farms of South China. Cotton textiles went chiefly in the form of "nankeens," named for Nanking, because the main center of the Chinese cotton textile industry was in the nearby region of Soochow and Sungkiang. These exports for the West were taken from the total Chinese domestic production, for which the principal market remained the Chinese public. Until well into the nineteenth century the chief import of the Country trade from India was raw cotton to supply China's own textile industry. The hong merchants served as funnels through which flowed out consignments of tea and silk collected by traveling merchants in the producing regions of Central China. The transport route by barge and by coolie carrier through Kiangsi to Canton was greatly developed. Despite its comparatively small volume, the Canton trade had become important as a center of growth, both in the accumulation of capital and in the creation of commercial mechanisms and an articulate commercial interest. The "Canton interest," in the person of merchant firms and imperial officials who profited from the Canton monopoly of Western trade, became a factor in Chinese policy considerations.

The Rise of the Opium Trade. The origin of a British opium trade between India and China lay partly in the growth of opium-smoking in China. Because opium is a habit-forming narcotic, it was a social evil even more serious than the gin that was considered an evil in contemporary Britain. The opium poppy had long been known in China and its product used as a drug, but the "smoking" (actually, inhaling water vapor) of opium began only after tobacco-smoking had spread to China from America by way of Manila in the seventeenth century. During the late eighteenth century, about a thousand chests of opium a year were being imported from India to China. From 1800 to 1821, the average was about forty-five hundred chests a year, but the annual total grew by 1838 to some forty thousand chests. (A chest usually contained 133 pounds.) The spread of opium addiction can no doubt be associated with other trends already noted—population pressure, the probable lowering of living standards, and the increase of corruption in government and of rebelliousness among the people. The spirit of the age, in short, was one of demoralization. Opium-smoking as a symptom of this frame of mind spread particularly among yamen underlings and soldiers, two groups who represented the government in contact with the populace.

Behind the growth of the opium trade also lay the basic fact that British India had become dependent upon it for 5 to 10 per cent of its revenues. While Bengal opium was cultivated under Company control and sold officially to private traders at auctions in Calcutta, opium in western India was grown not under Company control and at first competed with the Bengal product; but by the 1830's the Company had got control of the ports of shipment, like Bombay, which enabled it to levy a transit tax and profit accordingly. In the meantime, the competition between Bengal and

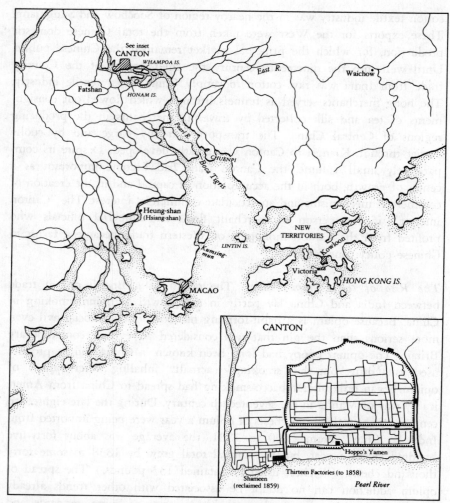

THE CANTON ESTUARY AND OUTER WATERS (19TH CENTURY)

western India had stimulated the production of more opium at lower prices.

Opium traders in China could make big profits, as prices fluctuated according to supply. A chest might sell for one thousand or even two thousand Mexican dollars before 1821, and for seven hundred to one thousand in the period of increased supply thereafter. This speculative trade created intense competition. Foreign merchants began to use the earliest type of clipper ships to get ahead of their rivals. They delivered cargoes to "receiving ships," which were heavily armed floating warehouses. The Chinese opium traders were organized in brokerage houses, usually composed of a score or more of partners, whose funds made up the capital for investment. Their smuggling boats, well armed and manned by sixty or seventy oarsmen (which gave them their Chinese names of "scrambling dragons" or "fast crabs") would normally take delivery of opium chests from the foreigners' receiving ships. By the 1830's one to two hundred such Chinese boats were taking deliveries from about twenty-five foreign receiving ships in the waters outside Canton. At first the domestic distribution of opium was along the routes of inland trade to the west and especially to the north of Canton, toward Central China, but eventually a new phase began with distribution by foreign ships on the coast of China northeast of Canton.

The incapacity of the Chinese government to stop the trade was illustrated by the opposite courses followed in Ch'ing policy and official practice. Selling and smoking opium had been prohibited by imperial edict as early as 1729, its importation or domestic production in 1796, and after 1800 these bans were frequently repeated. But official connivance had grown as the trade had grown. Opium paid its way, becoming a new source of corruption. To greed was added fear, for the opium distributors tied in with the secret societies, and could oppose with force those officials who would not accept bribes. The higher officials issued edicts of prohibition, while the lower officials connived at the trade, passing some of their ill-gotten gains on to their superiors, no doubt right up to the court. As the higher authorities became more vulnerable to exposure, blackmail, or censure, they found it safest to drive the contraband trade out of their immediate jurisdiction. In 1821 Governor-General Juan Yüan forced the receiving ships to leave the river anchorage below Canton and move outside to Lintin Island. Foreign traders began to seek outlets to the northeast at Namoa Island and Chinchew (Ch'üan-chou). This "coast trade," even less controllable than that in the Canton delta, began during the 1830's to import as much as Canton.

The opium trade was pushed from both sides. Not only had Britain's commercial expansion become dependent on opium; the trade had become entrenched in China as a powerfully organized smuggling system which corrupted the government as the number of addicts grew. The imperial household at Peking had been accustomed for over a century to drawing revenue from the Canton trade. Opium had merely increased the unofficial revenue and also strengthened the "Canton interest." Similarly, the British opium interest was a recent addition to the long-continued British desire for commercial expansion in China. It gave further impetus to British demands that had long been formulated.

To the list of British grievances was now added the financial inadequacy of the hong merchants. The most famous of these was the head of the Wu family firm, Houqua, who made a great fortune, trading and even investing abroad through his American friends of the Boston firm of Russell and Company. But Houqua was exceptional. Most of the hong merchants, constantly pressed for "contributions" to the government and short of capital themselves, regularly went into debt to the East India Company, which advanced the capital to buy up the next season's teas and silks. There was no legal machinery, however, for collecting debts owed to foreign merchants, and so unpaid hong merchant debts accumulated.

There was also the Western repugnance at the arbitary arrest and torture of accused persons, as practiced under Chinese criminal law. Antithetic assumptions concerning the rights and responsibilities of the individual underlay the Anglo-Saxon and the Chinese legal traditions, and so the British at Canton had refused to submit to Chinese jurisdiction in homicide cases after 1784, and the Americans after 1821. In practice a degree of extraterritoriality (foreign legal jurisdiction over foreign nationals) had grown up, but it was not explicitly assured from the Chinese side.

The British Crown Supplants the Company. Crisis came in 1834 when the proponents of free trade secured the abolition of the East India Company's monopoly of British trade with China and the British government sent an official Superintendent of Trade to Canton to oversee the commerce in place of the Company. This Scotsman (Lord Napier) had had no experience in diplomacy or in Asia. He was sent without adequate instructions, preparations, or support to attempt an all but impossible task: the opening of equal relations between Britain and China, which would bring to an end the ancient Chinese tribute system. The local officials predictably refused his demand for correspondence between them as equals. Soon they stopped the British trade, their usual device for curbing foreign merchants. Napier then circulated handbills in Chinese denouncing the Ch'ing officials' disregard for trade and its benefits. The officials in return cut off all supplies to the British. Lord Napier's two frigates forced their way through the principal mouth of the river and exchanged cannon fire with the Chinese forts. The emperor ordered that the English be made to submit or be expelled by force.

This wrathful confrontation was now somewhat palliated by the hong merchants on one side and the British free traders on the other, who pressed for a compromise. Napier retired to Macao, where he died of illness in October 1834, and for the next four years his successors pursued a "quiescent policy," while two schools of thought developed as to what the British policy should be. A majority group of merchants, headed by Jardine, Matheson and Company (a successor of earlier firms, which has retained this name since 1832), demanded that a British naval force repair the insults to Lord Napier and secure the opening of more ports. The rival group of merchants headed by Dent and Company preferred to reap the profits of trade quietly. The Canton officials demanded that England appoint a chief merchant to take responsibility.

By 1836 the Canton system had thus fallen apart. Trade was no longer confined to Canton, the Cohong no longer monopolized the Chinese side of it (in particular, the opium imports), the hong merchants were frequently insolvent, the Company monopoly had given way to competing private traders, and its function of controlling the British merchants had been assumed by an official who objected to taking orders from the hong merchants. The volume of trade and its lawlessness were both increasing.

The Opium War

No episode in modern history has provided more occasion for the charge of "imperialist aggression" than the First Anglo-Chinese War of 1839–1842—a war that was precipitated by the Chinese government's effort to suppress a pernicious contraband trade in opium, concluded by the superior firepower of British warships, and followed by humiliating treaties that gave Westerners special privileges in China. As patriotic Chinese of all camps have reviewed the story in recent times, it has given substance to their feeling of grievance at the forceful intrusion of the West and the subjection of China to "semicolonial" status for almost a century thereafter.

In addition to looking at the Opium War from this point of view, it is also necessary to see it in the context of major trends of modern history. By the nineteenth century, the Chinese position on foreign relations, like the contemporary seclusion policy of Japan, was out-of-date and no longer supportable. An industrializing West, moving rapidly ahead in technology, organizational skills, and military power, could no longer be dealt with like the Europe of the eighteenth century. A vast discrepancy in power relations had developed, and this would inevitably lead to a great change in China's relations with the outside world. Sooner or later the old order of tribute relations would have had to give way, not only because of China's relative military weakness, but also because of the currents of ideas—concepts of scientific learning, individual freedom, and economic growth, for example—which were beginning to sweep over the modern world. In demanding diplomatic equality and commercial opportunity, Britain represented all the Western states, which would sooner or later have demanded the same things if Britain had not. It was an accident of history that the dynamic British commercial interest in the China trade centered not only on tea but also on opium. If the main Chinese demand had continued to be for Indian raw cotton, or at any rate if there had been no market for opium in late-Ch'ing China, as there had been none earlier, then there would have been no "opium war." Yet probably some kind of Sino-foreign war would have come, given the irresistible vigor of Western expansion and the immovable inertia of Chinese institutions.

The Anti-Opium Movement. The British resort to warfare was precipitated when the Ch'ing court finally faced the opium-trade menace to its vital interests and strove, too late, to catch up with the situation at Canton. The anti-opium movement was a moral crusade which, as often happens in such cases, coincided with concrete interests.

Until the 1830's, neither the growth of addiction among yamen underlings and soldiers, nor the increase of barefaced smuggling and official connivance had roused Peking to a sustained effort at suppression. But meanwhile another problem had arisen. The opium inflow seemed to be causing an outflow or "drain" of silver that in turn seemed to be upsetting China's bimetallic currency system. The exchange rate began to change between the copper cash used in everyday transactions and the silver bullion (in the unit of weight and fineness known as the tael) used in government fiscal operations. Silver became dearer in terms of copper. This was a real crisis for the government because it imposed hardship at all levels—peasants had to pay more coppers to meet taxes, while tax collectors meeting their quotas in silver had less copper cash left over as private squeeze. In actuality, several factors lay behind this situation: first, a debasement of the copper coinage due to reductions in the size and weight of the copper cash by around one-third; second, the volume of cash officially minted every year was increased, and counterfeiting of cheap cash and hoarding of silver further increased this problem; finally, an actual outflow or "drain" of silver began sometime after 1821. Until then, China had consistently been a net recipient of silver in foreign trade—from Japan, Manila, England, the United States, India, and elsewhere. But, at least by the 1830's, China began to suffer a net loss of silver, mainly taken out to India as bullion to pay for opium. An apparent drain was noted long before the balance actually shifted, because Chinese observers saw silver paid out for opium but did not see its subsequent return to pay for tea exports. As a result they jumped to a simplified conclusion. In 1825 a censor connected the silver outflow specifically with the opium inflow, and soon it was generally accepted that the fiscal crisis caused by the shift in the copper-silver exchange rate was due to a drain of silver caused by the opium trade.

So great was the opium evil by this time that extirpation seemed an immensely formidable task. Some realists, especially a group connected with the academy that Juan Yüan had founded at Canton, counseled a policy of compromise: to continue to oppose smoking by scholars, officials, and soldiers, but to legalize the opium import under a tariff so as to discourage smuggling and at the same time to prevent the outflow of silver by letting opium imports be purchased only by bartering Chinese goods, not silver. In May 1836, while Juan Yüan was a Grand Secretary in Peking, this proposal was presented to the emperor, referred to Canton, and soon became known to the foreign traders, who for some time anticipated that legalization would occur. The Canton authorities gave their support to the proposal in September 1836. In Peking, however, the argument had meantime gone the other way and the legalization movement was dead within four months after it started. In 1837–1838 suppression of the Chinese part of the trade at Canton was attempted more vigorously, but smuggling continued on the coast and imports reached a new peak. In the latter half of 1838 a great debate of memorials from high officials all over the empire proved inconclusive. But the emperor at the end of 1838 finally decided on a root-and-branch attack upon the evil all along the line: against cultivators, distributors, and consumers, all of whom would be subject to the death penalty. This statute, issued in 1839, also provided the death penalty for foreign importers.

By this time the anti-opium campaign at Canton had destroyed opium dens, executed dealers, and depressed the trade, which in the winter of 1838–1839 was almost at a standstill. But this stimulated the coast trade and induced the foreign importers to take a more active and forceful role in armed smuggling operations. The position of the British government meantime was that it could not interfere "either by aiding or restraining the pursuits of the smugglers." Suppression would have to be effected by the Ch'ing government.

In the confused events of this period, one point stands out—that the Chinese government was attempting to do two things at once: suppress the opium evil and maintain the tribute system of foreign relations. The Canton authorities refused time after time to communicate with the superintendent of British trade except through the hong merchants, and demanded that the character "petition" head his letters, as it would those from an inferior to a superior. Any kind of trade agreement or cooperative effort between the two governments thus remained impossible. Two worlds stood in opposition. The Chinese struggle against the opium trade went forward in the context of the British struggle against the tribute system.

Commissioner Lin at Canton. The man selected to exterminate the opium evil, Lin Tse-hsü (1785–1850), was a practitioner of the school of "statecraft" and an incorrupt and effective administrator. After he reached Canton on March 10, 1839, he pioneered in obtaining translations from Western sources, for example, a passage from Vattel's *Law of Nations* concerning a nation's right to control its foreign trade. He also addressed two eloquent letters (never delivered) to Queen Victoria: "Suppose there were people from another country who carried opium for sale to England and seduced your people into buying and smoking it; certainly you would deeply hate it and be bitterly aroused. . . ."

Lin's program was to wipe out the Canton network of Chinese opium importers and distributors, and this he practically accomplished. It was not his aim to use force against the foreign traders, much less start a war with the British. But he soon found it necessary to coerce them into surrendering their opium stocks, and for this purpose on March 24 he confined the foreign community of about 350 men in the Thirteen Factories. Deprived of their servants but not of supplies, the foreigners spent six weeks in this detention. Lin released them when the British merchants delivered up their opium stocks, which he then publicly destroyed. Thus he secured delivery of some twenty thousand chests of British opium, but two things made this a hollow victory: first, the opium market had collapsed, while the supply on hand in China or in prospect from India had risen to some fifty thousand chests, so that the merchants' interest lay in getting whatever price they could; and second, the British superintendent of trade took personal responsibility for the surrender of the opium on behalf of the British government. As Matheson put it to Jardine at the time, "The Chinese have fallen into the snare of rendering themselves directly liable to the British Crown." Lin's coercion of British subjects and officials was entirely in keeping with the unequal nature of the traditional tribute system; but from the viewpoint of the modern international world it gave the British government a *casus belli.*

The traditional order in China's foreign relations was further brought into question in July 1839 when drunken English sailors killed a Chinese villager, who became a symbol in the dispute over legal jurisdiction. The Chinese authorities demanded that a culprit be delivered up. The British refused to admit Chinese criminal jurisdiction over British subjects. As the dispute widened, it highlighted the Sino-Western conflict over diplomatic relations and legal jurisdiction as well as over the opium trade.

Under pressure, the British community retreated successively from Canton to Macao and then in August 1839 to Hong Kong, a largely uninhabited island about thirty square miles in area, separated from the mainland peninsula of Kowloon by one of the world's best deep-water harbors. Hostilities began gradually, in small affrays intermixed with negotiations. The first naval battle was in November 1839. But the Canton trade survived even during wartime. The American firm of Russell and Company, working closely with their hong merchant friend, Houqua, handled much of the season's tea exports under the American flag on behalf of the British. Meanwhile, the coast trade in opium continued, well armed, beyond the reach of Commissioner Lin. When a British expeditionary force arrived in the summer of 1840, seized Chusan Island south of Shanghai, and then negotiated below Tientsin close to the capital, it was evident that Lin Tse-hsü had not succeeded in his twin efforts to suppress the opium evil and maintain the Canton system. In September the emperor recalled him in disgrace, while Britain prepared for a settlement by force of arms.

War and Negotiation.   The Ch'ing dynasty's unpreparedness for warfare was due both to the technological backwardness of its armed forces and to the decay of military administration. The army's training stressed form without content, a meaningless posturing with swords and spears. To make up a force against bandits or rebels, small detachments would be collected from a number of different garrisons. This prevented the development of large units as striking forces with high morale and continuous leadership. Troops were commonly rebellious. Without training or discipline, they lacked skill and courage in the field and would run before the enemy could arrive, being fearless only toward the helpless common people.

The decline of Ch'ing power was even more evident on the sea than on the land. The naval tradition included no concept of a mobile striking force constantly ready and able to apply sea power. Instead, each coastal province maintained flotillas of war junks to suppress disorder in certain assigned areas of coastal waters. Under separate provincial commands, trained neither for deep-water cruising nor for joint maneuvers, the Chinese "water forces" were a sort of water-borne constabulary. Pirates could therefore save themselves by using the same tactic as bandits—fleeing across jurisdictional boundaries, so that the province they had victimized would be unable to pursue them while the province they entered would have as yet no reason to do so. Chinese naval vessels remained small— about three hundred tons burden and one hundred feet in length, with one hundred men aboard and half a dozen cannon—in a period when trading junks might carry one thousand tons. They were in no condition to defend China against a nineteenth-century Western navy.

To chastise the Ch'ing government, Britain sent a small mobile force of a few thousand men with the latest devices of warfare, such as flat-bottomed, shallow-draft iron steamers that could defy wind, tide, fire-rafts, and fortresses. Chinese war junks with their archers and antiquated cannon proved as ineffective as the coastal batteries with their fixed emplacements and poor gunnery. The British reduction of Chinese strong points all along the coast from Canton to Shanghai was not difficult (see next page). The real problem was how to capitalize on this military superiority so as to create a new order in China's foreign relations. Britain had no territorial ambitions except for a commercial base like Hong Kong. Neither was it her aim to attack the Chinese populace, who, except at Canton, generally remained passive spectators of the fighting and supplied a coolie corps to work for the invaders' wages. But to make the Son of Heaven agree to a new status for the Westerners in China meant the end of an age-old set of beliefs and practices—in short, the destruction of the tribute system.

In the first phase of the war in 1840–1841, Lin's successor, a wealthy Manchu grandee, signed in January 1841 an abortive convention, which would have ceded Hong Kong, given diplomatic equality and an indemnity to Britain, and reopened Canton. But both governments spurned this attempted settlement. In May 1841, after the season's teas had been shipped,

THE FATE OF CHINA'S TRADITIONAL WATER FORCES. *Supported by boats from British warships, the East India Company's iron-hulled, paddle-wheel steamer* Nemesis—*184 feet long, 120 horsepower, with two 32-pounders on pivots fore and aft, but drawing only 6 feet of water—attacks a Chinese fleet in shallow water near Chuenpi on January 7, 1841.*

a small British force of twenty-four hundred troops attacked Canton, but withdrew from outside the city walls after securing a "ransom" of $6 million. Since local militia, mobilized under gentry leadership at official instigation, were threatening the British when they withdrew, this incident (at the village of San-yüan-li) was hailed as a victory of the Cantonese populace over the British forces. Some historians have viewed it as the first evidence of a modern spirit of nationalism among the Chinese masses.

In the second phase of the war in 1841–1842, the British seized positions all along the coast, in Amoy harbor, on Chusan Island (which they had earlier evacuated), and at Ningpo. Reinforced in the spring of 1842, they occupied Shanghai, took Chinkiang, where the Grand Canal crosses the Yangtze, and advanced to the outskirts of Nanking, having defeated every form of Ch'ing resistance. This resistance had had many aspects—the stoppage of British (but not other) trade, mobilization of militia at Canton, blocking of harbors and river mouths, building of war junks, and the assembling of troops from many provinces. In March 1842 a Chinese surprise attack was made on the British-held city of Ningpo. But this Chinese offensive in the traditional style was ineffective in command, organization, and armament alike. In defense, on the other hand, the garrisons of Manchu bannermen resisted the British with hopeless courage.

The new British plenipotentiary, Sir Henry Pottinger, negotiated only after the British attack had forced the Ch'ing court to consent to an entire new deal in Anglo-Chinese relations. The Manchu dynasty capitulated in order to preserve itself. As descendants of alien conquerors, the rulers at Peking were sensitive to the collaboration which so many "Chinese traitors" were giving to the invaders. Secret societies were active both in opium smuggling and at Hong Kong. Continued defeat by British arms would weaken the dynasty's hold on China. It had to make concessions to the British invaders in order to maintain its rule over the Chinese people. The Chinese reformer Lin Tse-hsü had failed to suppress the opium evil. Now another Manchu grandee, Ch'i-ying (died 1858), was sent to appease the British.

The First Treaty Settlement. Ch'i-ying signed the Treaty of Nanking with Pottinger on August 29, 1842. It prepared the way for a new order by abolishing the Cohong monopoly of foreign trade at Canton, promising a "fair and regular tariff," ceding Hong Kong to Britain, and opening five ports to British residence and trade—Canton, Amoy, Foochow, Ningpo, and Shanghai. An indemnity of 21 million Mexican dollars was to cover hong merchant debts, pay for the confiscated opium, and reimburse the British Indian government for the cost of the war. But three further treaties were necessary in 1843–1844 to complete the first settlement: the British Supplementary Treaty (October 8, 1843), amplified by the American Treaty (July 3, 1844) and by the French Treaty (October 24, 1844). Because of the "most-favored-nation" clause—a promise to each power that it would receive whatever privileges might later be given another—these treaties reinforced one another to form a single system of treaty law. Since China did most of the giving of privileges, the system has properly been called "unequal." It was not created in a day, however, and actually took eighteen years of continued trade, diplomacy, and eventually warfare to become established.

The first settlement was thus only an entering wedge. It placed British consuls in five ports where British residents were under their consul's legal jurisdiction, that is, they had the right of extraterritoriality. The protection of Western legal procedures covered not only the persons of merchants and missionaries but also their goods and property and sometimes extended in practice to their Chinese servants and assistants. Thus, Western and Chinese enterprises were relatively secure from the arbitrary exactions of officials. The printed treaty tariff, based on the rates of the old imperial tariff, ranged, very roughly, between 4 and 10 per cent. Chinese trade monopolies or guilds, like the Canton Cohong, were forbidden in the name of free trade. The American treaty, negotiated by Caleb Cushing and Ch'i-ying, improved upon the British in the provisions for extraterritoriality and gave Americans without a struggle all the privileges that Britain had fought for.

The "Opening" of East Asia:
Principal Treaties in the "Unequal" Treaty System, 1842–1943

Characteristic features: treaty ports, extraterritoriality,
most-favored-nation clause, tariff fixed by treaty.

Beginning	Development	Termination
CHINA		
Nanking (British) 1842, plus Suppl. Treaty of Hu-men-chai ("The Bogue") 1843	Wanghia (American) 1844, Whampoa (French) 1844	Germany, Austria-Hungary 1919, USSR 1924
	Tientsin (Br., Fr., Am., Russian) 1858	Tariff autonomy 1930 (ff. Washington treaties 1922, recognition treaties 1928)
	Chefoo Convention (Br.) 1876, ratified 1885	
	Boxer protocol 1901	New equal treaties (Am. and Br.) 1943
JAPAN		
Kanagawa, Perry (Am.) 1854 (Br. 1854, Russian 1855)	Harris (Am.) 1858	Brit. revision treaty 1894; extraterritoriality ended 1899; tariff autonomy 1911
VIETNAM		
Saigon (Fr.) 1874 (earlier Fr. 1862)	Hué (Fr.) 1883, protectorate confirmed (1885 China recognizes French protectorate)	"Freedom within French Union" 1946, independence of Repub. of Vietnam 1954
KOREA		
Kanghwa (Jap.) 1876	Shufeldt (Am.) 1882	(Japanese protectorate 1905, annexation 1910) Repub. of (So. Korea) 1948

Western Influence Through the Early Treaty Ports

Western contact, with its inevitable undermining of the traditional order, proceeded by stages from the first war and subsequent treaties, in 1840–

1844, to a second set of wars and treaties in 1856–1860. During this period the Ch'ing statesmen, whether Manchu or Chinese, found out too late what they were dealing with. The lead in learning about the Western invaders had been taken by Commissioner Lin at Canton. He turned the translations he had secured over to his friend, the scholar-official Wei Yüan, who produced in 1844 his *Illustrated Gazetteer of the Countries Overseas* (*Hai-kuo t'u-chih*). This collection of materials on world geography and Western conditions also contained a discussion of how to handle the "barbarian" problem. Wei Yüan's strategic thinking was a mixture of old and new. He combined the ancient theme of "using barbarians to control barbarians" (e.g., the French and Americans to control the British) with the new concept of "learning their superior technology in order to control them," specifically warships, firearms, and methods of maintaining and training soldiers. From this concept was to come the movement for the strengthening (*tzu-ch'iang,* literally "self-strengthening") of the Chinese state by borrowing Western devices and technology, a direct application, to the problem of Western aggression, of those ideas of "statecraft" which Wei Yüan and others had already advocated in dealing with domestic problems. The desire for knowledge of the West could be justified by quoting the Chou dynasty classic on the art of war, the *Sun-tzu*: "Know yourself, know your opponent; in a hundred battles, win a hundred victories." Unfortunately China was too big a country, with too many tradition-bound scholars annually moving into official life from the great reservoir of inland provinces, to be easily stirred by a marginal sea-frontier contact with foreign ideas. The stimulus of the Western example was largely confined to Hong Kong and the treaty ports.

Merchants and Missionaries. The British requests for legalization of the opium trade were refused by Peking, but the trade continued and expanded along the coast as far north as Shanghai without being mentioned in the treaties. Outside the five treaty ports there grew up double that number of "receiving stations," centers of unadvertised but regular and generally peaceable trade between the foreign opium importers and the Chinese opium distributors. Opium addiction increased. In the 1850's the import rose to fifty thousand and even sixty thousand chests a year, double the figure of the early 1830's at Canton. American opium merchants like Russell and Company, who had competed with the Indian supply at Canton by bringing opium from Turkey, now could compete directly with Jardine and Dent by acting as agents for shipments from India. American as well as Chinese, English, Scottish, and Indian Parsee fortunes were made from the trade. Cultivation of the poppy increased rapidly within China, foreshadowing the eventual supplanting of the Indian import. But during the mid-century decades, the few big firms, with their fast clippers, well-armed

TEA PRODUCTION AT A GLANCE. *Picked on the hillside (top left), tea leaves are dried, sorted, roasted, trampled, packed, weighed, and otherwise processed through successive stages until purchased by the three foreigners in top hats and tail coats (bottom left) and conveyed to their vessels (far right).*

receiving ships, accumulated capital, and superior facilities, maintained an oligopoly. Tea exports rose above 100 million pounds, silk increased similarly, but both were paid for mainly by the funds received for opium imports. The Chinese market for textiles and other British manufactures remained disappointingly limited, mainly because of the self-sufficiency and poverty of the Chinese peasantry, who still made their own textiles and had little money for purchases. This was not realized by the foreign merchants, perched on the rim of a vast subcontinent, and they continued to believe that the mills of Lancashire could be kept busy for a generation if only each "Chinaman" would add one inch to his shirt-tail.

The treaty ports, particularly Shanghai, represented an aggressive and highly dynamic new order based on organized competition. Some two hundred firms, mainly British and American, though united in chambers of commerce at Shanghai and Canton, lived or died by competing in all aspects of trade. Yet the five ports and Hong Kong formed a single community, protected by gunboats, mainly British, and inhabited by a young and mobile population. A similar degree of organized competition and a similarly expansive hope for the conversion of the "heathen" masses of China animated the early Protestant missionaries, who met similar frustration because of the slowness of the Chinese response. After the dissolution of the Jesuit order in 1773, French Lazarist fathers had taken the Jesuits' place at Peking. While leaving the missionaries untouched there, the Ch'ing government tried with some success to suppress Christianity elsewhere. From 1801 to 1829 only a few new missionaries were able to enter the country, except for the first Protestant pioneer, Robert Morrison, who lived in Canton from 1807 under the wing of the East India Company. Protestant missions had come out of that spiritual accompaniment of the rigors of industrialization, the evangelical movement in late-eighteenth-century Britain and parallel developments in New England. Robert Morrison succeeded in studying Chinese and translating the Bible. To avoid hostility at Canton, his colleagues opened an Anglo-Chinese training college at Malacca in 1818.

The first American Protestants, who reached Canton in 1830, were sent by the American Board of Commissioners for Foreign Missions, an agency founded in 1810 by several denominations but which eventually represented the Congregational churches. They founded an important monthly journal, *The Chinese Repository* (1832–1851) and one of its editors, S. Wells Williams, compiled an influential general account of China, *The Middle Kingdom* (1848). Peter Parker inaugurated medical missions by opening an eye hospital at Canton. Both Williams and Parker later served their government in diplomacy, just as Morrison and other British missionaries aided theirs. At first, however, their chief concentration was on spreading the word of the gospel in Chinese, particularly through tracts such as those written by the first convert, Liang A-fa (1789–1855). Intent on making the gospel available, they began to experiment with romanization (or transcription, i.e., writing the sounds of Chinese in the Roman alphabet). Yet for a long time converts remained very few, measured in tens rather than hundreds.

Meantime the revival of Roman Catholic missions went on both at the ports and in the interior. As the modern patron of Catholic missions, the French government secured from the Ch'ing emperor the issuance of imperial edicts of toleration, in 1844 and 1846, which made Christianity no longer a banned religion and restored certain churches. By working through its native hierarchy of Chinese priests and communicants, the Catholic Church was able to achieve a widespread growth. The Society of Jesus, which was restored in 1814, set up its main center at Zikawei (the ancestral home of Ricci's great colleague, Paul Hsü) in the suburbs of Shanghai. The Jesuit, Lazarist, Dominican, and other European missionaries, with their Chinese colleagues, vigorously revived the Catholic communities in nearly every province. This still illegal but extensive Catholic activity in the interior was more massive and better organized than the Protestant missionary effort, and yet represented a less acute cultural challenge to Chinese society. The Catholic priests dressed and lived in Chinese style, and

CANTON FACTORIES, CA. 1854. *The 15-man fast-boat (foreground) seems to be vying with two Westerners out for exercise in a shell (center). The American side-wheeler* Riverbird *lies off the open space in front of the factories, each of which has its own flagstaff. (Oil painting by a Chinese artist)*

their schools did not teach European languages, whereas the Protestants brought more of their secular culture along with them and attacked Buddhist and Taoist "idols" and Chinese religious and social customs more directly. Thus Catholic missions penetrated much further among the Chinese population, yet in the end the Protestants had the more revolutionary impact.

The Role of the Cantonese. Western influence was felt most directly through the Cantonese. Household servants, Chinese merchants in foreign legal trade, Chinese opium distributors, and Christian colporteurs (distributors of religious writings), all came at first from the regions of longest contact in the far south, particularly Canton. Speaking a strange "dialect" (actually a different language) and organized in their own community, the Cantonese who accompanied foreign merchants to Shanghai or Amoy constituted in themselves an unassimilable foreign element in competition with the local people. If they had established residence in Singapore or Hong Kong, they might carry certificates giving them the status of British subjects. If so, or if they were part of the foreign merchant "establishments" permitted at the ports by treaty, they could claim foreign protection under extraterritoriality. Often they wore Western-style clothes to advertise their privileged position.

In the late 1840's these Chinese in contact with foreign merchants helped to develop still another social evil in the form of the coolie trade, through which male laborers were shipped under contract, mainly from Amoy but also from Macao and other ports, to meet the demand for cheap labor in newly developing areas overseas, such as Cuba, Peru, Hawaii, Sumatra, and Malaya. Chinese emigration to Southeast Asia had been going on for centuries, but several factors now combined to speed it up. One was the worldwide effort to abolish slavery, which created a demand for contract labor as a substitute; another was the introduction of foreign shipping, both sail and eventually steam, which could transport large cargoes of coolies at very little cost. In this new trade under foreign flags, Chinese "crimps" (procurers of laborers) inevitably committed excesses while recruiting and keeping in depots (barracoons) the human cargoes for shipment, just as some foreign vessels came near to duplicating the conditions of the earlier African-American slave trade. The British government tried to prevent abuses by consular inspection of ships. The Ch'ing policy was at first to maintain the traditional ban on emigration.

Abolition of the Cohong at Canton led to the rise of a new type of Chinese merchant, the comprador, who was employed on contract to handle the Chinese side of a foreign firm's business with Chinese merchants, securing commercial intelligence and buying and selling. All this trained him to become a modern entrepreneur in the new Chinese business class which grew up within the protection of the treaty ports. Thus Chinese from the first participated in the modern economy of international trade that began to take shape on the coastal fringe of the Chinese empire.

The Rise of Rebellion

After 1850, peasant-based rebellions covered much of the eighteen provinces for the greater part of two decades. Considering the restricted scope of the Western impact before 1850, one can hardly conclude that it was the chief cause of these vast disorders. Their origins lay in the general condition of China, which by the late 1840's was plainly conducive to rebellion. Population, if we accept the trend of the official estimates, had continued to increase. Administration, judging by selected cases, had continued to deteriorate under the pressure of widespread official self-seeking in the face of ever-mounting problems. Thus, for example, the accumulation of silt in the Yellow River and Grand Canal was not offset by the maintenance of dikes. The canal became less usable for grain transport. In 1852 the Yellow River finally broke loose and began a long,

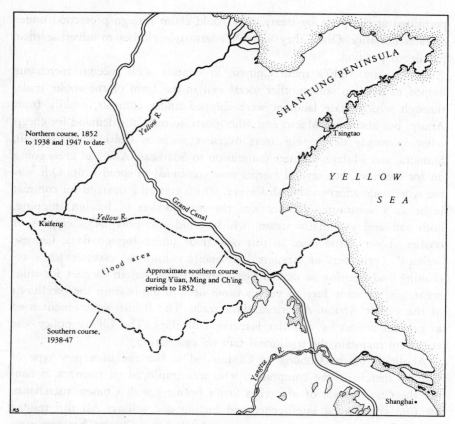

COURSES OF THE YELLOW RIVER

disastrous process of shifting its main stream from the south to the north of the Shantung peninsula, the first major shift since 1194. Pressure of numbers, flood, famine, poverty, corruption, and the resulting ineffectiveness of government were demonstrated in the increase of banditry, riots, and minor outbreaks in many areas.

As the Ch'ing power grew less effective, opposition was organized by secret societies. In general, these bodies were called *chiao* in North China, meaning a religious sect or doctrine, and *hui* in the South, meaning a society or association. Offshoots of the White Lotus Society (and forerunners of the Boxers of 1900) appeared in North China in 1813 and were quickly suppressed, but subversive activity was less easy to control in South China, where the main vehicle of unrest was the Triad Society, also known as the Heaven and Earth Society or Hung League and by several other names. According to legend, this society was founded in 1674 by militant Buddhist monks of a monastery near Foochow who had been victimized by corrupt officials. Under the slogan "Overthrow the Ch'ing and restore the

SECRET SOCIETIES. *Stages in the initiation ceremony for Triad Society members.*

Ming," it developed an elaborate secret ritual and became a blood brotherhood whose members were sworn to exterminate Manchu rule. The day-to-day functions of the Triad Society were more peaceful and prosaic, however. Like the Masonic orders of the West, it was a fraternal organization pledged to high moral principles and mutual help among members. It was particularly useful for persons who moved from place to place—traveling merchants, boatmen, transport coolies, petty officials, or smugglers. Use of the secret Triad signs and passwords could secure one protection in strange places on the routes of trade or in overseas centers like Singapore and Batavia.

Disorder became most widespread in the late 1840's in South China where imperial control was diminished by two factors. First, it was the part of China conquered last and least dominated by the Ch'ing, garrisoned by Manchu bannermen only at Canton. Second, it included the region which had been longest subjected to the disturbing influences of foreign trade and contact, culminating in the opium traffic and the war with Britain. Indeed, Canton was the seedbed of modern Chinese nationalism, the focal point most stimulated by the Western example of patriotism and nationalistic interests. Cantonese militia, armed to repel the British, felt in 1841 that they had done so. When later dispersed by the Ch'ing government, they harbored resentment against both the British and the Manchu appeasers of the British. Because Shanghai was closer to the districts of tea and silk production, its opening in 1843 had thrown transport gangs out of work on the routes to Canton. Finally, when the British navy began a program of pirate suppression in 1849, its success forced pirate gangs to move inland from the coast, up the West River and into Kwangsi province.

The Taiping Kingdom.   As in most popular rebellions, a religious cult provided the fanatical basis of organization for the rebel movement that finally emerged in Kwangsi. The founder, Hung Hsiu-ch'üan (1814–1864), and his chief collaborators were Hakkas, that is, members of a distinct linguistic group descended from North Chinese migrants who had settled centuries earlier in large communities in South China. They were not fully assimilated and sometimes became involved in local feuds with the "native" population. Hung was also a frustrated scholar, who had failed more than once in the Canton examinations. He was, finally, a mystic or, at any rate, an unstable personality, whose illness and religious experience convinced him that he was a new messiah. Hung's religious cult was based on the Protestant Bible, which reached him first in 1836 in the form of Chinese tracts written by the early convert Liang A-fa. Hung had a long delirium and saw visions. Subsequent reading of these tracts gave him the explanation: he had seen God and his own Elder Brother, Jesus Christ, for whom he, as the Heavenly Younger Brother, must now save mankind. Hung had some brief contact with Protestant missionaries at Canton, but he put together his own religion, borrowing chiefly the militant teachings of the Old Testament rather than the loving-kindness of the New. The Ten Commandments were taken intact, but not the Sermon on the Mount.

The military organization of Hung's followers, after he had spent several years preaching his new faith, was carried out in conditions typical of the period. As imperial officials lost their capacity to suppress bandits and settle disputes, local militia corps were commonly organized to maintain order. Usually they were paid and led by members of the gentry as the natural local leaders, but they could also be formed by secret societies or religious cults, who could develop sources of revenue from forced contributions, taxes, or rackets. The continued decline of central authority, however, soon set these local forces in competition against one another. Somewhat like tribes of the steppe before the rise of a Chinggis Khan, these militia units were susceptible to being swept up into a great expanding "horde."

The unit organized by Hung's followers in the late 1840's, called the "God Worshippers Society," attracted all manner of disaffected persons—Hakkas, Triad Society members, pirates, and homeless peasants. They began their armed resistance to imperial troops in July 1850 at a village near the West River in Kwangsi. Expanding rapidly, in September 1851 they captured the departmental city of Yung-an to the north and raised the banner of dynastic revolt. Hung took the title of Heavenly King of the "Heavenly Kingdom of Great Peace" (*T'ai-p'ing t'ien-kuo*). The term

"Great Peace" (*T'ai-p'ing*) had been used in the Classics, by earlier rebels, and as a reign title in several Chinese dynasties, in addition to its new use to translate a Biblical phrase. Another leader emerged in the person of a former charcoal dealer, Yang Hsiu-ch'ing (died 1856), who became the Eastern King and commander-in-chief, while others became the Northern, Western, Southern, and Assistant Kings.*

Besieged at Yung-an by imperial forces, the Taipings broke out in April 1852 and went north, acquiring cohorts as they went. Lacking artillery, they failed to take the provincial capitals of Kwangsi (Kweilin) and Hunan (Changsha) but seized the capital of Hupei (Wuchang) early in 1853 and descended the Yangtze in a great flotilla to Nanking, the second city of the empire, which they captured by assault in March 1853.

This remarkable military success was followed by a mixed record of ups and downs. An expeditionary force was sent toward Peking but it was forced westward to Shansi and back into Chihli, harassed by the North China winter, and was finally turned back near Tientsin late in 1853. Meanwhile the Taipings had not set up administrative control over the regions they traversed from Kwangsi northward. They lacked qualified personnel to install as local magistrates. Their forces entered sixteen of the eighteen provinces and captured some six hundred walled cities. But they could not administer what they conquered. Established in the rich heartland along the Yangtze, they set up the traditional Six Ministries of central government at Nanking, but they seem to have had little more than a military administration in the countryside.

In their military-religious society, during the early period, men and women were for a time strictly segregated in separate barracks. Chastity was prescribed for both sexes. Women were organized into labor and even military battalions. Equality of the sexes was manifest in the abolition of foot-binding and the appointment of women as officers and administrators. The Taipings' puritanical zeal also set them against slavery, adultery, witchcraft, gambling, alcohol, opium, and tobacco. Their religion and ideology were a fascinating mixture of Christian and Chinese elements. God's second son, Hung, was hailed as a new Son of Heaven, appointed by the Mandate of Heaven. His followers preached to crowds and offered sacrifices to God; they destroyed idols and temples, Taoist, Buddhist, and Confucian; and their first moral precept was reverence for God, Jesus, and Hung. But their second moral precept was filial piety. The brotherhood of men was combined, paradoxically, with a society of hierarchy and status.

Much of the Taiping system came in fact from Chinese tradition. Since the Bible did not provide a detailed blueprint, Hung and Yang found a

---

* *Wang*, the ancient term for king, had come to be used at Peking for imperial princes, as well as foreign rulers. In English the Taiping "kings" (*wang*) are sometimes called "princes."

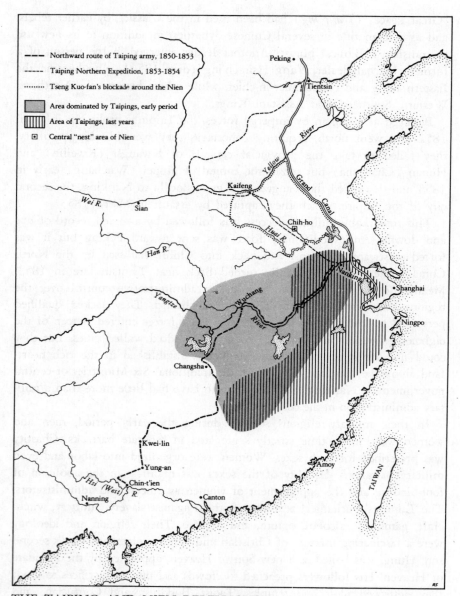

- —·—·— Northward route of Taiping army, 1850-1853
- ------- Taiping Northern Expedition, 1853-1854
- ·········· Tseng Kuo-fan's blockade around the Nien

Area dominated by Taipings, early period

Area of Taipings, last years

☒ Central "nest" area of Nien

THE TAIPING AND NIEN REBELLIONS

model in the classic *Rituals of Chou* (*Chou-li*), a work cited by radical reformers like Wang Mang (in power 9–23 A.D.) and Wang An-shih (1069–1074). The Chinese utopian tradition was reflected in a primitive economic communism. All persons were to contribute their possessions and services to a common treasury and receive their support from it. Both land and people were to be redistributed. Landholdings were to be classified in nine grades according to productivity, and farming households were to have equally productive allotments according to the number of household members. Every twenty-five families were to form a unit with a church and a public treasury under an officer who would be in charge of payments, as well as religion, education, the judgment of disputes, and the military organization. Ideally every farmer was also a soldier and the government hierarchy was at once both civil and military. (Equal landholdings, the groupings of families into mutually dependent units, and a peasant militia were of course all old Chinese institutions.) Since in fact the Taipings did not set up a territorial administration, it is uncertain how far the equalization of land use was carried out. Their blueprint was given effect mainly in the early years at Nanking. The egalitarian ideal was limited, for each king built up his own palace, administration, and military forces.

Since Hung stressed the role of a personal and transcendent deity, he envisioned something quite different from the traditional Chinese state, with its rather rational claim to be based on the immanent order of nature. The Taipings' fanaticism reduced their appeal. Their anti-Manchu attack was combined with attacks on Confucianism and the whole social order. They repelled the conservative scholar-gentry class yet failed to achieve an alliance with the rebellious Triad Society. The Taipings borrowed some Triad terminology and many Triads joined the ranks. But Nanking did not help Triads who engineered local rebellions at Amoy and Shanghai in 1853. The Taiping leaders underestimated the value of Shanghai as a source of foreign aid and made little effort to develop foreign trade.

Meanwhile, jealousy among the original founders of the movement proved its undoing. The Machiavellian Yang Hsiu-ch'ing had from the first gained power partly by going into trances and receiving visitations from God. The less devious Hung Hsiu-ch'üan, though he claimed to be the Son of God, did not claim to receive similar communications. At length Yang challenged Hung's superiority and in 1856 Hung got the Northern King (Wei Ch'ang-hui) to assassinate Yang. Wei went further and killed Yang's family and thousands of his followers. Hung soon felt obliged to have Wei assassinated in turn. His original lieutenants having been removed, Hung now appointed mediocre relatives to govern his kingdom. The movement gave way to profligacy and corruption and was kept going only by the emergence of a new military genius (Li Hsiu-ch'eng) who was given the title of Loyal King in 1859 and commanded the Taiping forces in their last years in the lower Yangtze.

With rebellion in every province in the 1850's, the Ch'ing dynasty was able to reassert itself because it continued to monopolize the trained administrative talent of those who knew how to govern in the Chinese Empire. The loyalty of these men was a tribute to the tradition of scholar government and to the achievement of K'ang-hsi and his successors in

*Defeat of Taiping forces by superior firepower of Ch'ing inland
navy (on left). A battle near Kiukiang reported by Tseng Kuo-fan
in January 1855.*

forging the unity of state and culture. The scholar class preferred Manchu
rule on traditional lines to Chinese rule by heterodox rebels. In the end,
the Taipings were suppressed by new Chinese armies under Chinese scholar-
official leadership, notably from Hunan.

The principal leader was Tseng Kuo-fan (1811–1872), whose career
illustrates the whole process. Tseng became a metropolitan graduate in
1838 and spent the next decade in high official and scholarly circles at
Peking. In 1852 he was given the task of organizing a militia army to
defend Hunan, his native province. He built his Hunan Army on Confucian
principles, to defend China's traditional society. Tseng had been an eclectic
scholar and an advocate of practical "statecraft" in administration. Not
brilliant, but persistent, he first enlisted local gentry as officers personally
loyal to himself. Then by discipline, training, and paternalism he built up
the morale of their troops, inculcating as cardinal virtues (1) respect for
superiors, (2) concern for the common people, and (3) cultivation of
good habits. The Hunan Army first grew from a defensive into an offensive force when sent to save situations in other provinces. Second, it built
and trained a naval arm for use on the Central China waterways. Third,

Tseng refused to move out of Hunan prematurely, until in 1854 his forces recaptured Wuchang. Yet even at this date there was still no unity of imperial command and rebellion was still spreading.

The Nien and Moslem Rebellions. Stimulated by the Taiping invasion of the Yangtze Valley in 1853, a separate rebellion emerged in that year in the area west of the Grand Canal between the Huai and Yellow Rivers. This region on the borders of four provinces (see map, page 294) had long harbored secret-society bandit gangs called simply *nien* ("bands"), whose origins can be traced back to the White Lotus Society. Lacking major cities but with easy access in all directions, the area had been plagued by salt smugglers, and by clan and village feuds, often involving a bellicose minority of Chinese Muslims, as well as by flood, famine, and refugees. The *nien* bands finally achieved a degree of coordination after 1853 by selecting a top leader. Several hundred local groups, based on their fortified, earth-walled villages, under clan and village leaders, supplanted the central government officials over a wide area. They accumulated arms and horses, levied their own taxes, and soon began cavalry raids to plunder adjoining regions. By 1855 the Nien movement was organized as an alliance of five main bands under yellow, white, blue, black, and red banners. It used secret symbols, blood oaths, and elaborate rituals in the secret-society fashion and also imitated the Taipings in wearing long hair. Nien and Taiping forces cooperated on many occasions. Yet the movement remained decentralized and never attempted to expand and take over big cities or set up a rival dynastic government. By degrees, however, the Nien leaders created an effective army, mainly cavalry, and established firm control, first over the local militia bands and then over the population and the food supply, in an area of perhaps 100,000 square miles. By 1860 they confronted the imperial government with the danger that the Nien and Taiping movements might join together.

An even more long-continued revolt against the Ch'ing arose in distant Yunnan. Islam had been firmly rooted in both Northwest and Southwest China ever since the Mongol period. The Chinese Muslim minority in Yunnan still formed a distinct religious community and not infrequently fought with their non-Muslim neighbors, particularly in mining areas, where the dwindling resources of copper, tin, lead, and precious metals extractable by premodern methods were a bone of contention. The Ch'ing officials in this faraway mountain plateau were few and impotent, quite unable to check disorders which began in 1855 under the leadership of the chief priest, a devout and learned man who had made his pilgrimage to Mecca and saw the Islamic faith as compatible with Confucian social teachings. In 1861 he was induced to return to an uncertain allegiance to the Ch'ing, but in western Yunnan the revolt continued for another dozen years under a vigorous fighter, Tu Wen-hsiu. In 1856 he had made Tali (once capital of the medieval kingdom of Nan-chao) the capital of his new Islamic kingdom, taking for himself the title of sultan. His regime managed to get some arms through Burma (it is sometimes called the Panthay Rebellion, using a Burmese term meaning Muslim), and in 1872 even sent a vain mission to London seeking British help. Meantime another violent Muslim rising, beginning in 1862, had convulsed Northwest China, while primitive Miao tribesmen in the mountains of Kweichow had been in rebellion ever since 1854.

Although these smaller movements—Nien, Muslim, and Miao—all lacked the size of the Taiping kingdom, they were a similar index to the collapse of the central power. The Ch'ing dynasty was now caught between the twin forces of "internal rebellion and foreign aggression." But while these inland rebels were proving unable to create institutions to supplant the traditional system, the Westerners in the treaty ports were energetically seizing the opportunity to create a new order on the coast.

Final Establishment of the Treaty System

Compared with the fratricidal slaughter of millions and the wholesale destruction of cities and farming capital (such as the mulberry trees essential for silk culture) which attended the great rebellions, the Opium War with its few thousands of casualties had been a very small affair indeed. Similarly the early opium trade, the missionary movement, and the first treaty ports all were on a small scale. They did not directly affect the lives of ordinary Chinese, but by calling the old order into question they began the long-term process of undermining the institutions of Chinese society. In the short term, however, the foreign diplomatic influence was not always revolutionary. On the contrary, one of the issues of China's modern history is the question how far the Western powers after 1860 may have inhibited political change by propping up the faltering Ch'ing dynasty. In the decade from the rise of rebellion in 1851 to 1860, the Western powers moved from a policy of negotiation with Peking to one of coercion and then, having secured a second treaty settlement, from coercion to cooperation with the dynasty.

During the 1850's the disintegration of the central government's control over the local scene, in the treaty ports as in the provinces of the vast interior, led to the rise of local power-holders. In the case of the ports, however, the foreign consuls, instead of creating Chinese-type administrative agencies of the kind set up by the various rebel regimes or the gentry leaders of the interior, created new Western-type agencies of their own. At Shanghai the foreign settled areas were flooded with refugees from the Taipings. In 1853, when Triads seized the walled city, the imperial custom house was put out of action and the imperial officials, from the taotai (intendant of circuit) on down, were ousted. The foreign settlement organized its own local militia of Western merchants, the Shanghai Volunteer Corps. In July 1854 the consuls of Britain, the United States, and France joined in getting the taotai's consent to regulations which set up a degree of self-government and formed the basis for the later growth of the International Settlement and French Concession, with their own powers of local taxation and upkeep of roads and municipal police. Thus the future center of China's modernization at the entrance to the Yangtze Valley became a semiforeign city run by the local foreign land-renters under the protection of their treaty rights of extraterritoriality.

Meanwhile, in the absence of the imperial custom house, the British consul had maintained the collection of duties due by treaty, so as to forestall Chinese collection of duties on foreign trade in the interior. The idea of a treaty tariff, known to all and equally enforced, had proved unworkable in the face of collusion between Chinese customs collectors and competing foreign merchants. Yet without equal taxation, free trade and the secure growth of legal commerce would be jeopardized. In July 1854, the British, American, and French consuls therefore arranged that their nominees should serve the taotai as his customs collectors, seeing to it that the foreign merchants were impartially assessed and also ensuring that the taotai would receive the revenue. From this beginning grew the Foreign Inspectorate of Customs. From 1855 an Englishman (Horatio Nelson Lay) was employed by the Chinese government, as a private individual, to assess the duties from China's foreign trade. Neither the International Settlement nor the Foreign Inspectorate would have been created in more normal times of strong Chinese administration. Under pressure of a crisis, they were a product of the British instinct for *ad hoc* arrangements and of Chinese resilience in cooperating with powerful aliens on the frontier.

The Anglo-French War with China. China's foreign trade in tea, silk, and opium increased even as rebellion spread more widely, but Canton lost its pre-eminence in trade and antiforeign feeling there mounted. Westerners were still excluded from the walled city, and this became an issue of "face" between Britain and China. By 1851 Britain was ready to coerce China again to gain broader trading privileges, but recognized that foreign agression might add to domestic disorder and so hinder foreign trade. It appeared unlikely that the Taipings would foster Western trade any more than the Ch'ing, and the Western powers therefore maintained neutrality toward the rebellion.

In 1854 Britain, the United States, and France tried to negotiate treaty revisions with Peking in pourparlers at Canton, Shanghai, and off Tientsin. But negotiation was refused or evaded, while occasional popular attacks on Western nationals raised the issue of foreign prestige. The Western nations, which at this same time were forcing trade treaties on Japan and other Asian countries, were in a mood to press their claims for further contact with China on Western terms. Convinced that the treaty system would deteriorate if not reaffirmed and extended, Britain found a pretext in 1856, when the consul claimed a British flag was disregarded on a Chinese-owned vessel registered at Hong Kong, the lorcha *Arrow*. (A lorcha was a vessel with Western hull and Chinese rig.) When a French missionary, seized as a foreign subversive in an area of rebellion, was executed in Kwangsi, the French found this a basis for cooperation with Britain to coerce the Chinese Empire.

The British knew what they wanted—the acceptance by the Son of Heaven of the Western concept of international trade and relations—but it took them four years to get it. After some delay, they captured Canton early in 1858 and installed the Chinese governor of Kwangtung as a puppet to govern the city under an allied commission.

Aiming at the emperor, the Anglo-French negotiators took their forces direct to Tientsin and there in June 1858 secured their treaties, which provided that their ministers could reside at Peking on terms of diplomatic equality. American and Russian plenipotentiaries went along to Tientsin as "neutrals" and secured almost identical treaties. Since permanent Western legations at Peking would end the ancient tradition of China's superiority, the Ch'ing court became increasingly determined not to concede this point, even though it had been accepted in treaty drafts. When the British and French ministers arrived off Tientsin a year later, in June 1859, to go to Peking and exchange treaty ratifications, they were refused passage. Trying to force a passage up the river, they were repulsed. Four British gunboats were unexpectedly sunk with many casualties. The British and French therefore had to return again in 1860 with stronger forces. For this final showdown the British brought to North China 41 warships, 143 troop transports, 10,500 troops, and a coolie corps of 2500 Cantonese. The French brought 6300 troops and more than 60 ships. The allies defeated much larger imperial forces under the Mongol commander-in-chief, Prince Senggerinchin, and entered Peking in October, while the emperor fled beyond the Wall to Jehol.

In the settlement at Peking, Anglo-French friction arose over the French thirst for national glory, in the absence of any commercial interest in China, while the British negotiator (Lord Elgin) had to restrain also the expansionist demands of the "old China hands." But when the chief British negotiator was seized while under a flag of truce and some twenty men in his party were executed before he was released, Elgin took reprisal against the emperor personally by destroying his summer palace of some two hundred buildings northwest of Peking (the Yüan Ming Yüan), which had already been looted by the invading forces and Chinese villagers. Short of ammunition and faced with the onset of winter, the allies had to get a quick settlement and withdraw. They signed new conventions with the emperor's brother, Prince Kung, who now represented the dynasty. These documents confirmed the treaties of 1858, increased their indemnities, and added certain other concessions. For example, Britain secured the Kowloon Peninsula opposite Hong Kong. France obtained by a subterfuge the right for Catholic missions to hold property in the interior.

This second treaty settlement had the general effect of opening the Chinese Empire to Western contact. Without introducing any radically new principles, it enlarged the scope of the foreign privileges that had been developed under British leadership at the five early treaty ports.

The Russian Advance in Manchuria. By the most-favored-nation principle, Russia also secured these privileges, but meanwhile her envoys had also been active elsewhere. By the Sino-Russian treaties of 1689 and 1727 the Ch'ing emperors had succeeded in keeping the Russians out of the Amur watershed and on the far outer frontier of Mongolia. This had diverted Russian expansion to other parts of Asia. Bering discovered Alaska in 1741, Russian posts were established on Kamchatka, and Russian contact began with Japan. In 1799 the Russian-American Company was chartered to keep up with the British East India Company by monopolizing Russian trade in the Pacific. From 1812 to 1839 it even maintained an outpost in California, not far north of that of the Mexicans at San Francisco. Meanwhile, from 1727 until after 1860, a regular Sino-Russian trade was carried on at the Chinese border town of Mai-mai-ch'eng in Outer Mongolia opposite the Russian town of Kiakhta (see page 252). Although trading missions ceased going to Peking, the Russian ecclesiastical mission had continued there with four priests and half a dozen language students. This mission became a center of Chinese studies, and was also a point of semiofficial contact.

The opening of the treaty ports had coincided with a continued Russian advance into Central Asia in the area soon to be known as Russian Turkestan (as opposed to Chinese Turkestan east of the Pamir massif). During the eighteenth century the Russians had steadily advanced, setting up fortified lines of outposts against the mobile Kirghiz and Kazakh tribes of the steppe. These outposts soon extended from the Caspian north to Orenburg and thence east along the Irtysh River. By degrees this arc was steadily pushed southward. On this frontier Russian trade developed with Chinese Turkestan as well as with the khanates of Khiva, Bokhara, and Samarkand (see map on page 347). In 1851 a Sino-Russian treaty was signed at Kuldja, the main city of the Ili region, to regulate trade there along the lines already established at the more easterly mart at Kiakhta. Russian trading caravans were to be carefully regulated as to routes, seasons, factories, residences, and the like, but were to be under the control of their own consul at Kuldja. The agreement was on terms of equality and reciprocity, such as seem to have characterized the contact between the Ch'ing and Russian Empires, particularly on this far frontier where both were conquering powers and had some community of interest against the warlike local tribes.

Stimulated by the British success in China, the Russians also began a second invasion of the Amur watershed, from which they had had to withdraw after 1689. This move was led by a vigorous proconsul, Nikolai Muraviev, who was appointed governor-general of Eastern Siberia in 1847. He sent Russian flotillas of barges down the Amur in 1854 and the years following, founding posts on the north bank all the way down to Khabarovsk, where the Ussuri enters the Amur. Russian troops and settlers soon created a position of strength. On May 16, 1858, even before the treaties were concluded at Tientsin, Muraviev secured a treaty at Aigun, which ceded to Russia the north bank of the Amur and left China and Russia in joint possession of the territory between the Ussuri and the sea, pending its further disposition. Muraviev's program of occupying sparsely populated frontier areas now won support from his own, hitherto reluctant, government in St. Petersburg (see map, page 252).

The Russian Treaty of Tientsin in June 1858, though it gained all the Western trading privileges, left the question of the east coast of Manchuria unsettled. It remained for a clever diplomat, General Nikolai Ignatiev, to consolidate Russia's East Asian gains in 1860 (all the more necessary after Peking in 1859 had rejected the Treaty of Aigun). In his negotiations Ignatiev used several stratagems. Reaching Peking in June 1859 after the Ch'ing victory over the British gunboats outside Tientsin, he took up residence at the Russian ecclesiastical mission and negotiated fruitlessly for several months. In 1860 he went to Shanghai and by his knowledge of Peking ingratiated himself with the other Western plenipotentiaries. After the allies had fought their way to the capital, with Ignatiev in their train, he was in a position to mediate between them and the Ch'ing court. The Sino-Russian Treaty of Peking of November 1860, signed after the British and French had departed, was his reward for mediating. It confirmed the Treaty of Aigun and in addition gave Russia the Maritime Province between the Ussuri and the Pacific, where Muraviev had already founded Vladivostok (meaning in Russian "Rule of the East") in July 1860. Thus the Ch'ing Empire had barely been opened to trade and evangelism by the Western powers when Russia began the process of its territorial dismemberment.

The Restoration of the Ch'ing Government

To overcome the evils of domestic disorder and foreign invasion, the Chinese state required strong leadership at the top, but for this exacting task the Taiping rebels had early proved unprepared and ineffective—Heaven's Mandate never really came within their reach. By 1860 the only hope of re-establishing peace and order seemed to be at Peking. Here a genuine "restoration" occurred, a revival of dynastic leadership such as had taken place before in Chinese history after devastating rebellions, notably in the founding of the Eastern Han and in the middle T'ang (see pages 85 and 120). This revival of imperial leadership coincided with several turning points in the struggles of the time—first of all, in the campaign against the rebels.

In 1860 the Great Camp of the imperial forces below Nanking was destroyed for a second time, by the vigorous Taiping commander Li Hsiu-ch'eng, and this disaster forced the Ch'ing court finally to give the Hunan scholar-general Tseng Kuo-fan unified command over the whole campaign of suppression. In August 1860 he was appointed governor-general and imperial commissioner with top military and civil authority over the middle and lower Yangtze provinces. He installed other Chinese scholar-generals as governors of provinces and finally began to hem in the rebel forces. Another corner was turned when the Anglo-French capture of Peking broke the back of the die-hard antiforeign party within the Ch'ing court, and the emperor's brother, Prince Kung, emerged to conclude the treaty settlement. Appeasement of the invaders by accepting the treaty system was now acknowledged to be the only possible way to save the dynasty. Finally, the Hsien-feng emperor died in August 1861, and by a *coup d'état* his brother, Prince Kung, and the young Empress Dowager, Tz'u-hsi, mother of the new boy-emperor, came into power. Executing rival princes who had been more antiforeign, they gave the new reign strong Manchu leadership along two main lines: to cooperate warily in the working of the treaty system and to give full support to the Chinese gentry leaders under Tseng Kuo-fan in the suppression of rebellion. As Prince Kung put it, the rebels were a disease in China's vitals, the barbarians an affliction only of the limbs. The new reign was called *T'ung-chih*, meaning "Union for Order."

Foreign Aid and the End of the Taiping Kingdom.   To assist his Hunan Army, Tseng had his able young disciple Li Hung-chang (1823–1901) build up the Anhwei Army, a similar regionally-based gentry-led striking force. Whereas the Hunan Army was already declining because of its long-continued losses and inadequate financial support, Li succeeded in April 1862 in moving his new Anhwei Army into Shanghai on foreign-rented steamers and with gentry-merchant support. Confirmed as governor of

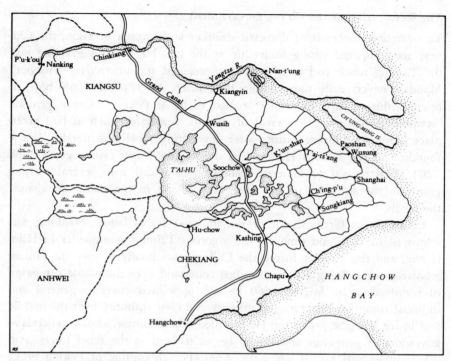

THE YANGTZE DELTA

Kiangsu, he gradually entrenched himself in the Yangtze delta. In addition to the tribute grain collections, he got some control over the new Maritime Customs revenues and other taxes on the commerce of the Shanghai area. Thus financed, he purchased foreign arms and built his Anhwei Army up to seventy thousand men, the most powerful force in China. He and Tseng set up arsenals to make Western guns and steamships and, in the process first of suppressing rebels and second of "self-strengthening," got their own personal supporters into power in a bureaucratic machine.

One impetus for adopting Western arms was given by the example of a foreign-officered mercenary force at Shanghai. This began as a local corps of foreign adventurers, paid by Chinese merchants and led by Frederick Townsend Ward of Salem, Massachusetts. When the last great outbreak of the rebellion brought Taiping forces to the outskirts of Shanghai early in 1862, Britain and France now abandoned neutrality in defense of the treaty ports of Shanghai and Ningpo. Instead of a foreign legion, Ward now trained a small Chinese force of about four thousand men, whose Western arms and use of amphibious tactics of maneuver on the waterways of the Yangtze delta won more than a hundred engagements and brought them the name of "Ever-Victorious Army." After Ward's death in 1862, Major Charles George Gordon, lent from the British army, eventually succeeded to the command, receiving, like Ward, Chinese military rank under Governor Li Hung-chang. "Chinese" Gordon and his small Sino-foreign army helped capture Soochow. A similar Franco-Chinese force helped recapture Hangchow.

Finally, in July 1864, Nanking was taken by Tseng Kuo-fan's younger brother, with no foreign assistance, after desperate fighting. Thus the rebel kingdom came to a bloody end. This massive movement, with all its early vigor and idealism, had lacked adequate leadership and had stumbled blindly into dissension, corruption, and final defeat. For several years the Taipings had had the opportunity to enlist foreign aid while the Western powers were, part of the time, actually at war with the Ch'ing government; yet the opportunity was never taken. In the end it was the large Chinese armies mobilized under Tseng that did the great bulk of the fighting against the rebels. Chinese use of foreign forces was kept carefully limited. As an imperial edict put it in 1862, "For the time being, we have to make use of foreigners to train our soldiers, as a scheme for self-strengthening...." Western aid to the Ch'ing cause came less through the intervention of foreigners than through the Chinese leaders' own use of foreign trade revenues and of Western guns, ships, and training, in the spirit of "self-strengthening." The Manchu dynasty was saved by Chinese scholar-officials who were loyal to it as part of the Confucian order, and who found Western aid useful for their own purposes in the final years of their long-continued effort. The other mid-century rebellions—of the Nien (1853–1868) and of the Muslims in the Southwest (1855–1873) and in the Northwest (1862–1873)—were all suppressed without Western participation but with some use of modern arms.

The Opening of China. China's acceptance of the second treaty settlement gave the Western powers a stake in the established order, for they were now part of it. In the early 1860's they moved to develop their opportunities. Eleven more treaty ports were eventually opened, including places in North China and Manchuria, on Taiwan, and up the Yangtze as far as Hankow. Foreign vessels continued to participate in the domestic carrying trade among China's coastal and river ports, a right denied foreigners in most countries. The import of opium was legalized on payment of a moderate duty. Foreign imports of all kinds were allowed to pass freely in the interior on payment of a further transit duty of 2½ per cent, which was roughly half the import duty. Thus they could compete with native products. The regulating of foreign trade was handled by an extension of the Shanghai Foreign Inspectorate, which created the Chinese Imperial Maritime Customs Service as a foreign-staffed arm of the Peking government. Travel in the interior under passport now gave the missionaries access to the entire population. Both Catholics and Protestants soon began to acquire and use new property in the interior.

Behind all these opportunities for merchant and missionary expansion stood the power of the Western nations, led by Britain. Their ministers at Peking, backed by gunboats in the ports, had the primary function of enforcing treaty rights. The result was a great intensification of the Western challenge. The new "barbarians" were now truly within the gates. The Chinese people, however, had not yet responded to this threat in nationalistic terms. The tribute system had been destroyed, but the treaty system, only a part-way step toward modern international relations, was curiously reminiscent of the Chinese traditional polity—under extraterritoriality, treaty-power nationals were added to, but did not displace, the privileged Manchu-Chinese ruling class. The traditional Chinese state and social order, which had accommodated alien rulers so often before, remained intact. The very competitiveness of the Europeans seemed to give the dynasty a chance to manipulate these aggressors against one another. After 1864 the Ch'ing dynasty thus had a reprieve and China an opportunity to modernize in self-defense with Western help.

11. China's Response to the West

Early Westernization in Self-Defense

The success story of Meiji Japan from 1868 to 1912 highlighted China's contemporary failure. Both countries had been saddled with unequal treaties that impaired their sovereignty and threatened their economic independence. For Japan to catch up with the modern Western world in all its complexities, and finally in 1905 to defeat Russia, a major world power, in a full-scale war—all in the space of a single lifetime—was an almost incredible feat. China's inability to do this is more understandable than Japan's success. Plainly one reason for Japan's achievement was its capacity to act as a nation with the same degree of patriotic mobilization that nationalism called forth among Western peoples.

As in Western countries, this intense nationalism also had its influence on the writing of history and our understanding of what happened. The Meiji period has been well documented by Japanese historians with a natural pride in Japan's accomplishments. In China of the same period the collapse of the old order left only a few loyal chroniclers and only a prolonged tragedy for them to record. Undoubtedly the parallel stories of Japan's rise and China's decline have come to us with a certain bias—or at least a fuller record—in favor of those who succeeded. Late Ch'ing history has remained less fully developed since 1912 also because revolutions, though they make history, give little opportunity to write it. In short, Japanese historical writing modernized with Japan, while in China, historiography, like so much else, remained longer in traditional channels.

For these and other reasons, we may expect our picture of China's response to the West to change as research progresses.

Our own view is that the major determinants of China's response lay within Chinese society, not outside it. Inertia, the most important of these, made efforts at Westernization superficial—temporary responses to immediate dangers, diminishing whenever danger receded. More broadly, we think traditional China never could have achieved modernization as Japan did because Chinese society was both so massive in size and so firm in organization that it could not be rapidly shifted to Western models of organization. In this view a modernized China could not be built up until much of the durable even if decaying structure of the old society had been torn down. This process was much slower than in Japan, which was far smaller and far more responsive, in addition to having characteristics that made Western institutions and ideas more readily accepted.

This explanation of China's slowness to modernize is sociological and institutional. It differs from the alternative explanation that traditional Chinese society was not distinctively different from the West, and that the slowness of modernization was primarily due to the baneful, depressive influence of Western "imperialism." In an extreme form this view regards all Western contact as having been injurious and a form of "imperialism." But this does not explain why so overwhelming an influence as "imperialism" produced such different results in China and Japan. We suggest that in both countries Western influence was at first slight, a stimulant more than a depressant, and that it stimulated Japan to respond rapidly and successfully. China's response was impeded by its size and inertia and also by certain distinctive features of the Confucian state-and-society such as the culturalism already described. By the time the depressive and exploitative influences of "imperialism" had grown and accumulated later in the century, it was too late for China to respond successfully. Even so, some of China's early efforts to modernize were vigorous and impressive. The contrast with Japan appeared only later. In the 1860's an outsider might well have bet the other way.

Two significant changes were made in 1860 in the Ch'ing political structure: first, the Anglo-French invasion of Peking forced the Son of Heaven to accept foreign potentates as equals, fatally undermining the monarchy's ancient claim to a universal kingship; second, the renewed Taiping threat in the lower Yangtze forced the Manchu court to entrust the military suppression of the rebels to the Chinese gentry leadership under Tseng Kuo-fan, which built up regional Chinese military power and weakened Manchu control. These were constitutional changes that led in the same direction Japan would soon be moving in: to make the Chinese Empire behave internationally like one nation among equals and base its military strength

Prince Kung (personal name, I-hsin; 1833–1898), brother of the Hsien-feng emperor, signer of the unequal treaties of 1860, head of the Grand Council and Tsungli Yamen.

upon the Chinese common people. Yet these results, so quickly to be achieved in Japan, were not realized until much later in China. Unlike the Meiji Restoration, which was a revolutionary fresh start, the Chinese reforms of the early 1860's were only the first step on a long road with many turnings.

"Self-Strengthening" and the Cooperative Policy. Since the Taiping campaign of 1860–1862 was defeated with Anglo-French aid around Shanghai and Ningpo, China in the early 1860's was quite aware of the military superiority of the West, and military Westernization was seen as a solution to both domestic and foreign problems. Tseng Kuo-fan quoted Mencius, "If you can rule your own country, who dares to insult you?" Prince Kung (see figure above) proposed to use suppression of the rebels as a means for securing Western arms. China's conventional wisdom invoked by Wei Yüan in the 1840's—use barbarians to control barbarians—was now seen to be inadequate. Instead, stress was put on Wei Yüan's statement, "Learn the superior technology of the barbarians in order to control them." Thus emerged the movement for "self-strengthening," which after 1861 followed several lines—diplomatic, fiscal, educational, and military. This program now began to supplant the outworn tribute system.

China's new foreign policy was welcomed by the Western ministers at Peking, who were now committed to a policy of cooperation both among

Britain, France, the United States, and Russia and between all of them and China. Diplomats like Rutherford Alcock (British minister 1865–1869), who had been a chief architect of the treaty system, tried to keep a balance between foreign treaty rights and China's legitimate interests and to check the aggressive demands of British merchants in the treaty ports. Alcock recognized that China's modernization involved "such a revolution as has never been seen since the world began." Progress could not be rapid. The "cooperative policy" of the 1860's was designed to help China modernize gradually.

To handle diplomatic relations with the West there was created in March 1861 a new "Office for General Management" or Tsungli Yamen, headed by Prince Kung. This was not actually a new ministry but only a subcommittee of the Grand Council which took the place of a foreign office until one was created in 1901. Decisions on foreign policy still had to come from the emperor, and the Tsungli Yamen was in charge of foreign relations only at Peking. In the coastal provinces there were appointed two commissioners for foreign affairs, who were also the governors-general at Nanking and Tientsin, reporting directly to the emperor. This decentralization suited the growth of regional power that had occurred during the struggle against the Taipings.

The Maritime Customs Service. Creation of the new order in foreign affairs was much influenced by the British negotiators. Horiatio Nelson Lay (see page 299) has been since 1855 the Chinese-paid "foreign inspector" vigorously administering the assessment of duties at Shanghai. His intimate knowledge of treaty relations and of the Chinese language had helped him play the key role, while on leave from his customs post, in browbeating the Ch'ing treaty negotiators at Tientsin in 1858. Later he had helped expand the new customs service. He was appointed Inspector General of Customs by Prince Kung and the Tsungli Yamen in January 1861, and soon after was instructed to procure for the Chinese government the ultimate weapon of the day, a fleet of steam gunboats. But Lay in England not only procured a fleet of eight ships with British crews, he also went further and tried to keep control of the fleet in his own hands. When this powerful flotilla reached China in 1863, both Prince Kung and Tseng Kuo-fan refused to accept Lay's arrangements, he was paid off, and the fleet was disposed of by the British. Lay had grandly considered himself to be working *for* the Chinese authorities, not *under* them. "The notion," he said, "of a gentleman acting *under* an Asiatic barbarian is preposterous."

Robert Hart (see page 311), who succeeded Lay in 1863, built the Customs Service on an entirely different basis. Hart was from northern Ireland and had come to China in the British service in 1854. He told his foreign Commissioners of Customs that "those who take the pay, and who

Sir Robert Hart at work. A drawing from a London periodical. ca. 1890, shows the Inspector General of Customs at his famous standing desk.

are the servants of the Chinese Government... are the brother officers" of the native officials and "in a sense, the countrymen" of the Chinese people. He had his foreign Commissioners oversee all aspects of customs procedure but they were nominally subordinate to the Chinese Superintendents of Customs (usually the local taotais) at each port, who received the actual payments of duties. Hart himself remained responsible for the entire foreign staff, which by 1875 included 252 employees from Britain and 156 from sixteen other Western countries. Thus he created with great tact, patience, and foresight an administrative arm of the Ch'ing central government which used foreign employees to handle the foreign merchants and also assisted China's efforts at modernization.

The new customs revenue, as well as Hart's discreet advice, supported a new institution at Peking, the Interpreters College (T'ung-wen Kuan) which aimed to free China's diplomats from dependence on foreign interpreters. As the Tsungli Yamen argued, "In any negotiations with foreign nations, the prerequisite is to know their nature and feelings." Or as Li Hung-chang said, "First understand their ambitions, be aware of their desires, and... their points of strength and weakness." Similar small schools were opened in Shanghai, Canton, and Foochow, but results were disappointing because the students appointed were mainly middle-aged Manchu bannermen.

A demand for Western scientific learning was created by the setting up of arsenals and shipyards. Tseng and Li finally combined all their efforts in the Kiangnan Arsenal at Shanghai in 1865. By 1868 its Chinese work-men had produced their first steamship, though they used a foreign-built engine. Translation of Western scientific treatises and manuals was an essential part of this development. At Foochow another arsenal and navy yard were set up in 1866 with French assistance.

Nearly all these steps in Westernization were dealt with at Peking through the new Tsungli Yamen rather than through traditional channels. The policy pursued during the 1860's was thus a mixture of old and new. The Western aggressors were appeased with trade and contact under the treaties, the secrets of their military strength were learned in order to ward off foreign attack and suppress domestic rebellion, but meanwhile efforts were made to revive the old Confucian type of government. Restoration of the traditional order, with its unity of state and culture, had actually been the major aim, Westernization in self-defense a minor aim.

The Restoration of Confucian Government

We have suggested that the Chinese state-and-society had achieved such an equilibrium and self-sufficiency among its political, economic, social, ideological, and other elements, that the whole might decline in vigor and yet remain impervious to outside influence. In the processes of government the need for order, the vested interests of the scholar-official and landown-ing classes, and the conservative ideology of Confucianism all met and reinforced one another. Consequently, China's basic response in the 1860's to the dual menace of foreign aggression and domestic rebellion was to reaffirm, or "restore," the old Confucian system rather than modernize it. The new was neither expected nor prized, least of all from abroad. As one arch-conservative put it, "Why must we learn from the barbarian foreigners? ... They are our enemies."

To this institutional and psychological inertia was added the political weakness of the Ch'ing central power after 1860. The Restoration, as a come-back of dynastic rule after serious rebellion, aimed in the traditional fashion at revival more than innovation. But the dynasty had been severely shaken. The emperor had to lead the way but the T'ung-chih emperor (reg. 1862–1875) was a weak boy, under a regency dominated by his mother, the Empress Dowager (1835–1908). This remarkable woman, usually called Tz'u-hsi from the first two characters of her long title, was clever and strong-willed but narrow-minded. As coregent for her son, she soon learned how to use the imperial prerogatives of appointment, promotion, praise, censure, dismissal, and punishment of officials to make herself the real ruler of the empire. She became entrenched in power, governing with the aid of palace eunuchs and trusted high officials, but she had no grasp of

China's problem of modernization. Consequently the revival of Confucian government on Chinese lines was energetic and partially successful, but steps toward modernization ran into trouble.

Suppression of the Rebellions. The capture of Nanking in 1864 had extinguished the Taiping Kingdom, the only real competitor for dynastic power, but large areas were still in revolt. The Nien rebels had developed a defensive strategy of "strengthening the walls and clearing the countryside" (see page 297), based on the fortified earth-walled villages of their "nest" area. This strategy concentrated both the farming population and the harvested crops from the fields within the earth-walled villages, so that invading imperial forces would find neither manpower nor food supplies. Meanwhile the Nien cavalry made hit-and-run raids into provinces to the north. The addition of Taiping remnants to the Nien forces prompted the appointment in 1865 of Tseng Kuo-fan to suppress the Nien.

Occupation of the nest area and leveling of its earthen walls had twice been achieved, but to no avail; the populace and chiefs of village militia corps had continued to support the Nien, and the earthen walls had been rebuilt. Tseng now tried a traditional strategy. He proscribed the Nien leaders, listing them for execution, but promised to pardon and protect their followers and the village chiefs who surrendered. Isolating the nest area by setting up four strong points and blockade lines (see map, page 294), Tseng's forces invaded it and carefully screened one earth-walled village after another, registering the populace in five-family groups for mutual guaranty and formally appointing village chiefs. Meanwhile they revived cultivation in devastated areas, recovered control of the people and food supply, and so cut off the Nien raiding forces from their source of manpower and provisions. "Strengthening the walls and clearing the countryside" was thus used against the rebels.

Late in 1866 Li Hung-chang took over the task of suppressing the Nien, since the principal force involved was the Anhwei Army which he had built up. Tseng Kuo-fan had formally disbanded his Hunan Army after the defeat of the Taipings, to get rid of urgent problems of finance, leadership, and discipline among the troops. Li's Anhwei Army took its place as the chief modern force in China. Supplied with arms from the new arsenal at Shanghai and with tribute rice from the rich Yangtze delta, the Anhwei Army soon had thirty thousand or more muzzle-loading rifles for its seventy thousand troops, together with cannon on barges, and seven thousand cavalry. After 1866 the Nien split into two mobile bands in the eastern and western sectors of the North China Plain. They were kept apart by blockade lines a thousand miles long, manned by 100,000 troops, along the Grand Canal and Yellow River, on the west and northwest borders of

Shantung. Gradually hemmed in, the eastern band was destroyed in January and the western in August 1868.

Southwest China, where Tu Wen-hsiu had set up his own Muslim state in 1856 (see page 298), saw an even longer struggle to reassert the central authority. Tu as a Muslim religious partisan apparently offered little leadership to the non-Muslim Chinese. The Ch'ing cause seems in the end to have offered a greater degree of orderly administration and nonpartisan justice to all elements of the mixed population. Some Ch'ing generals came from the local gentry as commanders of militia corps. Even Muslim Chinese found it advantageous to take the Ch'ing side. Through death and migration the population meanwhile had been reduced by more than one-half. Walled cities like Yunnanfu (modern Kunming) underwent long sieges. Muslim power at one time was based on fifty-three walled cities, which the imperial forces captured one after another, often with bloody massacres. Tali was finally captured in 1873, and Tu Wen-hsiu killed himself. In the same year the Miao tribesmen in Kweichow were also suppressed.

In Northwest China, in the arid "panhandle" strip of Kansu province that forms the corridor for communication with Turkestan, risings of Chinese Muslims had occurred in the 1780's, inspired partly by the fanatical sect known as the New Teaching. In the mid-nineteenth century a new rebellion seems to have arisen not against the Ch'ing so much as against corrupt local officials. A revolt broke out near Sian in 1862 and spread westward. The principal leader of the militant New Teaching built up his base near Ning-hsia. This northwestern region was of great strategic importance but its recovery had to wait upon the subjugation first of the Taipings in 1864 and then of the Nien in 1868. The task was given to one of the victorious gentry-generals of Hunan, Tso Tsung-t'ang, whose recovery of Shensi and Kansu took five years (1868–1873), precisely as he foresaw. His management of subordinates, maintenance of extended lines of supply, and revival of local civil administration all seemed to prove the efficacy of traditional methods. Systematic and indomitable, he advanced slowly, reducing rebel strongholds and killing as many rebels as possible. By 1871, as he wrote a friend, his wife had died, his hair was white, he had lost most of his teeth, he suffered from dysentery and malaria, and he was being criticized for his slowness. However, by 1873, though the population had been greatly reduced, peace reigned over the Northwest.

The Restoration of the 1860's was a triumph both of warfare and of civil government in the traditional manner. Tseng, Li, and Tso were preeminently scholar-administrators. Their success was due not only to hard fighting but also to their application of Confucian moral and political principles, encouragement of economic recovery, effective taxation and, in addi-

A PEKING HOUSEHOLD. *Peking official (ca. 1872) seated in his garden courtyard with his son; ladies, children, and servants above. Unidentified lady at far left.*

tion, some use of Western technology. Yet the Restoration did not bring China back to the status quo ante but rather to a new equilibrium in which the leading officials at the top of their provincial administrations, though loyal to the dynasty, had strong regional power. The dynastic central power owed its survival to, and henceforth had to contend with, this growth of regionalism.

The Economic Aftermath of Civil War. Like the United States, China in the late 1860's confronted an enormous task of reconstruction. Fighting had occurred over a longer period and in a larger area than in the United States, but the Middle Kingdom lacked a modern industrial capacity to bind up the nation's wounds. Serious losses of capital had occurred—for example, irrigation works in the Northwest and mulberry trees, essential for silk-worm culture, in Central China. Great numbers of homeless persons had to be fed and put to work. These problems were met principally by the fortitude and hard work of the common people. Leadership was exercised in each locality mainly by the gentry, with official encouragement. Transport and distribution of relief grain, establishment of soup kitchens, orphanages, refugee centers, as well as public works—"using work in place of charity"—were managed by gentry and officials together. Government action was mainly in the form of moral exhortation and direction, widespread remission of the land tax, reduction of tax rates, and occasionally the resettlement of farmers with seeds and tools. On the whole, these measures aided landlords more than tenants; the former might pay less land tax, but the latter seldom secured reductions of rent.

After the outbreak of civil war in the 1850's, the central government's treasury had been quickly exhausted, and land taxes from rich provinces were cut off. Peking increased the sale of rank and even office, thus inflating the gentry class, and issued new iron cash, paper, and other cheap forms of money, thus inflating the currency. But the revenue crisis could not be met by increasing the land tax, which had been set in established quotas for each area ever since the emperor in 1712 had optimistically decreed that tax quotas should "never thereafter be increased." Ch'ing finance had thus been cursed by inelasticity.

To meet this fiscal crisis there was instituted in Kiangsu in 1853 a small tax on merchants and traders, which became known as likin (*li-chin,* "a tax of one-thousandth"). This new tax had three important features: it was too small to be worth a great effort to avoid and hence was easy to collect; it was collected on articles of consumption, either as a transit tax on goods as they passed a likin barrier or as a sales tax where the goods were sold; and finally the likin revenues were mainly retained within the provinces, where the local gentry participated in administering the likin system. By 1860 it had spread to almost every part of China. Gentry and officials who were mobilizing troops collected likin to support them. By the time peace was restored, it could not be dispensed with.

The central government revenue before 1850 had been collected mainly from the agricultural sector of the economy (see table, page 317). By the end of the century the new taxes on commerce had more than doubled the revenue. Among these the portions of likin made available to Peking were at first the most important. But the new Maritime Customs revenue rose in the 1860's to about 7 million taels a year and subsequently much higher. It included the tax on foreign opium still being imported in increasing amounts from India. The government of China could no longer be financed by the ancient methods of a superficially centralized agrarian-bureaucratic state. The growth of regional armies and the spread of the likin system began a trend toward decentralization or regionalism which could not be reversed, although it was held in check by the reaffirmation of the Confucian ideology.

The Philosophy and Leadership of the Restoration. Western ideas played a remarkably small part in the revival of the 1860's. On the contrary, the

Estimates of Central Government Revenues

(receipts nominally expected at Peking, in millions of taels)

	Pre-1850	*Early 1890's*	*Early 1900's*
Land tax and grain tribute	30	32	33
Salt gabelle	5 or 6	13 (a)	13 (a)
Old-style customs	4	1	4
New Maritime customs	0	22	35
Likin	0	15 (b)	14 (b)
Sale of rank or office, misc.	1	5	4
Rough total	40	89	103

(a) including salt likin
(b) including native opium likin

Restoration leaders reaffirmed China's ancient morality and stressed its application to practical affairs through "statecraft" (see pages 268–269). The main ideas of this morality in action may be compressed into a series of propositions: that the harmony of Chinese society depended on hierarchic organization and performance of proper roles from top to bottom; that each individual should follow the social norms of conduct, the ancient Confucian *li* or "principles of social usage"; that the virtuous example of the superior man gave him moral authority; and that legal punishments and the use of force only supplemented government by virtuous moral example. Rebels had to be chastised, and either reformed or eliminated, but the use of force had to be followed up by an incorrupt, just, and benevolent government. Domestic harmony thus restored, prosperity would ensue. This philosophy was strongly elitist and hierarchic, opposed to the egalitarian trend of modern times. It looked for its model to the golden age of antiquity and had nothing like the modern concept of progress. The main emphasis of economic policy was not on increased production and revenue but on frugality, and the proper use of fixed taxes and resources. The Restoration's ideal was static harmony, not dynamic growth. Its vision was limited to the ancient Confucian model. This included a doctrine of cyclical change or "change within tradition," which could be invoked to sanction reform. But reform remained essentially conservative, restricted by two beliefs: that agriculture, providing the "people's livelihood" (*min-sheng*), was the basis

MILITARY MODERNIZATION. *Manchu bannermen with a small cannon, assigned to guard the British consulate at Canton, ca. 1870.*

of the state, and that a carefully selected elite of "men of talent" was the basis of good government.*

In the 1860's, the interests and ideas of Manchu and Chinese leaders became nearly identical, for both were bent on making the traditional system work again. Up to 1850 Manchus had supplied roughly half the officials at Peking, two-thirds of the governors-general and one-third of the governors in the provinces. But in the subsequent suppression of rebellion the new talent that emerged was almost entirely Chinese. They had always staffed the lower levels of bureaucracy. Now Manchus became even scarcer in the provinces. Meanwhile by the 1860's Manchuria was no longer tightly closed to Chinese migration, the Manchu banners were no longer a potent military force, the Manchu language was hardly used, and the ban on Manchu-Chinese intermarriage was no longer effective. The Manchu leadership had almost merged into the Chinese upper class. Until the new Chinese nationalism in the 1890's brought the dynasty under attack as racially alien, it functioned as a traditional Chinese institution. Modern critics who say that Chinese leaders, by remaining loyal to the Ch'ing in this era, "sold out" to alien rulers are applying a nationalist standard of loyalty anachronistically.

*See Mary Clabaugh Wright, *The Last Stand of Chinese Conservatism: The T'ung-chih Restoration, 1862–1874* (Stanford, Calif.: Stanford University Press, 1957).

The first step in finding the "men of talent" needed for the Restoration was to revive the regular examinations, reopen local academies, and get standard works reprinted. Another effort was to relate the examination questions to real problems of the day—for example, how could troops best be trained, distributed, and maintained? This element of practicality followed the school of "statecraft," stressing the more skillful use of traditional methods. One necessary measure was to restrain the sale of degrees. This practice, used in moderation, had had a double value: it provided quick revenue in times of emergency, and it assured the loyalty of the wealthy but nonscholarly man, by letting him buy his way into the scholar class without destroying the scholar's supremacy. "Irregular" degrees obtained by purchase were clearly distinguishable from "regular" examination degrees. In the first half of the nineteenth century the sale of degrees had regularly taken in more than a million, and often 2 million, taels a year. The "irregular" gentry by purchase, at the lowest level of rank, had formed roughly three-tenths of the whole gentry class, which up to 1850 totaled in any given year about 1,100,000 men throughout the empire.

The Restoration tried with some success to prevent any sale of office and to limit the sale of rank. But here again, it was not possible to go back to the status quo ante. The "regular" gentry had grown by an increase in the quotas of first-level degrees to be awarded by examination in the various provinces. As rewards for contributions, quotas were gradually raised during the Rebellion by about 18 per cent. Richer areas, by securing higher quotas, could get more of their young men into the gentry class. During most of the Ch'ing period the rich and cultured urban centers of the lower Yangtze had furnished a high proportion of the winners in the Peking examinations. About two-fifths had come from Kiangsu alone, where the Manchu court got its rice supply and most needed to have allies.

Meanwhile the "irregular" gentry increased even faster than the "regular." By the late nineteenth century the gentry totaled about 1,450,000, more than a third of them qualified only by purchase, an index no doubt of the movement of merchants into gentry status. Thus despite the revival of the examination system, its position as the font of Confucian government eventually grew weaker. Finally, the Restoration was least effective on the lowest level, that of the petty functionaries who normally lived on customary fees or "squeeze." Here the traditional morality was weakest. One could not select and train "men of talent" at this level, nor provide the technical specialization that modern government required.

The Reaction to Christian Missions

One positive result of the restoration of Confucian teachings, though similarly defensive in aim and spirit, was the anti-Christian movement aroused by increased missionary activity. Roman Catholic and Protestant missions were very different movements. The Catholics still had some 150,000 communicants scattered through the provinces in 1800, a foundation for the growth that came with the treaties. By 1870 their community numbered nearly 400,000 souls, ministered to by some 250 European Jesuits, Franciscans, Lazarists, Dominicans, and others, and by many Chinese priests and catechists. The Sino-French convention of 1860 promised the missionaries complete toleration and restitution of former properties, and through a French ruse, the Chinese text of the agreement also permitted them (and therefore all other foreigners too) to lease or buy land and erect buildings anywhere. Thus the Church became a landlord, renting out its properties, in addition to managing schools, seminaries, and orphanages. After its long history in China, Catholicism had become firmly rooted in Chinese society. Impressive ceremonies marked the stages through which a convert became first an adorer, then a catechumen, and finally was baptized. Festivals and pilgrimages, family worship, the teaching of moral conduct, the Church's support of its own, all bound the faithful into the Catholic community. The whole effort, tempered by the persecutions of the past, was carefully adjusted to Chinese ways.

The Protestant missionaries, in contrast, were still on the periphery of China. In 1850 they totaled only about 80 persons, representing a score of mission societies, and confined almost entirely to the five treaty ports, Macao, and Hong Kong. Lacking the tested methods of the Catholic fathers, the Protestant missionaries and their wives, many of whom were also missionaries, remained clearly a part of the Sino-Western treaty-port society (see figures on page 344). By 1870 there were 350 or more Protestant missionaries, but their converts probably totaled fewer than 6000 persons. No single agency, comparable to the Propaganda at Rome, coordinated their efforts, which were almost as fragmented as those of the Western merchants. Pioneer agencies like the London Missionary Society and the American Board of Commissioners for Foreign Missions (Congregationalist) had been joined by others in great profusion—Dutch Reformed, Gospel Baptist, Wesleyan Methodist, and many more. Protestant missionaries from northern European countries and North America were sharply marked off from the Catholic missionaries, who came mainly from Latin countries and regarded the results of the Reformation as dangerous heresy. To Protestants, Rome was anti-Christ, the Catholic faith a rival religion. Cooperation and even contact between the two branches of Christianity were minimal.

In 1866 a remarkable English organizer, Hudson Taylor, began the China Inland Mission, which eventually grew into the largest of all mission agencies, wholly devoted to the spreading of the gospel. Taylor had a straightforward belief in salvation through faith in Christ as the only alternative to eternal hellfire, and China had seemed to him a big problem. "*A million a month* were dying in that land," he said later, "dying without God." He recruited missionaries of any Protestant denomination, from any country, guaranteed them no fixed salaries, asserting "the Lord will provide," and sent them to inland centers to live simply among the people, dress in Chinese style, and lead Chinese souls to salvation. Making it widely known that he would not solicit support except by prayer, Taylor found contributions and recruits steadily forthcoming. Protestant mission stations gradually began to appear in the interior provinces where the Catholic Church had long been established.

Gentry Hostility. Since the days of Yang Kuang-hsien in the seventeenth century (see page 250), Confucians had criticized Christian doctrine as superstitious and heterodox: why, they asked, had an all-powerful and merciful God permitted original sin? Having been proscribed as heterodox in 1724, Catholicism remained so down to 1846. All this did not commend Christianity to the Chinese scholar class on intellectual grounds. To this were added urgent political considerations: the Taiping rebels claimed to be Christians, while the powerful barbarian invaders from the West also professed the Christian religion. Finally, the Chinese gentry now found the missionaries beginning to confront them as would-be rivals in the performance of their social functions.

First of all, the missionaries came as teachers, offered religious instruction, and set up schools, thus laying claim to membership in a scholar class which, however, was not Confucian. To convey the Christian message, missionaries found it necessary, at least by implication, to question the social order of which the gentry were the local protagonists. They competed with the gentry in practical affairs such as shelter of orphans, relief for the destitute, and aid in time of famine or disaster, thus tending to supplant the gentry in certain of their customary functions. Another important cause of friction was the privileged status claimed by missionaries, or thrust upon them, under extraterritoriality. Just as the gentry were set off from the Chinese populace by their immunity from corporal punishment and their privileged access to and influence with officials, so the missionaries were untouchably privileged, immune to official coercion, able to intercede with Chinese officialdom and, failing that, to call upon their own governments. Catholic bishops in particular assumed a quasi-official status with much pomp and ceremony. Having a privileged position, missionaries, like leading gentry, were often obliged to defend the interests of Chinese, primarily their converts, who regarded them as patrons and protectors. As friction developed between communities of Chinese Christians and non-Christians, missionaries were called upon to intervene with local officials, demanding punishment of culprits and payment of reparations. Hostility was not lessened by the fact that converts were sometimes opportunistic "rice Christians," or from among the underprivileged, those least committed to Confucian scholarship as a path of advancement. Christianity seemed bent on mobilizing the discontented.

Judging by modern standards of nationalism, it would be hard to imagine a more solid basis for gentry hostility to the incoming priest or evangelist, with his strange speech, uncouth ways, and apparently subversive aims. The missionary's purpose, expressed in terms of succor and salvation of his fellow men, was inevitably subversive of the traditional Chinese order. The hostility of the Chinese scholar class is not surprising. Chinese opposition was sufficiently violent to provoke thousands of small incidents and some 240 riots or attacks on missionaries between 1860 and 1899. Yet it was not adequate to check the missionary movement or to figure largely in the missionary literature that poured back to the West.

The anti-Christian movement was led sporadically by gentry here and there, who used traditional means to arouse popular hostility. Their first device was the printed word, which carried authority in a land where literacy was still an upper-class hallmark. Many traditional accusations were reprinted—that Christianity was only an offshoot of Buddhism and Islam, that communicants engaged in immoral and perverse practices, that priests administering extreme unction used the opportunity to extract a dying person's eyeballs for alchemic uses, and the like. In the 1860's scatological compilations vividly described the sexual promiscuity of Christian priests and believers in mixed congregations. This outright pornography attracted readers and discredited Christianity at the same time. Anti-Christian zealots next had recourse to the ancient practice of posting anonymous handbills in public to arouse action, especially in administrative cities at examination time, when thousands of tense degree candidates were concentrated for a week or more. Local issues might arise from missionary attempts to lease property, or build structures which adversely affected the local *feng-shui,* the geomantic "spirits of wind and water."

Disputes were seldom lacking, as well as rumors that exaggerated the facts. The most inflammatory were touched off by the willingness of Catholic Sisters of Charity (see page 323) to accept waifs and orphans and sometimes even to pay a small fee to encourage delivery of such unfortunates to their care. This charity, misinterpreted by popular suspicion, could be linked with the ancient folklore concerning kidnapers who mesmerize small children and lead them off. A few orphanages may actually have been exploited by Chinese kidnapers for the small fees involved. This was social dynamite. Overt action could be touched off by placards mobilizing all defenders of propriety to demonstrate at a given time and place. The local riffraff could be counted upon to create a mob. Riot, destruction, burning, beating, and even death might result. The more numerous and

A Roman Catholic orphanage in transit. A nun (center) inspects babies in process of transportation. Photographed in or near Kiukiang, ca. 1891, in the period of anti-Christian riots.

more vulnerable Chinese converts usually suffered more than the missionaries themselves. This pattern of events, repeated in many parts of China over many decades, must be seen as a largely unorganized defense of the old order, led by the less respectable members of that upper class which felt itself most threatened by Western contact.

The Tientsin Massacre, 1870. This incident undid the work of a decade by revealing the opposed and irreconcilable nature of Western and Chinese aims and attitudes. The British aim had been to put the responsibility for enforcing the treaty system on the Ch'ing central government, while helping it to inaugurate modernization. Yet peaceful suasion could not entirely supersede the threat of force, especially to protect the treaty rights of missionaries. For example, when Hudson Taylor, who had opened a station of the China Inland Mission at Yangchow on the Grand Canal just north of the Yangtze, was mobbed in August 1868, Minister Alcock had eventually sent four gunboats to Nanking to press Tseng Kuo-fan into cashiering the negligent Yangchow authorities. There were other cases of this sort, and Sino-French relations were much worse. Having no commercial interests to protect, French officials in China tended to use the protection of Christian missions as a means of expanding French political influence.

In asserting this protectorate, they used gunboats and negotiated missionary cases directly with the provincial authorities.

At Tientsin French Sisters of Charity had offered fees for orphans. Rumors spread and tension rose. On June 21 a mob gathered. The truculent French consul, demanding that it disperse, fired on the magistrate, missed him, and was himself torn to pieces. The mob then killed twenty other foreigners, mainly French, including ten nuns, and destroyed the Catholic establishments. The outraged and fearful foreign powers mobilized gunboats off Tientsin.

The crisis was laid in the lap of Tseng Kuo-fan, now old and ill, who nevertheless demonstrated once again his character and courage. He investigated and announced to his countrymen the unwelcome facts as he found them: that there was no real evidence of kidnaping by Chinese, or of scooping out eyes and hearts by missionaries. Simultaneously he resisted severe French demands and was finally helped by events in Europe, where France's defeat in the Franco-Prussian War left her powerless. Later in 1870 Li Hung-chang took over at Tientsin as governor-general of Chihli, backed by his Anhwei Army. The Tientsin massacre left Sino-Western relations even more embittered by resentment and fear.

Economic Developments under the Treaty System

The Western economic invasion was conducted so largely by Chinese merchants that it did not provoke as immediate and concrete a defensive response as did the earlier invasions of Western armed forces or the influx of missionaries. Yet China was slow to imitate Western forms of industrial development and the reasons for this pose a chief problem in the history of this period.

Extraterritoriality and the Treaty-Port Establishment. In the treaty ports, areas of land were leased in perpetuity by the British and French governments, which paid modest ground rents annually to the Chinese government; these were known as "concessions." In the 1860's, there were British concessions at Canton, Amoy, Chinkiang, Kiukiang, Hankow, Tientsin, and Newchwang; and French concessions at Canton, Shanghai, Hankow, and Tientsin. As time passed the number increased. Within these leased areas the foreign consulates in turn granted ninety-nine-year leases to land-renters. Under extraterritoriality they also exercised legal jurisdiction over their own nationals, and by degrees developed taxation, police forces, and other features of municipal government. Thus China's sovereignty, without being destroyed, was put largely in abeyance in the foreign quarters of the major ports. Meanwhile Shanghai created its own unique city government when

CHINESE LAW AND ORDER.
*A culprit in a cangue
sealed by the Shanghai
magistrate, 1872.*

in 1863 the British and American areas coalesced to form the Shanghai International Settlement. Among its two thousand or more foreign residents, the British were dominant with the Americans second. The foreign land-renters (or "rate-payers") were represented by an elected council which derived its authority from the foreign consuls and their extraterritorial powers. By degrees the Shanghai Municipal Council came to deal with all the problems of a large city—roads, jetties, drainage, sanitation, police, and recreation facilities such as the race course. Taxes were levied on Chinese residents without representation, as under a Chinese regime. Shanghai remained Chinese territory, but it was free from Chinese taxation and under foreign consular control within the treaty system.

With Western control came Western law with its special utility for commerce, such as legal incorporation and proceedings for enforcement of contract. Western nationals were subject to their country's consular court and could be sued by Chinese plaintiffs only in that court. Britain transferred her Supreme Court for China and Japan from Hong Kong to Shanghai to hear appeals from all her consular courts. But appeals from the French consular court had to go to Saigon, and those from the Spanish, Dutch, or Russian consulates to Manila, Batavia, or Vladivostok, respectively. This made it difficult for Chinese plaintiffs to appeal consular judgments. A new invention in 1864 was the Shanghai Mixed Court, presided

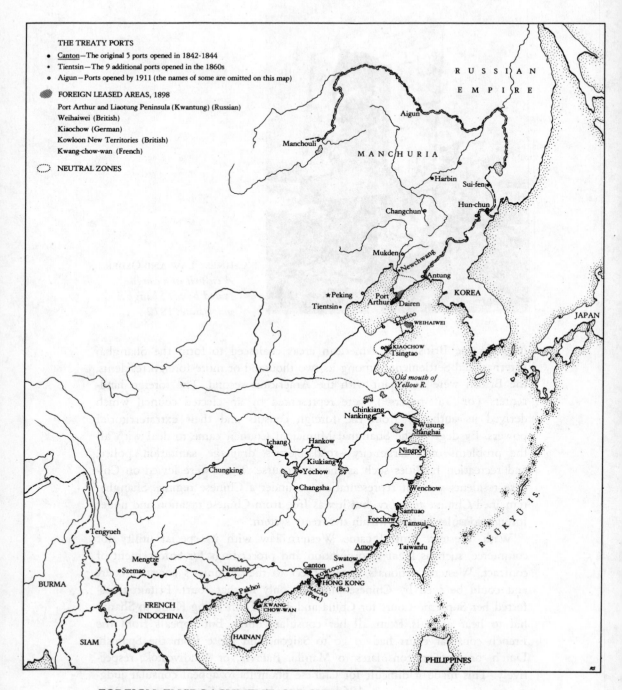

THE TREATY PORTS

- • Canton—The original 5 ports opened in 1842-1844
- • Tientsin—The 9 additional ports opened in the 1860s
- ∘ Aigun—Ports opened by 1911 (the names of some are omitted on this map)

▨ FOREIGN LEASED AREAS, 1898

Port Arthur and Liaotung Peninsula (Kwantung) (Russian)
Weihaiwei (British)
Kiaochow (German)
Kowloon New Territories (British)
Kwang-chow-wan (French)

⬭ NEUTRAL ZONES

RUSSIAN EMPIRE

Aigun

Manchouli

MANCHURIA

Harbin

Sui-fen

Changchun

Hun-chun

Mukden
Newchwang

Antung

KOREA

★ Peking

Port Arthur   Dairen
Tientsin

Chefoo
WEIHAIWEI

JAPAN

Old mouth of Yellow R.

KIAOCHOW
Tsingtao

Chinkiang
Nanking

Wusung
Shanghai

Ichang   Hankow

Ningpo

Kiukiang
Chungking   Yochow

Changsha

Wenchow

RYUKYU IS.

Santuao

Foochow   Tamsui

Tengyueh

Amoy   Taiwanfu

Mengtze

Swatow

Szemao

Canton

Nanning   KOWLOON

Pakhoi   MACAO
(Port.)
HONG KONG
(Br.)

BURMA

KWANG-
CHOW-WAN

FRENCH
INDOCHINA

SIAM

HAINAN

PHILIPPINES

FOREIGN ENCROACHMENT ON CHINA

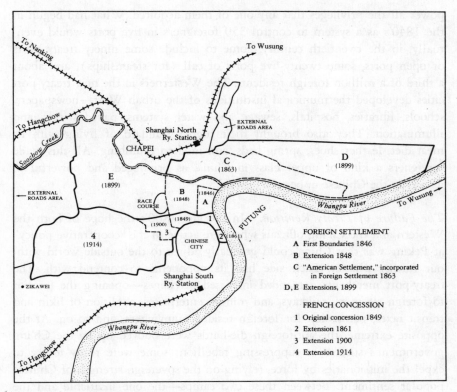

FOREIGN SETTLEMENT
A First Boundaries 1846
B Extension 1848
C "American Settlement," incorporated
   in Foreign Settlement 1863
D, E Extensions, 1899

FRENCH CONCESSION
1 Original concession 1849
2 Extension 1861
3 Extension 1900
4 Extension 1914

THE GROWTH OF SHANGHAI

over by a Chinese magistrate but with a foreign consular "assessor" sitting with him as a cojudge. Using Western procedure, it handled cases between local Chinese and cases in which Chinese were the defendants. Thus both foreign and Chinese defendants had rights of trial before judges of their own nationality, by the laws of their own countries.

Shanghai's business developed on the basis of extraterritoriality. As Chinese crowded in and real estate values rose, the foreign land-renters got high profits by subrenting the land they had leased. As Shanghai, Canton, Tientsin, Hankow, and other centers grew into great modern cities, the vested interests dependent on extraterritoriality grew correspondingly. What had begun as a legal device mainly to protect Western individuals against the Chinese custom of judicial torture became even more a device to protect foreign firms and corporations from Chinese taxation. Nationals of countries that lacked treaty relations with China secured extraterritorial privileges by becoming protégés of foreign treaty-power consuls. Thus, for example, the French consuls, instead of the Chinese government, exercised jurisdiction in China over citizens of Memel, Monaco, Persia, and Rumania. The most-favored-nation clause continued to give every treaty power all the privileges that any one of them acquired. What had begun in the 1840's as a system to control 350 foreigners in five ports would eventually, in the twentieth century, come to include some ninety treaty ports or open ports, some twenty-five ports of call (for steamships), and about a third of a million foreign residents. The Westerners in the new treaty-port cities developed the municipal institutions of the urban West—newspapers, schools, libraries, hospitals, sewage and water systems, paved streets, and illumination. They also brought their higher standard of living with its meat diet, leather shoes, spring beds, and modern plumbing. All this made foreigners a kind of upper class in China, as privileged and powerful in its way as the Chinese upper class itself.

The Failure of Treaty Revision.   In the late 1860's the hope of both the Western and the Ch'ing officials who were active in the "cooperative policy" at Peking was that China could gradually adjust to the outside world without further disaster. Each side had its opponents to contend with. The treaty-port merchants demanded increased privileges—opening the interior to foreign steamers, railways, and mining enterprises, abolition of likin and transit taxes, permission for foreign residence anywhere, and so on. At the opposite extreme, the antiforeign die-hards were buoyed up by the Ch'ing government's success in suppressing rebellion; some were ready to try to expel the missionaries by force, relying on the sovereign strength of Chinese popular sentiment. Between these two camps—the one insatiable and the other irreconcilable—the Western diplomats and the high Ch'ing officials tried to construct peace and security.

Proposals for reform to strengthen China were submitted in 1865–1868 particularly by Hart of the Customs and by Wade of the British legation. They put forward arguments which Chinese reformers were to use more fully in later decades. Western contact had created an unprecedented foreign problem which required an unprecedented solution by domestic modernization. "If policies are altered," wrote Hart, "China can become the leader of all nations; if policies are not altered, she will become the servant of all nations." Increased contact with the West seemed one of the best ways to help China remake her civilization. In 1868 the retiring American minister, Anson Burlingame, who had been a pillar of the "cooperative policy" since 1861, was sent as China's first envoy to the Western world. As an imperial appointee of the first civil rank, he and his retinue toured the Western capitals. In Washington he concluded a treaty on rather egalitarian terms. But Burlingame was also an orator. His proclamation that a new day of Westernization and Christianity had dawned in the ancient Middle Kingdom was premature and misleading. His mission ended with his sudden death in Russia in 1870.

Meanwhile, since the treaties could be revised after ten years, Alcock with Hart's help had conducted lengthy negotiations in 1868–1869, trying to reach agreement on concessions which would partly meet the demands of the British merchants and yet not be utterly rejected by Chinese conservatives. Signed in October 1869, subject to later ratification, the Alcock Convention's statesmanlike provisions would have put the British expansion and the whole treaty system in China on a more equitable basis for the future. But because Alcock was trying to restrict and so to stabilize the foreign impact on China, his draft treaty was violently attacked by the China trade interests in Britain. Consequently the British government refused ratification. On the Chinese side Prince Kung had consulted the court and Grand Council and high provincial officials. The Convention seemed a diplomatic victory for China and the imperial approval was considered final. Britain's unexpected rejection of it was therefore a damaging blow to the moderate "cooperative policy" of the 1860's. This setback, along with the more spectacular missionary incident at Tientsin in 1870, indicated how great was the gulf between Chinese and foreign interests in China.

Growth and Change in China's Foreign Trade. As the British position in China grew steadily stronger in the last decades of the century, the Maritime Customs Service under Hart performed a many-sided role facilitating trade under the treaties and also aiding Chinese efforts at modernization through new institutions. First of all, the Customs ensured to Peking a growing, reliable, and uncommitted source of new revenue and preserved the restricted imperial tariff against smuggling and corruption. To check the large-scale Chinese smuggling of opium, salt, and other commodities from the free port of Hong Kong into nearby Chinese territory, two measures were necessary: first, the old Portuguese port of Macao was formally ceded to Portugal in 1887, making it foreign territory; and second, the Customs set up offices in Kowloon and Lappa (close to Macao) to check the smuggling in Chinese junks. The Customs also completed the charting of the China coast, installed lighthouses, beacons, markers, and other modern aids to navigation, handled all the management of port facilities, and published trade statistics and commercial and scientific reports. Its foreign commissioners in the ports, like Hart at Peking, mediating between foreign treaty rights and Chinese interests, often performed quasi-diplomatic functions, while its Chinese staff provided a modern training ground for civil servants. From four hundred Western and fourteen hundred Chinese employees in 1875, the staff grew to seven hundred and thirty-five hundred in 1895, more than half the Westerners being British. In brief, Hart and the Customs were at the core of the treaty system, and their work was one of its most constructive aspects, however the whole system may be judged.

With the growth of the treaty ports into modern cities came the advances

*A Maritime Customs Assistant and his staff, 1892. W. Hancock
(Chinese name, Han Wei-li) rose from Third Assistant, Class B, in
1877, to Acting Commissioner in 1904. This photograph was
probably taken in Hanoi on his journey from Hong Kong
to the Yunnan border. Mr. Hancock's Chinese teacher, Mr. Lo,
on right, is with his two wives and their maids.*

in technology that brought China constantly closer to the outside world. In
1869 the Suez Canal halved the distance to Europe. In 1870–1871 cables
were laid connecting Vladivostok, Nagasaki, Shanghai, Hong Kong, and
Singapore, whence telegraphic communication went on around the world
via London to San Francisco. China was thus drawn further into the world
economy and became more subject to the vicissitudes of international prices,
business crises, and foreign competition. During the latter part of the nineteenth century the China trade was affected by the worldwide fall in the
value of silver, as silver output rose and many countries went on the gold
standard, demonetizing their silver. The treaty tariff had been set at fixed
monetary rates which in many cases represented 5 per cent in 1858 but
generally became lower as prices rose in subsequent decades. Foreign imports
and Chinese exports, as they passed in either direction between treaty ports
and the interior, were to pay an additional 2½ per cent (half the tariff
duty) as transit dues, and be subsequently free from all the likin and other
taxes that goods in China's purely domestic commerce might have to pay.
Similarly an additional 2½ per cent could be paid as "coast trade" duty to

*Commissioner of Customs H. F. Merrill (Harvard '74) at Ningpo,
about 1894, with his wife, daughter, and household staff: (from left)
amah, nurse-girl, number-one boy (in charge), number-two boy,
gateman, cook, number-two cook, wash boy, and four chairbearers.*

avoid all further taxes on Chinese goods carried in foreign ships from one
Chinese port to another. These arrangements prevented China from imposing a protective tariff, a considerable impairment of sovereignty, and
gave the foreign merchant a privileged advantage over his Chinese
competitor.

Foreign merchants, having looked forward to a rich opportunity, were
correspondingly frustrated when this Eldorado failed to materialize. During
the 1870's and 1880's China failed to provide the expected market for
Western products. By 1890 the total value of the China trade, both in and
out, was only 50 million pounds sterling, less than that of many small countries and was already surpassed by Japan's foreign trade. The chief reasons
for this stagnation were no doubt China's poverty, self-sufficiency, and conservatism. But British merchants ascribed it to a mandarin conspiracy
whereby transit taxes still prevented the "opening" of the China market.

In the content of the trade, the great staples of mid-century, opium
imports and tea exports, both reached their highest volume and then declined. Legalized and taxed under the treaty settlement of 1858–1860,
opium imports reached a peak of 87,000 chests in 1879, but thereafter
declined because production of opium within China (several times the quantity imported) increasingly supplied the still growing Chinese market.

Similarly tea exports to Britain rose, from 30 million pounds in the 1830's, to a peak of 150 million pounds in the 1880's but thereafter declined because tea from India and Ceylon, transplanted there from China in mid-century, began to take over the British market. China failed to modernize her tea industry. Indian tea was produced by large-scale methods on big plantations created by capital investment. It was carefully standardized and exported free of duty. Chinese tea was collected from individual farmers on a small-scale basis, its quality was not protected against adulteration by get-rich-quick dealers, and it was taxed both in transit and on export. China's silk, her most famous product, began to suffer a similar decline after 1900 because in Europe and in Japan scientific prevention of silkworm disease, mechanization of silk reeling, and modern market organization produced a higher quality standardized product. The Ch'ing government was unable to perform functions of commercial leadership and regulation which governments were performing elsewhere.

China's production of cotton, mainly in the Yangtze Valley, had supplied a large handicraft industry. After the second treaty settlement, imports of cotton goods up to 1890 failed to achieve the great increase that Britain hoped for. The principal growth was not in cotton textiles, but in cotton yarn, imports of which, mainly from India, increased twentyfold from 1872 to 1890. This was because machine-spinning of yarn was some eighty times as productive as hand-spinning, while machine-weaving of cloth was only about four times as fast as hand-weaving. Thus the cheaper cotton yarn from abroad crippled the native Chinese spinning industry but supplied Chinese weaving, which still continued for many years on hand looms in peasant households as before.

Opinions differ as to the net effect of foreign trade on nineteenth-century China. The classic Marxist concept, of machine-industry products disrupting the handicraft industries of a backward country's farm economy, seems to apply to China only in a limited degree, for China's involvement in the world economy was less than that of fully colonial areas in Southeast Asia. As tea and silk exports declined, China began to export diverse products (vegetable oils, tung oil, pig bristles, hides and skins, and soybeans) which were mainly by-products of cheap labor on small farms rather than on plantations or in factories.

Compradors, Bankers, and Entrepreneurs.   Unlike the rivalry of foreign missionaries and Chinese gentry, foreign and Chinese merchants needed one another. In the Canton trade the hong merchants had been the chief intermediaries between foreign traders and the great Chinese domestic market. In the treaty ports after 1842 their place was taken by the compradors. But where the hong merchants had been Chinese-style brokers licensed by government, the compradors were contractual employees of foreign trading firms who handled the Chinese side of their business. The compradors bridged the cultural, linguistic, and institutional gap between East and West. One of the most famous was Tong King-sing, who like most early compradors came from the Canton delta. Having got an English-language missionary education, he served as a Hong Kong government interpreter and then as a Maritime Customs clerk at Shanghai and in 1863 became Jardine, Matheson and Company's comprador there. Typically, he purchased degree status and so acquired membership in the official class, while also becoming a capitalist investor in treaty-port enterprises.

Comprador-merchants were only the most visible element in the growth of China's domestic trade. Another consisted of private banking that developed through chains of money shops centered in the coastal region at Ningpo and also, curiously enough, in certain cities of Shansi in the landlocked Northwest. Shansi had long been a strategic center of imperial control and a crossroads of trade routes—between Mongolia and Szechwan and between North China and Central Asia—as well as a transfer area between camel caravans and the canal transport of North and Central China. Shansi merchants already had widespread connections and a pawnshop business in other provinces, and had also begun to guarantee silver shipments by employing private mounted troops to convoy them. As the spread of banditry endangered the shipping of silver bullion, shippers began to use banking facilities. Where an armed convoy of silver would cost 2 or 3 per cent of its value, these private remittance banks charged a rate of only three-tenths of 1 per cent for drafts.

The pioneer Shansi banker in the period around 1800 was a dye-shop merchant, who had a shop in Tientsin, set up an office to buy materials in Chungking, and so got into the remittance business. The number of banking chains eventually grew to between twenty and thirty, organized in three main groups based in central Shansi. In order to be licensed by the Board of Revenue at Peking, new banks had to get a guarantee from others already in the business. The Shansi firms maintained a near monopoly by withholding their guarantee from extra-provincial capitalists. High provincial authorities, who were some of the greatest shippers of funds and who normally accumulated their personal fortunes through "squeeze," came to rely upon these private bankers in many unofficial ways. The banks not only transmitted their official funds to Peking, but specialized in dealing with the greedy functionaries who lined the route from the provincial treasuries to the Board of Revenue. The banks also advanced funds to officials expecting lucrative appointments. From the second quarter of the nineteenth century they helped the Canton trade transfer funds by draft to purchase teas and silks in Central China and pay for opium imports.

In the distribution of foreign imports Chinese dealers were aided by their guild organization and superior knowledge of local conditions. Foreign firms, which had originally set up branches in every port, began to close them and concentrate their business in major shipping centers like Hong Kong and Shanghai. In the interport trade, that is, from one treaty port to another in China's domestic commerce, Chinese merchants became the principal users of the foreign shipping, which was more secure and reliable than native shipping. In short, Chinese capitalists could also benefit from the security and facilities of the treaty system. Compradors who left foreign employment and became treaty-port entrepreneurs were only the most prominent representatives of this trend.

Shanghai's rise as the capital market of China was marked by the formation in 1865, mainly by British firms, of the Hong Kong and Shanghai Banking Corporation. It and other foreign banks financed Chinese merchants and Chinese banks, transferred funds between ports, handled remittances from Chinese overseas, and even issued their own banknote currency. Chinese capital was attracted to the ports by the security of investment in real estate, as well as by the need for local industries—to process goods; to provide public utilities and urban housing; and to support the shipping industry. This cooperative Sino-foreign growth attracted Chinese capital and talent. For example, in 1862 Russell and Company organized a steamship line by securing capital in roughly equal portions from partners in the United States, from foreign merchants in China, and from Chinese merchants and compradors. By securing shallow-draft American side-wheeler steamboats and setting up a regular twice-weekly service between Shanghai and Hankow, this American-led, Chinese-backed enterprise inaugurated the great era of steamboating on the Yangtze.

After 1870, economic growth in the treaty ports was creating resources of investment capital and entrepreneurial skill which, in favorable circumstances and in due time, might have been used to bring China through that critical phase of industrialization, the breakthrough into self-sustaining growth. But the treaty ports were only one sector of the Chinese economy. Contemporary experience in Japan showed that success in industrial modernization would have required more central support and more comprehensive scope. It would have needed a whole set of circumstances that were lacking in China outside the treaty ports—more clearly defined national political goals, a more stable framework of law and monetary practice, stronger leadership from the government, and a more independent style of entrepreneurship.

The Difficulties of Early Industrialization

During the quarter-century after 1870 the rate of China's economic modernization, though considerable, fell behind that of Japan and the West. Steamboating on the Yangtze imitated that on the Mississippi, but a subsequent era of railroading did not ensue, as it did in the American West. While industrialization was beginning to spread throughout Japan, it remained limited to a few small enclaves in China. China's slowness to industrialize may be attributed to a complex of factors—intellectual, psychological, social, economic, political, and administrative.

The Inadequacy of Government Leadership. The idea that the unequal treaties prevented China's industrialization, if we can judge by the Japanese example, is over-simple and does not explain what happened. Decision lay first with the Chinese government; only the government's default gave the treaty port its later dominant role. The restrictive effect of the treaty system was cumulative, and evils visible in its later years were by no means inevitable from the start. In short, the incapacity of government to take the lead was the first great fact in China's slowness to industrialize.

This incapacity of Peking was most evident in two sectors, finance and policy. Peking's antiquated fiscal system was still based on tax-farming— that is, provincial officials were expected to make certain tax quotas available to Peking while maintaining themselves and their administrations on the remainder of what they collected. Budgeting, accounting, central planning, and control were impossible. About 1890, Peking listed annual revenues totaling roughly 89 million taels (see table, page 317), but of these reported collections, only a part ever reached Peking, the greater part being allotted for provincial uses. However, the unreported collections were probably three to five times as great as those listed for the Peking record. Mobilization of fiscal resources was thus beyond the power of the central government.

In the provinces, industrialization was hindered by the purblind opposition of the official class. This intellectual conservatism was evident, for instance, in the economic views of Tseng Kuo-fan. In 1867 he noted with distaste that Western nations for centuries had been squabbling greedily over material gains; their merchants in the treaty ports sought profit at the expense of China; modern steamers, railways, and telegraphs, if managed by foreigners or by Chinese attached to foreigners, would threaten the livelihood of the common people (*min-sheng*); Confucian government must protect the people's livelihood, lest the wrath of the multitude be provoked. Tseng, though a leader in "self-strengthening," had no concept of modern economic development. Advocates of Westernization in the late nineteenth century are now blamed by some in retrospect for their failure to industrialize. At the time, however, they were attacked for attempting too many changes too rapidly. Their attackers, ignorant of the outside world, saw much innovation at home but could not see the larger paradox, that in spite of her considerable rate of change, China was steadily falling behind other nations. The Chinese upper class accepted neither the concept of progress (implying con-

The infant emperor Kuang-hsü (born 1871) on horseback.

tinual change and rejection of stability) nor the concept of nationalism (implying international competition on an equal basis).

Behind the inertia of the Ch'ing leaders lay their vested interests in maintaining the power structure of the day and in using modernization only for personal and political aims within that structure. During most of the period up to 1894 the court remained firmly under the control of the Empress Dowager Tz'u-hsi, who steadily built up her bureaucratic machine. She dominated the young emperor, and according to legend even encouraged him in a life of excess that brought on his death in January 1875 at the age of nineteen. To maintain herself in power the Empress Dowager now broke the sacred dynastic law of succession, which required that a new emperor always be chosen from the succeeding generation in order to maintain the ritual observances demanded by filial piety. Instead, she shocked propriety by having her own nephew (the son of her sister), a four-year-old boy of the same generation as his predecessor, selected emperor with the reign title of Kuang-hsü ("Glorious Succession," 1875–1908). Until he took on the imperial functions in 1889, she continued to rule. She removed Prince Kung from power in 1884. Officeholders all over the empire quietly contributed to her personal fortune.

The Empress Dowager's forceful personality was devoted to a conservative end, the maintenance of the dynasty by keeping an equilibrium between the traditional central power and the new regional interests. Regionalism was buttressed by the modernization projects of leading officials, their new arsenals and industries in provincial centers. The Empress Dowager could maintain the Manchu dynasty only by cooperating with and manipulating the regional leaders, all of whom with proper Confucian reverence still looked up to the Ch'ing throne for official appointment and for final answers, with no thought as yet of exercising the independent power of warlords.

Li Hung-chang's Industrial Empire.   Li Hung-chang's career (see page 303) illustrates the delicate balance between regional power and dynastic loyalty. During the quarter-century after 1870 he remained continuously in power at Tientsin, as governor-general of Chihli and commissioner for the northern ports, quite contrary to the tradition that even the highest official should be shifted every three, or at most six, years. Li's position was based on three elements: first, on his Anhwei Army, between twenty-five and forty thousand strong, stationed in Chihli and Shantung and for many years also in Kiangsu, supplied by arsenals at Tientsin, Nanking, and Shanghai; second, on his bureaucratic machine of some two hundred younger commanders, officials, and technical specialists, many of them from Li's native place (Ho-fei) in Anhwei, who worked under him as their patron; and third, on local provincial revenues plus those collected for defense of the metropolitan province of Chihli, mainly from lower Yangtze sources. In bringing Li to North China the Empress Dowager had evidently decided to join forces with, rather than oppose, his growing power. The two came to depend upon one another in matters both of policy and of profit. Li Hung-chang's machine, like that of an American city boss, utilized the flow of public funds through private hands. Thus his long leadership in Westernization had mixed motives, patriotic and personal, ideological and pecuniary.

In organizing new economic projects, Li and others used the formula "government supervision and merchant operation" (*kuan-tu shang-pan*), meaning that these were profit-oriented enterprises operated by merchants but controlled by officials. This followed the tradition of the salt monopoly, a fiscal device for milking official taxes and private squeeze from a monopolized staple for which there was an inelastic demand. This static, tax-farming tradition was antithetic to that of the dynamic, risk-taking entrepreneur who founds modern industries. It made for distribution of profits rather than their reinvestment, for profiteering rather than industrialization.

Li's first venture was naturally in steamships. Peking's food supply still depended on the lower Yangtze tribute rice which came by barge up the decaying Grand Canal and by seagoing junk around Shantung. Accordingly, the China Merchants' Steam Navigation Company which Li set up in 1872 was financed partly by an annual government subsidy for haulage of tribute rice. Li first appointed as managers men experienced, quite inappropriately, in the junk transport of tribute rice; but he soon turned to Jardine's English-speaking comprador Tong King-sing, who had been directing the operation of their steamships as well as some owned by himself and other Chinese. In the new company under Tong, the merchant shareholders generally became managers, with official titles. They secured perquisites and patronage, appointing relatives and friends to the staff. The enterprise was neither government-run nor private in modern terms, but a hybrid in which officials and merchants cooperated to get rich. Aided by the tribute rice subsidy, the China Merchants' line competed successfully with the foreign lines in Chinese waters. In 1877, it bought the larger fleet of Russell and Company, thus became the biggest, and thereafter maintained monopolistic rate agreements with the British lines. However, the latter reinvested their profits more prudently, while the China Merchants' managers took out the profits and let the fleet deteriorate. British ships eventually recovered their dominance in China's domestic carrying trade.

This company served as a prototype for other enterprises. The system of "government supervision and merchant operation" demonstrated in one enterprise after another that it was a traditional, not a modern, institution. First, it suffered from nepotistic and cliquish favoritism, squeeze, and lack of risk-taking initiative. Second, being under government control, managers were motivated to share profits immediately, rather than to save them for reinvestment in their enterprises, lest they be taken by the government. Finally, "government supervision" usually brought certain monopoly rights, originally granted to assist competition with the foreigner, but soon used as props to compensate for inefficiency.

Impelled by the logic of one industry demanding another, Li with Tong King-sing as his manager began in 1876 to develop a modern coal mine at Kaiping north of Tientsin. This aimed to supply fuel for China Merchants' ships and to give them a southbound cargo after they had brought tribute rice north. The use of modern pumps, fans, and hoists soon yielded profits from coal seams that old-style Chinese pit-miners had abandoned. With a dozen Western engineers and modern equipment, the new Kaiping Mining Company by 1883 had set up machine shops, produced its own engines, railway cars, and tugboats, and installed local telephones, telegraphs, and a railroad line seven miles long. It was soon producing 250,000 tons of coal a year. However, Tong King-sing died in 1892 and his successor was a Chinese bannerman close to the Manchu court, an expert in the art of squeeze, who milked the company of its resources. It became increasingly dependent on foreign loans and in 1900 was taken over by a British company, represented by an American engineer (later President), Herbert Hoover. After 1912 Kaiping was absorbed into the Sino-British Kailan Mining Administration.

Thus in North China, the steamship brought the coal mine, which required in turn a railroad. Early railway projects had been vetoed by officials determined to forestall foreign exploitation. A small, unauthorized Shanghai-

China's first railway, Shanghai-Wusung, a 30-inch narrow-gauge track built in 1876 by Jardine, Matheson and Company and others. At left: the first engine, the British-made "Pioneer"; note Chinese attendant wearing queue. Center: the 9-ton engine "Celestial Empire," with six 27-inch wheels. Line was purchased and destroyed by Chinese authorities in 1877.

Wusung line, opened by foreigners in 1876 (see figure above), was purchased the next year by the Nanking governor-general, who promptly had it torn up. The railway begun for Kaiping coal was extended only slowly—south to Tientsin in 1888, northeast to Shanhaikuan in 1894, and to the outskirts of Peking in 1896, about 240 miles in all. Except for a short line in Formosa, this was the sum of China's response to the railroad age after thirty years of agitation. The reasons for this retardation are instructive. First, the water transport network was well developed and offered severe competition except in North China. Steamships had penetrated China on waterways that went far into the interior, but railroads had to invade Chinese life much more directly, crossing canals and rice fields and disturbing grave mounds. Popular superstitions and xenophobic opposition could be easily aroused. High land values, when combined with popular sentiment, made any right of way a costly investment. Capital was not easily mobilized; government finances were weak, while bond issues and other devices for the creation of credit were underdeveloped. Peking's defensive strategy was to oppose both foreign-run railroads and big foreign loans for Chinese lines.

The mandarin-industrialist who rose to the top of Li Hung-chang's industrial empire was Sheng Hsüan-huai (1844–1916). After being assistant manager of the China Merchants' line, Sheng organized another "government supervised, merchant-operated" enterprise, the Imperial Telegraph Administration. Despite its official-sounding name, this company built up its capital of some two million dollars by selling shares to "merchants," particularly to Sheng and others in the management. The government made loans and policed the telegraph lines, to protect them against irate farmers fearful of the effect of the tall poles on geomantic forces of "wind and water"; but the profits went into annual returns of as much as 20 per cent to the shareholders. Until after 1900, when the company's lines were gradually nationalized, Li Hung-chang through his deputy, Sheng, controlled the telegraph administration all over the country, appointing its personnel and protecting them against charges of corruption.

In the industrialization of many countries, machine production of cotton goods had been the leading industry. Cotton mills were proving very successful in Japan in the 1880's. As early as 1878 Li began to sponsor a Chinese textile mill, the Shanghai Cotton Cloth Mill, to compete with foreign imports. The throne granted it tax exemption and a ten-year monopoly to produce cotton cloth and yarn; foreign machinery and engineers arrived. But merchant shares were subscribed in inadequate amounts, and the first manager invested the funds unwisely. After Sheng Hsüan-huai took over the project in 1887, he financed the mill with loans from the China Merchants' Company, which he also headed, and from Li Hung-chang's provincial government in Chihli. Beginning in 1890, some four thousand factory workers were soon turning out excellent cloth and yarn, and some 25 per cent was paid on shares in 1893, when the mill unfortunately burned down uninsured. Undaunted, Li and Sheng planned to set up eleven more mills, monopolize a new Chinese textile industry, and eliminate foreign imports. They had five mills in operation when the Sino-Japanese War of 1894–1895 cut short their hopes.

The Slow Progress of Modernization

The material growth of the treaty ports with their commerce and industry was of course accompanied by intellectual and cultural innovation. Yet the new ideas and attitudes got from Western contact remained minor elements in the broad stream of Chinese tradition. The wearing of the queue, the long gown of the scholar, the bound feet of women, marriage and funeral processions and the palanquins of officials passing through the crowded streets—the whole appearance of Chinese life remained unaffected by any vogue for things Western such as was sweeping contemporary Japan. Ideas of change were spreading, but very slowly. If we look at such new developments as the modern post office, the press, and the training of students abroad, we see a common pattern: in each case China's modernization was inspired by Western examples and yet had to be superimposed upon old indigenous institutions, which persisted so strongly as to slow down the need or demand for innovation.

Postal Services and the Press.　Robert Hart early began to work toward setting up a nationwide modern postal service, but it took him thirty years because he found China's needs already met, though at a premodern level of efficiency. First, there were the sixteen hundred or so official horse-post stations on the five main routes radiating from Peking over the empire. This ancient system moved official persons, correspondence, goods, and money but only for government purposes. Second, for the postal needs of the common people, commercial "letter hongs" forwarded private mail for small fees according to the distance and profitability of the route, without attempting, however, to reach all parts of China. By the end of the century there were some three hundred letter hongs registered in the twenty-four treaty ports and many more in the country as a whole. Finally, Western governments set up their own postal services between major cities in foreign trade and opened this facility to foreign residents. Eventually dozens of these foreign post offices operated in China.

To develop a modern national post, in the midst of all these vested interests, Hart used the resources of the Maritime Customs. Given the task of transmitting legation mail overland to Peking in wintertime, the Customs gradually built up a postal department. Eventually it got foreign steamers in Chinese waters to carry only the mail of the imperial post office, which was formally set up as part of the Customs in 1896. It became the agency for all steamer shipment of the mails of the private letter hongs and began to put its old-style competitors out of business.

The rise of professional journalism, another index of modernization, also had its venerable antecedents. The famous *Peking Gazette* dated back at least to the T'ang and reproduced official documents made public at the court, but it was not an official publication nor did it appear in one single form: private firms in Peking produced and distributed the so-called gazette on a commercial basis, disseminating court news and imperial documents among the scholar-gentry class all over the empire. In the cities news was also spread by commercial handbills or newsprints, produced as a sideline by printing shops and hawked in the streets. Price lists distributed by guilds and book publishing, usually under official or scholar-gentry auspices, were other traditional mechanisms for spreading printed information.

Protestant missionaries injected a revolutionary element into these ancient channels. Barred from the interior until the 1860's, they early resorted to print to spread the gospel in Chinese translation and in the vernacular, not the classical style. The London Missionary Society set up a press at Malacca in 1815 and published a monthly magazine in Chinese. Other missionaries followed this example. Besides the missionary periodicals in Chinese, there were English-language newspapers like the *China Mail* (Hong Kong, 1845–   ) and the *North China Herald* (Shanghai, 1850–   ) which served the trading community and became the immediate models for modern-style Chinese newspapers.

Chinese journalism finally rose above the purely factual level when men of literary talent began to publish editorial opinion—an activity strictly discountenanced by the dynasty and therefore possible only under treaty-port protection. The pioneer in this field, Wang T'ao, began life as a classical scholar, spent the 1850's in Shanghai as Chinese editor of the London Missionary Society press, and in the 1860's helped James Legge complete his monumental translations of the *Five Classics* (see pages 41–42). Two years of this period Wang spent with Legge in Scotland. After this long apprenticeship, Wang T'ao became in the 1870's an independent journalist, founding and editing his own daily newspaper in Hong Kong and publishing his own comments, enriched by his travels in Europe and Japan. Wang T'ao was a forerunner—at heart a nationalist, intellectually a critic of the Chinese scene. His Western contact generated ideas both of patriotism and of reform.

Training Abroad. A still greater stimulus for reform came from the experience of education in the West. The pioneer "returned student" was a poor boy from Macao, Yung Wing, who learned English in missionary schools and was sent by missionaries to the United States. He became a Christian and an American citizen and graduated from Yale in 1854. His Yale education revealed to him, he said, "responsibilities which the sealed eye of ignorance can never see." He conceived that "through Western education China might be regenerated, become enlightened and powerful." But not until 1872 was Yung Wing finally able, with the support of Tseng Kuo-fan and Li Hung-chang, to realize his long-cherished dream of sending an educational mission to the United States. Under this scheme 120 long-gowned Chinese boys, mainly from poor Cantonese families, went in four classes of 30 each to Hartford, Connecticut, where they were boarded out with families up and down the Connecticut Valley but came periodically to the mission headquarters for Chinese classical studies. Soon, however, they underwent "a gradual but marked transformation" in speech and dress, hiding their queues and developing athletic, exuberant, undecorous ways—becoming, in short, Americanized. Yung Wing, who had by now married an American girl and was more Congregational than Confucian in outlook, encouraged this acculturation but his conservative colleagues were appalled, and their outrage reverberated in Peking. The mission was expensive and an anti-Chinese movement had been growing in California, where Oriental exclusion was already a political issue. In 1881 the educational mission, for a variety of reasons, was given up. The students from Hartford who arrived

THE CHINESE EDUCATIONAL MISSION TO THE UNITED STATES.
*Above: Students on arrival in San Francisco en route to Hartford,
Connecticut, 1872. Below: Chinese students' baseball team
("The Orientals"), Hartford, 1878. The mission was recalled in
1881.*

AMERICAN PRESBYTERIAN PIONEERS: THE REV. CALVIN W. AND
MRS. JULIA B. MATEER. *In Tengchow, Shantung, Calvin Mateer
founded a secondary school, helped translate the Bible,
published many textbooks including the widely used* Mandarin
Lessons *(1892), and advocated higher education from the West to
undergird Christianity in China.*

back in Shanghai to kowtow before the taotai were greeted with suspicion as
a threat to the vested interest of all scholars in the unreformed classical
examination system. Consequently Yung Wing's boys contributed to China's
modernization mainly through Western technology or management, in the
navy, the telegraph and railroad administrations, the diplomatic service, and
the Kaiping mines. Only twelve became regular officials.

Protestant Missions and Modernization.   The same record of vigorous
pioneering and modest results, of great effort and much frustration, typified
the missionary movement. Foreign Catholic priests numbered about 250 in
1870 and about 750 in 1896, whereas numbers of Protestants arriving in
China roughly doubled every decade. Protestant mission stations increased
accordingly—from 35 in 14 places in 1860, to 498 in 356 places in 1900.
Yet by 1890, when the 1300 Protestant missionaries outnumbered the Catholics two to one, they had only 37,000 Protestant communicants, compared
with the half-million Catholics. The Protestant missionary force was composed for the most part of Americans and Britishers in roughly equal

numbers, mainly from the middle class or rural areas, and often without much higher education. While most Protestants remained committed to evangelism, an increasing minority began to see that good works might be more fruitful than evangelism alone. Reform came naturally to them. Their efforts to change individual conduct set them vigorously against many social customs—polygamy, child marriage, foot-binding, gambling, fortune-telling, the idolatry of other religions, and even Confucian reverence for ancestors, as well as infanticide and the opium evil. Literacy and therefore schooling were necessary to the reception of the gospel, and an educated native pastorate to its propagation. By 1877, when the first General Conference of Protestant Missionaries surveyed the scene, there were twenty theological schools with 231 students. Protestant primary schools gradually grew to secondary level, came to be called "colleges" (like St. John's College at Shanghai after 1879), and in time became counterparts, if not offshoots, of the denominational colleges in New England and the Middle West. Thus the missionary band from Oberlin College, in 1881, were forerunners of the Student Volunteer Movement for Foreign Missions that began to recruit American college youths for mission work. There was a parallel growth of medical missions, dispensaries, hospitals, and medical schools for Chinese doctors. By 1890, when the second General Conference of Protestant Missionaries met, they had a "Medical Missionary Association of China" in action parallel to their "Educational Association of China." There was no limit to the Christian opportunity for good works.

One Baptist who fought the terrible famine of 1877–1879 in Shansi was Timothy Richard, a Welshman of broad imagination who believed that Christianity, as the dynamic of Western civilization, could win China more effectively in proportion as China accepted the fruits of Western civilization in general. Human progress, Western-style, was part of God's plan, and good works, especially education, were necessary to progress. From 1891, as secretary of the SDK (Society for the Diffusion of Christian and General Knowledge among the Chinese), Richard sought to spread ideas of reform among the scholar and official classes. He had an ally in Young J. Allen from Georgia who had become a translator and editor, publishing from 1868 a weekly "mission news" for the Chinese Christian community. Allen expanded this into *The Globe Magazine* (later translated *Review of the Times*). This journal, ably edited by Chinese scholars, presented in literary Chinese a wide selection of Western ideas and information. It became in fact one source of the Reform Movement of the late 1890's.

Yet like Wang T'ao's editorials and Yung Wing's educational mission, missionary espousals of reform were peripheral to Chinese life, products of the new Sino-Western community in the port cities, remote from the peasants or scholar gentry. Until Japan's smashing victory of 1895, Chinese thinking remained for the most part firmly in the grip of tradition.

12. Imperialist Encroachment on China

Foreign Aggression on China's Periphery

Imperialist rivalry, nibbling at the periphery of the Chinese world, intensified after 1870 for a number of reasons. In Europe economic nationalism moved the democracies, Britain and France, to lead the way in colonial expansion. The literate citizenry of every European power, newly in contact with world events through the growth of the urban press, developed varying degrees of enthusiasm for national exploits overseas. These were rationalized by the doctrine of Social Darwinism—that races and nations necessarily compete for survival, and only the fittest survive. The religious enthusiasm of missionaries was echoed in the idealism of administrators conscious of the "white man's burden." Newspaper-reading publics became, psychologically, men-on-the-spot, alarmed or elated by the day's events and likely to clamor for action.

As the competition for colonies developed, it became apparent that the Chinese Empire had uncertain or unstable frontiers. Maps were usually unreliable, historical claims often conflicted, and the limits of Ch'ing authority came increasingly into dispute. To the uncertainties of terrain were added the vagueness and timidity of Peking's claims to suzerainty over tributary states. After all, the tribute system was mainly a defensive institution, based less on treaty law than on Confucian ethics, less on military domination than on cultural supremacy. When called upon either to take responsibility for disorders in tributary areas and recompense aggrieved foreigners or else to renounce suzerain jurisdiction, Peking's first impulse was to avoid responsibility and payment of indemnities. Thus the Ryūkyū

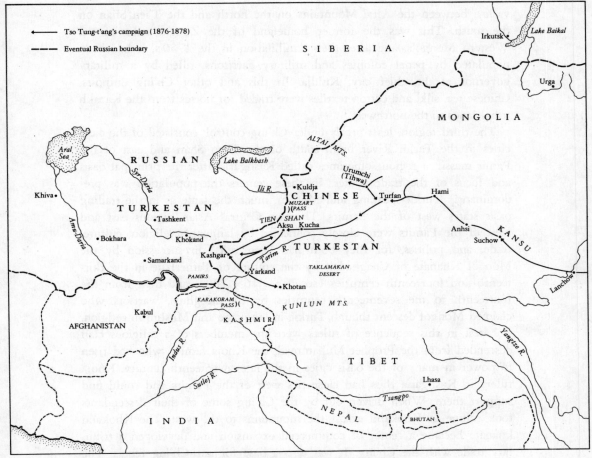

Legend:
← → Tso Tung-t'ang's campaign (1876-1878)
--- Eventual Russian boundary

CENTRAL ASIA IN THE NINETEENTH CENTURY

(Liu-ch'iu) Islands, Taiwan, Vietnam, Korea, and areas of Central Asia gradually became fair game for foreign colonial expansion.

Russian Pressure in Central Asia. The territorial integrity of the Ch'ing Empire was endangered in the 1870's on its farthest northwestern frontier, in Chinese Turkestan. Of the three principal areas there of concern to Ch'ing strategists, the first was the region around Hami (or Komul), which was the key point of ingress to Central Asia across the desert road from China's northwest province of Kansu. The Hami region and other nearby centers to the west, had been the Manchus' logistic base for military expeditions farther west and also a source of Turkic-speaking allies and administrators to assist in the Ch'ing conquest and rule of Central Asia.

The second strategic area centered on the grazing land of the Ili River valley, between the Altai Mountains on the north and the T'ien Shan on the south. This was the former homeland of the Zungar tribe of the Western Mongols, and after their annihilation in the 1750's, it had been populated by penal colonies and military garrisons, ruled by a military governor at the chief city, Kuldja. In this and other Ch'ing outposts, Chinese tea, silk, and cotton textiles were traded for horses from the Kazakh tribal lands to the northwest.

The third region, least firmly under Ch'ing control, consisted of the oasis cities in the Tarim River basin south of the T'ien Shan and east of the Pamir massif, a region sometimes called Kashgaria after the principal oasis and focus of the trade routes. In these centers the population was predominantly Turkic-speaking and Muslim, much the same as in the trading oasis states west of the Pamirs. The two Central Asian regions east and west of the Pamirs were closely connected by language, religion, culture, trade, and politics, for they both had been ruled in succession by the Mongol Khanate of Chaghadai; by the empire of Tamerlane in the thirteenth and fourteenth centuries (see pages 165, 200), and then from the fourteenth to the seventeenth centuries by the Moghuls, warriors who claimed Mongol descent though Turkic in language and Muslim in religion.

Latest in this sequence of rulers were the members of a religious clan descended from the Prophet Muhammad, the Khoja family, who had risen to power in many of the oasis cities in the late seventeenth century. Khoja rulers in Kashgaria thus had close ties west of the Pamirs and could find support there. When driven out by the Ch'ing some of their descendants took refuge in Khokand across the mountains to the west. The Khokand khanate became a center of commercial expansion and developed a tributary trade with the Ch'ing. It was also a base for anti-Ch'ing rebels. The Ch'ing governors in Kashgaria had conferred the title of *beg,* together with lands and serfs, on some 270 local chiefs who thus formed a local ruling class nominally beholden to Peking. Nevertheless, being on the farthest fringe of the Chinese world, they could not easily be kept under control.

By 1860, after only a century of Ch'ing rule, Chinese or Eastern Turkestan was of increasing interest to the expanding empires of Russia and Britain. The Russians in particular, encroaching steadily southward and southeast across the Kirghiz and Kazakh steppe, were about to take over Western or Russian Turkestan with its cotton production and its strategic access to the northern fringes of British India. Meanwhile Peking kept a tenuous hold on Kashgaria and Ili, at a distance of 3500 miles and six weeks by horse-post. This was dictated by a strong tradition of strategic, rather than economic, concern for the western borders of Mongolia.

In 1862 the Muslim rebellion in Northwest China led to a rising in Chinese Turkestan which got Khoja support from Khokand. A Khokandian general, Yakub Beg, soon seized power and ruled much of the Tarim basin as an independent Muslim state from 1865 to 1877. In 1871, to forestall Yakub and British influence, the Russians moved troops into the strategic Ili River valley and occupied the commercial center of Kuldja, where they had had a counsel and a regulated trade since 1851 (see page 302). The Russians promised Peking they would withdraw from Ili whenever Ch'ing control should be re-established.

By the mid-1870's Peking thus faced a crisis. Although Tso Tsung-t'ang's forces had suppressed the Northwest Muslims in 1873, his men were in Kansu province, roughly as far from Yakub's capital at Kashgar as Kansas City is from Los Angeles, on a route that crossed many hundred miles of desert and required ninety days' travel by caravan. At the same time China was embroiled with Japan over the Taiwan issue.

This crisis evoked two schools of strategy. Li Hung-Chang, and others concerned with "self-strengthening" and coastal defense against seaborne aggression, opposed the financing of a costly effort by Tso Tsung-t'ang to reconquer unproductive territory in far-off Central Asia. After a great debate in memorials presented to the throne, Tso won out and went ahead. Central Asia had bulked large in the dynasty's traditional strategy of defense against the Mongols; its recovery was necessary to show reverence for the imperial ancestors. Tso raised foreign and Chinese loans in Shanghai to buy Western cannon and operate an arsenal and a woolen mill at Lanchow. Meanwhile he fed and clothed his troops partly by making them farmers to grow grain and cotton. He built up a base area in Kansu, with advanced bases farther west. In 1876, Tso's troops dashed across the desert route, seized Urumchi and other strategic centers and mercilessly slaughtered the Chinese-speaking Muslim rebels of the northern region, treating them as domestic traitors. They then invaded the Tarim basin, treating the Uighur Turkish population more leniently as frontier rebels. Yakub died in 1877. By 1878 Tso had recovered all Chinese Turkestan except the Ili region.

This spectacular achievement led Peking to demand that Russia evacuate Ili. The first Manchu negotiator fatuously conceded so much to Russia that he was threatened with beheading. A great diplomatic furor and war scare ensued. But the crisis passed. Another treaty in 1881 exacted a larger indemnity from China but restored most of Ili to the Ch'ing. In 1884 Chinese Turkestan was made a province under the name Sinkiang, "The New Dominion." This happy outcome fostered a resurgence of Chinese self-confidence and confirmed the conservatives in their easy talk of fighting off foreign aggression while complacently opposing Westernization.

China's Slow Diplomatic Response. Why was Peking so slow to send abroad envoys who could observe the enemy's home circumstances and defend China's interests? Western ministers resided in Peking from 1861, but no Chinese diplomatic mission functioned abroad until 1877. This inertia had its roots in both psychology and politics. Traditionally, envoys had gone abroad in times of strength to spread the imperial prestige, but in times of weakness to beg peace from barbarian tribes. Once the imperial prestige had been shattered by the stationing at Peking of Western ministers who need not kowtow, foreign relations had become humiliating. This wounded pride was utilized in politics. The power of Westernizers like Li Hung-chang grew with Western contact but could best be checked and balanced by tolerating the shrill accusations of die-hard conservatives who condemned all association with foreigners as simple treason. The Empress Dowager accordingly gave ear to both sides and profited from the stalemate.

Foreign expansionists could also profit from Peking's indecisiveness, as the Japanese did in the case of the Ryūkyū Islanders killed by aborigines in Taiwan. Foolishly, the Tsungli Yamen did not contest Japan's suzerainty over the Ryūkyū Islands, which had been formally tributary to China although controlled by the Satsuma *han* of Japan since 1609. Worse still, to avoid paying Japan compensation, the Yamen disclaimed responsibility for the Taiwan aborigines, and so the restive Japanese samurai sent their punitive expedition to Taiwan in 1874. War was averted, but China had to pay an indemnity to get the Japanese to withdraw. Li and others made the point that a Chinese envoy in Japan might have averted this costly incident.

Another incident occurred when a British expedition went from Burma into Yunnan in 1875 to open a new overland trade route, and a British interpreter was murdered by armed Chinese. Britain demanded indemnity, apology, refinement of rules for Sino-foreign intercourse, and trade concessions, all of which were embodied in the final capstone of the treaty system, the Chefoo Agreement of 1876. As one result China's first resident minister abroad, Kuo Sung-tao, was sent to London in 1877 to apologize. Kuo was from Hunan, a Hanlin scholar and a friend of Tseng Kuo-fan. His reports from London praised railways, telegraphs, and mines and admired the two hundred Japanese whom he found learning British technology. Kuo's outspoken advocacy of Westernization roused the die-hards, whose denunciations forced him into retirement in 1879. By that time China had legations in the United States, Germany, France, Japan, and Russia as well as Britain.

China's predicament—not wanting to acknowledge the equality of foreign rulers by sending envoys to them—became a crisis when foreign powers took over states tributary to China. This happened especially in Vietnam, where all the elements of Western aggressiveness, the weakness of the tributary state, and China's incapacity to assert a Western type of suzerainty combined to destroy the old order of the tribute system.

China's Defeat by France in Vietnam

North Vietnam, centering in the Red River delta around Hanoi, had been annexed to the Han empire in 111 B.C. and remained a part of the Chinese state until 939 A.D. Even though the population spoke a non-Chinese language (Vietnamese has affinities to the Thai languages) and shared major cultural traits with other Southeast Asian peoples, still the structure of central administration together with the Chinese writing system, the Confucian Classics and family teachings, examinations, and a Chinese officialdom had all left a deep Chinese imprint. The rulers of Vietnam after 939 had regularly sent tribute to the Chinese court and continued to follow the Chinese model in law and learning. Vietnam was second only to Korea as a tributary.

The weakness of the Vietnamese state in the nineteenth century was due to many factors—first of all, to its size and elongated shape. The Hanoi delta in the North had been the ancient center of population, production, and power. The Mekong delta south of Saigon had been recently taken over and was less developed, a frontier of Vietnamese expansion, while the new capital of the Nguyen dynasty (1802–1945) at Hué, perched on the thin coastal strip of arable land, had the task of forging North and South into a unified state. Socially, unity was impeded by the presence of non-Vietnamese ethnic minorities. Lying on the cultural boundary between the Chinese and the Indian-influenced Southeast Asian civilizations, Vietnam had not attained the same degree of ethnic and social homogeneity as China, much less Korea or Japan. The Confucian state and its mandarinate overlay the rather different society of the villages, but could not rely on a classically indoctrinated rural elite or gentry class to dominate the countryside while remaining loyal to the throne. Syncretic religious sects easily arose and flourished, while regional overlords still maintained personal armies.

French Encroachment. In particular the Nguyen rulers found no way to keep out foreign influences, since the long coastal frontier was impossible to control, and this facilitated the steady growth of Roman Catholic Christianity aided by French missionaries. After two centuries of active proselytism, the Christian church had become an indigenous sect with more adherents in Vietnam than in all of China, deeply involved in Vietnamese politics, inter-village feuds, and occasional dissidence. As a regime based on Confucian principles of moral leadership through the imperial orthodoxy, the Nguyen rulers and their conservative supporters felt increasingly threatened by the foreign religion. They moved against it. In the dozen years up to 1860, some twenty-five European and three hundred Vietnamese priests and perhaps thirty thousand Vietnamese Christians were killed in persecutions. This gave French empire-builders the opportunity they had been seeking.

After much frustration in trying to keep up with Britain, when France lacked a comparable interest in foreign trade, the ambitious Napoleon III found an active East Asian role in championing Catholic missions. While joining with Britain against China in 1857–1860 (see pages 299–301), France also used her forces against Vietnam and in 1859 seized Saigon and then took over the three provinces around it. Soon there were Vietnamese risings against the French in the South. The local mandarins fled; hence the French, instead of being able to rule through them, had to undertake direct rule themselves and create their colony of Cochin China. Eyeing the possibility of trade with China up the Mekong, they also established a protectorate over nearby Cambodia in 1863–1864.

This French lodgement in South Vietnam was mainly the work of the navy, with missionaries playing only a secondary role and merchants almost unrepresented. The geographical exploration of the Mekong in 1866–1868 stirred the French public's appetite for an Indo-Chinese empire, but it proved that the Mekong could never serve as a trade route leading to Southwest China, and French interest now shifted to the Red River route through Tongking. On this frontier, French expansionists saw themselves reasserting France's vitality, competing with Anglo-American dominance, and helping lesser peoples.

The Sino-French War. By the 1880's sovereignty over "Annam" (as Vietnam was called in China and in the West) was claimed both by France, on the basis of a Franco-Vietnamese treaty of 1874, and by China, on the basis of some fifty tribute missions sent to Peking by rulers of Vietnam since 1664, most recently in 1877 and 1881. France, however, had control over her colony of Cochin China in the South and preponderant influence at the Vietnamese capital, Hué. Franco-Chinese hostilities developed on the Chinese border in the North, where Tongking had been in disorder for a decade. There was not only disaffection here against the ruling Nguyen dynasty of Vietnam, but also an infiltration of Chinese irregulars, remnants of the Taiping and Panthay rebels. The resulting turmoil prevented the French from using their new treaty rights, such as that of trade on the Red River. The Vietnamese ruler encouraged the irregulars against the French and invited in the Chinese army against both. Finally, in 1882 the French seized Hanoi, set up by treaty a protectorate over Annam, and at once had to send for reinforcements. China in 1883 sent regular troops from Yunnan and Kwangsi across the border into Tongking, where they met the French in pitched battles.

The concurrent Sino-French hostilities and negotiations in 1883–1885 confused observers at the time and have confused historians since. One complicating factor was the multiplicity of authorities, while the negotiators of both sides were harassed by compatriots whose clamor for war increased every time their side was defeated. A war party had emerged in the councils

FRENCH INDO-CHINA

of the Ch'ing government during the Ili crisis with Russia. The suppression of rebels in the 1860's and 1870's had left the Chinese bureaucracy sprinkled with old soldiers in the garb of civil officials, who took heart at the Ch'ing success in Central Asia. The most bellicose intransigence in foreign affairs was advocated at Peking by half a dozen younger scholars who were known as the "purification clique." Brilliant memorialists and sycophants of the Empress Dowager, they attacked the older advocates of "self-strengthening" as appeasers and supported a militant posture against Russia and France. In 1884 when French victories led to the dismissal of Prince Kung and the Grand Council, the "purification clique" came briefly into positions of power, only to suffer defeat and eclipse in turn through France's further victories. The most able member of this clique, and the only one to survive in power, was Chang Chih-tung (1837–1909), who became governor-general of Kwangtung and Kwangsi in 1884 and proved his practical capacity in support of the war effort.

Sino-French negotiations began almost as early as hostilities. Finally Li Hung-chang in May 1884 drew up with a French naval officer a settlement, known as the Li-Fournier convention, which provided that China should withdraw her troops and admit French trade through Tongking while France should keep Annam and her treaty rights there and claim no indemnity from China. For this deal the war party excoriated Li in forty-seven memorials, the court refused to accept the loss of suzerainty, and hostilities continued, sporadically but more violently, along with abortive negotiations. Robert Hart, being in the councils of Peking but not its politics, began secret talks. In 1885 he sent his London agent of the Maritime Customs to Paris and with the court's authority settled peace terms there on the basis of the Li-Fournier convention. Li signed the peace in June 1885.

The extra year of hostilities was costly for China. One French fleet attacked northern Taiwan in August 1884; another anchored in Foochow harbor alongside eleven small Foochow-built wooden steam warships, the Fukien fleet of the new Chinese navy. The eight French armor-clad vessels were bigger and had heavier guns. When, after five weeks' indecision, Peking let a French ultimatum expire on August 23, the French destroyed nine Chinese vessels in a few minutes and also the shipyard that had been founded in 1866 with the aid of French engineers.

On the land French superiority was less marked. Overconfident French troops were occasionally ambushed by Chinese with Remingtons in the Tongking jungle. The French took the delta around Hanoi and, advancing on the main route north to the Kwangsi border, eventually took Langson just south of Chen-nan-kuan. The unexpected Chinese recovery of this strategic spot in March 1885 caused the fall of the French cabinet and somewhat salved Chinese pride.

The war against France was China's first defensive action against a modern enemy since the beginning of the "self-strengthening" movement in the 1860's. It disclosed one major fact: modern arms are relatively ineffective without modern organization and leadership. The best European guns were useless in Chinese hands without adequate training, tactics, supply, communication, strategy, and command. The harbor at Foochow, for example, was some twenty miles from the sea through a narrow passage past forts armed with new Krupp and Armstrong cannon. Yet the command was so ill-informed, disorganized, and indecisive that neither the modern armament nor even traditional tactics of blockage and harassment were used with any vigor against the French. Again, China in 1884 had more than fifty modern warships, a majority built in Chinese yards, but they were of many sorts and under four separate commands. The Nanyang and Peiyang fleets, respectively under the Southern and Northern Commissioners at Nanking and Tientsin, were larger than the Kwangtung and Fukien fleets, but stayed defensively in their home waters. Caution and bureaucratic rivalry, each official saving his own, prevented a national war effort.

One result of the French war, however, was to call forth vigorous manifestations of nationalism, particularly in Kwangtung, the chief base area for the forces in Tongking. The long-standing antiforeignism of the Cantonese was heightened by several things—fear of a French attack, China's declaration of war after the Foochow debacle, and Chang Chih-tung's old-style offer of cash rewards for dead Frenchmen. Even without an invasion of the area, widespread riots and pillaging occurred, especially of Catholic and Protestant missions. The modern Chinese-language press in Hong Kong, which was now purveying inflammatory news to a social stratum of readers much broader than the scholar-literati class, seems to have helped this growth of an urban-centered mass nationalism.

China's Effort at "Self-Strengthening." After the conclusion of the Sino-French war in 1885, China enjoyed a decade of comparative tranquillity in her foreign relations. Her general effort to build up military and naval strength responded to the encroachments of Russia, France, and Japan in peripheral areas. These had roused a degree of nationalism and inspired many efforts to modernize in self-defense, yet in the absence of a strong central leadership, these efforts remained dependent upon the continuity of a reforming official in one post and the comparative weakness of local vested interests against him.

The vulnerability of this kind of personally sponsored development was illustrated in Taiwan, which was separated from Fukien and made a province in 1885. Gentry-based conservative interests were relatively weak, and the first governor, one of Li Hung-chang's lieutenants (Liu Ming-ch'uan), was able to get some impressive results during his six-year term: an arsenal at the capital, Taipei; a naval force based on the Pescadores Islands between Taiwan

WESTERNERS THROUGH CHINESE EYES. *Four sketches from a Shanghai picture magazine* (Tien-shih-chai hua-pao) *founded in 1884. Illustrated are Western sports (boat-racing and a paper chase), a cautionary tale of a French opium addict, and an instance of foreign medical skill. The Chinese explanations are summarized.*

"In the fair weather of spring and autumn, Westerners regularly hold boat races for high stakes. The little oars fly by like swallows crossing a screen; the shallow boats are like leaves, light as seagulls playing on water. Amid the waves the high-spirited participants don't mind getting wet. Spectators on both banks cheer them on. Their whole country is mad about it."

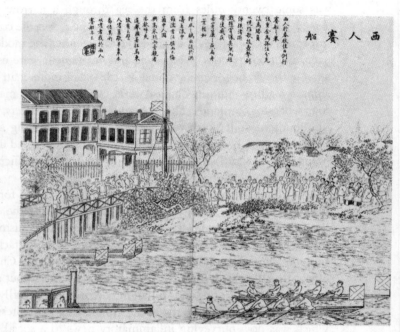

"In the fine weather of spring and autumn, on two occasions in each season and each time on three days only, Westerners compete in racing on horseback with high wagers. This autumn at Shanghai they have added paper-chasing: up to 50 or 60 riders gather in one place, one goes ahead scattering multi-colored paper strips, and the others follow, racing madly. Whoever first gets over the paper course is the winner."

"*Opium coming to China has become an evil beyond control. If it is not Heaven's will to stop it, there is no other way to save the situation. Heretofore it has been said that only we Chinese are opium smokers. Not so. A French addict in the prime of life, traveling with his wife, an English friend, and a French servant, lay down to smoke in a Singapore hotel but next morning became ill and died—the doctor said from smoking too much. How can one not be afraid!*"

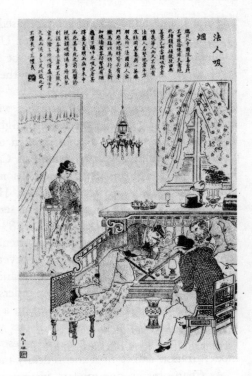

"*A foreign woman doctor, specialized in women's ailments and also in surgery, examined at the T'ung-jen Hospital in Hongkew a woman patient with a huge growth. Saying, 'This can be cured,' she took out a sharp knife, cut it off (it weighed one-fourth as much as the patient) and applied medicine, and after a month it was cured. The patient was fortunate to find this doctor, and the doctor fortunate to find this patient on whom to demonstrate such miraculous skill, which leaves Chinese doctors speechless and ashamed.*"

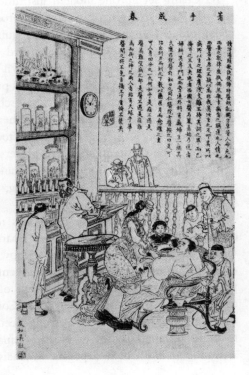

and the mainland; land-tax reform based on a land survey and population registration; and other modern services. Unfortunately, this governor was not a genuine Confucian scholar; rather, he had risen from the peasant-bandit level as an able commander against the mid-century rebels. Conservative critics effected his removal in 1891.

A more powerful regional reformer was Chang Chih-tung. Converted to modernization by bitter experience in fighting the French, he emerged after 1885 as Li Hung-chang's chief rival in regional influence and bureaucratic politics. Although governor-general at Canton in 1885–1889 and at Nanking in 1894–1896, Chang found his main regional base at the Wuhan cities (the joint name for Wuchang, Hanyang, and Hankow where the Han River enters the Yangtze). He served there as governor-general of Hunan and Hupei for fifteen years, 1889–1894 and 1896–1907. This long tenure helped him build up the appurtenances of regional power—his own staff of subordinates, local sources of revenue, military forces, industries, and political patronage. His scholastic brilliance and his record of antiforeignism made Chang less vulnerable than others to conservative attack when he embarked on modernization. Becoming a regional leader twenty years later than Li Hung-chang, he showed a less wide-ranging ability but a greater fiscal probity and a burning desire to establish a philosophical sanction for modernization and to fit it theoretically into China's classical tradition.

As Chang set up one modern institution after another, he confronted the fact that "self-strengthening" steadily eroded the underpinnings of the Confucian order. Defense, for example, required literate officers trained in academies, military men who also qualified as scholars. This broke down the ancient supremacy of *wen* over *wu*, civil over military. Again, the fact that military command required a mastery of practical military technology blurred the old distinctions between superiors (scholar-officials who "labor with their minds") and inferiors (artisans and other small men who "labor with their strength"). As Chang's defense effort took in more and more of Western technology, he constantly tried to preserve China's traditional learning and values. He became the leading spokesman for China's salvation through conservative reform by "self-strengthening," the use of Western devices for Chinese ends.

A major Chinese defense effort was to build a navy. After the French destroyed the Fukien fleet in 1885, a Board of Admiralty or "Naval Yamen" was set up at Peking as a gesture acknowledging that a navy must function as a centralized unit, but in fact the centrifugal forces of regionalism still perpetuated four fleets in four regions of the China coast. Li Hung-chang at Tientsin, as Northern (Peiyang) Commissioner, created the principal fighting force, known as the Peiyang fleet. He contracted with foreign firms to build forts and bases in North China, including a naval base at Port Arthur and a fortified depot at Weihaiwei. Instead of building his own vessels as Foochow continued to do, Li bought from the big British and German arms firms. A British naval officer served as his chief adviser until 1890. By then Li's Peiyang fleet of some twenty-five vessels had nine modern warships.

This late Ch'ing naval effort was starved by the court, which decided instead to build up the new Summer Palace northwest of Peking as a retreat for the Empress Dowager on her retirement in 1889. The famous marble barge in the big lake there epitomizes this story. It is reminiscent of the palatial extravagance of the Wan-li emperor that undid the Ming dynasty just four centuries earlier. The chief eunuch and other courtiers encouraged these expenditures to line their own pockets. The Imperial Household Department misused large levies from the provinces as "naval funds" and borrowed from Jardine, Matheson and Company. Thus, millions of taels went into the Summer Palace and no additions were made to the Peiyang fleet in the early 1890's, while intensive naval development was occurring in Europe and nine fast ships were being added to the Japanese navy. The fleet's smaller units even took to carrying passengers between Port Arthur and Chefoo. By 1894 Li realized his fleet was inefficient and did his best to avoid a showdown with Japan.

China's Defeat by Japan in Korea

Like North Vietnam, the northern part of Korea had been incorporated in the Han empire in 108 B.C., and the Chinese commandery at P'yŏngyang remained an outpost of Chinese civilization for four centuries thereafter. By the time Korea was unified in the seventh century, its culture was basically modeled on China. The Vietnamese variant of Chinese civilization had been mixed with Southeast Asian cultural elements; however, Korea adapted to her needs all the main features of Chinese culture. This made her China's number one tributary, even though the Korean people with their different language and history had a vigorous sense of their separate identity. With this went a deep political conservatism. The Koryo dynasty that reunified Korea in 935 had lasted 474 years, and its successor, the Yi dynasty (1392–1910), was almost as long-lived as the Ming and Ch'ing combined.

Where Vietnam temporarily fell victim to a European power expanding far overseas, Korea was fated by geography to lie where the three empires of China, Japan, and Russia met and clashed. Moreover, the blighting influence of imperial Confucianism in general and its tributary system in particular was more marked in Korea. For centuries the foreign relations of Korea had been limited to sending regular tribute missions to China and some to Japan. The Korean kings, though weak as domestic rulers, were vigorously hostile to all Western contact. They maintained a rigid policy of seclusion until it was almost too late to learn the art of diplomacy. The

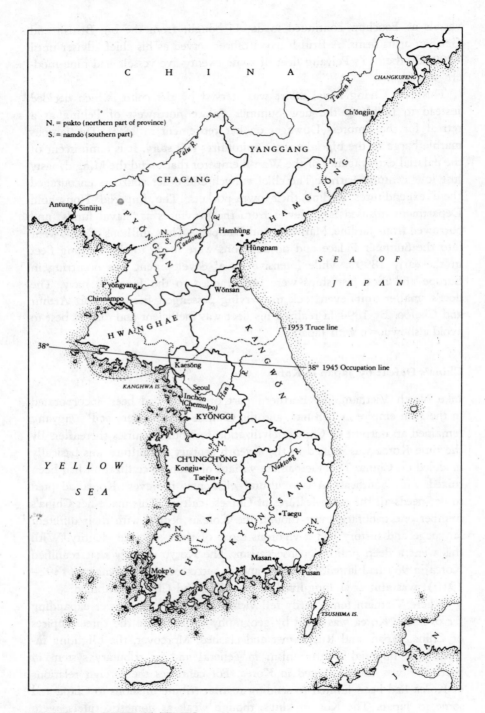

N. = pukto (northern part of province)
S. = namdo (southern part)

CHINA

CHANGKUFENG

Tumen R.

Ch'ŏngjin

YANGGANG

Yalu R.

CHAGANG

HAMGYŎNG

S. N.

Antung Sinŭiju

PYŎNGAN

N.
S.

Hamhŭng

Taedong R.

Hŭngnam

SEA OF JAPAN

P'yŏngyang

Wŏnsan

Chinnampo

HWANGHAE

KANGWŎN

—— 1953 Truce line

38°

—— 38° 1945 Occupation line

Kaesŏng

KANGHWA IS.

Seoul

Inchŏn
(Chemulpo)

Han R.

KYŎNGGI

S. N.

YELLOW SEA

CH'UNGCH'ŎNG

Kongju

Taejŏn

Naktong R.

KYŎNGSANG

Taegu

N.
S.

CHŎLLA

N.
S.

Mokp'o

Masan

Pusan

TSUSHIMA IS.

JAPAN

KOREA IN RECENT TIMES

reluctance and confusion of aim in Korea's response were major reasons for the disastrous outcome. For here, as elsewhere, imperialist expansion, though irresistible in its later phases, had seemed at first to be little more than an intellectual challenge on the outer horizon.

Rebellion and Restoration in Korea. The Korean state in the 1860's met a challenge on two fronts, foreign and domestic, just as China and Vietnam had done a few years earlier. On the domestic front there arose a large-scale peasant-based rebellion, led by a religious cult, the most serious revolt in several hundred years. Although primarily a protest against poverty and misgovernment, this rising was also inspired by the upsetting news of the Taiping rebellion and foreign invasion in China. In Korea, however, domestic rebellion and foreign religion had a different relationship from that they had in China.

Catholic Christianity had reached Korea first in the form of Chinese writings from the Jesuits at Peking and became known as the "Western Learning." The first Chinese Catholic missionary penetrated Korea only in the late eighteenth century. Gaining adherents, Christianity was soon persecuted, in 1801 and later, as a heterodox sect and also a foreign menace. It became perforce a secret society, ministered to by Chinese priests and, after 1836, by French priests who were smuggled into the country.

In the 1860's a syncretic religious cult known as the Tonghak or "Eastern Learning" arose in violent opposition to this "Western Learning," but also partly inspired by its example. Its teachings used concepts from Taoist, Buddhist, Neo-Confucian, and even Catholic cosmology, but with a strong admixture of native Korean shamanism and an apocalyptic emphasis on the spiritual union of the believer with the Creator. The new sect naturally appealed to the poverty-stricken peasantry, spread rapidly, and contributed to risings in southeast and south Korea in 1862–1863.

The rulers of Korea in the 1860's met domestic rebellion and the Western challenge by an anti-Christian policy of seclusion and a revival and reform of traditional institutions. The Tonghak movement was driven underground and a vigorous conservative reform program was pursued by the Korean regent of the decade 1864–1873, who was known by his title as the Taewŏngun or Grand Prince. This man was father of the boy-king Kojong (reigned 1864–1907); he was also quite prepared to challenge the whole establishment. He met the crisis in the domestic fortunes of the Yi dynasty by seeking reforms which would effect a "restoration" of the golden age of the dynastic founder.

But despite all his efforts to revitalize tradition and even use modern means to defend it, the Taewŏngun was vigorously exclusionist. When his execution of French priests brought on a French naval attack in 1866, his commander sternly lectured the invaders with Confucian righteousness:

"How can you tell us to abandon the teachings of our forefathers and accept those of others?" After the French had left (in defeat, as the Koreans assumed), the Taewŏngun kept on persecuting Christians, but by established custom he left foreign relations for Peking to handle.

The Opening of Korea. During all the alarms of the Ili crisis with Russia and the Tongking fighting with France, Li Hung-chang had kept his eyes on the danger closest to North China, the growth of Japanese power, particularly in Korea. Japanese trade had continued at Pusan on a restricted basis somewhat like the Dutch trade at Nagasaki, and occasional diplomatic missions went from Seoul to the shogun at Edo. Other than this, Korea kept her borders tightly sealed. The annual tribute ritual, conducted at Peking with the Board of Rites, continued down to the 1860's to be the only regular foreign contact.

In the nineteenth century, Western vessels, surveying or in stress of weather, more frequently visited the Korean coast. Korea regularly succored the shipwrecked, expelling them to China, but resisted violently all efforts to open trade or even negotiate. This excited a degree of rivalry to see who could emulate Commodore Perry and "open" Korea. In 1871 the American minister to China was sent with five warships to the river mouth below the capital. His surveyors proceeded upriver. Two Americans were wounded. He demanded an apology, in vain. In retaliation the American fleet destroyed five forts and killed perhaps 250 Koreans, yet in the end it could only sail away. Korea adamantly refused to negotiate and felt confirmed, by her apparent victories, in the old policy of seclusion.

Expanding powers in adjacent territory now began to pose more serious threats than Westerners who came from afar. By the mid-1870's some four thousand Koreans, refugees from hard times and harsh government, had defied the seclusion policy by settling in the newly formed Russian Maritime Province to the north. Meanwhile the provoking of a war with Korea had become a fixed aim of frustrated Japanese samurai. In 1873 their plans for invasion were forestalled by cooler heads in Japan, but Tōkyō was determined to try to open Korea and draw it away from China.

In 1875 a party of Japanese, landing from warships surveying the Korean coast, was fired upon. The Tōkyō government, still strongly opposed to an invasion of Korea, now determined to "open" Korea peacefully through moderate demands for intercourse backed by a show of superior force. The Tsungli Yamen and Li Hung-chang stuck to the old Sinocentric concept of China's moral but inactive suzerainty over a tributary state—"though Korea is a dependent country of China, it is not a territorial possession; hence in its domestic and foreign affairs it is self-governing." They finally advised Korea to negotiate. The Japanese warships and transports that anchored off Inchon thus secured in February 1876 an unequal treaty modeled on the

Western treaties with China and Japan. It opened three ports for Japanese trade—Pusan, Inchon (then known as Chemulpo), and Wonsan—and declared Korea to be an "independent state."

Sino-Japanese Rivalry.   The growth of foreign contact had violent repercussions within Korea, and China was soon obliged to play a more active role in Korea's government and politics. But China's reluctant intervention brought a Chinese program of moderate reform into competition with more radical modernizing influences from Japan.

Reform was complicated by the fact that both the Chinese and Japanese influences were violently opposed by die-hard conservatives like the Taewŏngun. Though out of power since 1873, he helped foment an antiforeign rising in 1882, during which a mob attacked the Japanese legation. Both China and Japan sent troops, but China sent larger numbers, kidnaped the Taewŏngun, and held him for three years in China. Japan was mollified by an indemnity, and Li Hung-chang now tried to develop preferential Sino-Korean trade relations, appoint advisers, and dominate Korean politics.

From 1880 China's relations with Korea had been removed from the control of the Ministry of Rites, which had traditionally handled tribute relations, and put under Li Hung-chang, who with Chinese and British advice had been developing a comprehensive policy. First, Li hoped through Chinese intervention in Korea's domestic affairs to foster "self-strengthening" concurrent with China's own development of naval and military power. Second, he hoped to protect Korea against Japanese or Russian absorption by getting her into treaty relations with all the trading powers, whose commerce would create vested interests in Korea's independence, a strategy of "using barbarians to offset barbarians." This new policy was followed when a United States naval diplomat (Commodore R. W. Shufeldt), again following the Perry tradition, tried first through Japan to negotiate a treaty, without avail, and then succeeded in doing so through Li Hung-chang at Tientsin in 1882. Li negotiated for Korea but failed to get into the treaty a clause describing Korea as "a dependent state of the Chinese Empire." Instead, the American treaty recognized Korea's independence. So did the treaties that followed in 1883–1886 with the other Western powers.

During the early 1880's the main threat to Korea seemed to come from Russia, which was also the power most feared by Britain. But as time went on, the basic rivalry for domination of Korea developed between China and Japan. At first China with British encouragement seemed to be ahead. But within Korea, the more radical reformers gravitated to the Japanese camp, because Japan was modernizing more vigorously than China. Korea's domestic struggles between radical and traditional reformers thus reflected the progress of modernization within her two big neighbors. But Korean conservatism and factional rivalries were still basic problems. China's removal of the Taewǒngun had left in power his enemies, the entrenched Min family, who were represented at court by King Kojong's queen (often referred to as "Queen Min"). The queen and her Min family faction now cooperated with China, undid some of the Taewǒngun's reforms, and similarly opposed the modernization efforts of those who wanted to follow the Japanese example. The lack of national unity, manifested in the curse of factionalism, continued to upset Korean efforts to achieve independence and modernization.

Foreign influences flooded into Korean politics. After cultural missions went in 1881 to both China and Japan, a Korean mission visited the United States in 1883, and another set up a legation in Washington in 1888. American influence, strong in Japan in the 1880's, also reached Korea through missionary-educators and sympathetic diplomats, who espoused Korean independence even though, as later with the "integrity of China," the use of force to support the idea was never contemplated in Washington.

Paradoxically, during the era of Chinese ascendancy at Seoul from 1882 to 1894, it was mainly contact with Japan that inspired a growing number of patriots with Western ideas of nationalism and reform. Japanese liberals, like Fukuzawa Yukichi who advised the young reformers Kim Ok-kyun and Pak Yǒng-hyo in the early 1880's, saw Japan inaugurating a new day in Korea much as the United States had done in Japan. But these Korean reformers, who wanted to Westernize on the Japanese model, found their hopes blocked by the ruling Min faction and the dominant Chinese influence, and so attempted a *coup d'état* in 1884. With the knowledge of the Japanese legation, they assassinated conservative ministers and seized the king, only to be thwarted by the vigorous young Chinese commander, Yüan Shih-k'ai, who defeated the Japanese legation guards and rescued the king. This crisis was settled in 1885 when Li and the Japanese statesman Itō Hirobumi negotiated at Tientsin the Li-Itō Convention, a mutual abstention agreement by which the two countries agreed to withdraw their troops and military advisers from Korea and in case of trouble notify the other party before sending them back.

Behind this stalemate lay a Japanese decision, following a great debate in Tokyo, to build up further national strength before becoming involved in hostilities abroad. Itō believed that time was on Japan's side, that to fight for Korea prematurely would only benefit Russia. Li, on his part, felt that historical tradition and geographical proximity favored China. Li went ahead with an active program of modernization, urging upon Korea many of the reforms that Britain had urged upon China twenty years before: a Korean Customs Service headed by Westerners lent from the Chinese Maritime Customs; an American adviser on foreign affairs; telegraph lines; and military training. Li's lieutenant in Seoul as Resident from 1885 to 1894, the young and overbearing Yüan Shih-k'ai, sought to preserve the forms of Chinese suzerainty, while American diplomats and missionaries, among others, benevolently fostered Korean independence. Meantime the decade after 1885 saw a steady increase of Japanese influence among young Korean patriots.

The Sino-Japanese War. The Korean government's halting efforts at reform did little to alleviate the misery of the populace, and the Tonghak movement continued to appeal to the oppressed. In 1894 conservative elements associated with the Tonghak and utilizing its popular organization rose in rebellion in South Korea, demanding reform of the corrupt and inefficient local administration under which the people were suffering. This rebellion precipitated Chinese and Japanese intervention. China sent a small body of troops at the Korean king's request, and Japan then sent in a larger force, demanded reforms of the Korean government, and finally seized control of it and had it declare war on China. War followed between Japan and China on August 1.

The ensuing hostilities were the first real test of the efforts at military modernization both China and Japan had been making for a whole generation. Most Westerners assumed that the Chinese giant would win through sheer size, but Japan quickly proved that its modernization had been more successful. Its armies seized the whole of Korea and then invaded Manchuria. But victory was largely determined by sea power, which in the absence of railways controlled even China's access to Korea. While the Chinese fleet was larger, the Japanese was qualitatively much better. On September 17 off the mouth of the Yalu River, the Japanese, using modern British naval tactics, severely crippled the Chinese fleet, which came out like cavalry, line abreast. The Japanese then captured the naval base of Port Arthur in South Manchuria and besieged Weihaiwei on the northern coast of Shantung, where the remainder of the Chinese fleet was bottled up. Weihaiwei fell, the fleet surrendered, and China had to sue for peace.

The terms of the Treaty of Shimonoseki, signed between Itō and Li on April 17, 1895, were relatively severe, though perhaps less so than they might have been had not a Japanese fanatic shot and wounded Li. China was obliged to cede Taiwan, the nearby Pescadores Islands, and the Kwantung Peninsula in South Manchuria; recognize Korea's independence; pay 200 million taels' indemnity; open more ports; and negotiate a commercial treaty. The latter, signed in 1896, gave Japan all the privileges that the Western powers had in China and added the further privilege of carrying on "industries and manufactures," using the cheap labor in the treaty ports.

Japan's triumph, however, was soon tarnished by a blatant power play by the Western nations. Russia, which itself had ambitions in both Manchuria and Korea, was alarmed by Japan's success. It persuaded Germany and France to join in a diplomatic intervention on April 23, 1895, "advising" Japan to give up the Kwantung Peninsula. Bowing to *force majeur,* Japan complied, receiving in compensation 30 million taels of additional indemnity.

Power Politics over China

The Impact of Japan's Defeat of China.   When the new Japanese navy unexpectedly defeated Li's Peiyang fleet off the Yalu in September 1894, it upset the power balance both within China and internationally. It had worldwide repercussions and inspired a rivalry among imperialist powers competing to expand at China's expense.

The rise of modern nationalism and industrialism in Europe and Japan had now reached the flash point where modern steam navies and railways, the ultimate devices of the day in firepower and logistics, could dominate distant areas of the globe. The great power rivals, expanding outward from Europe, had already laid claim to much of Africa and the Near East. The sudden rise of Japan as a military and naval power spotlighted the final collapse of the Ch'ing tribute system and the vulnerability of Britain's informal commercial empire based on the unequal treaty system. And so international relations in East Asia entered upon a full decade of ominous instability.

One way to bring some order into the confusing kaleidoscope of great power politics in the 1890's is to look at the Anglo-Russian rivalry all across the Asian continent, from the Near East and the Afghan border on the northwest approach to India, through Central Asia, Tibet, and Mongolia, to Manchuria and Korea. Britain was entrenched on the south as ruler of India, Malaya, and Burma and as the dominant trading power in Siam, China, and adjacent areas. Britain's particular rival in Siam and Burma had been France, and Anglo-French rivalry, which had been especially bitter in Africa, was compounded after 1893 by the Franco-Russian alliance. Thus one element intensifying European rivalry in the Far East was Russia's accelerated movement as a land power across the north of Asia.

After Muraviev's successful mid-century invasion of the Amur and the acquisition of the Maritime Province in 1860 (see page 302), Russian expansion had run into serious difficulties of food supply and transportation. The cossacks in the sixty villages that formed a communication route along the Amur could not grow enough crops in the unfavorable climate to feed themselves; in summer they could navigate upstream only with difficulty, and in winter they lacked draft animals for transport on the ice. With the sale of Alaska to the United States in 1867 and the decline of the sea-otter fur trade in the Pacific, even the Russian garrisons and naval forces in Northeast Asia were reduced. Finally, after 1869 the Suez Canal wrecked the Russian hope of developing trade via the Amur between China and European

LI HUNG-CHANG ON HIS WORLD TOUR, 1896. *Li at the age of 72 visited Russia, Germany, France, England, and the United States. Here he stands between the British prime minister, Lord Salisbury (left), and the later Viceroy of India, Lord Curzon.*

Russia. By 1880 the population of the Russian Far East was still less than 100,000; the combined immigration of Chinese, Tungus from Manchuria, and Koreans exceeded that of Russians; trade was mainly in non-Russian hands. The area's connections with European Russia were maintained more by sea than by land. Russia's position was weak and her policy passive. After the settlement of the Ili crisis in 1881 the Russians felt on the defensive in East Asia, where they faced the Ch'ing Empire's active colonization of Manchuria, Li Hung-chang's buildup of his Peiyang fleet and Port Arthur naval base, and the contemporary growth of the Japanese fleet.

However, in 1886 Tsar Alexander III concluded that all these weaknesses in the Russian position—in population, food supply, land transport, and naval power—could be overcome by building a trans-Siberian railway which would strengthen Russian land power in East Asia. Diplomatic isolation and frustration elsewhere made it easier to turn eastward again, and French capital was available. In 1891 work was started on the Trans-Siberian Railway from both ends, with completion scheduled for 1903. It became a key element in the Russian state program of heavy industry. Once under way, Russia's turning to the east was justified by ideologists of the time as a sacred "historical mission" to spread Western culture to the Orient.

As Russia's interest and power thus increased, her East Asian policy became more vigorous. Japan's victory in 1895 roused her to immediate action. After leading France and Germany in obliging Japan to restore the Liaotung

Peninsula to China, Russia pressed her advantage. In 1895 she got French and Russian banks to loan China about half the funds needed to pay China's indemnity to Japan. In 1896 Russia got Chinese permission to build the Chinese Eastern Railway 950 miles across Manchuria to Vladivostok, in order to avoid by this short-cut the costly tunnels and bridges which the trans-Siberian line would require on the 350-mile-longer Amur route. Li Hung-chang in St. Petersburg negotiated in June 1896 a secret Russo-Chinese treaty of alliance. It committed China and Russia to fight together against any Japan-ese expansion on the continent. After much maneuvering and confusion, Russia followed up this treaty by sending a naval squadron into Port Arthur in December 1897 and getting from China in March 1898 a twenty-five-year lease of the southern tip of Manchuria, the Liaotung (or Kwantung) Penin-sula, with the right to connect it with the Chinese Eastern Railway by a north-south line 650 miles long, the South Manchurian Railway.

The Scramble for Concessions.   This Russian success in acquiring her long-sought ice-free port, to be connected with Europe by rail, illustrated the novel methods of a new phase of imperialist penetration in China. The new approach used loans, railways, leased areas, reduced land tariffs, and rights of local jurisdiction, of police power, and of mining exploitation to create in effect a "sphere of influence." Great-power rivalry chiefly motivated the rapid maneuvers by which Britain, France, Germany, Russia, Japan, and to some extent the United States variously challenged, assisted, forestalled, and cooperated with one another to take advantage of the expected breakup of China.

The sequence of major events in the scramble went roughly as follows: because two German missionaries had been killed by bandits in Shantung, a German fleet occupied the harbor of Tsingtao in Kiaochow bay on the Shantung promontory in November 1897. Almost at once a Russian fleet seized Port Arthur on the south Manchurian (Liaotung) peninsula in De-cember, as already mentioned. By April 1898 a French fleet had occupied the harbor of Kwangchow, south of Canton and near Indo-China. Britain responded by leasing both the New Territories opposite Hong Kong and a naval base at Weihaiwei on the Shantung coast opposite Port Arthur. All these demands and seizures were legalized by treaties with China, usually through ninety-nine-year leases, and created what were called "spheres of interest" or "influence." Chinese sovereignty and customs collections were preserved but foreign domination and exploitation of key areas were also arranged. While the details of these maneuvers are almost as confusing to historians today as they were to diplomats at the time, certain patterns do emerge.

First of all, no power followed a single, straight course of action, because each was influenced by all the others and often by conflicting pressures at home. The Russian moves summarized above, for example, were only one thread in the tapestry and were partly responses to the moves of others. Thus both Germany and Britain in 1895–1896 had actively encouraged Russia to press forward in East Asia in order to lessen her pressure elsewhere; and Russia occupied Port Arthur in December 1897 only after Kaiser Wilhelm II had offered encouragement and set an example by sending his ships into Tsingtao in November. Russia's counsels were often divided, many of her efforts failed, events were often unforeseen, and bold action alternated with worried hesitation. So it was with the other powers.

Secondly, there was a certain degree of alignment among the European powers. The Franco-Russian allies, having little sea trade, encroached on China from their land-based positions on the south and north in Indo-China and the Russian Far East. France actually was the first to act, in June 1895, extorting a concession to open mines in Southwest China and to extend her railways there from Tongking. This success, after decades of Anglo-French competition in planning the railway penetration of Yunnan, was eventually followed by French construction of the narrow-gauge line from Hanoi up the Red River to Yunnan-fu (Kunming), completed in 1910. On their land frontiers, moreover, France and Russia secured reductions in the Chinese customs tariff. Working through a Belgian syndicate, they also secured in May 1897 the concession for a Peking-Hankow railway through the Chinese interior.

Britain and Germany, on the other hand, being trading and naval powers without important land frontiers with China, sought their spheres in the Yangtze Valley and Shantung respectively. They also had greater capital resources, and their bankers lent most of the funds that China required to pay the Japanese indemnity. Of these two maritime powers, however, the British were defending a long-established commercial position which gave them four-fifths of the foreign trade of China, while the Germans were newcomers and already Britain's chief trade competitors, aggressively seeking markets and naval bases. The Kaiser kept on friendly terms with his cousin the Tsar and, after prospecting for a naval base elsewhere, had won the latter's tacit consent for the German occupation of Kiaochow in November 1897. This move precipitated the general scramble.

In the ensuing melee, the British government, under vigorous pressure from the China Association and other spokesmen for the China trade and imperial expansion, pragmatically followed a policy of "compensation." While still espousing the traditional principle of the integrity of China, the Open Door, and equal opportunity for the trade of all comers, Britain nevertheless carved out her own "sphere," applying in effect the same two-power standard that she was applying in the naval race to keep abreast of any combination of two competitors. Thus, as it turned out, France acquired a "sphere" in Kwangtung-Kwangsi-Yunnan with a naval base at Kwangchow Bay (April 1898), while Russia got a "sphere" in Manchuria, and Germany one in Shantung, each with a leased territory enclosed by a neutral zone and with railways projected from the main port. But meanwhile Britain had kept pace with France by opening Southwest China to trade up the West River from Canton and by a projected Burma railroad (February 1897). Moreover, through a nonalienation agreement (that China would not cede the territory to any other power) Britain had got a claim to the entire Yangtze Valley—the whole hinterland of Shanghai, half the China market. Britain also got concessions to build some 2800 miles of railways, roughly equal to the combined length of the French (420 miles), Russian (1530 miles), and Belgian (650 miles) concessions. In addition Britain leased Weihaiwei, opposite Port Arthur, as a naval base and increased eightfold the territory leased on the mainland next to Hong Kong. She also tried to ensure the survival of the treaty system, which had been so largely a British creation, by securing the opening of more treaty ports in the southwest and northeast and a promise that the office of Inspector General of Customs would remain British-held as long as Britain's share of the China trade remained the largest. Yet this outcome tended to weaken Britain's position in China, since her taking "compensation" only confirmed the special positions of the other powers in Yunnan, Shantung, and Manchuria, contrary to her interests there.

The results of the scramble of 1898 were most evident in the political scene. It inaugurated a new and more ominous phase of the treaty system, because "spheres of influence" were plainly part-way steps toward making China into a congeries of outright European colonies. Up to this time the trading powers led by Britain had dominated China's foreign trade, ports of access, and internal waterways. Now, Germany and Russia were moving in to dominate entire provinces with new railways, mines, industries, and seaports. The leased territories and railway zones, to be governed and policed by foreigners in Manchuria and Shantung, would become quasi-colonial areas, much more extensive and more menacing to China's integrity than the old treaty-port concessions. In short, imperialism threatened the Ch'ing empire with extinction. It directly inspired both the Reform Movement and the Boxer uprising.

The Reform Movement

No one had been more surprised by China's defeat in 1894 than the conservatives who had opposed modernization. Remote from the scene of battle, shaken by its unexpected outcome, they were equally violent in accusing Li Hung-chang of treachery and in opposing the peace settlement. They clamored for the war to continue. Within a twenty-day period the throne received 130 memorials signed by some 2500 persons. This unprecedented outpouring of patriotic concern stressed that the indemnity, three times Peking's annual revenue, would put the empire in debt to foreigners while the other terms would weaken its prestige and power almost to extinction. In this atmosphere of concentration, a radical reformer from Canton, K'ang Yu-wei, led a group of more than 1200 provincial graduates, who were at Peking for the triennial examinations, in presenting on May 2, 1895, what became known as the "Ten Thousand Word Memorial" or "Memorial of the Examination Candidates." It advocated rejecting the peace treaty, moving the capital inland for prolonged warfare, and instituting a multitude of reforms. This inaugurated the Reform Movement which absorbed the attention of the scholar-official class during the next four years, while the imperialists' demands became constantly more menacing.

With China's defeat the dam had broken. The foreign powers moved toward dismembering the empire, "cutting up the Chinese melon," while the ruling class strove to save the traditional state-and-culture by something more than "self-strengthening"—namely, the "reform of institutions." The Reform Movement was an institutional innovation, for it led to political discussion by scholar-gentry who were not in office, quite contrary to the Ch'ing dynasty's established regulations. As early as 1652, mindful how factionalism had weakened the Ming, the emperor had forbidden degreeholders to put forward views on policy, or "to associate with large numbers of others, or to form alliances or join societies." The Yung-cheng and Ch'ienlung emperors had denounced all associations of officials as self-seeking "factions" (*tang*), incapable of any disinterested concern for policy, and had demanded that each official be personally loyal in the sense of taking the emperor's "likes and dislikes as his own will."

Although the nineteenth century had seen this authoritarianism modified in practice, the memorial of the examination candidates advocating myriad reforms was almost unprecedented. Even more revolutionary was the rise of scholar-gentry political associations or "study societies" (*hsüeh-hui*). The most famous was the "Society for the Study of Self-Strengthening" founded at Peking in August–September 1895. Branches of it and similar societies were soon set up in Shanghai and other major centers, with financial support from reform-minded high officials like Chang Chih-tung and Yüan Shihk'ai. Scholars once in politics quickly became journalists. The study societies began to publish journals and newspapers. When K'ang's junior colleague, Liang Ch'i-ch'ao, began in August 1895 to edit a daily for the Self-Strengthening Society, he at first borrowed the title of a missionary monthly (*Wan-kuo kung-pao* or *The Globe Magazine*) and reprinted many articles from it; indeed, the young Liang for a time actually assisted the reform-minded missionary, Timothy Richard. The Reform Movement began to use group organization, discussion meetings, and an active press, strongly reminiscent of missionary methods. With the spread of literacy, these methods could bring more than simply the scholar class into participation in political life.

The Ideology of Reform.   For scholars indoctrinated by their studies in the all-embracing social theory of Confucianism, change had to be sanctioned by ideas. The theory of reform had developed slowly over two generations, ever since men like Commissioner Lin Tse-hsü, believers in the administrative reforms of the school of "statecraft," had first urged the use of Western arms during the Opium War. But as the pressure to adopt Western ways in self-defense increased, so did the need to justify the process. How could one defend Chinese ways by adopting Western ways?

One answer was to make a distinction between what was defended and what was adopted, as between ends and means. Japanese reformers had used the phrase, "Eastern ethics and Western science." For China, the sanction for "self-strengthening" was finally summed up in the slogan popularized by Chang Chih-tung in the 1890's: "Chinese learning for the essential principles; Western learning for the practical applications." To a critical mind, however, this slogan was specious and misleading. It invoked a Sung philosophical distinction between *t'i* "substance" (literally, "body") and *yung* "function" (literally, "use"). This pair of terms designated the interdependence between the inner substance of any one thing and its outward functioning. It had been applied, for example, to the superior man's inner self-cultivation and outward governing of others, to the ruler's being a sage in spirit and a king in action. But Chang was now stretching the old ideology of Neo-Confucianism to cover the new practice of Westernization. This was decried by critics like Yen Fu, who in the 1890's was translating J. S. Mill, T. H. Huxley, Herbert Spencer, and other Western writers on evolution and utilitarianism and so knew something of both civilizations. Yen pointed out that "Chinese learning has its substance and function; Western learning also has its substance and function." The *t'i-yung* formula was a snare, for techniques will affect values, and means that are adopted will determine ends.

Another approach was to find the sanction for Westernization within China's own tradition. This was a variant of the customary practice of "finding in antiquity the sanction for present-day changes." Thus in the 1860's, Western studies in the Interpreters College at Peking had been justified by alleging that "Western sciences borrowed their roots from ancient Chinese mathematics." In the 1880's a vulgar apologetics for Westernization developed along this line—for example, tracing the origin of chemistry to the ancient theory of the "five elements" so as to make chemistry part of China's cultural heritage.

A further step was to find a doctrine of change in China's past. Thus the ancient idea of "change of method" (*pien-fa*) was gradually stretched by expanding the meaning of the term *fa,* which meant literally "method" but also, more broadly, "law" or "institution." The innocuous phrase "change of method" now began to cover "institutional change" of the most basic kind. For example, writers in the early 1890's advocated the inauguration of a parliament, which they justified by quoting classical aphorisms about "ruler and people being one body, superior and inferior being of one mind." But still there was no equivalent in Chinese tradition for the dynamic idea of progress, so dominant in contemporary Western works.

K'ang Yu-wei's Reinterpretation of Confucianism. K'ang Yu-wei, the radical petitioner of 1895, finally supplied the reinterpretation by which the Classics could sanction Westernization and Confucianism could include progress. He had been born into a distinguished scholar-official family of Canton and became a precocious student of the Classics. But soon he found them "all empty and lacking in substance." K'ang said later that his teacher "often cautioned me about my undue feelings of superiority," but nevertheless, at the age of twenty-one, while meditating upon the world, "in a great release of enlightenment I beheld myself a sage. . . ." He proceeded to act like one and remake the classical tradition.

First of all, he carried further the "new text" movement which had questioned the authenticity of the orthodox "ancient text" versions of certain Confucian Classics (see pages 66 and 267). To reformers committed to working within the classical tradition, the "new text" school of interpretation was very appealing because it broke the monopoly of the Neo-Confucian orthodoxy. K'ang synthesized the studies of the "new text" school, and in 1891 attacked the authenticity of several Classics. He concluded that the "Han Learning" was wrongly based, while "the Classics honored and expounded by the Sung scholars are for the most part forged and not those of Confucius." His devastating attack is not now generally accepted by scholars, but it was erudite, persuasive, and therefore most unsettling to the scholarly world of the 1890's. High officials had the printing blocks of his books burned in 1894, but they could not prevent K'ang's becoming a metropolitan graduate and Hanlin academician in 1895. He was now at the top of the establishment.

Having brushed aside the orthodox view, K'ang pushed further certain "new text" interpretations and in 1897 claimed that Confucius had himself created, rather than merely edited, the principal Classics as a means of invoking antiquity in order to make institutional reforms. This view, if accepted, would allow a near-revolution invoking the name of the Sage himself. Inspired by the example of Christianity, K'ang also proposed to exalt Confucius as the focus of a Chinese national religion. This was not all. Combining two classical sources, K'ang derived an evolutionary sequence, consisting of the Three Ages of (1) Disorder, (2) Approaching Peace and Small Tranquillity, and (3) Great Peace (*t'ai-p'ing*) and Great Unity (*ta-t'ung*). In this analysis, the world had been struggling in the Age of Disorder and with K'ang's reforms would now enter the Age of Approaching Peace and Small Tranquillity. Thus China's classical learning was made to encompass a theory of evolution and progress.

The Radical Reformers' Rise to Power in 1898.   Although K'ang Yu-wei had supplied the philosophic groundwork, the Reform Movement did not at once gain the ascendant. The panic that followed defeat in 1895 soon died down; the Self-Strengthening Society was suppressed in both Peking and Shanghai, though reform activities were pushed by officials and gentry in some provinces. Hunan, for example, though its gentry had held out against both Taiping rebels and Christian missionaries, now saw many innovations. With the blessing of Chang Chih-tung as governor-general, the provincial officials promoted modernization at the capital, Changsha—paved and lighted streets, steam launches on the river, telegraph lines to the outer world, a modern police system, colleges with modern curricula, a study society with lectures and discussions. These achievements of gentry-official cooperation were symptomatic of a growing movement in many parts of China.

When the imperialist powers revived the atmosphere of crisis in late 1897, K'ang Yu-wei got his chance. He was recommended to the emperor as a young expert on reform by moderates committed to orthodox "self-strengthening." By mid-1898, with the imperialist powers apparently ready to tear China apart, action seemed essential, K'ang was full of proposals, and the ardent young emperor, then twenty-seven, finally gave him his confidence. K'ang's first audience lasted five hours. "China will soon perish," he said. "All that is caused by the conservatives," replied the emperor. "If Your Majesty wishes to rely on them for reform," said K'ang, "it will be like climbing a tree to seek for fish."

K'ang's program called for the restructuring of internal administration on the grounds that China's traditional checks and double-checks, diffusion of power and surveillance of power-holders, had been developed to preserve the ruling dynasty against enemies arising from within. Now, against enemies from without, this cumbersome machinery was worse than useless. He therefore proposed a cabinet type of domestic administration, with a dozen ministers employing modern-trained experts, to supplant the clumsy Six Ministries and Grand Council. Like the Japanese, K'ang was impressed with the usefulness of parliaments not only to raise taxes, check corruption, and promote popular welfare as in Western countries, but also to strengthen the Confucian bond between ruler and people. He called for a national assembly, a constitution, and even local "bureaus of people's affairs" to carry out reforms with scholar-gentry participation. Among his followers all manner of wild ideas were current—democracy, simplification of the written language, even equality of the sexes and Western dress.

During the hundred days between June 11 and September 21, 1898, Kuang-hsü, with K'ang Yu-wei, Liang Ch'i-ch'ao, and others as advisers behind the scenes, issued forty or more reform edicts dealing with almost every conceivable subject: setting up modern schools and remaking the examination system; revising the laws as a preliminary to getting rid of extraterritoriality; promoting agriculture, medicine, mining, commerce, inventions, and study abroad; and modernizing the army, navy, police, and postal systems. Few of these orders were carried out, except in Hunan. Officials waited to see how the Empress Dowager, in retirement since 1889, would respond to this radical program. Conservative opposition was of course vociferous. All the reformers except the emperor were Chinese; the emperor's abolition of sinecure posts threatened many Manchu incumbents; and some feared he would dismiss all Manchus. The proposal to transform monasteries into schools terrified the monks, who had friends among the palace eunuchs. Military reform threatened the ancient Manchu banners and the Chinese constabulary of the Green Standard. The attack on the old examinations as qualification for office threatened all degree-holders who aspired to become officials. The attack on corruption affected nearly everyone in office. In short, as his program unfolded, the emperor found himself at war with the whole establishment, not least with his adoptive "mother," the Empress Dowager, who was still vigorous at sixty-three.

The issue in 1898 was not between reform or no reform, but between K'ang Yu-wei's radicalism and a continuation of the moderate "self-strengthening," which was now in its fourth decade of creeping Westernization. The aims of the latter were summed up in Chang Chih-tung's book, *Exhortation to Study,* which he published during the Hundred Days to state the antiradical position. This influential work, distributed by imperial order, aimed first of all to preserve the Manchu dynasty by a revival of the Confucian social order. It therefore upheld the "three bonds" (three of the *Mencius'* famous five relationships, namely, those between emperor and official, father and son, husband and wife) and vigorously opposed egalitarianism, democracy, constitutional monarchy, the doctrine of the "people's rights" (*min-ch'üan*), parliaments, the freedom of the individual, and civil liberties of the Western sort. Second, Chang aimed to save China by education. He proposed to reform the examination system; to set up a hierarchy of schools and colleges and an imperial university at Peking; and in the curriculum to stress both the Confucian Classics and Western technology. This program was modeled on Japan's. It would include the sending of students abroad and universal military service. Third, Chang hoped to save China by industrialization. For this his military "self-strengthening" effort at Wuhan was setting a practical example. One of its aims was to make China less dependent on imported steel. Having begun an iron foundry and arsenal at Hanyang (1890) and an iron mine at Ta-yeh in Hupei (1894), Chang advocated construction of a Peking-Hankow-Canton railway through China's heartland, by a central railway administration.

The Empress Dowager found her entire world threatened by K'ang Yu-wei's attack on those twin pillars of her regime, classical learning and organized corruption. She bided her time while opposition grew. Finally on September 21, 1898, with the help of the top Manchu military commander, Jung-lu, she seized the Kuang-hsü emperor in a *coup d'état* and began her third regency. K'ang and Liang escaped to Japan; but six of the reformers, including the brilliant young eclectic philosopher from Hunan, T'an Ssu-t'ung, were executed. The emperor remained in forced seclusion, and when the Empress Dowager finally died in 1908, he mysteriously predeceased her by one day.

The abrupt end of the Hundred Days restored most of the status quo ante, yet some moderate reform measures continued, such as the abolition of certain sinecures and the establishment of modern schools. The chief significance of 1898, however, was that the radicals' attempt at a revolution from above, in the pattern of the revolution effected in Japan by the Meiji Restoration, had failed. The Empress Dowager's countercoup, though it was followed by another decade of moderate reform, suggested that any really revolutionary change would have to come from below, presumably by violence. Thus gradualism, by being too gradual, made violent revolution more certain. Yet it was still in the future. The ease of the Empress Dowager's *coup d'état* suggests that China as a whole was far from ready for revolution in 1898. After sixty years of attack and stimulus from the Western world, the traditional Chinese order was still strong and capable of violent protest against modernization.

The Boxer Rising

The Boxer Movement. The radical reforms of 1898 had been a daring effort by Chinese scholars at the very top of the ruling class to respond to the foreign menace by modernizing the whole Ch'ing government. After its failure, the initiative shifted to a popular movement that was led by a traditional type of secret society. Its name, *I-ho ch'üan,* crudely translated by Westerners as "Righteous and Harmonious Fists," or more simply as "Boxers," indicates that this society under the name of Righteousness and Harmony (*I-ho*) practiced its own form of so-called Chinese boxing (*ch'üan*), which, through a sequence of postures and exercises, aimed to harmonize mind and muscle in preparation for combat. This was a magic art using Taoist sorcery and a prescribed ritual—members thrice recited an incantation, breathed through clenched teeth, foamed at the mouth, and became possessed by spirits who made them happily impervious to foreign bullets. The Boxers found their heroes in semifictional, semihistoric, operatic characters like those in *All Men Are Brothers,* in the ancient tradition of popular rebellion. Their original slogan early in 1899 was "overthrow the Ch'ing; destroy the foreigner."

Anti-Christian hostility was one obvious factor inspiring the Boxer movement, for the steady growth of missionary activity in the 1890's exacerbated all the problems that had accumulated during the previous decades. Some Christian converts flouted the sacred family relationships, refused to support the local festivals and deities, and got the missionaries to intervene and help them in their disputes. With French support, Catholic prelates could coerce local officials. Scurrilous anti-Christian diatribes continued to circulate.

The sudden rise of the Boxer movement was also fostered by economic and political conditions. Yellow River floods had led to widespread famine in Shantung in 1898. North China suffered generally from drought. Destitute country people were moving about as vagrants. To some degree the importation of foreign cotton goods and oil depressed local industries, while plans for new railways seemed to threaten the livelihood of carters and canal bargemen. The late 1890's, in fact, saw disorder, riots, banditry, or local risings in every one of the eighteen provinces, rather reminiscent of the late 1840's just before the Taiping upheaval. In sum, the Boxer movement emerged as a direct-action response to a deepening crisis in the lives of the whole Chinese people.

The movement received its prodynastic impetus in 1899 from the patronage of Manchu and Chinese officials. The hard core of conservative Manchu princes in the Ch'ing court had been educated in the palace with little experience of actual government or the outside world. These men accepted in 1899 the same purblind slogan that had roused the samurai of Japan forty years earlier—"Expel the barbarians!" In trying to use the Boxers against the foreigners, they were invoking the ancient idea, China's equivalent of Western "popular sovereignty," that the righteous indignation of the common people was the final arbiter of politics. An alliance between antiforeign officials and prodynastic Boxers began to take shape in the autumn of 1899, after government troops had defeated and seized some of the antidynastic Boxer rebels in Shantung. The Boxer slogan shifted to "support the Ch'ing; destroy the foreigner," which was pleasantly different from the usual anti-Ch'ing battle cries of secret societies.

Ch'ing officialdom was split into an ardent pro-Boxer faction, which eventually became dominant, and a much larger but frustrated anti-Boxer element, which despised the Boxers' superstitious fanaticism, and yet sympathized with their aims. In Chihli during the first five months of 1900, Boxer bands of hundreds and even thousands spread over the countryside, burning missionary establishments and slaughtering Chinese Christians. The Manchu princes seem to have persuaded the Empress Dowager that the

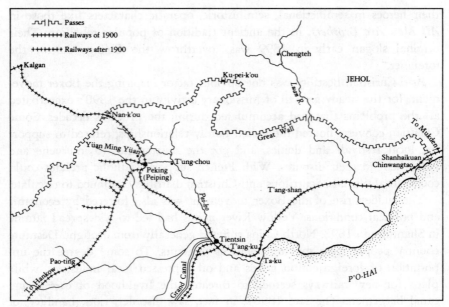

THE APPROACHES TO PEKING

Boxers' magic invulnerability was real. When repeated notes came from the diplomatic corps, demanding suppression, the edicts issued in response, in January and again in April 1900, were highly equivocal—the groups that attacked missionaries and their converts were "of different kinds"; officials suppressing them must "discriminate" between the good and bad elements. The diplomatic corps, so confident of Western superiority, was slow to recognize that the Empress Dowager, after decades of enforcing foreign privileges under the unequal treaties, was finally prepared to let this popular movement challenge the West by force.

The Siege of the Peking Legations and Its Aftermath.   With the court thus determined to appease rather than suppress the Boxer terror, further foreign provocation was hardly necessary to trigger the final explosion; the foreigners had been provocative for sixty years already. The final outbreak was precipitated from both sides. In June 1900 Boxers besieged the foreign communities in both Tientsin and Peking. The foreign powers concentrated naval forces and mounted a relief expedition. The Ch'ing dynasty declared war against them. In North China outside the capital some 250 foreigners were killed, most of them missionaries and mainly in Shansi province. Chinese Christians died in far greater numbers, although scattered communities succeeded in defending themselves.

This midsummer madness astounded the world. After a month of no news from the diplomats, the missionary leaders, Sir Robert Hart, and the

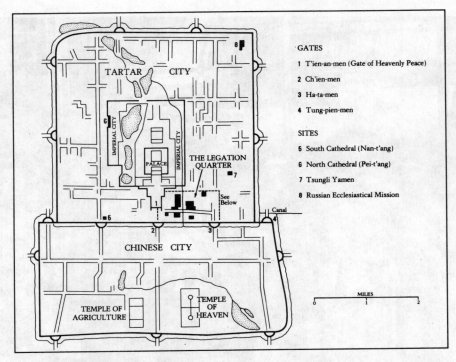

GATES

1 T'ien-an-men (Gate of Heavenly Peace)

2 Ch'ien-men

3 Ha-ta-men

4 Tung-pien-men

SITES

5 South Cathedral (Nan-t'ang)

6 North Cathedral (Pei-t'ang)

7 Tsungli Yamen

8 Russian Ecclesiastical Mission

PEKING IN 1900

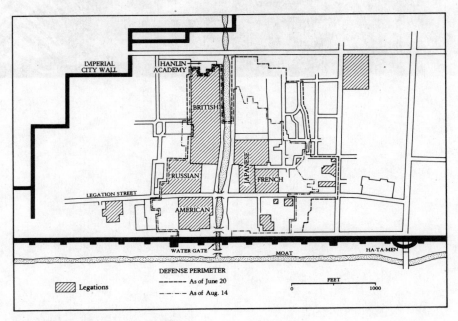

THE LEGATION QUARTER

大清國當今聖母皇太后萬歲萬歲萬萬歲

DYNASTIC DECLINE AT PEKING. *Left: The Empress Dowager transported by palace eunuchs in court dress, as photographed in 1903. In a mat-roofed Summer Palace courtyard under a dragon-embroidered umbrella, the Empress wears small shoes raised on gilt platforms. At right front is the chief eunuch, Li Lien-ying. Right: After the Boxer Incident, the Empress Dowager had to conciliate the foreigners. Here she is photographed with ladies of the diplomatic corps, who stand close about and over her, Western fashion. The Empress holds hands with the American minister's wife, Sarah Pike Conger, who had survived the siege of the Peking legations and was now deeply impressed by the Ch'ing ruler's "womanly tenderness" and "intuitive ability."*

others besieged in the Peking legations, they were credibly reported all massacred. The decentralized nature of the Ch'ing government meantime had proved of some practical use. While the benighted Manchus at court were trying extermination, the worldly-wise Chinese regional officials resorted to diplomacy to mitigate the catastrophe. Li Hung-chang, now governor-general at Canton in concert with Liu K'un-i at Nanking, Chang Chih-tung at Wuhan, and Yüan Shih-k'ai in Shantung, decided to ignore the dynasty's declaration of war. They proposed that if the foreigners would send no more warships into the Yangtze area, the governors-general there would maintain order. The effect of this was to neutralize all of China except the northern provinces. The convenient fiction was accepted that the Boxer outbreak was in fact a "rebellion," as it has since been called, and not an act supported by the dynasty.

Thus the Boxer War, the fourth and largest which China fought against Western powers in the nineteenth century, remained localized in North China while the provincial authorities elsewhere loyally represented the dynasty's interest in peace, corresponding by telegram with the court at Peking and letting the Empress Dowager eat her cake and have it too. She pursued simultaneous policies of extermination, as demanded by the Manchus dominant at court, and peace, as vigorously sought by her envoys abroad and her officials in South China. This ambivalence of Ch'ing policy was also evident in Peking. Seventy-six foreigners died defending the legations; the rest survived because the commander of one part of the imperial forces, though maintaining a noisy bombardment, did not use available artillery or press home the attack. International forces relieved the siege of the Tientsin concessions on July 14, and of the Peking legations on August 14.

As the Western invaders with the usual local assistance began to loot the city, which the Boxers had already despoiled, the Empress Dowager and the emperor left Peking by cart in disguise. At the age of 65, the Empress Dowager now had her closest contact with her people's problems of securing shelter, food, and protection against bandits and lawless troops. The court reached Sian and stayed there for more than a year. Li Hung-chang at the age of 77 was looked to as usual to save the situation. He temporized skillfully with the foreigners, who accepted his fiction that the hostilities had not been a war at all but a joint effort to suppress rebellion. Although the German minister had been the only German killed, the Kaiser demanded the right to name a commander-in-chief for the allied forces. The latter reached Peking only in October and devoted himself largely to punitive expeditions to dozens of North China cities, which continued for six months afterward. By late 1900, around 45,000 foreign troops were in North China, and Russia in a separate war had long since occupied Manchuria.

The Boxer Protocol was finally signed September 7, 1901, by a Manchu prince, Li Hung-chang (who died two months later), and the plenipotentiaries of eleven powers. It required the execution of ten high officials and the punishment of a hundred others; formal apologies; suspension of examinations in forty-five cities, half of them in Shansi, to penalize the gentry class; expansion of the Legation Quarter, to be fortified and permanently garrisoned; destruction of forts and occupation of railway posts to ensure foreign access to Peking from the sea; raising of import duties to an actual 5 per cent; and a staggering indemnity.

A British commercial treaty of 1902 tried with only modest success to improve various conditions of trade and evangelism. But abolition of likin taxes, which impeded trade, establishment of a national coinage, passage of legal reforms that would pave the way for abolishing extraterritoriality, and many other steps toward modernization which Japan had taken in the 1870's, all proved impossible to achieve. The Boxer rising and the Protocol marked the nadir of the Ch'ing dynasty's foreign relations and left little hope for its long continuance. Yet no alternative had emerged.

Imperialism and the Chinese Response

Foreign Financial Exploitation of China.   After 1901, the new imperialist domination was not confined to "spheres of influence" but extended to Peking's entire financial structure. Up to 1893, some twenty-five loans had been made to Chinese government agencies by foreign sources in China. But the total indebtedness still outstanding, all secured on the Maritime Customs revenue, had been inconsiderable. The Sino-Japanese war indemnity (230 million taels) came to about $150 million, and the big loans used to meet it in 1895, 1896, and 1898 were secured from the foreign banks on onerous terms: China received less than the face value to begin with (e.g., 94 per cent), had to pay rather high interest for as long as forty-five years, and also had to pay in gold, at the mercy of the gold/silver exchange rate. The Boxer indemnity of 450 million taels (about $333 million) was to be paid in bonds which bore interest at 4 per cent in gold, so that by the conclusion of payments in 1940, interest and principal repaid would total 928 million taels (or $739 million).

These Japanese and Boxer indemnities, unlike productive loans, were complete losses to China. Their payment drained off the Ch'ing government's revenue collected from foreign trade by the Maritime Customs, which had previously provided funds for armament and modernization. (Even this limited revenue had been further cut as the rise of prices gradually reduced the percentage value of tariff duties fixed in money terms in 1858.) Henceforth even large portions of the provincial revenues and of the likin and salt revenues on domestic trade would have to be added to the Maritime Customs revenue, just to pay the foreign bondholders.

To be sure, imperialism's bark was sometimes worse than its bite. The

Boxer indemnity illustrates this: in the end, the eclipse of Tsarist Russia and Imperial Germany during World War I and the remission of American, British, and other portions of the indemnity, as well as other changes, reduced actual payments to less than a third of the original assessment. Similarly, Japan's claim to a sphere in Fukien, obtained through a nonalienation agreement in April 1898, was never followed up. Italy's demand for a sphere in Chekiang in March 1899 was successfully refused. A number of the railway concessions made in the late 1890's were never actively pursued. That the "breakup of China" did not occur was partly owing to Chinese dexterity, as yet little studied, in balancing one imperialist power against another. Yet this era of financial imperialism, with its insatiable great-power rivalries and exploitative demands, has tended to overshadow the preceding decades of quieter commercial penetration and economic growth and has given patriotic Chinese ever since an indelible hatred for the whole treaty system as a "foreign imperialist yoke."

American Expansion and the Open Door.   Many Americans in the 1890's were righteously proud that the United States, unlike European powers, had never fought wars and seized colonies in Asia. To be sure, American missionaries and traders had enjoyed the special privileges secured and maintained there in large part by the British navy. Yet the fact remained that American activity, at least in the American view, had avoided "imperialism" in East Asia just as it avoided "entangling alliances" in Europe. By invoking Britain's own doctrine of most-favored-nation treatment and equal opportunity, the United States had got the benefits of Britain's free-trade empire without its odium or responsibilities. However, as the European race for colonies developed, new expansionist tendencies together with certain accidents of history brought the United States onto the East Asian scene as a great power also. The American people were more susceptible to the imperialist virus than they liked to think.

The expansion of the United States, like that of the European powers, was due to a mixture of causes—in its case, the rise of industries manufacturing cheap export products, the disappearance of the frontier at home, and a missionary tradition abroad. As the navy's great proponent of sea power, Captain A. T. Mahan, put it, America was "looking outward" in an era when doctrines of Social Darwinism and Nordic racial superiority provided a sanction for keeping up with other nations in the search for markets, colonies, and naval bases. Mahan's advocacy of bases overseas coincided with the decision of the Congress in 1890 to build a first-class battle fleet and with public agitation for a canal across Nicaragua so that the fleet could operate in both oceans. Meanwhile there had been a long-continued commercial interest in Hawaii, where the white sugar planters sought annexation to the United States.

The American expansion of 1898 in East Asia was triggered by the coincidence of the war with Spain over Cuba. Theodore Roosevelt, assistant secretary of the navy, had prepared Commodore Dewey and his American Asiatic Squadron at Hong Kong to attack the Spanish fleet at Manila. Dewey did so at dawn on May 1; by lunchtime the Spanish fleet was sunk or burning. Seeing no alternative, the United States occupied Manila with a force of eleven thousand in the summer of 1898, received the Philippines from Spain by a peace treaty in December, and at once became involved in suppressing a full-fledged Filipino struggle for independence. Hawaii had been annexed by Congressional action in July, and the western Pacific island of Guam had been taken from Spain. These American acquisitions, outstripping those of any imperialist power in China, gave the United States potential naval bases at Pearl Harbor, Guam, and Manila, as well as the Hawaiian Islands and the entire Philippine archipelago. It was right in the middle of this period, in September 1899, that Secretary of State John Hay issued his first Open Door notes.

Hay had recently been minister to London, where the British early in 1898 had consulted him on how to preserve the tradition of equal opportunity, an open door for trade, in the face of imperialist "spheres of influence" in China. He now got the advice of one of Robert Hart's chief commissioners in the Chinese Maritime Customs. As a result, the first American Open Door notes reflected the specific interest of Hart and the Customs in maintaining that original principle of the treaty system—the equal taxation of foreign trade in all treaty ports, inside as well as outside the new "spheres of influence." They requested, first, that each power not interfere with "any treaty port or any vested interest" within its "sphere"; second, that only the Chinese government should collect duties on trade at such ports, and only according to the treaty tariff; and third, that no preferential harbor dues or railroad charges should benefit the subjects of a power having a "sphere." In short, these first Open Door notes sought to preserve equality of trade in China, not the Chinese state. Britain, Germany, France, Italy, and Japan all agreed to accept these provisions if everyone else did. The Russian reply was rather negative and Hay's success was limited, but he made the best of it by blandly notifying all concerned that their unanimous acceptance of his notes had been "final and definitive."

As the Boxer rising brought foreign armies into North China and Manchuria in the summer of 1900, China's chances of survival as a state seemed more dubious than ever. Hay's second note, a circular of July 1900, therefore stated the American desire for a solution that would bring "permanent safety and peace to China, preserve Chinese territorial and administrative entity, protect all rights guaranteed to friendly powers by treaty and international law, and safeguard for the world the principle of equal and impartial trade with all parts of the Chinese Empire." Everyone agreed, and the Open Door became publicly established as the traditional American policy toward China. In time its essential concept became the preservation, not merely of foreign commercial opportunity, but of China's integrity as a nation. But in origin it was an effort by a maritime power at a distance to maintain the treaty system against the spread of colonialism. It was a statement of principle in words, put forward as a good thing in itself, without thought of forceful action to back it up. The United States was simultaneously acquiring a colony in the Philippines. It is safe to say that the Open Door policy seemed grander in the United States than elsewhere.

China's Weaknesses and Strengths.   When we try to interpret the events of 1900 it seems plain that the imperialist powers kept the reactionary Ch'ing dynasty in power the better to enjoy their special privileges; they had in fact cooperated with the established order throughout the six decades of the unequal treaties. Much evidence can be marshaled to show the inveterate stubbornness, if not rapacity, of foreign groups in defense of their interests in China—witness the failure of the Alcock Convention of 1869 (see page 329) or of the British treaty of 1902 to reform the treaty system for China's benefit. Great changes seldom seemed to the foreigners to be in their interest. They preferred to prop up the old order.

It is plain enough that China was victimized by the foreign powers. This theme is naturally attractive to modern Chinese patriots. It leaves unanswered, however, the underlying question: why did China not respond to foreign encroachment earlier and more vigorously? Where were those Chinese revolutionaries who could have met the Western aggression by modernizing the traditional Chinese state and expelling the imperialists? In the twentieth century such leaders appear; where were they in the nineteenth century?

The mid-century rebels, being anti-Manchu, were potentially nationalistic but lacked modern ideas. The strongest of them, the Taipings, after ten years' development proved themselves old-fashioned rivals for power and showed little capacity for remaking the traditional order. The "self-strengthening" movement thereafter was more defensive than creative, a conservative compromise avoiding radical modernization. The reformers of 1898, though their plans were potentially revolutionary, viewed themselves as loyal ministers of the dynasty, entirely dependent on the ruling power of the Son of Heaven. The empire's bankruptcy of leadership was finally demonstrated by those Manchu grandees who took up the inane atavism of the Boxers. Talent on a large scale was simply not devoted to purposes of real revolution or reform before 1900. No one appeared under the old order who had any solid prospect of making drastic changes in it. This weakness of the forces of change within China was less an achievement of Western imperialism than a tribute to the strength of the Chinese social order, state, and culture. It was the overall cohesion and structural stability of Chinese civilization that basically inhibited its rapid response to the Western menace.

In maintaining this Chinese momentum in established ways, no single factor was all-important. China's remarkable imperviousness to foreign stimuli resulted from a complex of factors, just as did Japan's equally remarkable and opposite capacity for change and modernization. At the highest level of generality, we have suggested that Japan already had the essential ingredients of modern nationalism, in a people ready to strive together for national ends, while China did not. Beneath this level of abstraction, each observer can select his own balance among many interacting factors.

On the material plane, for example, China had vast resources but they were being exploited in traditional ways. Modern methods could not easily be substituted. Japan, as it turned out, was far poorer in raw materials, like iron, necesary for modernization, but her people met the challenge with vigor and adaptability. The great size of the Chinese Empire, which made it potentially a world power, also retarded its response in many ways. Economically it was almost self-sufficient. Strategically it was well-nigh invulnerable to conquest, if not to defeat; sea power, to which Japan was so exposed, could dominate many Chinese cities but not the vast interior. The dense populations of interior areas like Hunan and Szechwan remained beyond foreign contact, reservoirs of traditional attitudes and of talent trained in the old style; instead of reading newspapers, the elite in these areas still studied the Classics and grew up intellectually almost untouched by the treaty ports.

Institutions, however, made an even greater difference than material circumstances. Japan's feudal order had already produced the loyal *han* administrators, the merchant capitalists, the scholars of Dutch learning, the patriotic individual samurai, who could create a nation-state to compete with other nation-states. China was in a different mold, above such competition. Her ancient institutions were finely balanced and well tempered to preserve an equilibrium among three strata—the monarch and his officials, the landlord-scholar-gentry class, and the illiterate farming populace. In this predominantly agrarian empire neither merchant-capitalists nor artisans, neither traders abroad nor inventors and investors at home, could create centers of disequilibrating growth. The Chinese people, in short, were in the grip of their past. Their national religion was in fact the worship of the past. The prime virtue of filial piety led to reverence for ancestors. The world of thought fostered reverence for the Confucian Classics. Rulers could not counter the injunctions of their dynastic founder. Precedent dominated administration. Social and economic life was ruled by old custom. Even rebels invoked the past, incapable of real revolution. China was under the spell of her own great historical tradition and ancient learning, both kept alive by the written language.

This backward-looking self-sufficiency of intellectual life gave China's leaders two major characteristics. First, trained to concentrate on the affairs of the Middle Kingdom, they were willfully ignorant and correspondingly

NON-CHINESE OFFICIALS IN CHINA. *Above: A Manchu official: Ch'ung-shan of the Bordered Red Banner. Inscription on right: "Tartar General of hereditary rank by receipt of Imperial Grace, with brevet rank of Board President and Peacock Feather bestowed for military merit," etc. On left: "Portrait of Ch'ung Yu-t'ing at 74 sui, 1905" (with his seals, "Yu-t'ing" and "Ch'ung-shan of the imperial family"). Below: Sino-foreign officials, Foochow, ca. 1905. Front row, from left: Customs Commissioner E. B. Drew (American) Salt Intendant Lu; Japanese Consul; Tartar General Ch'ung-shan; American Consul (Dr. S. L. Gracey); Grain Intendant Ch'i-yüeh; French Consul. In the back row are interpreters and officials.*

contemptuous of things abroad. Pride of culture, absorption in the Chinese universe, made them unresponsive to "barbarian" ideas. Secondly, as supporters of a universal state, China's leaders were immune to nationalism. The great empire of continental East Asia, though centered on the dense population of China, had long since had to take in the peripheral peoples of Inner Asia, particularly the nomads and seminomads of the steppe, whose warrior horsemen had played an ever greater role in China's domestic power politics. The Mongol and Manchu conquests were fundamental, not superficial, phenomena of the great empire's political life—despite the insouciance regarding them affected by some Chinese chroniclers. As the most sophisticated example of Sino-barbarian administration under an alien dynasty of conquest, the Ch'ing regime vigorously suppressed racist-nationalist sentiment. Through the examination system it recruited talented bureaucrats who had indoctrinated themselves in upward-looking loyalty; it avoided any formal doctrine that officials should represent bottom-level constituencies. Until the rise of treaty-port newspapers and missionary education, presenting a comparative view of other nations, the whole process of government remained highly elitist and lacking in the symbolism, vocabulary, and practices of modern nationalism. Among other things, the elite, trained in loyalty to the ruler and to the past, lacked a common sense of national purpose in making changes, and this inhibited the strong central leadership necessary for modernization. The Manchus could not afford to mobilize the Chinese people for participation in political life lest the dynasty become more obviously alien and dispensable and so be rejected.

In this specific and seldom understood political situation, China's response to the West was affected positively by one unusual and nonnationalistic factor, the tendency to admit "barbarians" to a peripheral participation in Chinese civilization and even to cooperate in joint enterprises with powerful invaders on the frontier. By their treaty-based privileges, special capacities and resources, the foreigners became a new element added into the old Chinese ruling class. This produced the long-continued role of the treaty ports, which is otherwise inexplicable. The ports were truly semicolonial phenomena in the sense that foreign governments dominated them locally while the dynasty continued to rule the broad interior of the empire as a whole. Sea power and land power, foreign ways and interests, and Chinese ways and interests met in the treaty ports in a peculiar, stalemated harmony that modern nationalism would never have tolerated. The Chinese and foreign officials divided their authority while the merchants shared their profits. In time the Chinese state, without changing its own nature, met its problems of Western contact by employing foreign administrators and advisers in the Maritime Customs and elsewhere. In the absence of a nationalistic spirit, this employment of foreigners was not used as an opportunity to learn from them quickly and get rid of them, as in Japan; it was more like those inveterate arrangements on the Inner Asian frontier where powerful "barbarians" who could not be defeated were given recognized status in the empire and so used, if possible, to control their fellows beyond the frontier. In their nineteenth-century foreign relations, as elsewhere, the Chinese were drawing on their past.

As a result, the antinationalistic Ch'ing regime, approaching the end of its dynastic cycle, was thoroughly on the defensive—strong enough to cling to tradition and suppress rebellion, yet too weak to provide leadership for change. The late Ch'ing record in diplomacy, dealing with the imperialist powers with considerable success from a position of weakness, is therefore all the more remarkable. China used her obvious weakness to motivate the foreigners to stultify one another's ambitions. The Ch'ing negotiators spread rumors and leaked secrets. They appeared panic-stricken and helpless. They accepted bribes while granting concessions. But China survived, and their diplomacy deserves re-examination as having been more effective than outsiders have realized.

13. From Monarchy to Warlordism

The Late Ch'ing Reforms

China in the early twentieth century was still absorbed in a process of incipient revolution such as Japan had gone through in the 1860's. The old order had begun to crack after Japan's attack in 1894–1895, but its political structure remained standing for another fifteen years.

The final decade of the Ch'ing dynasty from 1901 to 1911 was less a period of collapse than of new beginnings. Institutional and social change began early, political disaster came only at the end. Up to 1911, in fact, the Chinese state pursued a gradual reconstruction along lines that had been advocated unavailingly in the 1890's. The Empress Dowager and her conservative supporters, having thrown the Kuang-hsü emperor and K'ang Yu-wei out of power in 1898, proceeded to give effect after 1901 to most of their radical reform program. In truth, they had no alternative. The Boxer War had shown the bankruptcy of mere antiforeignism, while the threat of anti-Ch'ing rebellion goaded the regime into constructive action to save itself. Conservative reform was thus the principal movement on the Chinese public scene. The republican revolutionary effort grew up on the periphery, fragmented and inconsequential until 1905, and afterward still a minor eddy in the stream of change.

It was reformers, not revolutionaries, who mainly prepared the ground for revolution. Great changes were at last under way in Chinese life, and the alien Ch'ing dynasty, trying to guide these changes, could not avoid nurturing anti-Ch'ing and centrifugal forces that would eventually destroy it. Students the government trained abroad, new armies it trained at home,

391

merchants it encouraged in domestic enterprise, political assemblies it convoked in the provinces, all sooner or later turned against the dynasty. In political quicksand, the more the dynasty struggled to save itself, the deeper it sank. For modernization now meant Chinese nationalism, which implied the end of Manchu rule.

Along this one-way street leading to political disaster, however, the late Ch'ing reforms deserve study as attempted solutions to China's peculiar problems of modernization. Chang Chih-tung and Liu K'un-i, the Yangtze "viceroys" (governors-general respectively of Hunan-Hupei and of Kiangsi-Anhwei-Kiangsu), who in 1900 had dexterously remained both at peace with the foreigners and loyal to the dynasty, presented three memorials to the Empress Dowager in July 1901, outlining a broad program reminiscent of the Hundred Days of 1898. They understated a few blunt truths: "...popular feelings are not the same as thirty years ago. The people admire the wealth of foreign countries and despise the poverty of the Middle Kingdom." They admire foreign troops, the "fair play" of the Maritime Customs Service, the strict orderliness of foreign concessions. "Rebels are slowly emerging" and spreading subversive doctrines. Their catalogue of needed reforms was longer than ever, but it is significant that education, to create a new elite, was still first on the list.

Education: New Schools, New Scholars.   The general aim of the educational program was to train and select officials more effectively. Its aim was not mass education of the Chinese people, nor was it liberal education of the Chinese individual. The main problem was how to appease the contemporary generation of scholar-officials in office and the classically trained aspirants for office, all of whom had a vested interest in the classical examination system. The solution was a compromise: to set up a hierarchy of schools at all the territorial levels of government—county, prefecture, province, and imperial capital—parallel to and feeding into the traditional examinations. In time, after about ten years, the new schools, supported by contributions from the public, would supplant the old examination system. Meantime, it was hoped, the two systems could be used side by side. Candidates prepared in the new schools and candidates prepared privately in the traditional way would alike take the regular examinations, which would be somewhat modernized in content. As first steps, the "eight-legged essay" was abolished and the old-style academies (*shu-yüan*) were ordered converted into government schools.

Unfortunately it soon appeared that the traditional route to office of private preparation for the examinations would continue to be cheaper, easier, and more attractive than the new route, which led through years of costly schooling. The majority of old-style aspirants for office would shun the new government schools. On the other hand, among the restive, modern-minded youth, the new government schools faced competition from Christian missionary education in strategic urban centers. By 1905, Protestant missions had some 389 "intermediate and high schools and colleges" with fifteen thousand students. These institutions were setting a revolutionary example by fostering Christianity, individualism, education of women, and Western ways generally, all under the protection of extraterritoriality. They refused to have their students pay homage to Confucius or the emperor, as required in government schools. (Peking countered by barring mission school graduates from official careers.) Private Chinese modern education was also beginning. In 1904 an able young graduate of the Peiyang naval academy, Chang Po-ling, opened at Tientsin a middle school which acquired a campus and by 1909 grew into Nankai University.

Faced with this competition from the old-fashioned, who clung to the examinations, and the modern-minded, who flocked to missionary and private schools, Chang Chih-tung concluded in 1903 that the new school system could secure neither students nor popular financial support until the examination system ceased to exist as an alternative. In 1905 the leading provincial officials urged its immediate abolition, which was ordered to take effect the next year. The government's educational hopes now lay entirely with the new schools. A Ministry of Education was created in 1906 to supervise them.

The new system, modeled on the Japanese, called for specialization after middle school to produce specialists for government service. The massive and detailed regulations issued in 1904 followed Japan's example in leading students through higher elementary school (four years), middle school (five years), and higher school (three years, achieving the degree of *chü-jen*) to the Imperial University (three years, achieving the degree of *chin-shih*). The Imperial University had been created in 1898 with W. A. P. Martin, the American who had been head of the Interpreters College (T'ung-wen Kuan) from 1869 to 1895, as first dean of Western studies. In 1902 the university absorbed the Interpreters College. But below this top institution the new school system across the land lacked modern-trained faculties, buildings, equipment, funds, and leadership. It was easier to found colleges than middle schools, easier to inaugurate middle schools than primary schools. The system remained weakest at the base.

Provincial educators also found their chief inspiration in Japan. Chang Chih-tung sent two missions to study the Japanese system and buy textbooks. He began to see the need for general public education, in order to find talent among the people. Soon he imported Japanese professors, who could communicate with their Chinese colleagues and students at least in writing. He began to look to Japan as the best training ground for the new generation of Chinese schoolteachers—cheaper than the West because Japan was near at hand, easier because Japan's "language, literature, and customs" were close to China's and because many Western books had already been translated into Japanese. In addition, Chinese students could be supervised more easily in Japan by Chinese government inspectors.

The flow to Tōkyō of Chinese youth seeking modern education had begun by 1896. After the suppression of the 1898 reform movement, Chinese students in Japan rose to about two hundred in 1899, one thousand in 1903, thirteen hundred in 1904, roughly eight thousand by the end of 1905, and thirteen thousand or more in 1906. But the number who went exceeded by far the number who enrolled in serious academic studies, which in turn far exceeded the number who eventually graduated. Indeed, the Chinese graduates from reputable Japanese institutions before 1912 never exceeded seven hundred a year. Among the many thousands who went to Japan in the last decade of the Ch'ing, something like one-half were supported by Chinese government funds, mainly from provincial governments. They often prepared in new provincial schools and usually were sent in annual delegations to Tōkyō. There they followed the Chinese practice of organizing associations or guilds (*hui*) among fellow provincials, reminiscent of the regional guilds organized by officials, gentry, and merchants in Peking and other major cities over the centuries. As a result the new educational system brought young men and even some young women together more intimately, over a longer period and in circumstances more stimulating to group cohesion, than the old examinations had ever done. Just as the new student life in China nurtured provincial consciousness and provincial loyalties, so life in Tōkyō nourished nationalism.

In this way Chinese education was quietly revolutionized. Classical studies gave way to a mixed Sino-Western curriculum. Private preparation for triennial examinations on traditional themes gave way to school life day by day, a broader range of ideas, more social and intellectual contact. Instead of indoctrinated scholar-gentry loyal to Confucius and the Son of Heaven, the new system produced revolutionists. Chang Chih-tung could carefully prescribe light-blue gowns, hats with red tassels, a multitude of rules to foster decorum among his students, and an edifying song: "The Holy Son of Heaven plans for self-strengthening.... Hygiene makes the people strong and healthy.... Honor parents, respect rulers...." But once the examination system had been washed away, there was no checking the tides of change.

The intellectual content of the new education, in China as in Japan, now contained much from the West. Despite so many decades of increasing Western contact, it was only after 1900 that the Chinese scholar class really began to absorb Western ideas. A famous popularizer of Western fiction, Lin Shu, had already been turning out by hearsay (i.e., by listening to oral translations) his Chinese versions of Dickens, Dumas, Scott, Balzac, and others—156 works in all. To this continuing literary fare were now added Yen Fu's translations and interpretations of the classics of Western liberalism. Having joined the Chinese navy, Yen saw the world, especially England, in the 1870's and concluded that the secret of Western power was Western thought. He became a convert to Herbert Spencer's Social Darwinism: the individual's energetic self-realization must help his nation to compete and survive. Liberal principles, Yen Fu felt, were needed more to augment China's national wealth and power than to foster individual freedom. Democratic self-government would be premature. The translator tried especially to convey those ideas of Victorian Britain that seemed most meaningful for late-Ch'ing China. T. H. Huxley's *Evolution and Ethics* appeared in classical Chinese with Yen's commentaries in 1898, followed in the next decade by works of Adam Smith, J. S. Mill, Montesquieu, and others. Yen Fu's translations and commentaries, by exalting Western logic, law, science, and evolution, severely indicted China's sages as the cause of her backwardness, yet did it as an inside job, in classical Chinese addressed to the literati.

New Armies: The Rise of Yüan Shih-k'ai. By 1901 China had inherited from her distant and recent past three main types of military organization. The Manchu banner forces, still subsisting on their inadequate stipends, together with the decentralized Chinese constabulary ("Army of the Green Standard"), were effete and useles. A few thousand bannermen had been given modern guns and formed into the Peking Field Force in 1862. Later, selected units of the constabulary, especially around Peking, had received arms and training. But the officers were still chosen by their prowess in mounted and dismounted archery, sword-brandishing, pulling a powerful bow, and lifting a heavy stone, an antic ritual of no modern use. The old-style military examinations were abolished in August 1901, and new military academies ordered established.

The second type of military formation was the regional armies commanded by Chinese civil officials. Their prototype had been the precedent-breaking Hunan Army (see page 296) built up by Tseng Kuo-fan after 1852. Its peasant recruits had been officered by gentry and organized in battalions of 500 soldiers plus some 180 carriers for logistic support—nominally, one porter for every three soldiers. Despite Tseng's formal disbandment of the Hunan Army (see page 313), it had continued to exist, along with the Anhwei Army created by Li Hung-chang and similar forces organized by Tso Tsung-t'ang and others against the mid-century rebels. These gentry-led, regionally recruited armies were composed not of mere militia (*t'uan-lien*), in the sense of part-time farmer-soldiers, but rather of professional fighting men (*yung,* "braves"). With their own personal networks of leaders and sources of local support, they became vested interests, supplanted the bannermen and constabulary in the provinces, and came to be known generically as the Defense Army. The Anhwei Army (under Li at Tientsin) and the Hunan Army (led by Liu K'un-i at Nanking) had been the dominant rivals among these forces. Although usually equipped with modern rifles and artillery instead of the old matchlocks and smooth-bore cannon, they still lacked standardized armament as well as modern-trained officers and staff specialists, to say nothing of engineer, signal, quartermaster, modern transport, or medical services.

The third and most recent type of military organization had developed in response to Japan's aggression. Both Li and Chang Chih-tung had set up military academies in the 1880's and hired German instructors to train a new officer corps. Chang created a Self-Strengthening Army at Nanking in 1895 on the German model. Its three thousand men were carefully selected, well-paid country boys. A more significant unit developed under Yüan Shih-k'ai, a military more than a civil official, who had risen as Li's proconsul in Korea. Appointed in 1895 to train a new imperial army with German instructors to be financed by the Board of Revenue, he soon had seven thousand men in training near Tientsin, recruited from several provinces and well paid, with precautions against the usual corruption. Through his personal leadership of this new force, which came to be known as the Peiyang Army, Yüan laid the foundation of the "Peiyang clique" and became the "father of the warlords." Among his early officers were at least ten men who after the revolution were to become military governors of provinces, and five (in addition to Yüan himself) who became presidents or premiers of the Peking government under the republic.

The deaths of Li Hung-chang (1901) and Liu K'un-i (1902) left Yüan Shih-k'ai, in his mid-forties, the chief army-builder in the empire. Inheriting Li's position as governor-general of Chihli from 1901 to 1907, he worked closely with the top Manchu, the notoriously corrupt Prince Ch'ing, who had held the highest positions in foreign affairs at Peking ever since the dismissal of Prince Kung in 1884. Yüan's build-up of six divisions of his Peiyang Army, with its half-dozen diversified military schools, miniature general staff, well-drilled troops, and impressive maneuvers, was imitated, incompletely and less effectively, in most of the provinces.

For the Ch'ing Empire, still fragmented by regional-provincial interests, genuine military centralization was politically impossible. A reorganization in 1904 left China's armies still controlled essentially at the provincial level. The New Army blueprint called for thirty-six divisions, but it lacked the essential ingredients of centralized direction, adequate financing, and industrial support. The chief innovation was that new military academies, like that at Paoting near Peking, now produced a new class of scholar-officers, military activists imbued with patriotism, who combined modern military skills with the scholar's sense of responsibility for putting the empire in order. Japanese instructors, cheaper than Germans, were hired in increasing numbers, and Chinese officer candidates were sent to military

BOAT-TRACKING ON THE YANGTZE. *Photographed in the 1940's. The second junk is held inshore by four lines and hauled upstream by one line attached to 19 or more trackers, who pull with right arm and left shoulder-band.*

MAN-TRANSPORT IN SZECHWAN. *Porters resting with 298- and 317-pound loads of brick tea en route to Tibet, 1908.*

academies in Japan, where their patriotism was further aroused by the example of a foreign land. Chiang Kai-shek, of Chekiang, aged eighteen, attended Paoting in 1906 and went to Japan in 1907.

Administrative Reform: The Central-Provincial Power Balance. The Ch'ing administration, inherited from the early Ming and refined during more than four centuries, had served the agrarian-based Chinese Empire well enough until about 1800. But just as the mounted archer had been supplanted rather suddenly by the railroad and rifle, and the sailing junk by the steamship, so the imperial government had become outmoded. China now needed dynamic central organs to perform new functions with un-wonted initiative and speed, apply new laws and fiscal procedures, and be more fully acknowledged by the provinces as their superior and coordinator. But such a unitary national government would upset the ancient balance between Peking and the provinces. The provincial administrations still were a separate echelon parallel to the metropolitan administration, and they still reported directly to the emperor. The provinces were merely supervised and serviced, rather than directed and controlled, by the Six Ministries at the capital. Unfortunately for Peking, the late nineteenth-century growth of regionalism that began with Chinese gentry-led suppression of the rebellions, had also been helped by the growth of treaty-port industries, local trade revenues, regional armies, and personal bureaucratic machines. All these new things had strengthened the major provincial governments in the power structure, quite contrary to the increasing need for stronger government at the center. Centralization consequently faced both the bureaucratic inertia of old vested interests and the restive jealousy of new provincial interests.

Reforms at Peking were generally begun by new agencies set up along-side, within, or under the ancient organs of government; as the new organs grew stronger, the ancient ones withered. In 1901, as required by the Boxer Protocol, the Tsungli Yamen became a full-scale Ministry of Foreign Affairs (Wai-wu Pu). In 1905 a Ministry of Police was inaugurated, forerunner of a Ministry of Internal Affairs. In the reorganization of 1906, the new Ministry of Education took over the examining function of the Ministry of Ceremonies, while the old Ministry of War, customarily headed by civil officers, was expanded into the Army Ministry, headed by ambitious Manchu generals. Innovations started by "bureaus" (*chü*) in the coastal provinces also began to be pursued by committees or new ministries at Peking. After bureaus of commercial affairs had first promoted chambers of commerce, commercial newspapers, and business and industrial schools in leading provinces, a Ministry of Commerce was set up at Peking in 1903. It eventually absorbed the old Ministry of Works and became a Ministry of Agriculture, Industry, and Commerce, trying to promote railroad-building, in-dustrial exhibits, standard weights and measures, registration of firms, mining regulations, company law, farmers' associations, and other modern measures. Typically, it offered official rank as a reward for economic achievement.

New structures at Peking were easier to inaugurate than new processes over the empire. Legal reform, for example, was held by the foreign powers to be prerequisite, as in Japan, to any abolition of extraterritoriality. In 1904 a law-compilation bureau began work under Shen Chia-pen, a sixty-five-year-old scholar-veteran of the Ministry of Punishments. He began by trying to give modern expression to traditional social values but ended up proposing revolutionary changes. In 1907 Shen put forward a draft criminal code based on Japanese and German models which would have distinguished law from morality—that is, it would have made the Confucian rules of propriety, such as filial piety, legally unenforceable. By also making all persons outside the imperial family equal before the law, Shen would have dealt a blow to the five relationships and the whole hierarchic social order based on distinctions of status, age, and sex. His draft was rejected.

He also presented, however, a less drastic revision of the Ch'ing code which was finally promulgated in 1910 and remained in force until after 1928. It contributed to modernization by reducing corporal punishment and torture; abolishing branding, slicing, slavery, and public exposure of heads and corpses; substituting individual for collective responsibility; distinguishing between civil and criminal law; and enunciating certain general principles to guide the application of the numerous specific regulations or "supplementary laws" (*li*). These had accumulated during the dynasty to a total of about nineteen hundred items, a corpus of rather concrete but often mutually contradictory rules which magistrates could not apply with any degree of consistency or predictability. This ambiguity and uncertainty as to the law applicable to a case, added to the fact that law had been neither primary nor pervasive in Chinese society, had left the judicial function of magistrates stunted and undeveloped, to say nothing of the whole world of legal philosophy and phraseology and the legal profession itself. Though he reduced the number of *li,* Shen Chia-pen could not remake this situation.

Financial reform was even more difficult, not only because it threatened so many "rice bowls" (individual incomes) but also because the inherited fiscal system was so superficial and weak to begin with. Actual tax collections over the empire remained largely unknown, unbudgeted, and unaccounted for. Local tax collectors, as well as the provincial regimes above them, still had to live on what they collected. Moreover, the tax quotas officially received were not centralized in a "common purse." Instead, they were listed as fixed sums due from a multitude of specific sources and allotted to a multitude of specific uses. Revenues from a province were allotted in bits and pieces to meet needs in it or elsewhere. Of the eighteen provinces, thirteen regularly forwarded fixed allotments for specific purposes to other provinces. For example, the 7 million taels to maintain the bannermen in Peking came from fifty-two different sources over the empire. This *ad hoc* procedure tied the imperial revenues to an infinite number of vested interests, mainly the support of officials and soldiers. Finally, even at Peking there was no single fiscal authority. The imperial revenues about 1905 totaled on the books roughly 70 million United States dollars, a small sum for so large a country. Yet the new trade taxes—customs and likin— were earmarked for foreign indemnity payments, while the traditional land tax quotas remained inelastic. The Ministry of Finance, although reorganized in 1906, still could not achieve central control. Other ministries continued to receive and expend their traditional revenues and even set up their own banks, like the Bank of Communications (1907).

A novel effort to make a national budget began with nationwide revenue surveys in 1908 and the compilation of budget estimates in 1910, in which central-and-provincial government revenues and expenditures were differentiated from local. This produced estimates of total revenues (297 million taels) and expenditures (national-including-provincial, 338 million taels; local, 37 million taels) which presaged a sizable deficit (78 million taels). Unfortunately, planning and budgeting, collecting statistics, and setting tax rates, went on uncoordinated in both the central ministries and the provinces, with the provinces not subordinate to the ministries and yet expected to supply the revenues. This basic lack of centrality was deeply rooted in Chinese custom, political values, and social structure. It became apparent that the Ch'ing government, which had been superficial, passive, and indeed parasitic for so long, could become modern only by greatly expanding its functions and asserting central leadership. For an alien dynasty in an era of rising nationalism, this was impossible.

Constitutionalism, Provincialism, and Nationalism. When Japan's constitutional monarchy defeated Russia's tsarist autocracy in 1905, constitutionalism seemed to have proved itself as a basis for unity between rulers and ruled in a national effort. Even Russia now moved toward parliamentary government. Constitutionalism in China, it was hoped, might give the rising provincial interests a meaningful share in the dynastic government and so keep them loyal to it. Between 1906 and 1911 Peking actively pursued a dual program to combine administrative modernization and constitutionalism. Such changes, however, precipitated a struggle for power, both within the central government and between it and the provinces. At the capital, the Manchu princes succeeded in maintaining, or even enlarging, their grip on key posts while preventing really fundamental reforms. This pro-Manchu and therefore anti-Chinese coloration at Peking antagonized the rising spirit of nationalism in the rest of China.

The new nationalism produced in 1905 China's first modern boycott, against the United States' discriminatory treatment of Chinese, particularly the total exclusion of laborers. In this boycott, the old tradition of cessation of business by local merchant guilds was expanded nationwide to most of the treaty ports, especially Shanghai and Canton, where students joined merchants in mass meetings and modern press agitation. American trade was damaged for some months, and Peking hesitated to repress this popular antiforeign movement lest it become antidynastic also.

Under the pressure of rising nationalist sentiment, the court sent two official missions to study constitutionalism abroad in the first half of 1906. One visited mainly the United States and Germany; the other, Japan, England, and France. Prince Itō lectured the visitors to Japan on the necessity of the emperor's retaining supreme power, not letting it fall into the hands of the people. On their return they recommended following this Japanese view, that a constitution and civil liberties including "public discussion," all granted by the emperor, could actually strengthen his position because he would remain above them all. In September 1906 the Empress Dowager promised "a constitutional polity" after due preparation. In August 1908 she proclaimed a set of principles to guide a nine-year program to prepare for constitutional self-government. Consultative provincial assemblies were to be convened in 1909 and a consultative national assembly in 1910. Even this idea of a nine-years' tutelage imitated Japan, where in 1881 the Diet had been promised for 1890.

The Ch'ing regime was grievously weakened by the death of the Empress Dowager on November 15, 1908. For half a century the "Old Buddha" (*Lao Fo-yeh*), as she was respectfully called in common parlance, had been at the center of power, exerting a tremendous influence that is still almost unstudied. She was a great patron, for example, of the colorful, northern-style "Peking opera" but lacked the ability of a K'ang-hsi or Ch'ien-lung, in far different times, to be a leading connoisseur of art and patron of literature. On her death, the demise of the hapless but not unhealthy Kuang-hsü emperor was announced as having occurred on the preceding day. His mysterious death at thirty-seven destroyed China's best chance for a transition to a constitutional monarchy and left the throne in the hands of ignorant and vainglorious Manchu princes. The Empress Dowager had named as his successor her three-year-old grand-nephew, Pu-yi, who reigned as the Hsüan-t'ung emperor (1909–1912), with his father, the second Prince Ch'un, as regent. Sir Robert Hart, the Inspector General of Customs, returned to England in 1908, Yüan Shih-k'ai was forced to retire in January 1909, and Chang Chih-tung died in October.

The dynasty's reform effort, too grudging and too slow, now faced more problems than it could solve. For example, the new central administration reorganized under eleven ministries in 1906 needed coordination through a cabinet. But such an agency, if packed and dominated by the prime minister, might eclipse the throne as the source of executive action. The Ch'ing regency feared to create it.

By February 1910, representatives of all the sixteen new provincial assemblies gathered at Peking. Representing a vociferous, nationwide movement, they petitioned the throne to set up a national parliament. This was rejected, but the petitioning continued. The demand for government by a genuine parliament and cabinet became intensified after the consultative national assembly, consisting of one hundred appointees of the throne and one hundred of the provincial assemblies, convened in October 1910. Thus pressed, the regent promised a parliament for 1913 and meanwhile, in April 1911, at long last established a cabinet, but with incredible ineptitude he appointed eight Manchus, one Mongol bannerman, and only four Chinese!

The Railway Controversy.   Provincial conflict with the central power came to a head over railway-building. China's late nineteenth-century policy of avoiding foreign-financed and foreign-run railways had been smashed in the scramble of 1898. Foreign-controlled lines—Russian and Japanese in Manchuria, German in Shantung, and French in Yunnan—had now become tools of economic imperialism, preliminary to opening mines, extracting resources, and exploiting markets. Other lines, though nominally owned by the Ch'ing government, had been financed under contract by foreign banking syndicates, which commonly floated bond issues to raise funds as foreign loans to the Chinese government. They then built the lines and managed them as trustees for the foreign bondholders, holding a first mortgage on the railway as security for the original loan. China was thus entering the railway age with foreign financiers awaiting the profits.

Consequently a patriotic "rights recovery" movement arose in most provinces, where local groups demanded redemption of the foreign lines and formed companies to build Chinese provincial lines. With the moral support of provincial leaders in Hupei, Hunan, and Kwangtung, Chang Chih-tung got a British loan in 1905 and redeemed the American China Development Company's contract of 1898 to build the Hankow-Canton railway. But provincial resources proved inadequate to finance construction. Though doubly inspired by patriotism and hope of profit, these merchant-gentry railway companies found it difficult to raise the capital needed to purchase a right of way, pay the land tax on it, and buy foreign rolling stock. Speculation and corruption also handicapped their efforts, which in any case ran counter to the technological need for central planning and direction of any railroad network.

The chief proponent of railway centralization was Sheng Hsüan-huai, who had risen under the patronage of Li Hung-chang and Chang Chih-tung in turn (see pages 337 and 354) and by 1908 had got control over both the China Merchants' steamship line and Chang's industrial base around Hankow. In that year Sheng combined the Han-yang arsenal, the Ta-yeh iron mines (80 miles away in Hupei), and the coal mines at P'ing-hsiang (250 miles south in Kiangsi) to form the Han-Yeh-P'ing Coal and Iron Company. To finance it he had already become dependent on Japanese loans, just as Japan's steel works at Yawata, begun in 1896, had become dependent on iron ore from Ta-yeh. Already illicitly rich from his "official supervision" of textile mills, telegraphs, and other enterprises, Sheng now worked with the Manchu minister of finance at Peking to float foreign loans, in particular to build railways from Hankow to Canton and from Hankow into Szechwan. These were the so-called "Hukuang railways" (the line from Hankow to Peking had been completed in 1905). Thus railway-building had become a major political issue. Peking's technically necessary leadership in railway development, and the foreign loans needed for it, had got thoroughly embrangled with Sheng Hsüan-huai's well-known corruption, provincial opposition to central power, and anti-Manchu feeling in general.

Since railroad loans had become a chief tool of imperialist encroachment, the United States now became quixotically involved under the Taft administration in defending the Open Door through the contradictory method of "dollar diplomacy." Secretary of State Philander C. Knox made a vague proposal in November 1909 for "neutralization" of the railways in Manchuria. This, however, ran counter to the British policy after 1907 of acquiescing in the Russo-Japanese expansion in Manchuria. Knox's ill-conceived proposal only stimulated Japan and Russia to reaffirm secretly in 1910 their division of spheres in the Northeast. Meanwhile, in July 1909 President Taft had intervened in the Hukuang railway loan negotiations with a personal telegram to the regent at Peking, demanding "equal participation by American capital" so that it could promote "the welfare of China and ... her territorial integrity." This got the Morgan group of banks included in a four-power (French, British, German, American) banking consortium set up in 1910.

The final contract of the consortium, signed with Sheng in May 1911, coincided with an imperial decree, which Sheng had advocated, to nationalize, buy out, and put under Peking's control all provincial railway projects. This rebuff to provincial interests threw the fat in the fire. To patriots in the provinces it seemed that the Manchus and their corrupt henchmen were selling China to foreign bankers for their own profit. A "railway protection" movement sprang up, particularly in Szechwan, with mass meetings and anguished petitions to Peking, all in vain. The Szechwan movement intensified. Shops and schools were closed. Tax payments were stopped. Peasant support was mobilized. In September the government moved

MEMORIAL ARCH TO A
VIRTUOUS WIDOW. *Near
Chiung-chou, Szechwan, 1908.
Topmost inscription:
"Chaste and filial."*

troops, shot down demonstrators, and seized the gentry leaders. Typically, these men were degree-holders of means, with landlord-merchant backgrounds, who had studied in Japan, were now prominent in the provincial assembly, and had invested heavily in railway projects. Their antiforeign slogan, "Szechwan for the Szechwanese," represented the interest of the provincial ruling class, which had now become violently antidynastic.

Thus the decade of late Ch'ing reforms had seen the beginning of a social and institutional transformation. After the Boxer fiasco, the modern world began to flood into China and the pace of change accelerated. Missionary education and the Y.M.C.A. began to reach upper-class and city youth. The attack on footbinding marked the beginning of the emancipation of Chinese women. Two traditionally disesteemed professions, the merchant and the military, acquired new prestige. The nineteenth-century treaty-port mandarins and compradors who had specialized in dealing with foreigners at the ports began to be superseded by officials trained abroad and by merchant-capitalist entrepreneurs of broader background. Some landlord gentry, no longer oriented toward official examinations and imperial preferment, had developed local commercial and industrial interests. Basically conservative, this provincial elite had supported the constitutional movement in hopes that a parliament at Peking could link them with the ruling power, and that a cabinet responsible to parliament, holding the bureaucracy responsible in turn, could modernize China's finances, administration, and public services. After 1909 the provincial assemblies had become new political institutions, centers of policy discussion and political organization.

The modern press in the urban centers, most of which were treaty ports, served as the bloodstream of this new life of politics. Chinese periodicals had been started in large part by missionaries up to 1895, but most of the sixty or so publications begun during the next fifteen years down to 1911 were purely Chinese ventures that combined commercial journalism with reformist ideas. New dailies sprang up in Shanghai to join the pioneer *Shun Pao,* founded in 1872, which had reached a circulation of fifteen thousand by 1895. The Commercial Press, another pioneer in modern publishing, was founded in 1897 and spread new textbooks among the schools. By 1911 the provincial assemblies and the press provided a forum for both the "gentry" interests and the new class of young students and military officers—"Young China." Constitutional monarchy was still the slogan of the day, but the dynastic order had been fatally undermined by revolutionary ideas.

The Revolution of 1911

The Japanese Influence. New regimes in China have often started their conquest from an external base—witness the Khitan, Jurchen, Mongol, and Manchu conquerors between the tenth and the seventeenth centuries. In the early twentieth century the treaty ports, the Overseas Chinese communities in Southeast Asia and elsewhere, and the Japanese Empire all gave shelter to Chinese rebels. In fact, the Revolution of 1911 was largely made in Japan.

This idea of the formative role of Japan has been unpalatable and rather disregarded, both among Western peoples, whose forebears stimulated China's Westernization, and among Chinese patriots, who have suffered from later Japanese aggression. Nevertheless, the period from 1898 to 1914 saw a major Japanese impact on the course of Chinese history. Japan was alike the model of Ch'ing government reformers and until about 1907 the home base for anti-Ch'ing revolutionaries. Republican China went to school in Tōkyō. The Japanese stimulus to modern education, militarism, and constitutionalism in China, already noted, was part of a broader contribution to the rise of Chinese nationalism in general. Japan's influence in this brief period was more direct, profound, and far-reaching than that of Britain in the nineteenth century or of the United States from 1915 to 1949, or even, one may suspect, of the Soviet Union in the 1950's. One reason for this was Japan's cultural as well as geographical propinquity. Another reason was the historical circumstance that, in this dawn of their modern age, China was most eager to learn and Japan most eager to teach, as yet without serious conflicts of national interest.

Japan's coming of age as a great power between 1895 and 1905 made her the model for Asia in the eyes of patriots not only in other Asian lands but also in Japan. It fortified the dream of Japan's pan-Asian leadership toward modernization and against Western imperialism. Japanese interest in contemporary China was expressed in organizations like the East Asian Common Culture Society (Tōa Dōbun Kai) founded by political, cultural, and expansionist leaders in 1898. China was studied historically at Tōkyō and Kyōto, centers of contemporary research were established in Taiwan, at Mukden by the South Manchurian Railway Company, and at Shanghai. To promote Japan's continental expansion beyond Korea and against Russia, the ultrapatriotic Amur River Society (lit., "Black Dragon Society" from the Chinese name for the Amur), founded in 1901, encouraged Japanese adventurers to penetrate East Asia as students, travelers, and businessmen. The opposition leaders of the Liberal and Progressive parties also regularly demanded from the government, as a domestic political tactic, a more vigorous foreign policy. Some of them became actively interested in reform and revolution in China.

Japanese protection and shelter were accordingly given K'ang Yu-wei and Liang Ch'i-ch'ao in 1898 (see pages 373–376). K'ang stayed for a time with the Progressive Party founder, Ōkuma, who had been prime minister briefly in 1898 and who formulated Japan's growing interest in China in his so-called "Ōkuma doctrine": that Japan, having modernized first, should repay her ancient cultural debt to China by now guaranteeing her freedom and aiding her modernization. Ōkuma's follower, Inukai, cultivated the groups of Chinese political exiles. In 1898 he got Liang and the revolutionary leader Sun Yat-sen together to discuss cooperation between the radical reformers led by K'ang Yu-wei and the anti-Ch'ing revolutionaries represented by Sun. K'ang, however, not only refused to meet Sun unless he became a disciple; he also remained a monarchist, stubbornly loyal to his Kuang-hsü emperor. In 1899 he began to visit Overseas Chinese communities around the world to set up units of his Protect-the-Emperor Society, collect funds, and stimulate a reformist press. In his teacher's absence, Liang for a time contemplated joining forces with Sun, but K'ang prevented it. The Japanese effort at unity failed; and after 1900 the two Chinese exile groups, reformers and revolutionaries, though both patriotic and both proscribed by Peking, became bitter rivals. Of the many leaders who emerged in these years, two became especially well-known and have been most studied.

Two Protagonists: Liang Ch'i-ch'ao and Sun Yat-sen.   Liang visited Honolulu and Southeast Asia in 1900–1901, and the United States in 1903, but spent most of the decade in Japan. Already a master of classical learning, he absorbed modern ideas voraciously and wrote upon all manner of subjects in an eloquent, clear, and forceful style that soon made him the most influential writer of the period—the Chinese students' window on the world. The titles of his successive journals indicate the trend of his thinking— "Public Opinion" (1898–), "The Renovation of the People" (1902–), "The National Spirit" (1910–). Still only thirty in 1903, Liang soon left his teacher behind. K'ang Yu-wei was then forty-five, past changing, and Liang had already put him in his place by praising him as "the Martin Luther of Confucianism" and a great thinker of the period "before Darwinism came to China." As he absorbed modern learning in Japan, Liang began to put China's problems in a context of world history. To justify reform, he took up the then worldwide doctrine of Social Darwinism. He compared China's long development with that of other nations, compared Columbus and Vasco da Gama with Cheng Ho, Immanuel Kant with Wang Yang-ming, and looked back on the "new text" movement, of which he had been an ardent member in the nineties, as comparable to the revival of Greek learning in the Renaissance. In short, he got outside China's classical learning and began the modern reappraisal of Chinese history that is still going on.

Liang's hope for China lay in popular education for nationalism, a moral "renovation of the people." Echoing Fukuzawa and other Westernizers in Japan, he espoused an Anglo-Saxon ideal of self-respect, enterprise, and public-spirited citizenship. Denouncing China's political decadence, he urged the transfer of loyalty from ruler to nation, from Confucian personal relationships to principles of law and the establishment of new institutions—"a constitution, a parliament, and a responsible government." He also sponsored literary magazines, the writing of short stories and other fiction, and translations of world literature, mainly from Japanese versions, into Chinese. In politics, however, Liang refrained from blaming China's ills on the Manchu dynasty. Like any member of the gentry elite as well as most foreign observers, he believed his people unprepared for representative democracy. He remained therefore a gradualist and a constitutional monarchist, anti-republican and not actively revolutionary until the very end of the decade. The Political Culture Association (Cheng-wen She) which he organized in 1907 advocated orderly political processes and had great influence in the constitutional movement, although it fell into the usual liberal position— attacked from opposite sides by both the Ch'ing government and the anti-Ch'ing revolutionaries.

While Liang was an upper-class aristocrat of the intellect and a leader of thought more than of action, his fellow Cantonese Sun Yat-sen (formal name: Sun Wen) was one of the early professional revolutionaries of modern times. The two men approached China's problems from opposite social contexts, with antithetic preconceptions, and through different media.

While Liang was expounding the ideology of Chinese nationalism, Sun built up the structure of the early revolutionary movement. Sun had, or acquired, a remarkable list of qualifications for revolutionary leadership. He came from the district next to Macao, longest in touch with Westerners, farthest from Peking's control, home of the original "returned student" Yung Wing, of the early comprador Tong King-sing, and of countless emigrants to the Overseas Chinese communities abroad. Socially as well as geographically, Sun's origin was opportune. Son of a peasant, he was schooled by an uncle who had fought for the cause of the Taipings; its leader Hung Hsiu-ch'uan was his boyhood hero. Sun's early career was equally unoriented toward the emperor at Peking, for at thirteen he joined his elder brother in Honolulu, where he stayed three years and studied an English curriculum in a Church of England boarding school. He sang in the choir and accepted Christianity. Returning to his native village an iconoclast, he broke local idols and was sent away. He studied in Hong Kong, supported by his overseas brother, and after another visit to Honolulu, spent five years (1886–1892) in Canton and Hong Kong studying chemistry, physiology, surgery, and the like for his medical degree from a British misson hospital. In 1892 he began to practice in Macao but was forced out for lack of a diploma from Portugal. Having been concerned over the fate of China ever since her defeat by France in 1885, Sun submitted a reformist petition to the chief Westernizer of the day, Li Hung-chang, but got no reply. Thwarted as a doctor, disregarded by those in power, he now turned to a new calling—neither merchant, peasant, scholar, nor medical practitioner, but revolutionist, a man of no class, ready to work with all classes.

Sun had already made contact with that traditional rebel body, the Triad Society (see page 290). By 1894 he had a secret society of his own, the "Revive China Society" (Hsing-Chung Hui), with branches in Hawaii as well as in the Macao–Hong Kong–Canton area. In 1895 its first plot, to seize the Canton government offices, was discovered, and several of his fellow conspirators were executed. But Sun escaped to Japan, cut his queue, grew a mustache, and in Western-style clothes soon passed for a Japanese under the name of Nakayama (lit., "central mountain," which in its Chinese form, Chung-shan, would later be applied to public parks and thoroughfares, educational institutions, and even a style of clothing in Nationalist China). Now "wanted" by Peking, Sun went by way of the United States to London. There in 1896 he was recognized at the Chinese legation, "kidnaped," and held for twelve days preparatory to being shipped back to China for execution; but his old teacher of medicine (Sir James Cantlie) who had also taught him cricket in Hong Kong, mobilized British opinion and got him released. Thus at the age of thirty, already world-famous as the leading anti-Ch'ing revolutionary, Sun felt himself a man of destiny.

THE GROWTH OF HONG KONG.   *Top: Harbor, City of Victoria,
and the Peak seen from Kowloon on the mainland side of the
harbor in a painting of 1856. Bottom: The reverse scene one
hundred and twenty years later—from the Peak looking down
on the city and across the harbor to Kowloon, a photograph
of 1976.*

By the time he returned to Japan in 1897, and received the aid and advice of expansionists there, Sun had put together several ingredients of rebellion, some new, some old. New elements included financial support from Overseas Chinese communities which had grown up outside the traditional mainland society with nonconformist, commercial values, nationalistic but frustrated in their political loyalties; and leadership from a small group of semi-Westernized, sometimes Christian, patriotic youth who came like Sun from the Canton area, on the modernizing fringe of Chinese life. Old-style ingredients included the bands of armed rebels that could be assembled by the mainland secret societies; and the simple antidynastic aim of seizing local power somewhere by force, hoping thereby to set off a chain reaction that would topple the imperial government. In October 1900 a two-week rising was engineered with Triad Society aid at Waichow north of Hong Kong, but it petered out when Japanese arms and men from Taiwan failed to materialize. Combining traditional and modern means, Sun joined the American lodge of the Triad Society in Hawaii in 1903 and through it sought funds from Chinese all over the United States.

By this time, he faced a new problem: how to compete with other revolutionaries by appealing to the new generation of Chinese students, especially in Japan. For this purpose he needed a rationale of revolution. K'ang Yu-wei still had most of the support of the rather conservative Overseas Chinese merchants in Southeast Asia, and Liang Ch'i-ch'ao's writings were forming the ideas of the new student class. Meanwhile risings had been attempted by others, and revolutionary societies, schools, and journals were springing up in the treaty ports as well as in Japan. A group in Shanghai, led by classical scholars like Chang Ping-lin and Ts'ai Yuan-p'ei, attacked K'ang and Liang. In 1903 their inflammatory anti-Manchu paper (*Su-pao*) was suppressed amid great notoriety, and Chang was imprisoned for three years. In Hunan, Huang Hsing founded his "China Revival Society" (Hua-hsing Hui) in 1903 and tried to unite army officers, students, and secret society members for a rising, but as so often happened, the plot was discovered and broken up. Revolutionary activity was thus growing, but it lacked coordination, specific ideology, and a long-term program.

Facing this competition and opportunity, Sun Yat-sen now developed his own ideological appeal. In 1903 he wrote his first newspaper articles in Tokyo and Honolulu. By mid-1905, after organizing Chinese student groups in Brussels, Berlin, and Paris, he was back in Tōkyō again. Dedicated in aim but flexible, if not indeed opportunist, as to means, Sun now put together from his multicultural background from China, Japan, the United States, and Europe a set of ideas to justify and guide a republican revolution. This was the Three Principles of the People (*San min chu-i*): nationalism (*min-tsu chu-i,* a term connoting both people and race); democracy (*min-ch'uan chu-i,* literally, "people's rights"); and "people's livelihood" (*min-sheng chu-i,* a classical term that some later equated with socialism). These three protean concepts summed up much of the ferment of the age and yet could undergo much change in specific content. Nationalism was at this time both anti-Manchu, hence prorepublican, and anti-imperialist, though this latter aspect was not stressed by those seeking foreign aid for the revolution. Democracy implied an anti-Confucian egalitarianism to be guaranteed by a constitution (which stole Liang's thunder) with five powers—executive, legislative, and judicial as in the United States, plus examination and censorial or "control" powers drawn from Chinese tradition. This "five-power constitution" was apparently Sun's own invention. Finally, his "people's livelihood," to meet the new problems of industrial growth, involved no Marxist class struggle but instead followed Henry George's then popular idea of a single tax to appropriate future unearned increase of land values and thus check the enrichment of speculators and monopolists. Thus the ancient term "people's livelihood" in 1905 meant principally this urban "equalization of land rights" in the specific Western single-tax sense, not an agrarian land redistribution. The latter would as yet have kindled little enthusiasm among the sons of merchants and landlords, eager though they might be for a political revolution.

The T'ung-meng Hui and Its Vicissitudes.   All these ingredients—Overseas Chinese funds, secret society contacts, new student leadership, and revolutionary ideology—were finally combined in 1905 under Japanese encouragement. Bringing rival groups together, Sun's friends in Japan introduced him to Huang Hsing and others of the Hunan group. At a big Tōkyō meeting in August the T'ung-meng Hui ("United League," a typical secret society name) was founded with Sun as chief executive, Huang Hsing second in command, and Chang Ping-lin and others named to key posts. Overseas offices in Singapore, Brussels, San Francisco, and Honolulu were to be coordinated with branches in seventeen provinces. Among roughly a thousand early members, the largest group was from Hunan and Hupei (so long governed by that modernizer of education, Chang Chih-tung), while the Cantonese were second, and the Szechwanese and lower Yangtze contingents third and fourth in size.

Felt by many to be a magnetic personality, Sun at thirty-nine was not only the eldest but also the most famous, the most widely traveled, and the most experienced among this revolutionary band, with the greatest number of contacts in Japan and elsewhere abroad, although not in the Yangtze provinces. On the other hand, as a foreignized Chinese and not one of the scholar elite, a man known for conspiracy and desperate action rather than for literary production, and indeed intellectually rather superficial, he could not assume the role of modern sage to guide the thinking of his generation. And yet, given the multicultural confusion produced by the collapse of

China's great tradition and the variety of foreign models, probably no systematic thinker could have had even as much success as Sun Yat-sen.

The new ideology of republicanism was expounded by Sun's literary lieutenants in the T'ung-meng Hui journal *The People* (*Min-pao*). Attacking Liang's ideas of gradualist reform and constitutional monarchy, writers like Wang Ching-wei and Hu Han-min largely succeeded in winning Chinese student support for the attractive thesis that China could catch up with and indeed surpass the West by a quick revolution. "Men of determination," providing strong leadership (as in Japan), could intervene to speed up modernization. Gradual evolution and popular education to prepare for modern political life were unnecessary. *The People* backed Sun's three-stage program: (1) three years of military government, with local self-government beginning county by county; (2) six years under a provisional constitution, which later came to be known as a period of "tutelage"; and (3) eventual constitutional government with an elected president and parliament. These optimistic assumptions and over-simple promises soon proved more popular than the cooler rationality of Liang Ch'i-ch'ao, whose espousal of benevolent monarchy was in any case torpedoed by the death of the Kuang-hsü emperor in 1908.

Despite its new unity, the revolutionary movement suffered repeated frustrations. In the most rebellious province, Hunan, an independent revolt of the secret Society of Brothers and Elders (Ko-lao Hui) in October 1906, caused partly by famine, was joined by coal miners at P'ing-hsiang in Kiangsi but was suppressed in a month by government troops from four provinces. In 1907, Ch'ing protests led Japan to expel Sun Yat-sen. He and Huang Hsing moved to Hanoi in French Indo-China and in 1907–1908 staged six outbreaks in Kwangtung, Kwangsi, and Yunnan. But the friendly French soon found that the Chinese example stimulated Vietnamese unrest. They in turn expelled the T'ung-meng Hui conspirators. By 1909, Ch'ing arrests and executions, combined with the revolutionists' failure of coordination and lack of success, had discouraged Overseas Chinese financial support and led to dissension within the movement. It practically came to a standstill, and Sun went to the West again seeking funds. Others took up anarchism, advocated especially by a group of students from Paris, and, like Russian anarchists, resorted to assassination to dramatize their cause. In 1910 the handsome Wang Ching-wei tried to bomb the prince regent in Peking but was caught and imprisoned. Anti-Manchu feeling was rising, but the revolutionary movement seemed thoroughly frustrated.

Huang Hsing pursued the most hopeful course of subverting imperial New Army troops. An army revolt engineered at Canton in February 1910 was suppressed, but another overseas fund drive collected 187,000 Hong Kong dollars, mainly from Southeast Asia and Canada, and financed the smuggling of arms and "dare-to-die" attack forces into Canton in April 1911.

Like most earlier plots, this "Canton Revolution" was doomed, despite individual heroism, by a sequence of difficulties—inadequate secrecy, government precautions, last-minute changes of plan, lack of coordination, and general confusion. Huang Hsing's men in several groups tried as usual to seize the government offices, but one group mistook another's identity, and they dispersed each other with gunfire. Sun Yat-sen listed this as the tenth failure of his forces since 1895. Huang Hsing concluded that "in instigating revolution, dictatorship is imperative. Once a dissenting voice is permitted, the revolution is bound to fail."

All these risings had been more political than military in their ulterior purpose, to destroy the dynasty's prestige and claim to power. Outbreaks and assassinations, funds and arms from abroad, had been used for their destructive effect on that tacit popular acquiescence which constituted Heaven's mandate. But this was equally endangered by worsening economic conditions, manifested in peasant rice riots (as in Hunan in 1910) and by the frustration of gentry interests, which supported provincial "railway protection" movements (as in Szechwan in 1911). Both contributed to a rapid decline of the Ch'ing dynasty's central authority and therefore of the monarchy as an institution. By 1911 Heaven's mandate had indeed been withdrawn from the Manchus; they had lost the confidence and active support of the great part of the Chinese establishment—local officials and police, modern troops, and even their commanders.

The End of the Ch'ing Dynasty. When the denouement came, it was partly accidental, locally improvised, and out of T'ung-meng Hui control. Students and soldiers had organized a succession of revolutionary study societies in Hupei, the better to plot a rising. Their plot was as usual discovered (on October 9), and some of the New Army soldiers in Wuchang revolted in order to save themselves on October 10 (since celebrated as the "Double Ten," i.e., tenth day of the tenth month). Although fewer than three thousand out of a much larger body of troops rebelled, the Manchu governor-general fled the city, as did his military commander. Wuchang fell to the rebels. The foreign consuls declared neutrality. Since no revolutionary leader was on the scene, a brigade commander (Li Yüan-hung) was pressed into leadership. This anti-Manchu rebellion received spontaneous popular support locally. Within a few weeks it inspired anti-Manchu declarations in some two dozen other centers, usually backed by the T'ung-meng Hui, the New Army, and provincial assemblies. By early December all the southern and central and even the northwestern provinces had declared their independence, usually under Ch'ing army officers who became military governors and held power jointly with provincial assembly leaders of the constitutional movement. Fighting occurred in only half a dozen places.

LEADERS OF THE CHINESE REPUBLIC.
At Nanking, early 1912 (front, left to right): Ts'ai Yüan-p'ei, Minister of Education; Huang Hsing, Army Minister; Sun Yat-sen, Provisional President.

The Ch'ing court now recalled Yüan Shih-k'ai to power since the best troops were loyal to him, but he came on his own terms, as prime minister of a new cabinet government as well as commander of the armed forces. Meanwhile the rebellious provinces and the T'ung-meng Hui revolutionists joined forces in setting up a provisional government at Nanking. Sun Yat-sen, who had read of the Wuchang revolt in a Denver newspaper, had gone on to England seeking a loan and British help to prevent Japan's giving financial or military aid to the dynasty. He reached Shanghai just in time to be elected, as a senior figurehead, to the provisional presidency of the Chinese Republic. He was inaugurated at Nanking on January 1, 1912, but at the same time offered to resign in favor of Premier Yüan Shih-k'ai whenever the latter would support the new republic.

Although some sharp fighting occurred, particularly at the Wuhan cities, the 1911 revolution was singularly unviolent. It was also inconclusive, because its main aim was purely negative, to get rid of Manchu rule. There was a widespread consensus on a few positive points—that the provinces must be represented in a parliament; that Chinese unity was essential to forestall foreign, probably Japanese, intervention; and that Yüan Shih-k'ai was the one man with sufficient experience, ability, and backing to head a new government. Sun Yat-sen, Huang Hsing, and other revolutionists had generally agreed by late December that Yüan represented the chief hope of avoiding civil war, chaos, and foreign intervention. On his part, Yüan, backed by his military commanders, negotiated both publicly and secretly on various levels, from a central position, with the Ch'ing court on the one hand and with the revolutionists and their Nanking provisional government on the other, and gradually engineered a general settlement: on February 12, 1912, the infant Hsuan-t'ung emperor (later known as Pu-yi) bowed to "the Mandate of Heaven . . . manifested through the wish of the people" and abdicated, ending the Ch'ing dynasty, as well as the ancient Chinese monarchy and empire. Sun Yat-sen then resigned as provisional president and Yüan was elected his successor at Nanking. A violent army mutiny at Peking, however, necessitated Yüan's presence, and so he avoided moving the capital south. He was inaugurated on March 10 in his own bailiwick at Peking, to govern under a provisional constitution until a parliament should be elected and full constitutional government be established.

Yüan as president was later to "betray" the revolutionists who had elected him, just as he had "betrayed" the Ch'ing court that had made him prime minister. But in 1912 he had no rival of equal stature capable of holding power at that unprecedented moment when the Chinese leviathan had been decapitated and no Son of Heaven was left to perform the crucial imperial functions at the apex of state and society. In this great political crisis the Manchus might have tried to fight rather than be pensioned off; the northern armies might have been used against Nanking; and the Japanese, who were soon to become aggressive, might have seized this earlier opportunity. As it happened, however, Yüan had the skill and chicanery to oust the Manchus, court foreign recognition, beguile the revolutionists, and maintain an administration through a time of great uncertainty. The Japanese, with divided counsels, were unable to agree on an active policy. Britain pressed for Chinese unity. Sun and his republican colleagues, having neither armed forces nor large constituencies in the provinces, knew that China needed strong and unified rule, and that they could not provide it. With nationalist sentiments of every type calling for unity under a strong man, Yüan emerged as the sole candidate.

Thus when China's immemorial monarchy was abolished, the emergence of a power-holder cushioned the shock. But Chinese political life without the Son of Heaven inevitably deteriorated, because the chief of state now lacked the traditional ideological and ceremonial sanctions for the exercise of supreme power. While not exactly theocratic in Western terms, the Chinese ruler had been indubitably placed above mankind, as Yüan was not. Lacking the traditional sanctions and not yet having developed modern ones, the Son of Heaven's successors—both Yüan and the warlords—had to rely increasingly on military force. When new sanctions were eventually established, years later, they were not those of the Anglo-Saxon model of government, which the revolutionists had vaguely had in mind. In this way 1911 marked the beginning of a prolonged crisis of central power in the world's most ancient government.

The Republic's Decline into Warlordism

The great modern transformations of economy, politics, society, thought, and culture, which have swept about the world like tidal waves, had by 1912 begun to smash China's traditional civilization to bits and pieces. Chinese who have lived through the unprecedented era since that time have thus experienced chaos on every level, private and public, practical and theoretical. Nowhere has the search for a new order, a revival of national power, a remaking of the national life, been more prolonged or more frustrating.

Domestic Politics: Yüan vs. the Kuomintang.   The new provisional president, Yüan Shih-k'ai, having taken over the principal administrative functions of the extinct monarchy, soon became involved in a power struggle with the revolutionary leaders. To keep power from 1912 to 1916, he used bribery, military force, and assassinations, coerced the parliament, revised the constitution at will and finally tried to revive the monarchy. All these manipulations branded him an enemy of the people and their republic.

In March 1912 Yüan inaugurated the republican system of government by appointing his protégé T'ang Shao-i, a nephew of Tong King-sing who had been educated in Connecticut under Yung Wing (Tong and T'ang are variant romanizations of the same surname), to be prime minister and form a ten-man cabinet. It contained four T'ung-meng Hui members, among them Sung Chiao-jen of Hunan, a close colleague of Huang Hsing and a leading drafter of the new provisional constitution. This document had divided authority between president and parliament, and disagreement soon arose over which should control the cabinet and its administration. Prime Minister T'ang had no party organization, no patronage, no budget, and no control over his cabinet ministers. When he found that Yüan would not let him run the administration, he and the four T'ung-meng Hui members resigned (June 1912), and the cabinet thereafter became responsible to the president, not the parliament. President Yüan, however, avoiding a rupture, invited Sun Yat-sen and Huang Hsing to Peking, where each spent almost a month. Yüan saw them frequently, expressing agreement with their views, and appointed Sun director of railways to mastermind a great national railway system, all on paper. These older revolutionary leaders, unskilled in government, were unable to create or even demand party rule. Their ideas about it were vague, their aims uncertain, their counsels divided; the institution itself was untested on the Chinese scene. Political parties in fact were just taking shape, emerging out of two traditions.

One tradition was that of the clique or faction (*tang*) of scholar-officials, like K'ang Yu-wei's Self-Strengthening Society and the other political study groups formed after 1895. This element had contributed to the nationwide constitutional movement and now in May 1912 took shape in a Republican Party which generally supported Yüan's administration. After Liang Ch'i-ch'ao returned from Japan to a hero's welcome, he formed a Democratic Party and in May 1913 amalgamated these Republicans, Democrats, and other small groups into the Progressive Party, still generally in support of the government in power. The other source of party tradition came from the secret societies whose example had inspired the conspiratorial societies of revolutionists. Many political groups partook of both traditions. Some politicians belonged to several parties. No party was more than a congeries of upper-class individuals who were drawn together by personal ties or common background, but who lacked reliable electoral constituencies, politi-cal status, and experience. In short, the adaptation of Western methods of political association and agitation, such as had begun in Japan in the 1870's, was barely starting in China. Genuine issues of party policy could not be seriously debated because the institutional role of parties was itself still an issue.

Instead of a separation of powers under the supremacy of law as the central myth of the state, the Chinese monarch had traditionally integrated in his person all the powers of government. Yüan had got control over the cabinet and civil administration and was expanding it over the provincial military governors. Bearing these burdens of personal responsibility, he was unprepared by experience or tradition to countenance a "loyal opposition" that might attack his policies and thwart his power while professing a higher loyalty to the Chinese Republic. Nevertheless this was precisely what the Western model of parliamentary government seemed to call for; the way seemed open for an opposition party to try to dominate the parliament, and the attempt was made. This next phase of the power struggle was led by Sung Chiao-jen, who now ranked just after Sun and Huang among the revolutionists. He persuaded four small political groups in August 1912 to join with the T'ung-meng Hui in forming an open party, the Kuo-min Tang or "National People's Party." National elections, held on the basis of a very restricted and indirect franchise in each province, gave the Kuomin-tang a majority in the bicameral parliament by February 1913. Sung Chiao-jen thereupon campaigned widely in Central China, criticizing the adminis-tration and demanding that the Kuomintang should now control the cabinet, though Yüan should remain president.

This was a high point of parliamentary democracy in modern China, but Sung Chiao-jen's inauguration of electioneering had a denouement that spectacularly blighted this promising development. Yüan hired assassins, as the Shanghai Mixed Court later documented in detail, and on March 20, 1913, at the Shanghai railway station Sung Chiao-jen, not yet thirty-one, was shot down. Yüan temporarily confused the public with fabricated charges against Huang Hsing. Assassination had heretofore been a weapon of the anti-Ch'ing revolutionists out of power, but President Yüan had now developed its use in power, having already had various prorevolutionist generals assassinated or executed. The strategic murder of Sung asserted a principle (that the power-holder is above the law) and demonstrated a tactic (that an opposition movement can best be checked by eliminating its leader) which have been used to strangle democracy in China ever since.

The revulsion against Yüan was heightened by his getting money and recognition from the imperialist powers on onerous terms: while blasting party government at home, he seemed to be mortgaging China's revenues to the foreigners. This stemmed from his urgent financial needs. Although he now had personal control over the military governors who commanded most of the armies, having been their old commander, he was no more able than his Ch'ing predecessors to augment the land tax and other meager revenues flowing to Peking. The Ch'ing had staved off bankruptcy by borrowing 10 million pounds sterling in April 1911 for "currency reform and Manchurian industrial development" from the four-power consortium of British, French, German, and American banks. To this group Russian and Japanese banks were added in June 1912 to make a six-power consortium. Yüan had early begun to seek massive foreign funds, but the consortium, while maintaining its virtual monopoly over loans to China, demanded that China's salt taxes be the security and that they be collected, like the maritime customs, by a joint Sino-foreign administration. Patriotic Chinese of all persuasions protested these terms. President Wilson in March 1913, reversing Taft's position of 1909, refused to support American participation on the grounds that the conditions of the loan threatened China's administrative independence. But after fourteen months of negotiation the consortium contract for the Reorganization Loan of 25 million pounds sterling was nevertheless signed (April 26, 1913). This was done with the remaining five-power group banks, without the parliament's approval, and on the same day that the evidence was published concerning Sung's assassination. Since the bonds were floated at only 90 per cent with 6 per cent commission to the banks, China actually received only 84 per cent, or £21 million, and yet would have to repay principal and 5 per cent interest until 1960, a total of £67,893,597.

Yüan's success in smashing the idea of an opposition party and in borrowing foreign money to pay his armies was largely due to the widespread belief that only he could keep China united and at peace. In mid-1913 he was still backed by the Progressive Party, tolerated by much of the Kuomintang, and supported by the northern military governors, his own men of the Peiyang clique. He therefore spurned various concessions offered by the Kuomintang, dismissed the military governors who supported it in Central and South China, and moved troops against them. Reacting to Yüan's aggressiveness, during July and August 1913 seven provincial governments, though ill-armed, again declared their independence of Peking in the short-lived "second revolution." This movement lacked popular or foreign support and was suppressed within two months with little fighting. Sun Yat-sen, Huang, and other leaders, fleeing to Japan, found themselves back where they had started, while Yüan's generals of the Peiyang clique expanded their control over most of the remaining provinces.

The final phase of parliamentarism began when the Progressive Party, with moderate Kuomintang help, formed a cabinet at Peking in September 1913 which included some of Yüan's henchmen and also Liang Ch'i-ch'ao as minister of justice. Yüan's aim, now becoming more clear, was to get himself at last formally elected president by the parliament, by the agreed-upon procedure, and then dispense with it. Bribery and strong-arm intimidation bent the parliament to his will. On October 6 it finally elected him president. On the 7th he succeeded through diplomatic bargaining in getting the major powers to recognize the Chinese Republic. On October 10 he was formally inaugurated as its first president. Soon he destroyed it. In November he ordered the Kuomintang dissolved and excluded 438 members or former members from the parliament. In January 1914 he suspended the parliament and then the provincial assemblies. In February the cabinet resigned. Yüan, at fifty-four, was now dictator.

Though execrated by patriots of a later day, Yüan's piecemeal dismantling of the thin façade of parliamentarism seems to have been of great concern only to a minor part of the public, for the most part the sprinkling of would-be parliamentarians who had just begun to emerge in the treaty ports and provincial capitals. Neither the foreign powers nor the inarticulate common people nor the city merchant class offered much objection, while the administrative bureaucracy, the army, and most of the provincial governors simply favored stability under the one man at the top. Unlike the diffusion of responsibility in Japanese politics, the Chinese polity was accustomed to a single head who could balance the many conflicting interests and give final decisions. Yüan now did so, ruling through appointed organs and under a new document, the Constitutional Compact promulgated on May 1, 1914, which gave him comprehensive dictatorial powers. He muzzled the press, encouraged local "self-government" by gentry and elders, and revived the censorate and the state cult of Confucius. Alighting from his armored car, he conducted the ancient imperial rites at the Temple of Heaven. By the end of 1915 he was president for life.

Foreign Relations: The Republic vs. the Foreign Powers.   The new Chinese Republic began by losing control over two outlying regions of the old Ch'ing Empire. Tibet and Outer Mongolia broke away and became oriented more to Britain and Russia, respectively, than to Peking. Having cast out the Manchus in the name of national-racial self-determination, the Chinese revolution had little claim to Inner Asia. But Yüan Shih-k'ai, inheriting power at Peking, maintained the traditional claim nevertheless. Russia, Outer Mongolia, and China soon agreed on the formula: Chinese suzerainty and Outer Mongolian autonomy (which permitted actual Russian domination). Britain followed a similar formula: Chinese suzerainty and Tibetan autonomy (allowing a British permanent interest). Both Russia and Britain finally recognized Yüan's government on November 7, 1913.

This expansion of great-power influence in China's borderlands was paralleled by a further growth of foreign control over China's revenues at home. Hart's British successor as Inspector-General of Customs got the imperial government's agreement in November 1911 to a fundamental change in the handling of the Maritime Customs revenue, now fully pledged to meet China's foreign loan and indemnity payments. Previously the foreign commissioners had reported to Peking their accounts of revenues collected, but the Chinese superintendents of customs had actually received the funds. Now, as most of the provinces declared their independence, the unity of the Customs Service and China's foreign credit and debt payments were all preserved by arranging that the foreign commissioners should for the first time receive the revenue funds and transmit them through the Inspector-General to an International Commission of Bankers at Shanghai representing foreign creditors. The foreign position at Shanghai was further strengthened in the face of revolution when the consular body in late 1911 took control over the Mixed Court (see pages 325 and 327). This expansion of foreign control over Shanghai and the customs revenues, together with the modernization of the new Salt Revenue Administration under a British chief inspector, had the same ambivalence as many earlier aspects of the unequal-treaty system—infringing further upon China's sovereignty and yet in the short run helping its government. China's credit was sustained, facilitating foreign loans, and the salt revenues were greatly increased.

Another ambivalent merit of the treaty system had been that the rapacity of any one power was somewhat checked by the jealousy of all the others. World War I, however, diverted the powers' attention and let Japan embark on a course of aggression. In August 1914 China declared her neutrality, but the Ōkuma government declared war on Germany, flouted China's neutrality by landing troops on her territory, and took over the whole German position in Shantung. Japan followed this on January 18, 1915, by secretly presenting to Yüan Shih-k'ai Twenty-One Demands in five groups. The fifth group would have given Japan control over the Chinese government through a system of advisers and specific control over the police, arms purchases, arsenals, and the development of Fukien province. By the usual device of leaking these outrageous terms to the foreign press, Yüan obliged Japan to leave group five for "future discussion," but under a

Japanese ultimatum of May 7 he was forced to accept most of the first four groups. No Western power came to his aid, although the British minister opined that "Japan's action toward China is worse than that of Germany in the case of Belgium." The Sino-Japanese treaties of May 25, 1915, embodying these demands, confirmed Japan's dominant position in Shantung, and in South Manchuria and Eastern Inner Mongolia, long recognized as her sphere. In addition Japan was acknowledged to have a special interest in the Han-Yeh-P'ing industrial base in Central China, which had long been used as security to get Japanese loans, even by Sun Yat-sen in 1912. Although never ratified by a Chinese parliament, these treaties served Japan as a charter for continental expansion. The aim of the Twenty-One Demands, presented by a cabinet that represented Japan's new industrial interests, was basically economic. But the effect in China was mainly political, for they roused a new spirit of nationalism, expressed in mass rallies, strikes, boycotts of Japanese goods, and vigorous protests in the press.

Yüan's Monarchical Fiasco.   Yüan's stout anti-Japanism, for which he had been famous ever since his start in Korea, won him nationwide support in 1915, but his effort to govern China floundered in an ideological vacuum: the ancient Confucian ethical sanctions and the ceremonial forms of imperial rule had lost their potency, while modern beliefs and institutions of popular government, either parties in competition or party dictatorships, had not yet become established. Since Chinese society now lacked a clear political creed, Yüan governed in a rather "Legalist" tradition, by force and manipulation, with little faith even in himself, knowing only that human beings "fear weapons and love gold," as Liang phrased it.

This poverty of political belief was illustrated in Yüan's effort to revive the monarchy. In August 1915 he launched from behind the scenes a monarchical movement complete with a Yüan-for-emperor association to "plan for peace," nationwide "people's petitions," a unanimous vote by "elected" representatives, old-style memorials, and similar contrivances, all demanding his enthronement. In response to the demand thus manufactured, Yüan, after appropriate hesitation, consented in December 1915 to accept the throne. His reign title would be "Grand Constitutional Era" (*Hung-hsien*), to begin with 1916. All this came to nothing.

One factor in his failure was the disaffection of his generals, who bore him no love. Another was the opposition of the Japanese government, which mobilized an almost unanimous treaty-power opinion and "advised" against the monarchy. The precipitating factor was military opposition within China, sparked by men like Liang Ch'i-ch'ao, the antirevolutionist who still saw history as irreversible and now advocated the continuity of the Chinese Republic. He plotted with one of his Hunanese students, who had been military governor of Yunnan, the province farthest from Yüan's control, and on December 25, 1915, Yunnan declared its independence. There followed six months of limited fighting and intensive negotiation. By degrees eight southern and western provinces turned against Yüan, while he first postponed his enthronement, then renounced the throne, and finally died on June 6, 1916, a broken man.

In the background other forces, both ideological and geopolitical, had worked against the idea of monarchy. The sanction of power in China no longer came from an impersonal heaven, expressed in portents and in the tacit acquiescence of the populace. On the contrary, the idea had taken hold that the people, the body politic of the nation, were the active makers of history. The Son of Heaven as an institution had been gradually discredited in the long years leading up to 1911. For Heaven's Mandate had been substituted the concept of the people's will, the consent of the governed. The apotheosis of "the people" (*min*) permeated the new nationalist thinking—the "people's army" (*min-chün*), the "national people's party" (*Kuomintang*), the "three people's principles." Yüan the strong man had been too scornful of the modern idea of representation, even though it was demanded only by the upper classes, not the common mass. In traditional terms he had also been too disloyal to his followers to command their loyalty in return.

Geopolitics too worked against him because the provinces, distinct geographic, cultural, and administrative regions, had grown steadily more independent of Peking, in a process under way since the 1850's. There were also the ineradicable climatic, economic, and historical differences that produced divergent interests and outlooks between South and North China, such as had plagued every dynasty. After Yüan's death still other, foreign influences inhibited China's unity and continued to checkmate his successors in the struggle for power: first, the political sanctuary and strategic resources available to local power-holders in the treaty ports, beyond central control; second, the interests and capacities of the imperialist powers in their respective spheres of influence, which enabled them almost to dominate whole provinces; third, the power of the foreign banks, both in and outside the consortium, to make and unmake Chinese governments by giving or withholding loans; and finally, the constant inflow from abroad of new ideas and techniques, ranging from the anarchism of Kropotkin and the individualism of Ibsen to armored trains and bicycles, all of which contributed both to China's ongoing cultural revolution and to the disintegration of the old order.

The Nature of Warlordism.   Between 1916 and 1928 and in peripheral areas even longer, China was divided among a number of competing warlords, or local military leaders. These were essentially men in between. They were not in a dynastic interregnum, where "change within tradition" would bring forth a new dynasty. Yet they were not modernizers with a new order in mind. Their armies, newly swollen and modern-armed, using the new railways and river steamers, could now more easily dominate the terrain, yet they could not create a new polity. In 1911 the revolutionists, with a party but no army, had failed to gain power. Now the warlords, with armies but no parties, were equally incapable. Their repeated use and misuse of parliaments and slogans only highlighted their lack of adequate principles and institutions. Since 1913 the armies had proliferated and the parties had splintered. No one could integrate the new military power with a new political organization. Under the warlords, China's government deteriorated, the people suffered, and Chinese society after a century of decline reached a nadir of demoralization.

Behind the surface parade of hundreds of bemedaled commanders leading their shambling legions across the historical scene in these years, certain typical characteristics emerge. First of all, a warlord had to have a strong personality, subordinate officers, and troops. His problem was first to train them and win their personal loyalty, then to feed and supply them all. For this he needed support from the revenues of a great city, a province, a trade route, or railway, or from other militarists or a foreign power. The geography of a region might give him a strategic advantage, but its land and people could provide only food and manpower to be requisitioned, not a true territorial base in the modern guerrilla sense, with support among the peasantry. The typical warlord army had no roots among the local people but was a scourge upon them, exacting taxes, living off the villages, feared and despised. An army moving to a new province might therefore better itself, at least temporarily. It might be both parasitic and peripatetic.

In the second place, because military force created political power only when legitimized and mediated through institutions, the warlords sought formal appointments, seals of office, and documents properly signed by others, and also justified their every move by pronouncements in favor of the public welfare and patriotic principles. In short, they needed the help of civilian politicians and civil government. Warlordism did not substitute military force for the other elements of government; it merely balanced them differently. This shift in balance came partly from the disintegration of the sanctions and values of China's traditional civil government, already noted. Partly it came from the warlords' new technical military capacities, greater mobility and fire-power, which were not balanced by an equilibrating growth of new political institutions. This has become, of course, a major motif in modern world history—material technology, especially military, outrunning the growth of popular participation in government. In this respect warlordism was less an old Chinese custom, as foreigners have generally assumed, than a result of unbalanced modernization, armaments growing faster than political agencies capable of controlling them.

Finally, the nature of warlord politics has seemed remarkably confusing to everyone at the time and since, partly because the warlords were so venal and treacherous, so given to sudden shifts of allegiance and wily stratagems reminiscent of operatic characters in the *Romance of the Three Kingdoms.* However, while the old power structure was decapitated, its lower, regional levels continued to function, and tried to create nationwide organs at higher levels. The ultimate aims of the warlords were political, and they sought all manner of institutional means to bolster and expand their power, working with parliaments and assemblies, even convoking conferences of military governors. Being deficient in their capacity for modern political organization, the competing warlord groups could not rise above the regional level. Nevertheless they always acknowledged the existence of the Chinese state. Throughout this period the Peking government continued to function abroad diplomatically and maintained many of its services. No one ventured to proclaim a new dynasty. Times had changed. The struggle among the warlords, among the politicians in the parliament, and between the warlords and the politicians went through a sequence of phases with a general trend toward the weakening of the parliament and fragmentation of the country. In the first phase Liang Ch'i-ch'ao and others of the former Progressive Party formed a "Research clique," which generally tried to work with the Peking government and was opposed by the Kuomintang remnants from the South. As the Peiyang military governors who dominated a dozen northern and central provinces got more and more control over the government and parliament, this estranged the southern provinces. In the second phase, the defection of the Southerners from the Peking parliament in 1917 marked a turning point, for it gave another opportunity to Sun Yat-sen.

In Japan Sun had reverted to his earlier secret-society approach to revolution and in July 1914 had founded the "Chinese Revolutionary Party" (Chung-hua Ko-ming Tang) as a disciplined underground elite who were to be fingerprinted and sworn to personal loyalty to Sun. His aim was to overcome "that lack of party discipline . . . the cause of our failure." Huang Hsing and many others, however, refused to take the oath; this revived conspiratorial effort was plainly not democratic, nor did it appeal to the rising patriotism of the time, for Sun Yat-sen omitted from his new party platform of 1914 the principle of nationalism. Originally anti-Manchu, this principle (incredible as it may seem) apparently no longer held significance for him; his thinking was now pan-Asian, directed toward cooperation with Japan, not against imperialism. Out of tune with the times, Sun had contributed little to the frustrating of Yüan Shih-k'ai in 1916.

In 1917, however, Sun Yat-sen re-emerged and jumped into the warlord-parliamentary fray. In July he went to Canton along with other former Kuomintang colleagues and most of the Chinese navy. He convened some

WARLORDS. *Top: The quondam "Christian General," Feng Yü-hsiang, addressing his troops in 1928. Bottom: The "Marshal of Manchuria," Chang Tso-lin (in winter hat), saluted by the Fifteenth Regiment, U.S.A., then stationed in Tientsin, ca. 1927.*

250 members of parliament and formed a military government with himself as generalissimo, but the local warlords were the real power-holders. Sun at Canton, trying to team up with the local men in power, was like Liang Ch'i-ch'ao at Peking, trying to provide a civilian component for the warlord government there. After the Peking government declared war on Germany in August 1917, it financed its domestic warfare by borrowing enormous sums from Japan, the so-called "Nishihara loans," partly on the excuse of preparing to fight Germany. Peking now made a military alliance with Japan, imported Japanese military instructors, and worked closely with a pro-Japanese group of politicians and militarists known as the An-fu (Anhwei-Fukien) clique. Many patriots protested that the power-holders were again selling China to the foreigners in order to build their own military power. Liang Ch'i-ch'ao finally withdrew from politics in frustration.

In the South Sun Yat-sen's Canton parliament was also split. One element in it (the Political Study clique), cooperated with the warlords, who nevertheless began to assassinate Sun's men and forced him to retire to Shanghai in May 1918. A Kwangsi clique of militarists now dominated the South, much as the An-fu clique controlled the North. The end of World War I put North and South under pressure to patch things up, and in 1919 the two factions negotiated at Shanghai in a fruitless peace conference. During 1920, however, China's fragmentation entered a third phase: minority elements both north and south, seeking allies wherever possible, ousted the groups in power but still could not stabilize their own control.

After 1922 the disintegration of China's civil government entered still another phase and began to produce divergent results north and south. In the North the warlord melee cast up new leading personalities, less directly indebted to Yüan Shih-k'ai for their early careers. Three men eventually stood out; in the course of their triangular relations, each allied himself in turn with each of the other two against the third, and thus each was double-crossed by the others. These three were:

(1) Chang Tso-lin (died 1928), "Warlord of Manchuria," an ex-bandit who had risen as Japan's ally against Russia and been military governor at Mukden since 1911, buttressed by the resources of the Three Eastern Provinces and their strategic defensibility vis-à-vis North China.

(2) Wu P'ei-fu (1872–1939), who had been trained in the Confucian Classics and then by Japanese officers at the Paoting military academy, and who became the repository of many Chinese and British hopes for peace and order in Central China.

(3) Feng Yü-hsiang (1882–1948), a big, burly man of peasant origin, a soldier from the age of eleven and a graduate of Paoting, who was baptized by a Y.M.C.A. leader in 1913 and was known to his foreign missionary friends as the "Christian General" because he urged his well-disciplined troops to pursue Protestantism, austerity, practical education, and social

reform. Seizing Peking in 1924, Feng broke the power of the Peiyang war-lords and finally destroyed their façade of parliamentary government.

The intricate relations among these and other warlord figures defy detailed description. From 1922 to 1926 half a dozen inter-provincial wars erupted. They produced incalculable suffering among a populace oppressed by systematic pillaging and over-taxation. The material results of warlordism included inflation of the currency, disruption of trade, deterioration in railways and in public works for flood control and irrigation, and the recrudescence of the opium evil. The Ch'ing government in 1906 had begun a concerted attack on opium production and smoking, with such widespread patriotic support that the British Indian importation, already down to fifty thousand chests a year, was gradually reduced and stopped at the end of 1917. The much larger Chinese production, well on the way to extinction, was then revived by the simple warlord device of levying such high taxes on land suitable for poppy-growing that nothing but opium could meet the payments.

But the impact of warlordism with all its evils was greatest perhaps on the minds of patriotic youth. "In China today only cunning, crooked, vile, and ruthless people can flourish," wrote Liang Ch'i-ch'ao. Out of the desperation and humiliation of the period came a new revolution which began among the intellectual class.

14. The Rise and Decline of Nationalist China

The Revolution in Thought and Culture

Modern China has experienced demoralization and decline followed by revival and regeneration on a scale much larger than a mere dynastic cycle. If we compare the social ills of the early nineteenth century (of which increasing opium addiction was a symptom) with the moral fervor and dedication of the Maoist revolution of recent decades, we must conclude that an entire civilization has not only waned but also been remade. The decline reached its political nadir with warlordism after 1916, and revival began with the institution of party dictatorship. Ideologically the waning of Confucianism eventuated in Mao Tse-tung's adaptation of Marxism-Leninism. But in both politics and ideology there was a crucial transition period in which Western liberal models and ideas had an influence.

The warlord era was both chaotic and creative. This was no paradox, for in China's tradition-bound society, new ways could be tried out only after old patterns had been broken. In the decade after 1916 all sorts of ideas and practices, fads and experiments, bubbled forth unrestrained by authority. With political decline came a pluralism of intellectual, economic, and social developments. Underlying the intellectual ferment were processes of economic growth in the cities and of general social change.

The Economic and Social Background. While the decline of central power permitted the rise of disorder in the countryside, the decline of Western imports into China during and after World War I facilitated the rise of native industry in the foreign-administered treaty ports, protected from the warlordism which flourished in the provinces. A new merchant class, outside the ancient guild system, had been fostered by government policies after 1901. By 1914 there were over a thousand local chambers of commerce with 200,000 members. Large-scale enterprises, however, had been mostly British, but also American (particularly in Shanghai) and German (in Shantung until 1915). For example, China's paucity of petroleum resources had given a clear field to foreign imports of kerosene, to supplant vegetable oils for illumination, and of fuel oil, to compete with coal. These imports were dominated by Standard Oil subsidiaries and by the Asiatic Petroleum Company (A.P.C.), an affiliate of the Anglo-Dutch combine, Royal Dutch–Shell, formed in 1907. The long-continued import of cotton yarn and then of textiles had stimulated Chinese cotton-growing to supply British, Chinese, and Japanese mills in China. The market for cigarettes was first developed by an American-organized, London-based combine, the British-American Tobacco Company (B.A.T.), formed in 1902, which soon began through its compradors to lend seed and credit to North China tobacco cultivators. It set up a network of collecting points and curing factories to supply Chinese tobacco to half-a-dozen big B.A.T. cigarette factories, but Chinese firms, like Nanyang Brothers formed in 1905, were soon competing.

By 1914 a modern Chinese administrative and entrepreneurial class had emerged. (It was later stigmatized, anachronistically, as the "comprador class.") To be sure, it grew up under the wing of foreign educators, civil servants, and businessmen. This new class acquired experience in mission and other schools with mixed Sino-Western curricula, in the Maritime Customs, in the Post Office (which was separated from the Customs in 1911 and by 1918 employed a hundred foreigners and 27,000 Chinese), in the steamship lines, mills, shops, and general commerce of old treaty-port firms like Jardine, Matheson or Butterfield and Swire, or in new specialized concerns like the A.P.C. and B.A.T. This nascent middle class had learned modern economic ways in the treaty ports and from association with foreigners. They had accumulated the attitudes and skills necessary for economic development, and World War I gave them their opportunity.

Of the other ingredients needed for industrialization, Chinese capital had accumulated both in overseas communities and in the ports. It was now handled through modern Chinese banks, some of which grew up under government auspices and some as private concerns. These modern banks increased from 17 in 1914 to 102 in 1926, and put the old-style Shansi remittance banks out of business. Yet many factors still retarded the growth of financial resources. As an alternative to productive investment, old-fashioned moneylending, for instance, could still bring 12 per cent or often much more per year. Efforts at currency reform and unification had still not succeeded in abolishing the variable unit of account, the silver tael, even though silver dollars from government mints had come into general use under Yüan Shih-k'ai, most of them bearing his image.

A labor force meanwhile had been drawn to urban centers where cheap labor was needed to tend cotton spindles or sort tobacco, or to work in factories producing matches, flour, canned food, cement, and other mass-produced commodities. These opportunities for employment, newly accessible by railway and steamship, opened up alternatives to the closed routine of peasant life. Warlord taxation and conscription, population increase (presumably), and natural calamities stimulated migration to the cities. Urban life and factory work broke the bonds of the old family system. As wage-earning sons and womenfolk became financially independent, the family ceased to be a self-contained economic and social unit controlling the individual. Instead, the impersonal, universalistic criteria of function, not those of status or specific kinship ties, were applied in the urban labor market. In crowded slums and sweatshops, new values began to take over, and true proletarian factory workers began slowly to accumulate. By 1919 they numbered over a million, perhaps a million and a half.

Social change was evident not only in the rise of new capitalist and labor classes but also in a new status for youth and women. Young men had led the Revolution of 1911, and students now claimed the old privileged status of the scholar class. By 1915 the Ministry of Education listed 120,000 government schools of all sorts with about four million students—an increase over the old days, although only a few thousand reached the college level. Catholic and Protestant mission schools had perhaps half a million students in 1919. Protestant colleges set new standards in higher education. Missionaries had also pioneered in teaching girls, who were a sizable proportion of the thirteen thousand students in Protestant middle schools. In 1915 the first women's institution of higher education, Ginling College, opened at Nanking.

The emergence of these new social classes—merchant-entrepreneurs, factory laborers, and modern-style students—fostered the metamorphosis of Chinese society. Classical degree-holders (gentry in the narrow sense) gave way to younger men, students trained in the cities or even abroad. Landlords tended to become absentee city-dwellers, no longer presiding over the rural society. In short, the rise of city life, with its classes responsive to mass movements, was accompanied by a corresponding decline of rural life, where the leadership of the big households disappeared at the top and the peasant masses met grievous problems in the villages. Through improvements in transport and public health, China's rural population was probably increasing in numbers, but its standard of living was probably falling. Tenantry seems to have grown, as well as the landless peasantry—illiterate, rootless, jobless, and so available for banditry, warlord armies, or dirt-cheap coolie labor.

This collapse of the old society pressed the new student class to stand forth as leaders and saviors. Having inherited the tradition that scholars should advise the power-holders and serve the state-and-culture, they felt uniquely qualified by their studies to modernize and "save" the nation. Their motives and ideas sprang increasingly from foreign contact. Japan still took the largest number of students abroad (about two-fifths), but one-third now went to the United States. The remission to China in 1908 of $12 million (about two-thirds) of the American share of the Boxer indemnity had led to the establishment of Tsing Hua College at Peking, whence a steady flow of scholarship students to the United States began in 1911. (In 1924 the remainder of the indemnity was remitted, and the China Foundation for the Promotion of Education and Culture was established to use the remitted payments as they fell due.) To provide a labor force during the war in Europe, some 140,000 Chinese contract workers were recruited in 1916–1918 and sent to France, where Chinese student workers like James Yen (Yen Yang-ch'u) of the Y.M.C.A. began to develop methods of mass education. In France a work-and-study movement among Chinese students had already been initiated by Ts'ai Yüan-p'ei and others. All this experience fostered the long process of dissolving the ancient barrier between scholarship and labor.

France more than America became a source of political movements and doctrines among returned students in China. The industrial capitalism and factory labor class which gave socialism its *raison d'être* in Europe were still small-scale in China. But European theories of anarchism, especially the anarcho-communism of Peter Kropotkin, found a wide response. Kropotkin's *Mutual Aid: A Factor of Evolution* (1902) argued that mutual aid was as much a law of nature as mutual struggle, although restraints upon freedom must of course be destroyed before cooperation could flourish. Chinese students in Tōkyō and especially in Paris applied the anarchist teachings to China by opposing all elitist organizations and all government (hence nationalism itself), while advocating egalitarianism, mass movements, and direct action including assassination. This anarchist line of thought, combining puritanism, self-sacrifice, and the destruction of the established order with a utopian faith in the public will and voluntary association, was taken up by anarchist groups in major centers.

The New Thought at Peita.   The intellectual revolution centered at Peking National University (usually abbreviated as Peita) because of its prestige as the top of the educational system—only two other government universities as yet existed—and because of the faculty collected there in 1917 by the new chancellor, Ts'ai Yüan-p'ei. As a classical scholar, T'sai had risen to the Hanlin Academy at twenty-five, but later had joined the T'ung-meng Hui, studied Kant and other Western philosophers in Germany, and served as minister of education in the first republican cabinet under Sun and then Yüan in 1912. Returning from further study in Germany and France, he now set about converting Peita from a bureaucrat-ridden school that prepared officials to hold sinecures into a center of learning where ideas from all over the world might compete. His clarion call in 1912 for "education above politics . . . beyond political control," had been silenced by Yüan Shih-k'ai's authoritarian effort to revive Confucianism, and it would be muffled again by the rise of party dictatorship; in the long run, China's reconstruction would seek a new orthodoxy to buttress a new polity. But in the warlord era the very weakness of the political order (not its strength, as under a pluralistic rule of law) permitted freedom of thought to flourish for a time in a genuinely liberal fashion. Ts'ai encouraged the most divergent views at Peita and even the activity of professors and students, as individuals, in politics. The resultant intellectual flowering was a counterpart, on the plane of ideas, to the political revolution in 1911. This revolution in thought was carried on by men of a rare transitional generation, born generally in the 1880's, who had acquired a grounding in Chinese classical studies and then immersed themselves in Western culture abroad. They stood astride two worlds, as few have done before or since, and rejected China's traditional orthodoxy out of knowledge, not ignorance.

Ts'ai brought to Peita to be Dean of Letters a leading revolutionary journalist, Ch'en Tu-hsiu. Coming from a well-to-do official family, Ch'en had passed the classical examinations, studied in Japan and France, and participated in the 1911 revolution. He had become a zealous advocate of individual freedom in the style of the French Revolution—"liberty, equality, fraternity." He attributed China's decay to Confucianism: its family obligations enervated the individual; its disdain of commerce impoverished the economy. In the monthly he founded in 1915, *New Youth* ("La Jeunesse," *Hsin ch'ing-nien*), Ch'en called upon Chinese youth to "be independent, not servile . . . progressive, not conservative . . . dynamic, not passive . . . cosmopolitan, not isolationist . . . utilitarian, not emptily formalistic . . . scientific, not (merely) imaginative." At Peita, Ch'en continued to edit *New Youth,* which became a wide-open forum for discussion, printing letters to the editor, distributing as many as sixteen thousand copies, stirring up the student class all over the country.

Ch'en's principal ally at Peita was a younger man, Hu Shih, also from a scholar-official family and with an early training in the Classics. He had turned to philosophy at Cornell and under John Dewey at Columbia picked up the idea advocated by many revolutionists of using vernacular speech (*pai-hua*) for literary writing instead of the classical style (*wen-yen*). The vernacular novels of the Ming and Ch'ing (see pages 236–237) and also the missionary tracts had paved the way for writing *pai-hua*. Hu Shih, reflecting the "New Tide" in American poetry, pioneered in writing Chinese poetry in everyday words. He and a brilliant specialist in linguistics (Y. R. Chao) stated the case for written *pai-hua* and the movement was launched

Dr. Hu Shih in 1946, at Cornell University, lecturing on the history of Chinese philosophy. He was China's ambassador to the United States in the early war years 1938–1942.

with Ch'en Tu-hsiu's support in the pages of *New Youth,* which soon was written entirely in the vernacular.

This "literary renaissance" had several aims—first of all, to create a new written style to go with modern thought. "A dead language," declared Hu Shih, "cannot produce a living literature." His advocacy of Dewey's pragmatism and the scientific method led him to seek precision of statement, a new written language as a tool for critical thinking. A second aim was to reach the common people, both by making literacy easier for them and by creating a popular literature directly relevant to their lives. Ch'en Tu-hsiu wanted to abandon "stereotyped and over-ornamental" classicism in favor of "fresh and sincere" realism, to overthrow the "unintelligible literature . . . of the aristocratic few" and create a "plain, simple, and expressive literature of the people." A further aim of the movement was to emancipate the individual, by destroying the written language that had been "the repository of Confucian morality and Taoist superstition." A new literature of protest soon emerged. *New Youth* published in May 1918 a satirical short story, "The Diary of a Madman." In it the madman is convinced that people want to kill and eat him. He examines a history book: "Over every page were scrawled the words 'benevolence, righteousness, truth, virtue.'" Looking closer, however, he "discovered all over it a succession of two words between the lines: 'Eat men!'" This bitter indictment of the old society was typical of the author, Lu Hsün, whose short stories and essays soon made him the great pioneer figure in China's modern literature.

Thus by 1919 Peking University had become a meeting ground for manifold influences from abroad and from China's classical tradition. *New Youth* had been joined by other journals of discussion. In the resulting ferment, all the social and philosophical theories then current in the Western world and Japan were given expression, whether or not fully grasped—realism, utilitarianism, pragmatism, liberalism, individualism, socialism, anarchism, Darwinism, materialism, etc. Utilizing this armory of ideas, the wholesale criticism of the old society supported two principal protagonists, called by Ch'en "Mr. Democracy" and "Mr. Science." "Only these two gentlemen," he wrote, "can cure the dark maladies in Chinese politics, morality, learning, and thought." The ground was prepared, in ideas and means of communication, for a great explosion of intellectual energy in politics and learning.

The May Fourth Incident.   The phrase "May Fourth" derives from the 1919 student demonstration of that date in Peking, but has been taken in the Chinese numerary fashion to designate the whole intellectual movement roughly from 1917 to 1921 or even later, of which we have noted the beginning. The May 4 incident marked the emergence of nationalism as the dominant force in politics. This patriotic concern had been mounting ever since Japan's seizure of Shantung in 1914 and her subsequent Twenty-One Demands. China's entrance into World War I in August 1917 had been urged by some as a means of ensuring China's presence at the peace settlement in order to counter Japan's wartime expansion. However, Japan by secret notes had got British, French, and Italian agreement beforehand to her retaining the ex-German rights in Shantung, which also seemed implicit in the Lansing-Ishii agreement of November 1917 with the United States. The end of World War I in November 1918 brought jubilation in the West at the victory of democracy over militarism. But the Chinese delegation representing both Peking and Canton at the Paris Peace Conference in January 1919 soon found, like President Wilson, that his doctrine of self-determination and open diplomacy did not apply to East Asia. It developed that in 1918 the warlord government at Peking also had signed secret agreements confirming Japan's Shantung position. The arguments of China's able young diplomats were unavailing. Chinese public concern became unprecedentedly aroused. Hundreds of associations of Overseas Chinese, students, merchants, educators, labor unions, and political groups telegraphed their protests to Paris. As student indignation mounted at the Peking government's secret sell-out, news came of the Paris decision to leave Japan in Shantung. On May 4, over three thousand college students from thirteen institutions in Peking assembled at the Gate of Heavenly Peace (T'ien-an Men) and endorsed a manifesto. The subsequent demonstration erupted into violence when students beat one pro-Japanese official as a "traitor" and burned the house of a cabinet minister.

The historical impact of the May Fourth incident came from the students' subsequent program of political agitation. The Peking students organized a union, including girls as well as boys. They quickly secured nationwide support from the press and the merchants, from Sun Yat-sen and the Canton government, and from warlord rivals of the An-fu clique. Students in other cities, similarly organized, staged demonstrations, began boycotts of Japanese goods, and mobilized support with speeches in the streets. They stimulated a similar organization of the modern scholar class—professors, teachers, writers, journalists—for political action. In late May and early June student strikes closed the schools in more than two hundred cities. The students proved themselves a new force in politics, under the banner of anti-Japanese patriotism. The warlord Peking government, true to its belief in force, tried early in June to suppress the movement by imprisoning some 1150 student agitators, turning part of Peita into a jail. In response, girls now joined the boys in the streets. Shanghai merchants sympathetically closed their shops in a week-long patriotic strike. Workers struck for patriotic reasons in some forty Shanghai factories. This truly national movement, involving major classes and reaching a new level of popular activity, won the day. The Peking students marched victoriously out of jail. Three pro-Japanese "traitor" officials were dismissed. The cabinet resigned. China refused to sign the Versailles Treaty.

The New Culture Movement. Out of the political activity of the May Fourth incident came China's new nationalism of the 1920's, to be marked by the rise of party dictatorship, the growth of socialist thinking, and the struggle against imperialism. Meanwhile the intellectual ferment, out of which political activism had been generated, went steadily on—media of communication increased, Western ideas were eagerly sought after, old evils were more vigorously attacked and new values debated. This intellectual activity, in the year or two following May 4, 1919, generally stopped short of social and political action and was given the name "New Culture Movement." As its medium, several hundred new periodicals in the written vernacular made their appearance, though some only briefly. Newspapers, too, catered to the new thought and its re-examination of all values. Publication of books, including translations of Western works, rose sharply. By these means the intellectual revolution, begun by young professors in their thirties and students in their twenties, spread from Peita all over the country. Associations for innumerable purposes sprang up everywhere. Leading foreign scholars came to lecture. John Dewey spent two years in China and lectured frequently, often with Hu Shih interpreting. Bertrand Russell came for almost a year and, advocating state socialism, found a wide audience.

The attack on the old Confucian order of hierarchy and status denied the validity of the ancient "three bonds," the subordination of subject to ruler, of son to father, and of wife to husband. It denounced the three corresponding virtues—loyalty to superiors, filiality, and female subjection—as props of despotism in both state and family. The anti-Confucianists attacked the tyranny of parents, their arrangement of marriages, and the subordination of youth to family. The emancipation of women made great strides in this period, parallel with the movement for women's suffrage and equal rights in the West. The many conservatives who wanted to make Confucianism a state religion, which K'ang Yu-wei still advocated as he had in 1898, provoked increasing opposition. The Confucian proprieties or principles of social usage were denounced as fetters on the individual. Social harmony based on inequality of roles was anathematized. "Chinese culture," wrote Lu Hsün, "is a culture of serving one's masters, who are triumphant at the cost of the misery of the multitude."

The attack on Confucianism stimulated a critical re-evaluation of Chinese antiquity. Scholars at Peita, "antiquity-doubters," reappraised the authenticity of the Classics. Liang Ch'i-ch'ao, now retired from politics, and Hu Shih among others led a wide-ranging "reorganization of the national heritage," winnowing the grain from the chaff within the great tradition. Thus they restudied the ancient philosopher Mo-tzu, the history of Buddhism in China, the vernacular novels, the thought of the Ch'ing period. This concern for the national heritage was heightened by disillusionment with European "materialism" after World War I. Liang returned from the Paris Peace Conference convinced of the spiritual bankruptcy of Western civilization, which had become materialistic, withered, dry, and sick from a "spiritual famine." A whole series of controversies argued the merits of one issue after another. Religion was debated, defended, and widely decried. When the World Student Christian Federation met in Peking in 1922, a nationwide antireligious and anti-Christian movement was organized among students.

In proportion as the intellectual and cultural revolution triumphed over the traditional order, it lost its unity of aim. A split occurred between those inclined toward academic studies, reform, and gradual evolution and those inclined toward political action, rebellion, and violent revolution. People sorted themselves out, partly according to background and personal temperament. The pragmatic approach to recreating China's civilization was led by Hu Shih, who inveighed against "isms," both the various forms of socialism and other all-embracing creeds. Instead, he urged a concentration on "problems," to be analyzed by the "genetic method" and with "a critical attitude": "There is no liberation *in toto,* or reconstruction *in toto.* Liberation means liberation from this or that institution, from this or that belief, for this or that individual; it is liberation bit by bit, drop by drop." To many, this seemed inadequate to meet China's problems and emotionally unsatisfying as well. Hu's long-term program of education had no short-term political method. It could only produce liberal manifestoes asking warlord governments to guarantee civil liberties, all in vain. Chinese supporters of individualism could not appeal to a positive doctrine of individual rights and freedoms like that of Western liberalism. The latter had derived from the Western doctrines of natural rights and the supremacy of law, but these had no counterparts in China capable of supporting a genuine Chinese liberalism. Instead, the would-be liberal in warlord China, before he could "selfishly" demand his own civil liberties, had to help create a modern nation-state, as his new loyalty to country also demanded. For a time the focus of concern had been how to emancipate the individual. But after 1921 it shifted back to the more customary theme, how to strengthen the state. Nationalism took precedence over liberalism. Political movements soon arose that would again try to mobilize and control the individual and his cultural activity.

The Introduction of Marxism-Leninism. The May Fourth incident had shown what students could accomplish when organized for political action. This potentiality was plain to Sun Yat-sen, then in Shanghai, and he set about recruiting students as part of his general reorganization of the Kuomintang. Political action also appealed to the romantic temperament of Ch'en Tu-hsiu. Just at this point, the example and the doctrines of Soviet Russia came to hand in practical form. One whole wing of the New Culture movement, like some major Kuomintang leaders, soon felt they had found the action program they had been seeking.

The intellectual appeal of Marxism lay partly in its claim to being "scientific," in an age when science seemed to be the secret of Western superiority. Marx's concept of "historical materialism"—that society progresses through a sequence of stages (primitive, slave-owning, feudal, capitalist, socialist) by virtue of "class struggle" between ruling and exploited classes for control of the "means of production"—appealed to students in need of a system to explain "progress" and simplify the confusing events of history. The optimistic belief that class struggle and exploitation could be obviated by abolishing private ownership of the means of production was particularly attractive in an underdeveloped country where industrialization and all its problems were just beginning. Moreover, Marxism had been capped by Lenin's concept of the revolutionary vanguard, the disciplined intellectual elite of the Communist Party, and by his explanation of colonial imperialism as due to the growth of international monopoly capitalism. While European Marxism, originally prescribed for advanced industrial societies, had thus far been a very minor motif in China's intellectual history, Marxism-Leninism was something new. In the China of 1919 its messianic vision was made more credible by the startling Soviet success in seizing power. It seemed to offer an all-embracing solution to China's problems. On the theoretical plane, it provided a self-consistent, universalistic, and "scientific" view of world history which enabled one to reject the imperialistic West in the name of Western "scientific thought" and explain China's humiliating backwardness as due to her bondage to "capitalist imperialism" (e.g., Japan and the Western treaty powers), which had allied itself with "warlord feudalism" (e.g., the An-fu clique). On the political level, Leninism offered a new and tighter method of party organization and a technique for seizing power and using it to mobilize the populace and recreate society —actually, the latest step in borrowing political technology from the Western world. For the individual, finally, Leninism claimed to offer a way toward self-discipline and sacrifice for patriotic ends.

While these appeals would grow stronger with time, they made their appearance at a propitious moment, when patriotic fervor was seeking organized expression. China's "betrayal" at Versailles offered dramatic proof that the real national enemy was "imperialism." Henceforth nationalism and anti-imperialism seemed interlinked, just as Lenin said. Some leaders of the New Culture movement proceeded to political action. In the pages of *New Youth,* Li Ta-chao, a professor of philosophic bent much concerned for the Chinese peasants' liberation, had already hailed "The Victory of Bolshevism"; in May 1919 he edited a whole issue on Marxism. Study groups in Peking and Shanghai took up various kinds of socialist theory. (A Hunan student, Mao Tse-tung, who had assisted Li in the Peita library, returned to Changsha in March 1919 and led another such group.) By mid-1920 Ch'en Tu-hsiu and Li Ta-chao had wholeheartedly accepted Marxism-Leninism. Ch'en met with others in September to plan the founding of a Chinese Communist Party. By the time Mao and eleven others attended the Shanghai meeting of July 1921, now regarded as the founding First Congress of the Chinese Communist Party, small party branches existed also in Peking, Changsha, Wuhan, Canton, and Tsinan.

The Soviet contribution to this sudden development had begun with an offer to give up all privileges under the old tsarist unequal treaties, which aroused widespread pro-Soviet enthusiasm. Agents of the Communist International (Comintern, organized in March 1919) helped set up the first Communist organization in Shanghai, with its news agency, publications, and branches and also assisted at the First Congress of the Party. At this stage Comintern know-how was an essential ingredient. Activists among the worker-students in postwar France, many of them from Hunan, in 1921 set up their own Young China Communist Party in Paris. Chou En-lai, a graduate of Nankai University, became the most famous of the group of Communist leaders who returned from France.

After 1921 the growth of party organizations, both Communist and Kuomintang, confronted intellectuals with a painful choice, to pursue scholarship eschewing politics, or to subordinate learning to political action. When Hu Shih and Ch'en Tu-hsiu parted company early in 1921, after four years' collaboration, they symbolized the alternatives.

Writers soon faced a similar choice. As in the European Renaissance, the written speech of everyday life was just beginning to be used, tentatively and experimentally, in all the forms of literature. New styles and themes for novels, stories, essays, poetry, drama, criticism, all awaited fresh creation in Chinese. Many beginnings were made, many of them not yet studied. But for most writers the overwhelming preoccupation became the social revolution—the evils of the old order, the struggle to remake it. Writers believed that theirs was a didactic social function, to instruct their fellow countrymen and save China. Those who individualistically pursued romanticism or "art for art's sake," often on Anglo-American models, were soon overshadowed by those with a social purpose, like Lu Hsün, desirous of serving their country as spiritual physicians.

The most influential early group, the Society for Literary Studies, took over the editing of *Short Story* magazine published by the Commercial Press. They advocated a varied and realistic "humane literature," stressed the translation of Western fiction, and encouraged new talent, including several women. A rival group was the Creation Society formed by Kuo Mo-jo and others in Japan, dedicated at first to an all-out, rebellious romanticism. It published candid autobiographic confessions in which sexual desire and patriotic sentiment alike met frustration and left the hero usually remorseful and guilt-ridden. In the mid-1920's, however, the Creation Society turned with equal energy to Marxism. As Kuo Mo-jo wrote on his conversion in 1924, "I am now able to impose order on all the ideas which I could not reconcile; I have found the key to all the problems which appeared to me self-contradictory and insoluble"—a statement which epitomized the appeal of Marxism-Leninism and augured ill for the liberal-individualist approach to literature as art. Lacking a modern tradition and established artistic canons in a new medium, writers perhaps more readily accepted a primarily social function in the revolutionary process.

The Background of the Nationalist Revolution

The 1920's saw the height of warlord disorder and the rise of a revolution to overcome it. The first aim of the revolution was national reunification. Beyond this were other goals, foreign and domestic. In foreign relations, the revolution aimed to abolish foreign privileges and influence under the unequal treaties. Every patriot was anti-imperialist. On the domestic scene, however, interests diverged. Social revolution, through mass organization of factory labor and even of peasants in the villages, emerged as a possibility. But the main leadership eventually turned against social revolution, suppressed the mass movements, and consolidated its power on a platform of national unity and anti-imperialism. As a process the revolution first accumulated its various elements during a preparatory period from 1921 to mid-1925, came to high tide for two years thereafter, and then receded. As a step in China's political modernization, the rise of the Kuomintang meant that a new form of government, party dictatorship, had finally been devised to supplant the dynastic system. The treaty system also took on its final form, modified to permit more exercise of Chinese sovereignty. Yet both these developments stopped part way. The Kuomintang dictatorship did not get firm control over all the provinces of China. The revolution which brought it to power, mainly in the cities, also stopped short of the countryside. Similarly China's recovery of sovereignty failed to abolish extra-territoriality. Thus the Nationalist Revolution, like the Revolution of 1911, got limited results.

The influence of the West was also meeting its inevitable limitations. Neither Western entrepreneurs in the ports nor missionaries in the interior could deal with the problem of China's political order. No treaty-power government could offer China a model for her reorganization, or show how to harness her new nationalism for purposes of industrialization. The West had helped destroy the old order, but how could it now help build a new one? This question underlay the post–World War I diplomatic settlement of 1921–1922.

The Slowness of Treaty Revision. The treaty powers looked forward to China's developing a stable central government like any other nation. The treaty system had always kept open the possibility of its own liquidation, since the treaties were all made between two sovereign powers, one of which (China) accepted limitations on its sovereignty. Foreign diplomats and Chinese nationalists disagreed less on the desirability of China's recovering full sovereignty than on the speed and procedures with which to accomplish it. The principal effort by the powers to deal with the China problem was made at the Washington Conference (November 12, 1921–February 2, 1922). The settlement was in four main categories, although it lacked any means of enforcement, either in sanctions and operative clauses or in binding commitments of power politics.

In the first place, the Anglo-Japanese alliance, which might embroil Britain and the Commonwealth in any Japanese-American conflict, was now abolished, with no equally firm alliance to take its place. Second, limitation of naval armament in capital ships, one primary purpose of the conference, was accepted on a five-five-three ratio for Britain, the United States, and Japan, with the proviso that no British or American naval bases would be developed east of Singapore or west of Hawaii. Third, Japan agreed to withdraw from Shantung and also withdraw her forces from the Northeast Asian mainland, where intervention against the Bolshevik revolution in mid-1918 had brought Allied forces, especially Japanese, into the Maritime Province, northern Manchuria, and eastern Siberia. Thus, in return for an assurance of her naval domination of the western Pacific, Japan withdrew on the Asian mainland to her territorial position in 1905, except for Korea. Finally, the Nine-Power Treaty formally proclaimed everyone's support of the Open Door and the territorial integrity and administrative independence of China and moved toward gradual liquidation of the treaty system by calling for conferences on the Chinese customs tariff and on extraterritoriality.

As a consequence of these agreements, Japan withdrew from Shantung, and Britain eventually restored Weihaiwei. But the tariff conference was not held until 1925–1926, and even then failed to agree except on the important point that China might exercise tariff autonomy by 1929. Similarly the extraterritoriality commission, meeting in Peking only in 1926, achieved no result. Inhibiting this international effort to facilitate China's growth as a nation-state was the lack of an effective central government. Banditry and warlord excesses endangered foreign lives and property. The inability of the Chinese authorities to perform their international obligations undercut their claims to exercise rights of sovereignty. Thus China's internal disorder checked the proposed revision of the unequal-treaty system.

The Soviet Approach to the Chinese Revolution.   The Soviet impact on China in the 1920's was still another phase of Western influence. But in contrast with the treaty powers' halfhearted efforts at a gradual reform of China's foreign relations, Moscow offered China a working model of domestic revolution. As early as 1912, Lenin had suggested that the Communist-led proletarian revolution of industrialized Europe should support Asian nationalist revolutions that might be led by "bourgeois-democratic" movements against colonialism and imperialism. At the second Comintern congress in 1920 Lenin's "theses on the national and colonial question" argued that, just as Western capitalism had prolonged its life by exploiting the cheap labor and raw materials of its Asian colonies, so the Western proletariat could now, by a "flank attack," ally with the Asian bourgeoisie against their enemy, "capitalist imperialism," which was the economic exploiter of the colonial peoples and the political ally of the reactionary "feudal" ruling class in Asia. Lenin's theory of imperialism thus unified the world scene. It gave historical significance, within a single cosmology, to all the elements in Chinese politics. One's military rivals could be stigmatized as "warlords" representing the "feudal reaction" of a dying order. Urban merchants and middle-class individuals could be classified as the "national bourgeoisie," representing the capitalist stage of history, which it would now be possible to "leap over." With the use of Soviet aid and of the Chinese peasantry, a "united front" could be developed, led by the "proletariat" in the Communist Party. By this tactic the "bourgeois nationalist" movement could be supported to defeat foreign "imperialism" while at the same time (and this was essential) the "proletarian party" could be organized to seize power from within. Lenin foresaw a wide range of opportunities—Communist parties in Asia could make "temporary agreements and even alliances" with "bourgeois nationalist" movements in a united front, or alternatively, they could develop their own communist "soviets of workers and peasants" as centers of independent power.

This range of theoretical alternatives was inherited by Lenin's successors. Trotsky advocated independent soviets in China, while Stalin advocated a united front with the Kuomintang. In Marxist thinking a true party must represent a class, and so Stalin had to argue that the Kuomintang was only a coalition or "bloc of four classes": proletarian workers, peasants, petty bourgeoisie, and capitalists, later called national bourgeoisie. These alternatives gave the Soviet approach to China a built-in dualism—it could stress either a united front of all revolutionary classes against foreign imperialism and its "lackeys," or a class struggle within China, with soviets of proletarians and peasants fighting the Chinese bourgeoisie plus the feudal reactionaries, landlords, militarists, and their imperialist supporters. Between these two tactics lay a middle ground of coalition with some classes against others, for example, with the "petty bourgeoisie" but against the "national bourgeoisie."

In addition to this flexibility of doctrine, the Soviet government pursued a dual approach to China on the two levels of open diplomacy and revolutionary subversion. Diplomacy conducted by the Soviet foreign ministry had begun with the offer to give up the former tsarist privileges. Several missions to Peking led to hard bargaining and an actual reassertion of former tsarist aims in Northeast Asia. The eventual Soviet treaty with Peking in May 1924 provided for joint administration of the Chinese Eastern Railway and a dominant Russian influence in Outer Mongolia. Simultaneously, under the Soviet program of subversion, Comintern agents helped develop the Chinese Communist Party apparatus and a Communist-led labor movement, and also made contact with leading warlords in the North and with Sun Yat-sen in the South. By this time events in Russia had necessitated Lenin's introduction in 1921 of the New Economic Policy of retrenchment, a "temporary retreat" from Communism. This was the less extreme and less fearsome Soviet image presented to Sun and his followers.

The Kuomintang Reorganization and Comintern Alliance. Sun Yat-sen was groping for a party organization that could make the transition from a seizure of power to a civil government exercising "political tutelage" over the unsophisticated Chinese masses. The Soviet party dictatorship now seemed to be part of a broad trend of history, while fascism in Italy after 1919 offered an example of party dictatorship not based on class war. The May Fourth incident inspired Sun to revive and reorganize the Kuomintang, and new general regulations, party principles, and a manifesto, were all three issued on January 1, 1923. Reorganization was formally completed at the party's First Congress in January 1924. As part of this process, Sun gradually developed a working alliance with the Comintern.

Sun was pushed in this direction by several circumstances. The treaty powers had dealt only with the Peking government and had done little to liquidate the treaty system. His demand in September 1923 that they let his Canton government use the local Maritime Customs surplus was sharply refused; the treaty powers concentrated naval vessels at Canton to prevent his seizing the Customs. His repeated requests for Western aid got no response. His domestic vicissitudes had been equally disappointing. The Kuomintang rump parliament at Canton was as prone to splintering as the warlord parliament at Peking. Sun's uneasy cooperation with a local warlord had collapsed, forcing him to flee to Shanghai. He needed help.

The Kuomintang-Comintern alliance meant cooperation with the nascent Chinese Communist Party (CCP). The Second Congress of the CCP in mid-1922 favored an alliance with the Kuomintang (KMT) on a parallel or equal basis. However, instead of an alliance between parties, it was arranged on Comintern orders that Communist Party members would join the Kuomintang as individuals, and keep their own separate organization, thus forming a "bloc within" instead of a "bloc without." Sun permitted Li Ta-chao to retain his CCP membership when he joined the KMT. Ch'en Tu-hsiu then joined on similar terms and was given high KMT positions. Others followed.

With Soviet advice Sun now began the creation of a party army and sent his devoted military assistant, Chiang Kai-shek, to the Soviet Union to study its methods. The KMT began to be represented at Comintern meetings. After returning to Canton early in 1923 Sun began using CCP members in important posts. He took the technical guidance of an able Soviet adviser, Michael Borodin, who drafted the KMT's new constitution and soon had a political institute teaching propagandists how to organize mass support. On the Soviet model the KMT now set up local cells which in turn elected delegates at higher levels (county and province), each of which elected an executive committee, up to the national party congress, which chose a central executive committee, whose standing committee could now by "democratic centralism" dominate a centralized Leninist-type party.

On the Communist side of this marriage of convenience, the Third CCP Congress, in June 1923, by a bare majority acquiesced in the "bloc within" type of alliance. It agreed that the KMT should be the "central force of the national revolution." Mao Tse-tung, for example, as head of the CCP organization department, cooperated for a time with a KMT stalwart in "coordinating" the two party organizations. But the small CCP, with fewer than a thousand members, opposed close coordination as giving the KMT too much control over its membership. Their dual strategy was now to

Sun Yat-sen and his young wife, Soong Ch'ing-ling, a graduate of Wesleyan College for Women (Macon, Georgia), en route to Peking at the end of 1924.

capture the KMT from within while developing their own mass organizations outside it.

Sun Yat-sen's attitude in welcoming individual Communists into his party was both self-confident and practical. He saw how effectively students could organize workers and peasants. The few hundred members of the CCP were a mere handful compared with the scores of thousands of the KMT. While Lenin is said to have referred to Sun Yat-sen's "inimitable, one might say, virginal naiveté," Sun felt certain that his party could remain the principal Chinese partner of the Russians, who he felt would "not be fooled by these youngsters" of the CCP.

Kuomintang Ideology and the Party Army. To go with the new party apparatus, Sun Yat-sen needed as always a revolutionary ideology. While on the sidelines in Shanghai in 1918 and later, he had developed a theory of "psychological reconstruction." This included the idea that "knowing is more difficult than doing," an acknowledgment that the revolution thus far had lacked in ideas. In his own mind Sun did not accept the Leninist thesis that capitalism inevitably produces imperialism. He favored the struggle of oppressed nations against oppressing nations, but he did not link this with a class struggle inside each nation. Instead, in response to Borodin's request that the KMT be given a more formal ideology, he put forward his own

*Chiang Kai-shek as
superintendent of the
Whampoa Military Academy
in 1925, aged 38.*

revised statement of the *Three Principles of the People*. In these rather discursive lectures in the winter of 1922–1923, the principle of nationalism, which in 1905 had been anti-Manchu and in 1914 had been disregarded in Sun's platform, now stressed anti-imperialism. It also included self-determination both for the Chinese people and for minorities within China. The principle of people's rights, often translated as democracy, distinguished between popular sovereignty and the administrative capacity of the government. Sun piously hoped to "make the government the machinery, and the people the engineer," but this was to be done only through the devices of election, initiative, referendum, and recall (copied from the American Progressive movement of a bygone era), which had never become operative in China. The principle of people's livelihood (*min-sheng*) remained the vaguest of all, since Sun specifically denied the Marxist thesis of class struggle and reiterated his earlier concepts of the limitation of capital and the equalization of landholdings on the single-tax basis advocated by Henry George. Of the three principles, nationalism was the dominant core around which unanimity could be achieved.

Just as important as the party apparatus and its ideology was the indoctrinated party army. After Chiang Kai-shek's return from four months in the Soviet Union, he became head of a new military academy at Whampoa below Canton, aided by a corps of Soviet advisers. The leading CCP representative, Chou En-lai, was deputy head of the political education department, which Communists steadily infiltrated but without ultimate success. Soon two regiments of cadets constituted a KMT "party army," trained to fight for Sun Yat-sen's ideology.

Sun died unexpectedly on March 12, 1925, and his figure became the object of a revolutionary cult reminiscent of the ancestor reverence accorded a dynastic founder. His writings became a creed of "Sun Yat-senism." To carry on his cause, the Nationalist Government (Kuo-min cheng-fu) was formed at Canton on July 1 as a military-party dictatorship with Wang Ching-wei, one of Sun's principal political heirs, as its chairman, just as the revolution developed into a great mass movement.

The Kuomintang's Rise to Power

Labor Organization.   By the summer of 1925 the two revolutionary parties, the dominant KMT and the small CCP, faced an explosive opportunity: an upsurge of patriotic anti-imperialism combined with a militant anticapitalist labor movement. Each of these movements had its own rationale. Six years after the May Fourth movement, the treaty powers still exercised nearly all their accumulated privileges: the Japanese Kwantung leased territory and South Manchurian Railway dominated southern Manchuria. The South Manchurian Railway and the British-owned Kailan Mining Administration policed China's biggest coal mines. At Tientsin, concession areas were still governed by the British, French, Japanese, and Italians. Legation guards still paraded through Peking. Most of Shanghai was governed by the foreign (mainly British) rate-payers through the Shanghai Municipal Council. The trade of South China was largely dominated by Hong Kong. Foreigners still held the top posts in the Chinese Maritime Customs, Salt Revenue, and Post Office administrations, revenues from which went chiefly to pay China's foreign creditors. Foreign steamship lines and gunboats plied China's inland waters all the way into Hunan and Szechwan. Many modern industrial enterprises were foreign-owned.

Any middle-school student could add details to this humiliating picture of semicolonialism, which the competing warlords of North and Central China and Manchuria could not alter, some of them indeed being part of it. The stimuli for anti-imperialism were most visible in the great port cities— Shanghai, Canton, Hong Kong, Wuhan, Tientsin—where the new factory labor class was also heavily concentrated. The evils of factory work in China had become as great as the unlimited supply of manpower: a twelve-hour day, more or less; a seven-day week with a very few festival holidays; unskilled peasants paid by piece-work, with a high rate of turnover; child labor exploited along with that of mothers, their nursing babies often parked under the basins of boiling water in the silk filatures; uncontrolled hazards to body and health; friction with Chinese labor contractors and foreign managers and foremen; and pay so low that all family adults had to work—such conditions, reminiscent of Europe a century earlier, gave the Chinese labor movement its own impetus.

A modern labor movement required, of course, new forms of labor organization. In China's traditional handicraft guilds, shop masters still dominated the artisans and apprentices, and craft solidarity was stressed, not working-class solidarity. Nor were the old secret societies suited to leading a labor movement; in Shanghai the powerful "green gang" (*Ch'ing-pang*) and "red gang" (*Hung-pang*) could not rise above the underworld level of opium smuggling, prostitution, crime, and protection rackets. Some workingmen's benefit associations had been formed, mostly among miners or railway workers, but the most efficient early union was built up after 1914 among Chinese seamen in international shipping. With the May Fourth movement had come a wave of strikes. Thereafter the organizing efforts of anarchist, KMT, and other political groups were gradually overshadowed by those of the CCP, which initiated the first all-China congress of labor organizations at Canton in May 1922 and fomented strikes in Hunan, Hupei, and along the North China railways.

By 1925 the foreign treaty-port establishment and the provincial military governors seemed to much of the articulate Chinese public to constitute an evil partnership of "imperialism" and "warlordism." KMT and CCP alike saw these twin evils as the enemies of "nationalism." Chinese industrialists were the more ready to oppose them because of the recrudescence of foreign competition since World War I. In Shanghai early in 1925 union organization and strikes increased, and at the same time merchants in the Chinese General Chamber of Commerce protested against regulation and "taxation without representation" under the Shanghai Municipal Council. When its British-officered police killed thirteen demonstrators on Nanking Road on May 30, there ensued a nationwide multiclass movement of protests, demonstrations, strikes, boycotts, and militant anti-imperialism. This "May Thirtieth movement" dwarfed all previous antiforeign demonstrations. In similar fashion, on June 23, a demonstration on the Shaki bund, the roadway facing the consular island of Shameen at Canton, led to shooting between Whampoa cadets and Anglo-French troops and to the death of fifty-two Chinese. There then ensued a great fifteen-month strike and boycott against Hong Kong, crippling British trade in South China. These tumultuous events, with many smaller incidents and issues, afforded a great opportunity for student agitation and for mobilizing all classes in a great national cause. The CCP exploited this opportunity. Its young enthusiasts moved into the center of affairs. Its membership, including the Youth Corps, rapidly increased to about twenty thousand by late 1925. It bade fair to capture the leadership of the mass movement in the cities.

TREATY PORT LIFE. *Top: Returned students from Britain, France, and the United States. Bottom: Sikh policeman directing Shanghai traffic.*

The Northern Expedition and the KMT-CCP Split. The nationwide response to the May Thirtieth movement of 1925 marked the onset of high tide for the Nationalist Revolution. It also raised the question of the revolution's ultimate aims and began to strain the unity of the disparate groups that were working together at Canton. The growth of the CCP, which was abetted by the ambitious leaders of the left-wing KMT who now dominated the Canton government, put the right wing of the KMT on the defensive. Its major interest was anti-imperialism on a united, national basis rather than through class warfare. It wanted an ideology of national unity which would be multiclass and both anti-imperialist and anti-Communist. For the CCP and the Comintern, which controlled its party line, the choice was difficult—either to break with the KMT entirely, facing the danger of being overpowered by it, or to keep working with the still dominant left KMT against the right, hoping to split the two. The Communists were developing independent power in the labor movement, and were also leading peasant movements.

On balance, however, the trend of events seemed still to justify the KMT-CCP united front, and Stalin chose to continue it. The Second Kuomintang Congress of January 1926, at which the left KMT held the balance of power, also continued the alliance. It kept leading Communists in the KMT secretariat and organization bureau, and seven (constituting 20 per cent) on the central executive committee. This arrangement was approved by both Wang Ching-wei, the leader of the left wing, and Chiang Kai-shek, the principal military commander. Chiang's Whampoa cadets had already defeated local forces in the Canton area, but the militant organization for the Hong Kong strike and boycott had been taken over by the CCP and was creating at Canton an armed, Communist-led government-within-a-government. Communist influence was expanding within the KMT apparatus and mass organizations and practically took over the navy. Allegedly in self-defense, Chiang on March 20 staged a *coup d'état* at Canton, ousting part of the CCP leadership and some Soviet advisers, while simultaneously reaffirming his loyalty to the Canton-Moscow alliance. Thus in the spring of 1926 Chiang Kai-shek emerged as the principal proponent of China's military unification, and the CCP again faced the choice of continuing to work with the KMT or turning against it. Once again Moscow favored collaboration: Stalin needed his alliance with Chiang as a means of arguing against Trotsky, just as Chiang still needed a united revolutionary effort with CCP and Soviet support for a great Northern Expedition.

This great military campaign, long planned by Sun to smash the warlords and reunify China, was also aimed at rising above local conflicts at Canton and expanding the revenue area of the government. Launched in July 1926, the expedition, preceded by its newly trained propagandists, advanced rapidly and absorbed some thirty-four warlord armies or contingents by the time it reached the Yangtze. The Nationalist troops showed respect for the people and were welcomed. Only one regiment eventually proved to be under Communist control; CCP cells had not been widely established in the military forces. At the end of 1926 the Nationalist Government, still dominated by the left KMT, moved from Canton to Wuhan. The Comintern in Moscow followed Stalin's lead and ordered the CCP to stay with it. The CCP therefore continued as a "bloc within," largely prevented from exploiting peasant unrest or building independent military power.

As the Northern Expedition in the spring of 1927 continued its successful take-over of Central China, the Nationalist Revolution entered a phase in which the military forces played a larger role, and purely political manipulation of the movement as a result became less feasible. The preponderant anti-Communist view of the military soon fostered a split in which first Chiang and the KMT military joined the right KMT in turning against the left KMT and the CCP, and then the left KMT also turned against the CCP, eventually rejoining the right. Thus the Nationalist drive for unity and a new political order purged itself of the divisive Communist program for class struggle and social revolution.

These developments took place after Chiang Kai-shek had moved down the Yangtze to take over the rice basket and industrial base of the region around Shanghai. Just at this point, on April 6, 1927, Peking authorities raided the Soviet Embassy and seized incriminating evidence of subversion (Li Ta-chao and other Communist leaders were later executed). Then at Shanghai, on April 12, Chiang's forces with foreign concurrence supported local anti-Communist elements who destroyed the armed CCP organization and labor movement by a sudden coup and reign of terror. On April 18 Chiang set up his own government at Nanking with the support of most of the KMT central executive committee in defiance of Wuhan. In this crisis the Comintern representatives and CCP leaders at Wuhan were still instructed from Moscow to follow Stalin's line of cooperation with the left KMT. But the latter, finally disillusioned and alarmed, broke in July with its Communist colleagues and expelled them. On August 1 an uprising of Communist troops at Nanchang began an open civil war between the two parties. The Comintern blamed Ch'en Tu-hsiu, as secretary-general of the CCP, for the "opportunism" which had led to failure, "in complete contradiction to the instructions of the Comintern." (He was expelled in 1929, a scapegoat for Stalin's misjudgments.) Mao Tse-tung, who in a February 1927 report on the peasant movement in Hunan had advocated a peasant rising contrary to the Moscow directive of that period, now led a so-called "Autumn Harvest" insurrection in Hunan. It was soon suppressed. Communist putsches at Swatow and Canton both failed. The youthful CCP leadership was executed, driven underground in the cities, or forced into the countryside.

The way was open for Chiang Kai-shek and the right-wing KMT, with the support of the Chinese bankers and businessmen of Shanghai, to make peace with the left KMT and build up their Nanking regime as the central government of China. Warlordism was not yet wiped out, but China was more united than it had been for a decade. At last it had a government intent on building a modern nation-state and reasserting the national dignity.

The Revolution and the Foreign Powers. The response of the treaty powers to China's dramatic awakening to nationalism was to give ground and acknowledge many of its claims. After the May Thirtieth movement of 1925, Chinese were added to the Shanghai Municipal Council; municipal parks were eventually opened to Chinese residents; and the Shanghai Mixed Court was supplanted by a purely Chinese district court. The powers in 1926 permitted Canton to collect the customs surtaxes they had refused to Sun Yat-sen in 1923. Britain gave up concessions in Hankow and Kiukiang.

The fighting in 1925–1927 forced most of the Protestant missionaries to withdraw from the interior, while an international force of forty thousand troops gathered to defend Shanghai. When Nationalist troops, taking Nanking in March 1927, killed six foreigners, British and American gunboats laid down a protective barrage but later a settlement was worked out. Considering the passions and fears of the day, rather little Sino-foreign violence erupted. Like Britain, the American State Department maintained neutrality and refused to be obsessed by the Bolshevik menace, despite the conviction of the Shanghai foreign community that Chinese antiforeignism was a Moscow plot. The Western powers did little to prevent the rise or precipitate the fall of Soviet influence on the revolution.

Another Nationalist Northern Expedition in 1928 occupied Peking ("Northern Capital") and renamed it Peiping ("Northern Peace"). By the end of 1928 the Nationalist Government had received international recognition. The "Young Marshal" of Manchuria (Chang Hsueh-liang, son of the old warlord Chang Tso-lin), brought the Three Eastern Provinces into political union with the rest of China. China's unity was nominally complete. Led by a new generation of "returned students" who had studied mainly in the West, the government strove to consolidate national resources and abolish the unequal treaties. Extraterritoriality for the major powers continued, but Nanking issued new law codes and secured new treaties placing many minor foreign nationalities under Chinese jurisdiction. Tariff autonomy was fully recovered by 1933, as well as control over the Maritime Customs, the Salt Revenue Administration, and the Post Office. Foreign concession areas were reduced from thirty-three to thirteen.

This vigorous Nationalist foreign policy, whittling away treaty privileges, slowed down after 1931 because Japan's new aggression gave China and the Western powers a common defensive interest in preserving the Western legal position in China. As Nanking turned against Marxist-Leninist class struggle and confronted Japanese aggression, it toned down its attack on foreign privilege and found a community of interest with the foreigners, particularly the British, Americans, French, and Canadians, who continued to participate in Chinese life as privileged persons, maintaining colleges and hospitals, banks, trading firms, and investments.

The Comintern strategy of the 1920's seems in retrospect to have had little if any chance of success. The political organization of urban labor, in order to seize power as in Europe, was still a forlorn hope in China. Labor unions could develop strength only in the few port cities where the new Nationalist leadership and foreign interests were also most heavily concentrated. Lacking a party army, the CCP could not seize the cities. Nor could it seize the KMT from within, since the Comintern had given the KMT a centralized Soviet-style party structure, difficult to subvert. The peasantry meanwhile remained largely unexploited for political purposes in the 1920's. With the CCP so small and inexperienced and Moscow's directives coming from such an obfuscating distance, a Communist success was hardly to be expected. From their victory the KMT and Chiang Kai-shek drew the fatal conclusion, typical of the time, that national political power depended fundamentally on professional armies supported by industries. They remained blind to the potentialities of peasant organization as another source of political power, also capable of lending support to armies. This was the view of an entire generation, older than the Communists, with more ties to the cities and the landlord class than to the peasantry, whose ambitions did not include a social revolution in the villages.

The Decade of the Nanking Government

The Nanking period, from 1928 to the time of the full-fledged Japanese attack of 1937, forms a distinct epoch during which China faced toward the Western world, while the latter, unfortunately, was absorbed in its own problems. This decade saw the onset of Stalinism in the Soviet Union, the Great Depression in the United States, and Nazism in Germany. Japan's aggression against China was unchecked from outside the East Asian scene. Nanking thus balanced precariously among three major influences—the pervasive though somewhat superficial Western contact; the mounting aggression of Japan; and the unresolved problems of the Chinese countryside. The Nationalist regime looked for inspiration both to the modern West and to the Chinese past, but remained stuck in between. This bifocal dilemma, with all its false hopes and frustrations, may be typical of new nations modernizing late on the ruins of ancient empires. The old regimes and traditions seem bankrupt, but Western models do not fit the local scene—patriotic leaders look to both, but in vain.

One striking feature of Nationalist China was the comparatively small size and underdeveloped condition of the modern government and economy. Even at the end of the Nanking decade, the 400 or possibly 500 million Chinese were served by about the same mileage of modern highways as the 25 million people of Spain, less railroad mileage than Italy or the state of Illinois, less than a third the telegraph lines of France, less industrial production than the 8 million people of Belgium.

In seeking to promote China's national development, the generation of the 1930's for the most part turned to Western models, for neither Japan nor the Soviet Union were friendly sources of inspiration. This dependence upon Western models, which created the community of interest between Nanking and the West, helps to explain the superficial character of the regime. Its program of modernization verged upon Westernization, for Western-trained officials naturally tried to apply what they had learned abroad, and their efforts reflected the administrative institutions, technology, and values of life in the industrialized nations, where agricultural backwardness and peasant discontent were not dominant problems. Consequently Nanking often understood modern finance, foreign trade and exchange, transport and telecommunications better than it understood its own hinterland. Its modern-minded officials seldom felt at home in the villages.

The Kuomintang's weakness derived also from the way it came into power, first by absorbing into its ranks most of the time-serving local officialdom in areas taken over, second by killing off its younger and idealistic rivals in the CCP. Once in power the KMT abandoned the Soviet-type organizations through which it had begun to mobilize workers, peasants, youth, and women. It turned against student movements, ceased to scrutinize local administration, and lost its sense of mission. In short, the party became a wing of the bureaucracy, antirevolutionary.

Chiang Kai-shek. Despite the end of the monarchy two decades earlier, Chinese politics still required a single power-holder at the top to give final answers, which neither a presidium nor a balance of constitutional powers could supply. Unification (against warlords) and resistance (against Japan) were the dominant needs of the day; the power-holder had to be a military leader. Chiang Kai-shek became indispensable. He was a man of patriotic dedication and strong-willed determination, politically astute but with certain backward-looking intellectual limitations. To his early landlord background in Chekiang and an abiding respect for the virtues of Tseng Kuo-fan had been added some of the samurai ideals of the Japanese Military Cadets Academy and finally the experience of warlord politics in a period when armies counted heavily. From Soviet Russia, Chiang had learned more about armies than about mass movements. He did not believe in the efficacy of popular mobilization vis-à-vis military force. In any case, he faced the

GENERALISSIMO AND WARLORDS. *Chiang Kai-shek (center) in late 1928, after taking over North China, with two of his army commanders: the "Model Governor" Yen Hsi-shan (right), and the "Christian General" Feng Yü-hsiang (left, in common soldier's uniform). In 1930 Yen and Feng fought Chiang for power but were defeated.*

continuing problem of all holders of power: how to keep on holding it. Dealing with all possible rivals required the constant and jealous manipulation of personnel and resources. Chiang's dual task was to stay on top and simultaneously build up the military strength of the state.

After his marriage in 1927 to Soong Mei-ling, a Wellesley graduate and sister of Sun Yat-sen's widow, Chiang became like her a confirmed Methodist and maintained contact with the West through his wife, her brother T. V. Soong (a Harvard graduate), and her brother-in-law H. H. Kung (an Oberlin graduate). He used these relatives with American background in top financial posts, and long-time colleagues of Japanese background in military posts. In party politics, Chiang's major problem, as an outsider not of the old guard, was how to cooperate with and divide the KMT leaders descended from the early days of the party, especially Wang Ching-wei of the left wing and Hu Han-min of the right. During 1927 Chiang cooperated at different times with each against the other. Then for three years, he worked with Hu, leaving Wang out of power. When the two of them briefly joined up against him in 1931, Chiang proved more than ever indispensable as military commander against the Japanese. He then joined with Wang for four years. Hu died in 1936, and Chiang became Party Leader in 1938. Wang, who had considered himself Sun Yat-sen's heir, survived an assassination attempt in 1935, and in 1939 went over to the Japanese, evidently out of both personal and patriotic frustration.

In time the supremacy of the "Generalissimo" (the title used for Chiang Kai-shek by the foreign press) came to rest on a tripod of army, party, and government, in each of which he balanced his personal bureaucratic machine against regional or rival groups. The army was dominated by the "Whampoa clique" of officers who had been his students at Canton. They controlled the great military bureaucracy and the secret military police and held the balance against the Kwangsi militarists and other regional forces. In the party, Chiang relied on the "Organization clique" headed by the brothers Ch'en Kuo-fu and Ch'en Li-fu (hence commonly called the "CC clique"), who built up the Central Political Institute for training civil servants and the KMT central secretariat and Organization Ministry, with their personnel files, financial resources, and secret party police. Their major rivals were the "Political Study (or Science) clique" (Cheng-hsueh Hsi), a looser-knit group of politicians and administrators with business connections, partially descended from Liang Ch'i-ch'ao's "Research clique."

The Kuomintang never achieved a tight discipline over its members, whose effective number remained somewhere between 2 and 4 million. In its power structure a gradual expansion of membership was offset by a continual concentration of power at the top. The First Party Congress of 1924 had had 150 delegates; the Sixth in 1945 had 600, a catch-all of prominent personalities. The Central Executive Committee had begun in 1924 with 24 regular members and 17 reserves, but by 1945 totaled 222 regular members with 90 in reserve. Since it had only two or three meetings a year, power gravitated to its Standing Committee, which began as 8 persons but increased to 50, meeting more or less weekly. There being no institution of a loyal opposition, the tendency was to bring everyone of importance under the KMT aegis into a personal relationship with the leader. Since the party, not the people, controlled the government during the "period of tutelage" (1928–1948), the Political Council which usually headed the government was really a subcommittee of the Central Executive Committee of the party. Some party ministries—Organization, Information, Social Affairs, Overseas Affairs—functioned as part of the central administration. Party and government thus interpenetrated and became practically indistinguishable. China's first experiment in party government thus echoed many aspects of dynastic government—the separate military and civil bureaucracies were united only at the top, under a ruler chosen from a continuing body (the party) which retained the statutory power, and he was aided by open and secret supervisory personnel at all levels.

The Growth of Militarism.   Much can be said for the thesis that Japan's aggression changed China's history by necessitating military defense and distracting attention from domestic reform. When Japanese militarism was finally destroyed after continual aggression in China during fourteen years (1931–1945), the Chinese government, or what was left of it, had little but militarism with which to reconstruct the country. The Japanese militarists had forced it to go in the same direction, negating the Western influence of the 1920's and 1930's and destroying all chance of gradualism, reform, and evolution in meeting the problems of the Chinese people.

While not denying the validity of this view, one can also see domestic reasons for Chiang Kai-shek's rise as a military politician. After the 1927 split, Nanking was committed to unification and national development without class war. Kuomintang labor unions ("yellow" unions in Communist parlance) were promoted to compete with leftist unions, but peasant associations were generally suppressed. Forgoing mass mobilization at the village level as a source of power, the Nationalist Government had to compete with the remaining warlords pretty much on their own level. A post-unification conference in 1929 to disband the swollen armies reached no agreement. Warlordism died only slowly, and military unification was never achieved. An anti-Chiang wing of the KMT centered at Canton. In Yunnan, Szechwan, Shansi, Sinkiang, and other provinces, local militarists gave only lip service to Nanking. The Communists in Kiangsi until 1934 and in Shensi thereafter constituted a regionally based rebel power. The Japanese in Manchuria from 1931 and in Jehol and part of Hopei from 1933 became a foreign-based regional power. Year after year central government forces fought or negotiated in some part of the country in the name of national unity. Nanking's comparative success in this task was Chiang Kai-shek's success. Under him the Nationalist military establishment became less a Soviet-type party army controlled by the Kuomintang than a semigovernment under its own leader who had created it.

Having dispensed with the Soviet military mission in 1927, Chiang shifted to German advisers and aid and the German military structure, similar to that of Japan. The general staff was autonomous and separate from the minister of war under the Executive Yuan. The Nationalist forces remained independent of civil government and free from legislative interference. The Military Affairs Commission created more and more ministries for economic and political as well as strictly military purposes. In this enormous bureaucracy, Whampoa graduates held top posts without further training and expended the larger part of the Nationalist revenues on an unbudgeted basis. The central army, the best troops in China, soon grew to a crack force of 300,000. The Yangtze delta between Shanghai and Nanking was fortified. Arsenals produced German-type weapons. The German specialists got results, although they did not envisage cooperation with the peasantry or the eventual war of maneuver and "scorched earth."

The Economy.   During the Nanking decade the chief models of economic growth were provided by nations that were in varying degrees "totalitarian" —Nazi Germany, the Soviet Union, and Japan. However, the Nationalist Government, trying to inaugurate budgeting and auditing with the military out of hand, was never sufficiently in control of its finances, let alone the national economy, to pursue a plan of development. The United States was absorbed in the depression and the New Deal, and as yet had no concept of government-to-government programs of foreign aid.

Finance was the first focus of the government's economic effort. More than thirty foreign banks still operated in the treaty ports, monopolizing foreign exchange transactions, in some cases issuing their own bank notes, and generally serving as repositories for the private funds of Chinese politicians, militarists, businessmen, and speculators. Sometimes they held half the silver stock in Shanghai, where silver was the basic medium of exchange. The biggest foreign bank was the Hong Kong and Shanghai Banking Corporation, with assets of half a billion dollars. The hundred or so modern Chinese banks—government, provincial, or private—issued great quantities of depreciating bank notes and chiefly financed short-term commercial transactions or made loans to government agencies.

To finance the revolution, the Kuomintang had established the Central Bank of China at Canton in 1924 with T. V. Soong as manager. From 1928 it acted in Shanghai as a central bank of issue and a government treasury. Soon it was joined by the Bank of China (descended from the Board of Revenue Bank of 1905), the Bank of Communications (dating from 1907) and the Farmers Bank of China (1933). These four government banks now monopolized the issue of bank notes and formed a quadripartite equivalent of a European-type central government bank, dominating the scene with two-fifths of the capital and reserves, and over half the deposits, of all the modern Chinese banks.

As finance minister until 1933, T. V. Soong carried through a fiscal revolution—recovery of tariff autonomy and increase of customs revenue, suppression of likin taxes, and abolition of the ancient unit of account, the tael. These reforms brought the modern sector of the economy increasingly under the government's financial influence and made it possible to move toward government control of credit. From 1934 the American silver-buying program siphoned the silver currency out of China most disastrously. In self-defense China carried through a monetary reform in 1935 which substituted a managed paper currency for silver and backed the paper currency partly with reserves of foreign exchange. The effort was to stabilize the international value of China's money, and so build a banking system independent of foreign powers.

Despite this progress in the modern sector, it proved well-nigh impossible, even through credit cooperatives or the Agricultural Credit Administration set up in 1937, to make credit readily available to the farming population. Rural bank credit had still to be used for seasonal short-term needs, not for long-term productive investment, and merely competed with the usury of old-style moneylenders. Many fine rural programs were blueprinted, and some begun, for everything from land reclamation, reforestation, irrigation, and water conservancy to pest control, improved seeds and tools, and crop and animal breeding. Farm extension work, American-style, was introduced. But no sustained effort could be mounted at the critical level of the village to increase the farmer's productivity nationwide.

Public finance showed the same concentration of activity in the modern, treaty-port sector of the economy. Partly this was necessitated by the important fact that the Nanking Government had given up any claim to the land tax and left it for provincial administrations to exploit, thus making a virtue out of its initial inability to control large regions of the interior. This renunciation of the tax which had been the main resource of most dynasties was symptomatic of Nanking's tendency to avoid disturbing the rural scene. Instead, the National Government got about 50 per cent of its revenue from the Maritime Customs (as compared with about 1 per cent in the United States). In addition, it taxed the consuming public through consolidated excise taxes on staples like tobacco, kerosene, and flour, as well as through the salt monopoly. Since there was no income tax, this regressive taxation fell on the average consumer as heavily as on the wealthy and so tended to reduce mass purchasing power. Constant deficits were met by borrowing from the four government banks about 25 per cent of what the government expended. The four banks in turn sold bonds on the domestic market, debt payments on which soon exceeded the large payments still due to foreign creditors. Servicing all these debts took about a third of all expenditures. The domestic bondholders included many Nanking bureaucrats, and they often got high interest rates (up to 20 to 40 per cent if one allows for discounts they received on the purchase price). Such ill-gotten gains, paid to Chinese within the Chinese scene, were no doubt a good deal less odious than the enormous indemnity payments extorted by foreign powers after 1901. But Nanking's policy did not encourage production at home or capital loans from abroad, and achieved little saving and investment for long-term industrial growth. The nation's capital was not mobilized, while the available resources went mainly to support the military or to benefit what the Marxists called "bureaucratic capitalists."

Cultural Life and American Influence. Though living in the shadow of rebellion suppression and imminent invasion, those Chinese in the 1930's who felt themselves the intellectual inheritors of the May Fourth period re-

LIBERALS IN SHANGHAI 1933. *From left, the American journalist Agnes Smedley, George Bernard Shaw, Madame Sun Yat-sen (Soong Ch'ing-ling), Ts'ai Yüan-p'ei, then head of Academia Sinica, and Lu Hsün. Shaw was visiting China. The others had been founders of the short-lived China League for Civil Rights.*

mained divided into two main wings—reformist and revolutionist. Representative of the former were academically inclined scholars who fostered science, technology, and learning divorced from politics. Typical of the latter were activist-minded writers who tried to produce a literature of social revolution.

In literary circles Lu Hsün became a senior figure, encouraging younger writers, denouncing the Nationalist censorship and persecution of left-wing literature, and at the same time deploring the lowered, propagandist standards of the leftists. "Good literary works," he asserted, "have never been composed in accordance with other people's orders." As a rebel against social injustice, he became emotionally converted to the Communist cause although never a party member. In 1930 he joined with others to form the League of Left-Wing Writers. This broad organization with its many subsidized publications and polemical tactics marked the beginning of Communist ascendancy in the literary scene under the recently unfurled Soviet banner of "socialist realism." The KMT could neither prevent nor compete with this development, which increasingly gave student youth its view of the world.

American reformist influence in the 1930's was greatest among the non-revolutionary wing of the intelligentsia, those who were foreign-trained and worked in academic and scientific institutions. The dozen Christian colleges now got more than half their income from Chinese sources, and were controlled locally by Chinese boards of directors, with faculties two-thirds Chinese though largely foreign trained. Although they had only 6500 students, as compared with 41,000 in the hundred or so government institutions of higher education, they still were pacesetters in instruction as well as in standards of living and social life. The big national universities like Peita and Tsing Hua also had staffs largely trained abroad, mostly in the United States. American influence was similarly evident in the Geological Survey of China, the dozen research institutes of the central government's Academia Sinica, the National Agricultural Research Institute at Nanking, and the big Rockefeller-supported Peking Union Medical College at Peiping, as well as the national health service which benefited from its pioneer work. This institutional growth was the fruit of training Chinese students in the West. Some 2400 had entered American universities between 1901 and 1920; 5500 did so between 1921 and 1940, studying altogether in 370 institutions, primarily in branches of engineering or business economics—practical subjects. Returning to work in Shanghai firms or Nanking agencies or in institutions like those just listed, these modern-trained graduates were a new elite, who lived on a material and intellectual plane far above the poverty and illiteracy of the Chinese village. In the 1920's and 1930's, a new generation of Chinese scholars, stimulated by study abroad, achieved creative beginnings in many lines—for example, discovering Peking Man and the Shang dynasty capital at An-yang (see pages 5 and 19–20), finding previously unknown architectural monuments, publishing and using Ch'ing archives, and in general assimilating into Chinese the vocabularies and concepts of modern science.

The missionary response to China's problems, while still evangelical, had also taken on many practical forms. The thousand or so American missionaries of 1900, representing twenty-eight societies, had increased by 1930 to more than three thousand representing sixty societies. With the rise of nationalism, the effort now was to make the Christian church in China indigenous, led by a Chinese pastorate and partially self-supporting, with the foreign missionary only advising and assisting. With its lesser stress on the gospel and its direct concern for social service, the Y.M.C.A. attracted an able young Chinese leadership and now developed programs for literacy and social work among factory laborers. Christian compassion found other outlets. The North China famine of 1920–1921 led to the creation of the China International Famine Relief Commission. By 1936 it had used $50 million in foreign contributions for pioneer programs of rural improvement in cooperation with local authorities in famine areas—building wells, roads,

A Chinese Christian community leader of the Society of the Divine Word, Lanchow vicariate, Kansu, among paintings, scrolls, and statues of Chinese Christian art.

and river dikes, and setting up farm credit cooperatives in North China with some 200,000 members. As Christianity in China became increasingly concerned with social welfare, an interdenominational Protestant conference of 1922 organized the National Christian Council, partly to apply the social gospel, partly to promote the "indigenous" Chinese Christian church. In addition to its urban program, this body began to develop a rural program and encouraged agricultural research and extension activities. Christian missions were thus by the 1930's approaching the problems of "rural reconstruction."

A pioneer in this movement, James Yen, a graduate of Yale and the Y.M.C.A., began work at Ting-hsien near Peking in 1926 with subsequent support from the Rockefeller Foundation. Here his Mass Education Movement began with foreign assistance to attack the problems of the Chinese peasantry, pioneering in the application of agricultural science and the spread of elementary education. It soon confronted questions of farm credit, marketing, cooperatives, and farmers' associations. This last type of organization, when combined with literacy, could give voice to peasant grievances and eventually raise questions of land tenure and local politics. At this point, the gradualist approach of the social worker and educator ran into the vested interests of local power-holders, those remnants of the erstwhile "gentry" who now often functioned with the military support of militarists or secret societies. Thus "rural reconstruction" threatened the status quo.

Instinctively, government authorities moved to control and use it. Chiang Kai-shek through Madame Chiang, who was in close touch with church and Y.M.C.A. leaders, invited American missionaries to set up a model county administration among the peasantry in a part of Kiangsi recovered from the Communists, but little could be achieved in religious or community work in the midst of so much poverty. Chiang mounted his own program for China's regeneration in the New Life Movement, stressing the ancient virtues of moral conduct—propriety, righteousness, integrity, and the sense of shame—and using Y.M.C.A. methods. It exhorted the public through a network of thirteen hundred branches during 1934–1937. Behind this movement but unknown to the public was Chiang Kai-shek's secret Blue Shirt organization modeled on European fascism and devoted to militarizing the nation under his leadership.

Largely beneath the level of public notice or statistical knowledge in this period, the disintegration of China's ancient rural society was still proceeding apace. The great mass of the Chinese farming population in the million villages remained beyond the reach of the Nationalist Government or missionary reform efforts. Farm handicrafts were now suffering the full impact of factory production. Drawn inexorably into the money economy, farming remained undercapitalized. The cultivator was too poor to store his crops, improve his seeds or tools, or avoid borrowing from the usurer. Poverty and demoralization worsened in the villages, while the non-Communist prescriptions and programs for their remaking, largely Western-inspired, remained scattered and ineffective. The hope for rural reconstruction was in any case cut short by invasion and warfare.

Japan's Aggression in China

Japan in Manchuria and China's Response. Manchuria, China's Northeast, was a big, new frontier area, a quarter the size of China proper, yet containing less than a tenth as many people. Population had tripled from perhaps 11 million in 1900 to 34 million in 1930, partly through migration from North China, and was 95 per cent Chinese. But the Japanese military in Manchuria felt a sense of imperial mission. The rise of the Nationalist Government and its patriotic claims to Manchuria as racially, historically, and legally part of China clashed head on with the explosive militarism of the Japanese Kwantung Army. When Japanese officers arranged the "Mukden incident," of September 18, 1931, and proceeded to take over Manchuria, the Chinese patriotic reaction and boycott led to an "undeclared war" outside the foreign concession area at Shanghai (January 28–March 3, 1932). After seventy thousand Japanese troops had battled a surprisingly vigorous Chinese resistance, both sides accepted an armistice rather than expand the fighting. But meanwhile the successful coup in Manchuria had shattered the collective security system of the League of Nations. Neither the League nor the American policy of "non-recognition" of gains made by force could now stop the momentum of Japan's expansion.

Mindful of the old tradition of barbarian conquest of China with Chinese help, the Japanese set up a puppet government in Manchuria with Japanese advisers in indirect control. The state of Manchukuo ("Manchu-land") was proclaimed on March 1, 1932. Soon the last Ch'ing boy-emperor, Pu-yi, was enthroned as emperor. Local Chinese were brought into "self-government committees" proclaiming "national independence." The fiction of an independent state justified the exclusion of foreign interests as long as the powers did not recognize the new government. The army pro-gram for Manchukuo stressed industrialization. New companies were chartered with special inducements to mobilize private capital. A badly needed unification of the currency was achieved under a central bank; and communications, transport, and hydroelectric power developed rapidly. Strategic railroads were pushed toward the Soviet frontiers of Manchuria, and the formerly competing Chinese lines parallel to the South Manchurian Railway were incorporated with it into a single system. All this created in Manchuria an industrial base in competition with the Japanese homeland and required a heavy capital investment. Japan's economic gains were mini-mal, but the new strategic base on the continent provided the satisfactions of imperial glory and also a vested interest in further expansion.

Moving inexorably on North China, the Japanese created a demilitarized zone, just south of the Wall between Peiping and Tientsin, from which a Chinese puppet regime fostered infiltration of smuggled goods and narcotics into North China. In 1935 North China was made a neutral zone by agree-ment, whereupon Japanese officers tried to incite a separatist movement to make its five provinces into a puppet "North China-land" (*Hua-pei kuo*). This effort collapsed in December in the face of Peiping student demon-strations which dramatized Nanking's dilemma—when and where to resist by force.

China's nonmilitary resistance in the form of a boycott after the Mukden incident had been very effective, spreading over the whole country and overseas, inhibiting Japanese sales and even contact with Japanese banks or business concerns. The boycott was coordinated by the Kuomintang with much initiative from students and merchants. It operated underground in the treaty ports, using terrorism when necessary, and enforced its program elsewhere by public meetings, propaganda, inspection, fines, and actual punishment of malefactors. Japanese exports to China proper were cut in half. Japan's aggression was provoking a national response at a new level of public participation. Nanking, however, discounted the capabilities of nonmilitary and paramilitary (guerrilla) resistance. The Nationalist experts in firepower knew that unarmed civilians could not stop Japan's tanks and planes. The indubitable correctness of this view was confirmed by common sense as well as by military opinion in most of the world. Yet it overlooked what was later demonstrated in many countries: the effectiveness of popular resistance when mobilized in support of, and coordinated with, conventional firepower. Chiang Kai-shek expressed the conventional wisdom in his strategy of building up his German-trained army before committing it to battle. For almost six years after September 1931, with skill and tenacity, he temporized, negotiated, withdrew, and avoided a showdown with Japan. This was plainly a harsh necessity. Yet alongside his new army Chiang had little success in using mass organizations to mobilize the nation. On the contrary, opposed to the class war by which the Communists were rallying peasants against landlords (see pages 473–480), Chiang used his new army to follow a strategy of "unification before resistance" and so mounted five anti-Communist "extermination campaigns" in 1931–1934. Nanking's policy of fighting Chinese rebels but not Japanese invaders outraged noncommunist patriots and put the government under heavy pressure.

By 1936 the Communists had survived their Long March of 1934–1935 from Kiangsi and now had a territorial base in the Northwest. Both the CCP and the Comintern had proposed a second united front in August 1935, this time for national defense against Japan. This tactical shift aimed to take Japanese pressure off the Soviet Union and Nationalist pressure off the CCP. In late 1936 the formation of the Rome-Berlin Axis and the German-Italian-Japanese Anti-Comintern Pact heightened the danger of aggression. When Chiang was forcibly held or "kidnaped" in December at Sian by Chinese troops from Manchuria, who were more eager to resist Japan than to exterminate CCP rebels, Chou En-lai mediated to release him, whereupon the second united front gradually took shape.

The Second Sino-Japanese War. Japan's full-scale aggression in 1937, first near Peiping on July 7, then at Shanghai in August, really opened World War II, which in China lasted a full eight years, longer than the war in Europe. During the first four years, moreover, down to December 8, 1941, Free China fought alone while isolationist America until mid-1941 continued with a growing sense of guilt to sell essential oil and iron to Japan's war machine. By that time the Nationalist Government and its leader had shown both inspiring fortitude and the same limitations that had characterized their rule at Nanking. The regime, oriented toward foreign trade and contact, was progressively cut off from them and confined to the hinterland whose problems it had hardly begun to face. Chiang assumed, correctly, that Japan's fanatical aggressiveness would sooner or later bring other powers to China's aid. The war became a test of stamina. At Shanghai the new Nationalist armies fought the Japanese to a standstill but suffered severely. Once outflanked in late 1937, they withdrew westward, "trading space for time" and using "scorched earth" tactics to destroy many industrial installations that could not be transported inland. After a pause at Hankow in 1938 the Nationalist Government moved up above the Yangtze gorges to Chungking in the mists of Szechwan. Whole arsenals and factories, and faculties and student bodies of universities, migrated beyond the reach of Japan's tanks, though not of her planes.

Occupied China was soon divided between two puppet regimes, each with its own currency. In North China the Japanese forces, using the rail lines as invasion routes and seizing the cities, rather quickly overcame resistance except in the densely populated plains inside the rail network, where guerrilla movements began to take shape. Japan's North China army kept ahead of its Central China rivals by setting up a puppet Provisional Government of China at Peiping, using as figureheads old men who had been Japan-oriented in the warlord era. They urged a return to the classical virtues and pan-Asian cooperation, in press and school propaganda that was both anti-Western and anti-Communist. In Central China, Japan also installed a puppet Reform Government at Nanking in March 1938. After the fall of Canton and Hankow in October, Japan announced the creation of her New Order in East Asia, a paper scheme which would substitute Japan's overlordship in China for the Western treaty system. This induced the frustrated patriot and one-time student in Japan, Wang Ching-wei, to seek peace by defecting from Chungking and Chiang Kai-shek; and on March 30, 1940, after much negotiation, Wang became head of a Reorganized Nationalist Government at Nanking, a shadowy replica of the former Nanking Government, under the nominal control of the "Orthodox Kuomintang," a rump group of anti-Chiang KMT members who had defected along with Wang. These puppet façades at Peiping and Nanking, like Manchukuo, rested on force and fooled no one. Yet, as in Europe a bit later, the invaders' superior arms made urban resistance suicidal and collaboration almost unavoidable. Collaborators, moreover, could mitigate the conqueror's harshness even while working under him, and so were not wholly unpatriotic. The relative ease with which Japan recruited collaborators and governed a large part of China in the 1930's suggests that not all the Chinese people were as yet ready for mobilized popular resistance.

Beyond the southwestern periphery of Japan's invasion, the Nationalist Government survived in the less developed hinterland. This brought it into competition with the Communists. From mid-1937 began another period of KMT-CCP collaboration and scarcely veiled competition. Soon the KMT could see that the CCP would gain more from the social transformations of wartime, especially mass mobilization and the arming of peasants. It turned against such developments in the area under its control, and Nationalist troops, eventually 200,000 or more, blockaded the CCP in its base in the

MANPOWER TAXIS. *A family wheelbarrow with front and rear handlers, Hankow, late nineteenth century. A rickshaw puller evacuating a Nationalist officer from Nanking, 1949. A pedicab on Nanking Road, Shanghai, 1966.*

Northwest. The united front continued only as a façade of unity, to paper over the fact that two armed party dictatorships were rivals for ultimate power.

The Nationalist Government, while avoiding social change in the countryside, took measures to buttress its political power. A People's Political Council, chosen of broadly representative public figures, was created in 1938 to meet the demand for representative government, although it was given advisory powers only. Its questions did not have to be answered. From 1939 to 1947 the San-min chu-i Youth Corps under Chiang as chief built up a pyramidal structure parallel to the party. However, as the youthful membership grew older, it became a rival of the party, with no new ideas, and finally had to be absorbed back into it. A Central Training Corps, set up at Chungking as an indoctrination mill, brought together group after group of assorted magistrates, officers, professors, and administrators from all over the country. Each group, in two or three weeks of tightly scheduled lectures, calisthenics, and other exercises became informed on the Kuomintang's principles and heard and saw the Party Leader. Meantime in local government a "new county (*hsien*) system" was introduced in 1939. It aimed to invigorate economic and welfare activities at the county level, which proved difficult, and also to revive the ancient *pao-chia* mutual-responsibility and surveillance system, which proved of some effect in maintaining local order. This revival featured "self-government" through election of *pao* representatives in village administration, but there is little record of the election process taking hold in the back country.

All these measures, like Chungking's indomitable wartime performance as a whole, betrayed a poverty of ideas. The original leaders of the KMT still clung to power. The Military Affairs Commission took over more and more of the civil government's functions and had as many as 5 million troops under arms at one time. Yet the intellectual leadership of this massive effort was confined to the meager set of ideas put forth in *China's Destiny,* a treatise Chiang Kai-shek published in 1943. Its first theme was anti-imperialism, stressing the humiliations of foreign aggression, the manifold evils of the unequal treaties. The patriotic sense of grievance is plain whether or not one agrees that the many strains of modernization have all been due to Western victimization of China. The second theme was Chiang's proposal to revive the ancient virtues of the Confucian social order and subordinate the individual properly to the state. At the same time he would industrialize on a grand scale for national defense and collectivize the peasants to make them farmer-soldiers.

The sufferings of the government civil servants, the people from "down river," who had migrated to the crowded housing and consumer-goods shortages of wartime Szechwan, were capped by the continuing inflation, which destroyed their government stipends and living standards by a process

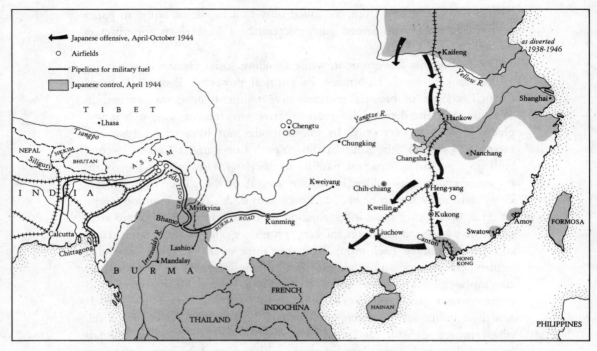

Japanese offensive, April-October 1944
Airfields
Pipelines for military fuel
Japanese control, April 1944

THE CHINA-BURMA-INDIA THEATER IN WORLD WAR II

of slow strangulation. Although it was in a self-sufficient agricultural region with a considerable food supply, the government failed to develop its tax revenues and relied heavily on note-issue to finance its needs. This left the rural subsistence economy relatively unaffected, but put the government's urban stipendiaries, the whole modern element in Free China, through an inflationary wringer. White-collar salaries never kept up. Books, clothing, furnishings went for food. Malnutrition produced skin disease, stomach ailments, tuberculosis. Poverty led many to the humiliation of surviving by corruption. The privileged few in business tended to hoard commodities or gold rather than invest their untaxed profits, but most of the modern stratum of Free China was enervated and demoralized, and eventually blamed the regime in power. This coincided in the universities with the KMT effort to both expand and control higher education for political purposes. The academic wing of the intelligentsia began to question the KMT leadership.

American Aid to China.   In the first two and one-half years of China's struggle, the Nationalist Government received far more help from the Soviet Union than from America, Britain, and France. An entire Soviet "volunteer" air force fought Japan in China. But Soviet aid died away after the onset of World War II in September 1939. At first Free China's cause

MANPOWER FOR AIRPLANES. *Thousands of peasants moving earth
and crushing rock to build an airfield near Chengtu for B-29's
to bomb Japan, 1942.*

won American public acclaim but little help. Except for the Indo-China rail
route from Haiphong to Kunming (until the fall of France in 1940) and
the Burma Road truck route over high mountains and deep gorges from
the rail-head in Burma to Kunming, Free China was practically cut off.

When the Japanese attack at Pearl Harbor in 1941 made an active ally
of Chungking, the United States Government through its military aid began
for the first time to play a major role in China's domestic affairs. The
wartime alliance brought to its highest point the American participation in
Chinese life that had been growing for a century past. Revision of the
British and American treaties in January 1943 formally ended the unequal-
treaty system; yet, ironically, the war effort created an American presence—
manifest in air forces and bases, training schools, supply and transport
services, and other wartime agencies with their radio networks and airlines
—greater than ever before. Most spectacular was the success of the Fourteenth U.S. Air Force under General C. L. Chennault in checking the
Japanese bombing of Free China's cities.

But American aid suffered a series of handicaps. First, Japan's quick
seizure of Burma in early 1942 cut the Burma Road supply route. The only
substitute was an airlift from India over the mountainous "hump" of

*Generalissimo and Madame
Chiang Kai-shek with Stilwell
at Maymyo in Burma, April
1942.*

northern Burma to Kunming—a costly route of very limited capacity (see map). Second, the Allied strategy, to defeat Germany before Japan, gave the distant China–Burma–India theater a low priority. Lend-lease aid to China amounted by early 1946 to $1.5 billion, but this was only about 3 per cent of the $50 billion lend-lease aid given to all countries in World War II. China was neither easy to help nor strategically of first importance. General Joseph Stilwell, designated Chiang Kai-shek's "chief of staff," tenaciously set about the difficult reconquest of North Burma to reopen a land route to China as the putative base for attacking Japan. By early 1945 a road and a pipeline accomplished this, but the naval campaign in the Pacific had long since carried the war directly to Japan.

Thus warfare outpaced diplomacy. The initial American policy aim, to help China become a "great power" capable of stabilizing East Asia after Japan's defeat, had been joined with a parallel military aim, to help the Nationalist Government build up its military capacity. If the Allied attack on Japan had indeed gone through China, conditions there after the war might have been more viable and less inviting to Communist rebellion. In fact, however, China was bypassed and became a sideshow. This exacerbated the inevitable frictions of any alliance and produced bitterness and recrimination between the Americans and the British, between Stilwell and Chennault, between Chiang Kai-shek and his allies—eventually between America and China. The American war effort, so concentrated on defeating Japan, expressed the outlook of a people accustomed to peace in a stable society, who had never themselves suffered invasion and who viewed the war overseas as a brief interlude. In China, on the other hand, the principal war effort had already been expended, to survive Japan's aggression since 1937. The KMT ideal of unifying China militarily and the CCP hope of seizing power for social revolution underlay Chinese politics. Americans eager to win the war pressed for a more unified KMT-CCP war effort, only to meet frustration. Partly over this issue, General Stilwell was recalled in November 1944. Once Japan was defeated in August 1945, the United

States quickly demobilized its powerful forces. But the arms it had provided made the Nationalist commanders overconfident of their capacity to suppress the Communists. Their government emerged from World War II economically debilitated and politically insecure but with superior firepower. This combination of circumstances led it into a civil war that proved its undoing.

The decline and fall of the Kuomintang, after its early promise, was a tragedy hotly disputed in the United States. Certain points may be suggested. First, the KMT-CCP rivalry was continuous from the very moment in 1923 when the KMT was reorganized as a Leninist-style party dictatorship. The potentialities for revolutionary change, such as the mobilization of the peasantry to take part in war and politics, steadily increased, yet the Kuomintang did not succeed in grasping and using them. Second, Japan's aggression after 1931 was an ever present fact in China's national life, even more immediately pressing than the potentialities of revolution. It diverted the government from many constructive tasks and led to its militarization. Third, American aid to the Nationalist Government after 1941, though it climaxed a century of American help toward meeting China's problems, came too late. If in the early 1930's substantial United States Government aid had gone to Nanking, as it has gone to so many regimes since 1941, Chinese history might have been altered. But American aid in wartime, coming late to a hard-pressed regime, served more as a crutch to lean on than as a means to cure its ailments.

Finally, Nationalist China's deterioration during eight years of wartime attrition reflected both the impact of overwhelming circumstance and an inadequacy of leadership, in proportions still being debated. For the Nanking Government, based on the coastal cities, removal inland was all but fatal. The Chinese Communists' comparatively successful wartime expansion was accomplished without the oppressive burden of frontal resistance and national responsibilities that exhausted Chungking's energies. Nationalist forces tied down most of Japan's troops in China, roughly half her armies overseas, and suffered the great part of China's 3 million or more battle casualties. Meanwhile the CCP regime built up its power on a more primitive level (see pages 473–480). Chinese tradition sees history in more personal terms than does modern social science. Chiang Kai-shek, who took responsibility as the holder of power, has been blamed by many for losing it. Study should show, however, that he was seldom master of Free China's circumstances. His inflexible rectitude mirrored the inertia of a whole political tradition, still in the shadow of the Confucian Empire. On the other hand, just as Western aid was unable to prevent Free China's deterioration, so Western models were of little use to the Chinese republic in wartime. Out of the war in China came something new, the greatest of all its revolutions.

15. The People's Republic

The Rise of the Maoist Leadership

The Chinese Communist party (CCP) like the Comintern had at first regarded peasants in orthodox Marxist-Leninist fashion as capable only of auxiliary action. But Mao Tse-tung's famous report on the peasant movement in Hunan in February 1927 asserted heretically that the "revolutionary vanguard" in China was not the proletariat but the "poor peasantry." Mao soon learned from experience the necessity of combining peasant mass organization with military power. With Chu Teh as military commander and a few thousand men he took refuge in the winter of 1927–1928 in the mountainous Ching-kang-shan region on the Hunan-Kiangsi border, where he developed a territorial base in the traditional fashion of rebels. But Mao kept his movement ideologically orthodox in terminology. The Chinese Soviet Republic was proclaimed at Juichin, Kiangsi, in November 1931 as a "democratic dictatorship of the proletariat and peasantry," using Lenin's formula of 1905 in utterly different circumstances. The nonexistent "proletariat" was favored by excellent labor laws on paper. The Red Army was specially privileged as a political class army. Land was violently redistributed, but collectivization was not pushed.

Mao Tse-tung's ascendancy to leadership came only by degrees. It was delayed when the CCP Central Committee, dominated by young Moscow-returned students, abandoned Shanghai for Kiangsi in the autumn of 1932. Chiang Kai-shek's first four extermination campaigns, in late 1931, May–June and July–October 1932, and again in 1933 were checked by guerrilla tactics that drew KMT columns into the mountains. In late 1933–1934,

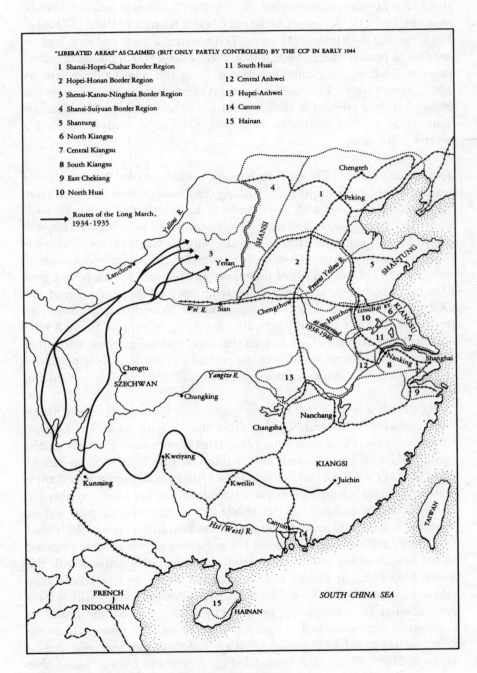

"LIBERATED AREAS" AS CLAIMED (BUT ONLY PARTLY CONTROLLED) BY THE CCP IN EARLY 1944

1 Shansi-Hopei-Chahar Border Region
2 Hopei-Honan Border Region
3 Shensi-Kansu-Ninghsia Border Region
4 Shansi-Suiyuan Border Region
5 Shantung
6 North Kiangsu
7 Central Kiangsu
8 South Kiangsu
9 East Chekiang
10 North Huai

11 South Huai
12 Central Anhwei
13 Hupei-Anhwei
14 Canton
15 Hainan

Routes of the Long March,
1934-1935

THE RISE OF THE CHINESE COMMUNISTS

however, a systematic, German-devised, KMT blockade and penetration along lines of blockhouses began to invade the Communist area. As a result, over 100,000 CCP personnel broke out of their Kiangsi redoubt in October 1934, moving swiftly by night on the Long March, a great and now legendary feat of human endurance that took them in one year some six thousand miles on foot, fighting continual battles along the way. Only in January 1935, when Chinese Communism was out of touch with Moscow, was the Moscow-trained element in the party obliged to acknowledge Mao's leadership. Even so, they continued to oppose his line in party councils for several years more.

The Yenan Period.   The CCP leaders and less than twenty thousand troops reached northern Shensi in 1935, making their headquarters at Yenan from the end of 1936. This arid, sun-drenched, dusty region of loess soil, fragmented by eroded gullies and not easily penetrated by wheeled vehicles, was defensible but generally lacking in water supply, surplus crops, and landlords. It formed a natural setting for a simple, egalitarian, do-it-yourself way of life, far from the ills of urbanism. The ten-year Yenan period gave Mao his opportunity, and he put his stamp on a whole generation of the CCP leadership. When an enterprising American journalist, Edgar Snow, interviewed Mao and his colleagues after the Long March, he found a self-confident and even jovial band of veteran revolutionaries, whose homespun earthiness and evident devotion to the peasant's cause, brilliantly portrayed in *Red Star over China,* captured the imagination of readers around the world.

By 1937 it was plain that Chinese resistance to Japan would divert Japan from attacking Russia and Nanking from attacking the CCP. The Chinese Communists therefore joined the Nationalist government in a new united front, following Japan's attack near Peiping on July 7, 1937. This second effort at KMT-CCP cooperation was little more than an uneasy armed truce that began in an atmosphere of patriotic enthusiasm but soon deteriorated. CCP power now expanded in the wholly new context of a national war of resistance that in itself provided an urgent sanction for peasant mobilization in patriotic self-defense. The bases for organized resistance were centered in the less accessible border areas between provinces, beginning with the Shansi-Hopei-Chahar Border Region set up in 1938. By 1945 there were said to be nineteen such bases, mostly called "liberated areas," with a total population of 70 to 90 million, protected by about 2 million militia and by Communist armies claimed to total 910,000 troops. The Chinese Communists had expanded as the most effective leaders of peasant resistance to Japan in North China. The Nationalist government at Chungking, unable to compete on this level, blockaded the Yenan area.

WOODCUTS FROM NORTH
CHINA IN WARTIME: THE
ARMY AND THE PEOPLE.
*"Support Our Common
People's Own Army."*
From top:
*Peasants bring in flocks for
food and pack animals for
transport. They welcome
soldiers with music and a
banner, stand guard, provide
hot water to drink, carry the
wounded, give new recruits a
send-off, and care for the
disabled. Matching placards
at the serviceman's door
read, "Fine clothing and
sufficient food; a
well-established household."*

*"Marriage Registration." A couple arrange their own marriage in
modern style and sign the register on the k'ang-table of a local
official. Right: brick cooking stove, folded quilts.*

During wartime the Communists temporarily abandoned their program of land confiscation in favor of rent reduction. Landlords were generally left in possession, guaranteed a reduced rent, and also allowed to vote in local elections. Instead of their former soviet system, the Communists announced direct elections by the so-called three-thirds system. They would confine their own representation to one-third of the offices and seek to retain Kuomintang and independent participation in the other two-thirds. The Communist movement and its Eighth Route Army prospered in proportion as the common people would willingly give them support in the free political competition of the war years, when the Japanese and their Chinese puppets as well as the Kuomintang offered some alternative to the Communist regime. The CCP's economic program included production drives both by troops and by farmers to achieve the self-sufficiency of each area in food supply. The improved seeds and techniques of Western-style scientific farming were largely lacking, but the Communists made up for this by their emphasis upon cooperation in land reclamation, labor exchange among farmers, mutual aid in transport, and small-scale industrial cooperatives. By bringing the farmers into associations for common ends and controlling these associations through leadership and propaganda, the CCP found a new road to political and military power.

Ideological Development.   Mao's three stated goals in 1940 were the pursuit of the united front with the KMT, armed struggle against Japan, and party building in the CCP area. A fourth goal, less advertised, was to build a million-man army. The overall problem was to maintain long-term revolutionary aims while finding as many allies as possible in the effort to compete with the Nationalists, fight Japan, and reform China. The CCP united-front tactics became sophisticated, flexible, and efficient. They tried to isolate enemies, separating out all possible allies and neutrals, appealing to their interests and caring for their specific needs almost like ward politicians, and yet never compromising the ultimate independence of the CCP. "United-front cadres" in the KMT areas posed as non-Communists and never expected CCP help. Free China's cultural and political life was infiltrated by able, dedicated, and hard-working members who kept their secret faith in China's Communist future. Similarly the "friendly armies" program penetrated the KMT forces with military men who rose by merit. But the united front also fostered a wartime attitude of friendly cooperation and exemplary sacrifice in the common cause. Armed struggle could be integrally combined with the united front, against either Japanese invaders or KMT diehards, once they had been sufficiently isolated.

The third ingredient of CCP power was party building. Membership grew from 40,000 in 1937 to 1,200,000 in 1945. Strenuous efforts were required to keep the CCP a disciplined, centrally controlled Leninist Party. It

TROOPS AT FARM WORK. *Soldiers threshing with flails and a stone roller, stacking the straw, and storing bags of grain. Note basketball hoop, right rear.*

EXPLAINING NEW METHODS OF CHILDBIRTH. *An instructress points to the chart, stressing principles of hygiene and proper preparation for delivery.*

was less than ever a party of the proletariat, even though peasants were now called "rural proletarians." Its activities were spread over a quarter of a million square miles. Control could be exercised only by Communists working with proper ideological coordination, and so it was essential to indoctrinate the new cadres. For this purpose party schools processed thousands of students at Yenan.

In 1942 Mao inaugurated an ideological reform movement for "correcting unorthodox tendencies" *(cheng-feng)* in thought, in personal relations inside and outside the party, and in speech and writing. Prolonged criticism and self-criticism in small groups, confessions of guilt and repentance in public meetings, became standard procedures. The aim was to maintain the party's militancy during a united-front period and so keep it prepared for future tasks. This took a strenuous effort to re-educate and discipline new followers still contaminated by a liberal background, an individualistic temperament, or traditional morality.

This rectification campaign also marked the final elimination from CCP councils of the Moscow-returned "internationalists," trained by the Comintern, who had opposed Mao's leadership. It was now agreed that Marxist-Leninist theory had to be tested in action, be applied to rural China's concrete realities, and become a Marxism that had "taken on a national form." This became the basis of "Mao Tse-tung thought." It represented the Sinification of Communism in China, two decades after the party's founding, in a period of wartime nationalism and minimal Russian influence. Henceforth it was no longer an alien creed. The principal achievement had been to build a Leninist party on a peasant base, demonstrating (contrary to Marxist theory) that the Communist order is in fact independent of the proletariat. This inversion of Marxism implied that a man's ideological tendencies did not come from his class affiliation, as posited by historical materialism. His class was now determined by his ideology; a bright peasant could become a "proletarian." This was a triumph of subjective and political considerations over the Marxist emphasis on the economic mode of production.

Mao's essay of 1940, "On the New Democracy," was a persuasive propaganda document that justified the united front as a temporary phase and yet reaffirmed the party's long-term mission. For the benefit of his non-Marxist audience Mao Tse-tung blandly claimed to have inherited the mantle of Sun Yat-sen and the May Fourth movement, while for Marxists he implicitly put himself on the level of Marx, Engels, Lenin, and Stalin as an original contributor to Communist theory. In actual fact Mao's "innovations" had been in the realm of practice, not theory. All his dicta could be found in earlier literature. His real contribution had been the creation of a party, an army, and mass support in a rural territorial base.

A new cult of the common people, stressing their "liberation," aimed at the awakening and activation of the Chinese peasant masses. The cultural movement stressed pictorial art in the form of the woodcut, which could be cheaply reproduced. Choral singing was combined with an ancient type of country dance to create a new art form in the *yang-ko* ("seedling song"), a poor man's opera that used folk tunes, a chain dance step, and the subject matter of everyday life to provide entertainment that indoctrinated as it liberated. The new creed of the common man embraced the revolutionary ideal that modern technology and a new social organization could be used to remake and enrich the life of the peasant. This cult of the common people animated the cadres and the military forces. The party worker had to live in the village, work with the peasant, eat his food, lead his life, think his thoughts. Only thus could he lead the masses in their regeneration. "Liberation" by the inexorable logic of events became also the sanction for the new party dictatorship: 1) the revolution aimed to give the masses a new life; 2) this could be achieved only through absolute political power, sufficient to change the old order; 3) political power could be achieved only through organization in a centralized party; 4) a party could be effective only if its members submitted to absolute party discipline. The party took on the character of an ongoing, living entity with a historic mission, transcendent over individuals.

The CCP's Seventh Congress in April–June 1945, the first since 1928, perfected its strategy for the postwar period by adopting the flexible line of "coalition government." After the New Fourth Army incident of January 1941, when Nationalist troops had fought a CCP force south of the Yangtze, the government had blockaded the CCP area more intensively. A general fear arose in China that World War II would be followed by civil war. Mao now declared that China needed a "new democratic government of a coalition nature embracing all parties and nonpartisan representatives." Depending on expediency, this could mean a coalition including the Kuomintang, as was proposed in 1946, or a coalition with minor parties and liberals against the Kuomintang, as was to be achieved in 1949. Meanwhile, this line appealed particularly to modern-minded but frustrated intellectuals.

The KMT-CCP Civil War. During World War II, General Joseph Stilwell as Chiang Kai-shek's nominal chief of staff had trained Chinese troops in India for the reconquest of North Burma, while United States airpower supplied by the Hump airlift had protected cities and harassed Japanese forces in China. But the Allied attack on Japan bypassed China, going more directly by sea, and the main result of American aid was to give the politically enfeebled Nationalist government superior armaments and a sense of overconfidence with which to face the CCP after 1945. General George C. Marshall as a special envoy to China mediated during

THE PROBLEM OF DISTRIBUTION IN CHINA IN THE 1940's. *The well-nourished woman sits in front of a grain shop; the beggar boy has come into town from a famine area.*

1946 to arrange a coalition government, but the Nationalist generals (and Stalin too) overrated the efficacy of Nationalist firepower, while Mao and the CCP pushed ahead with popular mobilization and civil war. After 1946 American forces were withdrawn, and Secretary of State Marshall in Washington abstained from intervention.

The Chinese civil war from 1946 to 1949 was one of the big struggles of modern times. At the beginning the Nationalists had about 3 million troops, mostly with modern arms including American-supplied trucks, tanks and planes. The main lack was a cause to inspire the common soldier. Chiang Kai-shek, contrary to experienced advice, persisted in reoccupying provincial centers in the North and Northeast, where his garrisons were soon cut off and became dependent on air supplies. The CCP infiltrated and mobilized rural support in the Northeast as they had earlier in North China. The CCP forces began with about a million men but gained steadily in men and American equipment from Nationalist surrenders. Maneuvering in the countryside, mobilizing the villages, destroying Nationalist rail communications, but avoiding unfavorable terms of battle, the CCP field armies grew in size and power. They were aided by the mobilized logistic support of some millions of peasants who could both destroy railways and substitute for them, as well as dig tank traps and report the results.

Less than a year after the People's Republic had been proclaimed, over 50,000 young people gathered inside the Forbidden City, now called the Imperial Palace, to welcome delegates of the World Federation of Democratic Youth.

The Nationalist debacle in 1947–1949 was a failure less of arms than of aims. Chiang's forces had superior arms but no capacity for economic revival, no program for popular mobilization, no new vision of China's future. Urban populations in the KMT areas were increasingly demoralized by skyrocketing inflation. The Nationalists reoccupying the Lower Yangtze acted like corrupt conquerors, seizing property and treating their Chinese compatriots as enemy collaborators. In the civil war, Nationalist military collapse came from many causes: Whampoa-vs.-Kwangsi jealousies among commanders, defensiveness and hoarding of resources in warlord style, corruption in handling of supplies, distrust between officers and men, the Generalissimo's determination to mastermind tactics from a distance. By mid-1948 the Communists equaled the Nationalists in numbers. In October they forced the surrender of the large garrisons in the Northeast, and,

by January 1949, of large forces surrounded on the Hsuchow plain north
of Nanking. In January the Communists entered Tientsin and Peking, in
April Nanking, in May Shanghai, in October Canton, in November
Chungking. By May 1950 their victory was complete. Chiang Kai-shek
and part of the KMT leadership withdrew to Taiwan. In the midst of these
events the People's Republic of China (PRC) was proclaimed at Peking
on October 1, 1949.

Founding the People's Republic

Political Organization.   After twenty-eight years of trial and error on
the road to power, the CCP had acquired the experience, vision, and self-
confidence to try to create a new China. The early 1950's recalled the
great epochs of reorganization in which a new dynasty such as the Ming
swept out foreign influence, surveyed the land and people, and put the
empire in order. Continuities with the past, however, were less striking
than innovations, creative adaptations of what the modern world, especially
the Soviet Union, had to offer. The first eight years of the PRC to 1957
were an era of vigorous innovation and apparent success.

The military takeover left in office most local administrators, since the
CCP had barely 700,000 persons to fill 2 million posts. The Communist
cadres gave the takeover a festive air, dancing the *yang-ko* in the streets,
proclaiming peace and liberation. It was a hopeful honeymoon period,
devoted to getting rid of the residual Kuomintang influence, supplanting
it with a coalition government, and reforming China's armies, foreign
relations, and economic system.

Mao defined the new government as a democratic coalition under Communist leadership at the same time that it was a dictatorship directed against
the reactionary classes or "enemies of the people." Thus the Chinese
"people's democratic dictatorship" would attempt in united-front style to
line up the broadest possible support for the regime and at the same time
eliminate its foes. Any individual could be transferred by a stroke of the
pen to the category of enemy of the people—a flexible system for sifting
out dissident members of the population. Many counterrevolutionaries
were executed.

The new central administration under Chou En-lai as prime minister
left several minor parties in existence, though without much following, and
gave posts of prominence to non-Communists in order to carry out the
idea of coalition government. It was essential to use the training and ability
of that major part of the upper class that had never been Communist.
Liberal intellectuals were therefore given scope for their talents and placed
in high positions, interlarded in the ministries with party members who

Chairman Mao and Premier Chou, photographed in 1952 watching a sports meet of the People's Liberation Army.

lacked their abilities but were more under control. The larger part of the scholars returned from the West as patriots, and were devoted to their country's future. Long since estranged from the Kuomintang, they saw no alternative but to cooperate with the CCP.

The Communists, like the Kuomintang, set up a tripod of power—party, government, and army, each forming a separate echelon but tied together by the Communist leadership. The party grew to 2.7 million members by 1947, to 6.1 million by 1953, to 14 million by 1959, to 17 million by 1961, and to some 28 million by 1973. (It would total 47 million in 1987.) The Central Committee grew to include ninety-four members and ninety-three alternates as of 1962, but power was exercised by its Political Bureau of nineteen members and ultimately by this bureau's Standing Committee of some seven persons. Below the Central Committee the party structure descended through roughly eight levels, the principal ones being 6 regional bureaus; 28 provincial or big-city committees; 258 special district committees; 2200 county *(hsien)* or similar committees; some 26,000 commune committees after 1958; and more than 1 million branch committees in the villages, factories, schools, army, or other units.

The party structure was paralleled by the government structure that its members interpenetrated. People's Representative Congresses were set up in a hierarchy from the village on up to the National People's Congress at Peking, first convened in 1954. These congresses were supposed to provide an arena for popular participation in government but had no real power. The government structure was reorganized in 1954 when the new constitution (to be distinguished from the new party constitution of 1956) diminished the role of non-Communists and strengthened that of the prime minister. Chou En-lai now headed a State Council that included as many as sixteen vice premiers and the heads of some seventy ministries or similar bodies. Administration was divided into major functional systems that handled political and legal (internal) affairs; propaganda and education (cultural matters); agriculture, forestry, and water conservation (rural work); industry and communications; finance and trade. Each of these systems was supervised both by an office of the State Council and by an office of the party Central Committee. "Vertical rule" extending downward through lower-level branch agencies was balanced by "dual rule" when such branch agencies were also coordinated through committees operating laterally at a given level in the hierarchy. Foreign affairs and military affairs were also handled by functional systems.

In all operations the party set the policy and the government agencies carried it out. The party also had its members in most of the key administrative posts, and its regional, provincial, and local party committees could supervise as they coordinated action at the various levels. Within each government agency party members had their own organization in committees and branches, and the leading party members formed a top group or "party fraction."

Parallel to the party and government were the new nationwide mass organizations. These had originated during the KMT-CCP collaboration of the 1920's, but the KMT had let them wither away. For example, the All China Federation of Trade Unions founded in 1922 claimed a membership of over 13 million in 1956. Similar organizations were set up for Democratic Women (76 million members in 1953); Democratic Youth (34 million in 1957); Cooperative Workers, that is, peasants in cooperatives (162 million in 1956); and for intellectuals, students, Young Pioneers, and so on. These mass organizations reached the individual in his professional or social role, among his peers, in ways that the government could not. Each had broad programs and an extensive administrative apparatus. Half the adult population was thus brought into one or another action group and its program of meetings, study, and agitation. Big training programs with schools and indoctrination centers served to recruit activist personnel. The mass organizations, bridging the immemorial gap between populace and officialdom, helped to politicize the formerly apolitical populace and applied the concept of the "mass line": that the CCP leadership must be guided by constant contact with the worker-peasant masses, first securing from the party workers full and accurate reports as to the masses' problems and opinions, then issuing policy directives to meet these problems, and finally getting the masses to adopt the policies as their own and carry them out. In effect, this was an effort to indoctrinate and manipulate the climate of opinion. When coordinated in each locality, this whole apparatus could bring to bear upon every individual a pervasive and overwhelming public pressure.

The mechanism to apply this pressure was the campaign or movement, which might appear to start spontaneously but developed only as the Central

Committee decreed. Campaigns quickly set in motion the enormous new apparatus of party, state, and mass organizations and directed hammer blows against one target after another among the various classes and their habits and institutions.

Standing behind this apparatus for revolutionary change were well-paid security forces and secret services. Local police stations also supervised the street committees, whose duty it was to promote not only welfare measures but also mutual surveillance and denunciation among neighbors and within families. The street committees disposed informally of conflicts arising among individuals. The police stations settled more serious cases or if necessary passed them on to the hierarchy of "people's courts," where criminal cases normally came to trial only after the accused had been thoroughly interrogated, without benefit of counsel, had fully confessed, and had denounced any others concerned. Since law expressed the revolutionary policy of the party, it remained largely uncodified and changeable. The legal profession was not developed. Justice was weighted on the side of the state, to be secured by applying universal principles to the circumstances in each case, with a minimum of procedure. Litigation was disesteemed, legislation unimportant. Although law codes remained unpublished, the norms of conduct were of course made known through political indoctrination. In all this there were many echoes of Chinese tradition. "Reform through labor" in state factories and work camps followed Soviet organization but reflected the ancient Chinese belief that individual conduct could be reformed through indoctrination and social pressure. But overall the state control of the individual was much greater than it had ever been under the more loosely organized regimes of the past.

Economic Reconstruction. In 1949 Mao proclaimed a "shift to the cities" and the need to learn from the Soviet example in industrialization. A first aim was to get production back to its prewar level. In the Northeast, the Soviet occupation had removed more than half the capital equipment, worth at least 2 billion American dollars. In China proper, railroads had been torn up, urban labor demoralized. Wartime blockades between city and country had increased rural self-sufficiency; market crops such as cotton had to be revived. Some 9 million persons were on government rations or payrolls (including minor Nationalist administrative and military personnel). The regime still had to expand its note issue to meet a budget deficit of perhaps 75 per cent.

The first move toward quelling the inflation was to get the budget more or less balanced by increasing revenue, first in the countryside by collecting agricultural taxes in kind, then in the cities through devices such as a sales tax on each major commodity and business taxes set by "democratic appraisal" of trade associations to squeeze money out of the more monetized sector of the economy. Secondly, the entire fiscal administration was reorganized to give the central government control over formerly local taxes, to eliminate the handling of official funds by private banks, and generally to reduce expenditures. By taking over the banks, the government got control of money and credit and set up six government trading corporations to dominate prices in major consumer commodities.

One device for restoring confidence was to express wages, salaries, bank deposits, some government payments, and bond issues in terms of commodity units (commodity "basket" values), defined in quantities of goods of daily use such as certain amounts of rice, flour, coal, and white shirting. As prices rose, the commodity-based unit would rise accordingly in money terms. Paid in this unit, one was protected against further inflation. Thus, by a variety of methods designed to achieve a balance between the supply of goods and the flow of money income, the inflation was conquered by mid-1950. It was an impressive achievement.

By 1952 the old economy had been given greater unity. Railway track had been rebuilt and even expanded from about 10,000 miles to 15,000, and highways had been reopened to make a total of about 75,000 miles. A centralized banking system and single uniform currency now covered the country. Budgeting could be attempted realistically for the first time. Private enterprise was permitted to continue in form, but in fact it was brought increasingly under state control. By controlling credit and raw materials and monopolizing key commodities, the state could now dominate production and commerce, in addition to having outright control of most heavy industry, railways, and foreign trade. The one other thing necessary was to achieve the traditional goal of controlling the surplus production of the land.

The nationwide land reform, begun in mid-1950 and completed by early 1953, applied the tried and true methods that the CCP had devised to establish its power in North China during the anti-Japanese war. The process was not merely economic in aim but also social and political. A work team of cadres coming to a village first identified out-and-out enemies, if necessary got them out of the way, and then explained the desirability of land reform to the poor peasantry and identified active elements to lead the forthcoming movement. After this preparation a period of "class struggle" was inaugurated. In "struggle meetings" the accumulated grievances of the populace could be brought forth in "speaking bitterness" or "settling accounts." Unpopular landlords or "local despots" could be either killed, expelled, or brought to confess and reform, while the entire community committed themselves to the new order by taking violent measures.

The next phase was to create peasants' associations that by a process of community assent could work out the definition of class status for each individual as landlord, rich peasant, middle peasant, poor peasant, or farm laborer and could carry on the classification, confiscation, and redistribution of landholdings. The resulting "equalization of land tenure" was in the old tradition of peasant rebellions. Generally the remnants of the landlord gentry were wiped out either in person or in status, while the party representatives established their authority. The tiller now had title to his land.

This "new democracy" phase of private ownership had been advertised in 1950 to last for a "rather long time," but in fact it lasted no longer for the farmer than it had for the capitalist. The regime moved without delay toward the construction of the new collectivist agrarian system. The reform moved gradually from north to south through a series of planned phases, first setting up temporary, usually seasonal, small-scale mutual-aid teams, then larger permanent ones, and then agricultural producers' cooperatives in which the peasants began to cultivate in common and share a common product in proportion to their pooled contributions of land, equipment, and labor. The cooperatives were still posited on private ownership of land and voluntary cooperation for mutual benefit. However, the goal began to shift. Soon it was argued that only full-scale collectivization could effect the increase in agricultural product necessary to pay for industrialization.

Social Change.   China's traditional ancestor reverence, family-clan cohesiveness, and filial piety had long been eroding. Communist "liberation" furthered the process. By the new marriage law of 1950, women were given full equality with men in rights of marriage, divorce, and property ownership. This acknowledged the portentous but little studied emancipation of Chinese women, a secular change that had been accelerating throughout the century. As a symbolic deathblow to the old family system, children were now commended for denouncing their parents, thus spectacularly reversing the ancient stress on filial piety as the highest virtue. Extended family ties were disparaged as feudal, and romantic love as bourgeois. The new state tried to displace the Chinese extended family system as the focus of one's primary loyalty, leaving the nuclear family as the norm, much as in industrial-urbanized societies.

Mobilization of the populace was made easier in late 1950 by the Korean War (see Chapter 27). Reports of China's early victories and later of alleged germ warfare by the United States provided a useful sanction for destroying the generally favorable Chinese image of America. Two major campaigns were mounted, to "resist America, aid Korea," and to "suppress counterrevolutionaries." They called for patriotic spying on relatives and neighbors, public denunciation even of parents, and consignment of enemies of the people to "reform through labor." Execution of such enemies, together with persons condemned by "people's courts" in the land reform, were in the hundreds of thousands, some say many millions. The honeymoon was over.

In this context of terror and patriotism, foreign missionaries were denounced as spies and jailed or expelled. A "three-self" movement was set going, for "self-government, self-support, and self-propagation" of the Christian church in China, free of the missionaries' alleged "cultural imperialism." "National churches" free of foreign ties were finally set up. By 1958, the "three-self" movement unified the worship of all Christian denominations in each locality.

The campaign mechanism for mobilizing public pressure against designated types of individual conduct was used more and more plainly for refashioning China's social structure. The "three-anti" and "five-anti" movements of 1951–1952 were organized very thoroughly with standardized methods. The "three-anti" campaign was directed against officialdom and was anticorruption, antiwaste, and antibureaucratism—plainly an attempt to weed out and invigorate the vast administrative apparatus inherited from the KMT and rapidly added to since 1949. The "five-anti" movement was a similarly concerted attack on merchants and manufacturers (the bourgeoisie) and was specifically against bribery, tax evasion, theft of state assets, cheating in labor or materials, and stealing of state economic intelligence. As in all campaigns, the public was mobilized, committees established, and appearances created of great popular initiative, righteous anger, and enthusiasm for the triumph of virtue. Confessions, apologies, and the reform or elimination of culprits by suicide, execution, or labor camp followed. Large sums were also squeezed out of the business class.

Building upon methods used in Yenan to Leninize the party (as well as to convert Japanese war prisoners), Liu Shao-ch'i and other organizers developed empirical procedures of thought reform to deal with every type of enemy or supporter. When Americans taken prisoner in the Korean War "confessed" to germ warfare and collaborated with their Chinese captors, they were responding to techniques developed through use with Chinese of all sorts, including party members. These so-called "brainwashing" procedures applied to prisoners were the extreme example of what in a more normal form was the real Communist effort at revolution, to change Chinese thinking and behavior.

Thought reform generally had certain common features: control of the individual's personal environment and of the information available to him (this was now true of the whole country); the stimuli of idealism and of terror intermixed; and a grim psychological experience, undergone with guidance through successive phases and intensified by the manipulation of one's sense of guilt or shame. The Chinese slang term "brainwashing" imparted perhaps too much mystery to a process visible elsewhere in religious crusades of the past, only now more thoroughly organized. Psychologists can explain how privation, prolonged insecurity, and tension, combined with extended fatigue and repetitive indoctrination, can shatter the individual's sense of inner identity and create pressures from which the only escape for many is submission to authority. For the Chinese student class, from whom the CCP had to get its cadres, this intellectual-emotional reconditioning was carried out in the big revolutionary colleges set up as part of the new educational system.

A center of this type containing about four thousand students might be subdivided into classes of one or two hundred and then into study groups of six to ten persons. A typical six-month course of thought reform might consist of three stages. First, group identification, a period of togetherness and considerable freedom and enthusiasm. During this stage major Marx-Lenin-Maoist concepts were studied, and a free exchange of views, with a feeling of common effort, led the trainee to expose himself freely in a "thought mobilization."

The second phase was one of induced emotional conflict within each individual. The daily schedule continued to be physically exhausting. The milieu, carefully controlled behind the scenes, now seemed to close in. The individual began to feel under pressure as criticism and self-criticism intensified and the dangers of being rejected became apparent. The evils within the old individual were now attacked, not merely the old society in the abstract, and the student strove to dig up his failings and correct them. He might struggle with himself and be "struggled with" by his group-mates over an excess of subjectivism or objectivism, of opportunism or dogmatism, of bureaucratism or individual heroism, and so forth. Each participant, whether or not he resisted, felt completely alone. He soon felt guilt (he should be punished) and also a sense of shame. He was thus prepared to achieve a psychological catharsis through confession and self-condemnation.

The third phase was that of submission and rebirth. When his final thought summary or confession had been gone over and accepted, the individual was likely to feel exhilarated, cleansed, a new person. He had been manipulated so that the wellsprings of his own nature had put him under intense emotional pressure, and the relief from this self-induced tension was associated with the external authority of the party, on whom he should henceforth be dependent. The party's aim was not only to secure control over disciplined activists but also to raise the quality of their performance by changing their goals and values. They renounced family and father, and accepted the party and the revolution in their place.

In the case of older intellectuals, particularly returned students from the West, criticism, self-criticism, and confession could only be an overlay of the formative experience of a mature person. When Peking professors denounced the corrupting influence of the bourgeois West, the net effect was perhaps less to change these individuals than to align them in the public eye as supporters of the new order. Thus the one class who might have represented a Western non-Communist influence neutralized themselves.

Out of the Chinese inheritance, authoritarian traditions could be invoked for modern purposes. One point of resonance was the concept of the unity of theory and practice. Lenin held that theory must be applied in activity, as an effort not only to understand the world but to change it. Or as Mao said, "We must unify appropriately the general truth of Marxism with the concrete practice of the Chinese revolution." Confucian scholars, particularly Wang Yang-ming (1472–1529), had attacked the dualism of knowledge and action, holding that the completely sincere man must express his moral perceptions in equally moral conduct. Confucianist self-cultivation meant that knowledge is realized in action and action contributes to knowledge.

While Confucian self-cultivation was not a group affair, it stressed the possibility of morally improving human nature, the ancient Chinese belief that through proper ethical instruction and exhortation, man can be made into a more social being. The gap between individual self-cultivation and group self-criticism is a very broad one in fact, but the two have something in common. Thought reform at Yenan made use of traditional Chinese terminology and invoked Confucian sanctions. The good Communist, according to Liu Shao-ch'i, must discipline himself through self-cultivation, through "watching himself when alone," so as to become flexibly and resourcefully obedient to the party's leadership. Thus where Confucianism had instilled loyalty to family, father, and emperor, Maoism now diverted it to the people, the party, and the leader. The Classics were quoted for this purpose.

Thought reform was carried on mainly among the educated minority, who formed the talent pool of potential elites. Among the great mass of peasants in the villages, social change would become most evident in the assignment of class status to each individual and the installation of a new leadership—the cadres or revolutionary activists. Representing the new authority of the CCP and its central government, this local managerial stratum would succeed to the position of the old lower gentry. But social change in the vast Chinese countryside came more slowly than in the cities.

The Korean War and Soviet Aid.   Mao Tse-tung early in 1949 proclaimed his policy of "leaning to one side" against "capitalist imperialism" and later spent nine weeks of hard bargaining in Moscow, where in February 1950 he signed with Stalin a thirty-year Sino-Soviet alliance treaty. Yet it seems unlikely that Peking expected to join in the Soviet-armed North Korean aggression of June 1950 against South Korea. Instead, the CCP may have hoped to seize Taiwan from the Nationalists, but this was prevented when President Truman ordered the American Seventh Fleet to stop invasion either way across the Taiwan Strait. As the Korean War developed, China's chief strategic concern was for the security of her principal industrial base inherited from the Japanese in south Manchuria.

When the United States forces crossed the 38th parallel in early October and pushed north toward the Yalu, they plainly expanded their aim from repulse of the Northern invasion to an ill-advised effort to reunite Korea by force. This military purpose, stemming from MacArthur's victory and acquiesced in by Washington, disregarded China's strategic need for a buffer state, so as to avoid having a declared enemy lodged on the frontier of her northeast industrial base. China issued a clear warning of intervention, and in mid-October massively organized Chinese Communist "volunteers," units of Lin Piao's Fourth Field Army, secretly began to cross the Yalu into North Korea. In late November, they surprised the Americans, whose forces were divided, and forced the troops to retreat all the way south of Seoul.

But China's attempt in her turn to use her vast resources of manpower to unify Korea by force was now contained by United Nations firepower, which eventually produced a stalemate on about the 38th parallel. Truce talks began in July 1951 and dragged on at the border post of Panmunjom for two years. During this period fighting continued and the Chinese forces in Korea were built up with heavy Soviet weapons. The People's Liberation Army also invaded Tibet in October 1950 and in a year-long campaign reasserted Chinese control. Afterward, China's military modernization used Soviet models and assistance. A professional officer corps was created in Soviet style to run a regular army of about 2.5 million men.

Soviet aid came only at a price. In 1950 Sino-Soviet "joint-stock" companies were set up, on the model used in Eastern Europe, for the development of mining in Sinkiang and similar purposes. However, after the death of Stalin in 1953 these were liquidated, and the Soviets also gradually gave up their special position in the Northeast on the main railway and at the Port Arthur naval base.

In industrialization the Soviet example and expertise were at first China's greatest inspiration. Thousands of Chinese trainees went to the U.S.S.R., and thousands of Russian technicians came to help with hundreds of industrial projects. Aided by Soviet loans, China's prewar pattern of foreign trade was reversed, flowing to the Soviet bloc instead of to the West and Japan. China received essential help in technology, unknown amounts of military hardware, and capital equipment but went into debt accordingly. The loans were repaid in raw materials.

China's capacity to follow the Stalinist Russian industrial model was inhibited by certain specific conditions. China in the early 1950's was actually closer to the Russia of 1900 than to the Soviet Union of 1928, when the five-year plans began. Russia in 1900 already had a higher per capita production of pig iron, steel, and cotton goods, and more railroad track per square mile, than China in 1952, together with a larger corps of modern-educated technical and professional manpower and a more developed educational system. The Soviet model, which stressed heavy industry at the expense of the peasant, was thus not really suited to China's situation. China's superabundance of people (estimated by the census of 1953 at 583 million and increasing about 12 to 14 million yearly), together with the comparative lack of new land for cultivation, meant that China's population would press upon the food supply even more than Russia's had.

The Struggle Toward Socialism

China's social revolution had tried, most basically, to make peasants into citizens, to bring the masses into politics. But the Chinese village was not yet part of automobile civilization. Its concerns had come down from a simpler age: how to produce enough to live on and how to distribute it. Next to famine and disease, the farmer's ancient enemy had been the ruling class—the privileged few whose education and connections gave them access to land and office. Since the ruling class generally governed the villages from the towns and cities, Mao's problem after taking power was how to reach the village to revolutionize it. If he could not reach and change them, the villagers would retain the ancient ideas that sanctioned the ruling class —for example, that acquiring an education qualifies one to rule others— and thus the old village would remain ready to accept a new ruling class. The Maoist revolution, to remake the society by remaking the people, thus became a semicontrolled process of struggle, between ideas, behavior patterns, and class interests.

One feature of the revolution was the fusion of morality and politics, such that a policy mistake was a moral crime, on the ancient Confucian assumption that conduct is character made manifest or, in Marxist terms, that theory and practice interact. This unity of ideas and action could be achieved (or at least aimed at), in the People's Republic as under imperial Confucianism, became moral-ideological authority and political power were combined. Since theory and practice in this Chinese view interpenetrate, ideology must also constantly shift in its application to events as they unfold.

Another feature of Mao's thought was a stress on contradictions as the stuff of the dialectical process of conflict: for example, contradictions of socialism and imperialism in the outer world, of the needs of industry and those of agriculture within China, of proletarian and bourgeois tendencies within oneself, of freedom and discipline, democracy and centralism, and so on in all aspects of life. Contradictions when perceived lead to struggle, eventual polarization, and resolution in a new unity. Thus one struggle only led to another without any end to the process, which Mao aptly called "continuing revolution," a way of life. What a contrast with the old Confucian ideal of harmony!

Agriculture versus Industry. Land reform together with controls over the urban and industrial sector put Peking by 1953 in a position to plan for both industrialization and agricultural collectivization. The swelling cities would increase their demand for agricultural products. Industrialization would also necessitate imports of Soviet-bloc capital goods, to be paid for again by agricultural products. To extract more from the farm economy, a squeezing mechanism had to be created in the form of true collectives. While these might lower incentives, they seemed the only sure way to enforce saving and check the revival of a "rich peasant" class.

The initial move toward collectivization got results faster than anticipated. Fifteen per cent of the farm land and families were in agricultural producers' cooperatives by mid-1955. Mao Tse-tung spent several weeks touring major provinces, testing local sentiment, and then called for 250 million peasants to form 2 million agricultural producers' cooperatives of fifty families each (say two cooperatives in each of a million or so villages). This bold plan, pushed by eager cadres, again went faster than expected. By May 1956, nine-tenths of the peasantry were reported to have joined cooperatives. They were quickly asked to move on to the higher level of socialized agriculture by giving up their shares in the cooperatives (which had varied according to their contributions) and becoming wage laborers on full collective farms. Unlike the disastrous Soviet collectivization of 1929–1932, collectivization in China did not lead directly to state ownership but to ownership by the individual cooperatives, which bought the land from the peasant owners. The program at its successive stages had evidently produced sufficient results to obviate resistance—at least very little was reported. China's peasantry saw no alternative but to have faith in Chairman Mao and the party, even though the New Democracy had now run its course in only five years. Unlike Lenin, Mao had begun with the villages, not the cities, and all anti-Communist leadership had been eliminated.

The cooperatives developed forthwith into fully collective farms. One or two to a village, they now served as the new focus of village life, undertaking the local public works and welfare activities that under the empire had been the function of gentry leadership. Where the local Confucian degree-holders of the big families—a conservative-minded and often exploitative elite—had traditionally taken the initiative to repair temples and bridges or maintain schools and charities, it was now the local cooperative or collective farm chairman, usually an enthusiastic party appointee, who initiated projects for reforestation, combating erosion, care of the aged, improving the local dispensary, introducing pumps or new plows, or pushing literacy. Ambitious plans set forth bright promises: to see cultural amenities introduced, the multitude of diseases and all flood and drought eliminated, forests widely planted, labor fully employed. For the farm boy just learning to read, this confident vision was undoubtedly inspiring. For doubters and dissenters there was plainly announced "reform through labor."

Meanwhile preparation for a Soviet-type forced-draft industrial development had gone forward with the nationalization of banking, industry, and trade. The conflict between the development of agriculture and industry, and the consequent subordination of the former, was apparent in the targets of the first five-year plan for the years 1953–1957. The targets were announced only in 1955: steel to be quadrupled, power and cement doubled, but cotton piece goods to be increased by less than one-half and food grains by less than one-fifth. The farmer's product would be taken from him indirectly as well as by outright collection of crops and taxes. Just as men had been cheaper than armament in Chinese warfare, so in her agricultural development China would have to stress capital-cheap, labor-intensive projects such as flood control dikes and irrigation ditches. Pigs could be multiplied to provide both food and manure, but chemical fertilizers were likely to be limited. Meanwhile capital investment was to be concentrated in heavy industry. The Maoist enthusiasts who now dominated the CCP Central Committee envisioned that the people's productive energies would be psychologically liberated and that incentive devices such as emulation campaigns would achieve "quantity, speed, quality, and economy" of production all at once. This forced-draft industrialization eventually did channel something like 30 per cent of the Chinese people's gross national product through the government, which used approximately one-half of it for investment. China's industrial growth seemed rapid and formidable—as of 1957, the fastest of any underdeveloped Asian country.

In this period also, the railroad was extended in the Northwest to Outer Mongolia and over the desert road to Turkestan. These lines, accompanied by migration, opened up the arid Inner Asian frontier for greater exploitation and also had political-strategic importance, strengthening the revived Chinese grip on Inner Mongolia and Sinkiang.

Intellectuals and Cadres. "Socialist construction" required the mobilization of everyone, including the thin stratum of about 100,000 technical, professional, and academic "higher intellectuals" who were still mainly Western

*At the Chinese People's University in Peking, students were formed
into study groups "in order to develop a cooperative outlook."*

oriented. The party heads believed, optimistically, that they had by this
time "spiritually transformed" this stratum and won its allegiance; but they
were concerned that the new party apparatus had stifled intellectual life.
Campaigns were therefore mounted in 1956–1957 to manipulate these two
strategic elements, intellectuals and cadres.

A campaign for freer criticism by the intellectuals of the cadres and bureaucrats was begun in May 1956 under the slogan "Let a hundred flowers
bloom together; let the hundred schools of thought contend." This was not
a clarion call for free speech. Criticism was not to overstep the implicit limits
of complete devotion to the party's final authority. In the aftermath of the
Hungarian rising of October–November 1956 and its suppression by Russia,
which coincided with signs of discontent in China, Mao announced in 1957
his doctrine of contradictions—some "antagonistic" as between the regime
and its "enemies," and some "nonantagonistic," normal and arguable, as
between the bureaucracy and "the people." Within this framework he hoped
that a continuing struggle over the execution of policy, using his method of
"unity-criticism-unity," could be healthily pursued and yet contained. As in
the Yenan period, this dialectical process would call forth criticism and then
would meet it. Repeated invitations eventually released in May 1957 a

surprising torrent of publicly expressed dissatisfaction on the part of intellectuals and the professionally trained elite with the CCP's totalitarian political system, its ideas, aims, and methods. This startled the party and was harshly suppressed. The recent critics were soon obliged to accuse themselves publicly and condemn one another.

Meanwhile the Central Committee faced the even more serious problem of controlling the enormous apparatus of cadres that executed its policies. The twin drives in agriculture and industry had achieved spectacular results. The face of the country was changed with new roads, factories, cities, dikes, dams, lakes, afforestation, and cultivation, for which the 650 millions of China had been mobilized in nationwide efforts of unparalleled intensity and magnitude. An enormous apparatus of many millions of activists was needed to do the party's work, yet it was largely unseasoned and inexperienced. Four-fifths of the party members probably lacked a high school education. Young cadres fresh from their indoctrination might easily fall into the evils of "blind optimism," "dogmatism," and "commandism," or of "conservatism," "empiricism," and "blind opportunism," instead of manipulating the peasantry correctly through discussion, logic, and persuasion. Cadres could be stimulated by Mao's ideological pronouncements more easily than they could be given wisdom, or saved from the corruption and false reporting that had inveterately characterized peasant-official relations in the past. Agricultural collectivization had in fact proceeded with considerable friction. The peasantry had been widely misled by the cadres' false promises.

Roused by the danger of being "out of touch with the masses," the CCP inaugurated in April 1957 a great ideological campaign for "rectification" of the party cadres' working style, parallel to the campaign to induce criticism from the intellectuals. In mid-1957 these two campaigns merged in a great "anti-rightist" campaign. The result was to stigmatize and put out of action one-half to three-quarters of a million of China's tiny educated elite—a serious disaster for the revolution. Both intellectuals and officials were also brought into a big campaign for "downward transfer," *hsia-fang*, to move teachers, students, and city cadres and functionaries into the countryside so that by manual labor among the villagers they could avoid "separation from the masses" and could also help agricultural production. From this time on, Mao's revolution began to run into a series of disasters.

The Great Leap Forward of 1958.   When the Central Committee met in September 1957, it faced a crucial problem. "Socialist transformation" had given the new state-and-party apparatus an effective control over the economy, and party committees at all levels now made economic decisions. But red tape had grown faster than production. Collectivization had not actually increased the agricultural product received by the regime, which faced a dire problem of agricultural stagnation. During 1952–1957 city population grew about 30 per cent, but government grain collections hardly grew at all. The Soviet model of taxing agriculture to build industry was facing a dead end.

To meet this crisis, the strategy of a Great Leap Forward was adopted in 1958 to achieve development in the modern industrial sector and the rural agricultural sector as two distinct though related processes. In the villages, mass mobilization would make use of rural labor never before fully employed: first, for irrigation, flood control, and land reclamation; second, to raise productivity per unit of land by using more hands; and third, to expand small-scale rural industries with materials and equipment locally available. It was hoped that this rural development, using China's abundance of manpower, would not need much help from the modern industrial sector, which would put its product into exports for securing capital goods or into investments in further plant construction.

The Great Leap was to take advantage of China's rural backwardness and manpower surplus and realize the Maoist faith that ideological incentives could get economic results, that a new spirit could unlock hitherto untapped sources of human energy. Since the professional economists, like other intellectuals, had suffered downgrading as a result of the anti-rightist campaign, the overambitious targets of the Great Leap were formulated in each locality, not by economists, but by cadres inspired by emulation and often contemptuous of experts. One spectacular way to localize industry was to set up small backyard iron smelters that would involve farmers in metallurgy (even though the metal produced usually turned out unusable). As the campaign developed, there was a general decentralization of economic planning and management. The central statistical bureau was broken up and localized. As a result of reporting by untrained local enthusiasts, the statistical bureau claimed that in 1958 production of food crops and cotton had nearly doubled in one year. The leadership became a captive of its own claims. The incredible figures that the Central Committee trumpeted abroad had to be humiliatingly withdrawn in the late summer of 1959.

The Great Leap got mixed results. Through sheer muscle power, it changed the face of China with tens of thousands of reservoirs, thousands of small hydroelectric power stations, hundreds of miles of railways, bridges over the great rivers, new canals and highways, more mines, more irrigated land. But this all-out effort at instant growth led to massive errors, such as the salinization of newly irrigated land, and a tremendous wasting of manpower, which was withdrawn from agriculture.

In 1958 the commune became an integral part of the Great Leap, based on the mass-line idea of the release of the "spontaneous initiative of the masses." A typical commune was formed by amalgamating a number of

*A people's commune shown in the first spring (1959) after the Big
Leap Forward.*

agricultural producers' cooperatives of the higher stage. The commune included local government functions, both military and security, as well as
local trade, finance, taxation, accounting, statistics, and planning, all under
party control. It was divided into production brigades composed of teams,
a production team corresponding to the old cooperative, perhaps half a
village. Private plots were taken over. Peasants were to eat in large mess
halls, although this was seldom achieved, and all labor was to be controlled.
Farmer battalions marched like shock troops to attack new production goals
while women took their places in the fields. This grandiose concept was
pursued with great fanfare and utopian fervor. The result, it was hoped,
would be a new type of agricultural city with the peasants proletarianized
and uprooted from their own land. Since land owning had been an inveterate ideal among China's farming families, peasants tended to drag their
feet in opposition to the communes.

    This revolution collapsed from general overwork and exhaustion, the
damaging of incentives, and the incapacities of management. When an
egalitarian wage system was instituted, paying each according to his needs,
it lowered productivity. So did shifting labor about like military platoons
within the commune. In December 1958 the Central Committee had to
transfer the center of decision making from the commune down to the level
of the production brigade. Wages were paid again according to labor done
and work points acquired. As the agricultural crisis worsened in 1960, the
commune was further decentralized and the production team with an aver-

age membership of about forty households that could work together became the basic unit. Private garden plots were reintroduced. The economic recession and industrial standstill after 1960 were greater than any that had occurred in the better-off Soviet economy. In the early 1960's China suffered both from adverse weather, producing poor harvests, and also from the withdrawal of Soviet technicians and aid. As a result China underwent several years of serious economic dislocation. Gross national product declined by perhaps one-third in 1960. Malnutrition was widespread. Mortality rose in 1959 by 25 million or more above normal. These were victims of mismanagement. The people were exhausted and apathetic. Transportation broke down. Industry stagnated. The regime acknowledged that agriculture, shortchanged for a decade, must now receive top priority. Mao and the CCP, using their political power, had made economic errors on a truly gigantic scale.

The mounting extremism of the Chinese revolution during the 1950's, the feverish tendency to accelerate campaigns and revise targets upward, had been continually encouraged by Mao and the Central Committee in the faith that the masses would respond to a Marxist-Leninist leadership that knew how to unleash the latent "productive forces" of society and free the "creative capacity" of the Chinese working class that had previously, it was believed, been held in check by domestic and foreign exploiting classes. This faith was not entirely frustrated but neither was it vindicated. By the 1960's the Chinese people had learned how to coexist with the CCP regime, as they had with autocracies in the past, but the initial enthusiasm of the revolution had been spent. Worse still, the rift had widened between the party's top organizers and their charismatic leader. In mid-1959, smarting from the economic debacle of the Great Leap, members of the Central Committee denounced Mao's romantic and extremist policies. Mao weathered their criticism, since he was still indispensable, but his infallibility was gone and he had to remove himself from day-to-day administration of affairs. From this time the domestic policy battle was joined; soon it was complicated by foreign relations.

Foreign Policy. The ethnocentric tradition that the Chinese Empire was all-under-heaven (*t'ien-hsia*) or mankind's "central country" (*chung-kuo*) had stressed China's self-sufficiency and nonexpansiveness, except on its strategic Inner Asian frontier. The revolution during the 1950's created a new Chinese nation that expanded over Inner Asia to include Tibetans, Uighur Turks, Inner Mongols, and two score other minorities within a vast realm that comprised the unheard-of total of 700 million or more persons. The preponderant Han Chinese majority had inherited an ideal of unified central government as the only guarantor of peace and prosperity against civil war and foreign incursion. Unlike European nation-states that all arose within the culture of Christendom, the Chinese had a sense of cultural or ethnic nationalism that demanded the unity of the whole Chinese realm. One principal aim of foreign policy was therefore the recovery of Taiwan, which Peking claimed to be an integral part of China "occupied" by American imperialism. Its recovery would end the Nationalist-Communist civil war and complete China's reunification.

The revolution at home fostered a militant attitude toward the outside world, stressing the universalistic theme of "American imperialism" as the enemy and China's "liberation" as the model for all ex-colonial and underdeveloped countries in a great worldwide struggle of the progressive "socialist camp" against the reactionary "imperialist camp." In these terms China's newly heightened nationalism found expression in a broader universalism, in which People's China relied upon the Soviet Union as its "elder brother." In this spirit, Peking during the 1950's utilized both coercion and persuasion in foreign policy, as on the home front.

The first phase, 1950 to 1954, began belligerently in an interaction with the United States containment policy, which was triggered specifically by the Soviet-backed North Korean invasion of South Korea in June 1950. As we have noted, this precipitated both the American-backed United Nations defense of South Korea and a resumption of American military-naval support of the Nationalist government on Taiwan. Soon after Chinese troops intervened in Korea and entered Tibet, Chinese military support aided the Viet Minh in Indo-China. After two years of negotiation, the Korean armistice was signed in July 1953; and after the defeat of the French at Dien Bien Phu, France's withdrawal from Indo-China was agreed upon, with China participating as a great power, at Geneva in July 1954. This expansion of Peking's influence, however, was paralleled by an expansion of American commitments. On this front of the Cold War, both sides sought security through military action. In September 1954 a joint defense system, the Southeast Asia Treaty Organization (SEATO), was created by the United States to include Britain, France, Australia, New Zealand, the Philippines, Thailand, and Pakistan. Washington also signed defensive alliances with Seoul (October 1953) and Taipei (December 1954). Thus, by the time the Communist-Nationalist confrontation over the offshore island of Quemoy outside Amoy harbor led to a crisis in early 1955, China's activity concerning four contiguous areas — Korea, Taiwan, Vietnam, and Tibet — was matched by an American-led and financed anti-Communist effort at containment.

After the militancy of these early years came a phase of greater reliance on diplomatic persuasion. At the Geneva conference of April–July 1954, Chou En-lai joined the foreign ministers of the other powers in an effort to create stability in Indo-China as France withdrew. In negotiating at this time with India and Burma, Chou enunciated five principles of "peaceful coexistence." These also formed his main theme at the conference held in April 1955 at Bandung in western Java by leaders of twenty Asian and African states. In tune with the "Bandung spirit," American and Chinese ambassadors began in August 1955 to hold periodic talks—in all they held seventy-three at Geneva and then fifty-eight during 1958–1966 at Warsaw.

Yet this soft line soon yielded to a hard one. Imperialism seemed to be on the defensive after Russia launched the first intercontinental ballistic missile (ICBM) in August 1957 and its first satellite orbited the earth in October. In November Mao went to Moscow, leaving China for the second time, to celebrate the fortieth anniversary of the Bolshevik revolution. Declaring that "the east wind prevails over the west wind," he called for a new belligerency in East-West relations. This soon became evident in the Taiwan Strait, where the American buildup of Nationalist military power had been resumed in 1951. The Nationalists increasingly harassed the mainland by espionage, reconnaissance and leaflet-dropping flights, and commando raids. They also strengthened the fortification of "the front" on Quemoy, committing to it a third of the Nationalist forces. Eventually, Communist bombardment in August–September 1958 created a second Quemoy crisis, which subsided but left Quemoy a bone of contention, still held by the Nationalists as a recognized part of the mainland.

Another area of renewed belligerency was Tibet, whose people were pressed toward a socialist revolution that would amount to Sinicization. A rising at Lhasa in March 1959, when the Dalai Lama fled to India, led to harsh repression by the Chinese. During the following summer Sino-Indian friction increased on both ends of the Himalayan frontier and finally erupted in brief hostilities in October 1962. China asserted control of the strategic route between Tibet and Sinkiang through the Aksai-Chin region. Although it later appeared that India had provoked China's brief but crushing counterattack, the People's Republic seemed to the Western public at the time to be the aggressor.

The Cultural Revolution

The Fall into Factionalism. Socialist transformation had bureaucratized Chinese life, but neither it nor the Great Leap and communes had met the people's economic expectations. As popular dissatisfaction mounted, it inspired within party councils a sharper struggle between alternative lines of policy. Once the CCP leadership had established its control of China, its unity began to suffer from the strain of decision making, and this strain

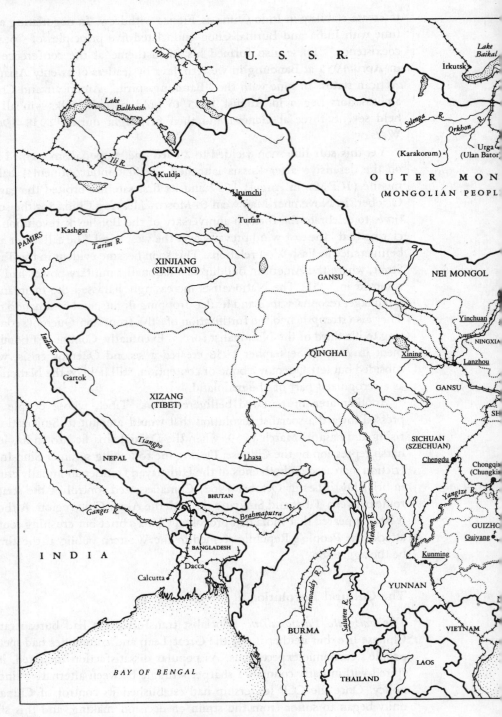

CHINA: THE PEOPLE'S REPUBLIC

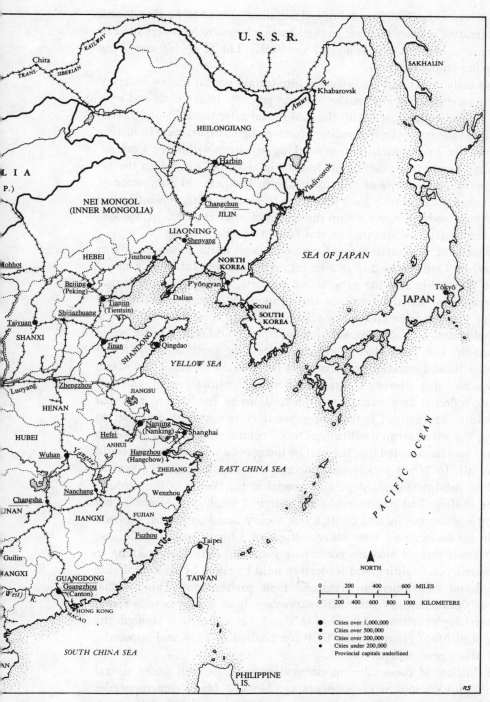

This map contains *pinyin* spellings of place names. To provide consistency from 1800 to the present, however, the text and most other maps use the old Wade-Giles spellings. The railroad to Lhasa in Tibet has not been completed yet.

increased when the Soviet model of industrialization had to be abandoned. The alternative policies inherent in the situation began to be represented by protagonists, Mao on one side and eventually Liu Shao-ch'i and Teng Hsiao-p'ing on the other.

Mao's early career had confirmed in him certain special traits—independence of view and concern for the common peasant. In the early and mid-1920's he had collaborated with the KMT, and after the split of 1927 he had learned the importance of military force and guerrilla tactics. In neither period was he an organization man working primarily within the Communist Party. The twenty years of his leadership after 1935 had seen the repeated success of his style of militant struggle. The personal dominance of Mao Tse-tung was steadily built up by the revolutionary movement's need for personal leadership, yet within the spectrum of alternatives he was distinctly the protagonist of one line and faction against another.

Two views of revolution were of course inherent in the European origins of Marxism. One saw history as a moral drama and revolution as a moral crusade. The other saw the progress of the arts, especially technological development in material terms, as the agent of revolution enabling new forces of production to create new classes. Pursuing these cognate themes, Mao could stress the moral pursuit of social equality and selfless virtue while Liu Shao-ch'i and Teng Hsiao-p'ing could stress the practical need of specialized skills and material progress. This latter strain of "scientific Marxism" assumed that a society's "superstructure" of political, social, and cultural life reflected its material base, the relations of production; and that these had to be changed before the superstructure could be changed. In contrast, the voluntarism (willfulness, not "volunteering") and populism espoused by Mao asserted that the will of the masses, once energized, could conquer all. In Mao's background one can also see the peasant's ancient hatred of ruling class privilege and special status. Early in the century, Chinese students had responded to the anarchist ideal, to abolish all government and capitalism, and create a free society based on mutual cooperation. In his background were other vestiges of China's past: the Chinese classics assert that all men are potentially good and only need teaching to realize their potentialities, and leadership must be taken by an ethical elite whose moral superiority can transcend their environment. This residual strain of Confucianism fostered the supreme role of a sage hero, whereas the more Soviet-oriented Liu Shao-ch'i and his colleagues omitted the "thought of Mao" from the new CCP constitution of 1956 and opposed a cult of Mao's personality.

The dualism of these inherent alternatives could be seen under several rubrics: 1) *Voluntarism versus planning*: Most of Mao's contemporaries favored the systematic effort of five-year plans, the accumulation of invest-

Chairman Mao talking to peasants at Yang-chia-ling near Yenan about 1940.

ment capital, and building up of industry. But Mao was less concerned with economics than with politics. Voluntarism was Mao's personal faith. It led him to favor decentralized local initiative versus central control, the people versus bureaucratism, the peasantry versus any revival of a ruling class. 2) *Leader versus commissar*: Mao had been the distant symbol of paternal compassion, whereas the party commissars under Liu had had to exercise local discipline. Mao stood above his colleagues, a figure apart, worshipped as the object of a cult not unlike an emperor. 3) *The mass line versus party building*: Mao stood for struggle. He wanted the cadres to serve the people, stir them up, and respond to their stirrings in the spirit of the mass line. Liu and other party builders preferred to keep struggle subordinate to party unity and stressed the training of cadres to be a new elite that could guide China's transformation. 4) *Village versus city*: Mao's concerns harked back to the simple existence of Yenan. He disdained city life. His ideal was the omnicompetent man of the soil, a combined farmer, craftsman, and militia soldier in a self-sufficient countryside. Organizers in the Central Committee, in contrast, saw the need of special skills for industrialization, the importance of the urban elite, the necessity of technical education. 5) *Red versus expert*: Finally, the most publicized of all these contrasts was that of the politically indoctrinated versus the professionally trained—in short, the party organizers versus the government specialists.

These different paths to China's future had not always been mutually exclusive but had been advocated as cognate principles (like the ancient *yin* and *yang*) in many Central Committee pronouncements. Liu and Teng had backed the utopianism of the distinctly Maoist Great Leap Forward. But its failure precipitated a hardening of attitudes. After December 1958, Mao "voluntarily" gave up his position as chief of state to Liu. The CCP leadership now confronted the question that comes to every revolution: when should change give way to stability? Alternatively, how can the revolutionary spirit be kept alive? In the final analysis, this was the problem of revisionism, a dilemma that the Soviet Union had also faced. This made the impact of Soviet revisionism on Chinese politics all the greater.

The Sino-Soviet Split.   Since the Chinese and Russian peoples had very different histories, self-images, needs, and goals, it is not surprising that a major split developed between them on several levels at once. Memory made them suspicious of each other: the Mongol horde of the thirteenth century had enslaved South Russia; Tsarist imperialists had encroached on China's Northeast, Mongolia, and Turkestan. Behind the Communist fraternal rhetoric, history provided few bonds of mutual admiration. Their collaboration, chiefly in the form of Soviet aid paid for by China, had followed the desires of their leaders, who could as easily disrupt it. Ideology had been the original bond, so it became the point of fracture.

Mao knew no foreign language. By the time he acquired a Marxist concept it had often been a bit Sinicized in the process of translation. Moreover Mao had begun with revolutionary action; he acquired ideology as he went along. He had to bend Communist doctrine to fit it to local needs. Russia had created a "dictatorship of the proletariat" as the only path to socialism. But the CCP set up a "people's democratic dictatorship" and claimed that a mere "hegemony of the proletariat" at the head of a united front and coalition government representing all "revolutionary classes" could lead China to socialism. Moreover, the CCP claimed to do it by a gradual, persuasive, nonviolent transformation, quite unlike the abrupt and violent change postulated by Lenin and Stalin.

In 1956 Soviet "de-Stalinization"—the exposure of Stalin's crimes— embarrassed the CCP at a time when it was still invoking Stalin's name. To be sure, Soviet premier Khrushchev's recognition of "many paths to socialism" accepted Peking's claim to be the model for Asia, but this concession also cut the ground from under Marxist-Leninist doctrine. From this time on, the split widened. Peking, like Moscow, was now an autonomous center of doctrinal authority. International Communism was no longer monolithic. Friction, if not rupture, was inevitable. Khrushchev, on the crest of the Soviet success in launching the first sputnik, denounced the Great Leap and the communes, with which Mao claimed to be surpassing Moscow, as left deviations, dangerous fanaticism. In return, Soviet "revisionism" was attacked by Peking as an opportunist sell-out to capitalism. Although Moscow had promised Peking nuclear weapon assistance in 1957, it was stopped. The Soviet technicians with their blueprints were suddenly withdrawn from China in 1960. A lively fear of Chinese fanaticism and expansion grew up in the Soviet Union, and by 1969 armed border clashes arose both along the Amur and in Central Asia. The Chinese built air-raid shelters on a massive scale.

As the Sino-Soviet split widened, Peking sought at first to capture the leadership of the Communist world revolution, exporting cultural missions and militant propaganda and supporting "national liberation movements" in Asia and Africa. Mao and his principal supporter in this period, General Lin Piao, pictured how the Chinese model of revolution could be applied to the underdeveloped two-thirds of mankind against the industrialized imperialist powers. The metaphor used in September 1965 was to "surround the cities from the countryside," but the advocacy of self-reliance for all people's revolutions meant that China could point the way but not itself achieve the world revolution by its own expansion. (One is reminded of the ancient theory of tributary relations: China was a model that other countries should follow but on their own initiative.)

Lin Piao's do-it-yourself prescription for world revolution was issued partly to forestall any effort by the professional military to intervene in Vietnam under Soviet nuclear protection, because this would sidetrack the Maoist effort at continuing revolution. In February 1965, the United States had begun continuous bombing of North Vietnam; this aggression on China's doorstep was accompanied by promises not to invade North Vietnam on the ground; and so Peking suffered the humiliation of impotence, unable to protect a neighboring ally. Meanwhile, 1965 brought other setbacks in Peking's foreign relations. China's effort to organize an Afro-Asian conference excluding the Soviet Union failed in June. And in October, an abortive coup in Indonesia was followed by the slaughter of the pro-Peking Indonesian Communist Party. These and other failures abroad helped turn China inward.

Problems within the Party.   Behind the civil strife of the late 1960's were deep strains and stresses. The first was among the people, where there was a gap between China's poverty and the expectations of her citizens, newly active in politics. To destroy the old order, the CCP had roused a whirlwind and now had to ride it. Where the KMT had been a small, superficial regime, the CCP had asserted its authority down to the very rice roots. Shortages before, in the old free market economy, had been no one's fault. Now they reflected poor planning.

Having taken on this staggering burden, the CCP had built enormous structures of administration. But administrators of collective units had tended to become bureaucrats, less concerned with common manual labor, closer to being an upper class. Opportunists interested in their own careers and families reappeared, seeking connections and special privileges, better education, private property. For example, party leaders of the Long March generation were not averse to special schools for their children. In short, "liberation" of the common peasant had intensified rather than diminished the competion for elite status. The new party-government-army power structure was an elite organization, intensely status- and security-conscious, controlled from the top down. The upper incumbents became more cautious and less revolutionary while the lower levels felt boxed in and frustrated. The axiom that revolutionaries supplant an *ancien régime* only to inherit its evils was evidenced in the wide gap between the cadres and the Chinese public. Mao could see that a new ruling class was taking shape, abetted by organization men such as chief of state Liu Shao-ch'i and the CCP secretary-general Teng Hsiao-p'ing.

Within the bureaucratic structure were further problems of morale and motivation. The party was responsible for the thought and behavior, loyalty and discipline, of all party members. They were set apart from nonparty members and deeply involved in the "party life" of constant meetings, criticism and self-criticism, reporting on subordinates, and trying to maintain a good record in the secret files of the personnel, control, and supervisory offices. Whether in the party or not, a cadre's personal dossier was almost more important than himself. He never saw it, but he knew it contained his own statement of his personal history and background, his ideological views, and all his family and other associations. Dubious individuals would be systematically investigated, and in campaigns, of course, a vulnerable individual might become a target. Where the ancient examination system had made for self-indoctrination, the Communist system made for self-intimidation. Quite aside from the specific evils attacked by a campaign, the eventual selection of certain human targets for systematic denunciation and public humiliation was sufficient to remind all observers that, but for the grace of the party, they too might be pilloried. These unnerving public spectacles strikingly reaffirmed the party's authority. Typically they moved individuals who felt threatened to denounce their pilloried colleagues with unusual vehemence.

As a result of all this, campaigns, the engines of social change, began to lose their efficacy in the 1960's. Cadres learned how to go through the proper motions in meetings without thorough commitment. They learned to avoid close friendships lest they involve themselves in subsequent denunciations in intimate detail. An activist discovered how to ride out campaigns, feigning a progressive enthusiasm in the mobilization phase, and becoming properly prudent and self-critical in the consolidation phase. The party establishment, in short, had learned how to protect itself against Mao's methods of continuing revolution, but it was thereby losing its capacity really to mobilize the people.

Thus the issue of revisionism arose from the fact that too many party members had lost faith in Mao's romantic, Heaven-storming approach to China's problems. Party bureaucrats like Liu and Teng opposed the Maoists' fanaticism and zealotry because they would only hinder economic recovery. Wrestling with practical problems, the bureaucrats dragged their feet when Mao called in late 1962 for yet another campaign, for "socialist education." The inadequate response to this campaign led Mao to turn to the army.

Bureaucratism had also appeared in the Soviet-type professional officer corps, established in 1955. The officers challenged the political commissar system and "politics in command," and favored the Soviet principle of unity of command. Party committees in the armed forces declined as did party membership. But after Defense Minister P'eng Te-huai was ousted in 1959, for criticizing the Great Leap and having had contact with the Soviets, he was succeeded by General Lin Piao, who now worked closely with Mao. New party members were recruited into the armed forces and company party committees re-established. A separate echelon of party members now had its own organization at successive levels down to the company and the squad. Indoctrination and surveillance were both pushed. Political officers kept this system functioning and prevented the formation of groups of like-minded dissidents. The army was thoroughly indoctrinated, so well that by 1964 it was possible to launch a nationwide emulation campaign to "learn from the People's Liberation Army." The army by the fall of 1965 provided the base from which Mao was able to move toward a new campaign that he called the Great Proletarian Cultural Revolution, or more accurately, the great revolution to create a propertyless class culture.

Chairman Mao's Crusade. This was a supercampaign that ran nominally from May 1966 to April 1969 but actually continued until Mao's death in 1976. It turned out to be a second revolution more than a controlled program. As Mao moved against outspoken critics, he found more party support for them than he had foreseen. As with the Hundred Flowers criticisms of 1956, opposition proved surprisingly widespread, but this time it was within the party. Mao responded with a vast new effort to mobilize support from outside the party. The public scene was soon filled with mass meetings, parades, and propaganda displays exalting Mao as "the red sun in our hearts." Tremendous excitement, even hysteria, among millions of youth led to exhaustion, apathy, and further surges of effort. Out of it all came a purge of the party by the leader. But where Stalin had purged his party from within, secretly and using the party apparatus, Mao purged the CCP

In 1967 during the Cultural Revolution, agricultural workers in Tachai erected boards with quotations from Mao along the paths leading to the fields.

from without, publicly and using mass organizations such as the Red Guard youth. Where Stalin used his secret police and killed millions of people, Mao relied on the People's Liberation Army and used methods of public humiliation, frequently accompanied by beatings and incarceration.

Mao's first move was to assure his control of the mass media at the center by attacking cultural and educational commissars and the Peking Party Committee. He went outside the party apparatus to field groups of teenage school students as Red Guards, calling upon them in a poster written in his own hand to "bombard the headquarters." They were to "learn revolution by making revolution." Also outside party channels, he set up a nationwide Cultural Revolution organization headed by a committee that included his wife, Chiang Ch'ing. During the fall of 1966, with logistic support from the army, some 11 million Red Guards came to Peking for a succession of mass rallies and then dispersed over the country to link up with others and carry out their own "Long Marches." In the public scene they violently attacked people and things that seemed to represent the "four olds" (old ideology, thought, habits, and customs). In January 1967, Mao escalated the Revolution still further to attack the party structure itself, inciting

*At a Peking mass rally in 1966, Mao (center) with Teng and Chou
(to the right) are surrounded by students.*

the "revolutionary masses" to seize power from below as in the Paris Commune of 1870. Many million copies of a little red booklet, *Quotations from
Chairman Mao Tse-tung,* brought every activist a wide range of axioms to
ponder and a talisman to wave in devotion. The cult of Mao dominated the
media. The party power holders were attacked piecemeal and had no way
to organize among themselves. As a result, the party establishment was
thoroughly shattered. Liu, Teng, and other leaders were purged as "persons
in authority taking the capitalist road."

To take the place of the old structure of authority, Mao eventually called
for "revolutionary committees" at all the levels of government. They were
to include "revolutionary masses" (new blood), army men, and old party
cadres who had been adequately revolutionized. The party establishment
fought back bitterly in one place after another, fielding their own Red
Guards, proclaiming their loyalty to Mao but defeating his forces. Eventually, local factions began to use firearms in their struggles. Civil warfare
reached a point where the army had to be called in more and more to restore order. By January 1968 revolutionary committees had been set up in
all the twenty-nine provinces and major cities, but an effective core of administration had not been built up within them. In the end, the attack on

the party gave civil power to an increasing number of army men, who were brought into key administrative positions and often continued to terrorize intellectuals and bureaucrats.

In the midst of all this frenzied turmoil, the universities and schools had remained closed for several years while intellectuals and experts were being attacked and students revolutionized in factional fighting. In the fall of 1968 Mao disbanded the Red Guards, and millions of student youth, including erstwhile Red Guards, were sent down to the farms. The Ninth Party Congress of April 1969 elected a new Central Committee with a preponderance of military personnel. A new party constitution named Lin Piao as Mao's successor.

In the 1970's universities slowly reopened with student bodies selected not by competitive examinations, which would still create an elite, but by popular nomination from their production units. Candidates for higher education had to have worked for two years after middle school and were expected to return to serve the communities whence they had come. This idealistic effort to make workers and peasants almost overnight into "proletarian intellectuals" failed simply from lack of literacy and schooling. The acquisition of learning could not be achieved by a quick fix. More successful was the effort to give elementary public health training to "barefoot doctors" who would work among the common people. Urban functionaries were meanwhile rotated regularly to "May 7 schools" (really farms), which gave them an experience of manual work on the land, in a continuing effort to break down the ruling class tradition. For city people, life on the land at the peasant level was a harsh experience. The Cultural Revolution did not disrupt the economy as severely as the Great Leap had done. But its ideological slant retarded development—for example, by demanding regional self-sufficiency in grain or forbidding a farmer's sideline raising of ducks and chickens.

Suddenly in September 1971 General Lin Piao, who had risen so high during the Cultural Revolution and the subsequent ascendancy of the military, was reported killed in a plane crash in Outer Mongolia. By degrees the story was put out that he had plotted usurpation and even the assassination of Mao and had attempted to flee when his dastardly plot was discovered. Whatever may have been the facts of this bizarre episode, the subsequent circumstantial exposure of Lin Piao's long-term perfidy made him out to have been a traitor to the Revolution much like his predecessor Liu Shao-ch'i. This posed again the question how one so evil could have risen so high. To outside observers the need to blacken the moral character of policy losers seemed a curious holdover from Confucianism. Within China, CCP prestige and credibility suffered a new blow.

Lin Piao's elimination was followed by a succession struggle between leaders of Mao's faction, who continued to dominate the media and preach

SCHOLARS ON THE FARM. *Peking Aeronautical Institute teachers and students helping Tungpeiwang Commune members with their July harvest, 1967. A hundred people using hand tools.*

class struggle, and the top CCP administrators, who followed Premier Chou En-lai and sought orderly economic growth. Before Chou died in January 1976 he effected the rehabilitation of Teng Hsiao-p'ing to become acting premier as well as head of the Military Affairs Commission. But after a public outpouring of esteem for the late Premier Chou on April 5, 1976, his understudy Teng was again removed from power by Mao's Cultural Revolution group, the so-called Gang of Four, headed by Mao's wife Chiang Ch'ing. These radical ideologues lost power only after Mao died in September.

As thus far studied, the Cultural Revolution is generally seen as "ten lost years" in China's modern development. The wanton destructiveness of ignorant teenagers; the reign of terror against members of the intellectual and official establishments; the harassment, jailing, beating, torture, and often killing perpetrated against something like a million victims were an enormous human and cultural disaster. Mao's hinging so much violence on the theme of class struggle was aberrant extremism; it was hardly compensated by the urban elite's fitful experience of peasant life and the greater understanding it brought.

Sino-American Normalization.   While the Chinese people had been going through the Cultural Revolution, the American people had been involved in a different turmoil, the Vietnam War of 1965–1973 (see Chapter 27). The American defeat in Vietnam after an expenditure of 58,000 lives coincided with several other factors to make possible President Nixon's dramatic renewal of Sino-American relations.

First, the American withdrawal from the Indo-China area (Vietnam, Cambodia, and Laos) followed the inauguration of a policy of détente or negotiation, rather than military confrontation in the continuing competition between Washington and Moscow. The resulting Soviet-American collaboration-cum-rivalry in trade, arms limitation under the SALT agreement (May 1972), and cultural exchanges modified the cold-war posture of these two superpowers. This in turn made Chinese-American contact highly desirable on the third side of the Sino-Soviet-American triangle.

Second, the American defeat in South Vietnam, where the war effort had always been limited by the necessity not to invade North Vietnam lest it provoke China's entrance as in Korea, led Mao Tse-tung to conclude that American capitalist imperialism was for China a "minor contradiction" as compared with the "major contradiction" of Soviet "socialist imperialism." This appraisal of Russia as the main menace led Peking to respond positively to the Nixon administration's measured efforts to restore relations.

The breakthrough, after twenty-two years of estrangement, was dramatic. In April 1971 Peking unexpectedly welcomed American table-tennis players and journalists in a gesture of "people-to-people diplomacy." Suddenly in July Mr. Nixon announced that his national security adviser, Dr. Henry Kissinger (later Secretary of State), had secretly visited Peking to prepare for a presidential visit. In October the Republic of China on Taiwan was expelled from the United Nations and the People's Republic admitted. In February 1972 President Nixon visited Peking, saw Chairman Mao, and with Prime Minister Chou En-lai signed at Shanghai a joint communiqué. This document stated the two parties' divergent views on several matters but agreed on a joint effort to develop commercial and cultural contact and to move toward normal relations. In May 1973 the two governments opened embryo embassies in the form of liaison offices headed by ambassadors in Peking and Washington.

Under this new order trade developed, dozens of delegations passed back and forth (mainly in fields of technology), and thousands of Americans (mainly ethnic Chinese) visited the People's Republic. On the Chinese side this was a large-scale government program of controlled contact that brought Americans into the channels of tourism within China that had already been established for other foreigners from all over the world. This foreign tourism was in fact added on to the massive domestic program by which

Chinese delegations were brought to exemplary demonstration sites where they could learn from model achievements such as those of the Shansi province Tachai brigade in agriculture and, in the northeast, of the Taching oil field in industry. American contact was thus fitted into the ongoing effort to remake China.

The Shanghai communiqué also defined the status of Taiwan when the American side acknowledged "that all Chinese on either side of the Taiwan Strait maintain there is but one China and that Taiwan is a part of China." The United States sought "a peaceful settlement of the Taiwan question by the Chinese themselves." Accordingly it would reduce American forces on Taiwan with the ultimate objective of their complete withdrawal. Implicit in this document and its acceptance of the one-China concept was the idea that Washington would eventually withdraw diplomatic recognition from Taipei in order to achieve "normalization," full diplomatic relations, with Peking. However, since two separate regimes had existed since 1949, each claiming to be the one China, it was plain that this potent phrase represented an ideal (in fact the central myth of the traditional Chinese state) rather than an actuality. This made the history and circumstances of Taiwan peculiarly important (see Chapter 27).

In the years following the Shanghai communiqué of 1972, American progress toward normalization was slowed by the distraction of the Watergate investigation, climaxed by the resignation of President Nixon in August 1974. Dr. Kissinger made repeated visits to Peking, and in December 1975 President Ford did so too, reaffirming the normalization policy. Yet Peking and Taipei both continued to be represented in Washington, as in few other capital cities and in no international bodies.

Another cause of delay was the succession struggle in Peking, where Teng Hsiao-p'ing won out and became "paramount leader" only in late 1978. Anti-communism was still a widespread public sentiment in America, but once the Teng leadership seemed securely in power, the Carter administration recognized the People's Republic in Peking as the government of China on January 1, 1979, just thirty years after its coming to power. Following Japan's example of 1972, the United States Congress in April 1979 passed the Taiwan Relations Act, which continued the legal arrangements that had supported American trade, investment, and cultural relations with Taiwan. Diplomatic recognition was withdrawn. The former embassy became the American Institute in Taiwan, staffed by former diplomats now on leave from the Foreign Service. In this way the United States finally acknowledged the patriotic Chinese theory of One China as well as the fact that Taiwan was a separate province, surrounded by water, with its own government and army. American military aid to Taiwan continued though it was promised to be on a diminishing scale.

Teng Hsiao-p'ing in 1983.

Reform under Teng Hsiao-p'ing

After Teng's accession to leadership in late 1978, the Chinese Communist slogan of class struggle gave way to that of the "four modernizations": in agriculture, industry, science and technology, and the military. The policies of the reform era made a startling contrast with those of the Cultural Revolution. As though a dam had burst, the anti-intellectualism and xenophobia, the austere ideological fervor and egalitarianism preached by Mao, were overwhelmed by a flood of new policies and programs. Within a few years the tenor of Chinese life became quite different.

These changes could be so basic because Mao's leadership had ended so bankrupt. In the name of the amorphous slogan of class struggle that only he could correctly invoke, Mao had attacked and damaged the major elements of the body politic: Intellectuals were capped as rightists by party zealots (1957). Peasant lives were squandered by the tens of millions through zealous mismanagement (1958–1959). Party and government officials were put out of action by Red Guards (1967). Feuding Red Guard youths were sent down to the villages by the army (1968). And army commander Lin Piao was destroyed (1971). Having broken all the eggs in the nest, Mao finally sat upon a shambles. The gargantuan Chinese state, dependent for its existence upon a unity of leadership and of ideology, had seen competing factions shouting discordant slogans. The reforms after 1978 had to begin within the party.

Reinvigorating the Chinese Leadership.   In order to reestablish its legitimacy, the CCP had to function as the nation's conscience and redress injustice. The cases of many hundred thousand, perhaps a million, victims of the Cultural Revolution were reexamined all the way back to the anti-rightist movement of 1957. The one-time chief of state, Liu Shao-ch'i, who had died neglected and alone in 1969, and many others were rehabilitated posthumously. Surviving professors, writers, party members, and others once stigmatized and ill treated came back into public life.

Second, Mao Tse-tung, who had been both Lenin and Stalin in China, had to be publicly judged by his successors if they were to govern the country with credibility. In June 1981 the Central Committee published its appraisal of the origins and course of the Cultural Revolution. It denied Mao's accusation of bourgeois revisionism within the Party and concluded that his great earlier contributions outweighed the grievous errors of his later years in a proportion of about 70 to 30. But the thought of Mao Tse-tung was hailed as the continuing guide to China's progress, along with the necessity of CCP dictatorship on the road to socialism.

A further need was to rebuild the party's personnel, a gigantic task. Of its 40 million members about half had been admitted during the Cultural Revolution. Often they lacked education, for which they substituted ideological zealotry. Such people could hardly lead in China's new day. Teng's twofold problem was to change both the leadership and the rank and file. A system of retirement was instituted, and aged leaders were invited onto an honorary but powerless Advisory Council, retaining their salaries and numerous perquisites—houses, servants, limousines, special supplies, and privileges. It was a slow process because a leader's influence based on his prestige and personal connections only grew with time. Only after nine years, when death had removed many Long March veterans, was the retirement program brought to success at the Thirteenth Congress of the CCP in October 1987. Teng Hsiao-p'ing at eighty-three led his elderly rivals into nominal retirement (though Teng remained head of the party's Military Affairs Commission). Under Chao Tzu-yang (*pinyin* Zhao Ziyang) as new party leader, men of the post–Long March generation now in their late fifties or sixties took over the Politburo and its standing committee of five persons at the pinnacle of power.

Meanwhile a rectification campaign had aimed to winnow the incompetent out of the party rank and file, but it was again a slow process. Though more than 200,000 were expelled and 325,000 disciplined, this was little more than 1 per cent of the membership. As death took its natural toll, the party's composition was changed through expansion of membership to 47 million in 1987. The proportion of party members who had received substantial education in school or even college rose from about a third to a half.

Reinvigorating the party was accompanied by a tremendous nationwide effort in education to make up for the "ten lost years" and foster the skills needed for modernization. The PRC faced a shortage of college-trained professional manpower. The drive to raise the quality of education so as to approach the standards of advanced industrial nations necessarily meant a return to elitism, the traditional search for outstanding talent. For this the Chinese had inherited great sophistication and so devised a complex system. In general, two streams of students were selected out at the senior middle-school level—a small elite who would go on to higher education and a majority who would get vocational education in useful skills and specialties. Among the university elite only a small superelite would attend the few comprehensive universities and get the broad education desirable for top leaders.

After 1978, revived government examinations became the absorbing annual target of middle school students. Instead of being arbitrarily assigned to specialties and institutions, as under Mao, student applicants now expressed their preferences, while institutions selected them increasingly on the basis of academic ability. At the same time, the schools and graduates were reduced in number to ensure high quality and to avoid the danger of having a large cohort of educated youth left unemployed. Children of officials and intellectuals had a head start in their early literacy at home that tended to make them into a new educated elite. Similarly, among the thousand or so institutions of higher learning only a few were selected to be "comprehensive universities." At the postgraduate level research institutes proliferated. Parallel to the central Academy of Sciences, an Academy of Social Sciences was set up at Peking, with affiliated bodies in major centers in the provinces. From this elite system, thousands of high achievers were sent abroad for advanced training, while in high-priority specialties such as business management both long- and short-term courses were also set up in China. (In the mid-1980's, however, the ten to fifteen thousand PRC students in the United States were no more numerous than those from Taiwan.)

Meanwhile, apart from the ordinary schools and universities, a variety of special educational institutions were established to meet the needs of Teng's four modernizations. Factories, local governments, and ministries set up part-time schools, correspondence schools, and institutes for tech-

nical training. Courses were offered on radio and television. The study
of English boomed; Japanese came next; and Russian was a distant third.
In this new age of education so many people sought so many kinds of
education in so many ways that the formal system of education was only
the tip of the iceberg. The changes that had transformed Japan and the
societies of the rim nations of Asia seemed at last to be under way in China.

For the People's Liberation Army (PLA), which had been politicized
during the Cultural Revolution, the need was to retire overage officers and
revive professional training. As in higher education, quality was improved
by reducing quantity. Troop strength was reduced by about one-quarter to
leave the armed forces still totaling almost 3 million men. Much equipment was updated, though the high technology of the superpowers was
unavailable. The armed forces were prepared more for defense than for
attack abroad. When China undertook to "teach Vietnam a lesson" in early
1979, the battle-hardened and partly American-equipped Vietnamese proved
very difficult to deal with. Yet China's space rockets, nuclear developments,
and ballistic-missile-firing submarines showed her military capability.

Problems of Economic Development.   During the rule of Mao the economy
had grown but so had China's population. Wages and consumption had
both stagnated while waste and inefficiency had increased. Part of the fault
lay in planning: in following the Stalinist model of investment in producer
goods through heavy industry at the expense of agriculture, Chinese plan-
ners had assumed the capital/output ratio (the productivity of investment)
would be unchanging; but in fact during the 1960's and 1970's the ratio
grew so that given increases of investment led only to smaller increases of
output. For example, during the fifth five-year plan of 1976–1980 it took
three times as much investment to produce a kilowatt hour of electricity as
it had taken during the third plan of 1966–1970. Although investment continued to be high, growth slowed down. The Maoist revolutionaries had
disesteemed both material incentives and foreign trade and technology.
They had even demanded regional self-sufficiency, thereby forgoing the
comparative advantage of letting each region do what it could do best. As
a result China continued to lag far behind other industrializing countries
of East Asia.

The reformers' new approach was to revive material incentives and open
China to foreign trade, investment, and technology. The revival of incentives was most impressive in agriculture, in the villages where 70 per cent
of the Chinese people lived. Under Maoist collectivism the guarantee of the
farmer's livelihood, the so-called "iron rice bowl," had dampened his
incentive and led to a decline in his productivity. Even with improved

strains of rice and new scientific methods, the collective farms had failed to produce much more than the old scattered family plots that had seemed so medieval.

The remedy of the eighties was the "responsibility" system. Under it each household contracted to produce its quota for the collective production team and then could sell any surplus on the market. Private plots were enlarged up to 15 per cent of the cultivated acreage, thus reviving the farmer's incentive. Farm production, largely on the private plots, amazingly doubled in volume, a proof that material incentives outweighed Mao's teaching to "serve the people."

Another change under Teng was to permit farm families to expand their sideline activities, formerly denounced by Mao as "incipient capitalism." Many results ensued. Something like a sixth of the farm families became active in such services as transport, repair, private food markets, and other ways of meeting consumer needs. These families were permitted to hire labor. The latent capacity for entrepreneurship among villagers brought some of them remarkable wealth. They built two-story houses and became figures of local importance. They were held up as models.

Entrepreneurial farmers soon cooperated with local party cadres. The cadres, to be sure, were not supposed to engage in economic activities or profit from the positions they held. But their contacts and influence were of use to the new entrepreneurs. So cadres and entrepreneurs emerged as the new local elite, a bit like the local gentry of earlier times. Opportunities for corruption abounded. Overall the new opportunities for economic innovation increased consumer goods and services and improved the villagers' standard of living. But the abolition of communes and deterioration of collective institutions in the new enthusiasm for profits created problems of livelihood for the less able.

New developments in industry were even more innovative and farreaching, though more difficult to achieve. In the Maoist era plant managers had had to work closely with party committees and meet production quotas set up by the state, for which the planned economy gave them a supply of resources but not always a means of distribution. The result was that a plant might work strenuously overtime to meet its periodic quota of production and then slack off until the next deadline. There was little incentive for cost efficiency, and the goods produced might deteriorate outdoors awaiting nonexistent purchasers. To better their record, some plant managers planned and built additional plants even when their contribution to the general economy remained uncertain. The iron rice bowl meanwhile inhibited increases of labor productivity. The incentive of bonus pay had been dropped. Labor discipline was slack, with much absenteeism.

The Teng reform was to put plant managers on a "responsibility" system, freed at least nominally from the close supervision of party committees.

Instead of quotas to meet, the managers were given state loans to be paid back from production. Thus they had an incentive to achieve repayment and reduce interest charges. This new focus on cost efficiency went along with a decentralization of planning control. Central command gave way partly to local administrative guidance. When Peking expected only payment of an income tax and repayment of loans, a manager had more chance to shape his product to local consumer demand and sell it at market rates. As the supply of materials from the central government was reduced, managers purchased their supplies in the market. This greater freedom to invest their funds gave them innumerable chances for personal deals and corruption but also stimulated development.

As enterprise grew, the need for credit expanded. The central bank therefore spawned a series of specialized banks. The People's Bank of China remained the central policy maker and superintended the specialized banks that dealt with such diverse activities as agriculture, industry and commerce, construction, insurance, international trade, and foreign exchange. This greatly enlarged banking network with branches all over the country used the making of loans and the setting of interest rates as means of guiding economic growth.

The state sector of the economy was the chief problem. In the mid-eighties it accounted for about 70 per cent of urban employment and industrial production, while the collective or cooperative sector accounted for around 25 per cent and the new private entrepreneurial sector for only 5 per cent. The reformers met their most severe challenge in trying to invigorate the big state enterprises, in which the allocation of resources and the setting of production quotas had been controlled by central government bureaucrats. To do away with waste and inefficiencies, the state enterprises were now encouraged to produce for the market. This meant buying raw materials at market prices, firing inefficient or lazy workers, and pricing goods competitively. But this competition opened the possibly of a factory going bankrupt. It aroused resistance, often expressed in ideological terms. Formerly the state had set most prices and, moreover, in traditional Chinese style had given local industrial plants monopolies over their local markets. Now the new free market prices set by supply and demand created a competition that threatened the bureaucrats' vested interests. Combining free market forces with a planned command-economy was very difficult. Would not a free market in goods call for free markets in labor and in capital (a stock market)? Where could one stop?

In the 1980's China moved toward a mixed bureaucratic-command and market system. Japan, South Korea, and Taiwan had all done this but with private industry dominant. In China, by contrast, instead of private ownership of most industries, state enterprises remained dominant. China was not going capitalist. Reliance on market forces to spur competition and productivity was part of China's new industrial strategy. The Teng reforms built up light industries to produce consumer goods. These could meet the domestic demand fueled by higher wages and private profits. Consumer goods such as textiles, clothing, or bicycles could also be exported to secure foreign exchange and imports of foreign technology.

The Open Door and its Consequences.   China's industrial boom in the early 1980's was helped by another reversal of Mao through Teng Hsiao-p'ing's policy of an "open door" for foreign trade and investment. Where Maoist China had kept capitalism outside the country at arm's length, Teng's reform program now invited it to come in and foster economic growth, which of course had been the experience of other states in the early course of industrialization. Undoubtedly the lack of this foreign help had held China back.

The new open door for trade and investment got spectacular though mixed results. The great enthusiasms for contracting foreign loans to develop China's resources and industries after 1978 led at first to a great overexpansion and then to a bust. Grandiose plans and large contracts with Japanese, U.S., and European firms had to be scaled back. To set up conditions that would attract foreign investors the PRC next created four Special Economic Zones. the most prominent of which was Shenzhen, next door to Hong Kong. Within such zones foreign investors were given special facilities for a foreign lifestyle while undertaking joint ventures with their Chinese counterparts. The zones were set apart from the Chinese economy in general. Along with them went the opening of fourteen ports specially suited to foreign trade—a bit reminiscent of the nineteenth-century treaty ports, though now China, not the foreigners, called the tune. In 1980 China resumed its participation in the International Monetary Fund and World Bank. Foreign loans built up her foreign exchange reserves.

Foreign trade also required the building up of a legal profession schooled in commercial law to handle contracts with foreign firms. In fact, however, growth of China's socialist economy, especially horizontal relations between government agencies, had already required new legislation regarding contracts, labor, enterprise, bankruptcy, and the like. The National People's Congress, meeting annually, accordingly took on a new importance as a forum for debating new legislation.

Once Teng opened the door to development many changes ensued within the Chinese government. For the sake of defense, Mao had tried to develop heavy industry in interior provinces but under the control of Peking ministries. This development now gave way to emphasizing growth in the port cities and in light industries that could sell products abroad. These projects were less under the control of Peking. Enterprise required decentralization, and Peking soon found it expedient to set up a great number of new corporations and commissions to coordinate widespread developments in various industries instead of relying on cumbersome central government ministries. For example, a number of government agencies were combined under an overall education commission, others under a petrochemical commission, and still others under a shipbuilding agency. Most innovative was the Chinese International Trade and Investment Corporation, headed by a former leading capitalist in Shanghai who developed worldwide operations in the style of a multinational firm. The open-door policy also led to the study and partial imitation of many foreign economic institutions, even a stock market. Thus Teng's China blossomed with vigorous economic growth in a variety of ways.

The problems of such growth were formidable. Both energy supply and transportation remained inadequate. Oil production grew but fell short of meeting China's needs. Coal was still the main fuel, yet the large deposits were inland—for example, in Shansi province—while the principal users were along the seacoast. The importation of foreign equipment was inhibited by limited foreign exchange. The need for modern industrial managers could partly be met by sending students abroad, but this took time. And all the while relentless population growth threatened China's agricultural self-sufficiency.

After China's first modern census of the early 1980's showed a population well over 1 billion with a great preponderance of people in the child-bearing age group, a national policy of one child per couple was officially pushed, even though it severely contradicted the traditional family system. The one-child policy achieved some success in the cities, but in the countryside a farm family prospering by its own efforts needed extra hands. The preference for boys as farm workers and to carry on the family surname encouraged some female infanticide. Since the one-child-per-couple goal could not be achieved in the countryside, despite the availability of contraceptives and abortions, future growth to a total of 1.5 billion Chinese by the mid-twenty-first century seemed unavoidable. In earlier centuries such growth would have been checked by wars and famines. But the combination of the green revolution and better transport opened up the prospect of a far larger population, industrialized but poor.

The PRC has been no exception to the rule that the early stages of industrialization are a dirty business. The long-time beauty of Peking as the world's most impressive capital of empire was destroyed by smog, the tearing down of old monuments such as the city walls and gate towers, and the construction of undistinguished high-rise housing for several million new residents.

The ills of urbanization had long been exemplified in foreign-run Shanghai. The initial Maoist attitude was to break Shanghai up and move

Peking street scene in 1985: The density of China's population is evident in this river of Sunday shoppers.

it inland as a disgraceful product of imperialism vulnerable to foreign naval power. When it proved to be a necessary base for industrial development, Shanghai was put to work on heavy industry with little buildup of infrastructure. Transport, housing, sewage disposal, and social services generally had received little attention and had become old and outdated, in need of basic renovation. In transport alone the reform program therefore built new bridges and under-river tunnels, started a subway, and expanded the port capacity and airport. New policies stressed light industries to meet consumer demand, special education facilities to foster high technology, and enhanced capacities for foreign trade and joint ventures with foreign capitalists.

Culture and Politics.   In the midst of so much openness and decentralization, how could the Communist party maintain control? As so often before, the danger of dissidence seemed especially great among writers, artists, and intellectuals in general.

In Chinese tradition the scholar served the state. The state propagated its own orthodox belief system, which scholars helped maintain. There was a craving for order. Disruptions or lack of order (*luan*) were seen as threats to the state. These views were buttressed by culturalism: the sense that Chinese art, literature, philosophy, and values were superior and things foreign inferior. Many of these traditional attitudes carried over into the modern era and occasionally have been reinforced by the Communist state. Dissent was seen as unconstructive and unpatriotic. Intellectuals were expected to be both loyal and orthodox. Marxist doctrines were as important to the Communist cadres as Confucian doctrines had been to scholar-officials.

Confronting this tradition, the party under Teng encouraged openness for the sake of economic growth. The reforms included the gradual relaxation of party control over literary expression. This allowed the Cultural Revolution's frightful attacks on writers and academics to be recorded in a literature of the "wounded," as though portrayal of individuals' sufferings could exorcise their traumatic effects—the demoralization of scientists and scholars and the cynicism of the youth. The relative lightening of the heavy hand of politics on art permitted a revival of cultural activities of every sort: traditional Chinese opera was again performed, hundreds of new magazines appeared, thousands of translations of foreign books and magazines were published, and Chinese were once again permitted to watch selected foreign films and TV shows. Writers and artists experimented with new techniques and delved deeper into China's problems. Tales of love, rape, corruption, injustice, and so on—topics hitherto suppressed— were given expression. It became evident that great works of literature and art would emerge from the Chinese people's searing experience of revolution.

To control the pace of change, a seesaw tilted within the reform movement between radicals and moderates. The conservative moderates were appalled at the new foreign fashions and lifestyles taken up by urban youth—disco dancing, women's body-building in bikinis, a craze for electronic gadgets, commercial advertising on all sides. To contain this explosion of individual self-gratification and materialism campaigns were launched: in 1979–1980 against the political restructuring through real democracy called for in posters on Peking's "Democracy Wall"; in 1980–1981 against "bourgeois liberalism" in literature and art; in 1983–1984 against "spiritual pollution"; and in 1985–1986 against "unhealthy tendencies." In all these policy fluctuations between permissiveness and repression Teng Hsiao-p'ing held the balance, by turns acknowledging the conservative reformers' fears of moral bankruptcy and social instability and then the radical reformers' demand for innovation and creative self-expression. In December 1986 student demonstrations again erupted into the streets, demanding that economic modernization must be accompanied by political modernization—a multiparty system, a free press, competitive elections, no official ideology. Such demands posed thorny problems of timing and control, such as the problem of grafting a more dynamic market economy onto a bureaucrat-ridden command economy.

The CCP under Teng gave ground slowly while stoutly defending its claim to final power. The annual National People's Congress began to play a greater role in policy discussion but remained only advisory. A move toward democracy was symbolized by nominating a few more candidates than could be elected to the party's central committee. But the CCP remained above the law, answerable to no one but itself. The party gave intellectuals the freedom to be creative only within the limits of the "four basic principles" set forth in June 1981. These were the preservation of Marx-Leninism and Mao Tse-tung thought, the leadership of the Chinese Communist party, the people's dictatorship, and the socialist road. These could not be questioned.

Perspectives on China's Revolution

The progression from Mao to Teng can be viewed first in its international environment. In the 1940's the Russia of Stalin dominated the Communist world. It was not surprising that China accepted the Soviet model and leadership for almost a decade. Mao had had no firsthand experience of the outside world. The treaty port China in which he grew up seemed to confirm Lenin's theory of imperialism. Mao accepted the notion that capitalist nations were subject to cycles of boom and bust and routinely exploited their workers. He distrusted economic relations with the non-Communist world and sought China's self-sufficiency, but the economy began to stagnate.

By 1976, when Mao died, and even more evidently in the decade that followed, a different world presented itself to China. Waves of reform and economic realism were breaking across the U.S.S.R. and other Communist nations. Eventually even Vietnam and North Korea were affected. In the meantime the East Asian Third World, those rim nations closest to China, had become autonomous and capitalist and were bursting with productivity and well-being. According to Lenin, this was not supposed to happen. Moreover, Marxism prided itself on being scientific. Science was the shibboleth of the Communist world. Yet Communist countries were scientifically backward; the Nobel prizes went to Western Europe, the United States, and Japan, and non-Communist East Asia was quickly catching up. After 1978, therefore, Teng's open-door policy aimed to use foreign trade and investment to invigorate the economy. Where Mao had been doctrinaire, Teng became pragmatic.

A similar counterpoint characterized the internal dynamics of China's growth and change. Modern innovations had to be harmonized with ancient traditions. The proportions of old and new, Chinese and foreign, might differ sector by sector. Thus in economic reform the Maoist desire for local self-sufficiency had to compromise with the need for national organization;

market forces had to be used as well as central controls; individual enterprise had to be fostered along with bureaucratic planning. In social life the emancipation of women and youth was limited by old values as well as new circumstances. The work unit vied with the family system to guide each person. Yet the claims of the collective group had to contend with a newly individualistic consumerism. A similar competition between new practices and old values was visible in politics. Revived examinations buttressed the old idea of government by power holders using a trained elite. How could the modern media and democratic election procedures bring the masses to participate in politics without manipulation by mass movements and thought police? Teng's patient and pragmatic reforms remind us of the long tradition of statecraft by which scholar-officials organized the people's lives in order to cope with their problems. The goal is still to create a more powerful and humane society, but step by step, not in a single great leap forward.

The new state and society now taking shape in China will continue to surprise us with innovations and yet may also appall us with apparent throwbacks to earlier times. History lies just below the surface of Chinese life, available to be called upon. Tendencies toward convergence between Chinese ways and those of the outer world are already apparent. Yet science and technology, similar products and mechanisms, all the gadgetry of consumerism in food, clothing, housing, transport, and communications will not succeed in wiping out the contrasts in our social structure, political history, and values. The differences between China and the United States in traditions as well as in ecological-demographic circumstances are so great that our two cultures will not be homogenized. Anchored in their own soil, the Chinese people will continue to live in the shadow of their past.

Illustration Acknowledgments

Chapter 1   p. 10, G. B. Cressey, *China's Geographic Foundations;* p. 13, *P'ei wen chai kung-chi-tu;* p. 14, *Tien-kung k'ai-wu collection* of 1637; p. 15, *T'ien-kung k'ai-wu.*

Chapter 2   p. 23, East Asian Library, Columbia University; p. 29, (left) Courtesy Museum of Fine Arts, Boston, (top right) Courtesy Museum of Fine Arts, Boston, (bottom right) Courtesy of the Smithsonian Institution, Freer Gallery of Art, Washington, D.C.

Chapter 3   p. 39, W. C. White, *Tomb Tile Pictures of Ancient China,* pl. LXXII, Courtesy of the Royal Ontario Museum, Toronto, Canada; p. 43, American Museum of Natural History; p. 45, (top) *Han Wu Liang Tz'u,* (bottom left) Shanghai woodblock, 1873, (bottom right) Sung painting by Chao Ming Chien.

Chapter 4   p. 58, restored by Wilma Fairbank from a rubbing; p. 64, Courtesy of the Royal Ontario Museum, Toronto, Canada; p. 67, restored by Wilma Fairbank from a rubbing; p. 70, restored by Wilma Fairbank from a rubbing; p. 74, *T'ien-kung k'ai-wu;* p. 77, restored by Wilma Fairbank from a rubbing.

Chapter 5   p. 89, Courtesy Museum of Fine Arts, Boston; p. 90, Osvald Siren, The Museum of Far Eastern Antiquities, Stockholm; p. 92, Nelson Gallery—Atkins Museum, Kansas City, Missouri; p. 97, Collections of the University Museum of the University of Pennsylvania; p. 110, Paul Pelliot; p. 113, (top and bottom) Nelson Gallery—Atkins Museum, Kansas City, Missouri; p. 114, Laurence Sickman and Alexander Soper, *Art and Architecture of China,* Penguin Books, 1936.

Chapter 6   p. 133, *Fa yüan chu-lin,* compiled by Tao-shih in 668, printed in 1124; p. 141, *Ch'ing-ming shang-ho t'u-chuan,* Peking, 1958; p. 144, Courtesy of the Smithsonian Institution, Freer Gallery of Art, Washington, D.C.; p. 145, Courtesy Museum of Fine Arts, Boston.

Chapter 7   p. 155, American Museum of Natural History; p. 156, The Museum of Far Eastern Antiquities, Stockholm; p. 175, *Shui-hu-chuan.*

Chapter 8   p. 183, *Chao Tzu-ku erh-shih-ssu hsiao shu-hua bo-pi;* p. 189, Sidney Gamble; p. 199, *Ming-jen hsiang-chuan;* p. 194, *Pin-feng-kuang-i.*

Chapter 9   p. 219, by permission of the Houghton Library, Harvard University; p. 221, (top) Charles Cutting, (bottom) slide in John K. Fairbank's collection; p. 224, *Ch'ing-tai ti-hou-hsiang;* p. 233, Nan-hsün sheng-tien; p. 236, *Ch'ing-tai ti-hou-hsiang;* p. 239, by permission of the Houghton Library, Harvard University; p. 247, (both) Nieuhof, *An Embassy from the East India Company of the United Provinces to the Grand Tartar,* Rare Book division, the New York Public Library, Astor, Lenox, and Tilden Foundations; p. 248, (top) Musée Guimet, Paris, (bottom) by permission of the Houghton Library, Harvard University.

Chapter 10   p. 264, *Shanghai Gazetteer,* 1871; p. 270, (top and bottom) *Hai-kuo wen-chien lu,* ca. 1730; p. 272. (both) *Huang Ch'ing chih-kung t'u,* Palace Edition, 1761; p. 282, Radio Times Hulton Picture Library; p. 286, Courtesy of the Peabody Museum of Salem; p. 288, Courtesy of the Peabody Museum of Salem; p. 291, *Ming-jen hsiang-chuan;* p. 296, by permission of the Houghton Library, Harvard University.

Chapter 11   p. 309, Radio Times Hulton Picture Library; p. 311, Drew Collection, Harvard-Yenching Library; p. 315, Thomson, *Illustrations of China and Its Peoples,* vol. 4, London, 1874; p. 323, Drew Collection, Harvard-Yenching Library; p. 330, Drew Collection, Harvard-Yenching Library; p. 331, Mrs. Helen Merrill Groff-Smith; p. 336, Courtesy of Essex Institute, Salem, Mass.; p. 339, Courtesy of Essex Institute, Salem, Mass.; p. 344, Drew Collection, Harvard-Yenching Library.

Chapter 12   pp. 356–357 (both) *Tien-shih-chai hua-pao,* 1844; p. 367, Radio Times Hulton Picture Library; pp. 380–381, Oriental Collection of the late Ernst von Harringa; p. 646 (top and bottom) Drew Collection, Harvard-Yenching Library.

Chapter 13   p. 397 (top), Dmitri Kessel, *Life* Magazine, © Time Inc., (bottom) Wilson, Arnold Arboretum; p. 404, Arnold Arboretum; p. 409, (top) Courtesy of the Peabody Museum of Salem, (bottom) Government Information Services, Hong Kong; p. 414, China Photo Service; p. 425, (top) Wide World Photos, (bottom) U.S. Signal Corps.

Chapter 14   p. 433, Cornell University; p. 444, Wide World; p. 445, Radio Times Hulton Picture Library; p. 448, taken from *China* by Marc Chadourne. Copyright 1932 by Marc Chadourne. Used by permission of Crown Publishers, Inc.; p. 454, Radio Times Hulton Picture Library; p. 459, Eastphoto; p. 461, The Bettmann Archive; p. 466, (top) Courtesy of Essex Institute, Salem, Mass., (bottom left) Henri Cartier-Bresson/ Magnum Photos, (bottom right) Emil Shulthess/Black Star; p. 469, General Library, University of California at Berkeley; p. 470, U.S. Army Photograph.

Chapter 15   p. 480, George Silk/*Life* Magazine, © Time Inc.; p. 481, Eastfoto; p. 483, Magnum Photos (courtesy Eve Arnold); pp. 495, 498, 505, 510, 511, 513, and 516, Eastfoto; p. 524, Wide World Photos.

Index

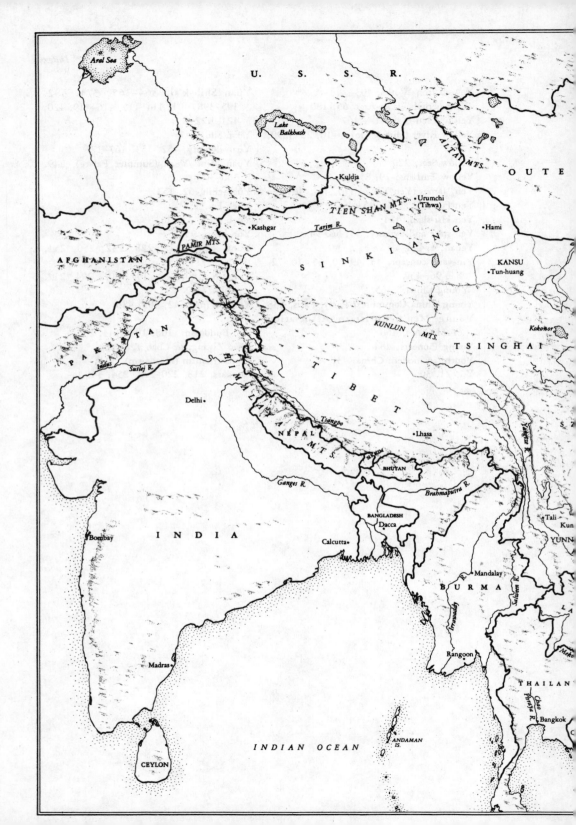

Irkutsk

Lake Baikal

Ulan Bator
(Urga)

MONGOLIA

INNER MONGOLIA

NINGSIA

SHENSI

SHANSI

HOPEI

Ta-t'ung•

•Peking
Tientsin•

Shanhaikuan

LIAONING

Mukden•

Ta-lien
(Dairen)

KIRIN

Ch'ang-ch'un
(Hsinching)

HEILUNGKIANG

•Harbin

Khabarovsk

SAKHALIN

HOKKAIDO
•Sapporo

KURIL IS.

MARITIME PROV.

Vladivostok

SEA OF

JAPAN

HONSHU

Sendai

Tōkyō
Nagoya•

SHANTUNG

Yellow

Loyang

Kaifeng

HONAN

Sian

Wei R.

Yellow

MTS.

HUPEI

Han

Wu-han
(Hankow)

Yangtze R.

Changsha

HUNAN

KIANGSU

Nanking

ANHWEI

Soochow

Hangchow•

Ningpo•

CHEKIANG

KIANGSI

Foochow•

FUKIEN

KWEICHOW

KWANGSI

Hu (West) R.

KWANGTUNG

Canton•

Shanghai

NORTH
KOREA
•P'yŏngyang

•Seoul
SOUTH
KOREA

Pusan

YELLOW SEA

KYŪSHŪ

Nagasaki

KYŌTO

Ōsaka

SHIKOKU

EAST CHINA

SEA

RYŪKYŪ ISLANDS

Taipei•

TAIWAN

HAINAN

SOUTH CHINA SEA

Hanoi
NORTH
VIETNAM

Hué

SOUTH
VIETNAM

Saigon

Manila•

PHILIPPINE

ISLANDS

PACIFIC

OCEAN

Great Wall

Modern Grand Canal

Provincial boundaries in
China proper

Sanderson

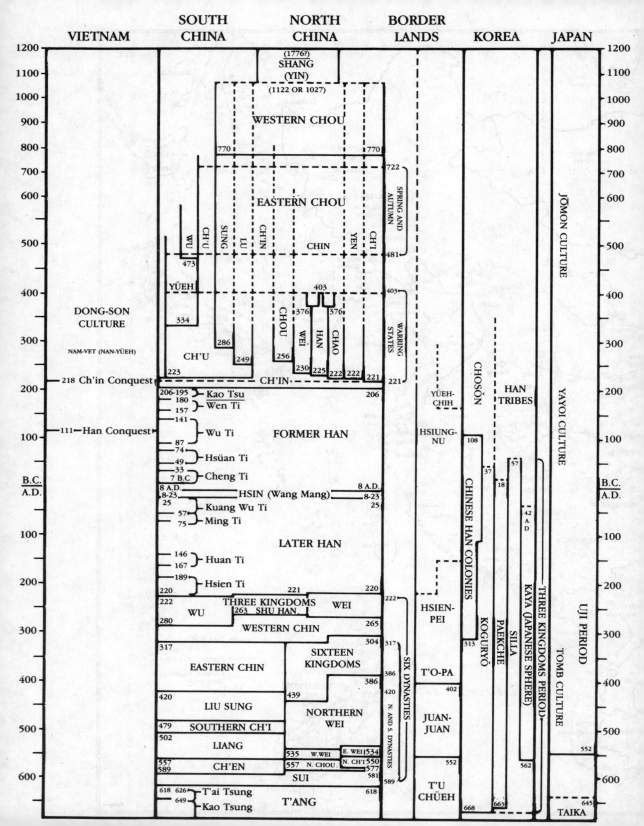

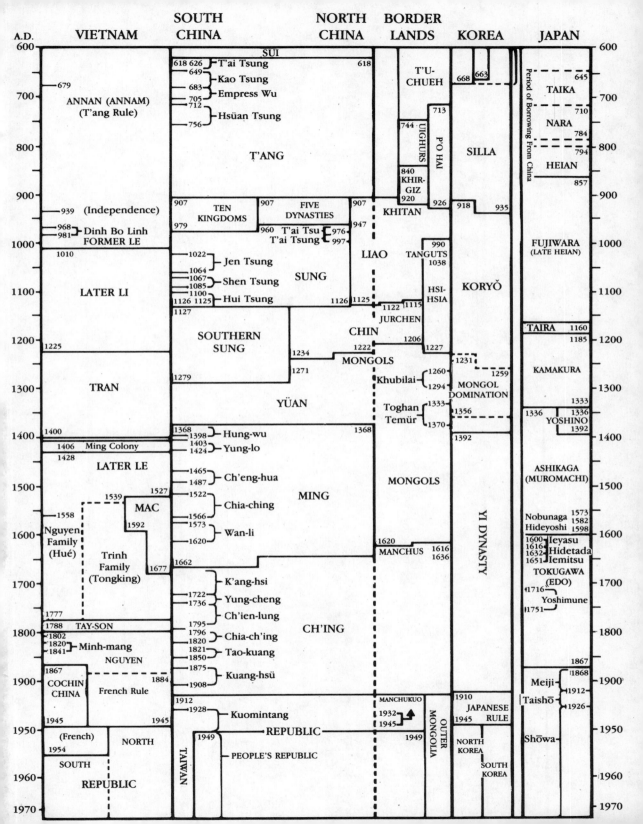